Chess Strategy in Action

John Watson

First published in the UK by Gambit Publications Ltd 2003

ISBN 1 901983 69 2

DISTRIBUTION:
Worldwide (except USA): Central Books Ltd, 99 Wallis Rd, London E9 5LN.
Tel +44 (0)20 8986 4854 Fax +44 (0)20 8533 5821. E-mail: orders@Centralbooks.com
USA: BHB International, Inc., 302 West North 2nd Street, Seneca, SC 29678, USA.

For all other enquiries (including a full list of all Gambit chess titles) please contact the publishers, Gambit Publications Ltd, P.O. Box 32640, London W14 0JN. E-mail: info@gambitbooks.com
Or visit the GAMBIT web site at http://www.gambitbooks.com

Edited by Graham Burgess
Typeset by John Nunn
Printed in Great Britain by The Cromwell Press, Trowbridge, Wilts.

10 9 8 7 6 5 4 3 2 1

Gambit Publications Ltd
Managing Director: GM Murray Chandler
Chess Director: GM John Nunn
Editorial Director: FM Graham Burgess
German Editor: WFM Petra Nunn

Contents

Chapter 3: The Pieces in Action

Part 2: Modern Games and Their Interpretation

Symbols

+	check
++	double check
#	checkmate
!!	brilliant move
!	good move
!?	interesting move
?!	dubious move
?	bad move
??	blunder
Ch	championship
Cht	team championship
Wch	world championship
Wcht	world team championship
Ech	European championship
Echt	European team championship
ECC	European Clubs Cup
Ct	candidates event
IZ	interzonal event
Z	zonal event
OL	olympiad
jr	junior event
wom	women's event
rpd	rapidplay game
tt	team tournament
corr.	correspondence game
1-0	the game ends in a win for White
½-½	the game ends in a draw
0-1	the game ends in a win for Black
(n)	nth match game
(D)	see next diagram

Dedication

To the Hummels: Paul, Carla, Patrick, and Christina, with love and appreciation

Acknowledgements

Thanks to: John Tomas for his insights; Eric Schiller for advice on technical issues; Jeremy Silman and John Donaldson for chess inspiration; and my editor Graham Burgess for help in every aspect of the book's preparation.

Preface

This book is a companion volume and continuation of my *Secrets of Modern Chess Strategy* (Gambit 1998). I will refer to that book often and use the acronym 'SOMCS' for that purpose. A premise of that book (one that I find almost self-evident) is that modern chess has undergone great changes both conceptually and philosophically since the time of the old masters including Nimzowitsch. The latter was, I fccl, a transitional figure who consolidated older theory and presented new ideas, some of which have survived to this day. My project in both books has been to identify and discuss the post-Nimzowitschian changes in chess middlegame theory. This involves an investigation of the nature of chess itself with an emphasis on experimentation involving an ever-widening set of ideas and positions which have gained general acceptance since his time.

As this book began to develop, I realized that it was beginning to resemble its predecessor in terms of its structuring, layout, and verbal discussions about theoretical issues. In other respects it was less like SOMCS than envisaged, both because I placed so much more emphasis on complete games and because I kept adding new material about concepts *not* discussed in the former volume. Thus the two books stand in a theory-to-practice relationship, but they also have a Volume 1 – Volume 2 connection, with the second volume filling in gaps in theory left by the first. I have also stressed recent games that reflect current practice and thought right up to the time of publication.

Before addressing structural and philosophical issues in the Introduction, I think that it might be useful here to give an explanatory overview of the contents of this book. Much as with SOMCS, it begins with a look backward emphasizing a couple of areas that have seen a constant but unpunctuated evolution over the years. As in most of this book, I have chosen to investigate topics that were relatively neglected in SOMCS. One such is the concept of the 'surrender of the centre', to which I devote a rather technical section describing its historical progress from the early part of the twentieth century to the present. Both that section and the next highlight the important relationship of space to the exchange of pieces, an area that has, I think, been inadequately addressed in the literature. Then the discussion moves forward in time to the extraordinary changes in the modern practice of and attitude towards development. To put bounds upon this immense topic, I concentrate upon recent ideas as well as methods of development in specific pawn-structures.

The centre has always been considered sacred territory with assumed primacy over other areas of the board. What if, after all of these years of investigating it, we would have to change or revise our most fundamental theories about the centre's nature? Surprisingly, that's exactly what's happening in a radical change that has accelerated dramatically even since the publication of SOMCS. In that work I cautiously discussed 'the new relationship of flank to centre'; but five years later I see that this considerably understates the case. We have experienced an explosion in the use of flank pawns in nearly every context and type of position, so much so that this must be considered the most revolutionary development of chess theory and practice in many decades. I have naturally devoted a lengthy section to this subject, but since that can only begin to touch upon the subject, examples appear throughout the book in many contexts, and of course in the games of Part 2.

Another subject that I skimped upon in SOMCS was the contemporary treatment of doubled pawns (as opposed to a history of conceptual changes in their use). That receives special attention, as does the ever-more-important subject of the positional pawn sacrifice. I touch upon other pawn issues such as majorities and minorities less extensively throughout various sections. One might note that pawn-chains are given considerable attention in the section on development, but not in the chapter on pawns itself.

The chapter on piece play initially deals with the controversial subject of knights developed to the edge of the board as well as elaborate knight manoeuvres. It includes a section on good and bad bishops in the context of their use as individual pieces, a topic I just touched upon in SOMCS. While the issue of two knights versus two bishops (minor-piece pairs) crops up repeatedly throughout the book, it was given extensive treatment in SOMCS, and I only added enough separate material here to give a taste of the subject. Exchange sacrifices pop up everywhere; they are played so routinely that they hardly seem a part of theory any more, but still have new and noteworthy aspects that may be seen throughout the book. I have included a section on the early development of the queen, another subject that is only lightly discussed by other sources.

The more general and/or abstract topics in SOMCS are incorporated into the text. Examples of prophylactic techniques, for example, appear throughout the book. Although philosophical issues appear in the Introduction, they are limited thereafter since the main body of the book stresses practice. In general, opening play receives a great deal of attention. There are two reasons for this. First, as has become a commonplace observation, opening theory now extends so far into the middlegame that it tends to determine the nature of the play that follows in terms of structure or piece placement or both. Thus the distinction between a study of middlegames and openings (never very clear anyway) fails to apply in many cases. Another motivation for talking about openings and early middlegames stems from the fact that anyone can pick individual middlegame examples and use them to say something like 'See? Capablanca was so classical in his thought' or to argue the contrary. But for openings and the pawn-structures which persist into the middlegame, we can clearly see overall trends, discuss the extent of their use in practice, and do statistical counts thereupon. Regarding the latter, I have compiled some statistics about the practices of leading players for various epochs. Assisted by Steve Solas's historical ratings research, I put together lists for the best players in four historical periods (with the number of such players in brackets):

a) before and including 1900 [12];
b) 1901-1935 [22];
c) 1936-1970 [32];
d) 1971-2002 [35], with a subcategory for 1985-2002 in one case.

Especially in the first few chapters, which tend to be more historically oriented, I have used statistics from these periods to try to identify trends. For the book as a whole this technique, inevitably inexact and subjective, has been kept to a minimum.

The games in Part 2 of this book are meant to unify the discussion and illustrate key concepts from both books. With luck, they will also provide an entertaining break from an ordered theoretical presentation. Selecting these games has been enjoyable and challenging. I have tried to avoid the temptation to include chaotic struggles that illustrate 6-10 modern strategic themes in one game, although such contests indeed exist. When too many 'counter-intuitive' moves are seen in a single contest, it is likely that the players employing them are doing so partly by accident! Good illustrations need a limited number of focal points, so the more typical game will involve three or fewer main themes. I have chosen a large majority of games from 1990 onwards, and within that time have tended to feature the play of leading grandmasters. Quite apart from the fact that they make fewer mistakes, top players tend to understand what they're doing! My notes are meant to be limited and non-obsessive. This is not a games collection. Others have authored such collections more skilfully and with greater depth than I have attempted here. The publishers of this book, for example, not too long ago put out both John Nunn's *Understanding Chess Move By Move* and Igor Stohl's *Instructive Modern Chess Masterpieces*, works involving more analytical detail than I have devoted to my Part 2 contests. I hope instead to have achieved a more casual presentation that focuses in upon conceptual issues and explains them in an accessible way.

Since the publication of SOMCS, I have been thinking about the times over which critical changes took place in the modernization of the game. Naturally all such changes assert themselves gradually and at no particular date. Nevertheless, I think that there have been three very softly bounded transitional periods since the mid-1930s. After an initial conflict between new and classical ideas, the creative experimenters of the 1940s broke through old barriers and by the early 1960s had established the pragmatic basis for modern play. This dramatic achievement was accomplished mostly in the old Soviet Union and was at first only partially absorbed into Western chess culture. Naturally there was no halt to the progression of chess thought in the late 1960s through to the early 1980s, including a steady growth in the use of positions and structures that were previously considered inferior on general principle; and the steady infusion of new dynamic ideas continued. But in my estimation the nature of that expansion changed as a sort of consolidation took place and new positional ideas began to appear. This emphasis was influenced by Petrosian's careful style, Fischer's technical proficiency, and Karpov's particular genius in less dynamic and (sometimes) more classical positions. Play in that era underwent a distinct evolution marked by a dramatic rise in the use of space-starved set-ups (with Western players fully contributing) and more subtle changes such as toleration for structural weaknesses (anathema to most earlier players, even the very best of them), an increase of purely prophylactic strategies, and a de-emphasis on rapid development and king safety.

Then, as Kasparov has pointed out, something very radical began to occur in the mid-1980s. An almost chaotic dynamism seemed to take over much of the game while the more orderly part was subject to extreme refinement and positional experimentation. This revolution has to do in great part with the rise of the so-called Information Age. We have seen the exponential increase and rapid dissemination of games and articles. The introduction of computers has had two major effects. First, the astonishing growth of information at players' disposal: portable laptops now carry hundreds of games by each opponent and thousands of examples of his or her favourite opening lines and middlegame structures. Then there has been what I feel is an even more significant change: that players on all levels are able to try out seemingly risky, paradoxical, and 'unprincipled' moves and strategies on a computer in order to confirm whether they are unsound, playable, or strong. Contemporary play has thus been marked by much greater openness towards both positional and attacking strategies that were previously considered anti-positional and/or unsound. Important contributions are thus not only multiplying at an accelerated pace but coming from players of all strengths.

Trying to make some sort of sense of this evolution is a daunting task. A book centred about practical play cannot begin to touch upon all of the relevant material. Every day in magazines, books, and on the Web, I would see interesting and worthwhile new games that were valid candidates for inclusion. We are experiencing so rich a time in chess that, in the end, choosing among such examples and even among topics seemed almost an arbitrary process. For the average reader, this means that you should be able to find the strategic themes described here in many if not most of the new games that come to your attention. I hope that this book will to help you to identify these and thus to understand the chess of our time.

John Watson
San Diego, California, 2003

Part 1: Theory and Practice Combine

Introduction and Philosophical Considerations

The goal of this book and its predecessor, *Secrets of Modern Chess Strategy* ('SOMCS'), is to describe modern chess and in particular the changes that the game has undergone over the years and is undergoing today. Right away it is important to stress that I have mainly concentrated on what players (especially masters) are *doing*, i.e., what strategies and ideas they are employing. To a lesser extent I am also concerned with what players are actually thinking when they employ these strategies. Therefore, although this Introduction deals mostly with philosophical issues, the heart of both books resides in the games and examples presented and not in generalities.

I must also stress that in this work I am not describing, much less promoting, any method of teaching. The book makes no claims about how the beginner should learn, nor how the 1200 player or 2200 player should improve. That clearly involves factors other than the ways in which advanced players think. So one can form virtually any kind of pedagogical theory based upon this work; but, since I emphasize ambiguities rather than certainties, I doubt that most teachers will find it more than partially applicable.

With those disclaimers, let me gingerly touch upon some philosophical matters. In SOMCS I introduced the phrase 'rule independence', which was meant to describe the attitude of modern players towards decision-making, and in particular with respect to certain topics in the book. I came up with that expression, an admittedly inexact phrase, as an abstract characterization intended to bring the reader some sense of unity with regard to *some* modern ideas and practices. Of course, as an abstraction it lacks essential force and is fairly meaningless without scores of specific examples and explanations, as given in SOMCS and now in this book. A similar case arises when a chess author promotes the virtues of 'harmonious play' or 'harmonious interaction of the pieces', as many middlegame writers have done. This is hardly useful by itself; I suspect that if you asked even beginners whether they thought that harmonious play was desirable, they would probably agree that it was. The author's task in that case would be to provide many examples of harmonious (and not so harmonious) play, describing what that means in each situation with as much detail as possible. In a similar fashion, I have discussed the ascendance of concrete thinking in modern chess, as opposed to reliance upon general considerations, by giving large numbers of annotated examples. Those examples with their corresponding explanations are the essence of the book, regardless of whether they fit into a general model. However, since the philosophical side of SOMCS attracted so much attention, I will try to expand upon and clarify a few points before getting to the core of the material.

Probably the most important distinction that I should make is between (a) the belief that valid rules exist and (b) the idea that there are specific generalities that are losing relevance in today's game because players don't think in terms of them. The former proposal is not of much interest because it is so vague and subject to various interpretations of the word 'rule'. But I have tried to show evidence for the latter claim, and to make the related point that the *movement* in modern chess is away from abstract theoretical thinking and towards a more open and realistic view of the board. To what extent that is true can be seen best by examining actual practice. I would suggest that when one considers the many specific changes that modern chess has undergone, a handy way to think about some of them would be in terms of the limiting influence that certain general and specific assumptions have had on players' thinking. Of course I am only describing an evolution of thought, not saying that older generations played largely by rules or that modern ones have abandoned them outright. But over time, the changes have been considerable indeed. I think that most observers will agree that there has been an exponential increase in positions and ideas that are now deemed at least satisfactory but were once (sometimes not even that long ago) considered laughable, ugly, and/or unthinkable. This and other evidence indicates to me that players are much more tolerant of ideas that used to be rejected 'on principle'. Such openness has been increasing throughout the last century; but recently it has accelerated, in part due to the availability of computer analysis. The latter resource has freed players to try out almost any absurd-looking set of moves in the hope of finding something effective. What continually surprises those of us who grew up thinking in terms of classical principles is how often those absurd-looking moves turn out to be strong! Similarly, one marvels at how much players can 'get away with' in terms of neglected development, voluntary weaknesses, exposed kings, casual sacrifices of pawns and exchanges, and so many more things that might seem counter-intuitive. It's true that strong young players, raised in a more open era, seem to take much of this in their stride. They are, in my observation, less weighed down by philosophical worries than the rest of us.

All this relates to the relationship between verbal explanations of play and actual master thought. My own view is that top players operate mainly from a basis of pattern recognition and calculation, and would have a very difficult time explaining in words why they made a complicated decision except by using some sort of radical simplification. By contrast, they frequently do provide a detailed explanation for a move by demonstrating variations, for example, in a post-mortem analysis. But in such an analysis, how can so much information be gleaned from a limited number of moves? Clearly there exists a large pool of shared information between any set of analysts involving chess patterns and associated assessments that are taken for granted by all parties. Referring to a study by the University of Constance that grandmasters have access to something like 100,000 stored patterns, Grandmaster Jonathan Rowson says: "In my view it's the brain that makes the patterns on the basis of experience, so all the grandmaster does is expose himself to chess information and lets the brain rack it up in its own mysterious way." This corresponds with the study's finding that in complex positions, grandmasters tend to rely on those parts of the brain that are used for long-term memory, whereas less experienced players work harder at 'encoding and analysing information'. Rowson continues "Moreover, we should not ignore the striking empirical fact that the vast majority of grandmasters started playing when they were quite young and continued to do so intensely until they became grandmasters. Thus they exposed themselves to chess when their brains still had a lot of 'plasticity' and the chess patterns could be near optimally organized. That said, all of our brain mechanisms are highly complicated and the question 'why did I play that move?' often remains unanswered, even for grandmasters."

Thus we have a sort of chess language that provides the detail and subtlety needed to make an over-the-board decision. It also provides the basis for intuitive judgements, which are informed by experience and verified by calculation. As Sosonko said: "Behind the word 'intuition' lies our subconscious experience or knowledge of games and ideas, either our own or those of others." One way of expressing this is that the master sees before he says, i.e., intuition and analysis precede words. For an example of this that has nothing to do with rules as such, take a standard King's Indian Defence, Pirc Defence, or Dragon Sicilian. These all involve a kingside fianchetto with ...g6 and ...♗g7. Now White often lines up his queen and bishop with ♕d2 and ♗e3; in that case playing ♗h6 to exchange bishops on g7 can be good for any number of general reasons, e.g. because Black has subsequent weakness on his dark squares, because White's centre will be protected in the case of an ...exd4 exchange, or because White's potential gain of space after d5 will be more effective. But the move ♗h6 may equally be bad, e.g., if it allows Black to exchange off his only bad piece and block the game, or if it diverts White's queen from the action, or if it helps Black to play ...c5 and attack a weakened centre. The reality is that such a decision tends to be very subtle, ultimately depending upon a great number of other less obvious factors; e.g., how quickly Black can play ...b5, whether a well-timed ...exd4 followed by ...c5 or ...♖e8 has tactical advantages, whether White's a3 will slow the attack or provide a target, what reorganizations of pieces are available to both sides, and so forth. From many years of analysing with top players, I believe that with the aid of calculation they assess this decision more or less instinctively based upon experience and judgement, without resorting to verbal reasoning. Later, the move can be explained to an audience using simplified generalities. But going the other way, from words to move, is extremely unlikely to produce the right decision. And it is particularly hard to act upon raw concepts. For example, one might trade off time or development to secure some other positional advantage (an outpost, doubled pawn for the opponent). But one question of many is: how *much* time/development can I give up before, e.g., a counterattack becomes a problem? This is solved by some combination of analysis and judgement, and very seldom by abstract reasoning.

People commonly interpret what I've said in terms of rules and exceptions, i.e., modern players know the rules and have discovered the exceptions. Or that a player should in fact learn the rules first and then learn their exceptions. But that's not what I'm saying at all. The point is not whether there are X exceptions to every Y instances in which the rule is true. Naturally

factors like space, outposts, and 'better' minor pieces will always correlate, however mildly, to winning percentage. Rather, I am asking:

a) Does a master *think* in terms of a given rule (and exception) at all?

b) Is it even useful to think in those terms when confronted with a specific position?

Granted, there are cases in which the simplest way to make my argument (and I have occasionally done so) is to point out that there are so many exceptions to a particular traditional rule that it becomes meaningless, and so by implication the modern player must not be using it. An extreme case is one examined in Chapters 1 and 2, where I'm not sure whether the rule 'The player with more space should avoid exchanges (and vice-versa)' is true even 50% of the time! But let's say that figure were 60% or 70%: it would still be terribly limiting to be thinking about a prospective exchange in terms of such a rule. Even when the rule expresses a situation that is true in many more cases than not (e.g., 'a knight on the rim is grim'), is it constructive to think in those terms? Or is it better to examine the concrete situation in all of its subtleties, without prejudice, using calculation and pattern recognition as tools? Which does the strong player do? In my observation and from many conversations and analysis with them, grandmasters don't think much in terms of rules and exceptions at all. Indeed, in some cases where they have done so, some quite playable positions have escaped deserved consideration because of they 'looked' bad on general principle. Increasingly, that attitude is being replaced by a pragmatic analytical approach.

Other models have been floated to deal with these issues. One such is the idea that rules are valid, 'other things being equal'. I won't go into detail here, but the question in practice is whether anyone can decide by explicit means to what extent other factors in a typical middlegame are 'equal'. Since the diverse considerations are interdependent and also time-dependent, and since they can be so unbelievably complex, the determination of what weight to give one abstract rule or another seems to me impossible in almost all cases. Then there is the idea of assessing and utilizing explicitly identifiable imbalances. But juggling and weighing the many and often subtle imbalances (and *anticipated* new imbalances) which are themselves interdependent, all to assess a particular move somehow, is just as complicated as trying to juggle and weigh the influence of rules and generalities. The reality is that a strong player is using previous experience and analysis to attend to the specific details of a unique position and to assess its implicit imbalances on some subverbal level. The same basic argument applies to the theory that the master is thinking in terms of trading advantages. Can we come up with realistic examples of how that might be done? I just don't find any of these models convincing as a reflection of actual thought over the board by even moderately advanced players.

Not surprisingly, the idea of playing according to concrete analysis of the position on the board instead of by rules and principles is not new. In SOMCS, I twice quoted Richard Réti from *Modern Ideas in Chess*, written in the early 1920s, with respect to the ineffectual application of 'so-called' rules to a given position. Without doing so again, I would bring the last sentence of his exposition to the reader's attention: "The source of the greatest errors is to be found in those moves that are made merely according to rule and not based on the individual plan or thought of the player."

Going even further back we have this wonderful quote from Mikhail Chigorin, which was brought to my attention by Macon Shibut: "I do not consider myself belonging to this or that 'school'; I am guided not by abstract theoretical considerations on the comparative strength of pieces, etc., but only the data as it appears to me in this or that position of the game, which serves as an object of detailed and possibly precise analysis. Each of my moves presents itself as a feasible inference from a series of variations in which theoretical 'principles of play' can have only a very limited significance. ... The ability to combine skilfully, the capacity to find in each given position the most purposeful move, soon leading to the execution of a well-conceived plan, is higher than any principle, or more correct to say, is the only principle in the game of chess which lends itself to precise definition."

That's about as accurate a description as can be wished for of the philosophy of the modern analytical school!

Richard Forster provides a third example. In a fascinating article about Simon Alapin, Forster presents him as 'more modern than the hypermoderns': "Alapin's general attitude is the same throughout: fewer words, but more variations! Whereas Tarrasch, according to Nimzowitsch, presents 'classical' principles, and Nimzowitsch tries to refute them by his 'modern' principles, Alapin time and again asks for concrete moves. He shows how all principles can have only relative validity and are even often contradictory... his refusal of a theoretical battle in terms of abstract principles alone, and his insistence on always examining the position at hand and giving concrete variations, makes him the most progressive of the trio ... Alapin was in fact the one closest to the modern point of view, which values nothing except practical examples and practical success."

Of course, such quotes have little to do with the actual practice of chess at these players' respective times. That can only be assessed by examining games and their common characteristics. Réti, for example, lived in pre-modern times and I don't believe that the philosophy expressed by him above had more than limited influence on his contemporaries; nor did he himself realize how thoroughly the invested intellectual tradition in chess would be changed as the years went along. His own play had only certain modern characteristics and I strongly suspect from his notes to games that he would have rejected a great deal of what we take for granted today. These considerations naturally also apply to the two earlier players. Alapin's play is impressively independent but not always modern in the sense that I have outlined in this book. At any rate, his influence on the chess of his era is not apparent. As for Chigorin, he was a very creative player, but his games show little evidence of a modern attitude towards development, flank pawn advances, exchange sacrifices, pawn-chains, backward pawns or any number of other prominent features of modern chess. He was also, as pointed out in SOMCS, wedded to a dogmatic view of knight play. Interestingly, he has been called an adherent of the Classical School and a disciple of Steinitz (e.g., by Romanovsky), but also the first 'computer player' (Spassky). Ultimately we must go by the games and to a lesser extent annotations and articles to form our own judgements about such things.

It's not difficult to see that individual statements of a philosophy, while they *could* be indicative of changing attitudes in general, are not necessarily so. Rather, ideas (and freedom from the grip of ideas) tend to work their way into the game slowly, traditionally by a player's observation or even imitation of others' new moves and strategies in the same or similar situations. Occasionally there is a wild and unforeseen breakthrough. But in either case, the new strategies eventually become second nature, so that nearly all strong players and not just a few innovators will partake of this kind of play. Thus I have referred to chess ideas as being in the 'everyday consciousness' of players. With regard to the masters quoted above, this book's description of how chess is actually played today simply doesn't apply to the times in which they lived. And of late, while the traditional process of assimilation is very much alive, it is also being bypassed and accelerated. This is due both to the increasingly pragmatic attitude towards the game and to the fact that players of all ratings have a greatly enhanced ability to experiment due to the availability of powerful chess engines.

Enough. There is more that I could say about these esoteric topics, but in the final analysis, one can only assess such matters on the basis of practice. It's therefore time to enter into the world of modern chess strategy in action.

1 Broader Issues and Their Evolution

1.1 Surrender of the Centre

The phrase 'surrender of the centre' usually refers to the classical situation after 1 e4 e5, in which White plays d4 and Black plays ...exd4 rather than trying to protect his e5-pawn. This arises, for example, in Philidor's Defence after 1 e4 e5 2 ♘f3 d6 3 d4 exd4, and in the Ruy Lopez after 1 e4 e5 2 ♘f3 ♘c6 3 ♗b5 ♘f6 4 0-0 d6 5 d4 ♗d7 6 ♘c3 exd4, among other sequences. Surrender of the centre can also occur when there are pawns on d4 and d5, such that after White's move e4, Black plays ...dxe4 rather than trying to shore up his centre. Nimzowitsch approved of this strategy in the French Defence line 1 e4 e6 2 d4 d5 3 ♘c3 dxe4; and the opening that perhaps most successfully employs the surrender of the centre is the Caro-Kann Defence: 1 e4 c6 2 d4 d5 3 ♘c3 dxe4. In fact, one could argue that the very existence of this last venerable line means that no universal condemnation of central surrender can be made.

Surrender of the centre is closely connected to the topic of space. The side that surrenders the centre gives his opponent influence over five ranks, i.e., he controls only three ranks securely, his opponent controls four, and his own fourth rank is disputed territory. For convenience, let's call the side that surrenders the centre 'Black' (as is the case in the above examples). In which cases is this justified? How should Black proceed? Which side benefits from exchanges? These issues are treated differently in modern chess from the way they were in classical times. Most significantly, the philosophy of when and when not to exchange pieces has changed, and the decision to cede territory to White depends more upon the immediacy of central counterplay.

Surrender in the Double e-Pawn Openings

Let's begin with examples of double e-pawn lines involving ...exd4 that were relatively more popular in the 19th and early 20th centuries: 3...exd4 in the Philidor Defence (1 e4 e5 2 ♘f3 d6 3 d4) and an early ...exd4 in the Ruy Lopez (1 e4 e5 2 ♘f3 ♘c6 3 ♗b5 with a later d4). To identify some trends, I will use databases of the top players who were at their best for various epochs, as described in the Preface. The Philidor Defence was of course more popular in earlier times. Among top players, it was used about twice as often in the 19th century as in 1901-1935, and about 8 times as often as in later years (it has a small but steady following today, with even top players dabbling occasionally).

1 e4 e5 2 ♘f3 d6 3 d4 *(D)*

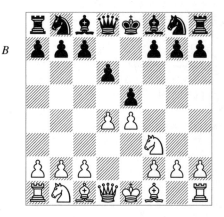

Black now faces a fundamental choice about whether to surrender the centre with 3...exd4

(or its transpositional equivalent 3...♘f6 4 ♘c3 exd4) or to support the e5-pawn by, for example, 3...♘f6 (3...♘d7 4 ♗c4 ♗e7 seeks to transpose via 5 ♘c3 ♘gf6, but allows an arguably more effective 5 dxe5) 4 ♘c3 (4 dxe5 ♘xe4 is theoretically sound for Black) 4...♘bd7, followed by ...♗e7 and ...0-0.

Black originally played 3...exd4 or 3...♘f6 4 ♘c3 exd4 with considerable frequency (this accounted for almost half of the Philidors among top players in the 19th century), aiming for the following type of position:

3...exd4 4 ♘xd4 ♘f6 5 ♘c3 ♗e7 6 ♗c4

This move probably presents Black with the most difficulty, although 6 ♗f4 is also popular. After 6 ♗e2 0-0 7 0-0 ♖e8, Black is cramped but has play against White's e-pawn and prospects for a timely ...d5.

6...0-0 7 0-0 *(D)*

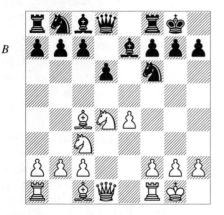

A close look at theory suggests that White keeps a moderate but definite advantage here; and indeed, his results have been good. On his Philidor Defence CD, Bangiev shows that Black fails to equalize after the active attempts 7...a6 and 7...c6, and he has difficulties with lack of a target in a line like 7...♖e8 8 ♖e1 ♗f8 9 a3 (or 9 ♗g5 c6 10 a3) 9...♘bd7 10 ♗a2! ♘c5 11 f3. One should compare such positions with those after ...exd4 in the Ruy Lopez, analysed in some detail below. There is nothing inevitable about such an assessment, and it may yet be that Black will find some way to get satisfactory play. In general, however, one can see why this kind of set-up has become less popular for Black.

It's important that specifics work in addition to the general logic. In this case, White may

sometimes have avoided the above move-order so as to side-step Black's attempt to destroy the centre by 7...♘xe4 8 ♘xe4 d5; but in that case 9 ♗d3 dxe4 10 ♗xe4 retains the freer play; e.g., 10...♗f6 11 c3 ♘d7 12 ♗f4 ♘b6?! 13 ♕c2 g6 14 ♖ad1 ♕e7 15 ♖fe1 gave White a large advantage in Lautier-I.Sokolov, Cap d'Agde rpd 1996. I think that one will find that with accurate play by White in the ...exd4 line with ...♘f6 and ...♗e7, Black remains somewhat cramped in a perhaps acceptable position, but one that would attract few top players.

Much later, in the 1970s and even up to the early 1990s, some very high-ranked players as Black played 3...exd4 4 ♘xd4 g6, to post the bishop on a more active square than e7 and gain King's Indian-like pressure on the dark squares. That has the drawback of leaving White's centre intact and allowing an attack based upon g4, h4-h5. Yet Black achieves concrete attacking chances on the queenside. This variation was finally worked out in some detail by means of pretty games, such as the following:

Hennigan – Westerinen
Gausdal 1995

1 e4 e5 2 ♘f3 d6 3 d4 exd4 4 ♘xd4 g6 5 ♘c3 ♗g7 6 ♗e3 ♘f6 7 ♕d2 0-0 8 f3 ♘c6 9 g4 ♗e6 10 0-0-0 *(D)*

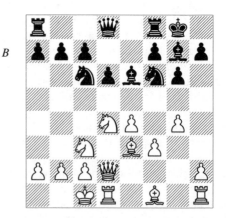

There are several move-orders that reach this position. Black still stands worse in the centre, and his only freeing move, 10...d5, will fall short after 11 g5 ♘h5 12 ♘xe6 fxe6 13 exd5 exd5 14 ♘xd5. So he exchanges and then launches a dynamic queenside attack, at the cost of leaving both the d5-square and the d6-pawn weak:

10...♘xd4 11 ♗xd4 c5 12 ♗e3 ♕a5 13 ♗h6 ♗xh6 14 ♕xh6

The exchanges have helped the side with more space, which is a theme of our discussion.

14...♗xa2

Alternatively, 14...b5!? 15 ♗xb5 ♖ab8 16 a4 a6 17 ♖xd6! axb5 18 e5 ♘xg4 19 fxg4 ♕b4 has been tested in no fewer than three games involving GMs, all leading to distinct advantages for White. One never knows what may be found, but this very concrete discovery accounted for the decline of the ...g6 plan to this day.

15 h4 ♗e6 16 h5 ♕c7

Black can't wait around with moves like 16...♖ae8? due to 17 hxg6 fxg6 18 g5 ♘h5 19 ♖xh5! gxh5 20 g6 ♕c7 21 ♖xd6!, etc.

17 ♘b5 ♕e7 18 ♘xd6 ♘d7 19 f4! ♗xg4 20 ♗c4! ♔h8 21 ♘xf7+ ♖xf7 22 ♗xf7 gxh5 23 ♗xh5

23 ♖xd7! ♗xd7 24 ♕xh5 ♕xe4 25 ♕h6 is even better.

23...♗xd1 24 ♖xd1 ♕f6 25 ♕xf6+ ♘xf6 26 ♗f3

White has an easily winning position. Eventually, losses like this discouraged most strong players from 4...g6.

An interesting example of forced surrender of the centre arises in the Scotch Game: 1 e4 e5 2 ♘f3 ♘c6 3 d4 exd4 4 ♘xd4. The difference between this and the Philidor Defence is that Black hasn't hemmed in his pieces with ...d6 and is able to play dynamically via 4...♘f6 or 4...♗c5. Peter Wells, who wrote a book on the Scotch, says "... it is no coincidence that most of Black's main choices in the Scotch are based on a strategy of disruption. Quite simply, other things being equal, the basic 'Scotch centre', a white pawn on e4 vs a black pawn on d6, constitutes a spatial plus for White which the defender wisely tries to avoid." The game he gives, Navara-Kallio, Leon Echt 2001, arose from a Pirc Defence but transposes to our Philidor 4...g6 line and provides another nice example: 1 e4 d6 2 d4 ♘f6 3 ♘c3 g6 4 ♗e3 ♗g7 5 ♕d2 ♘c6 6 f3 e5 7 ♘ge2 0-0 8 0-0-0 exd4 9 ♘xd4 (according to Wells, this is '± at least!') 9...♖e8 10 g4! ♗d7 11 h4 ♘e5 12 ♗e2 h5 13 gxh5! ♘xh5 14 ♗g5 f6 15 ♗e3 a6 16 ♖hg1 c5 17

♘b3 c4 18 ♘d4 b5 19 f4 b4 20 fxe5 bxc3 21 ♕xc3 fxe5 22 ♖xg6! exd4 23 ♗xd4 ♗f5 24 exf5 ♘f4 25 ♗xc4+ 1-0.

So it shouldn't surprise one that the surrender of the centre by 3...exd4 has become less appealing for most masters. As a practical matter, one notes that the ...exd4 lines have historically scored 61%-39% in White's favour (with equal opposition). Among today's stronger players, the 'closed' variation with ...♘bd7, ...♗e7, ...0-0 (i.e., without ...exd4) is the most popular choice in the Philidor, and among all players it scores about as well as any mainstream black defence. Black is undoubtedly slightly worse, but his position is very flexible and he can play a variety of plans in the centre or on the queenside. A typical example of the contemporary strategy is:

Vehi Bach – Cifuentes
Platja d'Aro 1994

1 e4 e5 2 ♘f3 d6 3 d4 ♘f6 4 ♘c3 ♘bd7 5 ♗c4 ♗e7 6 0-0 0-0 7 ♖e1 c6 8 a4 ♕c7 9 h3 b6 10 ♗g5 a6 11 ♕e2 ♗b7 (D)

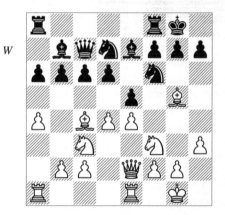

Now Black is ready to play ...b5, and ...d5 or ...♖fe8 and ...exd4 have to be watched for as well. So the game continued:

12 dxe5 ♘xe5 13 ♘xe5 dxe5 14 ♖ad1 b5 15 ♗b3 h6 16 ♗h4 ♖ad8 17 axb5 axb5

Black has full equality, since he controls key central points and can re-route by ...♗c8 when necessary. There are very many games with the same or a similar black set-up.

Thus we can see a theoretical and practical movement away from the ...exd4 strategy in the

Philidor Defence. In the meantime, top-level practice has shown an increased preference for semi-closed positions that do not surrender the centre (even after moves like ...c6, ...♕c7, and ...♖e8). This reflects a modern willingness to accept less space and fewer open lines in return for flexibility and more potential dynamic chances. But it's also a purely pragmatic matter. Note that the 3...exd4 4 ♘xd4 g6 plan above was also revived for the sake of dynamic attacking chances. Had it succeeded in generating sufficient counterplay, no one would be worried about the hypothetical disadvantage of surrendering the centre. As it turns out, the 4...g6 line seems to have narrowly failed in this precise form, and for concrete reasons.

To be sure, this very brief overview of Philidor's Defence reveals a trend in a rather obscure opening; but a similar and more pronounced trend can be seen in the most important of double e-pawn openings: the Ruy Lopez (a.k.a. Spanish Game) with 1 e4 e5 2 ♘f3 ♘c6 3 ♗b5. Here the movement away from surrendering the centre in modern practice shares the stage with other elements, including the reduced inclination to exchange pieces. In SOMCS, I made the remark that "the rule which states that 'a player with more space should avoid exchanges' is so riddled with exceptions as to have lost its usefulness." As with so many guidelines, I feel that this one is position-specific, as is its complement: a player with *less* space should strive to exchange pieces. Recognizing in which positions one wants to exchange pieces, and which ones to exchange, is a matter of knowledge and experience and is too subtle a decision to be assisted by such general advice. Nevertheless, one sees this rule quoted consistently in annotations by grandmasters even today, and of course in books on theory. While stated as a general principle, it is frequently conjoined with the historical development of 1 e4 e5 and 1 d4 d5 openings. Therefore it is useful to examine the issue in the context of those openings.

To examine the connection between space and the surrender of the centre, let's look at a couple of variations that were contested in the latter part of the 19th century through to 1930. The Ruy Lopez with an early surrender of the centre was played by just about all of the leading players of that time period, including Steinitz, Blackburne, Capablanca, Lasker, Alekhine, Bogoljubow, Nimzowitsch, Réti, Marshall and many others. To illustrate one line, I will follow one of the most famous games of chess history:

Tarrasch – Em. Lasker
Düsseldorf/Munich Wch (4) 1908

I examine this game at length in order to structure the issues involved in the typical early middlegame of the Ruy Lopez ...exd4 lines. Thus the many games in the notes are just as important as the main game. By using them, I hope to give a good indication of why the philosophy behind this mode of playing in these particular positions has proven to be a dubious one:

1 e4 e5 2 ♘f3 ♘c6 3 ♗b5 d6

Ignoring a few subtleties of move-order, 3...♘f6 4 0-0 d6 5 d4 ♗d7 transposes. That was the actual move-order of Tarrasch-Lasker. Instead, 3...♘f6 4 0-0 ♗e7 5 ♖e1 d6 6 ♗xc6+ bxc6 7 d4 exd4 8 ♘xd4 ♗d7, another example of the ...exd4 structure, resembles various examples below. Note that this is a conceptual overview and not a theoretical one.

4 d4 ♗d7

Of course, 4...exd4 and other variations with an early ...exd4 were also played at the time.

5 ♘c3 ♘f6

The characteristic drawbacks of exchanging via 5...♘ge7 and 6...♘xd4 were shown in Em.Lasker-Steinitz, New York Wch (1) 1894: 5...♘ge7 6 ♗c4 ♘xd4 7 ♘xd4 exd4 8 ♕xd4 ♘c6 9 ♕e3 (this position was reached three times in games between Lasker {White} and Steinitz in their 1894 match; White has more space and freer development, whereas Black's exchange hasn't helped to free his game; Lasker scored 2½ points) 9...♘e5 10 ♗b3 c6 (the alternative 10...♗e6 11 f4 ♘c4 12 ♕g3 didn't help much in their next encounter) 11 ♕g3 ♘g6 12 h4 ♗e6 (Black seeks simplification and in any case White's h5 cannot be met, since 12...h5 13 ♗g5 ♕c7 14 0-0-0 looks awful for Black) 13 ♗xe6 fxe6 (D).

14 ♗g5 (14 h5! really shows how cramped Black is; for example, 14...♘e5 15 f4 ♘d7 16 ♗e3 with a variety of ideas available such as 0-0-0, ♕h3, and ♘e2-d4, or perhaps simply

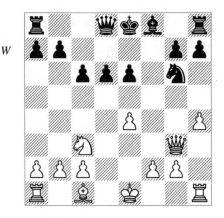

W

罝d1 and 奠d4) 14...奠e7 15 0-0-0!? (and here 15 h5 奠xg5 16 hxg6 h6 17 f4 奠e7 18 0-0-0 would tie Black down) 15...c5! (now things aren't quite as clear, because Black would like to occupy f4; hence White's next moves) 16 奠e3!? 0-0 (16...奠xh4 17 豐g4 is very hard to meet, since 18 g3 and 19 豐xg6+! is threatened) 17 ②e2 罝f7!? (perhaps Black should try 17...奠xh4 18 豐h3 豐c8 19 豐h2! 豐g4 with a messy position) 18 h5 ②f4 19 奠xf4 exf4, and now 20 豐d3 followed by ②d4 would maintain the advantage. As the game went, Black equalized but then played too passively and lost.

6 0-0

Tarrasch played and strongly advocated the white side of all positions involving ...exd4, almost never taking the black side. In *The Game of Chess*, he suggested 6 奠xc6 奠xc6 7 豐d3 exd4 8 ②xd4 *(D)* with the comment "White's position is appreciably better".

B

In SOMCS, we saw from Kasparov's notes to Nimzowitsch-Capablanca, St Petersburg 1914

that the highly desirable active move 8...g6? is dubious in view of 9 奠g5! (9 ②xc6 bxc6 10 豐a6 豐d7 11 豐b7 was played, and should have led to an advantage for White, albeit with difficulties) 9...奠g7 10 0-0-0 h6 (10...0-0? loses to 11 ②xc6 bxc6 12 e5) 11 奠h4 0-0 12 f4 罝e8 13 ②xc6 bxc6 14 e5 and White wins. Instead, Lasker in his 'Manual' suggested that 8...奠d7 was equal, giving 9 h3 奠e7 10 奠e3 0-0. However, White can get some advantage by several means, including the plan of b3 and 奠b2 as shown in the note to 7 罝e1.

Tarrasch was ultimately vindicated in his distrust of the ...exd4 lines, and in this same 1908 world championship match, he again demonstrated his prescience by twice playing (as Black) the modern 'closed' concept with 3 奠b5 a6 4 奠a4 ②f6 5 0-0 奠e7 6 罝e1 b5 7 奠b3 d6 followed by ...②a5 and ...c5. One could say that Tarrasch was the most clear-headed about the theory of these Ruy Lopez positions; but his match loss to Lasker obscured that reality. Was Tarrasch's dogmatic stance against the surrender of the centre thus an example of the triumph of general principles? Not at all. What did prove true is that the surrender of the centre was eventually shown to be unjustified (or at least too great a disadvantage to cope with in practice) in some very specific positions. But one cannot say this in general; as we shall see, a correct assessment requires the same case-by-case determination that applies with respect to any question about space, development, and central control.

6...奠e7

After 6...exd4 7 ②xd4 奠e7, 8 罝e1 transposes to the game, but White has an alternate plan that also illustrates his command of space and willingness to exchange pieces: 8 奠xc6 bxc6 9 b3 0-0 10 奠b2 罝e8 11 h3 (versus ...②g4) 11...奠f8 12 罝e1 *(D)* (12 豐f3 is also possible, but the text-move prevents 12...d5? due to 13 e5).

12...c5!? (trying to free his pieces by hook or by crook) 13 ②f3 奠c6 14 e5!? (clever, but 14 豐d3! would keep a solid grip on the position; the move e5 can then be prepared by 罝ad1 and perhaps 豐c4) 14...奠xf3 (after 14...②d7!, 15 ②e4 ②xe5 16 ②xe5 dxe5 17 豐g4 was probably Réti's intent, with ideas of 罝ad1 and perhaps ②g3-f5 or f4, but this is speculative) 15

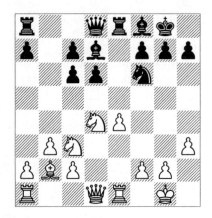

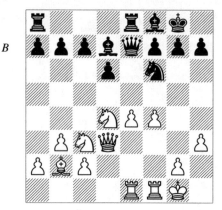

♕xf3 dxe5 (15...♖xe5 16 ♖xe5 dxe5 17 ♖d1
♗d6 18 ♘b5 with a slight advantage, according
to analysis given on ChessBase's Mega Database) 16 ♖ad1 ♗d6 17 ♘d5! ♘d7 (17...♘xd5
18 ♕xd5 ♕f6 19 f4! ♕xf4 20 ♖f1 ♕e3+ 21
♔h1 ♖f8 22 ♖d3 with an attack – this is also
from Mega Database) 18 c4 f6 (18...♖e6 19
♘xc7!) 19 ♘xc7! ♕xc7 20 ♕d5+ ♔f8 21
♕xd6+ ♕xd6 22 ♖xd6 ♗e7 23 ♖d5 (the bishop
is better than the knight, c5 is weak, and White's
rooks are more active) 23...g5 (versus f4) 24 g3
♖g8 25 ♖ed1 (25 ♔f1! is also strong) 25...♖gd8
26 f4 gxf4 27 gxf4 exf4 28 ♔f2 ♔e8 29 ♔f3
♔e7 30 ♔xf4 ♔e6 31 ♖d6+ ♔e7 32 ♔f5 1-0
Réti-Szekely, Debrecen 1913.

If fact, theory is not so completely one-sided
about some of these positions. The problem was
that even though Black found fully adequate
counterplay in several lines, White was always
able to avoid those with the proper move-orders.

7 ♖e1

The surrender of the centre after 7 ♗xc6
♗xc6 8 ♕d3 exd4 9 ♘xd4 (intending ♘f5)
looked very good for White in Pillsbury-Von
Bardeleben, Munich 1900: 9...♗d7 10 b3 (or
10 ♘f5!?) 10...0-0 11 ♗b2 ♖e8 (Steinitz also
lost to Pillsbury in a game with 11...c6 12
♖ad1) 12 ♖ae1 ♗f8 13 f4 ♕e7 14 h3 *(D)*.

14...c5 (without ...d5 and facing suffocation,
Black often feels that he has to resort to this
move) 15 ♘f3 ♗c6 16 ♘d5 ♗xd5 17 exd5 ♕d7
(17...♕d8? 18 ♖xe8 ♘xe8 19 ♘g5 g6 20 ♘xf7!
♔xf7 21 f5 is too strong) 18 ♗xf6 gxf6 19 ♘h4
and apart from Black's weaknesses, White's
knight dominates Black's bad bishop, and Pillsbury won shortly.

7...exd4 8 ♘xd4 ♘xd4

As was so common at the time in this line,
Black initiates a double exchange, supposedly
to neutralize White's space advantage.

9 ♕xd4

9 ♗xd7+ is straightforward, not losing time
with the c3-knight. Then 9...♕xd7?! (9...♘xd7!
is better, according to Réti, since Black cannot
enforce ...d5 anyway, and 10 ♕xd4 0-0, and if
11 b3?!, 11...♗f6 gives Black active pieces for
once) 10 ♕xd4 0-0 11 b3, when ♗b2, ♖ad1,
etc., led to a straightforward advantage for
White in Tarrasch-Schlechter, Leipzig 1894.

9...♗xb5 10 ♘xb5 *(D)*

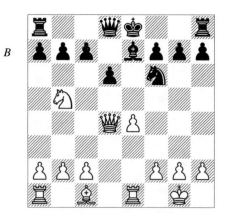

A test of Black's opening concept. He has
succeeded in exchanging two sets of minor
pieces and diverted White's knight, which will
take time to re-route. Surely Black is therefore a
step ahead of the variations cited above, but
will it lead to further simplification and equality? Réti considers the various treatments that
White gave this position to be indicative of the
evolving styles of his day.

10...0-0

Capablanca-Thomas, Hastings 1919 was an even more extreme version of the 'exchange pieces while cramped' theory: 10...a6 (this prevents Capablanca's ♕c3 and ♘d4 manoeuvre of the next note) 11 ♘c3 0-0 12 ♗g5 (12 b3! is a good alternative, as we have seen in similar positions) 12...♘d7!? (a third exchange of minor-piece pairs! 12...♖e8 or 12...h6 13 ♗h4 ♖e8 is more in line with Lasker's treatment) 13 ♗xe7 ♕xe7 14 ♘d5 ♕d8 15 ♖e3 (initiating a kingside attack) 15...♘e5 (something such as 15...♘c5 intending ...♘e6 was probably called for, but White would still have a large advantage in space and activity) 16 ♖g3 f6 (16...♘g6 17 f4 c6 18 ♘e3 isn't any better) 17 f4 ♘c6 18 ♕c3 *(D)*.

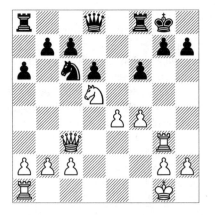

18...♖f7 19 f5 (19 ♖d1 leaves Black hard pressed for a move, but Capablanca wants to post a knight on e6) 19...♕f8 20 ♕b3 ♔h8 21 ♘f4 ♘e5 (21...♕d8? loses to 22 ♘g6+! hxg6 23 fxg6) 22 ♕xb7 ♖b8 23 ♕xa6 ♖xb2 24 ♖b3 (24 ♘e6 and ♖c3 is easier) 24...♖xc2 25 ♖ab1 h6? *(D)*.

The rest of this game is fun because of the famous tactical fiasco at the end. White is of course winning whatever Black plays. 26 ♘g6+ ♘xg6 27 fxg6 ♖e7 28 ♖b8 ♖e8 (Capablanca's idea was 28...♖c1+ 29 ♔f2! ♖c2+ 30 ♔e3 ♖c3+ 31 ♔d2 and White wins) 29 ♕a8??, and here Black resigned! In fact, instead of 29 ♕a8??, simply 29 ♖xe8 ♕xe8 30 ♕a4! would exploit the back rank and pick up the c2-rook, and 29 ♕b5! ♖xb8 30 ♕xb8 ♔g8 31 ♕b3+ is even better, defusing any ...♖xg2+ idea totally. But after Capablanca's 29 ♕a8??, Thomas could

have survived and more with 29...♖xa2!, as many books on tactics have pointed out. Nevertheless, this game is a merciless illustration of how exchanges can actually worsen Black's chances in a position like this.

11 ♗g5

An appealing positional alternative is 11 ♕c3!?, played by Capablanca versus an amateur in a game quoted with great admiration by Réti. White's idea is to eschew normal development, gain a tempo by hitting c7, and then follow up with ♘d4-f5, since Black has no safe way to dislodge that piece. This worked to a tee after 11...c6 12 ♘d4 ♘d7 13 ♘f5 ♗f6 14 ♕g3 ♘e5 15 ♗f4 ♕c7 16 ♖ad1. On the other hand, 11...♕d7! (*Hiarcs 8*) succeeds tactically after 12 ♕xc7 ♕xb5 13 ♕xe7 ♕c6!, and 12 ♘d4 d5! should equalize. So perhaps best is 12 ♕b3 c6 13 ♘c3 with only a small advantage.

Instead of all this, simply 11 ♗f4 (intending ♕c3) 11...♕d7 12 ♘c3 would also maintain a standard but small edge.

11...h6 12 ♗h4 ♖e8 *(D)*

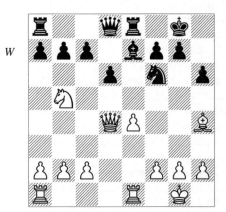

13 ♖ad1 ♘d7
Still another exchange!
14 ♗xe7 ♖xe7 *(D)*

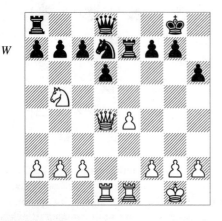

A position typical of the variation: Lasker never seemed too concerned about White's space advantage, since he felt that White didn't have enough pieces to take advantage of it before Black could reorganize (and perhaps even exchange into an ending). But I don't think that any modern player would want to get near this position – the simplification has made White's plans too easy to implement! And notice that the moves which would chip away at White's centre – ...d5 and ...f5 – are not available.

15 ♕c3!
15 f4 is also quite good, but the text-move implements the same idea as 11 ♕c3, without the annoying ...♕d7 tactic. Kasparov: "I think Tarrasch was quite happy with the opening results: White has a small but constant advantage, and there are chances to increase it without any risk. One would guess that Tarrasch expected something like 15...♘f8 and planned 16 ♘d4 with growing pressure. Lasker knew that his best chance to avoid a long, maybe painful defence was to take Tarrasch out of his confident mood by doing something very provocative (on the chess board, of course!). And so he moves his rook contrary to all rules of conventional wisdom:"

15...♖e5!?!?
Or perhaps '!!' for ingenuity. But objectively Kasparov's '?!' is probably more accurate. Regardless, Black's choice is not pleasant; 15...♘f8 16 ♘d4 (intending ♘f5) 16...♘e6 17 ♘f5 ♖e8 18 ♖e3!? ♔h7 19 ♖g3 g6? 20 ♘xh6!

is one of many possibilities for Black to go wrong.
16 ♘d4 ♖c5!? *(D)*

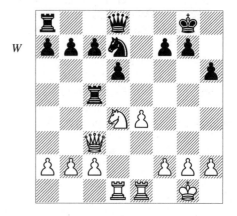

The last two moves taken together constitute one of the great creative ideas of the first part of the 20th century, and a tribute to Lasker's amazing imagination. The rook is placed on an absurd square and seems to serve no purpose at all! One is reminded of the rook moves along ranks that are featured in the present volume (and in SOMCS). But this particular manoeuvre probably lacks the soundness of those modern examples, and one has to wonder about Black's entire middlegame strategy if he is forced to play such an unlikely idea.

17 ♕b3 ♘b6 18 f4
Cutting off the rook. This is a good move, and Réti's comment here that Tarrasch's execution is on a lower lever than Lasker's seems unjustified.

18...♕f6 19 ♕f3 ♖e8 *(D)*
Réti describes this as an "aimless developing move of the old style", arguing that the rook has to return to d8 anyway, and that a better move was 19...a6. True, but 20 b3 would still be a strong reply.

20 c3?!
As Kasparov points out, 20 b3! is better (and much clearer) since c4 should be played soon anyway. White would save a move and maintain a clear advantage.

20...a5
Trying to weaken White's queenside.

21 b3 a4 22 b4?
22 c4! still leaves both the c5-rook and the b6-knight in bad shape. Then White has the

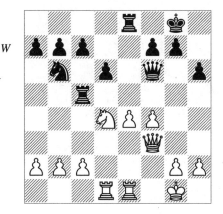

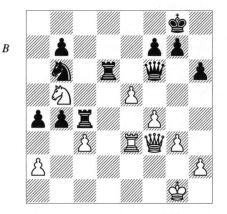

luxury of building up slowly, and the move ♘b5 can be dangerous, further hemming in the rook. For example, Kasparov gives 22...axb3 23 axb3 c6 24 ♘f5 d5 25 ♕f2 ♘d7 26 g4!, when one can quickly see how bad things have become for Black. Such variations are not comprehensive, of course, and I have not used all of the extensive analysis this game has received in so many sources. But regardless of the precise variations, I find it hard to believe that White isn't objectively better here, or that ...♖e5-c5 can justify Black's classical strategy of exchanging so many pieces in this type of structure.

22...♖c4

At least the rook has an outpost of sorts now, and White's c-pawn is weak. The rest of this famous game is not germane to our discussion, so I'll leave it as is with a few suggestions from Kasparov:

23 g3 ♖d8! 24 ♖e3?!

Kasparov gives 24 a3!. This renders ...c5 dubious, and thus retains some advantage. 24 ♕e3 has also been suggested in several sources, with the same assessment.

24...c5 25 ♘b5?

Kasparov observes that a better move was 25 bxc5 ♖xc5 26 ♖b1 ♘c4 27 ♖d3 with equality.

25...cxb4 26 ♖xd6 ♖xd6 27 e5 (D)

27...♖xf4!

Lasker had to see this well in advance of playing it, of course. The rest is not relevant to our topic.

28 gxf4 ♕g6+ 29 ♔h1 ♕b1+ 30 ♔g2 ♖d2+ 31 ♖e2 ♕xa2 32 ♖xd2 ♕xd2+ 33 ♔g3 a3 34 e6 ♕e1+ 35 ♔g4 ♕xe6+ 36 f5 ♕c4+ 37 ♘d4 a2 38 ♕d1 ♘d5 39 ♕a4 ♘xc3 40 ♕e8+ ♔h7 41 ♔h5 a1♕ 0-1

In what fashion did players eventually move away from the ...exd4 lines that sustained Black for so many years? For one thing, the top players of the last 70 years or so, including most world champions and elite players, established the superiority of playing certain closed variations with ...d6 and making the e5-pawn a protected strongpoint (superiority in the broader sense of achieving good results, as well as in the theoretical sense). But surely the great players of the late 19th and early 20th centuries had time and experience enough with this opening to come to the same conclusion? I think that there are several reasons that this took so long to happen, but one of them has to do with a philosophical notion that began to take over, i.e., one should only try to equalize or perhaps accept a small disadvantage with Black regardless of the dynamic chances one might forego thereby. It is true that the further back we go into the 19th century, the more outrageous were the swashbuckling attempts by Black to impose almost irrational dynamism into the play, in part with White's cooperation. One thinks of the way players treated the Evans Gambit, King's Gambit, Bishop's Gambit, Philidor Countergambit and others. However, with the arrival of Steinitz and the top-level adoption of his rational approach to chess, the leading players began to play less ambitiously in the opening and early middlegame, the Ruy Lopez positions being in the forefront of those which they treated in this manner. A second and related factor in the popularity of surrendering the centre was seen repeatedly in the games above: the limited idea that the side with less space could exchange pieces and render White's space advantage academic. What was not appreciated at the time and became obvious later was the large number of positions in which such exchanges actually increased White's advantage.

Let's look at some general figures about the surrender of the centre in both the Ruy Lopez and in the Philidor Defence. Here I am using databases including only the top players for each era. I have included cases of ...exd4 at an early stage in the Ruy Lopez while excluding lines involving c3 for White or ...exd4 exchanges such as occur in irrelevant or forcing situations like 1 e4 e5 2 ②f3 ②c6 3 ②b5 a6 and now 4 ②a4 f5 5 d4 exd4 or here 4 ②xc6 dxc6 5 d4 exd4. Combining the instances of a relevant ...exd4 in the Philidor and in the Ruy Lopez, we can compare the total number of those games as a percentage of the total of all games played in the two openings. Notice that this percentage will never be very high, because the latter total includes all sorts of Ruy Lopez favourites such as the Open Variation, the Berlin Defence, the Marshall Attack, and a very wide variety of closed systems such as the very main lines. One should also remember that an early d3 in the Ruy Lopez was quite popular in the classical period, following Steinitz's lead. Obviously, Black never has the option of ...exd4 in these cases. Nevertheless, by examining the figures, we find that the leading players of the period from 1900 and before chose a variation with ...exd4 in about 13% of all Philidor and Ruy Lopez games. During 1901-35, that figure rose to almost 16%. But from 1936-70, these ...exd4 systems were used only 3% of the time, a ratio that modestly declined to about 2.3% in 1985-2002, and even then only because the small number of those ...g6 Philidor's Defences mentioned above contributed almost half of the ...exd4 examples!

Nor do such figures merely reflect some sort of increase in irregular variations of the Ruy Lopez (and thus a skewing of percentages). Let us count only the current main line beginning with 3 ②b5 a6 4 ②a4 ②f6 5 0-0 ②e7 6 ②e1 b5 7 ②b3 d6 (D).

We find that it was played in approximately 1.5% of top-level Ruy Lopez games before 1900, 10.5% during 1900-1935 (mostly toward the end), 41.2% during 1936-70, and 37.7% during 1971-2002. In other words, modern play

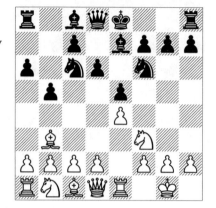

has seen a radical shift to closed or semi-closed variations.

I think that ultimately the world-class players concluded that these lines with ...exd4 were just too onerous and unrewarding. The 'surrender the centre and exchange pieces' approach was often even worse than the 'surrender the centre and batten down the hatches' approach, which at least made matters complicated and won some points. By the 1930s, after four decades of top-level use, other variations of the Ruy Lopez took over, and in the 1985-2002 database, for example, top players used a conventional ...d6 and early ...exd4 system in only 26 of 1,658 Ruy Lopez games. Yes, Lasker had managed to win some big-time contests with this strategy, but hardly due to the openings or middlegame structures. He also played the white side of these lines with pleasure and did very well against them. In any case, if you compare the ...exd4 Ruy Lopez lines with other 'surrender the centre' efforts (more to come), you see that they are similar in this respect, that is, in most cases Black's task is not eased by exchanges. And yet in the Ruy Lopez it is hard to do without them. In the type of cramped position that Black gets, with a few exceptions, his pieces don't have the dynamic potential that one sees in, say, the Hedgehog formations with ...cxd4, the King's Indian Defence lines with ...exd4, or the French Defence variations with ...dxe4. In the Ruy Lopez, Black's pawns are seldom threats to challenge White's centre as they are in those openings. Granted, the ...exd4 Ruy Lopez variations cannot be considered refuted; but very few players would want to take on the extended defensive task and lack of counterchances.

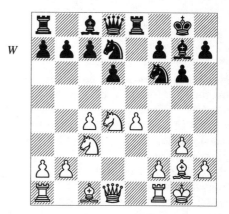

What then are the preferred modern approaches to the Ruy Lopez? Does Black aim for a closed position, as we suggested was the most successful Philidor Defence strategy? Of course that is the strategy involved in the main lines; for example, the Chigorin, Smyslov, Zaitsev, and Breyer variations. But modern players are more pragmatic than this: essentially, the philosophy is 'play what works', including both closed and open variations. Consider the extremely popular and effective Marshall Attack: 3 &b5 a6 4 &a4 ⁄f6 5 0-0 &e7 6 ⁄e1 b5 7 &b3 0-0 8 c3 d5 9 exd5 ⁄xd5 10 ⁄xe5 ⁄xe5 11 ⁄xe5 c6. This dynamic variation was considered rather marginal until it became clear that Black needn't prosecute his attack to checkmate if he was to avoid losing some pawn-down endgame. Instead, 8...d5 began to be used as a long-term positional pawn sacrifice, as is so common in modern chess (see Chapter 2 for other examples). Black also plays dynamically in the Arkhangelsk Variation, Open Defence, and other lines.

Examples in the King's Indian Defence

Returning to our topic, the surrender of the centre and exchanges, we find that the double e-pawn cases do not indicate a general philosophical shift that extends throughout chess thought. Instead, players decide on a case-by-case basis, using concrete analysis and pragmatic considerations as their criteria. Before turning to examples involving ...dxe4, let's look at another example of ...exd4, but this time arising from the King's Indian Defence. The following game provides a contemporary example of surrendering the centre:

Whiteley – Gallagher
Royan 1989

1 d4 ⁄f6 2 c4 g6 3 ⁄f3 &g7 4 g3 0-0 5 &g2 d6 6 0-0 ⁄bd7 7 ⁄c3 e5 8 e4 (D)
    8...exd4
    Black also plays ...c6 here or on the next few moves, thinking about ...exd4 in the near future. An example of this is 8...c6 9 h3 ⁄b6 10 ⁄e1

exd4. In such a position he will intentionally deploy his forces to avoid exchanging them. True, if he could ever achieve ...d5, it would tend to clear out the middle of the board, exchange pieces and equalize. But in choosing this kind of structure, both sides know that White can prevent that break with any type of reasonable play. Then Black has a cramped position, but his chances will lie in dynamic elasticity and not simplification. See the next game for a fine example of strategic manoeuvring in a similar context.
    9 ⁄xd4 ⁄e8 (D)

In this characteristic position, White has the move c4 in, which by comparison with the 1 e4 e5 examples above, further discourages ...d5 and ...b5. On the other hand, this also loosens the dark squares that Black's g7-bishop aims at and it weakens d3, a factor which seems irrelevant but will sometimes enter into play much later.
    10 h3

The main move, developed in the 1950s. It is both flexible and prophylactic. White doesn't commit to a piece placement until he has seen what Black is doing. He would like to centralize by means of 11 &e3 and not have to worry about a move like ...&g4.

10...a6!?

A very modern treatment developed by GM Joe Gallagher. It is still holding up well today. Black's play is ultra-flexible, as he doesn't commit his d7-knight to c5 or e5, he avoids ...c6 at least for the moment, and he prepares moves like ...&b8, ...c5, and ...b5. Recently 10...&c5 11 &e1 &d7 has also tended to equalize, but that's another matter.

11 &e1 &b8 (D)

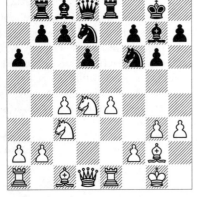

12 b3!?

By playing this modern-style system, Black also commits to dynamic play at the cost of weaknesses. A further example of the same trade-off is 12 &e3 (today, the flexible 12 &b1 is a common move, as is 12 a4, but I won't get into the extensive theory) 12...c5 (the point: Black weakens d5 and assumes a backward pawn on d6, but gains great activity) 13 &de2 &e5 14 b3 b5! 15 f4 &ed7 16 &xd6 b4 17 e5 (otherwise ...&xe4) 17...bxc3 18 exf6? (18 &xc3! &h5 19 g4 &f8 20 &d2 &g7 gives White unclear play for his piece) 18...&xe3 19 fxg7 &b6! 20 &d1 &be6 and White is completely tied up: 21 &c1 &f6 22 &c2 &e7 23 &f2 &f6 24 &cd1 &b7 25 &d5 &xd5 26 cxd5 &6e4 27 &d3 c4! 28 &xe3 &xe3 29 d6 &a7 30 &c1 &e4+ 31 &g2 &xg3+ 0-1 Hohler-Gallagher, Berne 1994. A typical modern King's Indian Defence game whose dynamism starkly

contrasts with the stolid and inferior black treatment that gave this opening a poor reputation all the way up to the late 1940s.

12...c5! 13 &c2 b5! 14 cxb5 axb5 15 &xd6 &b6! 16 &d1 b4 17 &a4 &be6

Suddenly all of Black's pieces are active. Soon he dominates the board, and particularly the dark squares. We will see this kind of long-term pawn sacrifice throughout this book.

18 &b2 &e7 19 &e3 &b7 20 f3 &h5 21 &xg7 &xg7 22 g4

Worse is 22 &h2? f5 23 exf5 &xe3.

22...&f4 23 &d2 &e5

Black threatens ...&xh3+ as well as ...&d8 and infiltration on d3. Look at Black's dominant knights and contrast White's horrible king's bishop and inactive pieces. Black won easily.

In the following game, Black surrenders the centre in a similar position, but uses a set-up with ...c6 instead of ...a6:

Salov – Kasparov
Linares 1991

1 d4 &f6 2 c4 g6 3 &f3 &g7 4 g3 0-0 5 &g2 d6 6 0-0 &bd7 7 &c2 e5 8 &d1 &e7 9 &c3 c6 10 e4 exd4 11 &xd4 &e8 (D)

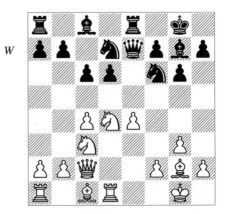

12 b3 &c5 13 f3 &fd7 14 &b1 &e5

Arriving at a typical middlegame position.

15 &ce2!

White refuses to weaken his centre; e.g., 15 f4 &g4, and if 16 h3?, 16...&f6.

15...a5 16 a3 h5! (D)

In contemporary play it's typical to use the rook's pawns to divert attention from the centre. In this case White has rendered ...a4 useless,

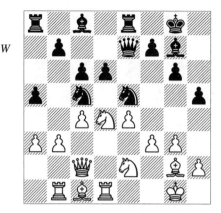

W

but now has to worry about ...h4 at the right moment. In addition, ...h5 serves as a prophylactic move versus f4.

17 h4

For example, 17 ♗e3 h4 18 g4 ♗xg4 19 fxg4 ♘xg4 20 ♗f4 ♗e5 is effective for Black, and 17 h3 h4!? 18 g4 g5 secures counterplay on the dark squares. In the latter instance Black plans ...♘g6, but even after 19 ♘f5 ♗xf5 20 gxf5, which prevents that move, Black plays 20...a4 21 b4 ♘b3 22 ♗e3 b5!, securing good play on the queenside *light* squares! Thus both rook's pawns are used to secure play on a colour complex. Notice that if White has to keep an eye on such moves as well as potential central breaks, his pieces tend to be very tied down to their posts, compensating Black for the fact that his own pieces are cramped from lack of space. This kind of dynamic balance in an elastic position is very similar to what happens in the modern 'hedgehog' structures that arise in many of the positions of the English Opening and the Sicilian and Modern Defences, among others.

17...♗d7

Now Black can develop this bishop, since 18 f4? ♘g4 would no longer win a piece for White (as it would have with the pawn on h3).

18 ♗e3

Calmly centralizing and anticipating long-term pressure against the queenside and the centre. Salov's play has been perfectly logical and beyond reproach. Now the position of the bishop gives Kasparov the chance to play one more undermining move that frees his game.

18...a4! 19 b4 ♘e6 20 c5!?

Still no exchanges, since 20 ♘xe6? ♗xe6 exposes c4. White's move looks a little too

ambitious, but otherwise he does have to be careful about moves like ...b5.

20...d5!

20...dxc5 21 ♘xe6 ♗xe6 22 ♗xc5 ♕c7 23 ♘d4 is not clear, but playing the thematic central break establishes control of the key c4-square.

21 exd5 cxd5 22 ♗f2 ♘c4

It's remarkable that Black has established such active play from an initially restricted position.

23 ♕c3 ♖ac8?!

The move 23...♘c7!, provided by the chess engine *Hiarcs*, is quite strong since it threatens ...♘b5 and in some cases ...♗b5.

24 ♖bc1 b6 25 cxb6 ♘xb6 26 ♕d3 ♘c4 27 ♖c1 ♕d6!? 28 f4! ♘b2 29 ♕d2 ♘c4 30 ♕d3 ♘b2 31 ♕d2 ♘c4 ½-½

The surrender of the centre was reasonable in this game due to dynamic play and the persistent threat of freeing moves for Black, something missing in the foregoing Philidor and Ruy Lopez examples.

As noted in the games above, Black would actually hurt his chances for activity by early exchanges. But once again, the precise verdict varies upon piece placement. For example, if White plays the main line of the King's Indian with 1 d4 ♘f6 2 c4 g6 3 ♘c3 ♗g7 4 e4 d6 5 ♘f3 0-0 6 ♗e2 e5 7 0-0, then according to theory neither lines with 7...exd4 8 ♘xd4 ♘c6, nor 7...♘bd7 and an early ...exd4 achieve full equality. Perhaps more importantly, Black often can't avoid early exchanges in these lines and isn't able to create the continued threat of credible game-freeing pawn breaks. By contrast, Black actually achieves ...d5 in the variation illustrated in this game:

Sashikiran – Thipsay
Calcutta 2001

1 d4 ♘f6 2 c4 g6 3 ♘c3 ♗g7 4 e4 d6 5 ♘f3 0-0 6 ♗e2 e5 7 ♗e3 exd4 8 ♘xd4 ♖e8 9 f3 c6 10 ♗f2

This is the juncture at which Kasparov famously sacrificed the exchange versus Karpov in the world championship (New York/Lyons Wch (11) 1990) after 10 ♕d2 d5 11 exd5 cxd5 12 0-0 ♘c6 13 c5 ♖xe3!?! 14 ♕xe3 ♕f8!, a shocking offer that helped to redefine what could be expected from long-term positional compensation.

10...d5 11 exd5 cxd5 12 0-0 ᐧc6 13 c5 ᐧh5 14 ᐃd2 ᐁe5 15 g3 ᐧg7 *(D)*

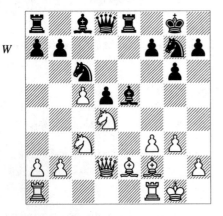

A fully pragmatic approach involving taking on the isolated pawn and fianchettoing a knight in order to return it to the centre. White is probably better in this position, but it hasn't been proven yet. In the game, Black is prepared to cede the bishop-pair in order to get two central pawns:

16 ᐃfd1 ᐁe6!? 17 ᐧxe6 fxe6 18 f4 ᐁf6 19 ᐧb5 ᐃf8! 20 ᐃab1

Here Black played 20...a6 and got some disadvantage, eventually drawing. Saving a tempo by 20...ᐃd7, intending 21 b4 a5 or 21 ᐧd6 ᐧe8, might have justified his strategy and kept White's edge to a bare minimum.

Old and New: Central Capitulation in the French Defence

We have seen the surrender of the centre in the context of the passive Ruy Lopez variations and the wild King's Indian Defence variations. The move ...dxe4 in the French Defence provides us with an up-to-date field test for the surrender of the centre in a middle-of-the-road setting, i.e. sound but not too ambitious. Grandmasters and international masters have revived the use of the variations 1 e4 e6 2 d4 d5 3 ᐧc3 dxe4 (or 3 ᐧd2 dxe4) 4 ᐧxe4 *(D)* and 1 e4 e6 2 d4 d5 3

ᐧc3 ᐧf6 4 ᐁg5 dxe4, with several subsystems in the play that comes afterwards.

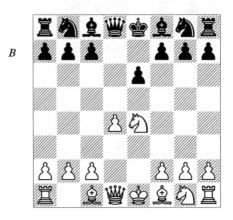

Before continuing, let's look at some historical trends. In the period 1900-1935, the leading players chose ...dxe4 on the 3rd and 4th moves in 26% of the French Defence games in which they had a chance to do so (i.e., games with 3 ᐧd2 and 3 ᐧc3 rather than 3 exd5, 3 e5, 2 d3, etc.). This reflected a friendly attitude towards the surrender of the centre, as we saw in the Philidor and Ruy Lopez. As time went on, however, the idea became less popular for all the classical reasons: lack of space and freedom for Black's pieces. In the period 1936-1970, with the rise of the Winawer and Tarrasch Variations with 3 ᐧd2 ᐧf6 or 3 ᐧd2 c5, the same figure plummeted to 12%. But from 1985 to 2002, leading players, given the opportunity, reversed course and chose 3...dxe4 or 4...dxe4 in 21% of the relevant French Defence games.

While this is still not a structure that French players absolutely rush into, such a degree of willingness by strong players to surrender the centre hasn't been seen for some time. What has happened, and what are the characteristics of the resulting positions? The first consideration we must deal with is Black's c8-bishop, which will need to be developed. In a manner analogous to the ...exd4 lines after 1 e4 e5, in which Black seldom achieves ...d5, Black will seldom be able to achieve ...e5 and free his queen's bishop. So to avoid the fate of passivity resulting from being stuck behind the e6-pawn, the c8-bishop will often have to be developed to b7 after ...b6, or to c6 via d7. This costs time, and the plan to go to b7 is sometimes not practicable due to moves like ♘e5 and ♗b5+ on White's part. Nevertheless, most of the time Black does succeed in activating this bishop within the next 6-8 moves. Another very interesting difference from the Philidor/Ruy Lopez version involves the counterattack on White's centre pawn on d4 via ...c5.

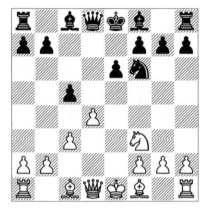

W

That move can be enforced by means of a knight on d7 and a bishop on f8 or e7. There is no real parallel to this in the ...exd4 lines stemming from 1 e4 e5, because the move ...f5 is blocked by a knight on f6; even were it achieved it would merely weaken the black king's protection and the e6-square.

If Black can succeed in playing ...c5 and either isolate or liquidate White's d-pawn, then the whole scheme begins to look more feasible. I think that it's fair to say that the modern treatment of ...dxe4 is more aggressive than in the early part of the last century. Very seldom are top players content to combine moves like ...b6, ...c6, ...♗b7, ...♕c7, and ...♘d7 before embarking upon central action. Now Black feels that he requires counterplay via the freeing moves ...c5 or ...e5, or by obtaining the two bishops (following ♗g5xf6, for example). Otherwise, once White consolidates his space advantage the play begins to resemble that of the ...exd4 Philidors and Ruys. Let's take a look at some concrete examples.

1 e4 e6 2 d4 d5 3 ♘c3 ♘f6

Not surprisingly, the viability of the ...dxe4 idea is a matter of specifics rather than general philosophy. For example, 3 ♘c3 (or 3 ♘d2) 3...dxe4 4 ♘xe4 ♘d7, the Rubinstein Variation, hasn't been quite as successful over the past few

years as the rather more dynamic lines resulting from 3 ♘c3 ♘f6 4 ♗g5. Of course, that can change: after all, Anand, Bareev, and M.Gurevich are not bad ambassadors for 3...dxe4 4 ♘xe4 ♘d7! The point is that variations which involve the same pawn-structure and associated issues may nevertheless result in different assessments.

4 ♗g5 dxe4 5 ♘xe4 ♗e7 6 ♗xf6 ♗xf6 7 ♘f3 (D)

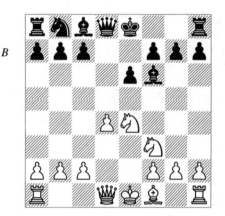

B

Here we have a fascinating example of symmetry with the Ruy Lopez variation 3...d6 4 d4 ♗d7 (the 'exact' analogy would be 4...exd4 5 ♘xd4 ♗d7 6 ♗xc6 ♗xc6) 5 ♘c3 ♘f6 6 ♗xc6 ♗xc6 7 ♕d3 exd4 8 ♘xd4. Why should this French instantiation be any more attractive for Black than that one? The answer lies mainly in precise moves and their playability rather than in general considerations. For example, let's go back to the note to 6 0-0 in Lasker-Tarrasch above. After 8 ♘xd4, the move that Black would most like to play is the active 8...g6 (instead of the passive 8...♗e7). I think that it's fair to say that a plan involving ...♗g7, ...0-0, and ...♖e8 would give him fully satisfactory play. But as we saw in that note, 8...g6? fails tactically. Now compare the (diagrammed) French Defence position. Black will generally succeed in playing ...b6 and ...♗b7, putting pressure on White's centre from both long diagonals. This has the further consequence that ...♘d7 can be played, both defending f6 and preparing ...c5. In the analogous Ruy Lopez position, Black's king's bishop uses up the e7-square, excluding the knight move to that square, and Black therefore has to be careful that White's move ♘xc6, doubling his pawns, is not at some point a good trade-off for White.

This availability of ...b6 and ...♗b7 (or possibly ...a6, ...b5 and ...♗b7) characterizes most of the ...dxe4 variations, whereas the analogous kingside fianchetto is bad in almost every ...exd4 Ruy Lopez variation. This relative advantage of Black's is probably more important than any disadvantage (for example, the fact that White's queen has direct control of d4 in the French example).

Here we might compare one of the few modern situations in which White himself surrenders the centre after 1 e4 e5, namely, 2 ♘c3 ♘f6 3 g3 d5 4 exd5 ♘xd5 5 ♗g2 *(D)*.

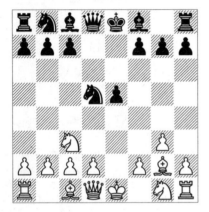

This has recently become a moderately popular line, played by the likes of Glek, Leko, and Morozevich. It often resembles a reversed Philidor Defence (with an extra tempo) after moves like ♘f3, 0-0, ♖e1, etc. Furthermore, the reverse 'freeing' move d4 can replace d3 in many situations. White's active fianchettoed bishop provides justification for such a strategy; White would be throwing away the advantage of the first move (at least) were it placed on e2.

7...0-0

Oddly enough, this natural move may be an inaccuracy. Black can get his pieces out as fast as possible and thwart certain white set-ups via 7...♘d7, as in the next game.

8 ♕d2

In line with the last note, 8 ♗c4! here has given Black considerable trouble, with the idea 8...b6 9 ♕e2 ♗b7 10 0-0-0 and White gets a clear advantage. See the next game for 7...♘d7 8 ♗c4, which is less effective for White.

8...♘d7 9 0-0-0 b6 *(D)*

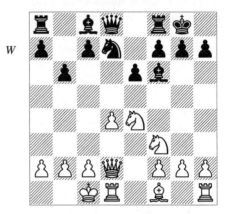

Here we follow the game...

Van den Doel – M.Gurevich
Hoogeveen 1999

10 ♗c4

After 10 ♕f4 ♗b7 11 ♗c4 ♗d5! 12 ♗d3 ♗e7, Black boldly keeps the bishops at loss of time. Now both ...c5 and ...f5 are ideas: 13 c4 ♗b7 14 g4 (to stop ...f5) 14...♘f6 15 ♘xf6+ ♗xf6 16 ♗e4 ♗xe4 17 ♕xe4 ♕e7! (planning 18...♕b4). This gave Black enough counterplay in Bologan-M.Gurevich, Belfort 1998.

10...♗b7!? *(D)*

In a couple of games Dreev has played 10...c6 to stabilize the centre and prevent White's next move.

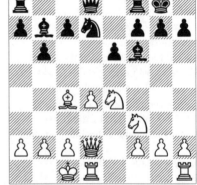

11 d5!?

The consistent move. Instead, 11 ♖he1 ♗d5 (11...♗e7!? is suggested by Hübner; or, since

White's king is committed to the queenside, 11...♗xe4 12 ♖xe4 c6 followed by queenside expansion would be another approach) 12 ♗d3 c5 13 c4 ♗b7 14 dxc5 gave White a very slight edge in Hübner-Short, Novi Sad OL 1990.

11...b5!?

This is more dynamic than Hübner's suggestion of 11...e5, although the latter should be fine. If then 12 g4!?, 12...a6 13 g5 ♗e7 gives Black quite as many queenside chances as White has on the kingside.

12 ♗b3 c5! *(D)*

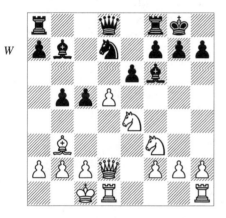

The point of 11...b5. Gurevich is interpreting this system in as dynamic a fashion as one can, which is possible only due to Black's active bishops.

13 ♘d6!

13 dxe6? loses material after 13...♗xe4 14 exf7+ ♔h8 15 ♕xd7 ♕xd7 16 ♖xd7 c4, and so does 13 ♘xf6+?! ♘xf6 14 dxe6? ♕xd2+ 15 ♖xd2 c4, etc.

13...♗xd5 14 ♗xd5 exd5 15 ♕xd5 ♘b6! 16 ♕e4

Not 16 ♕xc5? ♗xb2+!. In a later game Z.Almasi-Tukmakov, Croatian Cht (Pula) 2001 the players repeated all these moves and White deviated by 16 ♕f5 g6!? (or 16...♘a4) 17 ♕f4. Then probably the most straightforward solution is 17...♘a4 18 c3 (18 ♘e5?? ♗g5; 18 ♘c4 bxc4 19 ♖xd8 ♗xb2+ 20 ♔b1 ♖axd8 21 ♕xc4 ♖b8 is equal) 18...♗g7 19 ♖he1 ♕a5 with equality.

16...♘a4 17 ♘e5 ♕b6 18 ♕d5 ♖ad8! 19 f4!

White stabilizes his central position. Not 19 ♘exf7? ♗xb2+!.

19...c4

Black meanwhile continues his queenside assault.

20 ♔b1 ♕c7 21 ♖he1 a6 22 g4 ♗xe5 23 fxe5 ♘c5

This is a very unclear position. White's powerful knight on d6 and excellent centralization is balanced by his weaknesses; e.g., a black knight on e6 will be a strong piece as well. In the next few moves, inaccurately played, White wrongly allows an endgame.

24 ♖f1 ♘e6 25 ♖f3 ♕c5! 26 ♕xc5 ♘xc5

Black is better due to White's weaknesses. The game was nevertheless drawn.

Next comes another game by M.Gurevich, a leading expert on ...dxe4 systems.

Svidler – M.Gurevich
Esbjerg 2000

1 e4 e6 2 d4 d5 3 ♘c3 ♘f6 4 ♗g5 dxe4 5 ♘xe4 ♗e7 6 ♗xf6 ♗xf6 *(D)*

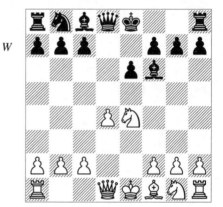

7 ♘f3 ♘d7 8 ♗c4

There are of course alternatives for White. 8 ♗d3 can be answered by 8...c5! intending 9 dxc5 (9 ♘d6+? ♔e7 will actually win material for Black) 9...♘xc5!. This was the idea of the always dynamic Alekhine versus Yates at Kecskemet 1927. The point is 10 ♘xc5 ♕a5+ 11 c3 ♕xc5, freeing his game and retaining the two-bishop advantage.

8...a6 *(D)*

A typical idea in these ...dxe4 variations. Black wants to develop as quickly as possible along the long diagonals, and foregoes the 'automatic' 8...0-0 to do so.

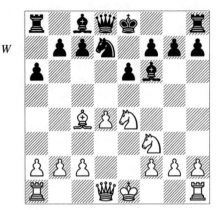

9 ♕e2

9 a4 0-0 10 ♕d2 b6, and the normal move without a4 in would be 11 0-0-0, but then 11...b5! gets Black's queenside attack rolling.

9...b5 10 ♗d5!

Stopping ...♗b7.

10...♖b8 11 0-0-0 0-0 12 ♗c6!

Now White has ideas of d5 with a very strong attack. Black finds a well-timed solution:

12...♖b6! 13 d5 exd5 14 ♗xd5 c6 15 ♗b3 c5! *(D)*

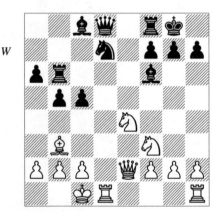

McDonald: "A brilliant example of the interaction of strategy and tactics."

16 ♗d5

16 ♘xc5? ♗xb2+! 17 ♔xb2 ♕f6+ 18 ♔b1 ♘xc5 would be very bad for White.

16...♕c7 17 ♖he1 ♗d8!

Now ...♘f6 is coming, and the resulting two-bishop situation is unattractive for White, so he forces the exchange of one and gains equality:

18 ♘eg5 ♗xg5+ 19 ♘xg5 ♘f6 20 ♕e5!
½-½

I'll close with two more illustrations of this variation, one successful for Black and the other for White. Naturally, both games are ambiguous with respect to the actual theoretical status of the lines involved.

Stefansson – Morozevich
Reykjavik ECC 1999

1 e4 e6 2 d4 d5 3 ♘c3 ♘f6 4 ♗g5 dxe4 5 ♘xe4 ♗e7 6 ♗xf6 gxf6 7 ♘f3 a6 8 ♗d3

Rather than 8 ♗c4 (aiming overtly for d5) or 8 ♕d2 (planning the aggressive 0-0-0), White simply develops his bishop. This move contains more venom than is immediately apparent.

8...f5

This initiates Black's natural freeing method, but things aren't so simple.

9 ♘g3 c5 *(D)*

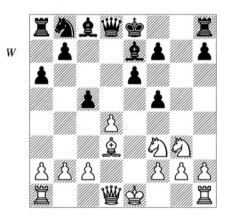

10 dxc5?!

White should have tried 10 d5!. This breakthrough looks impossible with the bishop on d3, but it is based on the tactical point 10...♕xd5 11 ♘xf5! when 11...exf5?? loses the queen to 12 ♗b5+. Also good for White is 11...♗f6 12 ♘e3. Therefore the key question is what happens after 11...c4! with the forced line 12 ♘xe7 (12 ♘e3? ♕a5+) 12...♘xe7 13 ♗e2 ♕xd1+ (13...♖d8 14 ♕c1!) 14 ♖xd1 b5 15 a4. It looks more or less equal, but White has some irritating pressure on the black queenside pawns; e.g., 15...♗b7 16 0-0 (16 ♘d4!? ♗xg2 17 ♖g1 ♗c6 18 ♖g5) 16...♖g8 17 g3 ♘c6 18 b3 (18 axb5 axb5 19 b3 cxb3 20 cxb3 ♖a3 21 ♖b1) 18...cxb3 19 cxb3 bxa4 20 bxa4 ♖g4? (20...♖ad8

21 ♖b1 ♖d7 22 ♖fc1 is also good for White; perhaps 20...♖ab8 is best) 21 ♖b1 ♘a5 22 ♖fc1 and Black is in trouble. Therefore the verdict is that Black might be OK after 10 d5, but then again he didn't play 6...gxf6 to end up in a slightly worse endgame with no winning chances!

10...♕a5+

Now everything goes smoothly for Morozevich. White centralizes his pieces, but then finds he has no constructive plan.

11 c3 ♕xc5 12 ♕d2 ♘c6 13 0-0-0

13 ♘h5!? is probably better, to threaten the kingside, though 13...♘e5! looks comfortable for Black.

13...h5!

Black rules out ♘h5 ideas. As White has no pawn advances to spearhead an attack, the obvious plan is to gear up for a line-opening piece sacrifice. However, Black's position is too resilient for such an approach to work. White therefore soon runs out of ideas. In the meantime Black's position improves with every move.

14 h4 b5 *(D)*

The game will now become a showcase for the bishop-pair's activity. White had to establish useful positions for his knights prior to this point.

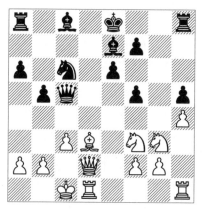

15 ♔b1 b4 16 ♖c1 ♗b7 17 ♕e2 ♕b6 18 ♘d2

White uncovers an attack on h5, but the situation on the queenside and in the centre has already grown critical.

18...♖d8 19 ♖hd1 bxc3 20 ♖xc3 ♔f8 21 ♖dc1 ♘b4 22 ♗c4 ♗xh4!

This clears g5 for the bishop.

23 ♖h1 ♗f6

This bishop has no rival and puts lethal pressure on the queenside.

24 ♖b3 ♕d6 25 ♖xh5 ♖xh5 26 ♘xh5 ♗e4+!

Now White's position collapses.

27 ♔c1 ♘xa2+ 28 ♔d1 ♗g5 29 f4 ♗xf4 30 ♘xf4 ♕xf4 31 ♖b6 ♕h2 32 ♕f2 ♕h1+ 33 ♗f1 ♗d3 34 ♕c5+ ♔g8 35 ♕e7 ♖c8 36 ♕g5+ ♔h7 37 ♖b7 ♖c1# (0-1)

Kasparov – Bareev
Sarajevo 2000

1 e4 e6 2 d4 d5 3 ♘c3 ♘f6 4 ♗g5 dxe4 5 ♘xe4 ♗e7 6 ♗xf6 ♗xf6

Bareev has played this solid variation for most of his career. Therefore Kasparov will need to find something special if he wants to set him new and unexpected problems.

7 ♘f3 ♘d7 8 ♕d2 0-0 9 0-0-0 ♗e7 *(D)*

Bareev prefers this to 9...b6, which is analysed in Van den Doel-Gurevich.

10 ♕c3!?

The idea here is to deter the freeing moves ...e5 and ...c5. Normally White develops with 10 ♗c4; for example, 10...♘f6 (10...a6! is Bareev's recent move) 11 ♘xf6+ ♗xf6 12 ♖he1 with a slight plus for White in Yermolinsky-Bareev, Lucerne Wcht 1997.

10...♘f6

Black seems to have enough chances after this, but a critical and positionally fascinating variation would be 10...c5 anyway! Then after 11 dxc5 ♕c7 Black regains the pawn with reasonable chances, as 12 b4 would be too weakening. The critical line is 11 ♗b5 ♕c7! introducing the kind of long-term positional pawn sacrifice we talked about in SOMCS, in which even the exchange of queens leaves Black's bishop-pair worth more than the pawn. A sample continuation might be 12 ♗xd7 ♗xd7 13 ♘xc5 (13 dxc5 ♗c6 14 ♘d6 b6) 13...♗c6 14 ♘d3 ♖ac8! 15 ♘de5 ♗d5 16 ♕xc7 ♖xc7 (D).

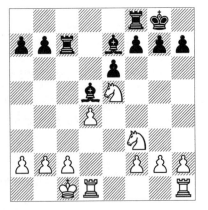

W

Despite White's extra pawn and lack of weaknesses, Black has full compensation and probably more. Notice that White's knights have no permanent outposts. Play might go 17 a3 (17 ♔b1 ♖fc8 18 ♖d2 f6 19 ♘d3 g5!, restricting the knights and preparing the simple minority attack with ...b5-b4, ...a5-a4) 17...♗b3 18 ♖d2 ♖fc8 19 c3 b5 20 ♘d3 a5 with a powerful minority attack; for example, 21 ♔b1 b4 22 axb4 axb4 23 ♘xb4 ♗xb4 24 cxb4 ♖a8! and wins, since ...♖ca7 follows.

11 ♘xf6+ ♗xf6 12 ♗d3 ♕d6 13 ♔b1 ♖d8 14 h4 a5 (D)

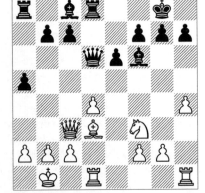

W

15 ♕e1!

The sort of simple solution that most of us would miss, preparing ♕e4 and avoiding ...♕b4. But at least Black still has the two bishops and the one on f6 does yeoman's work as the king's bodyguard.

15...♗d7

This leads to an inferior endgame, but Black is in trouble anyway: 15...g6 16 h5 b5? fails to 17 hxg6 hxg6 18 ♗xg6! intending 18...fxg6 19 ♕e4. Risky but playable seems 15...c5 16 dxc5 (16 ♘g5 cxd4) 16...♕xc5, when 17 ♕e4 ♕b4! saves the day and 17 ♘g5 h6 18 ♘e4 ♕e5 19 ♘xf6+ ♕xf6 20 g4! ♗d7 holds, even if it must favour White.

16 ♘g5 h6 17 ♗h7+ ♔f8 18 ♘e4 ♕e7 19 ♘xf6 ♕xf6 20 ♗e4 ♗c6 21 ♗xc6 bxc6 22 ♕e5!

Here White is happy to exchange queens as his potentially weak pawn on d4 disappears.

22...♕xe5

Or 22...♕xf2 23 ♖hf1 ♕xh4 24 ♕xe6 ♕e7 25 ♕xc6 with a nice advantage.

23 dxe5 ♖d5 24 ♖de1 ♖b8 25 ♖e2 ♔e7?

It was better to activate the queen's rook with 25...♖b4!, although White remains better.

26 c3 f6 27 exf6+ gxf6 28 ♔c2 ♖g8 29 g3 e5 30 ♖he1 ♔e6 31 ♖e4 ♔f5 32 ♖c4 ♖d6?

Kasparov says Black's last chance was to seek counterplay with 32...c5 33 ♖a4 ♖g4 34 ♖xa5 ♖e4 35 ♖xe4 ♔xe4 36 ♖a7 ♔f3.

33 ♖e3 h5 34 ♖f3+ ♔e6 35 ♖d3 ♖xd3 36 ♔xd3 ♔d6 37 b3 f5 38 ♖a4 c5 39 ♖xa5 ♖g4 40 ♖a4 f4 41 ♔e2 1-0

Black is already a pawn down and the pin on f4 will shortly cost him more material. A smooth win by Kasparov.

The line 3 ♘c3 ♘f6 4 ♗g5 dxe4 is popular at this time, and I think for some good reasons. Systems with ...gxf6 (after, say, 5 ♘xe4 ♗e7 6 ♗xf6) have led to dynamic and fun games, but not always so successfully for Black. Instead, 6...♗xf6 plans a set-up like ...♘d7 and ...c5 and/or ...b6 and ...♗b7. Black may be able to achieve active pieces as well as a freeing break like ...c5 or ...e5. Of course, White has more space and freer, more rapid development; these are characteristics of openings in which the opponent has surrendered the centre. It would be surprising if White wasn't a bit better, but perhaps no more than in any other opening. The difference between White's strategies and success versus 3...dxe4 as opposed to 3...♘f6 4 ♗g5 dxe4 indicates that the specific implementation of both sides' ideas is more important than a general philosophy about central structures.

The surrender of the centre has been our topic in this chapter, with an emphasis on its historical development and its relationship to the issues of space and exchanges. What can we conclude about this strategy? Above all, that its value varies from case to case. Small differences in piece placement and timing make a world of difference in the resulting assessments. Looking back upon the surrender of the centre via ...exd4 in the Philidor Defence and the Ruy Lopez, we can see that it enjoyed great popularity in both openings in the late 19th and early part of the 20th century, but then its status declined dramatically after it was found that White's space advantage was hard to contend against, and that exchanges tended to be of little or no value to the defender. By contrast, the mirror image lines of the French Defence are very popular today for a variety of reasons including the possibility of attacking the centre by ...c5 and the availability of a queenside fianchetto. Finally, a very different type of surrender of the centre was examined in the King's Indian Defence, where dynamism is the key ingredient in Black's strategy, so exchanges are therefore avoided by Black. These three dissimilar examples show that generalities do not apply well to this strategy. But the investigation has given us insights into the issue of space and exchanges, to which we turn next.

1.2 Space, Centre, and Exchanging on Principle

We continue our discussion of space and the centre, emphasizing the exchange of pieces, a topic which is conveniently amenable to direct comparisons from position to position. It takes exemplary games with modern openings to throw the issues of space and exchanges into stark relief, since one side (usually Black) very often stakes out relatively less claim to the centre, especially in terms of occupation by pawns. But I'll first continue from the last chapter with our examination of less radical examples from classical chess. The 1 e4 e5 and 1 d4 d5 openings are not clear-cut in regard to the issue of space, because their initial purpose is to establish a centre pawn on the fourth rank and thus an equal share of territory. Nevertheless, even if Black doesn't surrender the centre in the manner shown in the last section, the relative share of space can still become imbalanced in White's favour and has traditionally been met by a philosophy of exchanges by the weaker side. This is generally the case in the early middlegame of the orthodox lines of the Queen's Gambit Declined with ...e6 (1 d4 d5 2 c4 e6), and it is very instructive to see how these lines have evolved and been reassessed. Let's consider, for example, the current status of some of the very oldest main lines of that opening. Despite its appearance, this will not be a theoretical survey and shouldn't be treated as such. Rather, I am trying to present a series of illustrations of why modern attitudes have changed towards this kind of position:

Space and Exchanges in the Queen's Gambit

1 d4 d5 2 c4 e6 3 ♘c3 ♘f6

In the Exchange Variation line 3...♗e7 4 cxd5 exd5 5 ♗f4 c6 6 e3 ♗f5 7 g4 ♗e6 8 h4!?

c5, the strange-looking 9 ♗e5! ♘f6 10 ♗xb8! ♖xb8 11 g5 ♗e7 12 ♗g2 shows White's willingness to exchange pieces in positions where Black is cramped, even at the cost of ceding his two bishops. This continuation is seen in Part 2 in the game Dautov-Lputian, Istanbul OL 2000.

4 ♗g5 ♗e7 5 e3 0-0 6 ♘f3 (D)

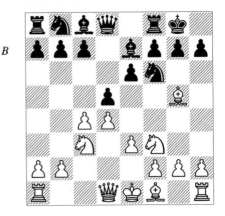

The basic position, in which I will examine only the three most popular variations from the Classical period, ignoring uniquely modern treatments. This is not a theoretical essay on all lines, but rather a selection of critical ones which illustrate the evolution of ideas regarding the centre and space.

6...♘bd7

The Classical Defence. 6...h6 will be seen in the next two games. After 6...♘bd7, White has a variety of moves, but the old main line was:

7 ♖c1 c6 8 ♗d3 dxc4 9 ♗xc4 ♘d5 10 ♗xe7 ♕xe7 (D)

This is sometimes called the Capablanca Variation, mainly due to his use of it (as Black) in his 1927 match versus Alekhine.

Can anything new be said about this venerable line? In general terms, Black first sets up the cramped formation with ...e6 and ...c6, and then

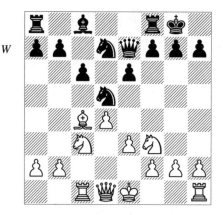

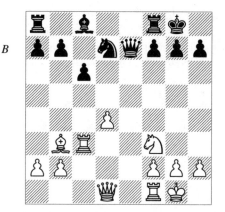

tries to exchange two sets of pieces followed by a central break, i.e. ...e5, to free his queen's bishop and his game. This is the same pattern that we shall see in the next game, via 6...h6 7 &h4 ♘e4 (Lasker's Defence). The philosophy bears some resemblance to the traditional recipe in the ...exd4 positions we saw in the last section.

11 ♘e4

This move at first seems to be avoiding exchanges, but actually just angles for a different set of exchanges in order to achieve the better endgame. In fact, 11 ♘e4 is probably even more damning evidence against Capablanca's line than the more common 11 0-0, because Black's counterchances are virtually nil after 11 ♘e4. Nevertheless, 11 0-0 has also discouraged players from entering this line as Black: 11...♘xc3 12 ♖xc3 e5 (all according to plan; as noted below, this position can also arise, with ...h6 and &h4 having been interpolated, in Lasker's Defence) 13 &b3 exd4 (another possibility is 13...♖e8 14 dxe5 ♘xe5 15 ♘xe5 ♕xe5 16 f4 intending f5, when Black's game is truly cramped) 14 exd4 *(D)*.

This is a well-known IQP position where even a glance shows that White has a nice attack, since he has much better development with ♖e1 coming, and the c3-rook is ready to swing towards the kingside. This doesn't mean that a very strong player couldn't defend the position with perfect play, just that very few would consider that a good bargain. Here are a few examples from modern practice: 14...♘f6 15 ♖e1 ♕d6 16 ♘e5! (threatening ♘xf7) 16...♘d5?! (16...&f5?! 17 ♘xf7! ♖xf7 18 &xf7+ ♔xf7 19 ♕b3+ and ♕xb7 is extremely strong; 16...&e6

is best, but not much fun after 17 &xe6 fxe6 18 ♕b3 ♖ab8 19 ♖ce3 ♘d5 20 ♖e4 ♖f6 21 ♘d3 b6 22 g3 with a small advantage for White, Khenkin-Sulskis, Koszalin 1998; Black has no counterplay) 17 ♖g3 &f5 (17...f6 18 ♘c4 ♕d8 19 ♕h5 {threatening ♖e4-h4} 19...&d7 20 ♘d6 with a large advantage for White) 18 ♕f3 &g6, Kahn-Almasi, Budapest 1992. At this point, Tsesarsky gives the following convincing analysis: 19 h4! ♕b4 (19...h6 20 h5 &h7 21 ♕g4 g6 22 hxg6 fxg6 23 ♘xg6 and White wins) 20 ♖d1 ♘e7 21 h5 &f5 and apart from other moves White has 22 ♖g5! g6 23 hxg6 hxg6 24 ♖xf5! ♘xf5 (24...gxf5 25 ♕g3+, etc.) 25 ♘xg6, winning. Fun stuff.

We now return to 11 ♘e4 *(D)*:

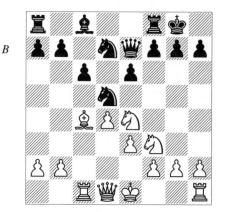

11...♘5f6

The immediate queen exchange 11...♕b4+ 12 ♕d2 ♕xd2+ 13 ♔xd2!, with a significant advantage for White, dates back to Alekhine-Capablanca, Buenos Aires Wch (6) 1927. Very few people have chosen to play this queenless middlegame since. White has a space advantage, dark squares, and a centralized king while Black still has the passive bishop on c8.

12 ♘xf6+ ♕xf6 13 0-0 e5 *(D)*

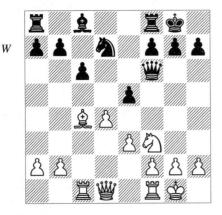

Black has now staked out a claim to the centre and freed a path for his previously miserable c8-bishop. Now 14 ♗b3 exd4 15 ♕xd4 ♕xd4 16 ♘xd4 gives White some advantage with his freer development and more mobile majority, but Black's position is difficult to crack and with care he may unravel his forces. Instead, a recent game is an example of the more direct approach that emphasizes White's space advantage:

Atalik – Zheliandinov
Podlehnik 2001

14 e4! exd4 15 ♕xd4 ♕xd4 16 ♘xd4 ♘e5 17 ♗b3 ♖d8 18 ♖fd1 ♗d7

Apart from having to watch for White's advancing central pawns, Black's problem is that there are few active squares for his pieces.

19 f4!

An accurate move. Black had drawn several games after 19 ♖c5 ♘g6, disentangling by means of ...♗e8, ...♖d7 and bringing the king to the centre. Atalik's new move is more dynamic, and already close to winning!

19...♘g6 20 f5 ♘e5 21 ♖c5! ♘g4

As Yusupov shows, 21...♖e8 22 ♘e6! eventually results in a large advantage for White after 22...♗xe6 23 fxe6 f6 24 ♖d7!.

22 h3 b6?!

Losing, but Atalik gives 22...♘f6 23 e5 ♘e4 24 ♖cc1 ♘g3 25 e6, also ending in a clear advantage for White.

23 ♘xc6! ♗xc6 24 ♖xd8+ ♖xd8 25 ♖xc6 1-0

In view of 25...♘e5 26 ♖c7 a5 27 ♖e7!.

These lines are rich with tradition. For many years, nearly every student would absorb the theoretical main lines as illustrative of White's initial space advantage and Black's subsequent liberation by freeing moves, achieving an equal game. But to a large extent, Black's dream of equality has turned out to be an illusion. As we shall see below, the Capablanca Variation is fast disappearing in top-level play. In my database, games with the move 14 e4 as played above have scored 79% for White with a 2796 performance rating for White versus a miserable 1940 for Black!

Next we look at the other renowned classical solution to the Queen's Gambit:

1 d4 d5 2 c4 e6 3 ♘c3 ♘f6 4 ♗g5 ♗e7 5 e3 0-0 6 ♘f3 h6

The move 6...♘e4 resembles what follows, and was more popular than 6...h6 7 ♗h4 ♘e4 in the early 1900s, but was ultimately discarded because of lines in which White would gain a tempo by attacking the h7-pawn.

7 ♗h4 ♘e4 *(D)*

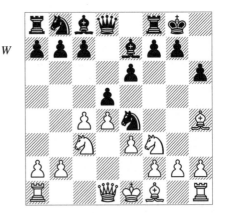

This is called Lasker's Defence (although Lasker seldom used it); it was at one time the textbook line in the entire Queen's Gambit Declined. Note the similarity to Lasker's own philosophy in those Ruy Lopez lines with ...d6 and ...exd4: first accept a cramped position, then free one's game by exchanging two sets of minor pieces (and hopefully some others soon thereafter).

8 ♗xe7 ♕xe7 9 ♖c1 ♘xc3 10 ♖xc3 c6

Passive, but there isn't much of an alternative to get Black's pieces out; e.g., 10...b6 11 cxd5 exd5 12 ♕c2.

11 ♗d3 dxc4 12 ♗xc4 ♘d7 13 0-0 b6 (D)

This move is a good idea. The natural continuation 13...e5 reaches a position extremely similar to the Capablanca Variation in the last game and expresses the essence of a classical philosophy. But with the additional weakness of ...h6, this is probably even more difficult for Black. The same treatment as shown above can result from 14 ♗b3!?; let's see two modern examples:

a) 14...exd4 15 exd4 ♘f6 16 ♖e1 ♕d6 17 ♘e5. Now the variations are very much as above; e.g., Karpov-Yusupov, London Ct (8) 1989 continued 17...♘d5? 18 ♖g3 ♗f5 19 ♕h5 ♗h7 20 ♕g4! g5 21 h4 with a very large advantage for White.

b) 14...e4 is a little depressing for Black after 15 ♘d2 ♘f6 but it at least limits the damage; e.g., 16 ♖c5 (16 h3 is also played) has the idea of ♖e5: 16...♗g4 17 ♕b1 ♘d7 18 ♖c3 ♗e2 19 ♖e1?! (Atalik's suggestion 19 ♖fc1! keeps Black more tied down) 19...♗d3 20 ♗c2 ♗xc2 21 ♕xc2, still with a small advantage for White due to his queenside pressure, Atalik-Zelčić, Bled 2000.

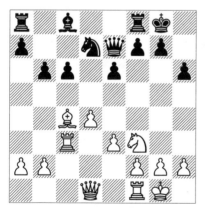

W

If only because 13...e5 is so difficult in concrete terms, the paradoxical 13...b6 is more likely to equalize. Black's idea is now ...♗b7 and ...c5. It looks ridiculous to prepare ...e5 and then switch to ...b6, and yet it caused a limited revival of the Lasker Variation by top players trying to draw with Black. Nevertheless, White found a general plan against it, and by now it

should not surprise the reader that, with more space, he tries to exchange pieces:

14 ♗d3

White's similar idea of 14 ♕e2 intending ♗a6 has generally given him a small advantage.

14...c5

Quite bad is 14...♗b7? 15 ♗e4 ♖fc8 16 ♕c2 and ♖c1.

15 ♗e4 ♖b8 16 ♕a4!?

16 ♕c2 is not much different in principle; e.g., 16...b5 (16...a5 17 ♖c1 ♗b7 18 ♗xb7 ♖xb7 19 dxc5 ♘xc5 20 ♘e5 ♕f6 21 ♘d3 ♖d8 22 ♘xc5 bxc5 23 ♕e2 and White was somewhat better in Karpov-Yusupov, Baden-Baden 1995) 17 ♖c1 b4 18 ♖d3 ♘f6 19 ♗c6 cxd4 20 ♖xd4 e5 21 ♖d2 ♗b7 22 ♗xb7 ♖xb7 23 h3 g6 24 ♕c6 ♖fb8 25 ♕d6 with a small advantage for White, Gelfand-Kramnik, Monte Carlo Amber rpd 2001.

16...♗b7 17 ♗xb7 ♖xb7 18 ♕c2! (D)

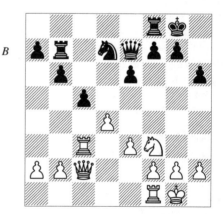

B

In this variation, the third minor-piece exchange has clarified White's small but definite technical advantage. He has nothing to fear at all, whereas Black has had to be careful in practice. For example, 18...a5 (after 18...♖c8 19 ♖c1 ♖bc7 20 b4 e5, as in Kramnik-Kasparov, Las Palmas 1996, Dolmatov suggests 21 bxc5! exd4 22 exd4 bxc5 23 ♖c4 ♘b8 24 ♖xc5 ♖xc5 25 dxc5 with a clear advantage for White) 19 a3 (Kramnik gives 19 ♖d1 cxd4 20 ♘xd4 ♘c5 21 ♘c6 ♕f6 22 b3 with an edge) 19...♖e8 20 ♖d1 with a small but definite advantage for White, Karpov-Yusupov, Dortmund 1997.

Still, one should not think that these difficulties are inevitable just because Black has chosen a simplifying strategy. In fact, such a sequence of exchanges came very close to levelling the game. The point is that one cannot reliably predict whether exchanges will help the side with less space to equalize or the player with more space to maintain an advantage. These are position-specific decisions that cannot be made on the basis of principle. Let's next turn to the solution that has replaced the lines above in modern players' favour:

Illescas – Short
Pamplona 1999/00

1 d4 d5 2 c4 e6 3 Ⓝc3 Ⓝf6 4 Ⓑg5 Ⓑe7 5 e3 0-0 6 Ⓝf3 h6

Just as 6...Ⓝe4 was much more popular than 6...h6 7 Ⓑh4 Ⓝe4 for some time, 6...b6 was the only version of the queenside fianchetto played by top players in the 19th century, and a clear majority of such games in 1901-1935 went 6...b6 rather than 6...h6 7 Ⓑh4 b6. By the 1930s and since then, 6...h6 7 Ⓑh4 b6 has taken over (it prevents a tempo-gain on h7 in some lines), and it is played in at least 50 times as many high-level games today.

7 Ⓑh4 b6 *(D)*

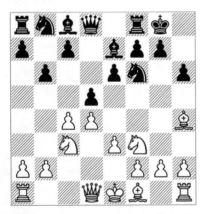

W

This is the Tartakower Defence, named after its earliest consistent practitioner. One might consider this philosophically analogous to Black's ...b6 in the French ...dxe4 lines in the last section, and to his ideal (but tactically unsound) ...g6 move in the ...exd4 Ruy Lopez lines. In the QGD, Black hasn't exchanged the d5-pawn and thus surrendered the centre. Thus we might provisionally expect him to have fewer

problems than in those lines. But he does have a cramped game, and by putting the bishop on the active long diagonal while reserving d7 for his knight, he follows a similar recipe to that of the 3 Ⓝc3 Ⓝf6 4 Ⓑg5 dxe4 French. Even the king's bishop may achieve activity along the h8-a1 diagonal, as also occurs in the French variation, if White chooses to play Ⓑxf6. Black's closed solution, with no rush to exchange anything, has become by far the most popular choice in the juncture following 6 Ⓝf3 among leading masters. Among its many adherents have been world champions Petrosian, Spassky, Karpov, Kasparov, and Kramnik, while players such as Beliavsky and Short use the Tartakower regularly and successfully. See also the figures below regarding its popularity. It has been so successful that it has chased White into increased use of the Exchange Variation (3 Ⓝc3 and 4 cxd5), Ⓑf4 systems, and the Catalan System with g3. Indeed, the Exchange Variation now outnumbers the Lasker, Capablanca, and Tartakower lines combined by well over 2 to 1!

On a practical level, Black retains more winning opportunities after 7...b6 by virtue of keeping more pieces on the board. It's true that White can himself force simplification by 8 cxd5 Ⓝxd5 9 Ⓑxe7, etc., but this has now been shown to be thoroughly harmless, and at the top level it is played almost exclusively by the peaceably minded; even then, Black wins his share of games. So let's look at some modern interpretations of the Tartakower in practice, again understanding that this is by no means a theoretical overview:

8 Ⓑe2

A recent example that reached the same type of position went 8 Ⓦb3 Ⓑb7 9 Ⓑxf6 Ⓑxf6 10 cxd5 exd5 11 Ⓡd1 Ⓡe8 12 Ⓑd3 *(D)*.

Now:

a) 12...g6?! (this is slow) 13 0-0 Ⓑg7? (inviting White to open up the position; Black should get developed via 13...c6 and ...Ⓝd7, although White will still succeed in playing e4) 14 Ⓡfe1 c6 (otherwise it's hard to develop) 15 e4 (now the knights are activated along with White's other pieces) 15...dxe4 16 Ⓑc4! Ⓡe7 17 Ⓝe5! Ⓑxe5 (there is no defence) 18 dxe5 Ⓦc7 19 Ⓝxe4 Ⓦxe5 20 Ⓡe3 (White can also win by 20 Ⓦb4 c5 21 Ⓝxc5 or 20 Ⓑxf7+! Ⓡxf7 21 Ⓝd6) 20...Ⓦg7 21 Ⓝd6 Ⓡxe3 22 Ⓦxe3 Ⓑa6

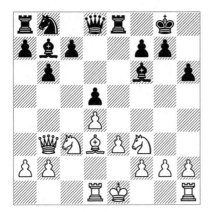

B

23 ♕e8+ ♕f8 24 ♗xf7+ ♔g7 25 ♕e6 1-0 Mitkov-Vasovski, Gevgelija 2002.

b) 12...c5! 13 dxc5 ♘d7! is an active solution. 14 c6! (14 cxb6 gives Black extremely active play after 14...♘c5 15 ♕c2 ♘xd3+ 16 ♖xd3 axb6) 14...♗xc6 15 0-0 ♘c5 16 ♕c2 (16 ♕a3 a5 is equal) and here Black has equalized with 16...♘xd3, 16...♕e7, and 16...♖c8, the last as in Beliavsky-Kramnik, Belgrade 1997. However, there is still play in these positions for both sides.

8...♗b7 9 ♗xf6

We're so used to this move that it no longer seems remarkable. And yet, consider that White retreated this bishop two moves ago only to exchange it at loss of tempo now! Furthermore, he cedes the two bishops in what doesn't look like a very closed position. The idea is that Black's bishop is in some ways worse on b7 than it was on c8! This modern, paradoxical solution came into its own in the 1970s and remains White's most popular approach to the Tartakower.

Incidentally, notice that there is no further exchange of pieces until move 21 of this game, nor until move 21 in the next game! Furthermore, in the Karpov-Ki.Georgiev game note on pages 42-3, you will see that the first piece is 'exchanged' on move 29 as part of the concluding combination. Dynamism and maintenance of tension in the position characterize the modern Tartakower QGD.

9...♗xf6 10 cxd5 exd5 11 0-0

In the next game we will see examples of 11 b4.

11...♕e7 12 ♕b3

This plan is less popular than expansion on the queenside by b4, but still very interesting.

The middlegame that we are entering has reasonably well defined characteristics. Without too much happening on that wing, White would like to restrain Black's move ...c5 by playing a rook to d1. Then he can either play for a bind and slowly expand with moves like a4-a5; or he can try to enforce e4 to get his knights activated.

12...♖d8 13 ♖fd1

In line with the last note, ♖ad1, ♖e1, and ♗d3 is the alternative plan.

13...c6 14 ♗f1 *(D)*

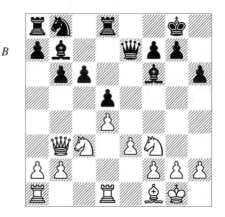

B

By contrast with the Mitkov game (note 'a' to White's 8th move), White is playing slowly and isn't preparing to open things up in either the centre or on the queenside. This is not terrible, but as discussed in SOMCS, time tends to favour the bishop-pair, since once Black catches up in development and reorganizes, he can himself open the position.

14...♘a6!

Planning a trip to the fine central square e6.

15 ♖d2 ♘c7 16 a4 ♘e6

A well-calculated move, anticipating that a5 isn't a problem. According to Short, it was also possible to play dynamically by 16...c5!? 17 dxc5 bxc5 18 ♕xb7 ♗xc3 19 bxc3 ♖db8 20 ♕c6 ♖b6 21 ♕xa8+ ♘xa8 22 ♖xd5 ♘c7, which he assesses as unclear.

17 a5 b5 18 ♕a2 a6 19 ♖c1?!

White overlooks Short's idea, although it is one that occurs quite a bit in the Tartakower. Donev suggests instead 19 ♘e2! ♖ac8 (19...c5 20 dxc5 ♘xc5 21 ♘ed4) 20 ♖c1 with equality.

19...c5! *(D)*

20 dxc5 d4! 21 ♘xd4 ♗xd4 22 exd4 ♘xd4

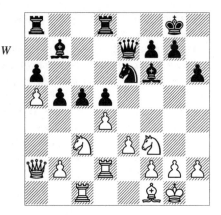

For a mere pawn, Black has activated his rook, bishop and knight and threatens the extremely hard-to-meet ...♘f3+.

23 ♔h1 *(D)*

23 ♖cd1?? ♘f3+! 24 gxf3 ♖xd2 25 ♖xd2 ♕g5+.

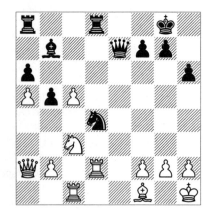

23...♘f3! 24 ♖xd8+

24 ♖dd1 ♕g5! threatens both ...♕f4 and ...♘d2.

24...♖xd8 25 c6 ♗xc6 26 ♘e2

White is lost here.

26...♕h4! 27 gxf3 ♕xf2 28 ♘f4

After 28 ♖xc6 Black wins with the pretty sequence 28...♕xf1+ 29 ♘g1 ♖d1 30 ♖g6 ♕xf3+ 31 ♖g2 ♕e4!! 32 b3 ♖xg1+ 33 ♔xg1 ♕e1#, as given by Short.

28...♗xf3+ 29 ♗g2 ♖d2 30 ♖g1 ♗e4! 0-1

This pretty game illustrates why the Tartakower appeals to players who desire more complexity and dynamism than is offered by the classical QGD defences. This is also true in the variation that follows.

Speelman – Lputian
Kropotkin 1995

1 d4 d5 2 ♘f3 ♘f6 3 c4 e6 4 ♗g5 ♗e7 5 e3 h6 6 ♗h4 0-0 7 ♘c3 b6 8 ♗e2 ♗b7 9 ♗xf6 ♗xf6 10 cxd5 exd5 11 b4

In this variation White tries to deny Black counterplay by discouraging ...c5. He may also attack on the queenside by b5 or a4-a5 at the right moment.

11...c6

Liquidating by 11...c5 has been played in many games, including several in the first Karpov-Kasparov world championship match. The usual continuation is 12 bxc5 bxc5 13 ♖b1 ♗c6 14 0-0 ♘d7 15 ♗b5 ♕c7, after which Black seems to achieve theoretical equality, but with minimal winning chances. The text-move is designed to create a complex and double-edged game, pitting White's space against Black's two bishops.

12 0-0 *(D)*

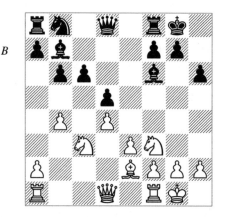

12...a5!

Gaining space. Black played the same plan in the following game, but his queen placement allowed White some other possibilities: 12...♕d6 13 ♕b3 ♘d7 14 ♖fe1 ♗e7 15 ♖ab1 a5 16 bxa5 ♖xa5 17 a4 ♖e8 18 ♗f1 *(D)*.

18...♗f8 (abandoning the long diagonal may not have been so smart, and now Black tries to regain it) 19 ♕c2 g6 20 e4! (but he is a tempo short; from here on, the game resembles the example in note 'a' to White's 8th move in the previous game) 20...dxe4 21 ♘xe4 ♕f4 22 ♗c4! ♗g7 23 ♖e2 c5 24 d5 ♖aa8 25 ♖be1 ♖ad8 26 ♕b3 ♗a8 27 g3 ♕b8 28 d6 (every white piece

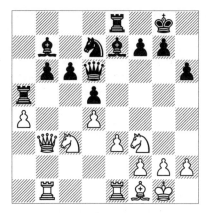

B

takes part in the attack) 28...♖f8 29 ♗xf7+ ♖xf7 30 ♘eg5 hxg5 31 ♘xg5 ♖df8 32 ♖e8 ♕xd6 33 ♕xf7+ ♔h8 34 ♘e6 1-0 Karpov-Ki.Georgiev, Tilburg 1994.

13 a3

This seems to maintain White's bind, but soon allows an interesting positional trick that seems to give Black equality.

Instead, 13 bxa5 ♖xa5 14 a4 is a common idea, restraining ...b5 and preparing to exert pressure against Black's queenside by ♕b3 and ♖ab1. Black then has a creative and paradoxical reorganization that maximizes the use of his pieces: 14...♗c8! 15 ♕c2 (15 ♖b1 ♗e6 16 ♕c2 ♘d7 17 ♖fc1 ♕a8 is equal, Alterman-Pigusov, Beijing 1997; Black is ready for ...c5) 15...♗e6 16 ♖fc1 ♘d7 17 ♗f1 ♕a8! 18 ♕d1 ♖c8 with equality, Beliavsky-Johannessen, Linares 2002.

13...♘d7 14 ♕b3 ♖e8 15 ♖ad1 axb4 16 axb4 b5! *(D)*

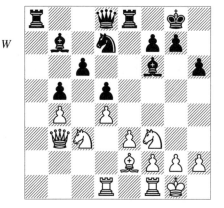

W

This is the point. Black gains c4 for his knight in return for c5. This mutual blocking

will make it hard for White to make progress against Black's lone weakness on c6. Still, Black's bishops are pretty awful, right? One is rendered ineffective by the d4-pawn, and the other is restricted by his own pawns. But wait a few moves...

17 ♘e1 ♘b6 18 ♘d3 ♗c8! 19 ♘c5 ♗f5 20 ♖a1 ♗e7! 21 ♖a2 ♖xa2 22 ♕xa2 ♗d6

Now everything is fine, and White even has to watch his kingside.

23 ♖a1 ♕h4 24 g3 ♕g5 25 ♗d3? *(D)*

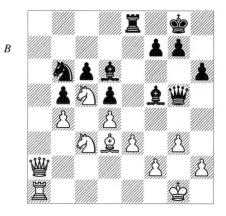

B

Tactically mistaken, but with ...♖xe3 threatened and the idea ...h5-h4 in the air, White was a little worse off anyway.

25...♗xd3 26 ♘xd3 ♖xe3!

Hardly an exchange sacrifice, since Black gets two pawns and yet another pawn falls soon thereafter.

27 fxe3 ♕xe3+ 28 ♕f2

28 ♘f2 ♕xc3 is no better.

28...♕xd3 29 ♘e2 ♗xb4 30 ♖a7 ♕b1+ 31 ♔g2 ♕e4+ 32 ♕f3 ♕e8 33 ♘f4 ♘c4

Black went on to convert his material advantage into victory.

The overall trends in this main line of the Queen's Gambit Declined can be clarified by examining some statistics. I will compare the frequency of the Lasker Defence (with ...♘e4), the Capablanca Variation, and the Tartakower Defence in databases of games by leading players. I have included the use of 6...♘e4 in the Lasker figures and 6...b6 with the Tartakower (both a small minority of total games except the earliest periods), because the difference between these lines and those with 6...h6 and

7...b6 reflects only the advancement of concrete theory and no philosophical change. Otherwise, for example, one might think that the Tartakower idea was hardly played until the post-1935 period, which would be very misleading.

Historical usage of these variations demonstrates the change in attitude towards them. In each case I will take percentages out of a total of QGDs with &g5 (representing a wide variety of black defences, so much of the game space is not filled by our particular lines). As before, I will first use the databases of the world's leading players in the time periods given. Although the figures that follow are slightly biased by the difficulty of separating out a given player's practice over decades in which he was not as dominant, the relative figures should be indicative anyway.

For leading players whose peak playing period was 1901-35, Lasker's Defence was used in 5.3% of their &g5 games, the Capablanca Variation in 10.6%, and the Tartakower (mainly 6...b6) in 12%.

For the period 1936-70, the Lasker figure goes to 11%, the Capablanca to 6.3%, and the Tartakower (almost all 7...b6) to 26%. It should be noted that I have not always split up the games of players whose play overlaps less dramatically into two periods, so in this case there is a moderate overstatement of the Tartakower figures. Still, a big leap in its use began in the 1960s.

In 1971-2002, high-level use of Lasker's Defence was 6%, the Capablanca dropped to only 1.6%, and the Tartakower Defence's popularity skyrocketed to 40%.

So we see that the Lasker and Capablanca variations have been to a large extent superseded by the Tartakower, in which Black keeps the pieces on the board rather than seeking exchanges. On the other hand, I was surprised to see that the Tartakower *idea* was fairly popular even going back into the 19th century (with 6...b6). This indicates that certain leading players at that time were willing to fianchetto their bishop (something that was still rare relative to modern times), and that they must have appreciated the greater scope for play this strategy afforded. Also noteworthy is that the Tartakower Defence proper (with 6...h6 7 &h4 b6) clearly

outperformed the Lasker and Capablanca variations in every time period. Over the last 30 years, it has scored almost exactly 50% as Black, with a dead heat in performance ratings. By contrast, the Lasker and Capablanca have done miserably; amazingly, Black hasn't scored a single win out of the 69 Lasker Defences in the 1971-2002 database of top masters! While the players split the point 46 times, it seems that Black can hardly hope for winning chances versus leading players in this line.

Hedgehogs and their Territoriality

The examples above are all based upon classical pawn-structures. In modern times, we find that the growing acceptance of openings that claim less space provides us with many illustrations of the flexibility that has arisen with respect to exchanges. In the theory of almost any opening we encounter examples of the side with less space seeking exchanges or avoiding them, depending upon concrete situations. The same applies to the player who controls more space. I will extend the discussion that I began in SOMCS of the structure that most cleanly illustrates this.

So-called 'Hedgehog' structures are characterized by black pawns on a6, b6, d6, and e6 with his c-pawn off the board, a sample skeletal structure being:

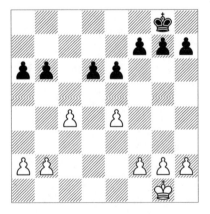

The white c-pawn can also be on c2 (as in the Sicilian Defence).

Hedgehog positions arise in many variations of the English Opening and still more in Sicilian Defences. For example, Frank Zeller's *Sizilianisch im Geiste des Igels* ('The Sicilian in the Spirit of the Hedgehog') provides a fascinating survey of a host of regular and irregular Hedgehog variants in the Sicilian (at least 30 independent ones!). I don't want to overdescribe the characteristics of this structure, which is covered in SOMCS, nor belabour the now-conventional point that Hedgehog positions exemplify a conceptual change in the attitude towards space, dynamism, and elasticity in modern chess. But by looking at some practical examples I hope to extend our discussion of the main theme of this chapter, that of exchanges in the context of space.

The 'original' Hedgehog move-order (i.e., from which it got its name) arises from the English Opening. Here is a well-known game (at least to those of my generation!) demonstrating both sides' strategy:

Polugaevsky – Ftačnik
Lucerne OL 1982

1 ♘f3 ♘f6 2 c4 c5 3 ♘c3 e6 4 g3 b6 5 ♗g2 ♗b7 6 0-0 ♗e7 7 d4 cxd4 8 ♕xd4 *(D)*

After 8 ♘xd4 ♗xg2 9 ♔xg2, Black has demonstrated that plans like ...♕c8 and ...♘c6 (to exchange another piece) as well as those with ...a6 and ...d6 equalize easily. Thus we have a case in which White's best attempt to maintain an advantage is by avoiding exchanges, in conformity with classical precepts.

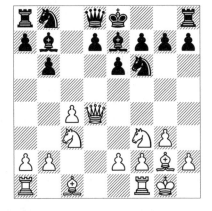

8...d6

9 ♖d1

However, after 9 b3 0-0 10 ♖d1 ♘bd7 11 ♗b2 a6 12 ♕e3 ♕b8 13 ♘d4 ♗xg2 14 ♔xg2, "Black must beware of endings" according to Dorfman, who queries Black's next: 14...♕b7+? 15 ♕f3 ♕xf3+ 16 ♘xf3 and White's space advantage gave him a considerable advantage in Karpov-Gheorghiu, Moscow Echt 1977. With too few pieces, Black's position loses its dynamism.

9...a6 10 b3 ♘bd7 11 e4

We look first at a traditional approach that was popular in the early days of the Hedgehog. White hopes to clamp down permanently on ...d5, but the trade-off is that he exposes his own centre.

11...♕b8

An elaborate move designed to prevent the exchange of pieces that White now aims for. 11...♕c8!? is also played with the same purpose. A classic example of what Black is trying to avoid (and has had to defend in many games) is Ribli-Ambrož, Baile Herculane Z 1982: 11...♕c7?! 12 ♗a3 ♘c5 13 e5 dxe5 14 ♕xe5 ♖c8 15 ♕xc7 ♖xc7 16 ♗c1! ♘fe4 17 ♗f4 *(D)* (a very *concrete* idea that justifies White's exchanges; otherwise Black would welcome them, as in the note to White's 12th move).

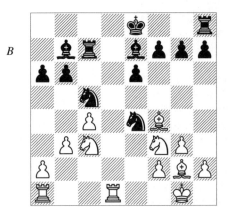

17...♖c8 18 ♘xe4 ♗xe4 19 ♗d6! (Wells: "Again, simplification seems to assist White in his cause.") 19...♗f6 20 ♘e5 ♗xg2 21 ♔xg2 ♗xe5?! 22 ♗xe5 (in just seven moves, most of the pieces have disappeared; note that ...b5 never became a problem for White) 22...f6 23 ♗d6 ♖c6 24 ♖d4 e5 25 ♖d5 ♘e6 26 f4! exf4 27 gxf4 g6 28 ♔f3 ♔f7 29 ♗a3 ♘c5 30 ♗xc5!

(Wells: "Again, despite the attraction of the bishop vs knight scenario from White's point of view, there is once more profit to be had from simplification") 30...♖xc5 31 ♖d7+ ♔e6 32 ♖ad1 ♖c6 33 ♖b7 h5 34 h4 ♖g8 35 ♖e1+ ♔d6 36 a3 ♖gc8 37 ♖g1, and Black had to give up the g-pawn in view of the disaster that would follow 37...♖g8? (37...♖8c7 was played) 38 f5 g5?? 39 ♖d1+ ♔e5 40 ♖d5#.

12 ♗b2

The point of 11...♕b8 instead of 11...0-0 is 12 ♗a3 ♘c5 13 e5 dxe5 14 ♕xe5 ♘cd7!, when Black has no problems with or without the queen exchange. Compare Ribli-Ambrož; this is the same structure and almost the same position, but, crucially, White cannot reorganize as he did there.

12...0-0 13 ♘d2!? *(D)*

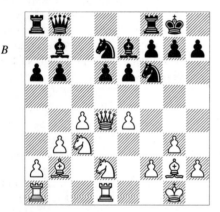

White's philosophy is a traditional one: when one has more space, concentrate upon preventing enemy freeing moves, and then slowly expand to put pressure upon the opponent's position. 13 ♘d2 prevents ...b5 by protecting the e-pawn and directs another piece at the d5-square.

13...♖d8 14 a4

Again, to prevent any trick with ...b5 followed by ...d5.

14...♕c7 15 ♕e3 ♖ac8 16 ♕e2

More pressure on b5, although the main point of this move is to prepare f4 without having to worry about ...d5 and ...♗c5.

16...♘e5 17 h3?! *(D)*

White has now played every classically restrictive move. He wants to play f4 without having to worry about ...♘eg4, and indeed, 17 f4?!

♘eg4 18 ♖f1 ♕c5+ 19 ♔h1 ♘e3! 20 b4 ♕xb4 21 ♕xe3 ♕xb2 22 ♖fb1 ♕c2 (22...♘g4!) 23 ♖a2 ♘g4! 24 ♕f3 ♕d3! 25 ♕xd3 ♘f2+ (Ftačnik) confirms this reasoning. But something goes wrong anyway, and it starts here. The best moves were probably just waiting ones like 17 ♔h1 or 17 ♖ac1. Nevertheless, Black would have no real problems.

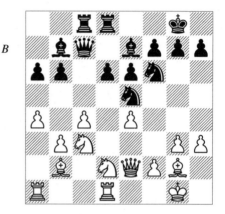

It seems amazing that 17 h3?! constitutes a serious weakening when most of Black's pieces are on the queenside and relatively passively placed. But Black's next move, defying all the rules about moving flank pawns in front of one's king, shows why:

17...h5!

Black intends to weaken White's kingside dark squares by ...h4 and ...hxg3, whereas in response to g4, ...♘g6 or even ...g5 and ...♘g6 can follow. This one-pawn attack turns the game around!

It is precisely the retention of pieces on the board that allows a flank attack like this to work. I wasn't aware of it at the time, but the two examples of the Hedgehog that I included in SOMCS, both wins for Black, had their first piece exchanges on move 35(!) and move 25 (in the second case two moves before resignation).

Wells expresses the concomitant thought from White's standpoint (that exchanges take the sting out of Black's flank attacks) in the notes to the next game.

18 f4 ♘g6 19 ♘f3?!

19 h4 allows ...♘g4. White should probably have acknowledged his problems and counterattacked by 19 f5!? ♘e5 20 ♘f3, although Black should stand better since he would control

the dark squares and White's g2-bishop is a sorry sight.

19...d5!

Polugaevsky's idea was 19...h4 20 f5!, when Ftačnik offers 20...exf5 21 exf5 ♗xf3 22 ♕xf3 ♘e5 23 ♕e3 ♕c5! (23...hxg3 24 ♕xg3 is awfully dangerous for Black given White's control of d5 and the g-file), claiming equality. But at this point *Junior* quite correctly suggests 24 ♖d4! with a significant advantage, since White threatens both g4-g5 and ♗a3; e.g., 24...hxg3 (24...♘c6? loses to 25 ♗xc6 ♖xc6 26 ♘d5) 25 ♗a3 ♕c7 26 ♕xg3 with an attack. One sees how potentially risky a weakening of the kingside like ...h5 might have been. But with accurate play, that thrust has diverted White from the centre, allowing 19...d5! and the explosion of Black's pent-up energy.

20 cxd5?! *(D)*

20 e5 ♘e4 highlights White's weaknesses, especially on g3. One line by Ftačnik goes 21 ♘xe4 dxe4 22 ♘d4 (22 ♘d2 ♖d3! and Black is well on top) 22...h4 23 ♗xe4 hxg3! (threatening f4) 24 ♗xg6 (24 ♕e3 ♗xe4 25 ♕xe4 ♘h4) 24...fxg6 25 ♕g4 ♗c5! 26 ♕xe6+ ♔h7 27 f5 gxf5! 28 ♕xf5+ ♔g8 29 ♕g5 (29 ♕e6+ ♔h8 and ...♖e8) 29...♕c6.

Ftačnik suggests that White's best move is 20 exd5!?, after which Black can only gain a small advantage following 20...♗c5+ 21 ♔h1 exd5! 22 cxd5 ♘xd5 23 ♘xd5 ♗xd5.

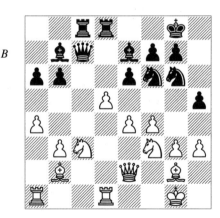

20...h4!

White's position is undermined by a series of pawn attacks that combine to activate every one of Black's pieces. Eventually, this kind of dynamic release of energy became routine in the

Hedgehog and no longer seems remarkable to the modern eye.

21 ♘xh4

21 dxe6? ♗c5+ 22 ♔h1 ♘h5, and it's amusing to compare the activity of Black's pieces with that on move 15.

21...♘xh4 22 gxh4 ♕xf4

Black is substantially better, perhaps already winning.

23 dxe6 fxe6 24 e5? ♗c5+ 25 ♔h1 ♘h:

Introducing a pretty finish.

26 ♕xh5 ♕g3 27 ♘d5

27 ♕e2 ♕xh3#.

27...♖xd5 28 ♖f1 ♕xg2+! 29 ♔xg2 ♖d2+ 0-1

Polugaevsky had had enough due to 30 ♔g3 ♖g2+ 31 ♔f4 ♖f8+, when mate follows.

After such torture became commonplace, many players with White decided to abandon the classical e4/c4 bind and try something more modest. Here's a recent game in which one of the great practitioners of the black side of the Hedgehog played White:

Suba – Nicholson
Malaga 2001

1 c4 ♘f6 2 ♘f3 c5 3 ♘c3 e6 4 g3 b6 5 ♗g2 ♗b7 6 0-0 ♗e7 7 d4

Because the pure Hedgehog that arises after this move tends to equalize for Black, one increasingly sees the sequence 7 ♖e1 d6 8 e4 a6 9 d4 cxd4 10 ♘xd4. This has its own extensive theory, and the sort of bizarre but instructive clash of ideas that we are seeing today is typified by the following game: 10...♕c7 11 ♗e3 0-0 12 ♖c1 ♘bd7 13 f4 h5!? (out of nowhere! The initial idea is ...♘g4) 14 h3 *(D)*.

Does this look familiar? But remember that in Polugaevsky-Ftačnik, the knight supported ...h4 from g6, so here ...h5 seems more suspicious to me. Nevertheless, Black survives both here and in other examples. 14...♖fe8 15 ♗f2 ♗f8 16 ♘f3 (putting the clamps on ...h4, but what's White's plan?) 16...♖ad8 17 ♕e2 g6 18 ♘g5 (18 e5 dxe5 19 fxe5 ♘h7 and White has to be careful about his e-pawn) 18...♘h7! (OK, at least now we know that it's *Black* who would like to exchange this time!) 19 ♘xh7 ♔xh7 20 g4 hxg4 21 hxg4 ♗g7!? (Nisipeanu analyses

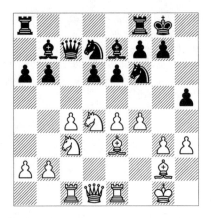

21...d5! out to some kind of dynamic equality; in that case, as above, Black's flank attack would again have diverted White sufficiently to allow the key central break) 22 ♗f3!? (22 g5! is Nisipeanu's suggestion, when of all things he wants Black to play 22...♕b8) 22...g5! (a sacrifice typical of both the Sicilian and King's Indian Defences; its main point is to secure the e5-square and reduce White's light-squared bishop to pathetic passivity; thus Nisipeanu considers White's next move forced) 23 e5 ♗xf3 24 ♕xf3 gxf4 25 exd6 ♕xd6 26 ♘e4 ♕c7 27 ♗h4 ♘e5 28 ♕h1 ♔g8 29 ♘f6+ ♔f8 30 ♘h7+ ♔g8 31 ♘f6+ ♔f8 32 ♘h7+ ½-½ M.Gurevich-Nisipeanu, Cap d'Agde 2000. A crazy game. As I say, no one seems surprised by this kind of thing any more!

7...cxd4 8 ♕xd4 d6 9 ♗g5 *(D)*

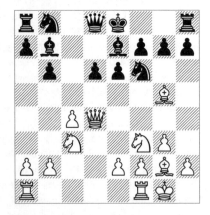

White increasingly turned to this move preparing exchanges after fiascos such as the one in the previous game. White intends to simplify regardless, even if it means sacrificing a few

tempi and the bishop-pair. The idea is that this will cut down on the dynamism of Black's position and the effectiveness of his ...d5 and ...b5 breaks. The particular line in this game, once played by Andersson and Karpov among others, has been around for some time. Black is theoretically able to come very close to equality, but it's not always comfortable for him. Suba, who is one of the world's leading Hedgehog experts and literally 'wrote the book' on it, is very complimentary of this system and is still happy to take White's side. It should be mentioned that White has many other systems based upon simplification, such as ones with ♘g5-e4 and queen moves followed by ♘d4, although they don't seem able to accomplish much against precise defence.

9...a6

To discourage ♘b5 in many variations. Black has now completed the Hedgehog set-up.

10 ♗xf6 ♗xf6 11 ♕d3 *(D)*

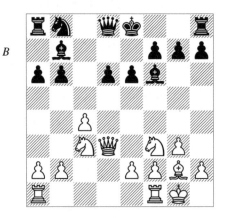

Thus White has prepared and gone ahead with the exchange of minor pieces and he will do so again on move 13. GM Peter Wells makes some insightful comments about the Hedgehog: "Ask most players what strategy should be employed when 'suffering' from a spatial disadvantage, and I strongly suspect the most common reply would revolve around the attempt to exchange pieces. Logical on at least two grounds – relative values of pieces in terms of their concrete potential – pieces could be simply seen as 'superior' in value to your cramped little victims of claustrophobia – and also simply when space is scarce, a reduction in wood eases the pain, leaving more space to share around. So far so good. However, let us, by way of plausible enough concrete example, take a look at the period of the rise to respectability of the 'Hedgehog' formation ... This is a black set-up which can be virtually defined in terms of White's spatial plus, but as we look at the evolution of White's strategy a very surprising development occurs. Respect for the flexibility of Black's passive pieces grows, and at the same time a number of White's more challenging attempts to demonstrate a plus involve White initiating simplification (!) – either the exchange of queens or at least a pair of minor pieces ... Interesting is Igor Stohl's take on this issue [that] 'without the queens on the board White often has more chances to advance his pawns on both flanks, thus emphasizing his space advantage without having to think about a devastating counterattack.' " The latter comment would apply, for example, to the Ribli-Ambrož example in the notes to the previous game.

11...Ia7

A multi-purpose move. It avoids 11...0-0? 12 ♘g5! ♗xg5 13 ♗xb7, when several games have demonstrated that White's space advantage is really starting to mean something. Black can also now swing the rook to c7 or even d7 if necessary. 11...♕c7 is a respectable alternative.

12 Iad1 ♗e7 13 ♘d4 ♗xg2 14 ♔xg2 ♕c8

Black needs to get his knight out; 14...♘d7 allows 15 ♘c6.

15 f4 ♘c6

15...g6 is actually the main move in theory, and it obviously leaves a lot of scope for double-edged play. Tal sacrificed dramatically and unclearly with 16 f5!? gxf5 17 e4 in two games, a strategy which is of course not compulsory!

16 If3

16 f5!? ♘e5 17 ♕e4 may give White a small advantage, but Suba doesn't want to allow counterplay.

16...0-0 17 ♘xc6 ♕xc6 18 f5 Ic7 19 b3 (D)

As is often the case, simplification has made it more difficult for Black to achieve ...b5 or ...d5.

19...Ib7 20 a4!?

Further prophylaxis. The direct 20 fxe6 fxe6 21 ♕e3! is even more attractive, I think.

20...Ibb8 21 ♕e3 Ibe8?

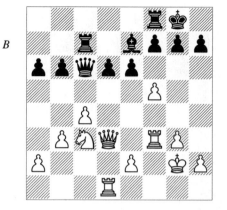

B

Black had to be patient and try 21...♗f6 22 ♕e4 (22 ♘e4!?) 22...♕d7!, when White has only a moderate edge.

22 fxe6 ♗f6 23 ♕e4! ♕xe4 24 ♘xe4 Ixe6 25 ♘xf6+ gxf6 26 ♔f2

Black has recovered his material, but his pawns are a wreck. The game ended as follows:

26...Ife8 27 Id2 ♔f8 28 Ifd3 ♔e7 29 Id5 Ig8 30 a5 Ib8 31 I2d3 Ie5 32 Ixd6 Ixa5 33 Id7+ ♔e6 34 Ia7 Ia2 35 Ie3+ ♔f5 36 Ixf7 ♔g6 37 Iee7

White is winning.

In the next game we return to a Hedgehog position that epitomizes the struggle between White's space advantage and Black's potential for dynamic counterplay. The particular line we look at has always scored well for Black, but here we see White getting in the first dynamic blows. It is noteworthy from the point of view of this section that neither side seeks exchanges nor even confrontations that might lead to them. In fact, the first exchange of pieces takes place on move 34!

Gavrikov – V. Lazarev
Switzerland 2002

1 c4 c5 2 ♘f3 ♘c6 3 d4 cxd4 4 ♘xd4 ♘f6 5 ♘c3 e6 6 a3 ♗e7 7 e4 0-0 8 ♘f3!?

White wants to clamp down on a potential ...d5. This goal is assisted by the pawn on a3, since after a pawn sacrifice by ...d5 and double capture by pawns on d5, Black doesn't have the counterattack ...♘b4 available.

8...d6 9 ♗e2 b6 10 0-0 ♗b7 11 ♗f4 Ic8 12 Ie1 (D)

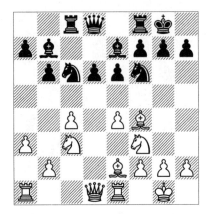

This position has arisen a few times recently. Black is setting up a pretty normal-looking Hedgehog, and in fact he could have completed it now by 12...a6. Instead he begins a massive reorganization of his knights while White manages to move most of his pieces several more times. Amazingly, the result of all this is a position right out of traditional Hedgehog theory.

12...♞g4!?

Given where this leads, one really wonders if Black has to use six extra moves to get his knights to d7 and f6! Presumably this is not easy or necessarily desirable to do directly because of lines such as 12...a6 13 ♖c1 ♞b8 (13...♛c7 14 ♞d5!) 14 ♛d3 ♞bd7?! 15 ♗xd6 ♗xd6 16 ♛xd6 ♞xe4 17 ♞xe4 ♗xe4 18 b4 with a small but definite advantage for White.

13 ♞d2

Now any attempt to pile up on the d6-pawn by doubling of the d-file is easily countered by ...♞ge5. Therefore, White switches to centralizing and protecting the central points e4 and c4.

13...♞ge5 14 ♗e3 ♞d7 15 ♖c1 ♞f6

Wait a minute: isn't Black's position familiar? Yet one might argue that White's pieces are no better placed than they were four moves ago either! It's interesting that Gavrikov, a 2580 player at the time, makes no criticism of Black's moves.

16 ♛a4 a6 17 ♖ed1 ♞b8 18 b4 ♞bd7 19 ♛b3

Both sides' pieces will continue to have trouble sitting still!

19...♛c7 20 f3 ♖fe8 21 ♞f1!?

Gavrikov doesn't like this, suggesting 21 ♞a4, since 21...d5? then fails to 22 cxd5 ♛xc1 23 dxe6!.

21...♛b8 22 ♔h1 (D)

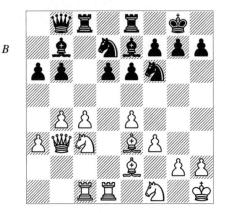

An amazing transformation. Something extremely close to this position can arise in various 'true' Hedgehog openings like 1 c4 c5 2 ♞f3 ♞f6 3 d4 cxd4 4 ♞xd4 b6 5 ♞c3 ♗b7 6 f3 d6 7 e4 e6, etc. This can also happen via a Sicilian Defence. Now Black plays a standard manoeuvre from this set-up:

22...♗d8!?

It's hard to believe that the bishop will actually be much better on c7 than on e7, but as we saw in examples in SOMCS, White's kingside can come under some real pressure due to the constant threat of ...d5. The safer and equally popular course is to play 22...♗f8, when the ideas expressed in Polugaevsky-Ftačnik above apply, i.e., that although Black cannot achieve anything dramatic, it is also hard for White to try anything substantial without allowing either a ...d5 or ...b5 break. The ...♗d8-c7 manoeuvre turns it more into a race between flank attacks, as we shall see shortly.

23 ♖c2 ♗c7 24 ♖cd2 ♔h8

Black now sets up the unlikely flank advance ...g5. It is particularly unconventional in that the kingside advance will be supported almost entirely by pieces stuck on the first and second ranks, and mostly on the queenside!

25 ♖b1!?

A very original idea (perhaps it could have been played earlier?). White would like to find a way to back up a queenside advance, and now both a4-a5 and c5 are possibilities since the b7-bishop hangs. The problem remains that any advance he makes runs the risk of unleashing the dynamic potential of Black's pieces.

25...h6!?

Small things make a difference. Black usually plays the same idea by means of ...♖g8 and ...g5, which leaves him more flexibly placed to play moves like ...♖g6 and even ...♖h6 without any further kingside weaknesses. This was the method we saw in SOMCS. Compare the note to Black's 26th move.

26 ♗g1

Perhaps 26 a4!? was worth thinking about, as was preparing c5. But in both cases it would be nice to have another piece controlling d5, so White arranges that.

26...g5 *(D)*

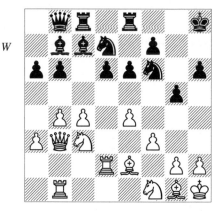

This is more or less the standard idea: Black wants to blast open lines on the kingside after ...♖g8 and ...g4 (often preceded by ...♖g6 and ...♖cg8, and sometimes with ...h5 in), followed by a ...d5 thrust that releases all of his pieces that are aimed at the kingside. All this sounds a bit idealistic, but it has worked in a lot of games. One difference here, as noted above, is that Black has substituted the rather strange ...h6 + ...g5 for ...♖g8 + ...g5. In addition to what I said above, it's sometimes nice to have the h-pawn on h7 for a while as a defender.

27 ♘e3 ♖g8 28 ♕b2!?

Irritating Black's king on the long diagonal. Generally speaking, White has had a difficult time countering Black's straightforward plan, so it's particularly interesting to see what he tries here.

28...♔h7 *(D)*

For example, 28...♖g6 could be met by 29 c5! (the point of ♖b1) 29...dxc5 30 bxc5 ♘xc5 31 ♘c4!, when b6 can only be defended by

31...♘cd7 allowing 32 ♘a4! with the double threats ♘axb6 and ♖xd7.

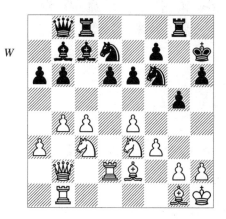

29 ♖bd1!?

White seems to be indecisive, and indeed 29 a4 might have been more consistent. But he has a new and probably better idea.

29...h5?

Now White gets his chance. Gavrikov queries this and suggests 29...♖cd8.

30 ♕b1! *(D)*

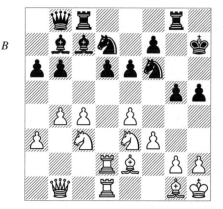

Again eyeing Black's king (31 e5+ is threatened).

30...♖g6?! *(D)*

At first 30...♘e5 looks logical but then White can take advantage of the knight's absence from d7 to play 31 c5! (31 a4 is also interesting, since direct attack by 31...g4 allows 32 f4 ♘g6 33 e5! dxe5 34 f5! exf5 35 ♕xf5 and the f6-knight can't be defended in view of 35...♗d8 36 ♖xd8 or 35...♘e8 36 ♕xh5+ ♔g7 37 ♘f5+) 31...dxc5!? (Gavrikov prefers 31...♖gd8 but

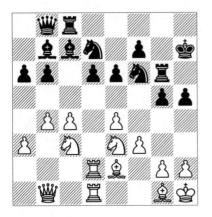

W

then 32 c6! ♗xc6 33 ♘ed5! {33 ♗xa6 is not bad either} 33...♘g8 34 ♗xa6 is very strong) 32 bxc5 b5 33 ♖b2!. This is Gavrikov's analysis. He suggests that White is better, with threats of 34 ♘xb5 and 34 a4, and it's hard to argue with that. Probably Black should just get out of the way of the queen by 30...♔h8, when White might try a similar idea with ♖b2 and c5 or a4-a5.

31 c5!!

In the race between flank attacks, White's has won out. Now ♘c4 is threatened and there's no safe way to capture on c5.

31...bxc5 32 bxc5 ♗a5

After 32...♘xc5, 33 e5 is promising according to Gavrikov, but easier seems 33 ♘c4! threatening 34 ♖b2!, 34 e5, and 34 ♘xd6.

33 ♖b2 ♘xc5 34 ♘a4! *(D)*

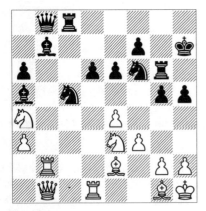

B

White is relentless. In what follows there is no defence.

34...♘xa4 35 ♖xb7 ♕a8 36 ♖xd6! ♘c3 37 ♕b2 ♘xe2 38 ♖xf7+ ♔h6 39 ♖xf6 ♘f4 40

♕e5 ♗c7 41 ♖xg6+ ♘xg6 42 ♕xe6 ♗xd6 43 ♘f5+ ♔h7 44 ♕f7+ 1-0

A fine strategic game that would probably look very strange to someone who was transported from the 1950s in a time machine!

A related line is the Double Fianchetto Variation, in which the character of the space advantage is changed by Black's more active bishop on g7. This is illustrated by:

Topalov – Gelfand
Monaco Amber rpd 2001

1 ♘f3 ♘f6 2 c4 b6 3 g3 c5 4 ♗g2 ♗b7 5 0-0 g6 6 d4

6 ♘c3 ♗g7 7 ♖e1 is an attempt to gain space by e4. Black can then follow the classical strategy of relieving his position through exchanges with 7...♘e4, or he can play for *two* exchanges via 7...♘c6 8 d4 ♘xd4 9 ♘xd4 ♗xg2 10 ♔xg2 cxd4 11 ♕xd4 0-0 12 ♗g5 h6 13 ♗d2 ♖c8, when he had no problems in Nezar-Jaracz, Metz 2002. This works because the active bishop on g7 is much better than its counterpart on e7 in the Hedgehog.

6...cxd4 7 ♕xd4 ♗g7 8 ♘c3 d6 *(D)*

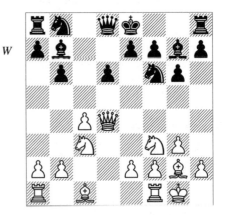

W

9 ♗e3

Decisions about exchanging are well illustrated in Pigusov-Ivanov, Moscow 2001: 9 ♖d1 ♘bd7 10 b3 0-0 (10...h6!?) 11 ♕h4 ♖c8 12 ♗h6 (first White wants to simplify, even at the cost of several queen moves) 12...♖c5!? 13 ♗xg7 ♔xg7 14 ♕d4! ♕a8 15 ♘e1 (White clearly believes that exchanges are to his benefit) 15...a6 16 e4 (or does he? This is a good move, and shows again that there are no simple rules) 16...♖cc8 17 ♘c2 ♘c5 18 ♘e3! and White is ready to play ♘ed5 with a standard advantage. His e-pawn is protected in view of 18...♘cxe4 19 ♘cd5! e5 20 ♕xb6 ♘xd5?! 21 ♘xd5 ♘c3 22 ♕xd6! ♘xd1? 23 ♕f6+ ♔h6 24 ♘e7! ♖xg2 25 ♘f5+ ♔h5 26 ♕h4#.

9...♘bd7 10 ♖ac1 a6 11 ♖fd1 ♖b8 12 b3 0-0 13 ♕h4

Again, White wants to exchange at least one pair of bishops, and maybe both, to limit the effectiveness of a black pawn-break with ...b5. Compare the Hedgehog games above. The g2-bishop will often be exchanged by ♘e1, but White can also explicitly avoid its exchange by ♗h3, allowing Black to double his pawns after ...♗xf3 in return for open lines and a strong bishop (this type of doubled f-pawn position is increasingly popular on both sides of the board; see Chapter 2, Section 2, on doubled pawns).

13...♖e8!?

But now it's the cramped side that avoids exchanges, very much as Kasparov did versus Kramnik in a similar situation. The reader may recognize this idea from the Dragon Sicilian.

14 ♗h6 ♗h8 15 ♗h3!?

Perhaps 15 e4!?, since 15...b5?! 16 cxb5 axb5 17 b4 seems to favour White.

15...b5!? 16 cxb5 axb5 17 ♕b4

Now 17 b4 is ineffective due to 17...♗xf3 18 exf3 ♘e5.

17...♗xf3 18 exf3 ♘e5 19 ♗g2 ♘c6 20 ♕h4 ♕a5 ½-½

The Philosophy of Exchanging in a Broader Context

In the last two sections I have been particularly concerned with the issue of exchanges with relation to space. In part this arose because in collecting master annotations, I have often noticed comments such as 'Since he commands more space, White (Black) avoids exchanges' or 'White (Black) follows the principle of seeking exchanges when one has less space'. On the other hand, I haven't seen the annotation 'Possessing more space, I sought simplification' or 'Confined to three ranks, Black avoids

exchanges that would reduce his counterplay', or anything similar. Yet in most of the games and notes above, we have seen exchanges favouring the side with more space. That is not to say that there aren't also plenty of examples that support the conventional wisdom. The point is that no generality can be applied.

An example of this attitude appears in Dvoretsky's book *School of Excellence 3: Strategic Play*. The author, a favourite of mine, is one of the most insightful of theoreticians when writing about opening and middlegame strategy. Nevertheless, even he is subject to classical oversimplification and, I think, errors about various old saws that we all grew up with. In his chapter on 'Advantage in Space', he advocates the classical notion: "The side who has an advantage in space can freely manoeuvre with his pieces, switching them from flank to flank, whereas his opponent often lacks scope for manoeuvring, and his pieces hinder one another. From this it is clear that, if you have an advantage in space, it is advantageous to retain as many pieces as possible, whereas in a cramped position, by contrast, you should aim for exchanges", soon adding "All these considerations are fairly obvious." But he then adds scant evidence favouring, and some contradicting, his own thesis. Dvoretsky gives a single game in which Black has surrendered the centre in a Pirc Defence resulting in a position structurally similar to those in the first chapter of this book. He criticizes Black, who has less space, for failing to exchange pieces and then White for encouraging exchanges on the very next move. Dvoretsky calls this "an astounding strategic mistake". That it is a mistake is clear, although White probably just missed the move sequence that followed the exchange and thus invalidated it. Be that as it may, one is left wondering whether this example by itself is meant to justify the broad claim quoted above. After all, we have seen many counter-examples, particularly in this type of pawn-structure. The obvious problem with Dvoretsky's reasoning is that exchanges may simplify the task of the side with space, whose pieces are still more easily transferred from flank to flank, in some cases with greater or decisive effect. In Dvoretsky's next few examples, the issue of exchanging to free a cramped game isn't essentially involved, since Black exchanges his bishop for a knight in order to create doubled pawns in White's position. That manoeuvre by no means frees his game, but has the usual effect of creating weaknesses and locking the pawn-structure to such an extent that White's bishop-pair is restricted and he can't make progress. Two draws result. This is followed by a game in which one side attempts to exchange his bad dark-squared bishop but lands in trouble, not a relevant test of the issue under question. Finally, in the last game in which exchanging is a theme, Dvoretsky shows White, with a huge advantage in space, avoiding an exchange; but he suggests that exchanging a piece at that point was a good option (it in fact looks better), in spite of his principle. Then a few moves later he finds that White definitely should have exchanged pieces rather than avoiding an exchange! This was not a grave error, and White's position remained very strong, but what became of the principle? To say the least, these examples provide only the thinnest of support to Dvoretsky's thesis. I think his presentation provides a good example of how a writer wedded to a lifelong conception can be blind to actual evidence one way or another. (Of course, that criticism applies to most writers, including the author of these lines.)

To conclude this discussion, I would like to talk in broad terms about a few contemporary pawn formations and get a feel for the philosophies of exchanging that seem to apply.

Continuing with the Symmetrical English Opening, one sees that both approaches apply depending upon the specifics. For example, as I was writing this I ran across the position after 1 c4 c5 2 ♘f3 ♘c6 3 g3 g6 4 ♗g2 ♗g7 5 0-0 e5 6 ♘c3 d6 7 d3 ♘ge7 8 a3 a5 9 ♘e1 ♗e6 10 ♘c2 d5 11 cxd5 ♘xd5 12 ♘e3 *(D)*.

This is from Smirin-Kariakin, Moscow 2002; the same type of middlegame has occurred in several forms and in particular with colours reversed. Black played 12...♘de7!, when Kosten says: "Thematic; Black avoids exchanges when he has extra space." He is right, and White tends to be a little worse in such positions. But in the similar traditional line with 1 c4 c5 2 ♘c3 ♘c6 3 g3 g6 4 ♗g2 ♗g7 5 ♘f3 ♘f6 6 0-0 0-0 7 d4 cxd4 8 ♘xd4, there are many cases in which the side with greater space should encourage

exchanges; for example, 8...♕a5 9 ♘c2 d6 10 ♗d2 ♕h5 11 e4! ♕xd1 12 ♖axd1 and White is better.

Let's turn to the Indian Systems with 1 d4 ♘f6 2 c4. In the Nimzo- and Queen's-Indian Defences following 2...e6, we often see an early simplifying ...♘e4 move to good effect, e.g. 3 ♘f3 b6 4 g3 ♗b7 5 ♗g2 ♗e7 6 0-0 0-0 7 ♘c3 ♘e4 or 3 ♘c3 ♗b4 4 e3 b6 5 ♘e2 ♘e4. By contrast, Black is much less inclined to exchange pieces in King's Indian positions after 1 d4 ♘f6 2 c4 g6 3 ♘c3 ♗g7 4 e4 d6 5 ♘f3 0-0, particularly when Black plays ...e5 and White plays d5. This is simply because White's extra space tends to give him superior endings, and exchanges can also reduce the risk from a kingside attack by Black.

In the main line of the Grünfeld Defence (another Indian System) consisting of 1 d4 ♘f6 2 c4 g6 3 ♘c3 d5 4 cxd5 ♘xd5 5 e4 ♘xc3 6 bxc3 ♗g7, one can find many instances of simplification aiding one side or the other; e.g., Black because he wins queenside squares or White because his centre can become so powerful in an ending. As for 1 d4 d5, we have seen the ambiguity of exchanges in the Orthodox Queen's Gambit Declined; but in the Exchange Variation of that opening as well, exchanges can help Black in his fight against White's centre, or they can hurt if White is pursuing a queenside minority attack.

We might add a couple of king's pawn examples for balance. Take the Maroczy Bind Sicilian line 1 e4 c5 2 ♘f3 ♘c6 3 d4 cxd4 4 ♘xd4 g6 5 c4 ♘f6 6 ♘c3 *(D)*.

There are several lines in which Black's queen goes to a5 and White's to d2 (after ♗e3 or

B

♗g5), and then after ♘a4 or ♘d5 the exchange of queens on d2 favours White, who has more space. By contrast Black very often makes the early exchange by 6...♘xd4 7 ♕xd4 d6 which makes it easier for him to get certain pieces out; for example, his queen's bishop to e6, or the same piece to c6 via d7. In the Pirc Defence, which features Black working with less space from the outset, we have the example of the Classical Main Line, 1 e4 d6 2 d4 ♘f6 3 ♘c3 g6 4 ♘f3 ♗g7. There Black often plays ...♗g4

and ...♗xf3 because it gives his pieces manoeuvring room. By contrast, in the line with 4 f4 ♗g7 5 ♘f3, the plan with ...♗g4 and ...♗xf3 tends to be undesirable because it helps White to prosecute a kingside attack.

And so it goes. Although there are patterns, we should remember that every pawn-structure allows for a variety of middlegame plans based on concrete factors. Thus the decision whether to exchange a piece can hang upon a seeming trifle, such as the position of a pawn on h2 or h3, or a king on g1 or h1.

Can there possibly be talk of a workable 'principle' here? Do good players, while at the board, actually think 'Well, I have more space, so I'll try to avoid exchanges'? Of course not; as discussed, one might even say 'I have more space, so I'll *seek out* exchanges' with equal or perhaps greater legitimacy. Either thought process is unfounded in reality and in any case impractical. In the end, any good player uses his or her knowledge of positions, combined with individual assessments of particular continuations, to determine whether a given exchange or general simplification is desirable.

1.3 The Development of Development

By the term 'development' various authors mean different things. Here I will be concerned with it in the simple sense of bringing one's pieces out, leaving questions of the quality of their disposition to be discussed case by case. SOMCS emphasized the increasing number of openings in which modern players choose not to bring their pieces out in order to achieve other goals such as establishment of a favourable pawn-structure. Increasingly, we see developmental patterns that defy traditional conceptions. For example, the same piece is moved repeatedly and ends up on a worse square (or even back at home) so as to provoke the opponent into a potentially vulnerable situation. Or pieces are developed to apparently awkward squares leading to inharmonious positions for purely pragmatic or prophylactic reasons. We also see pawn-grabbing sorties by the queen to the complete neglect of development, a strategy previously frowned upon by the textbooks.

Here I will be looking at these kinds of strategies, but also at the evolution of attitudes towards development in well-established positions. The latter is consistent with the idea of examining change that has become routine as well as that which is exceptional. We will discover an increasingly open-minded approach towards the problem of how to get the pieces out.

First, however, I want to make a brief historical digression. Some of the rules and dogmatic assessments that I discussed in SOMCS appeared in popular articles such as Steinitz wrote or in relatively elementary books such as Lasker's 'Manual' or in other general works such as those of Tarrasch. Others showed up in high-level annotations. This raises the question of whether the writers themselves weren't necessarily adherents of the views expressed, but were instead writing for the student. In fact, I think that it's fairly easy to distinguish as one reads these texts whether the author is expressing a fundamental belief or giving some oversimplified advice. We will always have instances of both. To this day, for example, fixed rules and principles are found in the annotations of advanced players, and yet increasingly we also find remarks about ignoring those rules. The play is the thing, and one can only use one's experience and judgement to discern the changes (or lack of them) over the years.

For all that, I think that the average player might be surprised how ingrained certain prejudices were in classical times. One cannot mistake the consistent aversion of top players to openings that failed to develop the pieces quickly or to challenge the centre. Along those lines, rules about how to conduct play took a long time to fade from players' consciousnesses. Réti, for example, is obviously serious when he talks about the prevalence in even the best of earlier games of "moves that seem self-evident and which the master of routine made without reflection, because such moves were founded on rules of such long standing as to have become part of that master's flesh and blood". In the same vein, he finds that in the games of the hypermodern players, "moves that were earlier held to be self-evident, that every good player made automatically, so to speak, must frequently be cast aside." As one of many illustrations, he emphasizes how the established developmental rules were changing. He cites, for example, the multi-faceted rule that apart from a few moves by central pawns, each move of the opening should develop a new piece, and it should be moved only once if possible (excluding captures, recaptures, and attacked pieces, of course). Réti finds counter-examples from young players of his time, and with hindsight we can see how the hypermoderns themselves, by comparison with players today or even Soviet players in the 1940s, were extremely modest in their deviations from the old rules of development. Today, Viktor Korchnoi can mischievously say "All obvious moves look dubious in analysis after a game".

Pleasure before Work!

The majority of master games played today follow standard and at least moderately well analysed openings. But it is instructive (and a lot of fun!) to look at some of the many experimental developmental ideas that have been played and investigated recently. The last 10-15 years have seen an explosion in the use of exotic irregular openings, for example. I personally find it a great delight when I see something new being played within just the first few moves of the game. One naturally thinks: how could this not have occurred to anyone before? Or if the move occurred once randomly in the past, why didn't it attract any interest then? Today's players are inclined to question everything and have few inhibitions about playing superficially unprincipled moves. This can lead to highly entertaining play, as illustrated by the following game fragments and the notes within them.

Gabriel – Korchnoi
Zurich tt 1999

1 ♘f3 d5 2 c4 d4 3 b4

A fairly normal move, but it introduces a surprising idea. A related example is Stefan Bücker's 3 c5!? *(D)*, which has a similarly irreverent feel:

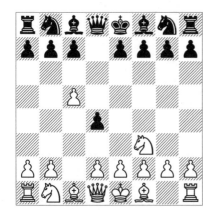

This looks more or less insane, using up a tempo to expose the c-pawn to attack and give up control of d5!. But there are some good points as well; for one thing, White has the concrete idea of 4 ♕a4+ ♘c6 5 b4!. M.Grünberg-Rahman,

Cairo 2000 continued 3...♘c6 4 ♕a4 (still intending b4-b5, followed by moves such as ♗b2 and ♘a3-c4) 4...♕d5 5 b4 e5 6 e3 ♗d7 7 b5 ♘d8? (7...♕xc5 8 ♘a3! ♘b4 9 ♗b2 dxe3 10 fxe3 ♗d6 11 d4 ♕d5 12 ♗c4 ♕e4 13 0-0-0 gave White rapid development in M.Grünberg-Popescu, Romanian Cht (Timisu de Sus) 1998) 8 ♗c4 ♕e4 9 ♘c3! ♕f5 (9...dxc3?? 10 ♗xf7+) 10 ♘d5 ♘e6 11 c6 bxc6 12 bxc6 ♗c8 13 0-0 and Black's position had fallen apart. In my database White has scored 5½/6 after 3 c5, with a performance rating of over 2700!

3...f6 4 e3 e5

So far, Black has played a normal solution to 3 b4, one which has discouraged players on the white side of this line for years. But now:

5 c5!?

This extravagant move has suddenly received some serious attention. It seems ridiculous to use a whole tempo to give up the key d5-square and expose oneself to a crippling ...a5. On the positive side, White stops ...c5 at all costs and temporarily prevents Black from castling after ♗c4 or ♕b3. At first thought, neither of these are terribly impressive goals, but there are concrete features as well:

5...d3!?

This intends to cut off White's f1-bishop and hamper his development for a long time to come. However, it's awfully ambitious, and Korchnoi himself (playing Black) was somewhat sceptical after the game. Quite fascinating play can follow the obvious 5...a5 after 6 ♗b5+! c6 7 ♗c4, and here Nikolaevsky-Savchenko, Kiev Platonov mem 1995 continued 7...♗g4! with unclear play. What good did White's check on move 6 do him? It turns out that, had Black played the natural 7...axb4, White could have played 8 ♘xe5!, intending 8...fxe5? (correct is 8...♘h6! 9 ♘f3 ♗xc5 10 0-0 with an unclear game) 9 ♕h5+ ♔d7 10 ♕f5+ ♔c7 11 ♕xe5+ ♔d7 (11...♗d6 12 cxd6+ ♔b6 13 ♗b2) 12 ♗e6+ ♔e8 13 ♗xc8+, etc. Note that if White had played 6 ♗c4 instead, then after 6...axb4, 7 ♘xe5?! would be inferior due to 7...fxe5 8 ♕h5+ ♔d7 (9 ♕f5+? ♔c6!). Very devious!

6 ♕b3!?

6 ♗b2 had been played before, so as to meet 6...a5 with 7 a3. The text-move is much more interesting, allowing the queenside to be shattered for the sake of concrete tactics.

6...e4 7 ♘d4 a5 8 ♘c3

This game caught the attention of a number of strong players. Here GM Pelletier gave 8 ♘e6 ♕e7 9 ♘xf8 ♔xf8 10 b5 ♗e6 11 ♕a4 f5 12 ♗a3 c6 with an advantage for Black, although Bücker then suggests 13 g4! to break up the pawn-chain.

8...f5 *(D)*

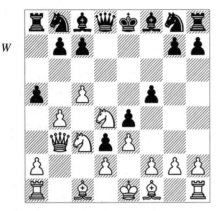

Black has now made eight straight pawn moves! Korchnoi demonstrates that there is more than one creative player in this game.

9 ♘e6!

This move was condemned at the time on account of the course of the game, but turns out to be correct.

9...♕e7?!

None of the annotators liked 9...♗xe6, but this is probably best. There could follow 10 ♕xe6+ ♘e7 11 b5 ♕d7 12 ♕c4 c6 13 f3! exf3 14 gxf3 ♘g6 15 f4 with a small edge for White.

10 ♘xf8?

Korchnoi recommended 10 ♕a4+!, which is very strong. White may not seem to have gained much after 10...♔f7 (10...c6? 11 ♘d5; 10...♗d7? 11 ♘xc7+ ♔d8 12 b5 is winning for White), but the queen belongs on a4 and the extra tempo makes a huge difference. Korchnoi gave 11 ♘xf8 ♔xf8 12 ♗a3 ♘f6 13 f3 ♔f7 14 fxe4 fxe4 15 g3 ♕e5 16 b5 ♖e8 17 ♗g2 ♔g8 18 0-0 ♗f5 19 ♕c4+ ♔h8 20 ♖xf5! ♕xf5 21 ♖f1 followed by capturing on e4 with a clear advantage for White.

10...♔xf8 11 b5?!

Korchnoi considered 11 ♕a4 better despite the fact that 11...♘a6! 12 ♕xa5 c6! gives Black the initiative.

11...♗e6 12 ♕a4

A vital tempo lost by comparison with the note to move 10.

12...♘d7

After this move Black was clearly better and went on to win. Such a game reminds us that chess is still wide open to new approaches.

In the following game we see another bizarre-looking idea that is rapidly becoming a main line:

Zurek – Hraček
Czech Cht 2001/2

1 b3 e5 2 ♗b2 ♘c6 3 e3 ♘f6 4 ♗b5

White develops his bishops before his knights, which tends to be an invitation to oddity. Now the e5-pawn is threatened.

4...♗d6!? *(D)*

Doesn't that block the d-pawn? There's a game Suhle-Anderssen, Breslau 1859 with this move, and then nothing that I can find for almost 120 years! Instead, Black has played 4...d6 here as a matter of course.

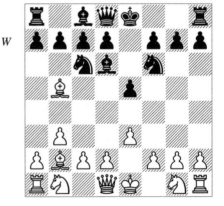

5 ♘a3!?

Knight to the rim! White answers claustrophobia with literal eccentricity, and would obviously like to play ♘c4. Anderssen's 1859 opponent played the drab 5 d3. Any such slow move allows ...0-0, ...♖e8, ...♗f8, and ...d5.

In Arencibia-Efimov, Saint Vincent 2001, White played 5 g4!?, which is quite in the spirit of things so far! But g5 really isn't much of a threat, and after 5...0-0 6 ♘c3!? ♗b4 7 g5 ♗xc3! 8 ♗xc3 ♘e4, Black was doing well.

In the daily e-zine *Chess Today*, GM Scherbakov tells a story. Sveshnikov was showing the move 4...♗d6 to some students at a lecture and was asked "What about 5 ♘a3?". Sveshnikov said that, "If you play such an ugly move then we have the right to play the same way", and showed them:

5...♘a5!

Very silly. Another knight saunters to the edge of the board. The game to this point has now been seen in several grandmaster contests. Nevertheless, I'm not sure that the average player, seeing their moves, would believe that the players involved were anything but rank amateurs (perhaps teetering on barstools!). In my database, the first person to play 5...♘a5 was GM Rainer Knaak in 1978, and it was taken up later by GMs Sveshnikov, Speelman, Hector, and Hraček. For the record, less fun but also satisfactory is 5...a6, which has tended to equalize; and Black can also try 5...e4!? with the idea 6 ♘c4 ♗e7, as Shabalov once did.

6 ♗e2!? *(D)*

Now threatening ♘b5. 6 ♘c4 and 6 ♘f3 have also been played.

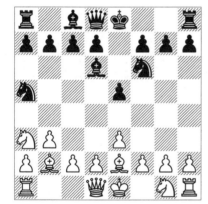

B

6...a6 7 c4

The end of Scherbakov's story is that Sakaev, who attended Sveshnikov's lecture, soon faced Sveshnikov himself over the board (Sakaev-Sveshnikov, Gausdal 1992). He took up the opportunity to play against 5...♘a5 and fared miserably after 7 ♘c4 ♘xc4 8 bxc4!? ♕e7 9 a4?! 0-0 10 ♘h3 (White puts yet another knight on the edge of the board to support f4, but after doubling his own pawns and wasting an extra tempo on a4, this is all too slow) 10...♗c5 11

f4? ♗xe3! 12 ♗xe5 (12 dxe3 ♕b4+) 12...♗a7 13 ♘f2 d6 14 ♗b2? ♖e8 15 d4 ♘g4 0-1.

7...0-0

Now it's probably about equal. A one-sided miniature followed:

8 ♘f3 ♖e8 9 ♘c2 e4 10 ♘h4!? ♘c6 11 f4?! ♗c5 12 ♘f5?!

White's knights are doing entirely too much hopping around to no purpose.

12...d5 13 cxd5 ♘b4! 14 ♘cd4 ♕xd5 15 a3??

A mistake, but 15 ♘g3 ♗g4! 16 0-0 ♘d3 is clearly better for Black.

15...♘d3+ 16 ♗xd3 exd3 17 b4

Or 17 ♕f3 ♕xf3 18 gxf3 ♗xd4 19 ♘xd4 c5 (ouch!).

17...♗xd4 18 ♘xd4 ♕xg2 19 ♖f1

White cannot be saved; e.g., 19 ♕f3 ♖xe3+ 20 dxe3 d2+ 21 ♔d1 ♗g4.

19...♗g4 20 ♘f3 ♘e4 0-1

Pytel – Piasetski
Buenos Aires OL 1978

1 c4 b6 2 d4 e6 3 e4

The English Defence was once a scruffy outsider but is now a member of the respectable classes. More than almost any other modern opening, it has provided eccentric ideas very early on in the game; for example, such things as 3 a3 f5 4 ♘c3 ♘f6 5 d5 ♗a6! and 3 e4 ♗b7 4 ♘c3 ♗b4 5 ♕c2 ♕h4!. When one side develops both bishops and the queen before any other pieces, the game will generally take an unusual course!

3...♗b7 4 f3

This has been fairly successful for White of late. 4 ♗d3 ♗b4+ 5 ♗d2 ♗xd2+ 6 ♕xd2 ♘h6!? intending ...f5 is another typical flank development.

4...e5!? *(D)*

At first sight, an utterly bizarre idea. Black moves his e-pawn for the second time in 4 moves, and even offers it up in the bargain! In all the games in my database with the relatively popular 4 f3, Pytel-Piasetski was the only early one in which Black answered 4...e5. The Canadians of the 1970s were investigating all kinds of modern opening set-ups (for example, they had an enormous influence in making 1 e4 g6 respectable), so it doesn't surprise me that

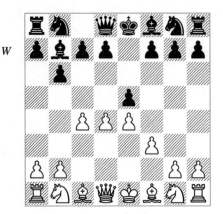

Piasetski played this way. But just recently 4...e5 has resurfaced, very likely because Daniel King made a case for it in his book on the English Defence. Again, once you see 4...e5 it makes perfect sense; but you have to be undogmatic enough to consider it in the first place. Black wants the a7-g1 diagonal, and if it means both losing a tempo and miserably shutting in his b7-bishop, so be it.

5 d5

What about 5 dxe5? Then Black probably plays 5...♘c6, and according to King gets good play following 6 ♗f4 ♗b4+ (or 6...g5!? 7 ♗g3 ♗g7) 7 ♘c3 ♕e7; instead, 6 f4 can be answered by a number of moves such as 6...f6, 6...d6, and 6...♗b4+ 7 ♗d2 ♕h4+ 8 g3 ♕e7, all of these needing tests. To continue with a little sub-theme, notice that 6 f4 would be the sixth consecutive pawn move for White.

5...♗c5

A fearsome bishop that compensates for Black's other problems. The fact that White's pawn is on f3 helps Black, because it makes the bishop hard to oppose and extends its scope. At this point it might be worth comparing two similar early ...e6-e5 attempts after 1 c4 b6 2 d4 e6 3 e4 ♗b7:

a) 4 ♗d3 ♘c6 5 ♘e2 e5!? 6 d5 ♘b4 7 0-0 ♘e7 8 ♘bc3 ♘xd3 9 ♕xd3 ♘g6, Lobron-Speelman, Bundesliga 1996/7. In this example White hasn't played the extra, weakening, f3, but Black is probably only slightly worse despite having only two pieces out, an absurd-looking bishop, and a space disadvantage!

b) 4 ♘c3 ♗b4 5 f3 e5!? 6 dxe5 ♕h4+!? (6...♗xc3+ 7 bxc3 ♘c6; King: "Then Black can consider playing the knight to e7.") 7 g3

♗xc3+ 8 bxc3 ♕e7 9 ♗e3 ♘c6 10 ♘e2 ♘xe5 11 ♘d4 0-0-0 with equality, Åkesson-Miles, Las Vegas FIDE 1999.

6 ♘c3!? a5

King offers the line 6...♗xg1 7 ♖xg1 ♕h4+ 8 g3 ♕xh2 9 ♖g2 ♕h1 10 ♗e3 with compensation.

7 ♘ge2 ♘a6 8 g3 ♘e7 9 ♗h3 0-0 10 ♘a4 ♗b4+ 11 ♘ec3 ♘c8

Has anyone noticed that very few of either sides' pieces are going to 'normal' squares in this game? Another option was going back home with the bishop following 11...d6 12 0-0 ♗c8, with equality. At any rate, the game was roughly equal after...

12 a3 ♗e7 13 0-0 ♘c5

...and Black eventually went on to win.

A similarly original dark-square grab has been played on move 3(!) of a well-established line, as in Kramnik-Leko, Tilburg 1998: 1 d4 ♘f6 2 c4 g6 3 f3 e5!? (3...d5 or 3...♗g7 had been played for most of the preceding century) 4 dxe5 (4 d5 e4!; 4 e4 exd4 5 ♕xd4 ♘c6 6 ♕d2 ♗g7 with activity and development; Black can aim for ...f5) 4...♘h5 5 ♘h3!. White finds his own way to utilize a knight on the rim. For the complete annotated game, see Part 2, Game 21.

There are also new things to be found in the old double e-pawn games, such as the following:

Labahn – Avant
corr. 2000

1 e4 e5 2 ♘f3 ♘c6 3 ♘c3 ♘f6 4 g3 d5 5 exd5 ♘d4!? (D)

Why not? 5...♘d4!? is a Belgrade Gambit Reversed, quite logical with g3 included, since that move is of debatable value in this new context. This simple move has been completely unknown to theory and as far as I can tell never even tried until now! The normal move had (naturally) been 5...♘xd5. My guess is that players shied away from even considering the move 5...♘d4 on the assumption that one should not offer gambits when undeveloped.

6 ♘xe5

The most critical move, but risky. Alternatives:

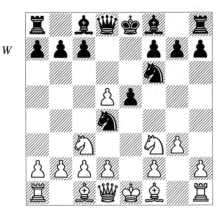

W

a) Labahn's analysis 6 ♘xd4 exd4 7 ♘b5 ♗c5 8 ♕e2+ ♔f8 9 ♗g2 a6 10 b4 ♗b6 11 ♘a3 ♗g4 results in an excellent position for Black in view of 12 f3 ♕d7! 13 ♔d1 (versus ...♖e8) 13...♖e8 14 ♕c4 ♘xd5, etc.

b) Bücker gives 6 ♗g2 ♗g4 7 0-0 (Labahn posits that 7 h3 ♗xf3 8 ♗xf3 ♘xf3+ 9 ♕xf3 ♗b4 10 0-0 0-0 is equal) 7...♗d6 8 d3 0-0 9 ♖e1 ♖e8 with equality.

6...♗d6 7 ♘c4 *(D)*

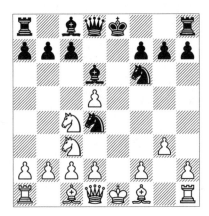

B

7...♗g4

Black can also play the amazing 7...♗xg3!? 8 ♘e3 (8 hxg3 ♗g4 9 ♗e2 ♗xe2 10 ♘xe2 ♕xd5 with a large, almost winning advantage for Black) 8...♗h4!? 9 ♗g2 0-0 10 0-0 ♖e8 and Black has enough compensation for the pawn. This is Bücker's analysis.

8 ♗e2 ♘xe2 9 ♘xe2 0-0 10 0-0 ♗c5?!

Much better is 10...♗f3! 11 d4 (11 ♘e3 ♘e4 12 ♖e1 ♘g5 13 d3 ♖e8, as given by K.Müller, "is very uncomfortable for White"; he also analyses 11 d3 ♖e8 12 ♗e3 ♘xd5 {or 12...♘g4}

with excellent play) 11...♖e8 12 ♖e1 ♕d7 13 ♘xd6 cxd6 14 c4 ♘h5 (or 14...♕g4 15 ♗e3 ♘h5) 15 ♕d3 ♕g4 (so far Müller's analysis) 16 h3 ♗xe2 17 hxg4 ♗xd3 18 ♖xe8+ ♖xe8 19 gxh5 ♖e1+ 20 ♔h2 ♗xc4 with a large advantage for Black.

11 ♘e5 ♗xe2

11...♗h5!? is probably best.

12 ♕xe2 ♖e8 13 c3 ♕xd5 14 d4 ♗d6 15 f4 c5 16 ♗e3 cxd4 17 ♗xd4 ♗xe5 18 ♗xe5 ♘d7 19 ♖ad1 ♕c5+ 20 ♕f2 ♕xf2+ 21 ♖xf2 ♘xe5 22 fxe5 ♖e7 23 ♖fd2 ♖ae8 24 ♖d7 ♔f8 25 ♖xe7 ♔xe7 26 ♔f2

White is much better because of 26...♔e6 27 ♖d6+! ♔xe5 28 ♖d7.

Sometimes players are so set on a particular formation that they neglect to consider changing the paradigm. This situation went on for years in a solid variation of the Pirc Defence:

1 e4 d6 2 d4 ♘f6 3 ♗d3 e5 4 c3

This system with c3 used to be very irritating for Black to meet, since White develops harmoniously and offers no targets. Pal Benko, for example, used it with resounding success. 4 ♘f3 exd4 5 ♘xd4 g6 6 ♘c3 ♗g7 was played in Lautier-Kramnik, Biel IZ 1993. The bishop doesn't look very well placed on d3 to me, so this should be equal; compare our discussion of 3...exd4 and ...g6 lines of the Philidor in Chapter 1.

4...d5! *(D)*

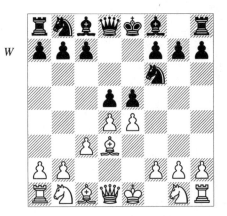

W

On the 4th move, Black moves his d-pawn a second time *and* makes a positional pawn sacrifice. For decades, 4...g6 was played nearly automatically here, or occasionally something like 4...♗e7, but in any case nothing that interfered with Black's dark-square strategy centred about the support of e5. To find and appreciate the move 4...d5 one needed, more than anything else, to be able to stop short and reconsider a preconceived idea of the position. This may have appeared singly at some point or other in chess history (I don't know), but if it did, strong players didn't recognize it for the solution it is. Sometime in the early 1980s the move surfaced with Chernin contributing key ideas. It is now a main line and has been played by numerous top-ranked GMs such as Kramnik, M.Gurevich, Beliavsky, Azmaiparashvili, etc.

5 dxe5 ♘xe4 6 ♘d2

Black's pawn sacrifice involves 6 ♗xe4 dxe4 7 ♕a4+ ♗d7 (another good set-up would be 7...♘c6 8 ♕xe4 ♗e6 9 ♘f3 ♗d5 10 ♕e2 ♕d7 and ...0-0-0) 8 ♕xe4 ♘c6 9 ♕g4 (to protect g2), and here Chernin suggests 9...h5, meeting 10 ♕g3 with 10...h4. Instead, 10 ♕h3 allows the simple 10...♕d7, but 10...g5! is more interesting; e.g., 11 ♘e2 g4 12 ♕g3 ♖g8!? 13 0-0 h4 14 ♕e3 h3 15 g3 ♕d5 with strong pressure.

Alternatively, the natural sequence 6 ♘f3 ♘c6 7 0-0 ♗g4 8 ♗f4 ♗e7 9 h3 ♗h5 offers Black at least equality: 10 ♗e2 (to untangle) 10...0-0 11 ♘bd2 ♘c5 12 ♘b3 ♗e6 13 ♗g3 f5! 14 exf6 ♗xf6 and Black had fine play in A.Sokolov-Chernin, 1984.

6...♘c6

Or 6...♘c5 7 ♗c2 ♘c6 8 ♘gf3, transposing.

7 ♘gf3 ♘c5 8 ♗c2 ♗g4

Black has excellent, active play. For example, Chernin offers 9 0-0 ♗e7 (or 9...d4) 10 ♖e1 d4 11 h3 ♗h5 12 ♘e4 d3! 13 ♘xc5 dxc2 14 ♕xd8+ ♖xd8 15 ♘b3 ♖d3! with an edge for Black.

Here's another example of early opening creativity by one of the world's leading players:

Topalov – Rozentalis
Batumi Echt 1999

1 c4 e6 2 ♘c3 ♘f6 3 e4 d5 4 e5 ♘e4

More and more often we are seeing piece development that 'looks ugly' but best serves the needs of the position. After 4...d4 5 exf6 dxc3 6 bxc3 ♕xf6, for example, the old main line of decades' standing is 7 d4, but this has been defused by the positional pawn sacrifice 7...e5!. The new main line, which has done very well, is 7 ♘f3 e5 8 ♗d3! *(D).*

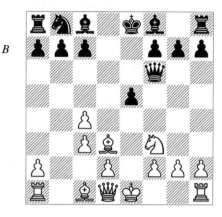

This move is pure and simply a pragmatic solution. It blocks the d-pawn and seems counter-intuitive, but thanks to a number of tactical and positional points, it manages to make the idea of 0-0, ♗e4, and d4 a real one.

5 ♘f3 ♗e7

A position has arisen that has been known for many years.

6 h4!? *(D)*

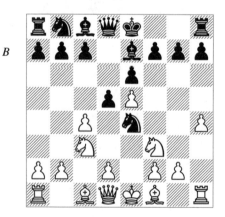

This peculiar flank thrust turns out to be a high-class waiting move as well as a prophylactic versus ...♘g5! The details and an explanation are given in Part 2, Game 1. I'll just give the bare moves with abbreviated notes here.

6...♘xc3

Or:

a) 6...♘c6 7 d4 f6 8 ♗d3 with some advantage; e.g., 8...♘xc3 9 bxc3 fxe5 10 ♘xe5 ♘xe5

11 dxe5 g6 (11...dxc4 12 ♕h5+ ♔f8 13 ♗xc4) 12 h5! (utilizing 6 h4!) and White is better.

b) 6...c5 7 ♕b3 (or 7 ♗d3 ♘xc3 8 dxc3 dxc4 9 ♗xc4 ♕xd1+ 10 ♔xd1 and White has an edge) 7...0-0 8 cxd5 ♘xc3 9 dxc3 ♕xd5 10 ♕c2 ♘c6 11 ♗g5 ♖d8 12 ♗xe7 ♘xe7 13 ♗e2 with an advantage for White.

c) 6...0-0 7 ♕c2 ♘c6 (no 7...♘g5 here!) 8 ♘xe4 ♘b4 9 ♕b1 dxe4 10 ♕xe4 ♗d7 11 ♘g5! g6 12 a3 ♗c6 13 ♕b1 ♘a6 14 b4 and White wins.

7 dxc3 dxc4 8 ♕a4+!? ♗d7 9 ♕xc4 ♗c6 10 ♕g4 ♗xf3 11 gxf3!

The opening has been an example of creativity mixed with pragmatism. White stands very well, and you can see more details about it and the rest of this exciting game in Part 2, Game 1.

There have been many such early-move bombshells. In SOMCS, I looked at 1 c4 ♘f6 2 ♘f3 e6 3 ♘c3 ♗b4 4 g4!? (D).

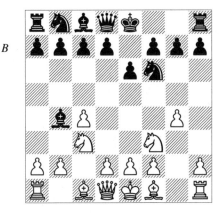

This move was first played by Zviagintsev in 1997, and discovered independently by Krasenkow. They have continued to play 4 g4 regardless of the opponent. Zviagintsev did so twice versus Adams in 2001, for example; those are battles between players with an average rating nearing 2700! The first justification is that the natural central counter by 4...d5 only creates problems for Black after 5 g5 (White has won all three games in my database). The non-traditional nature of White's development can be seen from the fact that ♖g1 will generally follow shortly; for example, 4...0-0 5 g5 ♘e8 6 ♖g1!, Vaïsser-A.Sokolov, France 2002; or 4...h6

5 ♖g1 and both 5...d6 and 5...b6 have been answered by the further flank advance 6 h4!?, although other moves are possible; e.g., 5...b6 6 ♕b3 (or just 6 d3) 6...♘c6 7 h4 ♗b7 8 g5 hxg5 9 hxg5 ♘g8 10 d4 with the advantage, Miroshnichenko-Kuzmenko, Kharkov 2000. With 4 g4, White is pitting space against development, and tries to argue that his apparently serious kingside weaknesses are not exploitable. An entertaining high-class struggle was Krasenkow-Romanishin, Lvov 2000, which featured White's bizarre-looking development versus Black's classical centre-grabbing approach: 4...0-0 5 g5 ♘e8 6 ♕c2 d5 7 b3!? ♗e7 8 ♖g1 c5 9 e3 ♘c6 10 ♗d3!? f5 11 gxf6 ♘xf6 12 a3 ♕e8!? 13 ♗b2 ♕h5 14 ♗e2! d4 15 ♘xd4 ♘xd4 16 exd4 ♕xh2 17 0-0-0 cxd4 18 ♘e4! with an attack, although after 18...♕f4!, Black still had reasonable defensive chances. The game continued 19 ♗d3 ♘xe4 20 ♗xe4 h6 21 ♗xd4 ♗f6? (21...♗xa3+ 22 ♔b1 e5 23 ♗e3 ♕xe4! 24 ♕xe4 ♗f5, as given by Ftačnik, leaves White only very slightly better) 22 ♗e3 ♕d6 23 c5 ♕a6 24 a4 ♕a5 25 ♗xh6 ♕b4 26 ♖xg7+!! ♗xg7 27 ♗h7+ ♔h8 28 ♗xg7+ ♔xg7 29 ♕g6+ ♔h8 30 ♕h5 ♖xf2 31 ♗e4+ ♔g7 32 ♖g1+ ♔f8 33 ♕h6+ ♔e7 34 ♖g7+ ♖f7 35 ♕g5+ ♔e8 36 ♖g8+ 1-0. A pretty combination.

A similar idea from another slow-developing positional opening was seen in the following game.

J. Watson – Dzindzichashvili
San Francisco 1999

1 d4 ♘f6 2 c4 e6 3 ♘f3 ♗b4+ 4 ♘bd2 0-0 5 a3 ♗xd2+ 6 ♗xd2 h6 7 ♕c2 d6 (D)

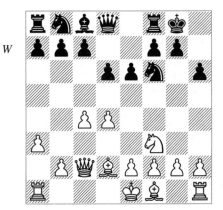

8 g4! e5!? 9 g5 hxg5 10 ♗xg5 exd4 11 0-0-0! ♘c6 12 ♖g1 ♖e8 13 ♘xd4 ♕e7 14 ♘b5! ♘e5

Here, instead of 15 ♘xc7!? ♕xc7 16 ♗xf6 ♘g6 17 ♗c3 ♗e6 with counterplay, a clear advantage was to be had from 15 ♗xf6 ♕xf6 16 ♘xc7 ♕xf2 17 ♖xg7+! ♔xg7 18 ♘xe8+ ♔f8 19 ♘xd6 ♕xh2 20 ♕e4.

Unquestionably, players going back to the 19th century sometimes employed radical strategies involving a break with the conventional wisdom. Witness, for example, the recent revival of 1 e4 c5 2 c3 ♕a5!?, an early queen sortie that was apparently invented by Tarrasch and also used once by Marshall. This move, designed to prevent d4, has been employed recently by players such as Movsesian, Kupreichik, and Romanishin. But such examples are hard to come by when investigating classical play, and those that did occur tended to be isolated affairs. What we see today is a very large and increasing set of rule-defying ideas that are often discovered simultaneously and quickly adopted everywhere. We are so used to this phenomenon that one seldom hears objections on general principle any more.

Many variations of the Trompowsky Attack demonstrate the uninhibited nature of development in contemporary chess. It's easy to forget that this well-established opening was extremely rare only 30 years ago. To give just one example between grandmasters, here is an example of what became a main line:

Hodgson – Wells
Copenhagen 1996

1 d4 ♘f6 2 ♗g5 ♘e4 3 ♗f4 c5 4 f3 ♕a5+ 5 c3 ♘f6 6 d5 ♕b6 7 ♗c1

White nonchalantly returns his bishop to base. This is considered better than creating weaknesses.

7...e6 8 c4 exd5

Remarkably, 8...♕b4+ 9 ♘c3 (9 ♗d2 ♕xc4 10 e4 is much better) 9...♕xc4 10 e4 ♕b4 11 ♗d2 ♕b6, risky as it may appear, has won a few games for Black recently, notably Agdestein-Bacrot, Bundesliga 2000/1. As discussed in SOMCS, pawn-grabbing raids by the queen

are on the upswing in many openings, perhaps a result of the concrete defensive preparation that a computer can provide.

9 cxd5 c4!?

9...d6 10 e4 g6 is safer, as in Wells-Nunn, British League (4NCL) 2001/2.

10 e3 ♗c5 11 ♔f2 *(D)*

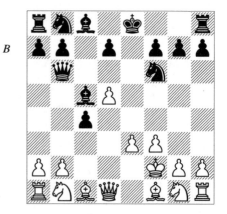

Does this game look eccentric to you? If not, it's probably because you've absorbed contemporary pragmatism into your world view. Taking stock: White has no pieces out after 11 moves, and has just moved his king! Oddly enough, this whole sequence (including the paradoxical ♗g5-f4-c1) may well be best play for White, probably favours him slightly, and has scored quite respectably.

Even the most innocent of traditional positions can contain good moves that defy common sense. A very common English Opening position arises after:

1 c4 c5 2 ♘c3 ♘c6 3 g3 g6 4 ♗g2 ♗g7 5 ♘f3 e6

For many, many years, White played the natural moves 6 0-0 or 6 d3 here, with an occasional 6 b3 or 6 a3. It took an experimental and open-minded attitude to take seriously the idea of giving up a precious centre pawn by:

6 d4!? *(D)*

Actually, 6 d4 is now so established and common that '!?' isn't really appropriate, but it reflects the initially speculative nature of the move. Chernin was the first to play this in a high-level encounter in 1981 and even then it took time to catch on. For one of my lengthy philosophical digressions about this move and

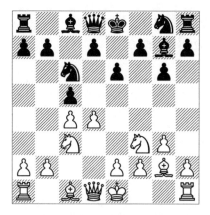

B

detailed analysis of the diverse continuations it engenders, refer to the Part 2 game Voiska-Alexandrova, Warsaw wom Ech 2001. Here I'll just mention a couple of bare-bones ideas here to indicate what logic lies behind it.

a) 6...♘xd4 7 ♘xd4 cxd4 (7...♗xd4 8 ♘b5 ♗e5 9 0-0 ties Black up) 8 ♘e4! d5 (8...♕c7?! 9 c5! ♘e7 10 ♗f4) 9 cxd5 exd5 10 ♕a4+! with fine play.

b) 6...cxd4 7 ♘b5 d5 (7...e5?! 8 ♘d6+ ♔e7 9 ♘g5! ♘h6 10 ♘ge4) 8 cxd5 ♕a5+ 9 ♕d2 (9 ♘d2!? ♕xb5 10 dxc6) 9...♕xb5 10 dxc6 ♕xc6 11 0-0 ♕b6 12 ♖d1 with a small advantage for White.

See the above-mentioned game for more details.

Notice that most of the above has been played by titled players. There are also all kinds of surprising developments at the grassroots; e.g., US master Brian Wall has been promoting 1 e4 c6 2 ♘f3 d5 3 e5, intending to meet 3...♗g4 with 4 d4!? *(D)*.

This is truly absurd, since Black usually needs an extra tempo to play the highly desirable ...♗g4 (via ...♗f5-g4) in lines such as 1 e4 c6 2 d4 d5 3 e5 ♗f5 4 ♘f3 e6 5 ♗e2 c5 (5...♗g4 has even been played here) 6 0-0 ♘c6 7 c3 ♗g4. However, returning to the diagram position, White's strategy can vary by 4...e6 5 c3 c5 6 dxc5, preventing a couple of natural moves by means of cheap traps, i.e., 6...♗xc5?? 7 ♕a4+ and 6...♘c6 7 ♗b5 ♗xc5?? 8 ♗xc6+ bxc6 9 ♕a4. This is not quite as dumb as it looks. Should Black avoid 5...c5, it can be that without a bishop on e2, White's lost tempo can actually help him in lines where ...♗xf3 can be answered by ♕xf3 (as opposed to ♗xf3, when the bishop is poorly placed), perhaps followed by ♕g3 with kingside pressure. A tempo lost can sometimes be a world gained.

Here's another case in which one can't help but think of play by a rank amateur, although we are dealing with very strong masters:

L. Aronian – Sulskis
Cappelle la Grande 2001

1 ♘f3 d5 2 g3 c6 3 ♗g2 ♗g4 4 0-0 h5!?

Out of over 1000 database games in the position after 4 0-0, I have no record of this move having been played until now. One might compare lines in the Leningrad Dutch like 1 d4 f5 2 ♘c3 d5 3 ♗g5 g6 4 h4!?, but there ...f5 is loosening. In the very different case before us White isn't even behind in development.

5 d3 *(D)*

What could be safer? 5 h3 ♗xf3 6 ♗xf3 h4 7 g4 e6 intending ...♗d6 would be double-edged.

B

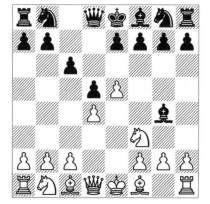

B

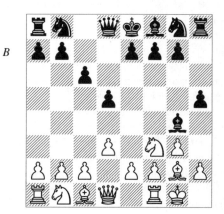

5...h4!!?

This is just beyond the pale, isn't it? Should we even take it seriously? Black has only one piece out versus his opponent's three and he gives up a pawn on move 5 for the sake of one open file. Worse, White hasn't the ghost of a weakness. And note that these are two 2500+ players!

6 ♘xh4 e5 7 ♘f3

Very logical. Does Black even have a threat? Probably not. One therefore has to call 5...h4 a positional pawn sacrifice! The difficulty for White is just getting his pieces out without permitting Black too comfortable a build-up behind his healthy centre. For example, Black would have plenty of play in a line like 7 ♘d2 ♗d6 8 c4 ♘f6 9 cxd5 cxd5 10 ♘b3 ♘c6. Ideas of ...♕d7 and ...♗h3 also have to be taken seriously.

7...♘d7 8 ♘bd2?!

I don't like this, since it blocks the queen's bishop. Sulskis suggests 8 h4!?, and 8 c4 followed by ♘c3 is logical as well, since ...♘gf6 can always be met by ♗g5. Black should probably switch to a plan with ...♘e7. The resulting positions are still very murky, however, and there's no obvious way to prevent Black from pursuing his attacking goals. What does this mean? Is there anything wrong with 4...h5? White's extra pawn just doesn't seem to be a factor unless he can make it to the endgame, which is a long way off.

8...♘gf6!?

I think that Black should strongly consider 8...♗d6 9 e4 ♘e7 with clear and difficult-to-meet attacking ideas.

9 e4 dxe4 10 dxe4

Or 10 ♘xe4 ♘xe4 11 dxe4 ♕f6 with compensation.

10...♗c5 11 ♕e1

Sulskis feels that 11 ♘c4! still gives White a small advantage. After Black's next two moves, he has at least sufficient play for the pawn.

11...♕e7 12 a4 0-0-0 13 ♘g5!?

A bad mistake would be 13 ♘c4? ♗xf3 14 ♗xf3 ♕e6 15 ♕e2 ♕h3 16 ♖d1 ♕xh2+ 17 ♔f1 ♘g4!. After 13 ♘g5, Black played 13...♘h5?! and his attack faltered after 14 ♘b3 (although he eventually won). Sulskis recommends either 13...♘h7 or 13...♘f8!?, with plenty of play in either case.

Revitalizing the Establishment

After that enjoyable walk in the wild, I want to turn to several more conventional situations in which the old ideas of development have changed in ways that we may not even think about. We take many such changes for granted because they have come about by gradual evolution and experimentation. Other new ideas burst suddenly upon the scene, but were so quickly absorbed that we are no longer aware of how blasphemous (or at least amusingly irrelevant) they would have appeared to earlier masters.

I'll begin with some familiar cases in which structure takes priority. When one player decides not to establish a classical central pawn presence (as in many modern openings), he or she obviously gets more leeway in terms of delayed development. This is simply because there are fewer immediate targets in his or her position, making it (at least initially) less critical to develop. In the Open Sicilian Defence, for example, Black may play a number of pawn moves like ...d6, ...e6, ...a6, and ...b6 or ...b5 with only a single minor piece out or perhaps just the queen, the piece traditionally admonished to stay at home in the opening. For example, in the Najdorf Sicilian (1 e4 c5 2 ♘f3 d6 3 d4 cxd4 4 ♘xd4 ♘f6 5 ♘c3 a6), there are lines such as 6 ♗c4 e6 7 ♗b3 b5 or 6 ♗e3 e5 7 ♘f3 ♕c7 8 a4 h6 or, famously, 6 ♗g5 e6 7 f4 ♕b6 8 ♕d2 ♕xb2, etc. The Kan/Paulsen Variation 1 e4 c5 2 ♘f3 e6 3 d4 cxd4 4 ♘xd4 a6 (often followed by 5...♕c7) is an even more extreme case in point. Black often plays moves like ...b5, ...d6, and sometimes even ...g6 in this variation before developing his minor pieces. In recent times there have even been variants in which Black's first piece move is ...♕b6; for example, 2...e6 3 d4 cxd4 4 ♘xd4 ♕b6, and if 5 ♘b3, 5...♕c7 6 ♘c3 a6 7 ♗d3 b5. And an exercise in structural change at loss of tempo is 1 e4 c5 2 ♘f3 e6 3 d4 cxd4 4 ♘xd4 a6 5 ♗d3 ♘f6 6 0-0 e5!? 7 ♘b3 d6, from McShane-Romanishin, Lippstadt 1999 and other games.

To emphasize how flexible the contemporary view of the Sicilian Defence has become, here's a sequence played mainly in the last few years: 1 e4 c5 2 ♘f3 e6 3 d4 cxd4 4 ♘xd4 a6 5 ♘c3 b5 6 ♗d3 d6!? *(D)*.

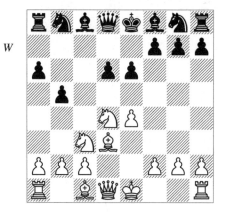

Six straight pawn moves! After 7 0-0, White has four pieces out to Black's none. I find 28 master-level games with this sequence since 1995 including quite a few with GMs, and Black scores +4 against only mildly inferior opposition! This particular move-order may or may not become a main line, but all the examples above contrast rather sharply with the older lines 1 e4 c5 2 ♘f3 ♘c6 3 d4 cxd4 4 ♘xd4 ♘f6 and 1 e4 c5 2 ♘f3 e6 3 d4 cxd4 4 ♘xd4 ♘f6 5 ♘c3 ♘c6 (or 5...♗b4). Those variations, with Black's pieces developed apace, are typical of the Sicilian Defences that gained early acceptance.

Let's see a recent example of pawn play between two experienced grandmasters who certainly know what they're doing strategically:

Tseshkovsky – Poluliakhov
Krasnodar 2001

1 e4 c5 2 ♘f3 e6 3 d4 cxd4 4 ♘xd4 a6 5 ♘c3 d6 6 g4 ♘e7 7 g5

It's a modern Sicilian Defence, so the odds are that we'll see g4-g5 (even without a target)!

7...d5 8 ♗g2 *(D)*

8...e5 9 ♘b3 d4

That's it! Black has made 8 out of 9 moves with the pawns! And he hasn't touched four of them. As if that isn't enough, he next moves his only developed piece and then advances another pawn. All of this appears completely sound.

10 ♘e2

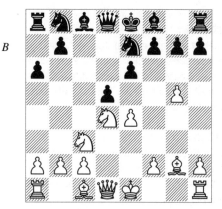

A cute trick is 10 ♘d5? ♘xd5 11 exd5 ♗b4+ 12 ♗d2? (12 ♔f1 0-0 and Black has the advantage) 12...♕xg5!.

10...♘ec6! 11 c3!?

Probably 11 0-0 is better, since this leaves him struggling a bit to stay even.

11...a5! 12 cxd4 *(D)*

12 a4 is more natural, when Poluliakhov gives a long variation leading to equality after 12...♗e6 13 cxd4 ♗b4+, but 12...♗g4! is probably an even more effective sequence: 13 f3 (13 cxd4 ♗b4+ 14 ♔f1 0-0! 15 d5 ♘e7 is not completely clear, but the f-file is about to be opened against White's king) 13...♗e6 14 cxd4 ♗b4+ 15 ♔f1 (15 ♔f2 ♕b6) 15...♗xb3.

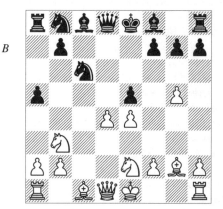

12...♗b4+?!

Too bad! Black could have made his tenth pawn move out of twelve by 12...a4!, which is quite good since 13 ♘c5 ♘xd4 14 ♘xd4 ♗xc5 15 ♘f5 0-0 (or 15...♕xd1+ 16 ♔xd1 0-0) slightly favours Black due to White's poorly-placed bishop on g2.

13 ♝d2 ♕xg5 14 ♜g1 ♝xd2+ 15 ♞xd2 0-0 16 d5 ♞b4

This is considered unclear by Poluliakov, but I'd rather be White after 17 ♞c4 because it seems to win either the e-pawn or a-pawn, and even without that leaves White with better development and nicely placed pieces; for example, 17...♕f6 (17...♕h4 18 a3 ♞4a6 19 ♞xe5; 17...f5? 18 a3 ♞4a6 19 ♞b6 ♜a7 20 ♝h3 and ♞xc8) 18 a3 ♞4a6 19 ♞xa5 (or 19 ♞g3). Black's lack of development finally hurts him; but that needn't have happened had he played 12...a4.

Of course there are historical precedents for such thinking (albeit in less extreme form). The Kan/Paulsen Variation was also played by Andersson and Paulsen himself in the 19th century; for example, Paulsen liked to play ...♕c7 and sometimes even ...b5 before ...♞f6. But such ideas were considered eccentric at best and weren't taken up by the leading players of the day or indeed by the next few generations after him. By contrast, the kinds of sequences described above no longer surprise us today. They appear in many contexts and are conceptually familiar even to average players.

The game that decided the 2002 British Championship illustrates Black's nonchalance with respect to development in the Sicilian:

McShane – Ramesh
British Ch (Torquay) 2002

1 e4 c5 2 ♞f3 ♞c6 3 ♝b5 e6 4 ♝xc6 bxc6 5 d3 ♞e7 6 ♕e2 f6 7 ♞h4 g6 8 f4 ♝g7 9 0-0 0-0 10 c4

An example of a very similar black structural strategy is 10 ♞f3 e5 11 fxe5 fxe5 12 ♝e3 d6 13 ♞bd2 h6 14 a3 ♜b8 15 b3 ♝e6 16 ♞c4 g5! and Black had a fine game in Shariyazdanov-Perunović, Subotica 2000.

10...d6 11 ♞c3 h6 *(D)*

Now Black has six pawns along his third rank, yet his idea is more than merely prophylactic, since he can finally claim space with a coming ...g5 and/or ...e5.

12 ♝e3 g5 13 ♞f3 gxf4

13...♞g6 would continue the theme of flexibility, with equal chances.

14 ♝xf4 e5

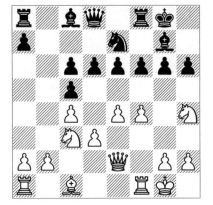

With 10 pawn moves out of 14, Black is now ready to activate his bishops, so White tries to shift the balance with a positional pawn sacrifice.

15 ♝d2 ♜b8 16 ♞h4!? ♜xb2 17 ♞d1 ♜b7

Second-rank defence. White has some compensation due to Black's pawn-structure, but it looks at most only sufficient.

18 ♞e3 d5 19 ♜ad1

So that the queen can move without ...dxe4 being a problem. Instead, 19 cxd5 cxd5 20 exd5 f5! would prevent occupation of the f5-square by a knight.

19...dxe4 20 dxe4

Now both 20...♜b2 and 20...♕d4 21 ♕f3 f5! are good.

Some creative treatments in accepted openings have become entrenched, and we forget how unnatural they must have looked when first introduced. The following apparently simple line only really caught on in the 1990s, and yet it immediately became a major threat to this variation of the Alekhine Defence:

1 e4 ♞f6 2 e5 ♞d5 3 d4 d6 4 c4 ♞b6 5 exd6 cxd6 6 ♞c3 g6

This system stretches far back to the early days of the Alekhine Defence and has always done well for Black. The main lines involve straightforward development via, for example, 7 ♞f3 ♝g7 8 ♝e2 0-0 9 0-0 ♝g4 10 ♝e3 ♞c6 11 b3 d5, or 7 h3 (to prevent ...♝g4) 7...♝g7 8 ♞f3 0-0 9 ♝e3 ♞c6 and ...d5 or ...e5. In both cases, Black has good play. Then perhaps ten years ago or so, someone realized the hidden strength of delaying development:

7 ♝e3 ♝g7 8 ♜c1!? 0-0 9 b3! *(D)*

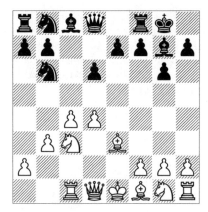

Once more it seems that an inexperienced player must be conducting the white pieces! He doesn't seem at all concerned about getting his kingside pieces out, which is particularly odd in a variation known for Black's dynamic play. As it turns out, White's strategy is purely prophylactic, i.e., Black is unable to play ...♗g4 and his standard central equalizer 9...d5 loses a pawn here to 10 c5 (since b3 has prevented the usual ...♘c4. Finally, White is prepared to meet Black's most natural move:

9...♘c6?!

In fact, 9...e5 is likely the best if slightly depressing chance. An endgame arises after 10 dxe5 dxe5 11 ♕xd8 (11 c5 has also been played, but is a less popular move) 11...♖xd8 12 c5. This has done well for White, but may be OK for Black if studied in advance and played precisely.

10 d5

Now that White has protected his c3-knight (8 ♖c1) and his c4-pawn (9 b3), he is able to make this move and disrupt Black's game. Thus White's opening set-up has also served as a prophylactic manoeuvre against 9...♘c6.

10...♘e5 11 ♗e2

Continuing a preventative policy: Black is denied ...♘g4 or ...♗g4 and White still doesn't commit his king's knight.

11...♘ed7

There are of course alternatives known to theory, but this move best illustrates the play.

12 ♘f3 ♘f6 13 h3

Here 13 ♘d4 has been played and is probably better, but 13 h3 continues with the theme of denying any squares to Black's pieces.

13...♘bd7 14 0-0 ♖e8 15 ♖e1 ♘f8 16 ♕d2

White controls the board. Black has no freeing move or counterplay, Nedev-Oney, Iraklion 1997.

One should also take note of fresh attitudes towards development in common but more tactical positions. There are hundreds of established lines in which creative new moves defy the traditional admonitions about getting the pieces out, so I've just picked a couple that caught my fancy.

1 d4 d5 2 c4 c6 3 ♘c3 ♘f6 4 ♘f3 e6 5 ♗g5 dxc4 6 e4 b5 7 a4 ♕b6 8 ♗xf6 gxf6 9 ♗e2 a6 10 0-0 (D)

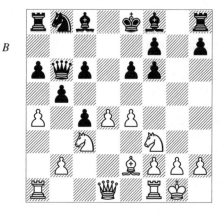

This is a well-known position in which at the very least Black has serious practical difficulties. He is a pawn up, but has only the queen out, is way behind in development, and is subject to attacks based upon d5 and b3. What's more, he has doubled pawns on the side of the board where his king will usually go. Surely it's time to get some pieces out?

10...♖a7!?

I mean, *minor* pieces? To understand this move fully, one first needs to realize that the concrete theory on 10...♘d7?! 11 d5!, and 10...♗b7 11 b3 (or 11 d5) is also very friendly to White. Thus 10...♖a7 is born from a pragmatic reaction to the difficulties found in the alternatives.

11 b3

Black's strategic goals and concrete variations outweigh developmental considerations here, as shown by these lines:

a) 11 d5 ♖d7 (the main point of ...♖a7: to pin the d-pawn, threaten ...b4, and get out of the way of the c8-bishop when it goes to b7) 12 axb5 cxb5 13 b3 cxb3 14 ♕xb3 ♗c5 with equality.

b) 11 ♕d2 ♖d7 is the archetypal position: so far Black has only the two major pieces out, the b8-knight has no moves, and the c8-bishop just one! Moreover, the line allows kingside weaknesses via ♗xf6. Nevertheless, the middlegame plan ...♖a7-d7 is considered a good one, perhaps the best available. Pedersen gives the additional moves 12 ♕f4 ♗g7, and this looks reasonably solid for Black.

11...cxb3! 12 ♕xb3 ♘d7 13 ♖fc1 ♖c7!

Yet another rook move, and this one to a closed file! Nevertheless, ...♖c7 gets out of the way when a bishop goes to b7, and strengthens the move ...c5.

14 ♖ab1 ♗e7 15 d5 ♘c5!? 16 ♕d1 b4 17 ♕d4 ♘d7 18 ♕xb6 ♘xb6 19 a5

19 ♘a2! is better according to Pedersen. There may follow 19...a5 with an edge due to the idea 20 ♖xc6 ♖xc6 21 ♗b5 f5!.

19...♘a8!

It's just that kind of game.

20 ♘a4 cxd5 21 ♘b6 ♖xc1+ 22 ♖xc1 ♘xb6 23 axb6

Kroll-S.Pedersen, Danish League 1995. Here 23...♔d7! 24 ♖c7+ ♔d6 "would have been very good for Black" (Pedersen). It's noteworthy that Pedersen annotates this game without any suggestion that it is an eccentric one.

A standard Modern Benoni position arises after:

1 d4 ♘f6 2 c4 c5 3 d5 e6 4 ♘c3 exd5 5 cxd5 d6 6 e4 g6 7 ♗d3 ♗g7 8 ♘ge2 0-0 9 0-0

Now a rather remarkable middlegame plan starts with:

9...♘g4!?

A move played and developed by Perenyi, and analysed in depth in my Benoni book. It is hard to explain, and its effectiveness depends upon very concrete ideas.

10 h3

Natural; the move ...♕h4 can be irritating to meet (e.g., 10 ♘g3? ♕h4 11 h3 ♘xf2!).

10...♘e5 11 ♗c2

I'm skipping the numerous alternatives at each juncture, of course. The positional charm of this variation can be seen in lines such as 11 ♗b1 ♘a6 12 f4 ♘c4 13 ♕d3 b5! 14 b3 ♘b4 15

♕f3 ♘b6 16 ♗b2 f5 17 a3 ♘a6 (or 17...fxe4 18 ♗xe4 ♘a6); this is based upon a Perenyi game and analysis by Kapengut. The knights move repeatedly only to get to the odd squares a6 and b6, and yet Black stands satisfactorily.

11...♘a6 12 f4 ♘c4

12...♘d7 is also played, but we follow Perenyi's idea.

13 b3 ♘a5! *(D)*

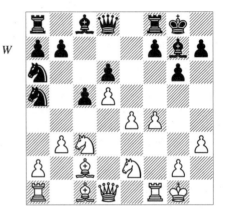

This is it: move the king's knight five times to put it on the edge of the board next to another knight also on the rim! In addition, the knight has no moves there. But the peripatetic piece proves to be quite useful in support of queenside play, since ...b5 is coming and White's a4 creates a weakness on b3 and can be met by ...c4 and ...♘b4 or ...♘c5. Nor can White be said to have merely overextended, because there are plenty of examples to show that his more conservative approaches are OK for Black as well.

14 a3 b5 15 ♖b1 b4 16 ♘a2 bxa3 17 ♗xa3 ♖b8 18 ♔h2 ♗d7

The game is equal, Serper-Nenashev, Novosibirsk 1989. This is certainly a high-level example. Perenyi's idea has been played quite a bit and has a perfectly good theoretical standing. The beauty of pure chess strategy has to impress one when such things are possible.

Further examples of the modern idea of development in sharp positions will be seen throughout this book. A striking example is the Caro-Kann system that begins with 1 e4 c6 2 d4 d5 3 e5 ♗f5 4 ♘c3 e6 5 g4 ♗g6 when White has a variety of outlandish-looking developmental strategies. See the chapter on flank advances for a detailed look at some of these. Also, Part 2 includes games such as Kasparov-Shirov, Horgen 1994, a famous example of how a strategic plan can be pursued at the cost of considerably delayed development. Finally, in part due to my strong leaning towards top-level players in this book, I would remind the reader that there are incredibly creative and unexpected ways of getting the pieces out in slightly less respected but perfectly playable openings to which I have unfortunately not paid attention. To name a few out of many such: the Leningrad Dutch (a goldmine of modern ideas), Pirc Defence, the 2 c3 Sicilian, 1 b3, and many variants of the Modern Defence. If you study or play these openings, you will see examples of just about every form of development (or non-development) that defies classical precepts.

Development and Pawn-Chains

Continuing with conventional openings, let's consider the 'semi-closed' variations of the French Defence, that is, ones in which White plays e5. These provide a setting in which, over the years, both moderately and radically different ideas have become routine over the years and been assimilated into our thinking. The d4/e5 structure is particularly relevant since it was the basis for Nimzowitsch's discussion of pawn-chains.

From the white point of view, relative neglect of development for structure reached new heights in the 1960s in lines such as 1 e4 e6 2 d4 d5 3 ♘d2 (the Tarrasch Variation) 3...♘f6 4 e5 ♘fd7 5 f4 c5 6 c3 ♘c6 7 ♘df3 ♕b6, when Benko and others found the idea of tucking the king away by 8 g3!? cxd4 9 cxd4 ♗b4+ 10 ♔f2 f6 11 ♔g2! *(D)*.

After 11 moves, White has moved his king twice and only has one piece out (versus five for Black after 11...0-0), but he stands quite well. He is finally ready to play moves like ♗d3 and ♘e2 (which generally would have failed tactically if played before this); and even if that reorganization is discouraged by Black, White can always play still *further* pawn moves such

as a3 and b4 and h4! The best way to understand how this sequence was previously neglected is to examine older tries with the more natural developing moves involving ♘e2-c3 and/or ♗e3, a3, b4, ♗b2, ♗d3, and similar ideas. These failed essentially due to ...0-0 and ...fxe5 with pressure down the f-file in conjunction with sacrificial ideas involving ...♘dxe5, ...♖xf3, and/or ...♘xd4. In view of those lines, it was counter-intuitive that one would choose a slow set-up like g3 and ♔f2-g2 that actually *increased* Black's development advantage. But this combination of moves quickly became the main line and single-handedly dragged f4 from relative disuse into a major variation.

That discovery (Benko-Schmid, Dublin 1957 is the earliest example I can find) fairly quickly caught on and was only the beginning of thematically similar ideas. For example, White now plays lines like 8 a3 (in place of 8 g3) 8...♗e7 (another example of purposeful non-development by White is 8...a5 9 b3 ♗e7 10 h4 ♕a7 11 h5) 9 h4 (this is not only aggressive, but has a prophylactic effect against ...g5) 9...cxd4 10 cxd4 f5 11 h5 *(D)*.

11...0-0 12 ♘h3 ♘db8 13 b4 ♗d7 14 ♘f2 ♘d8 15 g4 and here White has gone 15 moves with only two pieces out!

Still more common is the other flank pawn move 8 h4. The earliest games that I see with this move are in 1988, and yet it caught on immediately and became a main line. Now there are 226 examples in my database. A typical continuation is 8...cxd4 9 cxd4 ♗b4+ 10 ♔f2 ♗e7 11 ♔g3!?. The king heads for h2. I suspect that players in the first half of the last century would be a little shocked to hear that their

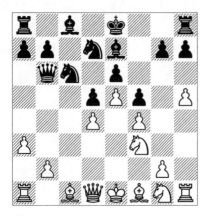

B

successors considered such sequences perfectly normal.

The oldest near-precedent for all this can be seen in this variation:

1 e4 e6 2 d4 d5 3 ♘c3 ♘f6 4 e5 ♘fd7 5 ♘ce2 c5 6 f4 ♘c6 7 c3 ♛b6 8 ♘f3 *(D)*

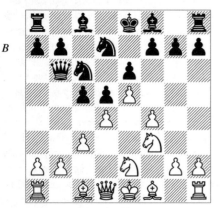

B

5 ♘ce2 has been around for a long time. It was introduced by Steinitz in the 19th century and has been played to some extent in every time period since. At least in this case, as opposed to the 5 f4 Tarrasch above, White has another piece out; and he generally doesn't go running around with his king (at least not voluntarily!). But even this position wasn't looked upon very favourably for White for many years until recently, when it has undergone a new interpretation more in line with the radical non-development philosophy that we are discussing. In the following game we see the intense clash between structural and dynamic priorities. Note that White and Black play on both sides of the board.

Anand – Shirov
Teheran FIDE Wch (4) 2000

8...f6

As White has increasingly turned to prophylactic pawn moves, Black himself has often moved away from brute force development (and subsequent sacrifices) to his own very untraditional methods. Lalić-Speelman, Hastings 2000 provides one example, continuing 8...♗e7 9 g3 a5 10 h4 a4!? 11 ♗h3 ♘db8!?. Here Speelman shows that White isn't the only one who can move backwards! His approach to this middlegame is philosophically opposite of what Black has mostly used for over 100 years. A similar reorganization is often seen in the f4 Tarrasch Variation, but with the solid defensive move ...f5 already in. Lalić-Speelman continued 12 h5 cxd4 13 cxd4 ♗d7 14 0-0 ♘a5 15 ♘c3 ♘c4 with a complex game that Speelman eventually won. I'm not sure whether this is an ideal approach, but at any rate Black took a clear lead in the anti-development competition!

9 a3 ♗e7 10 h4! *(D)*

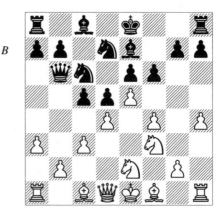

B

This additional pawn move supports attacking ideas involving h5 (or in some cases ♘g5), sets up the defensive/aggressive ♖h3, and significantly, it also acts as a prophylactic versus Black's undermining move ...g5.

If you look at games in this variation from the 19th century and most of the last one (many of them only in tournament books, of course), you see that beginning with move 9, White was almost never content to leave his pieces on their home squares for very long, preferring to develop with such moves as g3 and ♗h3, or ♘g3, or preparing ♗e3 by b3, ♕b3 or ♖b1. The plan Anand chooses emphasizes prevention over development.

10...0-0 11 ♖h3

Even when White *does* develop, it doesn't seem to be in the way that we learned as kids! The rook isn't going to g3; it's protecting against sacrifices on f3.

11...a5 12 b3 ♕c7 (D)

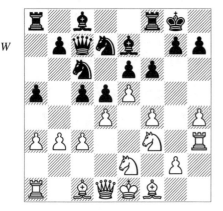

13 ♘eg1!

After all those pawn moves, it's finally the knight's turn ... to go backwards! Thus it has replaced its comrade by means of the route ♘c3-e2-g1, and the position is looking very similar to the 5 f4 Tarrasch Variation above. Paradoxically – and what are these kinds of middlegames if they aren't paradoxical? – White may even stand better than he did there, despite having taken two full extra moves to get his knights to exactly the same positions on g1 and f3!

13...a4!?

Anand suggested the restrained 13...b6.

14 b4

White's middlegame strategy looks too extravagant to be true: he still only has two pieces out after 14 moves, and one is the oddball rook on h3! Now Shirov felt that he could no longer resist trying to punish this impudence. But according to later analysis, the following sacrifice was unsound:

14...fxe5 15 fxe5 ♘dxe5?! 16 dxe5 ♘xe5 17 ♘xe5! ♕xe5+ 18 ♕e2 ♗xh4+ 19 ♔d1 ♕f6 20 ♘f3! ♕xc3 21 ♗b2 ♕b3+ 22 ♔c1

White has succeeded in consolidating. The rest was fairly straightforward:

22...e5 23 ♖xh4 ♗f5 24 ♕d1 e4 25 ♕xb3 axb3 26 ♘d2 e3 27 ♘f3 ♖ae8 28 ♔d1 c4 29 ♗e2 ♗e4 30 ♔c1 ♖e6 31 ♗c3 ♖g6 32 ♖h2 ♗d3 33 ♗xd3 cxd3 34 ♔b2 d2 35 ♔xb3 ♖g3 36 ♔b2 g5 37 ♔c2 ♖c8 38 ♔d3 g4 39 ♗e5 ♖c1 40 ♖h1 ♖xg2 41 ♘h4 1-0

Another semi-closed French Defence line is the Advance Variation, 1 e4 e6 2 d4 d5 3 e5, which is quite popular with top players right now. The conceptual changes in this opening in recent years have been dramatic and instructive. Traditional strategy used to consist of a fairly mechanical battle over who would control the d4-square, with both sides developing quickly to do so; for example, 3...c5 4 c3 ♘c6 5 ♘f3 ♕b6 6 ♗e2 cxd4 7 cxd4 ♘h6 8 b3 ♘f5 9 ♗b2 ♗b4+ 10 ♔f1.

In the last two decades or so, both White and Black have approached these positions differently, taking initially moderate and then more radical measures. First, White began to switch to structural ideas based upon queenside expansion:

Sveshnikov – Dizdar
Dubai rpd 2002

1 e4 e6 2 d4 d5 3 e5 c5 4 c3 ♘c6 5 ♘f3 ♕b6 6 a3

Instead of developing, White wants to gain space with b4, perhaps followed by ♗b2 or ♗e3 to protect d4. In practice, this often leads to strange and in every respect non-traditional play.

6...♘h6 7 b4 cxd4 8 cxd4 ♘f5 9 ♗b2 ♗d7 (D)

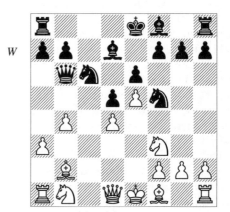

10 h4

White seems more interested in pawn moves than getting his pieces out. Sveshnikov, who played this move, has been and probably still is the world's greatest expert in the Advance Variation. His philosophy is very much what we have been describing: the establishment of space on the wings without much concern about normal development or king position. This and the next two games are also illustrations of the new love affair with flank moves before the completion of development. We repeatedly see, for example, b4, g4, and h4-h5.

Two heavyweights faced off in this position in Ivanchuk-Bareev, Dubai rpd 2002, again combining flank moves and tactics: 10 g4!? ♘fe7 (10...♘h6 is also played, when White can throw caution to the winds via 11 ♖g1 f6 12 exf6 gxf6 13 ♘c3 ♘f7 14 ♘a4 ♕c7 with unclear play, Savić-Lputian, Neum 2002) 11 ♘c3 ♘a5! 12 ♘d2 (12 ♘a4 ♕c6 is unclear) 12...♖c8 13 ♖c1 *(D)*.

13...h5!? (a deep move that anticipates the following sequence, although 13...♘g6! is safer and perhaps even slightly advantageous for Black; it threatens to go to f4 in many lines, prepares ...♗e7 and ...0-0, and by covering d6, prevents White's next idea) 14 ♖c2! ♘c4! 15 ♗xc4 dxc4 16 ♘ce4 (threatening ♘d6+ and the c4-pawn) 16...♘d5 17 ♘xc4 ♖xc4 18 ♖xc4 a5 (a long-term positional exchange sacrifice: for a pawn and exchange, Black has control of the light squares and play against the weakened king position, whereas White has to suffer because of his bad bishop on b2; nevertheless, Black's position is also loose and White can

give back the exchange in many lines) 19 0-0! axb4 20 axb4 ♕d8 21 ♗c1! (21 g5 ♗b5; 21 ♖e1) 21...♗b5!? (21...hxg4 22 ♗g5 ♕b8) 22 ♗g5 f6!? 23 exf6 gxf6 24 ♖c5! (or give back two exchanges! White comes out on top here) 24...♗xc5 25 dxc5 ♗xf1 26 ♘xf6+ ♔f7 27 ♘e4 ♕c7?! 28 ♘d6+ ♔g8 29 ♕xf1 ♕g7 30 ♕e2 ♕g6 31 h4! and Black's king was awfully weak; he was fortunate to draw. The general impression here is that White's early loosening pawn moves turned out to be sound, and pragmatically effective, in spite of Bareev's ingenious sacrifice. Compare the game.

10...♖c8 11 g4?! ♘h6 12 ♖g1 *(D)*

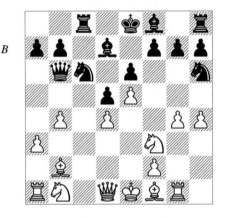

Everything that White does is aimed at maintaining or increasing his space advantage. On the other hand, his pieces lack mobility.

12...♗e7 13 ♘c3 ♘a5! 14 ♘a4 ♕c6 15 ♘c5 ♘c4 16 ♗c1

Back again.

16...♘g8!

Likewise.

17 ♗d3 ♗xc5! 18 dxc5 b6

Now White's elaborate kingside advances are going to haunt him.

19 ♗xc4 dxc4 20 ♗e3 ♕e4!? 21 ♖c1 b5 22 ♘g5!? ♕b7 23 ♘f3 ♘e7 24 h5 h6 25 ♔e2 ♖d8 26 ♖g3 ♗c6

Black is much better, although White eventually drew.

An even bigger change has come about when Black simply abandons the idea of attacking d4 and sets his sights upon e5 instead. As described in SOMCS, this contradicts the textbooks' old advice about attacking the base of the pawn-chain. In this section, we particularly want to look at the recent and unstereotyped ways in which Black is reorganizing his pieces to carry out his strategy. As for White, development is increasingly taking a back seat to pawn moves aimed at prevention of his opponent's ideas. Let's look at a couple of typical games:

Timman – Nikolić
Amsterdam 1999

1 e4 e6 2 d4 d5 3 e5 c5 4 c3 ♗d7 5 ♘f3 ♘c6 6 ♗e2 ♘ge7 7 0-0 ♘g6 *(D)*

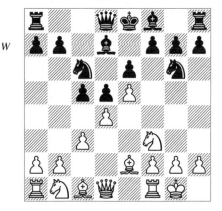

Here it is: a move considered anti-positional for a century or so, simply because it attacks the 'wrong' part of the chain (e5), and to a lesser extent because it is subject to harassment from h4-h5. In this and the next game, Black plays as though he couldn't care less about the d4-point.

8 g3!?

A slightly odd but logical move, covering f4 and preparing a space-grabbing kingside advance. It acknowledges that simple development won't stop Black's plan; e.g., 8 ♗e3 ♗e7 9 ♘a3 0-0 10 ♘c2 cxd4 11 cxd4 f6 12 exf6 ♗xf6 with plenty of activity.

8...♗e7!?

The direct 8...f6 has also been played successfully. These notes will indicate ideas and not represent high theory.

9 h4

The point of 8 g3, but Black is ready:

9...0-0! 10 h5 ♘h8 *(D)*

Voilà! The apparently immobile knight is actually well placed in the corner. It supports the

attack against the head of the pawn-chain by ...f6 and ...♘f7. Korchnoi first employed this typically imaginative strategy in Hjartarson-Korchnoi, Amsterdam 1991, which continued 9...cxd4 10 cxd4 0-0 11 h5 ♘h8 12 h6 g6 13 ♘bd2 f6. The interpolation of 9...cxd4 is perhaps inaccurate here because White gains the option of ♘c3 and ♘a4, although whether that matters isn't clear to me.

11 h6 g6

11...g5!? also looks playable, with ideas like ...f6 and ...♘g6 or ...♘f7.

12 dxc5!

White's 'pawns before pieces' strategy is very logical. The move h6 loosened up Black's kingside, which might end up exposed after the necessary freeing move ...f6. And now the further pawn move c4 will destroy or immobilize Black's centre. Thus Black has to move quickly and exploit his lead in development.

12...f6!?

12...♗xc5 13 c4 f6 is another idea; e.g., 14 cxd5 ♘xe5 15 ♘xe5 fxe5 16 ♘c3 ♕b6 17 ♘e4 ♗d4. None of this is very clear, and dynamic equality seems the fairest assessment.

13 exf6

A little greedy; 13 c4 will probably transpose into the last note. Either move, incidentally, means that White has made 10 pawn moves out of his first 13.

13...♗xc5 14 ♗g5!? ♘f7 15 ♗h4 ♕c7

White is a pawn up, but Black is active with a potentially mobile centre.

16 ♕d2

16 ♘bd2? g5! intending 17 ♘xg5 ♘xg5 18 ♗xg5? ♕xg3+.

16...♘ce5 17 ♘xe5 ♕xe5

Again Black threatens ...g5, which is getting awkward to meet.

18 ♔h2

Now 18...g5! would have favoured Black: 19 f4 ♕xf6 (or 19...gxf4 20 gxf4 ♕f5) 20 fxg5 (20 ♗xg5 ♘xg5 21 fxg5 ♕xf1! 22 ♗xf1 ♖xf1 wins for Black) 20...♕e5 21 ♗d3 ♕e3! 22 g6 ♘e5! 23 gxh7+ ♔h8 24 ♕xe3 ♗xe3, when Black recovers his pawns with advantage.

These strategies are now standard procedure for both sides. In the same variation, White can bolster d4 and get a piece out by ♘a3-c2. But as in the following examples, he still tends to rely upon flank advances to protect his centre:

Movsesian – Nikolić
Istanbul OL 2000

1 e4 e6 2 d4 d5 3 e5 c5 4 c3 ♘c6 5 ♘f3 ♗d7 6 ♗e2 ♘ge7 7 ♘a3 ♘g6

Again aiming at the head of the pawn-chain. The other treatment ends up being just as unconventional. It begins with 7...cxd4 8 cxd4 ♘f5 9 ♘c2 and now:

a) 9...♖c8 10 0-0 ♕b6 11 g4! ♘fe7 12 ♘h4! ♘g6 13 ♘g2 (this g4 + ♘h4-g2 manoeuvre has occurred repeatedly in master play) 13...f6 14 exf6 gxf6 15 ♔h1 ♗d6 16 f4, Sveshnikov-Atalik, Bled 1999. Despite White's rather miserable-looking pieces he stands better, since his f5 idea is going to compel ...f5 on Black's part.

b) 9...♗e7 10 0-0 g5! (Black can play on the flank as well) 11 g4 ♘g7!? *(D)*.

Another fianchettoed knight, this time without a single square to move to! Yet there is more

than enough for it to do. First, it can be effective in supporting ...h5 and/or ...f5: 12 b4 a6 13 ♖b1 f5!? (this opens more lines with unclear effects; 13...h5 looks good) 14 exf6 ♗xf6 15 a4 h6 (now the maligned knight protects e6; maybe we should extend the principle enunciated by Suba, 'Bad bishops protect good pawns', to 'Bad knights protect good pawns'!) 16 ♘ce1!? 0-0 17 ♗e3 (finally developing; now Black activates his d7-bishop) 17...♗e8 18 ♘d3 ♗g6 with equality, Dvoirys-Zakharevich, Elista 2001.

8 h4

Trying to kick the knight before it can get to the coveted h8-square! 8 ♘c2 ♗e7 9 g3 0-0 10 h4 cxd4 11 cxd4 f6! 12 h5 ♘h8 13 h6 g6 is a better version for Black of the previous game (White doesn't have c4): 14 exf6 (otherwise Black plays ...fxe5 and ...♘f7) 14...♗xf6 15 0-0 ♘f7 (Black is slightly better) 16 ♘e3!? ♘xh6 17 ♘xd5 exd5 18 ♗xh6 ♖e8 19 ♖e1? ♗g4! with the strong threat of ...♖xe2, Jonkman-I.Botvinnik, Tel Aviv 2000.

8...cxd4 9 cxd4 ♗b4+ *(D)*

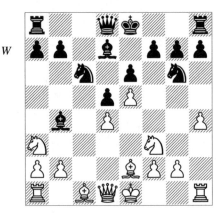

10 ♔f1

This tries to maintain the advantages of White's spatial plus. 10 ♗d2 ♕b6 11 ♗xb4 ♕xb4+ 12 ♕d2 0-0 13 h5 ♘f4!? 14 ♗f1 g6 15 hxg6 fxg6 is only equal.

10...h6!

The knight says: 'If you won't let me get to h6, I'll go to h7!'. Now 11 h5 ♘f8 helps him along the way to that square and perhaps to g5 afterwards.

11 ♘c2 ♗e7 12 h5

McDonald suggests 12 g3, although 12...0-0 13 ♔g2 ♘h8! and ...f6 switches effectively to the plan from the last game. 12 &d3 was played by Ehlvest, to discourage ...f6. But Black can still go in for 12...0-0 13 &e3 (13 ♘g5!? ♘xh4!) 13...f5!? 14 exf6 ♖xf6 with activity.

12...♘f8 13 ♖h3 ♘h7! (D)

The point. Now Black has the idea ...♘g5 in addition to the usual ...f6. For a game 13 moves deep, there haven't been many traditional ideas by either side!

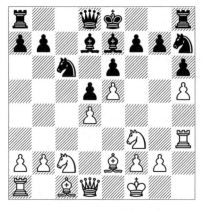

W

14 &d3 0-0 15 ♖g3 ♔h8 16 &f4 f5! 17 exf6

Instead, McDonald gives 17 ♕d2 &e8 18 ♖h3 ♘g5, which looks better for Black. But the h-pawn has been humbled and remains a problem for White regardless:

17...♘xf6 18 ♘e5 ♘xe5 19 &xe5 &e8 20 ♖h3 &d6 21 ♘e1!?

A harmless-looking move like 21 ♕e2 allows 21...&xe5 22 dxe5 ♘e4! 23 &xe4 dxe4 intending 24 ♕xe4 ♕d2.

21...&xe5 22 dxe5 ♘e4! 23 ♘f3 ♖f5 24 ♕e2 (D)

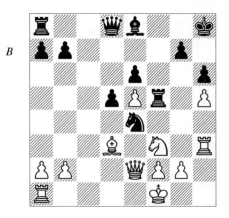

B

24...♖xh5 25 ♖xh5 &xh5 26 &xe4 dxe4 27 ♕xe4 ♕b6

Black's king is safer, his pieces are better, and ...♖f8 is coming. Nikolić went on to win the game.

Taken as a whole, this chapter offers a simple message: to come to grips with the play of modern grandmasters, it is necessary to discard the traditional view of development and replace it with one more flexible and pragmatic. There has been an incredible explosion of games involving previously unconsidered or rejected ideas. In my opinion, these new approaches cannot be considered merely exceptional because they permeate the theory and practice of most types of positions played today.

2 Modern Understanding of Pawn Play

Introduction

Every book on the general theory of chess has to place the pawns at the forefront of discussion. In the end, pawns are fundamentally more important to strategy than their more powerful cohorts. They are indeed still the soul of our game. The nuances of and changes in pawn-structures determine where, how, and with what effect the pieces can manoeuvre. Accordingly, I devoted more space to pawn play in SOMCS than to any other topic. In this book I will concentrate heavily upon three aspects of pawn play that have been of revolutionary importance to modern chess. In addition, but with much less detail, I will expand upon some other pawn issues raised in SOMCS.

Reuben Fine's *The Ideas Behind the Chess Openings* has always been a very popular book and in some sense a chess student's textbook for openings. Fine was of course one of the world's very top players in the late 1930s, using a classical style with tremendous success. He superficially revised his book in 1989 but kept most of his old ideas and claimed that opening theory "had reached its full maturity in the period from 1930 to 1945". It is very risky to use quotes from players as evidence for one's case, but sometimes the phrasing strongly indicates a genuine belief and or at least reflects an attitude of the time in which they played. Fine's 'old school' comments about pawn moves are therefore of interest. In the Sicilian Defence, he sets forth the rules "for all variations". Here are two: "(1) Black must never allow White to play c4 because he then has no counterplay on the c-file and is thereby doomed to passivity; (2) After White has played d4, Black must not

move ...e5, leaving his d-pawn backward on an open file." Obviously both of these are logical by classical theory, but they have been proven wrong by modern practice. In the Caro-Kann Defence, Fine says that 3 e5 (after 1 e4 c6 2 d4 d5) is "entirely useless", because unlike the French Defence case with 3 e5, Black can put his bishop on f5, outside the pawn-chain, following up with ...c5 at some point. Frankly, that was my own instinctive attitude towards 3 e5 in the Caro Kann for many years, so it's not as though the idea isn't rationally grounded in principle. As it turns out, however, 'bad' bishops are often as useful as 'good' ones; and more importantly, a very complex set of specific moves and responses has ultimately demonstrated that White can get promising play by at least two systems of development after 3 e5 ♗f5. Citing such examples, Bill Kelleher says of Fine: "He seems never to have fully realized the implications of the new ideas introduced by [the Soviet chess revolution]."

By contrast, Dražen Marović builds a modern model of the evolution of pawn play in his *Dynamic Pawn Play in Chess*. He divides chess history into very approximate theoretical periods in which masters successively learned how to play:

a) Open pawn centres, which were understood early on.

b) Closed pawn centres, the principles of which began to be grasped after Steinitz through the play of Rubinstein, Capablanca and others, but the broad understanding of which awaited the players of the 1960s and after.

c) Piece-controlled centres of the hypermoderns.

d) Fixed pawn centres, the 'underlying mechanisms' of which he thinks were understood through most of the 20th century.

e) The 'dynamic' pawn centre of modern times, gaining importance in the 1940s and still being expanded upon today.

He points out that the dynamic pawn centre has become the most important one both in frequency and for exploration. "Everything we knew about the dynamic pawn centre half a century ago has been questioned and re-examined. We owe the fascinating process of our time to the spirit of experimentation, readiness to enter the unknown and to take risks, but first and foremost to a new attitude borne out of conviction that all is possible if supported by concrete calculation. That seems to be the only general maxim the modern interpreter of the dynamic centre is ready to accept without reservation, to play and live by." Needless to say, these sentiments are very much in line with my own observations. I also tend to think that there has been some fundamental change in understanding and playing several of the other centre types, especially the closed and fixed ones, as may be seen in examples throughout this book.

Note that Marović's emphasis on the centre is the traditional one. But while that sector has always attracted most of the attention and respect of theoreticians, a change is underway. Of late, flank play has taken on a life of its own, no longer subservient to or dependent upon central structure but in a mutual relationship on equal grounds or sometimes even one of controlling influence. This development is the most dramatic and fastest changing in modern pawn play. I believe that as late as the 1990s and into this century, a whole new understanding has arisen about flank pawn advances. This continues the trend I discussed in SOMCS but brings it to such an extreme that it will become a major theme in all parts of this book, including the section that follows.

In a sentiment echoed by many, Marović says: "The boundaries between opening and middlegame, invisible but felt clearly by an experienced player, show a tendency of disappearing to such an extent that many a time only at reaching an endgame does a player become aware that he is out of the opening ... The subtle relation of marching pawns on different wings, the undefined centre offering both sides numerous options, the variety of pawn advances and tactical blows make assessments increasingly difficult. Each position, as if evading general principles, must be assessed on its own more than ever." I think that explains a great deal about why opening theory, now extending well into the 10s and 20s of moves in many openings, serves as the best way to make comparative observations about middlegame strategy. With the pawn-structures retaining some essential character and yet subject to various changes that resemble each other from game to game, we are able to gain an appreciation of what is truly new in contemporary play. By contrast, the random and chaotic nature of late middlegames arising from these dynamic pawn centres that Marović talks about inhibits strategic discussion. That is, philosophical changes are hard if not impossible to demonstrate in the sense of adducing multiple examples of them.

Getting back to this book, the reader may have noticed to what a great extent I have already stressed pawn play. The surrender of the centre, for example, is a subject based upon pawn-structure. More radically, the section 'The Development of Development' contained one after another discussion of pawn play and structure. It presented, for example, many examples of the use of multiple pawn moves to establish structure, with an often extreme neglect of development. We also saw numerous examples of early flank pawn advances (see the large section below). Most importantly, there was a lengthy segment on pawn-chains, a subject that I will forego here for that reason.

What I emphasize in this chapter therefore will be a limited number of fascinating new strategies of pawn play. These will often spring from known structures, some of them repeated in characteristic openings. Others will appear more or less out of the blue and demonstrate the uninhibited attitude that pervades contemporary practice. I will follow this with short comments upon other pawn subjects discussed in SOMCS.

2.1 The Flank Pawns Have Their Say

Introduction

The single biggest change in opening and middlegame strategy in the last two to three decades has been in the area of flank pawn advances. Traditional theory was extremely wary of using the a-, b-, g- and h-pawns to attack or grab space except under specified circumstances. The overall cautionary precept was that pawn moves tend to create weaknesses and thus should be avoided without strict justification. The particular rule that applied was that a stable or, better yet, locked centre was a precondition for flank pawn advances. This was held to be especially true for kingside pawn advances, and thus for any early thrust of the wing pawns when the king's eventual position was as yet unsettled. In game notes one would often see a disadvantage or loss ascribed to some attack on the wing when the centre was not yet stabilized. Naturally players sometimes indulged in exceptions to these guidelines, especially when in a particular position practice revealed that the dangers were merely apparent. But it wasn't until the middle of the 20th century that the prevailing attitude gradually began to change; and with the current generation of players, the whole framework seems to have been thrown overboard. As ever in modern chess, pragmatism reigns. Advances on the wing can sometimes be permanently weakening, of course; but they are very often positionally desirable and/or necessary, whether or not the central situation is resolved. The most dramatic indication of the change that has taken place can be seen from the flank pawn advances in very early stages of the game. The reader will find considerable overlap here with the section on development in Chapter 1.

This is an area in which choosing material is almost impossible because the matter under discussion saturates modern chess. A single issue of *Informator*, TWIC or CBM would probably provide enough material for a lengthy article. In the interest of communicating the main themes coherently, I shall mostly limit my examination to positions involving the kingside advances g4, h4, ...g5, and ...h5. These will include recognizable structures whose rapidly-evolving treatment exemplifies the overall trend in philosophy.

Before plunging into examples, it's worth considering what the main reasons are for playing on the flanks early in the game. There are a variety of ideas here, and any particular example of a flank advance will probably involve more than one of them, but here is a short list:

1) The most obvious motivation is direct, immediate attack upon the king. This was the most common reason that players in pre-modern chess hurled their flank pawns forward, feeling that a successful attack justifies weaknesses. I am concerned with strategy and don't want to spend too much time discussing what amount to tactical issues. Still, it is noteworthy when we see strong players resort to brute force attack in violation of the traditional principles of central play. It may turn out that the defensive reaction to direct attack will involve concessions in the positional battle that follows.

2) Another reason for early flank advances is to drive back enemy pieces, in order to release pressure on one's own position, remove defenders, and/or hamper the coordination of the enemy pieces.

3) Increasingly, flank moves are prophylactic in nature, i.e., they prevent undesirable or troublesome pawn or piece moves on the part of the opponent.

4) A major positional reason for pawn-thrusts on the wing is to establish space, regardless of whether there is an attack in sight, and regardless of the internal weaknesses created thereby. With the control of space may come greater ease of development and mobility for

the pieces on that wing. Previously, central space has been regarded as the absolute key to greater freedom and mobility for one's pieces; and of course it remains a vital factor. But as we have seen, the necessity of defending central pawns and preventing their undermining can tie down one's own pieces as well. Space grabs on the wing implicitly express the idea that piece movements under the protection of pawns on one side of the board can sometimes have just as much or more effect as those supported by central pawns. Naturally, such considerations are too broad to analyse outside the context of particular positions, and they are necessarily in some kind of competition with other important factors. Nevertheless, I think that it's obvious that the gain of flank space is far more aggressively pursued today than in the past. This is a tendency that one can see gradually increasing since the 1950s, but which has become dramatically ubiquitous in contemporary play.

General Examples from Practice

While the most exciting changes have taken place over the past 10-15 years, let's first turn to a couple of precedents for such pawn advances from Botvinnik, one of the most positionally creative players in history. We begin with a classic game that is worth seeing again in the context of later ideas:

Botvinnik – Smyslov
Moscow Wch (2) 1954

1 d4 ♘f6 2 c4 e6 3 ♘c3 ♗b4 4 e3 b6 5 ♘e2 ♗a6 6 a3 ♗e7 7 ♘f4 d5 8 cxd5 ♗xf1 9 ♔xf1 exd5 10 g4! *(D)*

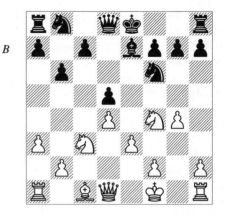

Peter Wells commented upon this famous move, which seems to expose the wing upon which White's king resides: "It's all here: space; driving/restricting pieces, even the pawn-storm – even prophylaxis. The implied threat to d5 will discourage Black from ever considering counterplay in the centre (with ...c5) and hence the 'fixed centre' which encourages White's wing ambitions looks here to stay. It also has, crucially, timing. If Black had a tempo either to castle or to play ...c6, he would be able to organize his knights optimally. As it is, they are likely to impinge on each other's space since they both need to land on d7. Thus are space advantages driven home."

The hard thing to realize (or remember) is how original and daring this move appeared at the time it was first played. Today it might well be the first move that a strong master would consider.

10...c6 11 g5 ♘fd7 12 h4 ♗d6

Black is cramped and lacks ideas, so he tries to exchange pieces. Now White can keep a comfortable edge by 13 ♕g4, but correctly decides to switch to attack mode:

13 e4! dxe4 14 ♘xe4 ♗xf4 15 ♗xf4 0-0 16 h5 *(D)*

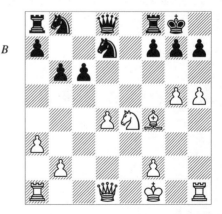

Completing the cramping, space-gaining plan started by 10 g4. Black can hardly move.

16...♖e8

Against most other moves 17 d5 will be decisive.

17 ♘d6 ♖e6 18 d5! ♖xd6 19 ♗xd6 ♕xg5 20 ♕f3

20 ♖c1 would probably win more quickly, but Botvinnik simplifies into a safely winning endgame. The rest is easy:

20...♕xd5 21 ♕xd5 cxd5 22 ♖c1 ♘a6 23 b4 h6 24 ♖h3 ♔h7 25 ♖d3 ♘f6 26 b5 ♘c5 27 ♗xc5 bxc5 28 ♖xc5 ♖b8 29 a4 ♖b7 30 ♖dc3 1-0

Another Botvinnik idea that we briefly mentioned in SOMCS has recently had some original and creative interpretations:

Vaiser – Timoshchenko
Tashkent 1987

1 d4 d5 2 c4 e6 3 ♘c3 ♗e7 4 cxd5 exd5 5 ♗f4 c6 6 e3 ♗f5 7 g4!?

This is pure and simply a space-gainer, especially in the following line:

7...♗e6 8 h4

8 h3 is the more common move, as played by Botvinnik versus Petrosian, and later by players such as Geller, Korchnoi, and Petrosian himself. But both Kasparov and Karpov have played 8 h4, so it is to be taken seriously.

8...♘d7

After 8...c5, the strange-looking 9 ♗e5! ♗f6 10 ♗xb8! ♖xb8 11 g5 single-mindedly continues with White's flank advance. This was the course of the game Dautov-Lputian, Istanbul OL 2000, which is discussed in Part 2.

9 h5 *(D)*

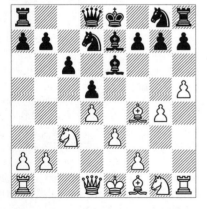

B

Remarkably, White ignores his development for the sake of mere territorial gain. Now after

9...♘gf6 10 f3, White prepares g5 and Black has no kingside counterplay.

9...♘h6!

This move solves the problem of how to get Black's pieces out, since ♗xh6 would leave White's dark squares terribly weak. It also leaves open the idea of ...f5.

10 ♗e2 ♘b6

The immediate 10...f5 probably leaves White with some advantage after 11 ♕b3 (as ...♕b6 will allow g5) or 11 ♗xh6 gxh6 12 gxf5 ♗xf5 13 ♗g4.

11 ♘h3!?

Kasparov-Karpov, Moscow Wch (21) 1985 featured 11 ♖c1. Note that he was unconcerned with losing the queenside castling rights; in so many of these early flank attack lines, the king remains in the centre or eventually castles by hand. The game went 11...♗d6 12 ♘h3 ♗xf4 13 ♘xf4 ♗d7 14 ♖g1!? g5!? 15 hxg6 hxg6 16 ♔d2!? (the king moves to connect queen and rooks! Nevertheless, simply 16 ♘d3 intending ♘e5 seems to favour White somewhat) 16...♕e7 17 b3 g5 18 ♘d3 0-0-0 19 ♖h1 f6 20 ♕g1 ♘f7 21 ♕g3 ♕d6 22 ♕xd6 ♘xd6 23 f3 ♖dg8 24 ♘c5 (or 24 e4!?) 24...♔d8 25 ♗d3 and White had the advantage.

11...g5!

Black can play with the flank pawns as well. This puts an end to g5 and makes White's advances useless unless he consents to open Black's h-file.

12 hxg6 hxg6 13 f3! ♗h4+ *(D)*

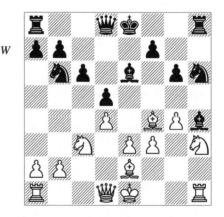

W

14 ♔d2

An eccentric move for an eccentric game. Also extremely interesting is 14 ♘f2 g5! (for the second time!) 15 ♗h2 ♕e7 16 e4 dxe4 17 fxe4?? (17 ♘cxe4 hits d6 and threatens ♗e5; then both sides have chances) 17...♘c4 18 ♗xc4 ♘xg4 and Black was winning in Turov-Vaganian, Moscow 2002.

14...g5

Another flank pawn move. Black locks in his own bishop but prevents recentralization by ♘f4 at some point.

15 ♗h2 f5 16 gxf5?!

An inaccuracy. White would do better to chase the rook now by 16 ♗e5 ♖g8, and then perhaps 17 ♘f2!?, with the knight trying to work its way to g4.

16...♘xf5 17 ♗e5 ♖h6! 18 f4?

Missing Black's next. 18 ♕g1 is better, to protect e3 and think about ♕h2 or ♘f2.

18...g4! 19 ♘g5

19 ♗xg4?? ♘c4+ wins for Black.

19...♗xg5 20 fxg5 ♕xg5 21 ♗f4 ♖xh1 22 ♕xh1 ♕g7!?

22...♕f6! 23 ♕h5+ ♔d7 is the way to keep the advantage.

23 ♗e5

And here 23 ♖g1! is correct, in view of 23...g3 (23...♘xd4 24 ♗h6!; 23...♘e7 24 ♕h5+ ♔d7 25 ♗xg4) 24 ♗xg3 ♘xg3 25 ♕h2 with equality. Now Black was content to draw:

23...♕h6 24 ♗f4 ♕g7 25 ♗e5 ♕h6 26 ♗f4 ½-½

Moving still further ahead in time, the following game features a surprising wing thrust that has the direct-attack philosophy:

Miezis – Smirin
New York 1998

1 c4 ♘f6 2 ♘c3 e5 3 ♘f3 ♘c6 4 g3 d5 5 cxd5 ♘xd5 6 ♗g2 ♘b6 7 0-0 ♗e7 8 ♖b1 g5!? *(D)*

This shocking move was introduced to top-level play by Korchnoi in 1993, although Baumgartner had employed it the previous year in a correspondence game. Black's idea is a primitive one: to play ...h5-h4 and ...hxg3, either before or after driving the knight back from f3, and then playing for mate on the h-file! Failing that, Black feels that trading weaknesses for a gain of space on the kingside will be a good deal, and that the time lost by White in retreating his knight will compensate for the time he

has spent on the exotic ...g5-g4. I think that most experienced players at the time looked askance at the move, which appears both amateurish and overoptimistic. But then it was taken up by others and is considered playable and almost normal.

Black's opening, incidentally, is a case of a reversed position that makes more sense for the player with a tempo less. I discussed how this occurs in SOMCS and quite a few other writers have been discussing the idea of late. Here the move 8...g5!? is especially jolting because Black is after all a full tempo down on a standard white position in the Classical Dragon Sicilian. Imagine being able to play this way for mate against the Dragon! But of course White's extra move in that opening is 0-0, with the result that there will be neither mates nor even a rook on an open file should he embark upon g4 and h4-h5.

9 d3

This is the natural response, but no longer the most popular move. The two alternatives perfectly illustrate classical and modern approaches to early flank advances:

a) 9 d4!? follows the traditional rule that a flank thrust should be met by central action, but grandmasters have only seen fit to try it once. After 9...exd4 10 ♘b5 ♗f5 11 ♖a1, Korchnoi gives 11...d3 (11...♗e4!? was played in Claesen-M.Gurevich, Antwerp 1994) 12 exd3 a6 13 ♘c3 g4 14 ♘h4! (in view of 14 ♘e1 ♕d7 and ...0-0-0, which Korchnoi assesses as giving Black a large advantage); then Black has his share of play after 14...♗xh4 15 gxh4 0-0 (safest, hitting d3 and h4); e.g., 16 ♗f4 ♖c8 17 ♘e4 ♕d4 with equality.

b) 9 b4!? is White's move of choice today, a dynamic counterattack on the other wing that is both a flank thrust and a positional pawn sacrifice: 9...g4 10 ♘e1 ♘xb4 (D).

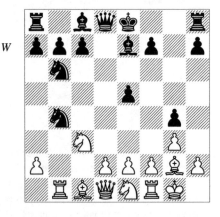

11 ♘c2! (calmly bringing his forces out; 11 f4? exf4 12 ♖xf4 ♘4d5 13 ♘xd5 ♘xd5 14 ♖f1 ♘e3?? 15 ♕a4+ occurred once, but 14...♘c3! 15 ♕b3 ♘xe2+ is extremely strong) 11...♘c6 (11...♘xc2 12 ♕xc2 c6 13 a4! gives interesting compensation) 12 ♗xc6+ bxc6 13 d4. A typically obscure position for this line. Two games have gone 13...f6!? 14 dxe5 (14 ♕d3!? has had split results) 14...♕xd1 15 ♖xd1 fxe5, when 16 ♗a3! of Khalifman-Lutz, New Delhi FIDE 2000 is the best try for a very slight advantage. But 13...exd4 14 ♘xd4 ♕d7! is not at all clear either. Black plans moves like ...0-0 and ...c5, and ideas with ...♗b7 and ...0-0-0 are also possible. The balance between White's much better pawn-structure and Black's extra pawn and two bishops is hard to assess, but I doubt that Black is any worse.

9...h5 10 ♗e3

Another complicated try is 10 a3 h4 (!?; with hindsight, this move might be too hurried; just 10...g4! looks fine, and 11 ♘e1 h4 or 11 ♘d2 a5 with ...h4 still in the air) 11 b4 hxg3!? 12 hxg3?! (12 fxg3! ends up helping White by giving him the f-file and some space; then Black should play something like 12...a6, since 12...g4 is met by 13 ♘d2!, when 13...♕d4+?! 14 ♖f2 ♕xc3 15 ♗b2 traps the black queen, and otherwise 14 ♘de4 is coming) Serper-Korchnoi, Groningen PCA 1993, and here Korchnoi gives the direct and promising attacking sequence 12...♕d6 13 ♘b5 ♕h6! 14 ♘xc7+ ♔f8 15

♘xa8 ♘xa8, consistent with the philosophy behind 8...g5.

In the next few moves, Black builds up a nice attack. Note that Smirin isn't shy about further opening up his own king position:

10...g4 11 ♘d2 ♘d4 12 ♖c1 h4 13 ♘c4 ♘xc4 14 dxc4 c6 15 ♕d3 f5! 16 ♖fd1 ♗f6 17 f4 gxf3 18 exf3 (D)

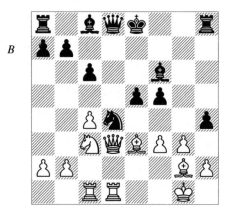

18...♔f7!

Very nice. The idea is ...♕g8 and ...♕h7.

19 ♕f1?

This logical defensive try ends badly, although Smirin shows that Black stands well in lines like:

a) 19 f4 e4 20 ♕d2 c5 21 ♘b5 hxg3 22 hxg3 ♕g8 23 ♘xd4 cxd4 24 ♗xd4 ♕xg3 25 ♗xf6 e3! 26 ♕d5+ ♗e6 27 ♕xb7+ ♔xf6 28 ♕f3 ♕xf3 29 ♗xf3 ♖ag8+, etc.

b) 19 ♗xd4! ♕xd4+ 20 ♕xd4 exd4 21 ♘e2 c5 22 b4 b6 with a small edge for Black.

19...hxg3 20 hxg3 ♕g8! 21 ♕e1 ♕h7 22 f4 ♗e6! 23 ♘d5!? cxd5 24 fxe5 f4!!

Mobilizing Black's last attacking piece.

25 ♗xd4

A pretty line is 25 ♗xf4 ♘f3+!! 26 ♗xf3 ♕h2+ 27 ♔f1 ♗h3+.

25...f3! 26 exf6 fxg2 27 ♔xg2 ♖ae8 28 ♗e5 ♗g4 29 ♕e3 ♕h2+ 30 ♔f1 ♕h1+ 0-1

In Part Two of this book we will examine the game Shirov-Kramnik, Novgorod 1994 with a similar theme: 1 e4 c5 2 ♘f3 ♘c6 3 ♗b5 g6 4 ♗xc6 dxc6 5 h3 e5 6 d3 f6 7 c3 ♘h6 8 ♗e3 ♘f7 9 0-0 g5! (who's that playing Black? Oh yes, the current world champion...) 10 ♕e2 (probably the most remarkable aspect of Black's

9...g5 is that the thematic 10 d4 may not even equalize after 10...g4 or 10...cxd4 and 11...g4; see the game in Part 2 for details) 10...h5 11 ♘e1 ♗e6 (11...g4 12 h4 f5 would make Black's pawns-only approach more extreme) 12 a3 a5 13 ♘d2 b6, when 9 of Black's 13 moves have been with pawns. The move 9...g5 is currently in excellent theoretical shape.

The reader is also referred to Part 2 for the exciting and attractive game Salinnikov-Miroshnichenko, Ukraine 2000, featuring the modern opening 1 e4 c5 2 ♘f3 d6 3 c3 ♘f6 4 h3!? ♘c6 5 ♗d3 e5 6 0-0, when we see an even earlier instantiation of the idea by 6...g5!. A particularly entertaining game follows that move.

Another kingside advance with ...g5, this time with barbaric attacking intentions, has appeared in what was once a thoroughly uneventful main line, as shown in Bruzon-Dominguez, Havana 2002: 1 ♘f3 d5 2 c4 c6 3 d4 ♘f6 4 cxd5 cxd5 5 ♘c3 ♘c6 6 ♗f4 ♗f5 7 e3 e6 8 ♗b5 ♘d7 9 0-0 ♗e7 10 ♕b3, and now 10...g5! 11 ♗g3 h5 12 h3 g4 13 hxg4 hxg4 14 ♘d2 a6 15 ♗e2? (Bruzon suggests the alternative 15 ♗xc6 bxc6 16 e4 ♗g6 17 ♖fe1) 15...♗d6! 16 ♖fe1, when Black would have been virtually winning after 16...♕f6!! intending 17 ♗xd6 ♕h6 18 f4 ♕h1+ 19 ♔f2 g3+. Bruzon also demonstrates a clear advantage for Black after White's alternatives on move 17. The real point is that such an apparently unsupported attack could be so devastating.

One may have noticed that Black doesn't have to be developed in order to lash out with his flank pawns, nor does the centre have to be stabilized. The following game illustrates a variation of the English Opening that has been fully respectable for 30 years or so:

Hulak – Z. Almasi
Pula 2001

1 c4 e5 2 g3 ♘c6 3 ♗g2 g6 4 ♘c3 ♗g7 5 e3 d6 6 ♘ge2 h5

This early flank advance becomes particularly relevant to our discussion if White responds in classical fashion to the 'premature' flank attack as follows:

7 d4 h4 *(D)*
8 d5

White nearly always plays this and it is the consistent move to stake a claim to superiority in the centre. Trying to open the game by 8 dxe5? ♘xe5 merely empowers Black's g7-bishop to no good effect and to make things worse, both ...♗g4 and ...h3 are then threatened.

8...♘ce7 9 e4 f5 10 ♗g5 h3 11 ♗f3

11 ♗f1 has also been tried, keeping an eye on the h-pawn at the cost of development. Then Black can try 11...♗f6 12 ♗e3 (not 12 ♕d2? ♘xd5!) 12...g5!?. The main line 11...♘f6 is safer, when theory suggests 12 ♕d2 although simply 12...fxe4! 13 ♗xf6 ♗xf6 14 ♘xe4 ♗g7 gives Black two bishops and options for his pieces like 15 ♘2c3 ♘f5! intending ...♘d4, or 15 0-0-0 ♗f5 followed by ...♗h6.

11...♘f6 12 0-0 0-0!

A rook's pawn advance (even one involving opening one's own rook's file) is often followed by castling on the same wing. Thus we see that what is apparently an attacking idea can also be used for positional purposes. In this position Black has cramped his opponent's kingside and forced the light-squared bishop to an awkward square. This goes well with the opening of the bishop's file that potentially follows ...f5.

13 ♕d2 ♘h7! *(D)*

Now White's bishop (too important to give up for a knight) faces a difficult choice.

14 ♗e3?!

Almasi gives 14 ♗h6, then suggesting the continuation 14...♗xh6 15 ♕xh6 g5!? (as given by Almasi, who assigns it an '!'). Play could continue 16 exf5 ♘xf5 17 ♕xh3 (17 ♕g6+ ♔h8) 17...g4! 18 ♗xg4 (but not 18 ♕xg4+?? ♘g7) 18...♘g5! 19 ♕g2 ♘e3! 20 fxe3 ♗xg4 leading to obscure complications. Perhaps even

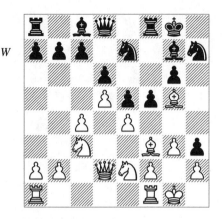

14...f4!? can be played: 15 ♗xg7 ♔xg7 16 gxf4 exf4 17 ♘xf4 ♘c6!; this is unclear, but 18 dxc6 ♕g5+ 19 ♔h1 ♕xf4 20 ♕xf4 ♖xf4 should be fine for Black. In general, we see that the ...h5-h4-h3 idea coordinates well with Black's positional and tactical ideas on the kingside. This is also true in the play that follows.

14...f4! 15 gxf4 exf4 16 ♗d4

And not 16 ♗xf4? g5!.

16...♗h6 17 c5

After 17 e5, a simple idea is 17...dxe5 18 ♗xe5 ♘c6! winning the valuable dark-squared bishop; for example, 19 ♗xc7 ♘g5! 20 ♗h1 ♕xc7 21 dxc6 bxc6 with the advantage.

17...♘g5 (D)

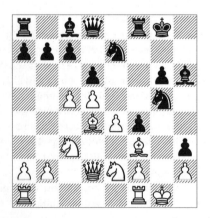

18 ♗h1

After 18 ♕d3, Almasi shows a remarkable line beginning with 18...♘f5! 19 exf5 ♗xf5 20 ♗e4 ♘xe4 21 ♘xe4 ♗xe4 22 ♕xe4 ♕g5+, leading to an advantage, but Black has even better with the sequence 18...dxc5! 19 ♗xc5 ♘c6! and now ...♘e5, giving Black a very large

advantage, can't be stopped since 20 ♗d4? loses to 20...♘b4.

18...♘f7!?

Almasi prefers the continuation 18...dxc5! 19 ♗xc5 b6! intending ...♘f7 with ideas of ...♘xd5 and ...♕g5+ as well as simply ...f3 or ...♗g7.

19 cxd6! cxd6 20 ♕d3 ♔h7?!

Better was 20...g5! with the idea 21 e5!? dxe5 22 ♗c5 g4 23 ♘e4 ♗f5 and Black has a clear advantage according to Almasi. A centre-versus-flank position!

21 ♖fe1 ♘e5!? 22 ♗xe5 dxe5 23 ♖ad1 ♘g8 24 d6 ♘f6 25 ♗f3! ♗d7!? 26 ♘d5 ♘xd5? 27 ♕xd5

We have reached a position that is no longer relevant to our theme. White is somewhat better but after great complications Black went on to win.

Flank Attacks, Space, and Weaknesses

Today there are a variety of early g-pawn and h-pawn advances whose purpose is primarily attacking, particularly those directed against a fianchetto position. But theoretically, the big change has come with the introduction of many new flank attack strategies that try to cramp the opponent and win by virtue of greater manoeuvring room and mobility, regardless of the weaknesses created thereby. The purely tactical impression that these variations give can sometimes arise when the defender strikes back in the centre, and this natural response can obscure the positional subtext of the line. Take, for example, this dynamic variation in the conservative Caro-Kann, one that we take completely for granted now:

Shabalov – Times
Foxwoods 2001

1 e4 c6 2 d4 d5 3 e5 ♗f5 4 ♘c3 e6 5 g4

Again this thrust. Larsen's old saying "When in doubt, push a rook's pawn" may be in danger of being replaced by "When in doubt, push the g-pawn"!

5...♗g6 6 ♘ge2 (D)

B

This has been all the rage for over a decade now. These moves went untried by a lengthy list of the world's elite for a century or more (although it should be said that Korchnoi actually played this once in 1951). For some reason, serious investigation of this line by top players didn't begin until around 1980, and didn't truly explode until around 1990. Now my database has over 800 games beginning with 5 g4, many featuring the world's top grandmasters such as Topalov, Shirov, Anand, and Khalifman.

What's going on and why did it take so long to appreciate White's possibilities? I'm supposed to be explaining some things about modern chess, but the fact is that I continue to find it amazing that White can achieve anything in this way. He throws his g-pawn forward and wants to play h4-h5; this is a plan? Surely Black, free of weaknesses and logically developing his bishop outside the pawn-chain, has done nothing to deserve so much trouble from a raft of nondeveloping pawn moves. In many openings, Black would gladly give his opponent such weakening flank moves for free! In fact, I admit that when 5 g4 stormed onto the scene, I was sure that a positional refutation would be found, or at least a solution that rendered it boringly harmless. Then we would get back to playing rational lines like 3 ♘c3 dxe4 4 ♘xe4 or 3 exd5 cxd5 4 c4. But that hasn't happened – quite the opposite. In 2001, Kasparov himself used 5 g4 to beat Anatoly Karpov with apparent ease. This had doubly symbolic value regarding the respectability of the variation, since Karpov is arguably the greatest Caro-Kann player in history. It's perhaps not surprising that we're seeing a lot of the move 4...h5 these days!

This opening highlights the pragmatism that pervades modern chess. Of course there is some logic to 4 ♘c3, 5 g4 and 6 ♘ge2, otherwise it wouldn't be effective. But the justification for these moves depends heavily upon concrete move-orders and tactics, specifics that are not apparent by considering the position in a detached way, however grounded in principle one may be. So to begin investigating this variation as a potentially serious weapon and have faith that they weren't wasting their time, the developers of 5 g4 had to be free of and/or willing to ignore some traditional prejudices. Quite apart from the taboos against early flank pawn moves, 4 ♘c3 itself isn't consistent with a conventional view of the d4/e5 pawn-chain, which would require c3 to bolster the centre against ...c5. That might seem to be a particularly devastating argument against ♘c3 in combination with g4, since it is usually true that when such a centre is broken up (e.g., by ...cxd4 and perhaps even ...♘xe5), the interior weaknesses created by advanced flank pawns are exposed. And there are various other arguments that one could adduce based upon the lack of targets in Black's position and the poor prospects for a piece like the c3-knight (where is it going?). But by playing moves with specific attacking and space-grabbing ideas, White can find both positional and tactical justification for his set-up.

6...♘e7

The most popular move at the top today. As an outsider to this variation, the main lines after 6...c5 7 ♗e3 or 7 h4!? (for two more games with these moves, see Shirov-Nisipeanu in Part 2 and the game Grishchuk-Shirov, which is imbedded in it) still strike me as unclear, but both White's results and his theoretical standing seem to be getting better and better as time goes along. The variations with 6...c5 put into relief one of the compelling issues in modern chess: right at the beginning of the opening, the centre is compromised for the sake of the flank. Naturally, the degree of that compromise and the compensation on the flank will vary from case to case, but it's no wonder that these lines didn't catch on in more conservative times. Sometimes both sides play in both spheres and everything starts to look like trial and error; e.g., some recent analysis by Nisipeanu goes 6...c5 7 ♗e3 cxd4 8 ♘xd4 ♘d7 (8...h5 9 ♗b5+ ♘d7 10 f4!? ♕h4+ 11 ♔d2 and White is slightly better; that is a remarkable sequence) 9 h4 h5 *(D)*.

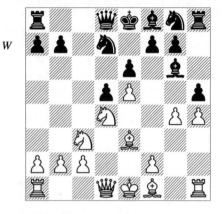

W

10 f4!? hxg4 11 f5 ♖xh4! (11...exf5 12 e6) 12 ♖g1 'with compensation' (!). It would be an understatement to call these lines dynamic, and the fun part is that all these variations are still expanding instead of being fully worked out. In fact, just in the last months since I wrote these lines, some of the most amazing games of recent years have appeared in precisely this variation.

7 f4 *(D)*

I think that I said something about White's plan being h4-h5? But the recently popular 7 f4, which hardly springs to mind in a first look at the position, demonstrates that White's position has a certain flexibility. The move 7 ♘f4 intending h4 has been the only move until recently, when again White sacrifices the centre for dynamic possibilities: 7...c5 8 dxc5!? (8 h4 cxd4 9 ♘b5 ♘ec6 10 h5 ♗e4 11 f3 a6 12 ♘d6+ has been played a number of times) 8...♘ec6 9 h4 ♕c7 10 ♗g2 (10 h5) 10...♕xe5+ 11 ♔f1 ♗xc5 12 h5 ♗e4 13 f3 (13 ♘xe4 dxe4 14 ♕e2 was another game between the same players) 13...f5 14 fxe4 fxe4 15 ♔e1, Sakaev-Bareev, Moscow FIDE 2001, is assessed as unclear by Bareev.

7...h5

This is completely natural, to secure the f5-square, and in fact it would seem almost automatic. But the game continuation results in a position that is at any rate difficult for Black to play in practice. Another try is 7...♘a6 8 ♘g3 ♘b4 9 f5 exf5 10 a3 f4 (10...♘a6 11 ♘b5! cxb5 12 ♗xb5+ ♘c6 13 ♗xc6+ bxc6 14 gxf5 ♗e7

15 0-0 and White is clearly better according to Sutovsky; there are alternatives to look at here, but so far they haven't appealed to Black) 11 axb4 fxg3 12 hxg3 ♘c8 (12...a6 13 ♗g5 ♕b8!? 14 ♗d3 ♕a7 15 ♘e2 looks better for White, who went on to win in Svidler-Galkin, Russia 2001) 13 b5 ♗b4 14 bxc6 bxc6 15 ♗d3 *(D)*.

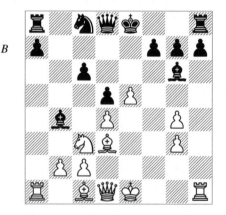

B

The end of a wild sequence. Having made 11 pawn moves out of 14, White finally gets another piece out and stands better! His pawn-structure turns out to be favourable due to tactics and three open files: 15...♘e7 16 ♗g5! ♕d7 (16...0-0 17 ♕e2 ♗xd3 18 cxd3 and the threat of ♕h2 is too strong) 17 ♗xe7! ♗xe7 18 ♗xg6 fxg6 19 0-0 with a large advantage for White, Sutovsky-Dautov, Essen 2001. There's no good place for Black's king.

Just to emphasize the importance of positional goals here, note that in Topalov-Bareev, Dortmund 2002, White made even one further kingside pawn move via 7...c5 8 h4!? h5 9 f5! exf5 10 g5 to secure a middlegame bind similar to that in the main game: 10...♘ec6!? (10...cxd4) 11 ♗g2 cxd4 12 ♘xd5 ♘d7 13 ♘xd4 ♘dxe5 14 ♘b5, and White had good-looking compensation for the pawn.

8 f5! exf5 9 g5 (D)

This positional pawn sacrifice is the point; White hopes that Black's sorry bishop on g6 will compromise his game for some time to come.

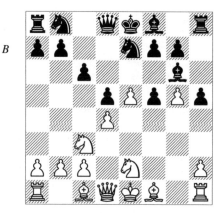

9...♘a6

9...h4!? prevents White's consolidation via h4 and looks best: 10 ♘f4 ♘a6!? 11 ♗xa6 bxa6 (Sutovsky thinks that White is somewhat better here but says that Dautov disagrees; I don't know who could ever understand this position!) 12 ♘a4?! ♘c8 13 ♖g1 ♕a5+ 14 c3 ♘b6 15 ♘xb6 ♕xb6 16 ♕c2 ♖b8 and at the very least, Black's position looks easier to play, Brinck-Claussen – S.Andersen, Roskilde 1998.

10 ♘f4 ♘c7 11 h4 ♕d7

Black was awfully tied up after 11...♘e6 12 ♘ce2! ♕d7 13 ♗h3 0-0-0 14 0-0 in Nataf-Grabarczyk, Hasselbacken 2001.

12 ♗g2 ♘e6 13 ♘ce2 c5 14 c3 0-0-0 15 ♗e3 ♔b8 16 0-0 ♘c7?!

Better was 16...cxd4 17 ♘xd4, but Black still lacks counterplay.

17 dxc5! ♘c6 18 ♗d4

Black can hardly move; White went on to win.

Here's an elementary prophylactic use of a flank pawn advance (*see following diagram*):

White has the two bishops and is obviously better on the queenside. Instead of the natural a4 and b5, Ljubojević turns his eyes to the kingside with:

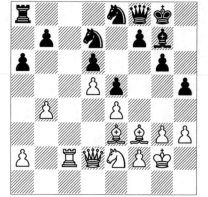

Ljubojević – Hausrath
Enschede 2002

24 g4!

Simple once you see it, but easy to miss. Given his way, Black intends to implement a plan that has served strong players well in this position: he intends to play ...♔h7 and ....♗h6, after which White's best bishop disappears and the queenside becomes much easier to defend, whereas ...f5 can follow on the kingside. The move 24 g4 will meet that idea by g5, and White's apparent kingside weaknesses after g4 prove to be no problem.

24...hxg4 25 hxg4 ♕e7 26 g5 f5 27 gxf6 ♘dxf6 28 ♘g3 ♕d7 29 ♗e2

Now White's bishops are actively aimed at the queenside, which guarantees a win in almost every endgame.

29...♖c8 30 ♖xc8 ♕xc8 31 a4 ♘g4 32 ♗g5 ♗f6 33 ♕c1! ♕d7 34 b5 axb5 35 ♗xb5 ♕h7?

Not even very good as desperation, but after 35...♕d8 36 ♗d2! Black is in awful shape.

36 ♗xe8 ♕h2+ 37 ♔f3 ♘xf2 38 ♗xf6 ♘d3 39 ♕e3 ♘f4 40 ♕f2 ♕h3 41 ♗g5 1-0

Flank pawn-thrusts are showing up more and more often in slower positional openings. The next few games will illustrate this.

Mozetić – Tiviakov
Belgrade 1993

1 d4 ♘f6 2 c4 e6 3 ♘c3 ♗b4 4 ♕c2 c5 5 dxc5 ♗xc5 6 ♘f3 ♕b6 7 e3 ♕c7 8 b3!

A recent and similar game Sashikiran-Sulskis, Calcutta 2002 continued 8 ♗e2 b6 9 g4!?, although here Black equalized rather easily after 9...♘c6 10 g5 ♘g4 11 h3 ♘ge5 12 ♘xe5 ♘xe5 13 f4 ♗b7 14 ♖f1 ♘g6.

8...a6 9 ♗b2 ♗e7 *(D)*

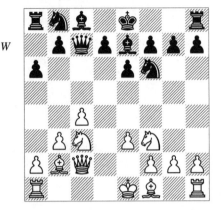

In this nice quiet position one expects extended manoeuvring. All of a sudden comes:

10 g4! d6

The tactical point is 10...♘xg4 11 ♖g1 ♘xh2 (11...f5 12 h3 ♘f6 13 ♖xg7) 12 ♘xh2 ♕xh2 13 ♖xg7 with threats along the long diagonal.

11 0-0-0 ♘c6 12 g5

Again, a simple space gain to disturb Black's development and in this case set up a tactic.

12...♘d7?

12...♘g4 improves, but White is obviously better.

13 ♘d5! exd5 14 cxd5 ♘de5 15 ♘xe5 dxe5 16 dxc6 ♗g4 17 ♗g2! *(D)*

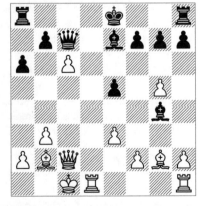

An almost automatic exchange sacrifice these days, once one takes a look at White's dominating bishops.

17...♗xd1 18 ♖xd1 ♖d8

19 ♖d7 was threatened.

19 ♖xd8+ ♗xd8 20 f4 exf4

What else?

21 ♗xg7 ♖g8 22 ♕xh7 ♖xg7 23 ♕xg7 fxe3 24 g6 fxg6 25 ♕xg6+ ♔f8 26 ♕h6+ ♔f7 27 ♗d5+

...and White won shortly.

The idea in the following game breathed life into a rather boring line.

Loginov – Skachkov
St Petersburg 2002

1 c4 c5 2 ♘c3 ♘c6 3 ♘f3 ♘d4 4 e3 ♘xf3+ 5 ♕xf3 g6

This variation has become very popular for Black. In spite of moving his queen's knight three times, he tries to show that White's queen is not very well placed on f3. For one thing, White's most attractive move, d4, isn't supported by any piece. Indeed, in the early games with this line White would sometimes play the move ♕d1, just to enforce d4. Here he just chooses to develop instead:

6 b3 ♗g7 7 ♗b2 d6 *(D)*

After 7...♖b8 Ribli queries 8 g4 due to 8...b6 '∓', but 9 ♗g2 ♗b7 10 ♕g3 ♗xg2 11 ♕xg2 looks better for White, who still has a bind on the kingside and can contemplate central expansion or h4-h5.

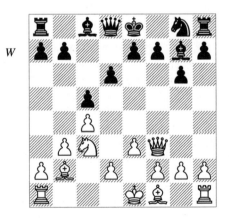

8 g4!

Here's the point at which White had played moves like 8 ♗e2 and 8 g3 without success, an instructive example of the latter move going

8...♖b8 9 ♗g2 ♘h6! 10 h3 ♘f5 11 ♕e2 a6 12 0-0 b5 with equality, Gabriel-Lalić, Pula Echt 1997. The previously main line with 8 ♕d1 gave Black no problems after 8...e5 (or 8...♘f6) 9 ♗e2 ♘e7 10 0-0 0-0, with equality, in Galliamova-Kramnik, Kazan ECC 1997.

By contrast, 8 g4 (called "eccentric" by Ribli) contains a completely different philosophy. It is a prophylactic versus ...♘f6, but also just a space gainer which maintains flexibility. In some cases g5 can cramp Black, in others h4-h5 is contemplated. A new idea just a decade ago, 8 g4 has become the most important move in this line.

8...♖b8

Normally played, to free the queen's bishop. 8...♘f6!? is a direct challenge to White's philosophy: 9 g5 (9 h3!? ♖b8 10 ♗g2 is also possible) 9...♘d7 10 h4 ♘e5 11 ♕g2 ♗g4 12 ♗e2 ♗xe2 13 ♔xe2 *(D)*.

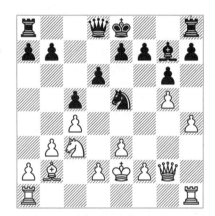

B

A perfectly good position for the king, which connects rooks and covers the light squares. To begin with, White is ready for further expansion by h5 and/or f4. The game continued 13...♘c6 (13...♕d7 14 h5 with a small edge) 14 ♖ab1!? (to exchange the g7-bishop which protects the dark squares; 14 h5 is also promising and somewhat better for White) 14...h5 15 ♘d5 0-0 16 f4! ♗xb2 (16...♕a5 17 f5! has the idea 17...gxf5? 18 ♘f6+ ♔h8 19 ♕f3) 17 ♖xb2 e6!? 18 ♘f6+ ♔g7 19 a3!? (19 d3! has the exotic plan ♖d2, ♔f1, ♖d1, and ♕b2!) 19...♖b8 (19...♕a5!? 20 ♖a1 ♖ad8 21 ♕h1 ♕b6 22 ♕c1! intending ♕c3) 20 b4 cxb4 21 axb4 and White had a nice advantage in Van Wely-Akopian, Enghien les Bains 2001.

9 h4!?

Another flank advance. White chooses space and attacking potential over development. Both 9 ♗e2 and 9 ♗g2 have been played numerous times. An example of White's strategy with 9 ♗g2 went 9...♗d7 10 ♕e2 a6 11 g5 b5 (11...h6 12 h4) 12 d3 ♕a5 (12...e6? loses to 13 ♘xb5) 13 ♖c1 h6 (13...e6 14 0-0 threatens ♘xb5, which is surprisingly awkward to counter) 14 h4 ♖h7!? 15 ♗a1 hxg5 16 hxg5 ♖xh1+ 17 ♗xh1 b4?! (17...e6!?) 18 ♘e4 and White is better, Krasenkow-Macieja, Plock 2000. Black is passively placed without a plan.

9...♗d7 10 ♕g3!?

10 ♗g2! probably gives White a small advantage; e.g., 10...♘f6 (10...♗c6 11 ♕g3) 11 g5 ♗c6 12 ♘d5! ♘xd5 13 ♗xg7 ♘h4 14 e4 ♖g8 15 ♕c3.

10...♘f6 11 f3

11 g5 ♘e4 is not what White is after.

11...h6!

The most pertinent alternative is 11...♗c6 12 h5, when 12...gxh5 (12...0-0 13 ♗e2 ♕d7 14 0-0-0) 13 g5 ♘d7 14 ♖xh5 ♘e5 15 f4! gives White the advantage.

12 ♗d3 a6 13 ♖b1

Again, White wants to exchange Black's best piece, the g7-bishop.

13...b5 *(D)*

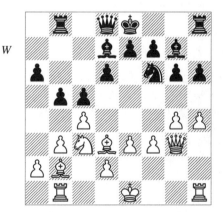

W

14 ♘d5!?

Here 14 h5! g5 15 ♘d5 e5 16 ♘xf6+ and 0-0 is the best sequence, and slightly better for White. After this, the quality of the game goes downhill for a few moves.

14...e5 15 ♗xe5?

Unsound. 15 ♘xf6+ is better.

15...dxe5 16 ♕xe5+ ♗e6?

Perhaps Black feared 16...♔f8! 17 ♕d6+ ♔g8 18 ♘e7+? ♔h7 19 g5 (19 h5 ♗e8!), but then 19...♖b6! 20 ♕xc5 ♗f8 finishes things.

17 ♘c7+ ♔e7

17...♔f8 18 ♘xe6+ fxe6 19 ♗xg6 gives White three pawns and an attack for the piece.

18 ♘xe6!?

Here 18 ♕xc5+! looks very strong: 18...♕d6 19 ♕xd6+ ♔xd6 20 ♘xa6, for example, and 20...bxc4 (20...♖b7 21 cxb5 makes a total of five pawns!) 21 ♘xb8 cxd3 22 ♘a6 ♘d5 23 b4 ♖a8 24 ♘c5 ♖xa2 25 ♘xd3.

18...fxe6 19 ♕xc5+ ♔f7

Not 19...♕d6? 20 ♕xd6+ ♔xd6 21 ♗xg6, when White is clearly better.

20 ♕a7+ ♕d7 21 ♕xd7+ ♘xd7 22 cxb5 axb5 23 ♖c1

White has a slight edge because Black's pawns are a little hard to defend. He went on to win, but with accurate defence the game should probably have been drawn.

Another variation of the English Opening had a reputation for dry manoeuvring until it recently occurred to somebody (or somebodies) that space-gaining flank advances in this line don't have to be heavily supported or even initiated on the side of the board where the advancer's pieces are directed. We see this clearly in the next game fragment.

Gulko – Hector
Copenhagen 2000

1 c4 ♘f6 2 ♘c3 e5 3 ♘f3 ♘c6 4 g3 ♘d4!? 5 ♗g2 ♘xf3+ 6 ♗xf3 ♗b4 7 ♕b3 ♗c5 8 d3

Instead of the usual 8 0-0. White keeps his options open.

8...h6!?

For thorough commentary on these moves, refer to the complete game in Part 2. The important thing to note is that Black wants to avoid 8...0-0 9 g4! followed by g5 and h4. I also analysed a game in the notes with the similar 8...c6 9 g4 d6!? (9...d5 10 g5 dxc4 11 ♕xc4 ♘d7 12 h4 ♕e7 13 ♘e4! ♗b4+ 14 ♗d2 ♗xd2+ 15 ♔xd2! is another interesting line) 10 g5.

9 h4! (D)

White strikes out in a seemingly random fashion on the kingside, but this limits Black's options. Because he can't play 9...d6? 10 ♗xb7,

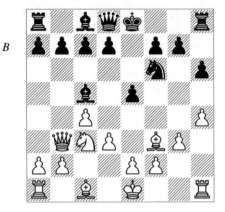

he would like to prepare ...d6 by 9...0-0. But then 10 g4! is particularly strong because of the support that the h4-pawn gives to the coming 11 g5. For the details on this flank attack and notes to the entire game, please refer to Part 2.

The next example involves another slow opening (a reversed Colle):

M. Gurevich – Kallai
Bundesliga 2001/2

1 c4 c6 2 ♘f3 d5 3 e3 ♘f6 4 ♕c2 e6 5 b3 ♘bd7 6 ♗b2 ♗d6 7 ♘c3 0-0 8 ♗e2 a6 9 ♖g1!?

White is willing to take two tempi to expand immediately on the kingside.

9...b5 10 g4 b4 11 g5 ♘e8 12 ♘a4 ♕e7 13 h4! (D)

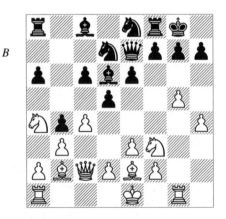

13...♗b7 14 h5 c5 15 cxd5 ♗xd5 16 0-0-0 ♖a7 17 ♔b1 ♘c7?

But White was clearly better now in any case.

18 e4 ♗c6 19 e5 ♘d5 20 exd6 ♕xd6 21 ♗d3 g6 22 ♗e4 1-0

Nor are slow positional variations of the Sicilian immune from the bug:

Macieja – Kempinski
Glogow 2001

1 e4 c5 2 ♘c3 d6 3 f4 a6 4 ♘f3 e6

A sophisticated move-order designed to prevent White's standard Grand Prix Attack with ♗c4 and f5. Black is perfectly happy to play the Najdorf/Scheveningen position that arises after 5 d4 cxd4 6 ♘xd4 ♘f6. Now 5 g3 with a Closed Sicilian is nearly always played, if only for lack of alternatives.

5 g4! *(D)*

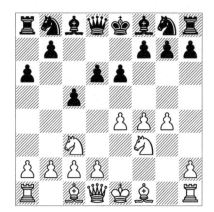

B

Already on move 5! White's mobile pawn-mass reminds one of Nimzowitsch's play in the very last game of this book. This advance is soundly based and not at all speculative; in fact, after most natural continuations White will stand somewhat better. For one thing he can usually return to the Closed Sicilian by ♗g2, when the move g4 can usefully gain a tempo on White's normal Closed Sicilian strategy of g3 followed by g4. Furthermore, moves like h4 and g5 are just as cramping and irritating as in the Open Sicilians to which, it should be added, White can still return by d4 in many lines.

If moves like 5 g4 are legitimate, one has to wonder where players have been all these years. I would argue that such moves 'looked' over-committal and premature to the player growing up with traditional strategic theory. I know that

I certainly felt that way, and I was always happy when someone (usually a much lower-rated player) would toss out such a loosening move. It is only recently that so wide a variety of positions both quiet and tactical are being invigorated by fearless creativity on the flanks, and at risk of repeating myself, I feel this to be the single most important development in chess over the last few decades.

5...d5

Central responses are not always ideal versus flank advances, as we have seen; but here I like this move, even if it is the fifth consecutive one with pawns and the second with the queen's pawn! Basically the reason rests with White's specific range of answers to the serious positional threat of 6...dxe4.

6 d3!?

As in so many of the lines that we're looking at, there are plenty of interesting alternatives; for example:

a) 6 exd5 exd5 7 g5!? would be strange-looking but has its good points. Then ♕e2+ is an idea, or just ♗g2 and 0-0. White's lead in development might well give him a small advantage.

b) 6 e5 is also quite playable, especially since 6...h5!? 7 g5 is a promising trade-off of space and development for the weakness on f5.

6...♘f6

Kempinski argues that 6...dxe4 7 dxe4 ♕xd1+ 8 ♘xd1 ♘f6 9 ♘f2 favours White slightly. This is hard to assess, but White's pieces will come out very smoothly. Nevertheless, this was probably Black's best course since things soon become very difficult for him.

7 g5 dxe4 8 ♘e5!

Extremely strong. White keeps the queens on and establishes a bind.

8...♘fd7

8...♘d5? fails to 9 dxe4 ♘xc3 10 ♕xd8+ ♔xd8 11 ♘xf7+, etc.

9 ♘xe4! *(D)*

This offers a pawn sacrifice that has both positional and tactical elements.

9...♘xe5

Black accepts the pawn now, since 9...♕c7 10 ♗g2! ♘xe5 11 fxe5 ♕xe5 12 0-0 is worse for him than the game continuation. It's hard to find another move.

10 fxe5 ♕d4 11 ♗g2

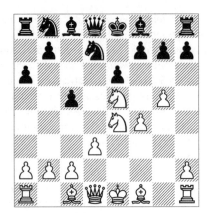

B

Suddenly White has a sustained initiative worth well more than a pawn. The other possible sacrifice by 11 ♗f4! is perhaps even more promising. Kempinski analyses 11...♕b4+! (after 11...♕xb2 12 ♗g2 White has compensation, according to Kempinski; even with two extra pawns, that would be hard for Black to play after something like 12...♘c6 13 ♖b1 ♕xa2 14 0-0 ♗e7 15 ♘c3!? ♕a5 16 ♗xc6+ bxc6 17 ♘e4) 12 ♗d2 ♕xb2 13 ♗c3 again 'with compensation'. That seems to me an understatement, as White has wonderfully active moves like ♗g2, 0-0, and ♕f3 or ♕h5 or ♘d6+ coming up.

11...♘c6

11...♕xe5 12 0-0 can only transpose at best.

12 c3! ♕xe5 13 0-0

Threatening ♗f4.

13...♕c7 *(D)*

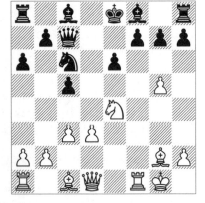

W

14 ♗e3

14 ♕h5! is *Junior*'s suggestion. Computers are supposed to be materialistic, but all of my engines are happy to be White here.

14...♘d8

Depressing, but perhaps best because it covers f7. Kempinski can only offer up 14...b6 15 d4! and 14...♗d7 15 ♘xc5 (15 ♕h5!); 14...♗e7 15 ♕h5 ♘d8 is the other way to try to limit White's growing advantage.

15 d4!

An embarrassment of riches. It's hard to argue with 15 ♕f3 either.

15...cxd4 16 cxd4 ♗e7?

Now there's no stopping the attack. Kempinski proposes 16...♗d7 17 ♖c1 ♗c6, when Black has at least countered the immediate threats.

17 ♖c1 ♕a5 18 ♗f4! ♘c6!

Black must stop 19 ♗e5.

19 ♕h5 0-0 *(D)*

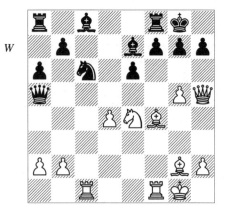

W

Now it looks like Black's position might just hold together. But there follows the trademark exchange sacrifice:

20 ♖xc6! bxc6 21 ♗e5

And the game is suddenly beyond saving. The execution is not so easy, however!

21...♕b4! 22 a3!

22 ♘f6+?! ♗xf6 23 gxf6 ♖d8 24 fxg7 f5 is not totally clear, as Black will defend by ...♖a7.

22...♕b3! *(D)*

Another clever defensive try.

23 ♘c3!!

A pretty conclusion to the combination. The knight, which looked beautifully placed and poised to land on f6, actually takes itself out of the attack and makes room for the still more deadly bishop. It also blocks a check on e3 and covers one on d1! Surprisingly, the obvious 23 ♘f6+?? ♗xf6 24 gxf6 ♕e3+ 25 ♔h1 g6 leaves White searching for an idea.

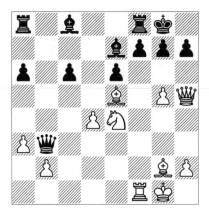

W

23...f5

Also losing is 23...♗xg5 24 ♕xg5 f6 25 ♖xf6 ♖xf6 26 ♗xf6 ♖a7 27 ♗e5.

24 gxf6 ♗xf6

24...gxf6 25 ♗e4 ♖f7 26 ♗xh7+! ♖xh7 27 ♕e8+ ♗f8 28 ♖xf6 and mate will follow shortly. The rest isn't perfect, but it's good enough:

25 ♗e4 g6 26 ♗xg6 ♖a7 27 ♗xf6 ♖xf6 28 ♗xh7+! ♔g7 29 ♖xf6 ♔xf6 30 ♕g6+ ♔e7 31 ♕g7+ ♔d8 32 ♕xa7 ♕xb2 33 ♕c5 ♕c1+ 34 ♔g2 e5 35 ♕b6+ 1-0

Seemingly anomalous flank pawn moves occur in a number of Kasparov games, for example in this innocent-looking position:

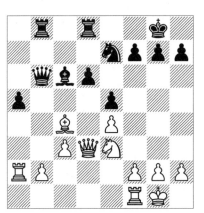

W

Kasparov – Van Wely
Wijk aan Zee 1999

The reader may recognize the pawn-structure from the Sveshnikov Variation of the Sicilian. White has an edge on the queenside and optical control over d5. Nevertheless, Black's pieces are active enough and his play on the b-file is as good as White's on the a-file. This is the kind of position Sveshnikov defenders are reasonably comfortable with.

22 b3 ♕c5 23 ♖fa1 ♖a8 24 h4!

Out of the blue, White switches to the kingside. One point as usual is to grab space, and White would also like to get a pawn to h6 followed by targeting weaknesses on Black's kingside dark squares. So Black naturally takes steps to prevent this:

24...h6

Kasparov thinks that this is not best, but he also shows that 24...h5 25 ♕e2! ♗xe4 26 ♕xh5 ultimately favours White.

25 h5! ♗b7 26 ♖d1 ♗c6 27 ♖da1 ♗b7 28 ♗d5! ♗xd5

White ends up with a large advantage after 28...♘xd5 29 exd5 ♖e8 30 ♕d2.

29 exd5 ♖dc8 30 b4 ♕xc3 31 ♕xc3 ♖xc3 32 ♖xa5 ♖b8 33 ♖a7 ♔f8 34 ♖d7 ♘c8

Kasparov gives 34...♔e8 35 ♖xd6 ♖xb4 36 ♖da6 with a clear advantage for White.

35 ♖d8+ ♔e7 36 ♖g8 *(D)*

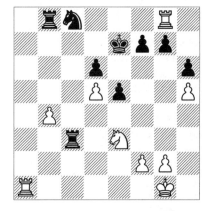

B

In a sense this is the completion of White's strategy begun by 24 h4! and 25 h5. Of course, the weakness on g7 might have been attacked differently or not at all depending upon the many variables of the play.

36...♖xb4 37 ♖a8! ♔d7

No better is 37...♖c1+ 38 ♔h2 ♔d7 39 g3!.

38 ♖xg7?

A slip near the time-control. 38 g3! wins.

38...♖c1+ 39 ♔h2 ♖f4 40 ♘g4 ♘e7

Kasparov observes that 40...♖f5!? isn't any better due to 41 ♔g3 ♘e7 42 ♘xh6 ♖xh5 43

♜xf7 ♜xh6 44 ♜a7+ ♜c7 45 ♜xc7+ ♔xc7 46 ♜xe7+ ♔d8 47 ♜a7 ♜h1, when White still has a clear plus.

41 ♜a7+ ♔e8?

Kasparov analyses the best but insufficient try: 41...♜c7 42 ♜xc7+ ♔xc7 43 ♞xh6 ♜h4+ 44 ♔g1!? ♜xh5 45 ♞xf7 ♔d7 46 g4 ♜h3 (46...♜h4 47 ♔g2) 47 ♞g5 ♜d3 48 ♞e4 ♔d8 49 ♞xd6 ♜xd5 50 ♞e4 with a large edge for White.

42 g3 ♜f5 43 ♜h7 ♔f8 44 ♜a8+ 1-0

The following case of space-grabbing contains some instructive points:

Kasparov – Csom
Baku 1980

1 d4 ♞f6 2 c4 e6 3 ♞c3 ♝b4 4 e3 c5 5 ♞ge2 cxd4 6 exd4 0-0 7 a3 ♝e7 8 d5 exd5 9 cxd5 ♜e8 10 g3 ♝c5 11 ♝g2 d6 12 h3!

Avoiding 12 0-0 ♝g4!.

12...♝f5!?

It's hard to believe that this can be so bad, smoothly developing all of Black's pieces to active squares (for example, ...♞bd7-e5 or ...♝b6 and ...♞bd7-c5) while White's queen's bishop and rooks are passive. The possible tempo gain by g4 seems harmless with Black aimed at White's loose central squares such as d3. But 12...a6 13 0-0 ♞bd7 turns out to be a better way to play.

13 0-0 ♞bd7?!

Kasparov preferred 13...♞e4, and upon 14 ♞a4, 14...♞d7, when White is only slightly better.

14 g4! ♝e4?

Black probably prepared this a few moves back; how much trouble can he get into with his remaining pieces already developed? In fact, the way to play was 14...♝g6 15 ♞g3 ♞e5 16 g5 ♞fd7 17 ♞ce4 f5! (Black gets some territory of his own) 18 gxf6 ♞xf6 19 ♝g5 and White has only a small advantage.

15 ♞g3 ♝xg2 16 ♔xg2 *(D)*

Suddenly what looks like a normal distribution of forces is extremely difficult for Black in view of White's idea of a simple pawn advance on the kingside and consequent attack. In view of this, Black tries to strengthen his dark squares on the kingside, but the c5-bishop is cut

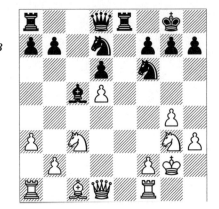

off from the action. Also, Black needs to clear a square for his f6-knight.

16...♞f8 17 g5 ♞6d7

If Black could get ...♞g6 in, his position would be looking up.

18 h4!

Now it looks almost too simple.

18...♞e5

This gives up protection of f6, but White had all kinds of fun planned by h5, b4, ♝b2, h6, ♞ce4, etc.

19 h5 f6 20 ♞ce4! fxg5 21 ♝xg5 ♛b6 22 h6 ♞f7 23 hxg7 ♞d7 24 ♞f6+ ♞xf6 25 ♝xf6

Threatening 26 b4, but that's the least of it.

25...♛b5 26 ♜h1 ♝b6 27 ♛f3!

Kasparov is a master at achieving positions in which all his forces are on one side of the board while his opponent's are cut off from defence.

27...♞e5 28 ♞f5! ♞f7 29 ♜xh7! 1-0

On his video biography, Kasparov shows this game and makes some comments about how many grandmasters expressed scepticism over White's strategy involving g4. He thinks that professional players of that time (1980) were in general too cautious and "scared to push pawns [in front of their king]". Maybe this isn't the perfect example, but I think he's basically right, especially in cases where White hasn't even completed his development. It's easy to forget how unusual such games looked because White's play all looks so natural now.

Knight's Pawn Advances

As should be obvious from the above, a great deal of attention is being given to knight's pawn moves. Although new modes of play with b4 and ...b5 are constantly being found, the moves g4 and ...g5 are more striking because they occur on the side of the board where the kings will usually reside or want to reside. Before moving on to a more focused discussion (g4 and ...h5 in Sicilian Defences), let's take a look at some statistics involving g4 in different eras. Here all the usual qualifications about statistics apply, perhaps even more so. For example, there are base positions in which a knight's pawn move is routine but unremarkable. An extreme case is the extraordinarily high use of ...g5 in the years previous to 1900; it turns out that the great majority are due to ...g5 in the King's Gambit, which merely defends a pawn. Since there are few such instances applying to g4, I have chosen to count all the games in which that move is played up to move 10. In my databases with only leading players from each era, I find that g4 is played (up to move 10) as follows:

a) Up to 1900: in 1.55% of all games, and not too effectively, since White scores only 43%.

b) 1901-1935: 1.2%, with White scoring 63%.

c) 1936-1970: 1.3%, with White scoring 57%.

d) 1985-2002 (the period Kasparov gave as involving a change in chess practice): 3.1% with White scoring 61%.

Since 55% is the average overall winning percentage for White, the choice of g4 has apparently been well motivated (the sample size is 772 games with g4 in the latter case, for example). Comparing recent play in a much broader spectrum of strengths, we find that in the TWIC database for 2001 to the present, White plays g4 up to move 10 in 3.6% of all games, scoring 57%.

A full 38% of these TWIC games with g4 up to move 10 involved Open Sicilians. We already discussed in SOMCS the explosion of White's early g4 moves in most variations of the Sicilian Defence. In particular White's early flank attack with f3 and g4 has suddenly become routine in many new Sicilian settings. Not long ago, it appeared almost exclusively in the Dragon Variation, and was considered harmless versus such defences as the Najdorf, Scheveningen, and Richter-Rauzer. Now it appears in numerous subvariations and even the main lines

of those variations. I think that this change came about primarily because White discovered that, contrary to the stereotype, playing two extra pawn moves on the kingside (f3 and g4, sometimes even with h4) did not in fact allow the classic Black response in the centre by ...d5 (or ...e5 and then ...d5). Once a pawn gets to g4, the possibility of permanently cramping Black's game by g5 arises, so the move has positional as well as attacking points. In general, this is often referred to as the 'English Attack', and it has spread to both Najdorf and Scheveningen lines, as well as to one of the very main lines of the Rauzer Defence. For example, Black has been hard-pressed recently to find anything that doesn't give White a clear advantage (much less the usual small edge) in the variation 1 e4 c5 2 ♘f3 d6 3 d4 cxd4 4 ♘xd4 ♘f6 5 ♘c3 e6 6 ♗e3 ♘c6 7 f3 ♗e7 8 ♕d2 0-0 (or 8...a6 9 0-0-0 0-0 10 g4) 9 g4. How times have changed! In 7 consecutive games of *Informator 83*, for example, there are 9 Sicilians with an early g4, 7 of them in different and mostly new variations. Here's an extremely accelerated version of the g4 idea that was even effective against Kasparov:

Ivanchuk – Kasparov
Moscow Russia vs RoW rpd 2002

1 e4 c5 2 ♘f3 d6 3 d4 cxd4 4 ♘xd4 ♘f6 5 ♘c3 a6 6 ♖g1!? (D)

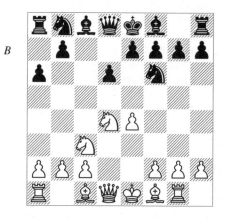

Who would have dreamed a few decades ago that a game between two of the world's greatest players would begin in this fashion? White's move is incredibly committal at so early a stage of the game. As so often, we see a determination to play g4 at all costs. This particular instantiation of that strategy is all the more remarkable because the rook is 'developed' to a closed file before either bishop is moved!

6...g6

I can't resist tossing in the following game. OK, it may not have tremendous strategic significance, but I'll claim author's prerogative:

6...♘c6 7 g4! ♘xd4 8 ♕xd4 e5 (8...♗xg4? 9 ♖xg4 ♘xg4 10 ♕a4+ with a huge advantage in view of 10...b5 11 ♘xb5 or 10...♕d7 11 ♗b5 axb5 12 ♕xa8+ ♕d8 13 ♕xb7; Rogozenko gives 8...♘xg4'?!' 9 ♘d5 'with compensation') 9 ♕a4+ ♗d7 10 ♕b3 b5 11 g5 ♗e6 (D).

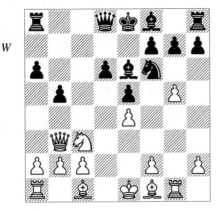

12 gxf6!!? ♗xb3 13 axb3 (White has two pieces for a queen and after the next move, a pawn; his compensation? The magnificent d5-square for his knight, two bishops, and some immediate tactics against Black's king – it's enough!) and now:

a) 13...♕xf6? 14 ♗g5 ♕g6 15 ♖xa6! ♖b8 16 ♖a8! f6 (16...♖xa8 17 ♗xb5#) 17 ♖xb8+ ♔d7 18 ♗xb5+ ♔c7 19 ♗e8! 1-0 Handke-Murdzia, Hamburg 2002. The queen is trapped. White was winning anyway, but what a pretty finish!

b) 13...gxf6 is a complete mess, with some beautiful lines; there are two reasonable white moves: 14 ♖xa6 ♖xa6 15 ♗xb5+ ♔e7 16 ♘d5+ ♔e6 17 ♗xa6 f5 (17...h5 18 ♗e3!) 18 ♗c4 fxe4 19 ♗g5 ♕a5+ 20 ♔e2! is unclear (Rogozenko). This would be hell to play for Black, even if it's defensible; the other option for White is 14 ♘d5!? ♕c8! (14...♗e7? 15 ♗xb5+; 14...♖b8? 15 ♖xa6 ♕c8 16 ♖a7) 15

c3!? (15 ♗d2 ♕xc2 16 ♘xf6+ ♔e7 17 ♘d5+ draws) 15...♗e7 16 ♘b6 ♕c6 17 ♘xa8 ♔d8 18 ♗e3!? ♕xa8 19 ♗xb5 ♕xe4 20 ♖xa6, assessed as unclear by Rogozenko. Then a draw would result from 20...♕b1+ 21 ♔e2 ♕xg1 22 ♗b6+ ♔c8 23 ♗c6 ♕g4+ and Black escapes with a perpetual check.

In an article in *New in Chess Magazine*, Rogozenko points out that Black has no fewer than eight moves after 6 ♖g1. Very relevant to this chapter is the radical prevention of 7 g4 by 6...h5!?; see below for similar ideas. He also quotes games to show that 6...h6, 6...b5, and 6...e5 are all playable, and lead to complex, dynamically balanced play.

7 g4 ♗g7 8 ♗e3 ♘c6

8...b5 9 f3 ♗b7 10 ♕d2 ♘c6 11 0-0-0 was Ivanchuk-Gelfand, Cap d'Agde rpd 1998. When one compares the analogous position from the Dragon Variation White would seem to have the best of it.

9 f3 e5!?

A little nervous. Perhaps just 9...0-0 is better. The problem, however, is that White can then play a normal anti-Dragon attack in which the move ...a6 isn't very helpful. So Kasparov tries to build a big centre.

10 ♘xc6 bxc6 11 ♕d2 ♗e6

Black's central freeing idea always runs into trouble because of g5; for example, Shipov thinks that 11...d5? is playable, but 12 exd5! (Shipov gives only 12 g5, and 12...d4 13 gxf6 ♗xf6 14 ♗f2 dxc3 15 ♕xc3 0-0, or 12...♘xe4!? 13 fxe4 d4, "in both cases with a slightly inferior but probably defensible position") 12...cxd5 (12...♘xd5 13 0-0-0 {or 13 ♗c5} 13...♗e6 14 ♗c4 is very unattractive for Black) 13 g5 d4 (now 13...♘e4? loses to 14 ♕xd5) 14 gxf6 ♗xf6 15 0-0-0, and Black's situation is dire; e.g., 15...♗e6 (15...dxc3 loses to 16 ♕xc3, while 15...dxe3 16 ♕xe3 is also winning for White due to the possibility of ♘d5, which was not available after Shipov's 12 g5) 16 ♘e4 dxe3 17 ♕c3 and White wins.

12 0-0-0 ♗f8 13 ♘a4 h5 14 h3 ♘d7 15 ♕c3 hxg4 16 hxg4 d5!

Kasparov's active attempt to avoid suffocation. Shipov gives the entertaining variation 16...♕c7 17 f4! ♘f6 (D).

18 fxe5! ♘xe4 19 exd6! ♘xc3 20 dxc7 ♘xa4 21 ♗g2 "and despite his extra piece Black stands

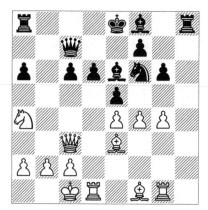

W

badly". This is starkly confirmed after the forced 21...♗d5 by the further sacrifice 22 ♖xd5! cxd5 23 ♗xd5: 23...♖c8 24 ♗c6+ ♔e7 25 ♗xa4, etc.

17 ♕xc6 d4 18 ♗d2! ♖c8 19 ♕b7!?

A move-order inaccuracy. 19 ♕xa6 ♖a8 20 ♕b5 would have avoided the next note.

19...♖b8

Now Black had 19...♗xa2!, as recommended by Shipov, without allowing 20 ♗c4.

20 ♕xa6 ♖a8 21 ♕b5 ♗xa2

21...♖b8 22 ♕a5 favours White.

22 ♗c4!? ♗xc4 23 ♕xc4 ♕f6?!

Black has played with resourceful energy, but it was now time to bail out by 23...♖c8 and a probable repetition.

24 g5! ♕d6

Black loses after 24...♕xf3? 25 ♖df1 ♕xe4 26 ♖xf7!.

25 ♔b1 ♖h3 26 ♖gf1

Or 26 b3 ♖xf3 27 ♖df1! with an advantage. The text-move just retains the extra pawn, and White went on to win. 6 ♖g1 was hardly responsible for this outcome, but it certainly appears viable!

Practically as I write this, the parade of new g4 ideas in the Sicilian continues. For example, here are two games from the 2002 Russia versus the Rest of the World rapidplay match:

Anand – Zviagintsev
Moscow Russia vs RoW rpd 2002

1 e4 c5 2 ♘f3 e6 3 d4 cxd4 4 ♘xd4 ♘c6 5 ♘c3 a6 6 ♗e2 d6 7 ♗e3 ♘f6 8 0-0 ♗e7 9 f4 ♗d7 10 ♗f3 0-0 11 ♘b3 b5 12 g4!

Brand new, as far as I can tell, and effective! Note that this sort of thing wasn't even counted

in my statistics above, since those involved g4 only up to move 10.

12...h6!

12...b4 is inferior due to 13 ♘a4 with the point 13...e5? 14 g5 exf4 15 ♗b6.

13 a4!?

Shipov proposes 13 ♕e1! and calls it "quite good". White has the easier game to play and Black's queenside expansion looks rather slow. White can thus play ♖d1, threatening e5, and then shift to the kingside.

13...bxa4 14 ♘xa4 ♖b8 15 ♘c3 a5 16 ♖f2

Shipov suggests 16 h4, when 16...♘h7!? 17 h5 e5 looks unclear. Another possibility is 16 ♕e2!?.

16...♖b4 17 ♖d2 ♕c7 18 h4 (D)

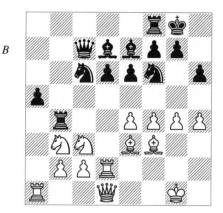

B

18...h5!

Meeting the flank attack with another flank move. This pawn sacrifice is familiar from the King's Indian Defence and a couple of other Sicilian lines.

19 g5

Since this works out so badly, 19 gxh5 should be considered.

19...♘g4 20 ♗xg4 hxg4 21 ♕xg4 a4! 22 ♘c1

Fruitless is 22 ♖xa4 ♘e5! 23 fxe5 ♗xa4 24 ♘xa4 ♖xa4 25 exd6 ♗xd6.

22...♖xb2

Black is clearly better.

Ponomariov – Zviagintsev
Moscow Russia vs RoW rpd 2002
1 e4 c5 2 ♘f3 e6 3 d4 cxd4 4 ♘xd4 ♘c6 5 ♘c3 a6 6 ♗e2 d6 7 ♗e3 ♘f6 8 f4 ♗e7 9 g4!? (D)

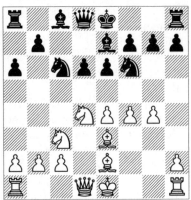

B

Another example of trying to rush ahead with g4-g5 before Black can set up his defences.

9...d5!?

The classical central response to White's primitive advance. 9...h6 is a logical alternative.

10 e5 ♘d7 11 g5!

Unthematic but effective; g5 has the prophylactic effect of preventing standard ideas such as ...f6 and ...g5, both destroying White's fragile structure (e.g. 11 0-0 g5!). However, Black has an obvious and tempting reply:

11...♘xd4 12 ♕xd4 h6

Shipov mentions 12...b5!?.

13 g6!

Leaving his king in the centre is a small price to pay for the attack.

13...♗h4+?

This allows White to connect rooks. Better is 13...♗c5 14 gxf7+ ♔xf7 15 ♕d3 ♕h4+ with unclear play, as given by Shipov.

14 ♔d2

The point, connecting rooks! This had to be anticipated on move 11.

14...fxg6

14...f5 may look more solid, but it also dooms Black to a position with no space or counterplay, whereas with time White has the queenside to exploit. After the text-move, White wins by virtue of space, open lines, and superior pieces:

15 ♖hg1 ♘f8 16 ♗d3 g5

16...♔f7!? is a little saner.

17 ♖af1

It's turning into a slaughter. The two extra pawn moves g4-g5 seemed to lose time but White is way ahead in development as a result.

17...♗d7 18 ♔c1 ♕e7 19 f5! ♗c6 20 f6?

20 fxe6! ♘xe6 21 ♗g6+ ♔d7 22 ♕d2! wins.

20...gxf6 21 ♖xf6 0-0-0 22 ♖gf1 ♗e8?

The last mistake. 22...♕c7 is correct.

23 ♕a7 g4 24 ♗xa6 1-0

Radical Preventative Measures

In most variations, White isn't completely giving up upon king safety by playing g4, because he normally has the move 0-0-0 in reserve, even if his king can be rather vulnerable on the queenside. Black, on the other hand, can normally play ...0-0 at some point because he seldom castles queenside in these Sicilian lines. So by traditional theory, Black should be even more reluctant to push pawns on the kingside in cases where their advance doesn't come with tempo or with tactical intent. Nevertheless, Black has recently turned towards the surprising move ...h5, which is both weakening and nondeveloping. It is nevertheless quintessentially pragmatic, i.e., it prevents g4! The advance ...h5 dramatically violates the traditional strictures against unforced and weakening pawn moves, especially those on the side of the board for which the king is most likely destined. But there is a growing nonchalance about early castling when one's own positional goals (normally on the queenside) can be given some extra time to develop. What's more, a little space on the kingside can prove useful. I will give a considerable number of examples of this now common prophylactic idea:

Hraček – Ftačnik
Czech League 2000/1

1 e4 c5 2 ♘f3 d6 3 d4 cxd4 4 ♘xd4 ♘f6 5 ♘c3 a6 6 ♗e3 e5 7 ♘b3 ♗e6 8 f3

A standard position of the 6 ♗e3 Najdorf. White's f3 + g4 plan was the impetus behind the revival of White's 6th move.

8...h5! *(D)*

'!' for the surprise. It took an undogmatic player to come up with this idea, particularly since the idea of waiting for g4 and then playing ...h6 was the normal and natural way of discouraging g5 in such positions without an early loss of tempo. But the g4 vs ...h6 scenario

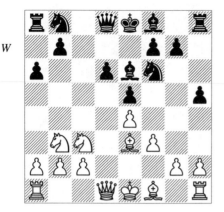

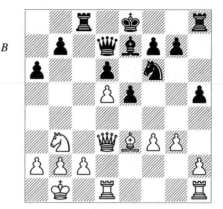

involves some special problems, including the idea of h4 and g5 (and sometimes g6).

9 ♕d2 ♘bd7 10 0-0-0

Black's idea is to make all of his useful moves before concerning himself about his king. This is illustrated by 10 a4 ♕c7 11 a5 ♖c8 12 ♗e2 ♕c6!? 13 ♖d1 ♗c4 14 0-0 ♗e7 (only now, when d5 has been covered) 15 ♖f2 0-0 16 ♗xc4 ♕xc4 17 ♕d3 ♖fe8 18 ♖fd2 ♘f8 19 ♖a1 ♕xd3 20 cxd3 d5! 21 ♘xd5 ♘xd5 22 exd5 ♖ed8 with excellent play, Farakhov-Asanov, Russia 2002.

10...♗e7 11 ♔b1 ♖c8

Black is in no hurry to commit the king. With g4 prevented, he reasons that there are plenty of useful moves on the queenside and that he has time to make some.

12 ♘d5

Probably the best move. White tries to change the pawn-structure and undertake action on the queenside. It's interesting to see how difficult it is for him to make progress by other means without g4. For example, 12 f4!? b5 13 ♗d3 (13 f5 ♗c4 with equality) 13...♕c7 (13...exf4 14 ♗xf4 0-0 also looks OK, with ...♘e5 to come; the h5-pawn never seems to be a weakness in view of the action on the queenside and in the centre) 14 h3 ♘b6 15 ♗xb6 ♕xb6 16 ♘d5 ♗xd5 17 exd5 e4 18 ♗e2 h4! with equality, Bologan-Zhang Zhong, Shanghai 2001.

12...♗xd5 13 exd5 ♘b6 14 ♕a5

The game thus far was repeated in Balcerak-Ftačnik, Lübeck 2001, which went 14 ♗xb6 ♕xb6 15 ♗d3 0-0 16 ♗f5 ♖c4 17 g3 ♖e8 with equality.

14...♘c4 15 ♗xc4 ♖xc4 16 ♕d2 ♕d7 17 ♕d3 ♖c8 18 g3 *(D)*

18...0-0

After all! It has become remarkably common in the Sicilian for Black to castle on the kingside after making moves such as ...h5 and ...g5. In this case he feels that the weakness of d5 and his own play along the c-file will become the centre of attention well before White can attack the weakened kingside.

19 h3 ♕a4 20 ♘d2 ♕b5!?

Also possible was 20...b5 with equality.

21 c4 ♕b4 22 a3 ♕a4

Now White has secured the d5-pawn, but Black still has good play with ...♖fd8 and ...b5 in mind.

23 c5! ♖fd8?!

Better was 23...♘d7 or 23...dxc5 24 d6 ♖fd8 25 ♘c4 ♖c6.

24 ♘c4 ♕b5 25 ♖he1 ♘d7 26 ♘xd6 ♕xd3+ 27 ♖xd3 ♗xd6 28 cxd6 ♔f8

Black went on to draw but he needn't have allowed White even this kind of small advantage.

The same idea but leading to a different strategy is seen in the following game:

Kobaliya – Pigusov
Dubai rpd 2002

1 e4 c5 2 ♘f3 d6 3 d4 cxd4 4 ♘xd4 ♘f6 5 ♘c3 a6 6 ♗e3 e5 7 ♘b3 ♗e6 8 f3 ♗e7 9 ♕d2 h5 10 0-0-0

In Morozevich-Sadler, Reykjavik ECC 1999, Black demonstrated a strategy against slow play by White: 10 ♗e2 ♘bd7 11 0-0 ♖c8 12 a4 g6 13 a5 h4!? (I like this move, which gains space and discourages g3 and f4, with ideas of a possible ...♘h5) 14 ♘c1 ♕c7 15 ♖d1 ♔f8 16 ♗f1 g7. Neither side seems to have a great deal to do in this position, but Black can keep threatening to play ...d5 and should have no real problems.

10...②bd7 (D)

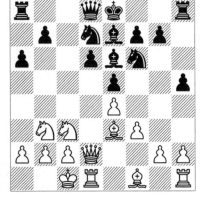

11 ⌂b1

Black played some creative moves in an opposite-coloured bishops situation in Anand-Sadler, Tilburg 1998: 11 g3 ♖c8 12 ②d5 ♗xd5 13 exd5 ②b6 14 ♗xb6 ♕xb6 15 ♗h3 ♖c7 16 ⌂b1 h4 17 ♕e1 ⌂f8 18 f4 exf4 19 gxf4 ♖h5! 20 ♗g2 ♖c4 21 ♖f1 ♖f5! 22 ♕xh4 ②h5 23 ♕h3 g6 24 ♖fe1 ♗f6! (this is equal) 25 ♗e4 ♖xf4 26 ♕d3 ♖c7 27 ♗f3 ♖h4 28 ♕d2 ⌂g7 29 c3 ♗e5 30 ♖xe5 dxe5 31 d6 ♖d7 32 ♕e1 e4! 33 ♕xh4 ½-½, in view of 33...exf3 and ...♖xd6.

11...♖c8

A recent example went 11...♕c7 12 h3!? h4 13 f4 b5! 14 ♕e1 ♖c8 15 ♗d3 b4 and Black had the initiative in Lanin-Kariakin, Moscow 2002.

12 h3

Covering g4 in anticipation of f4, although this allows a dark-square bind. Black has got satisfactory play from this position, a straightforward example going 12 ②d5 ②xd5 13 exd5 ♗f5 14 ♗d3 ♗xd3 15 ♕xd3 g6 16 g3 ♕c7 17 f4 f5 18 h3 ♕c4!? (or 18...e4 19 ♕d2 ♗f6 {with the idea ...②b6-c4} 20 ②d4 ②c5) 19 ♕d2 ⌂f7 20 ♕g2 ♗f6 21 ♖hf1 e4 22 ♖fe1 a5!? 23 ♕e2 ♕xe2 ½-½ Zhang Zhong-Short, Beijing 2000.

12...h4 (D)

13 f4 g6!?

Rather ambitious. 13...exf4! 14 ♗xf4 ②e5 is a natural and consistent strategy; e.g., 15 ②d4 ②h5?! 16 ②xe6?! (16 ♗h2 ②g3!? 17 ♗xg3

hxg3 18 ♕f4 ♖xc3!? 19 ②xe6 fxe6 20 bxc3 ♕b6+ 21 ⌂a1 ♕c5 with good compensation) 16...fxe6 17 ♗xe5? (17 ♗h2 0-0 with dark-square pressure) 17...dxe5 and apart from his dark-square advantage, Black's bishop is much better than its counterpart.

14 ♗d3

14 ♗e2 would discourage ...②h5.

14...exf4 15 ♗xf4 ②h5 16 ♗h2 ②e5 17 ♗e2 ②g3 18 ♗xg3 hxg3 19 ♕e1 ♗h4 20 ②d5 0-0 21 ♕b4 b5 22 ②f4 ♗c4!? 23 ②d4?!

Critical is 23 ♕xd6 ♕xd6 24 ♖xd6 intending 24...♗g5 25 ②d3!.

23...♗xe2 24 ②fxe2 ②c4 25 ②f4? ♖e8 26 ♖he1 ♗g5! 27 ②d5 ②d2+! 28 ♖xd2 ♖c4 29 ♕xc4 bxc4 30 ♖de2 ⌂g7 31 c3 ♕a5

Black is winning.

John Fedorowicz, a Rauzer Sicilian expert who feels that White's f3 systems are starting seriously to challenge that variation's status as a whole, believes that in various critical positions, the ...h5 move is Black's best chance. Here is an example that he cites:

A. Mista – Czarnota
Polish jr Ch (Trzebinia) 2002

1 e4 c5 2 ②f3 d6 3 d4 cxd4 4 ②xd4 ②f6 5 ②c3 ②c6 6 ♗g5 e6 7 ♕d2 a6 8 0-0-0 ♗d7 9 f3 ♕c7 10 ⌂b1 ♗e7 11 h4 h6 12 ♗e3 h5!?

Fedorowicz: "This forces White to play in the centre which is one good thing. White's play with g4 has got very routine."

13 ♗d3 ②e5 14 ♗g5 b5

"I feel if Black keeps the e5 ideas under control the position should be OK."

15 f4 *(D)*

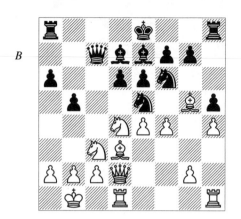

B

15...♘eg4

Fedorowicz again: "Keeping an eye on e5 shots. 15...♘c4!? walks the high wire: 16 ♗xc4 ♕xc4 17 e5 b4 18 exf6 bxc3 19 fxg7 ♖g8 20 ♕xc3 ♕xc3 21 bxc3 f6 22 ♗h6 ♔f7 23 ♖he1 ♖ae8 seems OK for Black."

16 ♖hf1 ♕b7 17 ♖de1 ♕b6 18 ♘f3 b4 19 ♘d1 e5!? 20 fxe5 dxe5 21 ♘e3 ♘xe3 22 ♗xe3 ♕c7 23 ♘g5 0-0

Fedorowicz feels that "Black's kingside is in decent shape". He soon gained the advantage.

Of course in the Dragon Variation itself after 1 e4 c5 2 ♘f3 d6 3 d4 cxd4 4 ♘xd4 ♘f6 5 ♘c3 g6 6 ♗e3 ♗g7 7 f3 (the oldest established f3 line) 7...0-0 8 ♕d2 ♘c6, we are used to seeing ...h5 in numerous lines such as 9 ♗c4 ♗d7 10 0-0-0 ♖c8 11 ♗b3 ♘e5 12 h4 h5, which at least discourages g4. This might even be called the main line of the Dragon, although it was considered practically revolutionary in the early 1970s due to the weakening of Black's kingside. White can also choose to accelerate g4 by playing 9 g4, for example. So it's amusing to see a couple of top masters playing the sequence 7 f3 ♘c6 8 ♕d2 h5!?, an otherwise meaningless move that prevents g4 already! This may be going too far, but it is worth keeping an eye on this and similar positions.

The evolution of ...h5 in the Sicilian was investigated by Curt Hansen in a fascinating article for *ChessBase Magazine* a couple of years back. He found the remarkable game Yates-Bogoljubow, Moscow 1925, a very modern-looking one at that: 1 e4 c5 2 ♘f3 e6 3 d4 cxd4 4 ♘xd4 ♘f6 5 ♘c3 d6 6 ♗d3 ♗e7 7 0-0 ♘bd7

8 ♔h1 a6 9 f4 ♕c7 10 ♕e1 b5 11 a3 ♗b7 12 ♕g3 g6 13 ♗d2 h5 14 ♖ae1 h4 15 ♕h3 ♘c5 16 f5 gxf5 17 exf5 e5 18 ♘b3 ♘xb3?! (18...0-0-0!) 19 cxb3 d5 20 ♗g5 e4 21 ♗b1 ♖h5 22 ♗xf6 ♗xf6 23 ♘xe4 (or 23 ♘xd5 ♗xd5 24 ♕f3 h3 25 g4!) 23...dxe4 24 ♕f3 h3 25 ♗xe4? (White misses 25 g4! 0-0-0 {25...♖h7 26 ♗xe4 0-0-0 27 ♖c1} 26 ♗xe4 with a clear advantage for White) 25...hxg2+ 26 ♕xg2 0-0-0 27 ♖e2 ♔b8 28 ♗xb7 ♕xb7 29 ♕xb7+ ♔xb7 30 b4 ♖d5 31 ♖ef2 ♖h3 32 ♖c2 ♖hd3 33 ♖ff2 ♗h4 34 ♖f1 ♖d2 35 ♖c3 ♗f6 36 ♖h3 ♗xb2 37 ♖e1 ♖xf5 38 ♖e7+ ♔c8 39 ♖e1 ♔d7 40 ♖h6 ♖ff2 0-1.

But Bogoljubow's idea didn't catch on. After that game, the next instance Hansen finds of ...h5 in the Sicilian was not until the 1960s in a game by Simagin! Hansen thinks that Simagin, who tried out the idea several times, was the first to understand that ...h5 could be primarily a positional and not just an attacking move. This notion was taken up by Filipowicz and a few others in the 1970s, with a gradual increase in interest thereafter that took off in the 1990s.

The game Ponomariov-Zviagintsev, which we discussed above, provides one example from the Scheveningen, the set-up that Bogoljubow employed. Here is another:

Zwanzger – Podzielny
Bechhofen 1998

1 e4 c5 2 ♘f3 e6 3 d4 cxd4 4 ♘xd4 a6 5 ♘c3 ♕c7 6 ♗e2 ♘f6 7 0-0 d6

Now we're back to a Scheveningen set-up.

8 f4 b5 9 ♗f3 ♗b7 10 ♕e2

A fairly conventional Sicilian Defence thus far. At this point one would expect Black to develop by ...♘bd7 or ...♘c6, or even just ...♗e7. But for one thing, he is aware of White's tendency these days to play a quick g4-g5 with devastating effect, and for another, he wants to establish an active response to the move e5. Hence:

10...h5!? *(D)*

A remarkable prophylactic move. Black not only wants to prevent g4, but to establish a pseudo-outpost on g4 for his knight. He also plays to gain space on the kingside, unconcerned about where his own king will end up.

11 ♔h1

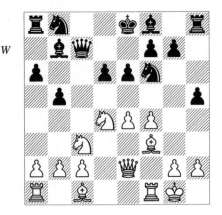

11 e5 can now be met by 11...dxe5 12 fxe5 ♗c5 13 ♗e3 ♘g4!, taking advantage of 10...h5, since 14 ♗xg4? (White should play 14 ♗xb7, when Black can choose 14...♕xb7 15 ♖ad1 ♕c7!, or even 14...♕xe5) 14...hxg4 15 ♕xg4?? loses to 15...♕xe5.

11...♘bd7 12 a3 ♗e7 13 ♗e3 *(D)*

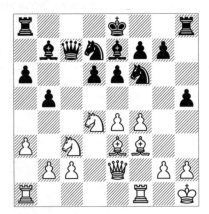

13...♖c8!?

This is another noteworthy idea, in that Black seemingly strands his king in the centre for the mere sake of pressure along the c-file! I'm not sure that this is the only or best way to continue, but it looks playable. Podzielny is not blind to the issue of the relative king placements, as we shall see.

14 ♘b3! ♕b8

Black clears the way for a potential ...♖xc3 (which is threatened) or ...♖c4.

15 ♗g1 ♗a8

In similar positions, Black has played 15...h4, contemplating ...g6 and ...♘h5.

16 ♖ad1 *(D)*

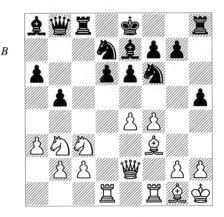

This position has potential for both sides. Again, 16...h4 is 'normal', whereas 16...g6! prepares the same idea of ...h4 and ...♘h5. That second strategy was the most thematic and probably best. Instead, Black played 16...♘g4?!, looking for speculative play based upon 17 ♗xg4 hxg4 18 ♕xg4 ♘f6 with very reasonable compensation for the pawn, especially in view of 19 ♕g7? (19 ♕f3 d5!) 19...♖g8 20 ♕h6 ♘xe4. But after Zwanzger's calm 17 ♖fe1! (protecting the critical e-pawn) 17...♘df6 18 ♕d3, Black seemingly lacked a useful plan and stood worse. A later pawn sacrifice by ...g5 to win the e5-square led to a rather lucky win for him. In any case, the position after White's 16th was quite playable for Black.

Here are a few game fragments from other Sicilian Defence variations to compare with those above. Some new themes appear:

Kudrin-Benjamin, USA Ch (Modesto) 1995: 1 e4 c5 2 ♘f3 e6 3 d4 cxd4 4 ♘xd4 ♘c6 5 ♘c3 ♕c7 6 ♗e3 a6 7 ♗d3 b5 8 0-0 ♗b7 9 a3 ♘f6 10 ♔h1 h5 (a practical and space-grabbing move intending ...♘g4) 11 f4!? ♘g4 12 ♗g1 g5! (to win e5) 13 ♗e2 gxf4 14 ♗xg4 hxg4 15 ♕xg4 0-0-0 with good chances on the dark squares and kingside.

Janošević-Matulović, Majdanpek 1976: 1 e4 c5 2 ♘f3 ♘c6 3 d4 cxd4 4 ♘xd4 ♕c7 5 ♘c3 e6 6 ♗e2 a6 7 0-0 ♘f6 8 ♔h1 ♘xd4 9 ♕xd4 ♗c5 10 ♕d3 b5 11 f4 h5 *(D)*.

12 ♗e3 ♗xe3 13 ♕xe3 b4 14 ♘a4 ♗b7 15 ♗d3 h4 16 h3 ♗c6 17 ♘c5 d6 18 ♘b3 ♕a7! with equality.

Prandstetter-Mokry, Trenčianske Teplice 1985: 1 e4 c5 2 ♘f3 d6 3 d4 cxd4 4 ♘xd4 ♘f6

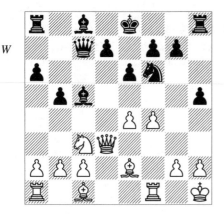

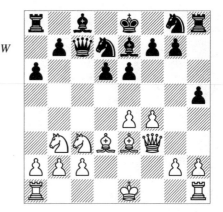

5 ♘c3 a6 6 ♗e2 e6 7 0-0 ♘bd7 8 a4 b6 9 f4 ♗b7 10 ♗f3 ♕c7 11 ♕e2 ♖c8 12 ♗e3 h5 (the ...♘g4 idea again forces concessions) 13 h3 c5 14 ♘b3 ♗e7 15 ♖ad1 0-0! (daring White to try something) 16 f5 ♖fe8 17 g4 hxg4 18 hxg4 d5 (in a turnabout, Black counters White's flank attack by his own in the centre) 19 g5 d4!? (or 19...♘xe4 20 ♗xe4 dxe4 21 f6 ♗b4) 20 gxf6 ♘xf6 21 ♘xd4 exd4 22 ♗xd4 ♗c5 23 ♖f2 ♕f4 with equality.

Agnos-Miladinović, Ano Liosia 1995: 1 e4 c5 2 ♘f3 ♘c6 3 d4 cxd4 4 ♘xd4 ♕c7 5 ♘c3 e6 6 ♗e3 ♘f6 7 ♗d3 a6 8 0-0 h5 (threatening ...♘g4) 9 h3 b5 10 a3 ♗b7 11 ♕e2 h4! (now Black has gained space and intends ...♘h5-f4 in many cases, or ...♗d6) 12 f4 ♘h5 13 ♕f2 ♗e7 14 ♖ad1 ♖c8 (as usual, Black doesn't seem worried about his king) 15 e5!? ♘g3 16 ♖fe1 ♘xd4 17 ♗xd4 and now Miladinović's 17...♗c5!? was unclear and very slightly better for White. Probably better was late castling on the 'weakened' kingside by 17...0-0! with ...d6 soon to follow. Black may have feared 18 f5, but 18...♘xf5 19 ♗xf5 exf5 20 ♕xf5 ♕c6 21 ♖e2 ♕e6 retains the bishop-pair with a fine game.

Finally we have an ultra-modern interpretation: ...h5 as a sophisticated prophylactic against g4, but before White has committed his king and before Black has even developed beyond the second rank!

Åström – Agrest
Sweden tt 1998

1 e4 c5 2 ♘f3 e6 3 d4 cxd4 4 ♘xd4 a6 5 ♗d3 ♗c5 6 ♘b3 ♗e7 7 ♘c3 d6 8 f4 ♘d7 9 ♕f3 ♕c7 10 ♗e3 h5!? *(D)*

At first sight this looks way beyond the pale, and yet Agrest is a 2600 player who has used this line at least three times.

11 0-0-0

Another answer is 11 h3 h4 12 0-0-0 ♘gf6 13 g4 hxg3 14 ♕xg3 ♘h5 15 ♕f2 b5 16 f5 ♘e5 17 ♔b1 ♗d7 18 fxe6 fxe6 19 ♖df1 and although Black won after the extremely risky 19...♖c8!? in Kjartansson-Agrest, Reykjavik 2000, the dark-square strategy we saw above is safer: 19...♕d8!? 20 ♗b6 ♗h4 21 ♕d4 ♕b8, etc.

11...♘gf6 12 ♖he1 b5 13 e5 ♗b7 14 ♕g3 dxe5 15 fxe5 ♘g4

with an unclear and dynamic position. Black went on to win after complications.

Of course, we also see the defensive ...h5 idea versus g4 and h4 in many King's Indian Defence variations, for which I would need another section. Rather than ignore those entirely, I'll give a single well-established example to conclude this chapter:

Ioseliani – Gallagher
Biel 1990

1 d4 ♘f6 2 c4 g6 3 ♘c3 ♗g7 4 e4 d6 5 ♗e2 0-0 6 ♗g5 ♘a6 7 ♕d2 e5 8 d5 c6 9 f3 cxd5 10 cxd5 ♗d7

A typical modern Averbakh King's Indian variation. Now White launches the standard attack:

11 g4 ♕a5 12 h4 h5!

A counter-thrust right in the face of the attack, and it even allows White to open up the kingside.

13 ♗xf6 ♗xf6 14 gxh5 ♔g7! *(D)*

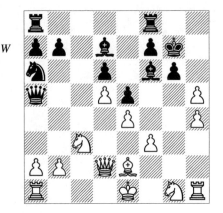

Suddenly, by investing a pawn, Black gets his own kingside chances involving ...♖h8; if the position gets closed on that side of the board, he will still have the advantage on the queenside.

15 hxg6

Black played dynamically after 15 0-0-0 in Hoang Thanh Trang-Shaked, Budapest 1997: 15...b5! 16 b3 ♖ac8 17 ♔b2 ♖c5 18 ♗d3 ♖fc8 with a lot of pressure (...b4 and ...♖xd5! is one theme).

15...fxg6 16 h5 ♖h8 17 h6+ ♔h7 18 ♘h3 ♗xh3 19 ♖xh3 ♖ac8 20 ♔f1 ♘c5 21 ♖b1 ♕d8

Black threatens ...♗g5. His bishop is much better than its light-squared counterpart, and he has plenty of compensation for the pawn.

The vast and rapidly growing realm of flank advances is one of the most exciting developments in modern chess. New ideas in this area are sweeping away the excessive caution and stale misconceptions of the past. To illustrate this, I have tried to emphasize thematic situations and types of positions that weren't already covered in SOMCS. But one should remember that such pawn advances are appearing in well-known older structures as well as in uniquely modern openings. I urge the reader to keep an eye out in his studies for more examples reflecting this changing philosophy. I don't think that you will play over too many games in contemporary chess before running into instances of flank pawn advances that most players would hardly have been contemplated until the last 10-20 years, and quite a few that were unheard of before the last five.

2.2 Doubled Pawns In Action

The treatment of doubled pawns has become increasingly complex in our times. As a broad characterization, we can say that the unifying factors of the modern treatment are retention of maximum structural flexibility and a general open-mindedness. More than ever, players are willing to enter into positions in which they have doubled pawns, even when it means retaining them for much of the game without prospect of liquidation. Conversely, players are more willing to sacrifice positive tactical and positional factors in order to create doubled pawns in the opponent's camp. Those factors might include time, development, the bishop-pair, safety and the like. It's all a matter of specific context, and there don't seem to be many general guidelines. Specific structures and formations may allow of doubled pawns while others tend to suffer from them. Yet even in those cases, delicate issues of timing and initiative can intervene and make general assessments unreliable. In short, the ideas are in the moves themselves.

What is clear is that the stronger players are expert at drawing upon their vast experience to assess which side they favour and thus when to enter into a doubled-pawn situation. Opening structures are as usual important teachers. Of course, most opening variations do not involve doubled pawns early on, if only because the opposing forces do not engage one another for some time. It also takes two to tango, so both the doubler and doublee must see advantages in their positions. Normally there must be a planned effort to create or provoke the creation of doubled pawns early on, and that's precisely what we are seeing more and more of today. In many situations, players no longer view doubled pawns as weaknesses to be compensated for but as natural or even positive features of the position. Because doubled pawn play has become so widespread, I will concentrate upon a few illustrative structures and some ideas that weren't discussed in SOMCS.

The Extension of Doubled Pawn Theory

I can't give enough credit to GM Peter Wells's subtle and extended discussion of doubled pawns in *ChessBase Magazine 80* (CBM is a collection of games and articles on CD), in which he brings forth theoretical details that weren't discussed in SOMCS and that haven't been covered in any other book or source that I know of. Remarkably, his many excellent examples were taken from a single issue of the magazine, an indication of how common these ideas are! I will borrow a couple of these first before moving on to my own selection of themes and games.

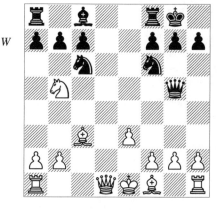

Rogozenko – Morozevich
Istanbul OL 2000

In this position, Black threatens to continue ...♗g4 and bring his rooks to the central files. So White demurs from taking pawns in order to develop. At the cost of a certain weakening of his kingside, he drives Black's queen to the side of the board and prepares to castle by hand.

11 h4 ♛h6 12 ♗e2 ♖d8 13 ♕c2 ♘d5 14 ♖d1 ♗e6 15 a3 ♖d7 16 ♘d4

Black is ahead in development and can double on the d-file whereas White will have to use a tempo to play the weakening g3 in order to bring his king to safety. White's advantage is his better-placed queen, which can operate well in conjunction with the minority attack and c-file. Morozevich enters into a forced sequence that most of us would blanche at.

16...♘xc3 17 ♕xc3 ♘xd4 18 ♖xd4 ♖ad8 19 ♖xd7 ♖xd7 20 ♗f3 b6 21 g3 *(D)*

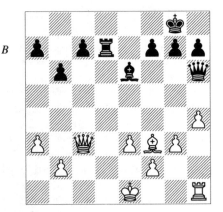

Things don't look that bad for White.

21...♕f6!

The point. Instead of worrying about 'weaknesses' that will never be attacked, Black exchanges off White's best piece.

22 ♕xf6 gxf6

Wells: "What I wonder is how many players simply would fail even to seriously examine 21...♕f6! because taking on such doubled, isolated pawns goes against deeply ingrained instincts. In fact, these pawns easily contain White's majority, while Black obtains total control on the other wing." This is one of Wells's themes: doubled pawns can be excellent restrainers of a majority. After all, when one pawn is exchanged the other takes its place! Conversely, he makes the (better-known) point that "a doubled pawn on the majority side is in general a far greater burden since it profoundly complicates the task of creating a passed pawn."

As for Wells's question of how many players would consider ...♕f6, I'm pretty sure that I wouldn't! On the other hand, it's easy enough to imagine this move from any number of positionally-minded grandmasters (and surely top ones like Kramnik or Karpov), particularly since the taboos against doubled pawns even in simplified positions is disappearing.

23 h5

White has to activate his rook.

23...h6 24 ♖h4

The computer, indoctrinated with classical principles, assesses White as better here. Wells more accurately sees this as a clear black advantage. White would normally push his kingside pawns, say, by g4-g5 in order to activate his pieces if nothing else. Now that can't be done. By contrast, Black's queenside majority is strong: not because it is on the queenside (White's king is not far away), but because it is mobile and will eventually produce a passed pawn. It is also very important that White will be tied to defence of d1 and d2 and thus rendered relatively immobile.

24...c5 25 ♗e2 ♗b3 26 ♖f4 ♔g7 27 g4!?

It's hard to know what to do. 27 ♖g4+ ♔f8 28 ♖f4 ♖d6 doesn't help.

27...♖d6 28 ♖e4 ♔f8 29 ♖f4 a5 30 ♖e4 ♖d8 31 ♖f4 ♔e7 32 ♖e4+ ♔d6 33 ♗d1 ♗e6 34 ♗e2 f5

Liquidated at last!

35 gxf5 ♗xf5 36 ♖f4 ♔e5 37 ♖f3 b5! 38 e4

The idea is 38 ♗xb5? ♗g4.

38...♗e6 39 ♖c3 c4 40 f3 ♔f4

Yikes! OK, Black was better, but who would have guessed that *this* could happen?

41 ♖c2 ♖d4 42 ♗d1 b4 43 axb4 axb4 44 ♗e2 ♔e3 45 ♖c1 ♖d2 46 ♗xc4 ♖h2 47 ♗f1 ♖h1 48 ♖c2 ♗h3 0-1

Another Wells example is a lesson in fighting against the doubled pawns:

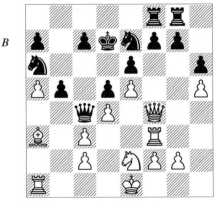

Hraček – Kallio
Istanbul OL 2000

Here White seems to have quite reasonable play based upon his active pieces. Black finds an effective continuation, requiring excellent calculation, which turns the game on its head.

17...c5! 18 dxc5

Black was threatening ...b4.

18...♕xf4 19 c6+?!

19 ♖xf4 ♘c6 20 ♘d4 is correct, although Black can limit White's bishop and keep the tripled pawns under control by 20...♘c7 21 ♖b1 a6 22 ♘xc6 ♔xc6.

19...♘xc6 20 ♖xf4 ♘xe5!

Most of us know by now that the exchange for a piece and pawn isn't all that much of an advantage, and when you throw in White's weaknesses and Black's outpost on c4, there can be no doubt that this is sound as long as the particular dynamics hold up.

21 ♗xf8 ♖xf8 22 ♘d4 ♘c7 23 a6!

Otherwise Black plays ...a6 and advances his centre pawns at his leisure.

23...f5!?

23...f6 is a more natural continuation; e.g., 24 ♔e2 (24 ♖b1 ♖b8 and ...♔d6-c5 is one plan) 24...♘c4 25 ♖g4 ♖g8 26 f3 ♘d6! and ...e5.

24 ♘f3?!

This makes it too easy. 24 ♔e2 is preferable, intending 24...♘c4 25 g4 ♖f6 26 ♘b3, although Black is still better.

24...♘xf3+ 25 ♖xf3 ♖f7 26 ♖b1 ♔c6

Black has a clear advantage positionally, with the immediate idea of ...♔b6 to boot.

I present the following position because it so echoes the game Botvinnik-Sorokin, Moscow 1931 given in SOMCS. The key here is unstereotyped thinking (*see following diagram*):

It's hard to tell if White has any advantage here, or how to make progress. After 19 g3?! ♘h3+ 20 ♔g2 ♘g5 Black threatens ...♗h3+ and can be happy with his position. The move Kholmov chooses is both elegant and surprising:

19 ♕e3!! ♕xe3

This move makes clear what the idea behind 19 ♕e3 was. The actual game went 19...♕e7 20 ♘b3 ♗e6 21 ♗xe6 ♘xe6 22 ♖d2 c5 23 ♖d5 c4 24 ♘c5 ♖fc8 (24...♘f4 25 ♖d7 ♕g5 26 g3 ♖fc8 27 ♖fd1) 25 ♘xe6 ♕xe6 26 ♖fd1, when "White has a significant positional advantage, which he successfully converted and won" (Dvoretsky).

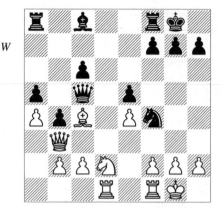

Kholmov – Suetin
USSR Ch (Leningrad) 1963

20 fxe3 ♘e6

20...♘g6 21 ♘b3 is no better.

21 ♘f3 ♗a6 22 ♗xa6 ♖xa6 23 ♘xe5 ♘c5 24 ♘d7!

White has a large advantage (Kholmov). By covering the key central squares (d4, d5, f4, and f5), White's doubled pawns played a key role in protecting his advantage.

Doubled Pawns in Pairs

Increasingly often we see the assumption of two sets of doubled pawns by one side. This subject deserves its own article. A decision to take on such an apparent burden is usually based upon the same pragmatic considerations as with one pair of doubled pawns. The possibility of direct attack aside, one can acquire additional open files, protect key squares, and gain space. In SOMCS, we showed two examples of Botvinnik playing with one set of doubled pawns. With that kind of play he and his contemporaries brought a key part of modern positional strategy to the forefront. In the following example, White engages in a more radical version of these ideas.

Botvinnik – Levenfish
USSR Ch (Moscow) 1940

1 c4 e5 2 ♘c3 ♘f6 3 ♘f3 ♘c6 4 d4 exd4 5 ♘xd4 ♗b4 6 ♗g5 ♗xc3+ 7 bxc3 ♘e5 8 e3 h6 9 ♗h4 ♘g6 10 ♗g3 ♘e4 11 ♕c2

It's interesting but perhaps going a little far to cede both bishops in the service of White's strategy as occurred in Paschall-Baginskaite, USA Ch (Seattle) 2003: 11 ♗d3 ♘xg3 12 hxg3 ♘e5 13 f4 ♘xd3+ 14 ♕xd3 d6 15 ♔f2. White did win, but here the play seems about equal, as White has space but with so many pieces off Black has chances of reaching a good ending.

11...♘xg3 12 hxg3 d6 (D)

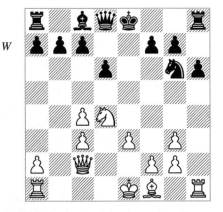

The basic position. White has assumed *two* sets of doubled pawns as well as a weak a-pawn. For his part, Black has a compact and weakness-free structure and he has retained his good bishop. White's play may thus appear thoroughly anti-positional, but it has its own positive points, such as three open files versus one and the prospect of gaining space in the centre and on the kingside. Also, some of what he is doing is purely pragmatic and position-specific, as we shall see.

13 f4!

A typical Botvinnik space-grab. This stops Black playing ...♘e5, and Botvinnik assesses his newly-created backward pawns as relatively unexploitable. The stem game Levenfish-Botvinnik, Leningrad 1934 had these opponents on the reversed side of things, with the creative Levenfish holding his own after 13 ♗e2 ♘e5 14 ♖d1 (contemplating 15 c5) 14...♕e7 15 ♕e4!? a6 16 ♖h5!? ♘d7 17 ♕f4 ♘f6 18 ♖a5, when a strange position had arisen that led shortly to a draw. See also the section on 'sleepless knights' in Chapter 3.

13...♕e7 14 ♔f2 ♘f8?

Intending to bring the knight to c5 via either d7 or e6. This is a positionally flawless idea,

but Black's timing is bad and White achieves a vital pawn break. A game Krutti-Palliser, York 2000 saw Black fix White's doubled c-pawns but relinquish the possibility of a later ...♘c5: 14...c5!? 15 ♘f3 ♗d7 16 ♗d3 0-0-0!? 17 ♖ae1 ♘f8 18 ♗e4! ♖e8 19 ♗d5 with extremely unclear play.

15 c5! (D)

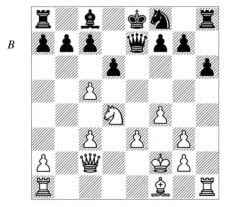

One of White's many potential ideas in this structure. Botvinnik activates his f1-bishop and liquidates one of the doubled c-pawns.

15...dxc5?

Black should prevent ♗b5+ by 15...a6, although White has the nice choice between 16 ♕a4+ ♗d7 (16...♕d7 17 ♗b5) 17 ♕b3 ♗c8 (after 17...♖b8, 18 c6 ♗e6 19 ♕a4 is extremely strong) 18 cxd6 ♕xd6 19 ♖d1, and 16 cxd6 ♕xd6 (16...cxd6 17 ♗d3! and it's hard for Black to move) 17 ♖d1 ♕e7 18 ♗e2 with a large advantage; e.g., 18...c5? 19 ♕a4+ ♗d7 20 ♘f5! ♗xa4? 21 ♘xg7#.

16 ♗b5+ ♘d7?!

Conceding White the critical f5-square, but 16...♔d8 leaves Black too exposed after 17 ♖ad1! cxd4 18 ♖xd4+.

17 ♘f5 ♕f6 18 ♖ad1 g6 19 ♘xh6 ♖f8 20 g4!

Now the advantage in space comes into play. Black is helpless against the attack.

20...a6 21 g5 ♕e6 22 ♗e2 ♘b6 23 ♘g4

All the key squares have fallen.

23...♔e7 24 ♘f6 ♕c6 25 ♖h7 ♗f5 26 e4 ♗e6 27 f5 1-0

Here's a recent example in which dynamism and the bishops only just cancel out an horrendous pawn-structure:

Khalifman – Leitão
New Delhi FIDE 2000

1 c4 ♘f6 2 ♘c3 e6 3 e4 d5 4 e5 d4 5 exf6 dxc3 6 bxc3 ♕xf6 7 ♘f3 e5 8 ♗d3 ♘a6 9 0-0 ♗d6 10 ♗c2 ♗g4 11 d4 ♗xf3

A trick that several strong players have fallen for is 11...0-0-0? 12 ♗g5! with a significant advantage for White in every line.

12 ♕xf3 ♕xf3 13 gxf3

Now White has two sets of doubled pawns.

13...0-0-0 *(D)*

The alternative is 13...exd4 14 ♖e1+, and now 14...♔d7 or 14...♔d8, when theory gives a modest edge for White.

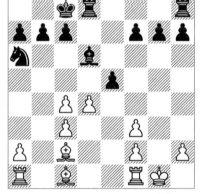

14 c5

White got stuck with the doubled pawn pairs and four(!) pawn-islands after 14 ♖b1 c5 15 ♗e4 b6 16 dxe5 ♗xe5, although he still held on: 17 ♖b3 ♘b8 18 ♗e3 ♔c7 19 ♖fb1 ♘c6 20 ♗d5 ♖d7 21 f4 ½-½ Gelfand-Yusupov, Erevan OL 1996.

14...♗f8 15 c6

Vaulin-Zontakh, Bosnia 2001 went 15 ♖e1 exd4 16 ♗f5+ ♔b8 17 cxd4 g5!! 18 ♖b1 ♗g7 19 ♗e4 b6 20 cxb6 axb6 21 d5 f5! and the game was equal. 17...g5 is the sort of move that is impossible to explain or justify without a detailed look at the alternatives, which would take up too much space.

15...exd4 16 cxb7+ ♔b8 17 cxd4 ♘b4

Zontakh and Shishin analyse 17...♖xd4! to equality after 18 ♗e4 ♘c5 19 ♗e3 ♖b4 20 a3 ♖a4. But the text-move is also satisfactory.

18 ♗e4 ♘d5 19 ♖b1! ♘c3 20 ♗g5 f6 21 ♗e3 ♘xb1 22 ♖xb1

A remarkable exchange sacrifice, and the only way to keep the balance in view of White's weaknesses. Among other ideas, White would like to play ♗c6, d5, and ♖b5-a5.

22...♖d6! 23 ♗f4 ♖b6

Protecting all the squares. Now Black is ready to play ...♗d6 with a simple material advantage. But White has another resource:

24 ♗xc7+! ♔xc7 25 ♖c1+ ♗c5 26 ♖xc5+ ♔b8 27 ♗c6 ♖d8 28 d5

White still has four pawn-islands, but Black is totally tied up and faces the prospect of White's king marching up the board. So he gives back the exchange and achieves equality, but unfortunately slips up in the ending:

28...♖xb7! 29 ♗xb7 ♔xb7 30 ♔g2 a6 31 a4 ♖d7 32 ♔g3 ♔b6 33 ♖c6+ ♔a5 34 d6 ♔xa4 35 ♖c7 ♖xd6 36 ♖xg7 h5 37 ♖h7 ♖d5 38 ♖h6 ♖g5+?

Black has no problems drawing after 38...a5 39 ♖xf6 ♔b4.

39 ♔f4 ♖g2?

Here 39...a5 40 ♖xf6 ♖b5 should be tried.

40 ♖xh5 ♖xf2 41 h4 a5 42 ♖h8 ♔a3 43 h5 ♖h2 44 h6 a4 45 h7 ♖h5 46 ♔g4 ♖h1 47 f4 ♖h2 48 ♔f5 ♖h4 49 ♔e4 ♖h5 50 f5 ♔a2 51 ♖a8 ♖xh7 52 ♖xa4+ ♔b3 53 ♖a6 ♖e7+ 54 ♖e6 ♖f7 55 ♔d5 ♔c3 56 ♖e8 ♖a7 57 ♔e6 ♖a6+ 58 ♔f7 ♔d4 59 ♖e6 1-0

Voluntary Undoubling of the Opponent's Pawns

A very common pattern discussed in SOMCS is that in which one side concedes the bishop-pair in order to double the opponent's pawns, and then paradoxically undoubles those pawns shortly thereafter! Sometimes this is done in order to establish outposts for the knight-pair, but not always. We often see such a pawn break to further one's piece coordination or to open lines against a vulnerable point in the enemy camp. An older game illustrates this idea:

Stein – Matulović
Sousse IZ 1967

1 c4 c5 2 ♘c3 ♘c6 3 ♘f3 g6 4 d4 cxd4 5 ♘xd4 ♗g7 6 ♘c2 ♗xc3+ 7 bxc3

See below for some brief comments about this most common of all doubled pawn-structures in modern chess.

7...♘f6 8 f3 ♕a5 9 ♗d2 d5! *(D)*

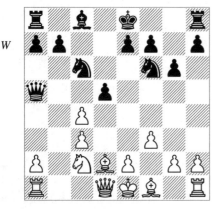

The simplest and probably even the best solution. Although White's pieces look passive, his bishops could have come alive rapidly after e4, and the idea of ♘b4-d5 would be particularly awkward to meet.

10 cxd5 ♕xd5 11 e4 ♕c5

This is equal. Black is ahead in development and is making it hard for White to get castled. 9...d5 is an example of how when one possesses the knight-pair one should often open the position quickly. But it is also an example of liquidating a forward doubled pawn both to challenge its grip on a square and to expose the weakness of the pawn behind it.

12 ♕e2! 0-0 13 ♕e3 ♕xe3+ 14 ♘xe3 b6 15 c4 ♗a6 16 ♗c3 ♖fd8! 17 ♘d5

17 ♗xf6? exf6 leaves the dark squares undefended and favours Black, who ironically has forced White to undouble his pawns and then allowed his own to be doubled!

17...♘e8 18 ♖c1 ♖ac8 19 ♗e2 e6

A cool-headed procedure would be 19...f6 intending ...♔f7 and ...e6.

20 ♘f6+ ♘xf6 21 ♗xf6 ♖d7

with equality, in view of White's weak c-pawn. The game was eventually drawn.

Another more interesting and ambitious example of this strategy arises in the extremely popular structure resulting from 1 e4 c5 2 ♘f3 ♘c6 3 ♗b5 Sicilian positions in which ♗xc6 follows shortly. The treatment of doubled pawns

in this variation is exceptionally interesting. The revival of White's enthusiasm for ♗b5 and ♗xc6 has come in part because of the discovery that one needn't pursue traditional ideas with respect to either minor-piece treatment or majority/minority issues. I want to compare a number of examples with these themes.

Glek – Lemmers
Belgium 1995

1 e4 c5 2 ♘f3 ♘c6 3 ♗b5 g6 4 0-0 ♗g7 5 ♖e1 e5 6 ♗xc6 dxc6 7 d3 ♘e7

In general Black has a solid position that is difficult to attack. If White tries to enforce d4, he will run into the ...c5 + ...e5 bind along with pressure down the d-file.

8 a3

This move intending b4 is the key idea we will investigate, one that White here initiates before developing any other pieces. It has been quite successful in practice, and I believe that it is superior to the other plans more frequently employed in these types of positions.

8...0-0 9 b4 cxb4 10 axb4 *(D)*

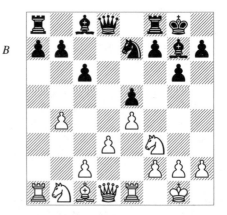

So Black has got rid of his only weakness and the game has been opened. Doesn't this favour his bishops? After all, White cannot even be said to have exposed any weaknesses in his opponent's position. But in fact, White has acted quickly before Black can reorganize his pieces and exploit the two-bishops advantage at his leisure. Notice that the e7-knight and g7-bishop are restricted. With 9 b4, White opens up the a-file and can put pressure on the queenside. Just as importantly, the moves ♗e3 or

♗b2 allow him to open the position still further with d4 if Black allows it.

10...♗e6 11 ♗e3

Provoking queenside weaknesses. The other standard plan here, also played in the reverse English Opening position, is 11 ♗b2 ♕d6 12 ♗c3!? ♖fd8 13 ♕c1 b6 14 ♕b2 f6 15 ♘bd2 with the idea d4, although in this particular instance Black can activate his bad bishop by 15...♗h6 and claim his own chances.

11...b6

11...a6 12 ♘c3 and ♘a4 is awkward for Black.

12 ♕c1 ♕d6 13 ♖a4

Preparing to double on the file. Black is now well developed, so the battle will revolve around whether White can get pressure on the queenside combined with threats of d4.

13...♔h8

A little slow. 13...f5 is more pointed, although similar to the note to Black's 14th.

14 h3!?

Also too conservative. 14 ♕a3! is direct and good; e.g., 14...♘c8 15 ♘bd2 h6 (15...f5 16 ♘c4 ♗xc4 {16...♕c7 17 exf5} 17 dxc4 f4 18 ♗d2 with an advantage for White) 16 ♘c4 ♗xc4 17 dxc4 and c5 next. This would have been the course of play consistent with White's positional goals.

14...♘c8

Black's position is a bit loose after 14...f5 15 ♕a3 fxe4 (15...♕c7 16 ♘c3 f4 is probably smarter) 16 dxe4 ♕c7 17 ♘bd2 intending ♖a1.

15 ♘c3 ♗d7

Glek gives 15...♖b8 16 ♖d1 intending d4, White's other main thematic idea in the position. In general Black's play has been rather slow.

16 ♖d1 ♕e7 17 d4! (D)

Finally! Note that all of White's pieces are active.

17...c5

The game has turned tactical and White is better developed. Alternatively, 17...exd4 18 ♗xd4 ♗xd4 19 ♖xd4 can lead to the cute variation 19...c5 20 ♘d5!? ♕d8 21 bxc5 bxc5 22 e5!, with 22...cxd4? 23 ♘f6 ♖g8 24 ♕h6 ♖g7 25 ♖xd4 winning for White due to ♖h4 next.

18 ♘d5! ♕d8 19 dxe5!!

This introduces a pretty combination that should have given White a very large advantage.

B

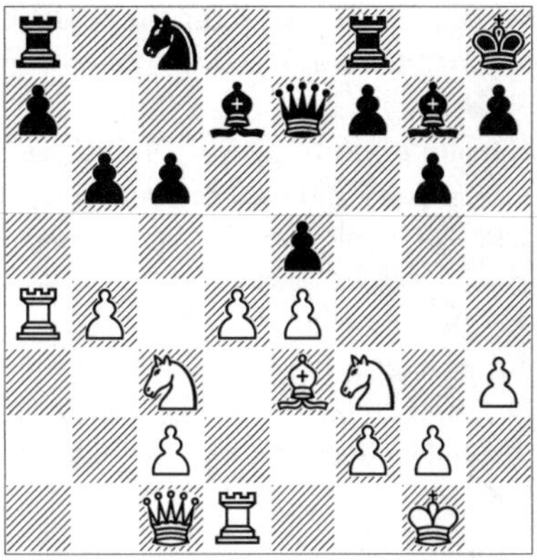

Although not terribly relevant, it's hard to resist showing just a few of the many ideas:

19...♗xa4 20 ♗g5! ♕d7 21 ♗f6!

Intending ♕h6 followed by ♘g5.

21...♕c6

21...♔g8 22 ♘f4 ♕c6 23 ♘h5! and White wins.

22 ♕a1!

Black's idea was 22 ♕h6? ♕xf6!, turning the tables. But now White threatens 23 e6.

22...♗xf6 23 exf6?!

Glek demonstrates at great length that 23 ♘xf6! with the idea e6 ultimately wins. One typical line is 23...cxb4 24 ♕c1!! (24 e6?? ♕c3) 24...♔g7 25 ♘d4 ♕c5 26 ♘f5+ gxf5 27 ♕g5+ ♔h8 28 ♕h6.

23...♘d6!? 24 ♘e5! ♕b7

Glek recommended 24...♕c8, based on 25 ♕xa4 ♕e6, but 25 ♘e7!, with the point 25...♕e6 26 ♘5xg6+ hxg6 27 ♕c1, looks very strong.

25 ♕xa4 ♘xe4 26 b5! ♘g5

On 26...♘d6, 27 ♕f4 threatens ♘e7 and ♕h6.

27 ♕h4 ♘e6 28 ♘e7 ♕c7?

But 28...g5 29 ♕g4! sets up ♖d7, and if 29...♕c7, 30 ♘xf7+ ♖xf7 31 ♕xe6 ♖af8 32 ♖d7 wins.

29 ♖d7! ♕xe5 30 ♘xg6+! 1-0

Poluliakhov – Lanka
Koszalin 1999

1 e4 c5 2 ♘f3 ♘c6 3 ♗b5 g6 4 0-0 ♗g7 5 ♖e1 e5 6 ♗xc6 dxc6 7 d3 ♕e7

A common move. Black doesn't like the knight's prospects on e7 (see the last game), so he protects e5 to prepare ...♘f6. This makes

White's method of the opening the position still more appropriate:

8 a3 ♘f6

The position after 8...a5 9 a4 ♘f6 10 ♘a3 ♘d7 11 ♘c4 0-0 is accurately described by Pedersen: "playable for Black, but positions like this are just a lot more pleasant for White".

9 b4! *(D)*

As in the preceding game. 9 h3 (to prevent ...♗g4) 9...0-0 10 ♘bd2 h6 11 b4, with similar ideas, was played in Enders-Cao Sang, Budapest 1996.

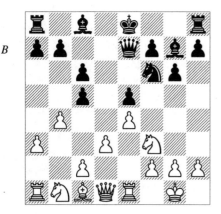

9...0-0

Let's see exactly what White is or should be up to by looking at alternatives and examples:

a) At this point 9...cxb4 10 axb4 just encourages ♗a3 or ♗e3.

b) 9...♘d7 is a logical way for Black to treat the position, refusing to surrender his centre pawns unless White allows his pieces activity. Timman-Reinderman, Wijk aan Zee 1999 continued 10 ♘bd2?! (there should be no hurry to develop when structure is so important; 10 bxc5! ♘xc5 11 a4! 0-0 12 ♗a3 is consistent with White's open-lines policy, and play might go 12...b6 13 ♘bd2 ♗e6 14 ♘b3 ♗xb3 15 cxb3 with some advantage; e.g., 15...♖fd8 16 ♖c1) 10...0-0 11 ♗b2?! (again, 11 bxc5 seems preferable) 11...♖d8 12 ♘c4 ♘b6! 13 ♘a5?! (13 ♘cxe5 ♘a4 14 ♕b1 ♘xb2 15 ♕xb2 ♖e8 16 d4 cxd4 17 ♘d3) 13...♘a4 14 ♗c1 ♕c7 and in this instance Black was better.

c) 9...♗g4 10 ♘bd2 0-0 11 h3 ♗xf3 12 ♘xf3 ♖fd8 13 ♗d2 ♘h5 14 ♕b1 ♘f4 15 bxc5 ♕xc5 16 d4 ♕e7 17 ♗xf4 (or 17 ♕b4) 17...exf4 18 e5 b5 19 c3 with a nice advantage for White,

Sedlak-Velimirović, Subotica 2002. White is ready to play a4.

10 ♘bd2

Again, 10 bxc5 ♕xc5 11 a4 is promising: 11...♖e8 12 ♗a3 ♕a5 13 ♘bd2 ♗e6 14 ♘g5 ♘d7 15 ♘xe6 ♖xe6 16 ♘c4 ♕c7 17 ♕d2 with a small advantage for White, Glek-Rabiega, Zillertal 1993. This may be the way to go in view of the note to Black's 11th move.

10...♖d8 11 ♘c4 ♘d7

Poluliakhov suggests 11...♗g4!? intending 12 ♘cxe5 ♕xe5 13 ♘xe5 ♗xd1 14 ♖xd1 ♘xe4 15 ♗b2 ♖e8 16 f4 ♘g5! 17 bxc5 ♘e6 with equality.

12 ♗d2 f6 13 h3 b6 14 ♕b1 ♗a6 15 ♘e3 ♘f8?!

This turns out badly. Poluliakhov suggests 15...cxb4 16 axb4 ♗b7.

16 bxc5 bxc5

Suddenly White has a classical target in the blockaded, unsupported pawns. How he converts this clear advantage is very impressive, but for our purposes it's enough to present the moves uncommented upon:

17 ♕b3+ ♘e6 18 ♕a4 ♕b7 19 ♖ab1 ♕c8 20 ♘c4 ♔h8 21 ♖b2 ♘d4 22 ♘xd4 cxd4 23 f4! ♗b5 24 ♕b3 ♗h6 25 ♖f1 ♕a6 26 ♘a5 ♕c8 27 ♘c4 ♕a6 28 ♘a5 ♕c8 29 a4 ♗a6 30 ♕f7 ♖f8 31 ♕e7 c5 32 ♖fb1 ♗g7 33 fxe5 fxe5 34 ♘b7! ♖e8 35 ♕d6 c4 36 ♕xa6 c3 37 ♗xc3 ♕xc3 38 ♘d6 ♖f8 39 ♕c4 ♗f6 40 ♕xc3 dxc3 41 ♖b7 ♔g8 42 ♖c7 ♖d8 43 ♖xc3 ♗b6+ 44 ♔h2 ♖f2 45 ♘c8! ♗e3 46 ♘e7+ ♔g7 47 ♘d5 ♗d2 48 ♖c7+ ♔h6 49 ♔g3 ♖af8 50 ♖bb7 1-0

Finally, a different positional result arises from the same basic idea in the following example:

Short – Pierrot
Buenos Aires Najdorf mem 2000

1 e4 c5 2 ♘f3 ♘c6 3 ♗b5 g6 4 0-0 ♗g7 5 c3 ♘f6 6 ♖e1 0-0 7 h3 e5 8 a3 a6?!

This encourages White to make a move that he would normally want to play anyway. The continuation illustrates important positional themes associated with this structure.

9 ♗xc6 dxc6 10 d3 ♕c7 11 ♕c2 h6 12 ♗e3 b6 *(D)*

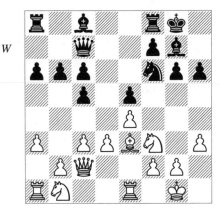

W

13 b4!

Once again opening up the position for the knights and cooperatively liquidating Black's doubled pawns. Wells's comment is: "This helps to explain a phenomenon, which otherwise appears quite paradoxical ... As in the Exchange Variation of the Spanish, White, facing the doubled pawn and the two bishops decides to open the position, in this case even liquidating the doubled pawns into the bargain. Practice has shown us that time and again the knight-pair make little headway against the doubled pawns in a closed position." After 13 b4 in this game, Black's interior weaknesses are exposed, although as we have seen in other examples it tends to be a good move whether or not a specific target is created.

13...cxb4 14 axb4! ♗e6 15 d4!

Yet another line-opening move. This opens the c-file and strengthens White's dark-square bind. White will soon exploit both factors, with a winning advantage.

15...exd4 16 cxd4 ♕b7 17 ♘c3 ♖fe8 18 ♗f4 ♘d7 19 ♗d6 ♗c4 20 e5

Now things are clear. Black manages to transform one weakness into another, but he is already without salvation here.

20...♖e6 21 ♘d2 ♗d5 22 ♘xd5 cxd5 23 ♖ec1 ♗f8 24 ♗xf8 ♘xf8 25 ♘f1 ♖ee8 26 ♘e3 ♖ec8 27 ♕a2 ♖d8 28 f4 ♘e6 29 ♕d2 ♘g7 30 ♖f1 ♕e7 31 ♖f3 ♖a7 32 f5 ♕g5 33 ♕f2 a5 34 h4 ♕e7 35 f6 ♕xb4 36 fxg7 ♕xd4 37 ♖f1 1-0

One should remember that the games above represent successful illustrations of a particular strategy and not the overall state of the opening; otherwise we would not see Black playing 2...♘c6 and 3...g6 at all!

Examples from Modern Play

Sticking with the 3 ♗b5 Sicilian Defence and doubled pawns, the following game contains a number of themes from this book:

Sergeev – Moroz
Ordzhonikidze 2001

1 e4 c5 2 ♘f3 ♘c6 3 ♗b5 e6 4 ♗xc6 bxc6 5 d3 ♘e7 6 h4! *(D)*

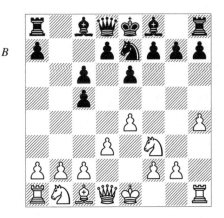

B

This move could be included in our discussion of flank pawn advances. Here the main idea is prophylactic: Black's plan in this position is ...♘g6, ...0-0, and to meet e5 by ...f6. Now 6...♘g6? runs into 7 h5. Conceivably White might also want to expand further by h5-h6 in the right circumstances.

6...h5

Sergeev offers 6...f6!? 7 ♗e3!? d6 8 c3 'intending d4 with a small advantage'. As usual, White will liquidate his opponent's doubled pawns by d4 both to open lines and use his mobile centre to create outposts for his knights. Here he has more time than usual because Black's pieces are so cramped and the knight won't be happy on g6; for example, 8...♘g6 (8...♖b8 9 ♘bd2! with the idea 9...♖xb2? 10 ♘b3) 9 d4 cxd4 10 cxd4 h5 (10...♗e7 11 h5 ♘f8 12 ♕c2) 11 ♕c2 with good prospects.

7 e5!?

This is the more traditional strategy of fixing Black's doubled pawns and making c4 and e4 into at least pseudo-outposts for his knights. Black normally successfully contests this via

...f6 and eventually ...0-0, but the inclusion of h4 and ...h5 will make this difficult.

7...♘g6 8 ♘bd2 f6 9 ♘c4 ♗a6

For example, the normal 9...♕c7 attacking the e-pawn can now be met by 10 ♕e2 fxe5 11 ♘fxe5 ♘xe5 12 ♘xe5, and ♘g6 is threatened.

10 ♕e2 ♕c7?!

10...♗xc4!? is generally anti-positional, but here it allows Black to break up the centre by 11 dxc4 (11 ♕e4! may be better because 11...♗xd3 12 ♕xd3 f5 13 ♗d2 gives White quite a bit of play for the pawn; note how in every line the h4/...h5 trade-off is coming in handy) 11...♕c7 12 exf6 gxf6 13 ♗d2 and with ideas like 0-0-0, g3 and ♗c3 White has some advantage, but it's not much.

11 ♕e4! ♔f7 12 ♗f4 ♘xf4 13 ♕xf4

Now it's a case of two knights versus two bishops. White has better development, but without a permanent outpost he needs more than just space.

13...♔g8!?

Not necessarily best, but Black has a clever plan to free his bishops.

14 0-0-0 *(D)*

Sergeev proposes 14 ♖h3!? with the idea ♖g3, but 14...♖h6 15 ♖g3 ♔h8 still looks equal.

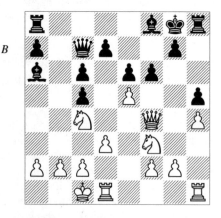

14...♖h6!

The idea is ...fxe5 and ...♖f6, with a bishop coming to d6 and all of Black's pieces suddenly active.

15 ♖h3?!

Here 15 ♖hg1! would prepare 16 g4 and exploit White's only real advantages: space and Black's vulnerable kingside. Then Black's plan in the game seems to fall just short: 15...fxe5

(15...♔h8 16 g4 hxg4 17 ♕xg4 f5 18 ♕f4 with a clear plus) 16 ♘cxe5 ♖f6 17 ♕e4 d5 18 ♕e2 ♗d6 19 g4! c4 20 dxc4 (20 gxh5!?) 20...♖b8 21 gxh5 ♕b6 22 b3 and White's attack is faster than Black's.

15...fxe5 16 ♘cxe5 ♖f6 17 ♕e4 d5!

Positionally undesirable, but that won't matter as Black develops quickly with threats.

18 ♕e2 ♗d6

Now White has the e5 outpost, but no kingside attack.

19 ♖e1 ♖af8! 20 ♖g3?!

It's not clear what's best, however, since 20 c4 ♖f5! doesn't improve the situation.

20...c4! *(D)*

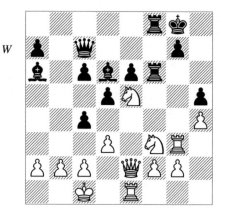

Black has taken over the initiative with his active bishops and rooks. If White plays 21 d4?, 21...♕a5 22 ♔b1 c3 and ...cxb2 gives Black a strong attack and activity. This example epitomizes the most common situation with the knight-pair versus bishop-pair: if the side with knights can open lines quickly before the bishops coordinate (here by 15 ♖hg1!), there's a good probability of success. But if the bishops get enough time, they will usually find a way to become the better pieces, as happened here.

The most common case of giving up a bishop to create doubled pawns has always been the one where those pawns were also isolated in the process; e.g., 1 c4 c5 2 ♘c3 ♘f6 3 g3 d5 4 cxd5 ♘xd5 5 ♗g2 ♘c7 6 ♕b3 ♘c6 7 ♗xc6+ bxc6 *(D)*.

This pattern occurs so often on both sides of the board that I don't need to go into any detail here. It also has a firm grounding in historical

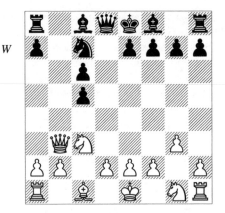

W

play. In Curt Hansen's terrific *ChessBase Magazine* article called 'Inventors of Modern Chess 2', he finds 13 examples of giving up the bishops for such pawns previous to 1935, with a real explosion in the 1950s that has yet to cease. Remember that those pre-1935 examples are for a period in which the database selection is notoriously limited. On the other hand, if we look at those examples the doubling of pawns sometimes proved unsuccessful, and several of them were purely pragmatic captures with an instant reward, and thus nowhere near as committal or risky as those we see today.

Without going any further, it might be worth just listing a subset of the openings in which this particular creation of such doubled *isolated* c-pawns commonly arise:

a) The Accelerated Dragon Sicilian with, e.g., 1 e4 c5 2 ♘f3 ♘c6 3 d4 cxd4 4 ♘xd4 g6 5 c4 ♗g7 6 ♘c2 d6 7 ♘c3 ♗xc3+ 8 bxc3, and the Hyper-Accelerated Dragon Sicilian with 1 e4 c5 2 ♘f3 g6 3 d4 ♗g7 4 dxc5 ♕a5+ 5 ♘c3 ♗xc3+ 6 bxc3.

b) Its cousin the Rubinstein Variation of the English, given above, with 1 c4 c5 2 ♘c3 ♘f6 3 g3 d5 4 cxd5 ♘xd5 5 ♗g2 ♘c7, and now many versions including 6 ♕b3 and 6 ♘f3 ♘c6 7 d3 e5 8 ♘d2 ♗e7 9 ♘c4 f6 10 ♗xc6+ bxc6.

c) A large number of King's Indian formations, an older one being 1 d4 ♘f6 2 c4 g6 3 ♘c3 ♗g7 4 e4 0-0 5 ♗e2 d6 6 ♘f3 ♗g4 7 0-0 ♘fd7 8 ♗e3 ♘c6 9 d5 ♗xf3 10 ♗xf3 ♘a5 11 ♕a4 ♗xc3 12 bxc3 b6, a formation occurring in Geller and Spassky's games. Also, many ideas such as 1 d4 ♘f6 2 c4 d6 3 ♘c3 g6 4 e4 ♗g7 5 f4 0-0 6 ♘f3 c5 7 d5 e6 8 ♗e2 exd5 9 exd5 ♘h5 10 0-0 ♗xc3 11 bxc3 ♘g7.

d) English lines related to the Grünfeld such as 1 c4 ♘f6 2 ♘c3 d5 3 cxd5 ♘xd5 4 g3 g6 5 ♗g2 ♘b6 6 d3 ♗g7 7 ♗e3 ♘c6 8 ♗xc6+ bxc6.

e) Various Sicilians; e.g., 1 e4 c5 2 ♘f3 ♘c6 3 ♘c3 g6 4 d4 cxd4 5 ♘xd4 ♗g7 6 ♘b3 ♗xc3+ 7 bxc3 ♘f6.

f) The famous Pirc Defence from the Spassky-Fischer Reykjavik match with 1 e4 d6 2 d4 g6 3 ♘c3 ♘f6 4 f4 ♗g7 5 ♘f3 c5 6 dxc5 ♕a5 7 ♗d3 ♕xc5 8 ♕e2 0-0 9 ♗e3 ♕a5 10 0-0 ♗g4 11 ♖ad1 ♘c6 12 ♗c4 ♘h5 13 ♗b3 ♗xc3 14 bxc3, and numerous Modern Defences and Benoni Defences.

An early example of a modern doubled pawn position arose in the next game. The creation of this particular type of position was ahead of its time; as we shall see, the issues that arise are remarkably similar to the analogous position played today with colours reversed. On the other hand, we also see that these lines can only be assessed by very exact analysis, and that little changes make big differences.

Sakharov – Reshko
USSR Cht 1966

1 c4 ♘f6 2 ♘c3 e6 3 g3 d5 4 ♗g2 d4 5 ♘b1 c5

White's move-order is not popular due to his loss of time. A curiosity at this point: 5...e5 transposes to a Hyper-Accelerated Dragon Sicilian position (1 e4 c5 2 ♘f3 g6 3 d4 ♗g7 4 d5) with colours reversed! But the tempi are the same, since White has wasted two moves (♘c3-b1) and Black has wasted just one (...e6-e5).

6 d3 ♘c6

This isn't so bad, but why give White any opportunity to justify his tempo losses?

7 ♗xc6+! bxc6 8 f4 *(D)*

White clamps down on ...e5, hoping to fix Black's pawns Nimzo-Indian style by means of ♘f3 and then play something along the lines of ♕a4, ♘bd2-b3, ♗d2 and 0-0-0. Black's two bishops are hard to activate, although some sort of ...e5 move or sacrifice may exploit the hole on e3. First, however, he tries to open kingside lines.

8...h5 9 ♘f3 h4! 10 ♖g1

White doesn't want to deal with 10 ♘xh4 ♖xh4! (10...♗e7 11 ♘f3 ♘g4 12 ♕a4 ♕c7 is unclear) 11 gxh4 ♘g4 12 ♕a4 (12 e4!? ♕xh4+

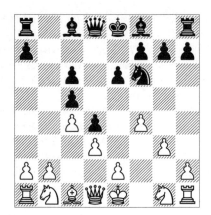

B

13 ♔d2 ♘e3 14 ♕f3 e5 gives Black an ongoing attack; for example, ...g6 might be played next) 12...♕xh4+ 13 ♔d1 ♗d7 and Black obviously has a lot of play in this unclear position.

10...hxg3 11 hxg3

At this point, it's worth making the comparison with a line that has maintained a small but fairly steady following in the last 15 years or so: 1 d4 g6 2 c4 ♗g7 3 ♘c3 c5 4 d5 ♗xc3+ 5 bxc3 f5 6 h4 ♘f6 7 h5 ♖g8 8 hxg6 hxg6 (D).

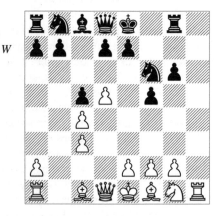

W

In our main game, Black actually has the extra move ...e6 in and White has d3, but Black is on the move. Moving to this modern position, I would argue that 9 ♘f3 is not the best move, as it encourages ...♘e4; Black is of course committed to ...♘f6 in the older game. Furthermore, White's c1-bishop is not cut off by a pawn on e3, so it might go to g5 or f4 in the right circumstances (not too often, however, because ...♘e4 and ...♕a5 creates immediate pressure). For all that, the possibility of a quick ...♗d6, ...♘g4 and ...e5 might make that extra

...e6 worth as much as any other factor. I would be hesitant to judge between White's 7 ♗xc6+ in the main game and Black's 4...♗xc3+ in this note, but both are at least playable. The only certain thing is that the side with the doubled pawns has to open the position fairly early on before too much simplification occurs.

11...♘g4 12 ♕a4 ♕c7 13 ♘bd2 (D)

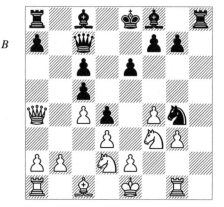

B

13...♗d7!?

13...♖b8 14 ♘b3 ♗d6 seems better, aiming for ...e5 more quickly. But 13...♘e3?! 14 ♘e4 is a poor trade-off for Black, since ♗xe3 is already threatened.

14 ♘e4?!

This makes it harder both to defend b2 and to develop, and it may also run into a problem based upon ...f5. I would prefer to both attack on c5 and cover a5 by 14 ♘b3! ♗d6 15 ♗d2 e5 16 0-0-0.

14...♖b8

Black might also play the aggressive continuation 14...f5 15 ♘eg5 (or 15 ♘f2 ♘xf2 16 ♔xf2 ♗d6) 15...♗d6 16 ♗d2 e5 17 fxe5 ♘xe5 18 0-0-0 ♘g4! when he should have some advantage.

15 ♕c2 ♕b6 16 b3 ♗e7?!

Drifting and allowing White to consolidate. Again, 16...f5! 17 ♘eg5 ♗d6 was a good idea. White gets a serious bind after the text.

17 ♗d2 f5 18 ♘f2 ♘xf2 19 ♔xf2 ♗f6 20 ♖h1 ♔f7 21 ♕b2! ♖be8 22 ♕a3

Threatening to win a pawn by means of ♗a5. White's structural advantage now dominates other factors as the position becomes simplified and any active options are eliminated.

22...a6 23 ♖xh8 ♖xh8 24 ♖e1

White is ready to play e3, opening the e-file with a large advantage. Apparently realizing how dire his situation has become, Black plays a desperate sacrifice that doesn't make much sense:

24...e5? 25 fxe5 ♗e7 26 ♗g5 ♕d8? 27 ♕c1?

Missing 27 e6+!, which wins because of 27...♔xe6 (27...♗xe6 28 ♘e5+) 28 ♗xe7 ♕xe7 29 e3. But White hardly throws away his advantage thereby.

27...♖h2+?! 28 ♔g1

There's no need to fool around with 28 ♘xh2 ♗xg5. The rest is easy.

28...♖h5 29 ♗xe7 ♕xe7 30 e3 ♗e6 31 exd4 cxd4 32 ♘xd4 ♕d8 33 ♕e3 g5 34 ♘xc6 ♕e8 35 ♘d4 f4 36 gxf4 ♕h8 37 ♕f3 ♖h3 38 ♕b7+ ♔g6 39 ♕g2 ♗g4 40 f5+ ♔h5 41 ♖e4 ♖h4 42 ♘f3 1-0

I should also make brief mention the truly radical ♗g2xc6 and ...♗g7xc3 ideas that double but don't isolate the c-pawns. As mentioned in SOMCS, this was a Larsen speciality; as early as the mid-1970s, he played three games along the lines similar to 1 g3 g6 2 ♗g2 ♗g7 3 c4 c5 4 ♘c3 ♘c6 5 b3 e6 6 ♗xc6 bxc6 7 ♗b2 (D) of Larsen-Andersson, Las Palmas 1974:

This is certainly the ultimate in the 'fianchettoed bishop captures knight' philosophy, because Black's pawns protect one another and he has no exploitable weaknesses. Meanwhile, White's own kingside light-square problems look serious, and it is remarkable that he could have good play. Nevertheless, Black's bishops can ultimately be neutralized by a prophylactic policy. His desirable structure with ...d6 and

...e5 can be prevented by f4, and moves like d3, ♕d2, and ♘e4 can exchange the g7-bishop and challenge Black's kingside dark squares. The result may be that the c8-bishop is imprisoned and White can slowly build up on the kingside or in the centre. I refer the reader to SOMCS for a complete example (Larsen-Betancourt, Lanzarote 1976). It might be of interest that Hansen finds precedent for this ultra-modern strategy in games by both Portisch and Smyslov; e.g., 1 c4 c5 2 ♘c3 g6 3 g3 ♗g7 4 ♗g2 ♘c6 5 ♘f3 d6 6 0-0 ♗d7 7 d3 ♕c8 8 ♖e1 ♗h3 9 ♗h1 h5 10 ♗f4 ♗xc3 11 bxc3, Golombek-Portisch, Zagreb 1965.

For those cases in which the doubled pawns aren't isolated, Wells makes the important distinction between:

a) unsupported doubled pawns, such as in the numerous Nimzo-Indian lines with ...♗xc3 which leave c4 weak (1 d4 ♘f6 2 c4 e6 3 ♘c3 ♗b4 4 a3 ♗xc3+ 5 bxc3, for example); and

b) supported doubled pawns with no such glaring weaknesses, as arises after 1 c4 ♘f6 2 ♘c3 e6 3 ♘f3 ♗b4 4 g3 ♗xc3 5 bxc3, for example, when a pawn on d3 can defend against any threat to c4.

Note that the ♗g2 + ♗xc6 examples in the preceding paragraph only created supported doubled pawns that were easily defensible, which makes the idea all the more remarkable. Regarding the various situations, let me make the obvious explicit: to the side that creates the doubled pawns, the case of isolated doubled pawns is the most attractive, followed by the case of unsupported pawns, and lastly the case of supported pawns. What's interesting, however, is how very popular it has become to inflict even supported doubled pawns upon the opponent, as we shall see below. Let's turn to some particular structures to illustrate the ideas involved.

Doubled f-Pawns

The various instantiations of supported doubled pawns present a broad and fascinating field. Today, for example, the occurrence of doubled f-pawns has risen dramatically in a wide variety of openings both classical and modern. In particular, players are more willing to defy traditional precepts and capture away from the centre by exf3 or ...exf6. This type of capture will be my main concern. But before directing your attention that way, I should point out that even f-pawn captures towards the centre are an increasing modern era phenomenon. Take, for example, the Sveshnikov Variation of the Sicilian (1 e4 c5 2 ♘f3 ♘c6 3 d4 cxd4 4 ♘xd4 ♘f6 5 ♘c3 e5 6 ♘db5 d6 7 ♗g5 a6 8 ♘a3 b5 9 ♗xf6 gxf6 (D)) and various related lines.

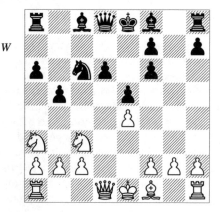

W

Note that these f-pawns are unsupported. When one takes that into account, and then factors in Black's backward d6-pawn on an open file, it's not surprising that the old masters (or even ones up to the 1970s) weren't disposed to get anywhere near the Sveshnikov, which is now an extraordinarily popular and effective variation. Other Sicilian variations, notably the Rauzer and the Najdorf with ♗g5, often involve doubled, supported, f-pawns after ♗xf6 and ...gxf6, since Black's e-pawn will be either at e7 or e6. Today we see things like 1 d4 d6 2 ♘f3 ♗g4 3 c4 ♗xf3 4 gxf3 or variations with ...b6, ...♗b7, ...♗xf3 and gxf3 with increasing frequency. Numerous examples arise in a main line of the French Defence Tarrasch Variation that goes 1 e4 e6 2 d4 d5 3 ♘d2 c5 4 exd5 ♕xd5 5 ♘gf3 cxd4 6 ♗c4 ♕d6 7 0-0 ♘c6 8 ♘b3 ♘f6 9 ♘bxd4 ♘xd4 10 ♘xd4 with an early ♗g5 and ♗xf6 answered by ...gxf6 (those pawns are supported ones when and if ...f5 is played). Even relatives of the very old French Burn Variation with 1 e4 e6 2 d4 d5 3 ♘c3 dxe4 4 ♘xe4 ♘f6 5 ♗g5 ♗e7 6 ♗xf6 gxf6 (similarly supported) are being reinvestigated. And so forth.

Nevertheless, captures *away* from the centre are particularly radical in the sense that the majority of them wouldn't have been allowed by one side or the other in the not-too-distant past. These new lines constitute the material for the latest debates over the advantages and disadvantages of doubled pawns. Such captures, after all, involve a crippling of one's own majority, which one would think would be a more serious defect than the analogous doubling of c-pawns:

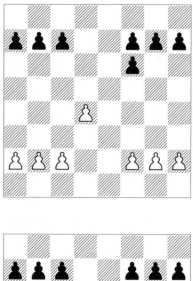

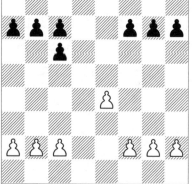

The diagrams clarify this: when one takes on the doubled f-pawns it is normally with the approximate resulting structure in the first diagram. One has then allowed the opponent a rather dangerous mobile majority, and without good prospects of a queenside minority attack in return, because ...c5 can so often be answered by d5. In the case of doubled c-pawns, we know from experience that the opponent's kingside majority will have a difficult time advancing since the king (in this case White's) would be exposed thereby. Hence, by the way, one motivation for White's paradoxical a3 + b4 queenside plan versus the 3 ♗b5 Sicilian earlier in this section: his prospects reside in a central rather than a kingside majority. Thus the possessor of the doubled f-pawns needs to justify his choice and establish his chances earlier in the middlegame. Some examples below will illustrate this difference.

Doubled c-pawns that arise from capture away from the centre occur in many openings, including classical ones such the Ruy Lopez, for example in the Exchange Variation and the recently revitalized Berlin Defence. One could even see 1 e4 e5 2 ♘f3 ♘c6 3 ♗b5 a6 as a bold challenge to White to inflict doubled pawns on Black's position, ones that cripple his majority after ...dxc6. The Scotch Game provides us with a knight exchange resulting in the same structure after 1 e4 e5 2 ♘f3 ♘c6 3 d4 exd4 4 ♘xd4 ♗c5 5 ♘xc6 ♕f6 6 ♕d2 dxc6. The reverse-colour situation with White playing dxc3 is also common, e.g., after ...♗b4 and ...♗xc3 in various lines of the English Opening, and we also see dxc3 variations after the exchange of a knight on d5 for one on c3.

But the theoretical superiority of the doubled c-pawn-structure over that of the f-pawns (diagrammed above) hasn't necessarily led to more success with the former, as illustrated by the widespread use of openings with the latter structure. This is the case even when the doubled pawns have no prospect of being liquidated in the short term. Here are just a few of the openings (many of them unknown or unpopular before modern times) in which strong players intentionally head for doubled f-pawn positions:

a) Nimzo-Indian Defence with 1 d4 ♘f6 2 c4 e6 3 ♘c3 ♗b4 4 ♕c2 d5 5 cxd5 ♕xd5 6 ♘f3 ♕f5 7 ♕xf5 exf5.

b) Trompowsky Attack with 1 d4 ♘f6 2 ♗g5 d5 3 ♗xf6 exf6, normally followed by ...f5.

c) Modern Systems with 1 d4 d6 2 ♘f3 ♗g4 3 c4 ♘d7 (or 3...♗xf3 4 exf3) and now 4 g3 ♗xf3 5 exf3 or 4 ♘c3 ♗xf3 5 exf3.

d) Slav Defence with 5 a4 ♗f5 6 ♘h4 e6 7 ♘xf5 exf5.

e) Caro-Kann Defence with 3 ♘c3 dxe4 4 ♘xe4 ♘f6 5 ♘xf6+ exf6.

f) French Defence with 3 e5 c5 4 c3 ♘c6 5 ♘f3 ♘ge7 6 a3 ♘f5 7 ♗d3 soon followed by ♗xf5 and ...exf5.

g) Dutch Defence with 1 d4 f5 2 ♘c3 ♘f6 3 ♗g5 d5 4 ♗xf6 exf6. Here a standard strategy for White is to undouble these pawns by h3 and g4, while Black prevents that by ...h5.

In each of these cases Wells's phrase 'supported doubled pawns' applies due to the adjacent g-pawn. It is worth noting that in a large database, openings with this f7+f5 structure score 52% for White and 48% for Black, with only a 40-point rating difference in performance. This is better than Black normally does. In databases of top masters only, the result varies dramatically by the specific line employed; e.g., the Nimzo-Indian 4 ♕c2 d5 5 cxd5 ♕xd5 6 ♘f3 ♕f5 has done very well (50%-50%), but the overall result with all such doubled f-pawn pairs for Black is better than normal for White at 58%-42%, indicating that in some positions these pawns are simply a disadvantage. Reversing the colours, however, we find that in positions with white pawns at f2 and f4, also among strong players, White has a nice 55%-45% score. Both results include fewer draws than usual, so it's fair to say that these figures mainly demonstrate that the lines are unbalanced, and that if one includes *all* occurrences of this type of doubled f-pawns, they will prove disadvantageous in only slightly more cases than they prove to be helpful. This is surely a remarkable conclusion for such traditionally frowned-upon 'crippled' pawns. It turns out that they have compensating qualities that are not apparent at first. One of them is the ability of the rear pawn to cover extra central squares, and to fulfil the same functions as the forward pawn in cases where that pawn has been exchanged.

Such an abstract discussion needs to be supplemented by actual play. I will present a few examples of some better-established strategies and then turn to something a little more experimental.

The Trompowsky Attack with 1 d4 ♘f6 2 ♗g5 d5 3 ♗xf6 exf6 (followed by some formation with ...f5) has been played by many leading players. Kasparov has won two games with it as Black, and Almasi, Tiviakov, Korchnoi are among others who have used it. An unexciting but typical continuation is seen in the following game:

Krasenkow – Schmidt
Glogow 2001

1 d4 ♘f6 2 ♗g5 d5 3 e3 c6 4 ♗xf6 exf6 5 c4 dxc4 6 ♗xc4 ♗d6 7 ♘c3 0-0 8 ♘f3 f5 9 ♘e5 ♘d7 10 ♘d3 ♕e7 11 0-0 ♘f6 12 g3 ♗e6 13 ♗xe6 ♕xe6 *(D)*

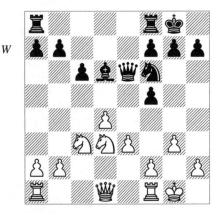

It's probably a good sign that Black has exchanged White's most dangerous bishop, even if his own wasn't so bad given the lack of central pawns to restrict it.

14 ♕e2 ♖ac8 15 b4 ♖fe8 16 ♖ac1 h5 17 ♕f3 g6
with equality.

The Nimzo-Indian line mentioned above has served Black well. In the next example, both players both demonstrate a flippant disregard for classical thinking about doubled pawns:

Kharlov – Timman
Saint Vincent Ech 2000

1 d4 ♘f6 2 c4 e6 3 ♘c3 ♗b4 4 ♕c2 d5 5 cxd5 ♕xd5 6 ♘f3 ♕f5 7 ♕xf5 exf5 *(D)*
The basic position. Black's pawns look quite awkwardly placed, but he counts upon his increased grip on e4 and the new-found activity of his otherwise bad bishop once it comes to e6. The open e-file can also be handy. White's unopposed central majority is of no real consequence because, as Wells points out, the e-pawn would have to get past not only the guard at f5 but also

that on f7. So even playing f3 and e4 on White's part doesn't give him a passed pawn. Even if White gets the bishop-pair (by 8 a3 ♗d6 9 ♘b5), world-class games have shown that Black's control of e4 and d5 equalizes. So effective has this 'anti-positional' doubling been that White switched to 6 e3 as his main weapon!

8 a3
The game that inspired Black's strategy (and to some extent the acceptance of this pawn-structure in so many other openings) was Beliavsky-Romanishin, Groningen PCA 1993: 8 ♗d2 c6 9 e3 ♘bd7 10 ♗d3 ♘b6 11 ♘e2 ♗d6 12 0-0 ♘e4 (or 12...0-0 13 ♖fc1 a5 with equality) 13 ♗a5 0-0 14 ♖fc1 ♖e8 15 ♘d2 ♘xd2 16 ♗xd2 a5! with equality.

8...♗d6
8...♗e7 has generally equalized in top-level play. After 9 ♗g5 ♗e6 10 e3 c6 *(D)*, here are two typical examples:

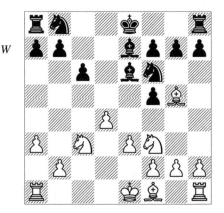

a) Relatively harmless is 11 ♗d3 ♘bd7 12 0-0 h6 13 ♗h4 a5 14 ♖ac1 0-0 15 ♘e2 g5 16

♗g3 ♘e4 17 ♘c3 ♘xc3 18 ♖xc3 ♘f6 19 ♖cc1 ♖fd8 20 ♖fd1 ♖ac8 ½-½ Kasparov-Kramnik, Linares 1999.

b) 11 ♘e5 (imagine how difficult it would be for White to establish a central pawn roller here) 11...h6 12 ♗h4 a5 13 ♗c4 ♗xc4 14 ♘xc4 ♘bd7 15 0-0 ♘d5 16 ♗xe7 ♔xe7 with equality, Seirawan-Adams, Bermuda 2000.

9 g3!?

Against 9 e3, the formation ...c6, ...♗e6, and ...♘bd7-b6 has done well.

9...c6 10 ♗f4! ♗xf4 11 gxf4

An amusing symmetry has arisen. White must be very slightly better because of his prospects of attacking on the queenside, but his advantage is largely abstract.

11...♘bd7

Or 11...♗e6 first, with ...h6 and ...♘bd7 to follow.

12 ♗g2 ♘b6 13 ♘e5 ♗e6 14 0-0 ♘fd5 15 e3 ♘xc3 16 bxc3 f6 17 ♘d3 ♗c4 18 ♖fd1 ♘a4

An alternative and satisfactory course would be 18...♗xd3 19 ♖xd3 0-0-0.

19 ♘c5!

A surprising move that suddenly transforms the position. Otherwise Black's initiative was beginning to give him the advantage.

19...♘xc5

After 19...♘xc3, 20 ♖d2 has the ideas of ♘xb7 and ♖c2, although 20...♘e4 21 ♗xe4 fxe4 22 ♘xb7 ♗d5 should hold, since White has only a modest advantage.

20 dxc5 *(D)*

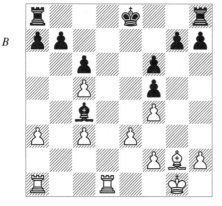

Ironically, White tries to get the advantage against the doubled f-pawns by taking on *two* sets of doubled pawns himself! As in many doubled pawn positions, the open b- and d- files are factors as important as the structural weaknesses, especially with the assistance of the forward c5-pawn, which both restrains and secures d6. Nevertheless, the resulting position should be OK for Black, especially since his bishop can defend the slightly vulnerable queenside.

20...♔e7?!

This makes things difficult. It's easier and better to anticipate White's next by 20...♖d8! 21 ♖d4 ♗b5; for example, 22 ♖b1 ♖f8 23 ♗f1 (23 a4 ♗a6 denies White the opportunity for ♖a4) 23...♗xf1 24 ♔xf1 ♖f7 25 ♖a4 a6 26 ♖ab4 ♖dd7 and White's initiative has dissipated.

21 ♖ab1 ♖ab8

Avoiding 21...♗a6!? 22 ♗f1!, although even then taking on yet *another* pair of doubled pawns after 22...♖ab8 23 ♗xa6 bxa6 24 ♖xb8 ♖xb8 25 ♖d6 ♖b1+ 26 ♔g2 ♖a1 still may be playable!

22 ♖d4

Now White's initiative is getting serious.

22...♗a6 23 ♗h3!

A far-seeing move that puts h7 under attack in those lines where a white rook gets to the 7th rank.

23...g6 24 ♗f1 ♗xf1 25 ♔xf1 ♖hd8!?

Black could temporarily defend all of his queenside pawns by 25...♖hc8 26 ♖a4 a6 27 ♖ab4 ♖c7 28 ♖b6 a5, but White can still play ♔e2 and ♖a6 with the advantage.

26 ♖a4 ♔d7!?

There may be a way to gain counterplay here, but it's not easy. The alternative 26...a6 27 ♖ab4 ♖d7 28 ♖b6 ♔e6 29 c4! ♖c7 30 ♖xa6 doesn't look much better.

27 ♖xa7 ♔c7 28 c4!

Preventing ...♖d5.

28...g5

28...♖d2 29 a4 ♖c2 30 a5 ♔c8 31 ♖b6 ♖xc4 32 a6 ends up in White's favour after 32...♖xc5 33 ♖axb7 ♖xb7 34 ♖xb7 ♖a5, when 35 ♖xh7 ♖xa6 36 ♖g7 shows the advantage of White's 23rd move!

29 fxg5 fxg5 30 a4

White has the idea of a5 and ♖b6 followed by a6. He is clearly better and went on to win. But this game is not a simple condemnation of Black's doubled pawn strategy; rather, it shows how conflicting approaches can lead to entertaining and dynamically balanced play.

Here are some examples featuring the same pawn-structure in the Slav Defence. This is a variation that was used rarely and very unsuccessfully up to the 1990s, when players realized that it had a number of desirable positional characteristics, in particular the restraint of White's centre. In some early games, Black tried to exchange off his doubled f-pawn via ...f4, which actually weakened his position. Now he simply brings his pieces out and finds the doubled pawns quite useful. This variation has been taken up by players at the highest level and has gained full respectability.

Poluliakhov – Kobaliya
Moscow Geller mem 1999

1 d4 d5 2 c4 c6 3 ♘f3 ♘f6 4 ♘c3 dxc4 5 a4 ♗f5 6 ♘h4 e6 7 ♘xf5 exf5 8 e3 ♗b4

An instructive illustration of the role of the two f-pawns in neutralizing White's centre is 8...♗d6 9 ♗xc4 0-0 10 ♕f3 g6 11 h3 h5 12 0-0 ♕e7 13 ♖e1 ♘bd7 14 e4 fxe4 15 ♘xe4 ♘xe4 16 ♖xe4 ♕f6 17 ♗f4 ♘b6 18 ♗b3 ♘d5 with equality, Rõtšagov-Lastin, St Petersburg 1998.

9 ♗xc4 0-0 *(D)*

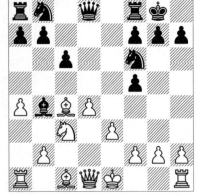

This version of the doubled f-pawns isn't quite as safe as that of the Nimzo-Indian example above because the queens remain on the board and White has some attacking ideas. But in the best-played games, Black holds his own because the f5-pawn exerts important influence over e4 in conjunction with an open file. The knight-pair is not a serious disadvantage, since both e4 and d5 are pseudo-outposts created by Black's pawn-structure. This is an example of

how doubled pawns don't have to be looked upon as burdens, but can justify themselves independently. As Wells says, "...the discussion [of doubled pawns] tends to focus on the 'compensation', important for sure, but liable to blur rather than clarify the characteristics of the pawns themselves."

10 0-0

In a manner reminiscent of the moves a3 and b4 versus Black's doubled pawns at c6 and c5 in the ♗b5 Sicilians above, White can play 10 h3 and aim for g4, voluntarily liquidating Black's theoretical weakness! This is associated with a direct attack, but also has to do with loosening Black's grip on e4; for example, 10...h5? (10...c5! 11 0-0 ♘c6 12 ♘a2 a5 13 ♘xb4 axb4 14 dxc5 ♕xd1 15 ♖xd1 ♘a5 with equality, Bunzmann-Pelletier, Bad Wörishofen 2000) 11 g4! hxg4 12 hxg4 ♘xg4 13 f3 ♘h6 14 e4 with White having both the centre and an attack for a pawn.

10...♘bd7 *(D)*

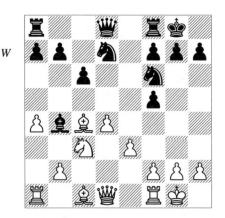

11 ♗d2

A direct approach played by some leading grandmasters is 11 ♕c2; for example, 11...g6 12 f3 (12 ♖d1 ♘b6 13 ♗e2 a5! 14 ♗f3 ♖e8 with equality, Korchnoi-Zhu Chen, Roquebrune 1998) 12...♖c8 13 ♔h1 ♘b6 (13...c5 14 d5 ♘b6 15 ♗a2 c4 16 e4 fxe4 17 fxe4 ♘g4 with equality, Lautier-Sakaev, Las Vegas 1999) 14 ♗b3 c5 15 a5 cxd4 16 axb6 (apparently a forced draw!) 16...dxc3 17 bxa7 cxb2 18 ♕xb2 ♗c3 19 ♗xf7+ ♖xf7 20 ♕xc3 ♖xc3 21 a8♕ ♕xa8 22 ♖xa8+ ♔g7 ½-½ Kramnik-Bareev, Dortmund 2000.

11...g6 12 f3!?

The central expansion idea again. But this is precisely what Black's set-up is directed against. Probably better is 12 ♕b3 or 12 ♘e4 ♕a5 13 ♗xb4 ♕xb4 14 ♕b3 ♕xb3 15 ♘xf6+ ♘xf6 16 ♗xb3, as in Cvitan-Hübner, Swiss Cht 1995.

12...a5 13 ♗b3 ♘b6 14 ♔h1 ♖e8 15 g4?!

Although it has a good idea behind it, the specifics of this move fail White. Better was 15 ♖e1 or 15 ♕e1.

15...fxg4 16 fxg4 ♗xc3 17 bxc3 ♘bd5 18 ♕f3

The position that White was counting on. He has ideas of e4 and g5 with a powerful two-bishop attack.

18...♘e4!

But this fine pawn sacrifice turns everything around.

19 ♕xf7+ ♔h8 20 ♗xd5 ♖e7!

This is Black's point. Now White has to enter a terrible ending or allow positional compensation.

21 ♕g8+?

The wrong choice. White had to try 21 ♗xe4 ♖xf7 22 ♖xf7 ♕e8! 23 ♖f4 g5 24 ♗f5 gxf4 25 e4 with unclear play (this is Hübner's analysis, supplementing Kobaliya). Instead, 21 ♕f3? loses to 21...♕xd5 22 ♗e1 ♖f7! 23 ♕xf7 ♘f2+ 24 ♔g1 ♘h3#.

21...♕xg8 22 ♗xg8 ♘xd2 23 ♖f2 ♘e4 24 ♖f7

Now 24...♖ae8? kept some advantage in the game, but 24...♖ee8! 25 ♗xh7 ♘g5 26 ♗xg6 ♘xf7 27 ♗xf7 ♖xe3 would have won outright.

Sometimes it seems that a player is intent upon inflicting doubled pawns from the outset of the game. The ultra-modern and flexible opening 1...d6 is often played with that attitude against d- and c-pawn openings involving ♘f3. Black's early ...♗g4 and ...♗xf3 will pose a new set of problems for both players, and in this case White will frequently opt for quick development via exf3 over gxf3. Here's one example:

Grabarczyk – Tella
Stockholm 2000

1 d4 d6 2 ♘f3 ♗g4 3 c4 ♗xf3 4 exf3 g6 5 ♘c3 ♗g7 6 ♗e2 ♘c6

After 6...♘h6!?, Spassov-Solozhenkin, Berga 1993 continued 7 0-0 ♘f5 8 d5 0-0 9 ♗d2 c6 10 ♗d3 ♕d7 11 ♖e1 ♖e8 12 ♖b1 ♘a6 13 b4 ♘c7 14 ♗e4 cxd5 15 cxd5 ♖ac8 16 ♖c1 ♘a8! 17 a4 ♘b6 18 a5 ♘c4 (Black is slightly better) 19 ♗d3 ♘d4 20 ♗xc4 ♖xc4 21 ♘e2 ♕b5 22 ♖xc4 ♕xc4 and Black retained the advantage. But I think that White has to accept the pragmatic character of the position and be unafraid of the flank thrust 7 g4! *(D)*, which purely and simply prevents ...♘f5.

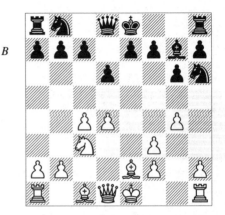

His pawn-structure is optically suspect, but he has that combination of the two bishops and space that makes any pawn break by Black unlikely to succeed. White's space grab continues in a line like 7...0-0?! (but Black has no easy solution to his problems; e.g., 7...♘c6 8 d5 ♘e5 9 ♗e3 and ♕d2; or 7...♘d7 8 ♗e3 e5 9 dxe5 dxe5 10 ♕d2 ♘g8 11 0-0-0) 8 h4 f5 (8...f6 9 ♗e3 e6 10 ♕d2 ♘f7 11 h5) 9 h5 ♘f7 10 hxg6 hxg6 11 gxf5 gxf5 12 ♗e3 ♘c6 13 d5 ♘ce5 14 ♕c2 ♕d7 15 0-0-0 and Black is helpless in the face of ♖dg1 and attacks on g7 and f5.

7 d5

7 ♗e3 e5 8 d5 ♘d4 isn't clear either.

7...♘d4 8 0-0 ♘xe2+ 9 ♕xe2!

Double daring Black to doubly double his pawns!

9...♗xc3

Which he does. But even with four doubled pawns, White has bishop versus knight, and as so often, the side with the knight needs to open lines to activate his pieces, ideally creating a knight outpost. This doesn't happen.

10 bxc3 *(D)*

10...♕d7 11 ♖e1 ♔f8 12 a4 a5?!

Blocking the position isn't consistent with the need for open lines. Black could try for

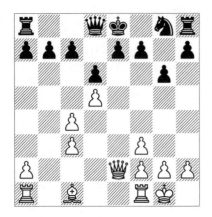

B

activity along the c-file; e.g., 12...♔g7 13 a5 (13 ♗e3 e5) 13...c6 14 ♗f4 ♖c8 15 ♕e3 a6 16 ♕d2 h6 with ...cxd5 and ...♘f6 to follow. Black would at least have some space and outposts on c5 and c4.

13 ♗e3 b6 14 ♗d4 ♘f6 15 ♕e3

At this point a pawn-storm with g4 and/or f4 would be strong.

15...h5!?

15...h6 may improve slightly. But Black is awfully cramped. The doubled pawns have simply given White the time to consolidate his advantage.

16 ♕f4!?

16 ♕g5! is very strong: 16...♔g7 (16...♕f5 17 f4!) 17 ♖e4! threatening ♖f4.

16...♕f5

16...♔g7 17 ♖a2 ♖ae8 18 ♖ae2 ♔h7 is also unpleasant for Black, but he can try to unwind by ...♖hf8 and perhaps ...♘g8.

17 ♕xf5 gxf5 18 ♗xf6 exf6 19 ♖e3

Now it's two sets of doubled pawns versus a set of tripled ones! The latter are much weaker, and most pure pawn endings win for White. I give the rest of the game without notes.

19...♖e8 20 ♖ae1 ♖xe3 21 ♖xe3 h4 22 ♖d3 ♔g7 23 ♔f1 ♔g6 24 ♖e3 h3 25 g3 ♔g7 26 ♔e2 f4 27 ♖e7 ♖c8 28 ♖e4 fxg3 29 fxg3 f5 30 ♖h4 ♖e8+ 31 ♔d2 ♖e5 32 ♖xh3 b5 33 cxb5 ♖xd5+ 34 ♔c2 ♖e5 35 ♖h4 ♖e3 36 ♖c4 ♖xf3 37 ♖xc7 ♖f2+ 38 ♔b3 ♖xh2 39 ♖c6 d5 40 ♖d6 ♖h3 41 b6 ♖h1 42 ♔a2 ♖h2+ 43 ♔a3 **1-0**

A few ideas about how to treat these kinds of positions appear in the following game fragment and the notes to it:

Ivanchuk – Speelman
Debrecen Echt 1992

1 d4 d6 2 ♘f3 ♗g4 3 c4 ♘d7 4 g3 ♗xf3 5 exf3 g6 (D)

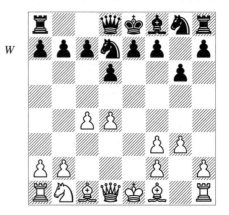

W

As above, Black doesn't want to give any targets for White to advance his pawns against; in particular, he avoids ...e5 for some time, since it would allow a timely f4.

6 ♗g2

Probably too cooperative, as this allows Black to win the d4-square. White should probably put his bishop on h3 to control f5:

a) 6 ♘c3 ♗g7 7 ♗e3 ♘h6! 8 ♗h3! ♘f5 9 ♗xf5 gxf5 with only the slightest of advantages for White; e.g., 10 ♕b3 b6 11 0-0-0 e6.

b) 6 ♗h3 ♗g7 7 0-0 ♘gf6 (this time 7...♘h6 can be met by 8 ♕d3; e.g., 8...c5 9 d5 0-0 10 ♘c3 ♘e5 11 ♕e2 ♘f5 12 ♗xf5 gxf5 13 ♔g2 and White is somewhat better) 8 ♘c3 0-0 9 ♖e1. White's pieces are active and he has a small edge, although Black stands solidly enough.

6...♗g7 7 0-0 ♘h6 8 f4

8 ♗xh6 ♗xh6 gives up the bishop-pair and is harmless. The most critical move is 8 g4, to prevent ...♘f5, but in this particular position Black is well positioned to control key squares: 8...0-0 9 ♗e3 f5 10 ♕d2 (10 g5 ♘f7 11 f4 c6 12 ♘c3 e5 13 h4 exf4 14 ♗xf4 ♕b6) 10...♘f7 (securing equality) 11 h3 (11 gxf5 gxf5 12 ♘c3 e6! 13 ♔h1 ♕h4 leads to equality) 11...e5?! (11...e6! and ...♕h4 is fully satisfactory; that would keep White's g2-bishop in the doldrums) 12 dxe5 ♘dxe5 13 ♘a3 with an edge for White, Klebel-Mirschinka, Bundesliga 1997/8.

8...♘f5

A dynamic solution. Black could also play 8...c6 9 ♘c3 ♘f5 10 d5 c5 with equality.

9 ♗xb7 ♖b8 10 ♗g2 ♘xd4 11 ♘c3 0-0 12 ♖b1 c6 13 b3 ♕c7 14 ♗b2

The game is equal.

All of the examples above have to do with bishop's pawns. As we move out towards the edge of the board to the knight's and rook's files, capturing away from the centre is much less common. Nevertheless, pragmatic players are not disposed to reject such captures when useful. In the Sicilian Defence, for example, we very often see the move cxb3 (after, e.g., ...♗xb3 or ...♘xb3) holding up Black's queenside attack, a factor that is often of decisive importance after White plays 0-0-0. An analogous situation is in the Nimzo-Indian/Queen's Indian line that goes 1 d4 ♘f6 2 c4 e6 3 ♘c3 ♗b4 4 ♘f3 b6 5 ♗g5 h6 6 ♗h4 ♗b7 7 e3 g5 8 ♗g3 ♘e4, when ...♘xg3 is sometimes answered by fxg3, since that not only opens up the f-file, but can make it easier to counter potential advances on the kingside (on the downside, ...g4 and ...♕g5 now gains a tempo).

Doubled Pawns on the Rook's File

Finally, doubled pawns that result from captures of pieces on the rook's file (all away from the centre, obviously) are quite a fascinating topic. I discussed in SOMCS the familiar ...bxa6 pawn recapture of a bishop that has taken a knight on a6. This opens the b-file for Black and can often lead to active piece play in addition to winning the bishop-pair. The idea is found in openings such as the Benoni, Pirc, and King's Indian. One might also note the recurrent theme of ...b6 and ...♘a5 in the Sicilian Defence, usually when White has a knight on b3. The idea of ...♘a5 to set up the useful move ...♘c4, but after ♘xa5, the recapture ...bxa5 opens the b-file to good effect. Even the forward doubled a-pawn covers b4 and can often advance to create further queenside problems for White. Needless to say, doubling and isolating the a-pawns while eliminating the minority attack by ...b5-b4 looks outrageously anti-positional to traditionalists, and was hardly

considered for many years. But then forty to fifty years ago this idea burst into popularity and has remained a standard stratagem ever since. Here are some examples:

Topalov – Anand
Las Palmas 1996

1 e4 c5 2 ♘f3 d6 3 d4 cxd4 4 ♘xd4 ♘f6 5 ♘c3 a6 6 ♗e2 e6 7 0-0 ♘c6 8 ♗e3 ♗e7 9 f4

Two good examples of the basic ...♘a5 strategy occurred after 9 a4 ♕c7 10 f4 0-0 11 ♘b3 b6 12 ♗f3 ♖b8 *(D)*:

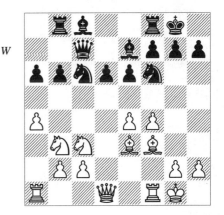

a) By transposition, the very first game that I can find with the ...♘a5 idea was Foltys-Benko, Budapest 1948, which went 13 ♔h1 ♖d8 14 ♕e1 ♘a5! (Benko himself pointed out that ...♘b4 had been the strategy in such positions) 15 ♖d1 ♘c4 16 ♗c1 b5 17 axb5 axb5 18 ♘d4 b4 19 ♘ce2 e5! 20 ♘b3 d5! 21 fxe5 ♘xe5 22 exd5 ♘xf3 23 ♖xf3 ♘xd5 and Black was better due to his bishop-pair.

b) 13 ♖f2 ♘a5! 14 ♖e2 (already White was getting shy about opening the b-file; see other notes and the next game; instead, 14 ♘xa5 bxa5 would activate Black's pieces, and even if White could reach an ending, it's not clear that he could exploit Black's optically weak pawns; sticking with the middlegame, play might go 15 ♖b1 ♖b4 16 ♕d3 ♘d7 17 b3 ♘c5 18 ♕e2 ♗b7 with pressure on e4 and ...♗f6 next) 14...♘c4 15 ♗c1 b5 (with a typical minority attack, although 15...♗b7 may be even better) 16 axb5 axb5 17 ♕d4 (17 ♕d3 ♗d7 18 ♘d4 b4 with Black having a small plus) 17...e5 18 ♕f2 b4 19 ♘d5 ♘xd5 20 exd5 ♗f6 (20...f5! would have retained the advantage) 21 fxe5 ♗xe5 with equality, Muhana-R.McLellan, corr. 1978.

9...♕c7 10 ♔h1 0-0 11 ♗f3 ♖e8

Another fairly early example saw White taking on a5: 11...♗d7 12 a4 b6 13 ♘b3 ♖ab8 14 ♖f2 ♘a5 15 ♘xa5?! bxa5 16 ♖b1 ♖b4 17 ♕d3 ♗xa4!? 18 ♘xa4 ♖xa4 19 b3 ♖a2 20 g4?! d5! 21 exd5 ♘xd5 22 ♗xd5 exd5 and Black has active pieces and kingside targets, Hennings-Unzicker, Kislovodsk 1972.

12 a4 ♗d7 13 ♕d2 ♖ab8 14 ♘b3 b6 15 g4 ♗c8 16 ♕f2 ♘a5 (D)

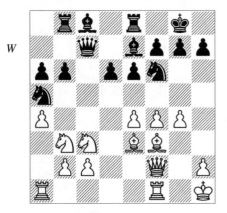

17 ♖ad1

Now standard stuff. The remarkable thing is that if you look at all the similar lines in *ECO*, you will very seldom even see White's option of ♘xa5 mentioned! It is assumed that Black has adequate play for the doubled pawns. This is a typical example of how ideas that originally look suspect are assimilated.

17...♘c4 18 ♗c1 b5 19 g5 ♘d7 20 axb5 axb5 21 ♗g2 b4 22 ♘e2 ♘c5

Black has good queenside play, so White tries to drum up something on the kingside:

23 f5 ♗f8 24 g6!? ♘xb3 25 cxb3 ♘e5 26 gxf7+ ♕xf7 27 ♘d4 exf5 28 exf5 ♗b7

Black is comfortably equal.

Here are two games in the Sicilian Accelerated Dragon Variation with the same basic idea:

Kupreichik – Kapengut
USSR 1972

1 e4 c5 2 ♘f3 ♘c6 3 d4 cxd4 4 ♘xd4 g6 5 ♘c3 ♗g7 6 ♗e3 ♘f6 7 ♗c4

The same position is arrived at with a move less after 7 ♗e2 0-0 8 f4 d6 9 ♘b3 ♕c7 10 0-0 b6, when ...♘a5 is an idea in many lines; for example, 11 ♔h1 ♗b7 12 ♗f3 ♘a5 13 ♘xa5 bxa5 14 ♕d2!? (14 ♗d4) 14...♗c6 (thinking about moves like ...♕b7 and ...a4) 15 a4 ♘d7 (D).

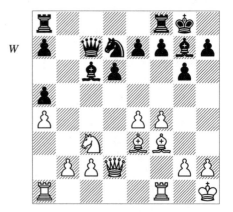

16 ♖ad1 ♖fd8 17 b3 (one idea after 17 ♗d4 is 17...e5 18 ♗e3 exf4 19 ♗xf4 ♘e5) 17...a6 18 ♘e2 ♖ac8 19 ♗d4 ♗a8 20 ♗xg7 ♔xg7 21 c4? ♘c5 22 ♘g3 ♖b8 23 ♖b1 f6 24 ♕c2 ♖b4, Breider-Silman, New York 1991. Black has taken over the dark squares and the game.

7...♕a5 8 0-0 0-0 9 ♘b3 ♕c7 10 f4 d6 11 ♗e2 b6 12 ♕d2 ♗b7 13 ♖ad1 ♘a5 14 ♘xa5 bxa5 15 ♗f3 ♖fb8?!

15...♖fd8 is more accurate, so that 16 ♗d4 can be answered by 16...e5 17 ♗e3 exf4 18 ♗xf4 ♘e8, with equality.

16 ♖f2 ♗c6 17 b3 a4 18 ♗d4 axb3 19 axb3 ♖d8

Again with the idea ...e5.

20 ♘d5 ♗xd5 21 exd5 a5 22 ♕e3 ♖e8 23 ♖a1 ♘d7 24 ♗xg7 ♔xg7 25 ♖a4 ♕c5

With White's restricted bishop and Black's occupation of the dark squares, Black should be able to handle White's intention to attack via f5.

A similar idea occurs in the King's Indian Defence, where a somewhat riskier but well-known strategy is for Black to play ...g6 and ...♘h5, leading to ♗xh5 and ...gxh5. This time the compensation consists partly of the open g-file against White's king, but also of the two bishops and removal of White's valuable defensive piece, his light-squared bishop.

Here is an example of both the ...♞a6 capture and the ...♞h5 capture in one game:

Ward – Mortensen
Copenhagen 1999

1 d4 ♞f6 2 c4 g6 3 ♞c3 ♝g7 4 e4 d6 5 f3 0-0 6 ♞ge2 c5 7 d5 e6 8 ♞g3 exd5 9 cxd5 ♞h5!?

A recent and literally eccentric idea in this position introduced by Igor Glek. Sometimes Black inserts ...a6 first, inducing a4, and that is fine, but it ruins the aesthetic effect created when Black brings the other knight to the edge of the board as well!

10 ♞xh5 gxh5 *(D)*

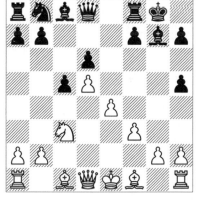

This kind of manoeuvre allowing the doubled and isolated pawns in front of one's king has become common enough that advanced players don't react much one way or another upon seeing it. The thing is to see whether the concrete lines work out for one side or another. But we forget how shocking such an idea was even to many GMs as recently as 1972, when a famous Spassky-Fischer game from the Reykjavik World Championship match went 1 d4 ♞f6 2 c4 e6 3 ♞f3 c5 4 d5 exd5 5 cxd5 d6 6 ♞c3 g6 7 ♞d2 ♞bd7 8 e4 ♝g7 9 ♝e2 0-0 10 0-0 ♜e8 11 ♛c2 ♞h5!? 12 ♝xh5 gxh5, an idea of Boleslavsky's that gained Fischer a precious point. That particular version turned out to be of marginal value, but the publicity surrounding the game inspired many other analogous ideas which then became respectable parts of mainstream theory. One such move, like the 9...♞h5!? of our main game, was a brainchild of Glek: 1 d4 ♞f6 2 c4 g6 3 ♞c3 ♝g7 4 e4 d6 5

♝e2 0-0 6 ♝g5 ♞a6 7 ♛d2 e5 8 d5 ♛e8 9 ♝f3 (or 9 ♝d1) 9...♞h5!? 10 ♝xh5 gxh5 *(D)*, as played in Petursson-Glek, Belgrade 1988 and later games.

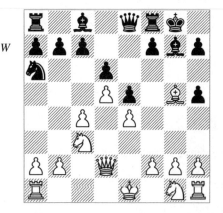

In this example, after White's light-squared bishop captures on h5, Black can play ...f5. Then after exf5 and ...♝xf5, he could justifiably expect to gain put pressure upon White's weakened light squares such as d3. In the Fischer game, White didn't allow that, but ultimately it was Black's unopposed light-squared bishop that won the game. But going back to our main game, Black doesn't even have the two bishops! So can he possibly expect real counterplay? Yet he has achieved it in practice for several reasons: White's dark squares are weak due to the move f3; Black has good development; and the ...f5 break can potentially compromise White's centre or activate more pieces. Finally, the forward doubled pawn can be useful in attacking White's kingside, perhaps in conjunction with the g-file. Whether the theoretical verdict will match the practical one remains to be seen.

11 ♝d3

Without going into the theory, 11 ♝e3 f5 also gives Black plenty of play.

11...f5 12 exf5 ♝xf5 13 0-0

13 ♝xf5 ♜xf5 14 0-0 is answered by the further flank development 14...♞a6; this is followed by ...♞c7, when we see that Black's pawns aren't the only weak ones!

13...♞a6!?

Mortensen feels that 13...♝xd3 14 ♛xd3 ♞d7 is also reasonable.

14 ♝xa6!? bxa6 *(D)*

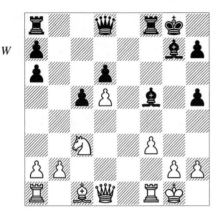

W

Someone's having a fun time with the rules here! Both of Black's knights were developed to the edge of the board, and he's now playing with two sets of isolated doubled pawns! But he has the bishop-pair, open lines, and active piece-play.

15 ♗e3 ♖b8!?

Later it was suggested that either 15...♖e8 or 15...♕h4 is more accurate, but this imprecision doesn't negate the general fact that Black has his share of the chances.

16 ♕d2 ♕f6 17 ♖ac1 ♕g6?!

At this point, 17...♖fe8 18 b3 h4! would keep up the pressure, since 19 ♗g5?! ♕g6 20 ♗xh4? ♖b4! is very strong; e.g., 21 ♗g3 ♖d4 22 ♕f2 ♖d3 23 ♘e2 ♖d2, etc.

18 b3 h4 19 ♘e2!

White aims at e6 and gains some advantage, especially when Black simplifies.

19...♗d3 20 ♘f4 ♖xf4 21 ♗xf4 ♗xf1 22 ♔xf1

Mortensen points out that 22 ♖xf1 is met by 22...c4! followed by ...c3 in several lines.

22...h3

The doubled pawn has come a long way and now loosens up White's kingside.

23 g3 ♖f8

Threatening ...♗e5.

24 ♖e1!

24 ♕e2 ♖e8 25 ♕xa6 ♗d4! intends ...♕h5 with a killing attack, as ♕d3 is met by ...♗e3.

24...♗e5 25 ♗xe5 ♖xf3+ 26 ♔g1

26 ♔e2? ♕g4 is too strong.

26...dxe5 27 ♖xe5

Correct is 27 ♕e2!, when 27...♕d3 28 ♕xd3 ♖xd3 29 ♖xe5 ♖d2 may hold, but White has the chances.

27...♖xg3+ 28 hxg3 ♕xg3+ 29 ♔h1 ♕xe5 30 d6 ♕e4+

The game is drawn, since 31 ♔h2 ♕e5+ 32 ♔xh3 ♕h5+ 33 ♔g3 ♕g6+ leaves no escape from perpetual check or win of the d-pawn.

To conclude this section, we look at a surprising acceptance of doubled pawns by Black that is combined with a positional pawn sacrifice. This idea has been taken up by several strong players. It typifies the dynamic treatment we are seeing today in apparently positional lines:

Nikolić – Piket
Wijk aan Zee 1997

1 ♘f3 ♘f6 2 g3 d5 3 ♗g2 g6 4 0-0 ♗g7 5 d4 0-0 6 c4 dxc4

Exchanging a centre pawn for rapid development.

7 ♘a3 ♘c6 8 ♘xc4 ♗e6 9 b3 a5 10 ♗b2 ♗d5

White was threatening to play 11 ♘g5 and if 11...♗d5, 12 e4.

11 ♖c1 a4 *(D)*

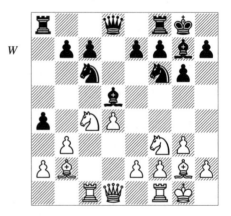

W

A typical middlegame position from this Grünfeld-like set-up. White has control of e5 and hopes for pressure down the c-file, while Black has active pieces and is attacking along the a-file.

12 bxa4

White voluntarily doubles his pawns, which gains him time to increase his queenside pressure. He is also a nontrivial pawn to the good.

12...♖a6!

Both defending c6 and preparing to double along the a-file.

13 ♘fe5 ♗xg2 14 ♔xg2 ♕a8 15 ♘xc6

Critical. There was a much earlier game Pomar-Gheorghiu, Siegen OL 1970 which continued with the slow 15 ♔g1 ♖xa4 16 a3 with equality. And 15 a5?? would be a blunder, allowing 15...b5!, which both attacks c4 and opens up the long diagonal to White's king.

15...bxc6! *(D)*

The key point. 15...♖xc6 looks natural, but it is inferior for timing reasons: 16 ♔g1 ♖a6 17 a5 and White is happily a pawn to the good.

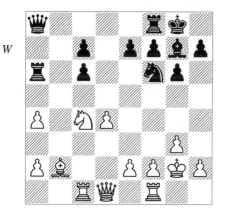

Instead of rejecting the variation on that basis, Black opts for a pragmatic solution based upon dynamic counterplay. His willingness to sacrifice a pawn and then take on these doubled and isolated pawns (along an open file) may not make sense in some abstract view of things, but the particular continuations that result show compensation in terms of either activity or structure.

16 a5

This is probably the most challenging response. Black's dynamic play is also evident after 16 ♔g1 ♖xa4 17 a3 and now:

a) Smooth and simple is 17...♘d7 18 ♘e5 ♘xe5 19 dxe5 ♖b8 20 ♖c2 e6 21 ♕d7 ♖a5 22 e3 ♗xe5 23 ♗xe5 ♖xe5 24 ♖xc6 ♖a5 25 ♖xc7 ♖f8 ½-½ Karpov-Piket, Tilburg 1996.

b) 17...♖b8 is also equal; e.g., 18 ♗a1 ♘d7 (18...♘e4 and 18...♘d5 have also been played with success) 19 ♕c2 c5 20 ♖fd1 cxd4 21 ♗xd4 ♘b6 22 ♘xb6 cxb6 23 ♗xg7 ♔xg7 24 ♖d7 ♖xa3 25 ♖xe7 ♖a7 with equality, Antunes-Atalik, Pula Echt 1997.

c) 17...♘e4 (the most ambitious) 18 ♘e5 ♗xe5 19 dxe5 ♖d8 20 ♕c2 ♖d2 21 ♕b3 c5 *(D)*.

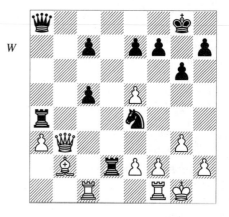

Black's pieces are terrifically active here: 22 f3 c4! 23 ♖xc4 ♕a7+ 24 ♔h1 ♘f2+ 25 ♔g2 ♖xc4 26 ♕xc4 ♘d1! (threatening ...♘e3+) 27 ♖xd1 ♖xd1 28 e6 fxe6!? (28...f6 29 ♗xf6 ♕e3!) 29 ♕xe6+ ♔f8 30 ♗e5? ♕b6 31 ♕c8+ ♔f7 (with a clear advantage) 32 ♕xc7? ♕g1+ 33 ♔h3 ♕f1+ 34 ♔g4 ♕xe2 35 ♕c3 ♖d5 0-1 Csom-Romanishin, Lippstadt 1995.

16...c5+ 17 ♔g1 ♖d8

Here we shall see that Black exerts at least enough pressure on the centre in return for the sacrificed pawn.

18 e3 cxd4 19 exd4 *(D)*

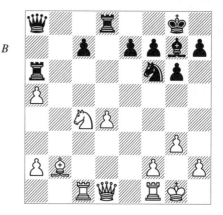

Already White's isolated d4-pawn and passive b2-bishop indicate that all is not well.

19...♘e4

Another instructive game continued 19...h5!? (harking back to our discussion of flank pawn advances that take place on the wing not yet contested; Black would like to play ...h4-h3 in some lines) 20 ♖e1 e6 21 h4 ♘g4 22 ♖c2 ♖d5! (this rook-lift looks awkward, but has ideas like ...♖f5 and ...g5, whereas ...e5 and ...c5 are always in the air) 23 ♕a1?! (White escapes the pin and intends ♖ec1, but a1 is a passive square) 23...g5!? 24 hxg5 ♖xg5 25 ♕c1 ♗h6 26 f4 ♖g6 (everything has switched to the kingside; the position is hardly clear, but White is on the defensive) 27 ♖g2 ♖c6 28 ♗a3!? h4! 29 gxh4? ♖xc4! 30 ♕xc4 ♕xg2+ 31 ♔xg2 ♘e3+ 32 ♔f3 ♘xc4 33 a6 e5! 34 dxe5 ♖xa6 35 ♗b4 ♖a4 36 ♖b1 ♖xa2 and Black was winning easily in Pingitzer-Topakian, Austrian Cht 1996.

20 ♕f3

Returning the pawn. Black was threatening ...♘g5!, winning on the spot. 20 f3 (perhaps best) can be answered by 20...♘g5 21 ♔g2 and either 21...♘e6 or 21...♗xd4!? 22 ♗xd4 ♘e6.

20...♗xd4 21 ♗xd4 ♖xd4

The problem is that now ...♕d5 is coming, and White can't challenge the file with 22 ♖fd1? due to 22...♖f6.

22 h4

A cute line given by Piket is 22 ♖c2 ♖f6 23 ♕e3 ♘xf2!! 24 ♖cxf2 (24 ♕xd4?? ♘h3#) 24...♖xc4 25 ♖xf6 exf6 26 ♖xf6 ♖c2 27 ♖f2 ♖xf2 28 ♔xf2 ♕xa5 with a large advantage.

22...♖f6 23 ♕e2 ♕a6 24 ♖c2 ♖e6 25 ♘e3 ♕xa5

Now Black is just a pawn up with more active pieces.

26 ♖b1 h5 27 ♖b8+ ♔g7 28 ♔g2 c6 29 ♖c8 ♘xg3! 30 fxg3

On 30 ♔xg3, 30...♕e5+ (or 30...♖g4+ 31 ♔h3 ♕a4!) 31 ♔g2 ♖xh4 32 ♕f3 ♕h2+ 33 ♔f1 ♖xe3! is soon decisive.

30...♖de4 31 ♖8xc6 ♖xe3 32 ♖xe6 ♕d5+ 33 ♔h2 ♕xe6 34 ♕b5 ♕g4 35 ♖g2 e5 36 a4 ♖e1 37 ♖f2 ♕e4 38 ♖g2 ♖a1 39 ♕b6 ♖xa4 40 ♖f2 ♕d5 0-1

I have necessarily simplified a complex subject by concentrating upon some types of structures that players are showing new and different attitudes towards. The broader lesson is that players are well served to be open-minded about doubled pawns, both as to the desirability of inflicting them upon the opponent and the strengths doubled pawns may exhibit. Sometimes, as a number of the most modern openings demonstrate, it's worth going to quite a lot of trouble in terms of time, space, or piece quality to create doubled pawns in the enemy camp. At other times one can happily accept doubled pawns which serve various useful functions such as covering key squares. It is important to note, as Wells does, that in such cases it need not be merely a matter of 'compensation' for doubled pawns, e.g. in the form of open files, the bishop-pair, space or whatever – they may be of superior value in and of themselves. What can be said with confidence is that modern players are taking both sides of a rapidly increasing number of positions with doubled pawns. Considerable experience with particular positions and related ones only accelerate this trend, and we should certainly expect it to continue for years to come.

2.3 The Positional Pawn Sacrifice

In a fashion similar to the phenomena of early flank attacks and exchange sacrifices, the frequency of positional pawn sacrifices has increased almost beyond belief. Kasparov talks about the new attitude towards material among younger players, a movement that he claims to be a leader of. Indeed he consistently enters into pawn sacrifices in positions where the compensation would have previously been regarded as insufficient or too abstract; and many, many leading masters (including older ones!) seem to have changed along with him. Grandmasters are finding positions of all types in which they are willing to invest a pawn for long-term compensation, sacrifices that would have seemed *too* long-term just 30-40 years ago. This is one of the most obvious trends that one will run into as one compares eras. One will also find a great increase in pawn sacrifices that lead directly to attacks, but those are readily understandable and not so much in the realm of strategy, so I won't be examining them here.

In a recent interview Spassky answers a question as to what the differences are between the chess of the 1950s, 1960s, and 1970s from that of today. He says "Nowadays the dynamic element is more important in chess – players more often sacrifice material to obtain dynamic compensation. Of course, such players were in my generation too and they existed before (for example, Alekhine), but then fewer people played like that than now." In my opinion, players in the 1950s, 1960s, and 1970s were already playing much more dynamically than in the 1900-1930 period, and it was indeed Alekhine who began to break down barriers with respect to material imbalance. Probably that movement slowed (but didn't stop) during the 1950s under the influence of Botvinnik and Smyslov; and developed more rapidly during the next few decades. But one didn't see the almost routine positional pawn sacrifice take over until recent times.

I believe that this is an extremely important subject for understanding modern chess, but it is almost impossible to illustrate sufficiently, since the instantiations are so varying and ubiquitous. I will therefore show a set of pawn sacrifices, mostly unspectacular, that caught my eye in the course of gathering material recently. While various modern openings involve early positional pawn sacrifices (e.g., the Benko Gambit, which I discuss in SOMCS), I will concentrate mainly upon middlegame positions. I will also discuss a type of opening complex that was considered rather dull but has been enlivened in modern times by long-term sacrifices. The reader is strongly encouraged to look for further examples, which he will find in abundance just by playing through random master games. If you have ChessBase, one can facilitate this task by using the search mask and the 'Material' theme key.

Assorted Examples

Many positional pawn sacrifices involve gaining the advantage of the two bishops. This game was played in the mid-1960s and seems in the style of Botvinnik. Gligorić demonstrates his faith in the bishop-pair even in a simplified position with weaknesses:

Gligorić – Matanović
Titograd 1965

1 d4 ♘f6 2 c4 e6 3 ♘c3 ♗b4 4 e3 c5 5 ♗d3 0-0 6 ♘f3 d5 7 0-0 dxc4 8 ♗xc4 ♘bd7 9 ♕e2 b6 10 d5 ♗xc3 11 dxe6 ♗a5 12 exd7 ♕xd7 *(D)*

A position once thought to be satisfactory for Black. This pretty game discouraged its further use.

13 ♖d1! ♕g4 14 h3! ♕h5 15 e4 ♗b7 16 e5! ♗xf3 17 gxf3!

The end of an original and far-seeing sequence that incorporates a dynamic view of the

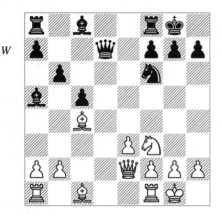

game. White accepts doubled pawns and sacrifices another one! Only this unusual-looking continuation exploits the offside position of Black's a5-bishop. Furthermore, the point of h3 becomes clear: were the queen on g4, White would be compelled to play ♕xf3 and allow ...♕xc4.

17...♖ae8 18 ♗f4

18 f4 ♕xh3 is not clear at all.

18...♕xh3 19 ♗h2! *(D)*

With 18 ♗f4, White has temporarily doomed his bishop to passivity, but White's sacrifice was for long-term advantages which become clear soon.

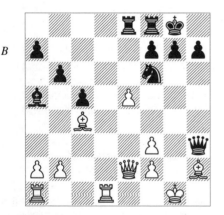

19...♔h8!?

Even a pawn down with his suspicious structure, White with the two bishops would welcome 19...g6 20 ♕f1! ♕xf1+ 21 ♔xf1 ♘h5 22 ♖d7 and his activity puts him on top; for example, 22...♘g7 23 ♖ad1 ♘e6 24 ♖xa7 ♖d8 25 ♖d6!. The text-move is a slightly inferior version of this.

20 ♕f1! ♕xf1+ 21 ♔xf1 ♘g8 22 ♖d7 f5

White is much better after 22...f6 23 e6.

23 f4 ♘e7 24 ♖ad1 ♘c6

Hoping to simplify with ...♖d8. White's h2-bishop appears bad, but it will soon appear on h4.

25 ♖1d6 ♖e7 26 ♗d5 ♖xd7 27 ♖xd7 ♘b4 28 ♗f7 g6

Still hoping to blockade the e-pawn after e6.

29 ♗g3! ♔g7 30 ♗c4+ ♔h6 31 ♗h4 1-0

A typical example of how the two bishops can be worth more than a pawn in a queenless middlegame, even though here there were additional factors for both sides.

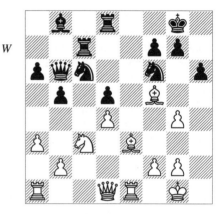

Karpov – Morović
Las Palmas (1) 1994

Here's an example I find quite remarkable. White, in an optically good position that is nevertheless hard to make progress in, sacrifices a pawn for one outpost and gradual pressure. Recovering the pawn is of little concern to him:

21 a4! b4 22 a5! ♘xa5 23 ♘a4 ♕d6 24 g3

Plenty of time.

24...♖a7 25 g5! hxg5 26 ♗xg5 ♘c6 27 ♖c1 ♘a5

Karpov gives 27...♖e7 28 ♖xe7! ♘xe7 29 ♗f4 and White wins. The queen is trapped, and 29...♕xf4 30 gxf4 ♘xf5 31 ♕d3 ♗xf4 32 ♖c6 hardly provides compensation.

28 ♖c5!

Seemingly allowing the knight back into play and foregoing ♘c5, yet both knights are better placed where they are.

28...♘c4

Not 28...♘c6?? 29 ♗f4, whereas 28...♘b7 29 ♖c2 ♘a5 30 ♘c5 ♘c4 31 ♖ce2 shows the point of the subtle ♖c5 manoeuvre.

29 b3 ♘a3 30 ♔g2!

Suddenly the h-file comes into play. Black's extra pawn was never an issue.

30...♖e7 31 ♖h1 ♖de8?

Allowing a nice finish, but 31...♖a7 32 ♖h4 is also winning for White, since ♕h1 follows.

32 ♖h8+! ♔xh8 33 ♕h1+ ♔g8 34 ♗xf6 ♕xg3+ 35 fxg3 ♖e2+ 36 ♔h3 gxf6 37 ♔g4 1-0

Short – Akopian
Madrid 1997

1 e4 e5 2 f4

There are so many modern pawn sacrifices in the openings that it's fun to turn to a traditional gambit. The King's Gambit has always had a certain following, with Nigel Short and Alexei Fedorov being the most prominent practitioners in the 1990s. The modern approach, emphasizing positional gains over all-out attack, gained currency with David Bronstein's adoption of the opening, and for the most part continues today. In this game and many others, White turns the gambit into a long-term positional pawn sacrifice.

2...exf4 3 ♘f3 d6 4 d4 g5 5 h4 g4 6 ♘g1 ♗h6 7 ♘c3 c6 8 ♘ge2 ♕f6 9 g3 fxg3 10 ♘xg3 ♗xc1 11 ♖xc1 ♕h6 *(D)*

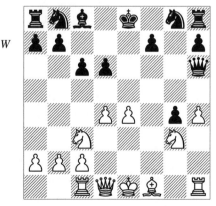

12 ♗d3!

Allowing the following simplification. In Fedorov-Kharitonov, Moscow 1995, 12 ♗g2 was met by the developing move 12...♘e7!, when White found nothing better than 13 ♕d2

♕xd2+ 14 ♔xd2 ♘d7 (compare the game: there White is better developed; here he has plenty of compensation, but Black's weaknesses are balanced by his extra pawn) 15 ♖cf1 ♘b6 16 b3 ♗e6 17 ♘ce2 d5 18 e5 0-0-0 19 h5 ♖dg8 20 ♘f4 (Bangiev suggests 20 ♖f4!? ♘d7 21 ♖hf1 ♖g5 22 ♖1f2 with a small advantage) 20...♖g5 21 ♘fe2 ♘d7 22 ♖f2 ♘f5 23 c4 ♘xg3 24 ♘xg3 (same story: Black keeps his pawn, White his positional advantages; it appears roughly equal) 24...♖f8 25 cxd5 cxd5 26 ♔e3 ♔d8 27 ♘e2 f6 28 ♘f4 ♗g8 29 ♘xd5 fxe5 30 ♖xf8+ ♘xf8 31 ♘f6 exd4+ 32 ♔xd4 ♗f7 33 ♗xb7 ♔e7 34 ♘d5+ ♔xd5 35 ♗xd5 ♘e6+ 36 ♗xe6 ♔xe6 (finally: equal pawns, equal game!) 37 ♔e4 g3 38 ♖g1 g2 39 ♔f4 ♔f6 40 ♔f3 ♖xh5 41 ♖xg2 ½-½.

12...♕e3+?!

This apparently logical move loses time and helps White reorganize. Black could consider 12...♘e7, as in the previous note.

13 ♘ce2 ♘e7 14 ♕d2! ♕xd2+ 15 ♔xd2 *(D)*

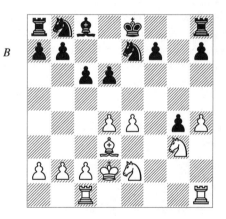

Black is still a pawn up and has managed to exchange queens, but White is happy to use his space advantage and worry about material later. Compensation in queenless middlegames is a theme of this section.

15...d5!?

Staking a claim to the centre, but it allows White a direct attack along open lines. Bangiev analyses 15...♗e6 16 c4 ♘a6 (16...c5!? looks interesting, since e5 would be a nice defensive square for a knight) 17 a3 ♘c7 18 ♖cf1 with the ideas of h5, ♖hg1 and eventual capture on g4. Again, this is a very relaxed approach that emphasizes long-term advantages. White might also want to play moves like d5 and ♘h5 or ♘d4. He certainly has enough play for a pawn.

16 ♖ce1 ♗e6

The e-file must be blocked.

17 ♘f4 0-0

Finally giving the pawn back. The obvious alternative is 17...♔d7 18 ♘xe6!? (18 ♘gh5 dxe4 19 ♘f6+) 18...fxe6 19 ♖hf1 h5 (19...♘a6 20 ♘h5) 20 c3!? (20 ♖f7 also looks simple and good) 20...♘a6 21 exd5 cxd5 22 ♖e5 (this is analysis by Bangiev); White has a big advantage.

18 exd5

18 ♘f5!? is another reasonable idea.

18...♘xd5 19 ♘xe6 fxe6 20 ♖xe6 ♘d7 21 ♘f5 ♔h8 22 ♖f1 ♖ae8 23 ♖xe8 ♖xe8 24 c4 ♘5f6 25 ♘g3

White has regained his pawn with an obvious advantage. He went on to win.

Hector – Wedberg
Skara 2002

1 e4 e5 2 f4 exf4 3 ♘f3 h6 4 d4 g5 5 ♘c3 ♗g7 6 g3 fxg3 7 hxg3 d6 8 ♗c4 ♗g4 9 ♖f1 ♕d7

Another example of compensation for a pawn with the queens off was seen after 9...♘f6 10 e5 dxe5 11 ♗xf7+! ♔f8! 12 ♗b3 exd4 13 ♕xd4 ♕xd4 14 ♘xd4 ♘bd7 in Fedorov-Almasi, Pula 2001.

10 ♕d3 ♗h5 11 ♗e3 ♘e7 12 0-0-0 ♘bc6 13 ♖d2! a6 *(D)*

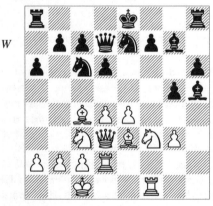

14 a3

Notkin expresses it very clearly: "This is the modern way of playing the King's Gambit. White pretends nothing has been sacrificed at all and simply improves the positions of his forces."

14...♕g4 15 ♖df2 ♖f8 16 ♕d2 ♗g6 17 ♘h2 ♕d7 18 g4!

Notkin: "White seals up the kingside. Black's extra pawn doesn't mean so much." White certainly has very active and coordinated play for the pawn.

18...f6 19 ♕e2 ♖h8? 20 ♖xf6! ♗xf6 21 ♖xf6 ♘d8 22 ♕f3 c6 23 ♗f2!

Threatening ♗g3.

23...b5 24 ♗b3 h5 25 ♗g3 hxg4 26 ♕e3 ♖h3?! 27 ♕f2! ♕a7 28 ♗xd6 g3 29 ♖f8+! ♔d7 30 ♕f6 1-0

Another example of the long-term positional pawn sacrifice, this time yielding some combination of space and activity, is the line we saw in Chapter 2, Section 1 (about flank pawns). The following game is also an illustration:

Topalov – Bareev
Dortmund BGN 2002

1 e4 c6 2 d4 d5 3 e5 ♗f5 4 ♘c3 e6 5 g4 ♗g6 6 ♘ge2 ♘e7 7 f4 c5 8 h4 h5 9 f5! exf5 10 g5 *(D)*

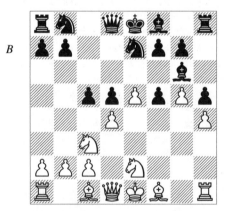

White has established a space advantage and temporarily shut out Black's g6-bishop. As Lutz points out, both ways of freeing the bishop have their disadvantages: ...f4 returns the pawn and still allows White great activity, whereas ...f6 weakens Black's kingside. Bareev takes a third path: to decimate White's centre.

10...♘ec6 11 ♗g2!

Now the players exchange all of the centre pawns. Assessing the effects of this trade is difficult, requiring a very concrete set of lines, but it turns out that White maintains his positional pressure.

11...cxd4 12 ♘xd5 ♘d7 13 ♘xd4 ♘dxe5 14 ♘b5 ♖c8 15 ♕e2

Pretty much forced thus far. Now Black gives up his dark-squared bishop in favour of rapid development:

15...♗d6!?

Another and probably better idea was to play 15...♗c5.

16 ♘xd6+ ♕xd6 17 ♗f4 0-0 18 0-0-0 ♕c5 (D)

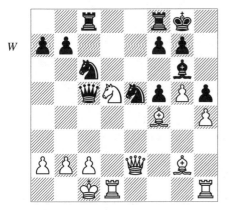

19 ♖h3!

Now it's obvious that White stands better, since his rook can both attack and defend on the queenside and all his other pieces are active.

19...♖fe8

It may well be better to try for an endgame by 19...♘g4!? 20 ♖c3 ♕f2. In that case, White's activity would still guarantee him the advantage.

20 ♖c3 ♕a5 21 ♖a3 ♕c5 22 ♖e3 ♘d4?

A mistake. Lutz suggests 22...♖e6, although 23 ♖d2! avoids all tricks, keeps Black's bishop imprisoned on g6, and leaves White with his two active bishops. Then 23...♖ce8? fails to 24 ♘c7!.

23 ♖xd4 ♕xd4 24 ♖xe5

White has won two pieces for a rook and retains the superior position. He went on to win. It's worth noting how this seemingly casual pawn sacrifice was justified despite a complete transformation of the original central pawn structure.

Another initially double-edged line is tamed by an extremely long-term sacrifice in the next example.

Moskalenko – Campos Moreno
Spain 2001

1 d4 ♘f6 2 c4 e6 3 ♘c3 ♗b4 4 e3 0-0 5 a3 ♗xc3+ 6 bxc3 c5 7 ♗d3 ♘c6 8 ♘e2 b6 9 e4 ♘e8 10 0-0 ♗a6 11 f4 f5 12 d5 ♘a5 (D)

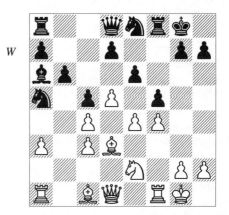

A standard Nimzo-Indian Sämisch Variation in which the progress of Black's familiar attack on c4 seems to be well ahead of White's attacking chances (which are not obvious in any case). White's bishops are passive, and his centre is in danger of falling apart.

13 e5!

This changes the nature of the game completely. White will end up a pawn down for as far into the future as one can imagine, but he establishes a bind in return.

13...♗xc4

Moskalenko gives the very rational alternative 13...d6 14 dxe6 ♕e7 (14...dxe5 15 fxe5 hits the f5-pawn) and now I think that White should try 15 g4!?, which looks a bit crazy, but determinedly pursues the light squares; e.g., 15...fxg4 16 ♘g3 ♕xe6 17 ♗e4 ♗b7 18 ♗d5 ♗xd5 19 cxd5 ♕d7 20 e6 ♕b7 21 f5 ♘f6 22 ♗g5 ♘xd5 (22...♘c4 23 ♗xf6 ♘e3 24 ♕e2 ♘xf1 25 ♖xf1 ♖xf6 26 ♘h5) 23 ♕xg4 with an excellent attack. Although not forced by any means, this illustrates how 13 e5 has changed the dynamics of the game.

14 ♗xc4 ♘xc4 15 d6 ♕c8 16 ♕d3 ♘a5 17 ♗d2!

Intending c4. White is in no hurry.

17...c4 18 ♕f3 ♕b7 19 ♕xb7 ♘xb7 20 ♗e3 *(D)*

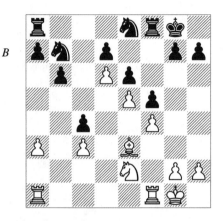

We have seen these pawn-down queenless middlegames before, both here and in SOMCS. Black's problem is securing squares for his knights. White is making progress before his opponent unravels. This is a truly long-term investment.

20...g6 21 ♖fb1 ♘g7 22 a4 ♖fc8 23 ♘d4 h6 24 g3 ♔f7 25 ♔g2 ♘a5 26 ♔f3 ♘e8 27 ♖a2 ♖c5 28 h3

Dubious, according to Moskalenko, who prefers 28 ♖b5! with the initiative.

28...♖d5 29 ♖b5 ♘g7

29...♖xb5 30 axb5 ♘g7 appears better, when White can still play for ♘c2-b4-a6 and a possible sacrifice on a5.

30 ♖ab2 ♘c6? 31 ♘xc6 dxc6 32 ♖5b4 ♔e8 33 ♖xc4 ♔d7 34 ♖cb4

White has finally regained his pawn (20 moves later!) and in spite of his opponent's weaknesses, Black has little to do versus c4-c5 or if ...c5, a4-a5.

34...♖a5 35 ♖a2 g5 36 c4 g4+ 37 hxg4 fxg4+ 38 ♔xg4 ♘f5 39 ♗f2 c5 40 ♖b5 ♖a6 41 ♖b1! ♖g8+ 42 ♔f3 h5 43 ♖h1 ♖h8 44 ♖aa1 ♔c6 45 ♔e4 1-0

The move g4 will soon follow, so there is no reason to play on.

Elianov – Turov
Kharkov 2001

1 ♘f3 ♘f6 2 c4 g6 3 ♘c3 d5 4 cxd5 ♘xd5 5 h4!?

A little flank-pawn lunacy to go along with our theme from earlier chapters.

5...♗g7 6 h5 ♘xc3 7 bxc3 ♘d7 8 e4 e5 9 ♗a3 ♘b6 10 ♗e2 ♗g4 11 h6 ♗f6 12 0-0 ♗e7 13 ♗c1 ♗f6 14 ♗a3 ♗e7 15 ♗b2!? ♗xf3 16 ♗xf3 ♕d3 *(D)*

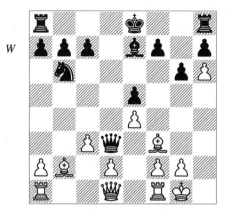

Here White's bishops are restricted and doing little, whereas Black has pressure down the d-file and the threat of ...♘c4. All this turns around in a flash when White offers a pawn.

17 ♗e2! ♕xe4

Otherwise d4 and other active moves can follow.

18 ♗f3 ♕c4

After 18...♕d3!? 19 ♗xb7 ♖d8 Wells suggests the unlikely-looking 20 ♖e1!? (or 20 ♗c6+ ♔f8), which is based upon 20...♕xd2 21 ♕xd2 ♖xd2 22 ♗c1! ♖d3 23 ♖xe5 ♔d7 24 ♗f4 ♗d6 25 ♖e3 ♖xe3 26 ♗xe3 with the bishops still a potent factor.

19 d3! ♕e6 20 c4!

Opening up the long diagonal for the b2-bishop. As with our other examples, White is not interested in the mere recovery of his pawn by ♗xb7.

20...0-0 21 ♖e1 f6 22 a4!

White restricts Black's knight, which would also be the standard technique in a normal middlegame with even pawns.

22...c6 23 a5 ♘d7 24 a6 b6 25 d4! ♖fd8?!

Probably 25...♕xc4 had to be tried, although 26 ♖c1 ♕a2 27 ♖e2 ♕xa6 28 ♖xc6 is terribly difficult for Black in view of ♕b3+ and dxe5.

26 d5

Now everything is becoming clear.

26...♕d6 27 dxc6 ♘c5

After 27...♕xd1 28 ♖axd1 ♘c5 29 c7 White wins, since 29...♖xd1 is met by 30 ♗xa8!.

28 ♗d5+!?

28 ♕xd6! ♗xd6 29 c7 is easier and presents few technical difficulties. White plays for the attack instead, and succeeds in breaking down Black's central structure.

28...♔h8 29 ♕f3 ♖f8 30 ♖e2 ♕c7 31 ♕g3 ♗d6 32 ♖ae1!? ♖ae8

32...♘xa6 33 f4! is even better.

33 f4 ♘e6 34 ♔h1 ♖f7 35 fxe5 ♗c5 36 ♖d1

White has a winning advantage.

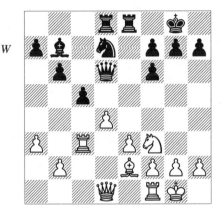

W

V. Georgiev – Aleksić
Cutro 2001

Wells draws attention to this fairly innocent-looking position. Black's doubled pawns are not yet a problem.

15 b4!

Suddenly White offers a pawn; with the immediate threat of taking on c5 Black must react.

15...cxb4

15...cxd4!? 16 ♘xd4 secures an advantage, partly due to the pawn-structure (e.g., the knight is unassailable due to the doubled f-pawns), but also because Black can't put his knight on c5.

16 axb4 ♕xb4 17 ♖c7 ♗xf3 18 ♗xf3 a5

It looks as though White has ceded a pawn and allowed his opponent powerful queenside passed pawns just for a seventh-rank rook. The surprise comes next:

19 ♕b1!

But it's not really a surprise to anyone any more that such outside passed pawns are often weak when pitted against a strong centre. One

need only study the many lines of the 8 ♖b1 Grünfeld Exchange Variation (in which Black grabs White's a-pawn) to verify this. We looked at this briefly in SOMCS.

19...♕d6

After 19...♕xb1 20 ♖xb1 ♖e6 21 ♗g4 ♖d6 22 ♖xd7 ♖8xd7 23 ♗xd7 ♖xd7 24 ♖xb6 ♔f8 25 ♖a6 ♖d5 26 ♖a7, bringing White's king to the centre will win.

20 ♖fc1 ♘b8 21 ♕b5

Black cannot improve his position.

21...g6 22 g3 ♖d7 23 ♖7c4?!

23 ♖b7! wins a pawn and then more.

23...♖dd8 24 ♔g2 ♔g7 25 ♖c7 ♖d7 26 ♖1c6! ♘xc6??

But after 26...♕b4! 27 ♕xb4 axb4 28 ♖xd7 ♘xd7 29 ♖c4! b3 30 ♗d1 b2 31 ♖b4 White will eventually win due to the better pawn-structure and bishop versus knight.

27 ♖xd7 ♘a7 28 ♖xa7 1-0

Kasparov's Pawn Sacrifices

Now I will perhaps bore you with too many examples from the king of the modern pawn sacrifice. But we'll actually be examining just a sample of the multitudinous pawn offers from the games of Kasparov, normally both positionally and tactically motivated. These are chosen from early in his career up to the present. The sacrifices very often lead to winning attacks, but they are also fundamentally strategic in nature.

Kasparov – Marjanović
Malta OL 1980

1 d4 ♘f6 2 c4 e6 3 ♘f3 b6 4 g3 ♗b7 5 ♗g2 ♗e7 6 0-0 0-0 7 d5!?

Still quite new at the time, this sacrifice invented by Polugaevsky illustrates well the long-term nature of positional compensation that can arise even when White has to give up a key central pawn and his opponent has no weaknesses.

7...exd5 8 ♘h4 c6 9 cxd5 ♘xd5 10 ♘f5 *(D)*

Kasparov notes that the idea of this pawn sacrifice is not a question of development, but of the concrete ideas of e4-e5 and ♕g4 with an attack. He adds, admitting a touch of exaggeration, that "a knight on f5 nearly always justifies a pawn sacrifice"!

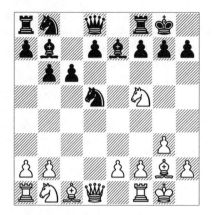

10...♘c7 11 ♘c3!

The immediate attempt to tie Black down by 11 e4 ♘e6 12 e5 allows counterplay after 12...f6!.

11...d5 12 e4

Now d5 is subjected to pressure, and White's queen can get into the act via g4.

12...♗f6

For example, 12...dxe4?! 13 ♘xe4 ♘d5 14 ♕g4 with a large advantage, according to Kasparov.

13 exd5! cxd5

13...♘xd5 14 ♘xd5 cxd5 15 ♘e3 wins the pawn back with some advantage, since ♘xd5 threatens a discovered check and also targets various points in Black's position, e.g. after ♗f4.

14 ♗f4 ♘ba6 15 ♖e1

White is content to improve his position, challenging Black to find productive moves.

15...♕d7?

15...♘c5 is better, when Kasparov gives possible continuations such as 16 ♗d6 ♖e8 17 ♖xe8+ ♘xe8 18 ♗xc5 bxc5 19 ♘xd5 ♗xd5 20 ♗xd5 ♖b8 21 ♕f3 ♖xb2 22 ♖d1. Then Black is still a pawn up, but the opposite-coloured bishops help White; e.g., 22...♕d7 23 ♗c4 ♖d2 24 ♖xd2 ♕xd2 25 ♕c6!.

16 ♗h3!

This "looks unnatural", says Kasparov, who nevertheless shows that it is the best way to a winning position. White of course threatens ♘h6+ and ♘e7+.

16...♔h8

Black cannot successfully contest the long diagonal: 16...♕c6 17 ♖c1! ♘c5 18 ♗e5! d4 19 ♘e4 ♖ae8 (19...♗xe5?? 20 ♘e7+) 20 ♘xd4, winning (the queen is trapped!).

17 ♘e4! *(D)*

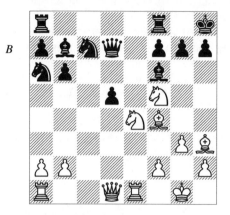

17...♗xb2?!

Natural, but losing. On the other hand, allowing the doubled pawns by 17...♘e6 18 ♘xf6 gxf6 is hopeless after 19 ♕g4 ♖g8 20 ♕h4.

18 ♘g5!

Ignoring the a1-rook. Now Black's king is attacked by too many pieces and the rest is simple.

18...♕c6

Or 18...♗xa1 19 ♕h5 h6 20 ♘xh6 and mate follows shortly.

19 ♘e7 ♕f6 20 ♘xh7! ♕d4 21 ♕h5 g6 22 ♕h4 ♗xa1 23 ♘f6+ 1-0

Kasparov – J. Přibyl
Skara Echt 1980

1 d4 ♘f6 2 c4 g6 3 ♘c3 d5 4 cxd5 ♘xd5 5 e4 ♘xc3 6 bxc3 ♗g7 7 ♘f3 b6 8 ♗b5+ c6 9 ♗c4 0-0 10 0-0 ♗a6 11 ♗xa6 ♘xa6 12 ♕a4 ♕c8 13 ♗g5 ♕b7 14 ♖fe1 e6 15 ♖ab1 c5 *(D)*

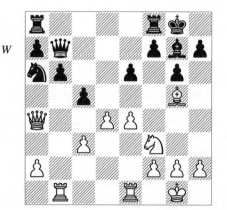

16 d5!

Giving up a pawn for the sake of a single soon-to-be-isolated passed pawn. Kasparov remarks that pawn sacrifices of this type are frequently seen in GM games today as opposed to traditional chess and even in contrast to the partially Karpov-influenced style of the 1980s. In his words, "the new generation says that initiative can be worth material and that this is more appreciated than before." He claims that he himself "contributed to the changing philosophy". Indeed, I remember being surprised time and again by Kasparov's early pawn sacrifices, which were quite unlike ones that I was used to. But these are fast-moving times, and today such a sacrifice looks almost routine and is often passed over without even an '!', so deeply have such ideas penetrated our thinking.

16...♗xc3 17 ♖ed1

No hurry.

17...exd5 18 exd5 ♗g7 19 d6 f6?!

Black wants to consolidate by bringing a rook to d8 and perhaps follow with ...♘b4-c6. A better try was 19...♘b4, although 20 d7 f6 21 ♕b3+ ♔h8 22 ♘e5! fxe5 23 d8♕ ♖axd8 24 ♖xd8 ♖xd8 25 ♗xd8 still gives White the advantage, one Kasparov considers substantial.

20 d7!! *(D)*

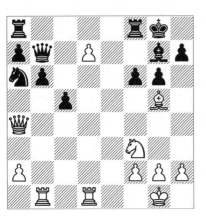

This piece sacrifice is the real justification for 16 d5!, a fact that emphasizes the need for calculation. It 'cuts the board in two', a favourite Kasparov theme.

20...fxg5

A typical line given by Kasparov is 20...♖ad8 21 ♕c4+ ♔h8 22 ♘e5 fxe5 23 ♗xd8 ♖xd8 24 ♕e6! (24 ♕f7 ♕c6!) 24...♕b8 (versus ♕e8+)

25 ♖b3 c4? 26 ♖h3 ♘c5 27 ♕xg6 h6 28 ♖g3 and White wins.

21 ♕c4+ ♔h8 22 ♘xg5

Interestingly, the same fellow making this sacrifice argues that most of Tal's combinations would be refuted today by top grandmasters "because the defensive technique is on an absolutely different level". Although some grandmasters of the time doubted its soundness, Kasparov's sacrifice was later shown to be airtight. That has proven true of most of his gifts throughout the years.

22...♗f6!

White wins after 22...♗d4? 23 ♖xd4! cxd4 24 ♕xd4+ ♔g8 25 ♘e6.

23 ♘e6 ♘c7! 24 ♘xf8 ♖xf8 25 ♖d6! *(D)*

A key move, and hard to find. White has to anticipate Black's next.

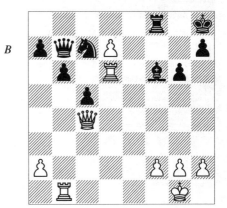

25...♗e7

After the two obvious alternatives, Kasparov shows that White can directly attack on the kingside: 25...♕b8 26 ♖bd1 ♕d8 27 ♖c6! ♗g7 28 h4! ♗d4 29 ♖xd4 cxd4 30 ♕xd4+ ♔g8 31 ♕c4+, winning; and 25...♗d8 26 h4 b5 27 ♕c3+ ♔g8 28 ♖e1! ♗xh4 29 ♕d3! ♗xf2+ 30 ♔h1 ♗xe1 31 d8♕, also winning.

26 d8♕!!

Giving up the pride of White's position, but for concrete attacking purposes, in spite of the reduced material.

26...♗xd8

Or 26...♖xd8 27 ♖xd8+ ♗xd8 28 ♖d1! (originally Kasparov gave 28 ♕f7 ♕d5 29 ♕xd5 ♘xd5 30 ♖d1) 28...♕c8 29 ♕f7 and it's all over.

27 ♕c3+ ♔g8 28 ♖d7 ♗f6 29 ♕c4+ ♔h8 30 ♕f4!

White is very much on top here.

30...♕a6??

Kasparov gives 30...♗g7 31 ♕xc7 ♕xc7 32 ♖xc7 ♗d4 33 ♖f1 a6 (33...a5 34 a4! with a large edge) 34 ♖c6! ♖f6?! 35 ♖xf6 ♗xf6 36 ♖e1! and White wins.

31 ♕h6! 1-0

Kasparov – Ivanchuk
Linares 1999

Here, White combines a tactically-based pawn sacrifice with a positionally decisive result.

1 d4 d5 2 c4 dxc4 3 ♘f3 e6 4 e3 c5 5 ♗xc4 a6 6 0-0 ♘f6 7 ♗b3 ♘c6 8 ♘c3 cxd4 9 exd4 ♗e7 10 ♖e1 0-0 11 a3 ♘a5 12 ♗c2 b5 13 d5! *(D)*

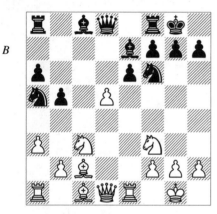

An innovation. The themes are familiar, and now second nature in similar positions; but since White isn't even threatening dxe6, this is a bit more difficult and he will have to reckon with capture of the pawn over the next few moves.

13...♘c4

The specifics are important. After 13...exd5, 14 ♕d3! is difficult to meet due to the threat of 15 ♖xe7 and 16 ♘xd5, and the simple ♗g5 can also make Black's life miserable. Less obviously, Kasparov gives 13...♘xd5 14 ♘xd5 exd5 15 ♕d3 g6 16 ♗h6 ♖e8 17 ♕c3 f6 18 ♘d4, which when you look at it utterly ties Black up. Finally, 13...♖e8 was tried later by Anand and although he lost, it may well be that Black can defend with extremely precise play. That could be debated either way.

14 ♕d3 ♖e8

Other moves are weaker; e.g., 14...♘b6 15 ♘g5.

15 a4!

Launching an attack on the wing where it's least expected. This is a patient move that emphasizes positional aspects over tactical ones. Kasparov gives a long line with the obvious 15 ♘g5?! exd5! 16 ♘xh7 g6, eventually leading to equality.

15...exd5 16 axb5 a5 17 b3 ♘d6 18 ♘d4 ♗b7 19 f3! *(D)*

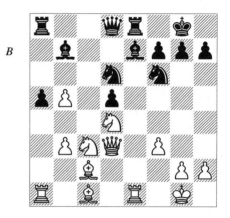

White covers e4 and thus establishes a clear positional advantage. Ivanchuk defends with great resilience, but in the end it's too much.

19...♖c8 20 ♘a4! ♗f8 21 ♗g5 g6 22 ♕d2!

Simply aiming at squares like f4 and a5.

22...♖xe1+ 23 ♖xe1 ♘de8 24 ♖e2

Tactics take precedence. White avoids the obvious 24 ♖xe8? ♕xe8 25 ♗xf6 owing to 25...♗b4 26 ♕c1 (26 ♕f2? ♗e1) 26...♗a3! 27 ♕d2 with equality.

24...♗b4 25 ♕e3 ♖c7 26 ♗d3 ♖e7 27 ♕c1 ♖xe2 28 ♗xe2 ♕e7?!

Kasparov suggests 28...♗d6!?, but this isn't going to help much.

29 ♕e3! ♕xe3+ 30 ♗xe3

White is winning, but the end of the game is marred by mutual time-pressure:

30...♘d7 31 ♘c6! ♗xc6 32 bxc6 ♘b8 33 ♗b6 ♗d6 34 ♘c3 ♗c7 35 ♗f2??

A real oversight. 35 ♗c5! d4 36 ♘d5 wins.

35...d4 36 ♘d5 1-0

Here Black's flag fell. White would still have a large advantage due to his two bishops after 36...♘xc6 37 ♗b5 ♘b4 38 ♘xb4 ♘d6 39 ♗d3 axb4 40 ♗xd4.

Kasparov – Anand
Amsterdam 1996

I already dealt with the first part of this game in SOMCS in the context of prophylactic play. Here I want to use it as another example of Kasparov's practice of the positional pawn sacrifice. The game also contains themes of two bishops and a favourite Kasparov attacking motif.

1 e4 c6 2 d4 d5 3 exd5 cxd5 4 c4 ♘f6 5 ♘c3 ♘c6 6 ♗g5 e6 7 ♘f3 ♗e7 8 c5 h6?! 9 ♗f4! ♘e4 10 ♗b5 ♘xc3 11 bxc3 ♗d7 12 0-0 0-0 13 ♖c1!

I gave an explanation of the prophylactic function of this brilliant move in SOMCS, but didn't look at the actual game.

13...♖e8

Kasparov gives this an '!', although White remains better. It avoids his main line 13...b6 14 c4!.

14 ♖e1 ♗f6 15 ♖b1

Arguably better is 15 ♗d3 b6 16 cxb6 axb6 17 ♗b1! with an attack by ♕d3 in store. This was suggested by Anand.

15...b6 16 ♗a6 ♗c8 17 ♗b5 ♗d7 18 ♗a6 ♗c8 *(D)*

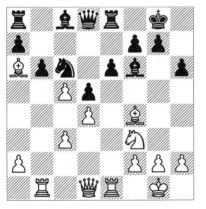

19 ♗d3!

This is the positional pawn sacrifice. It is particularly interesting because a certain degree of simplification can ensue at several junctures and therefore everything has to be deeply calculated.

19...bxc5 20 ♘e5! ♗d7?!

This move proves to be too passive because it leads to the invasion of White's rook to the 7th rank. A huge point behind the pawn sacrifice is if Black tries to simplify by 20...♘xe5!? 21 dxe5 ♗g5. Then 22 ♗xg5 ♕xg5 (22...hxg5 23 ♕h5) allows White to change direction by 23 ♗b5! with the dual threats of ♗xe8 and ♗c6!. Kasparov calls this simply winning, although Black would play on by 23...♖d8 24 ♗c6 ♗a6 25 ♗xa8 ♖xa8. He then has some chances with his bishop and pawn for the exchange, although White's pieces are more tive and he must stand better.

Best is 20...♗xe5! 21 dxe5 f5!, when 22 ♖e3 is suggested by Kasparov, but Stohl points out that 22...♕h4! 23 ♕a4 ♗d7 24 ♖h3 ♕e7 is fine. So White would have to play 22 exf6! ♕xf6, when Stohl suggests 23 ♗b5 ♗d7 24 ♗d6 intending 24...♕xc3 25 ♖c1 with more than enough for a mere pawn (two bishops with every piece being active).

21 ♖b7! *(D)*

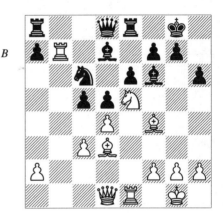

21...♗xe5

The alternative was 21...♘xe5 22 dxe5 ♗c6, when Kasparov intended 23 ♖xf7! (a necessary move, and indicative of how fragile White's compensation is) 23...♗xf7 24 exf6 ♕xf6 25 ♗e5 ♕g5 (25...♕h4 26 ♖e3) 26 f4 ♕e7 27 ♕h5+ ♔f8 28 ♕g6 with a very scary attack which will inevitably yield White some advantage.

22 dxe5 ♖b8?

To get rid of the powerful rook, but it doesn't work. Stohl shows that 22...f5 23 exf6 ♕xf6 24 ♗xh6! ♕xh6 25 ♖xd7 was the only chance, with a nice advantage for White, but no direct win.

23 ♖xb8 ♕xb8 24 ♕g4 ♔f8 25 ♖e3 *(D)*

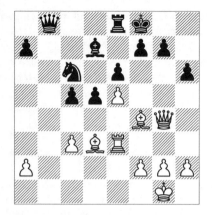

B

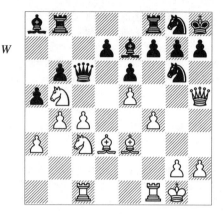

W

Very instructive: once again Kasparov has 'cut the board in two': none of Black's pieces defend the kingside! The way he now wins involves some wonderful tactics in the variations, but I'll just show the remaining moves:

25...♕d8 26 h4! ♕a5 27 ♖g3 ♚e7 28 ♕xg7 ♚d8 29 ♕xf7 ♕xc3 30 ♗b5 ♕a5 31 ♖g7?!

White is still winning after this, but much easier was 31 ♗xc6! ♗xc6 32 ♗xh6.

31...♘e7 32 ♗xd7 ♚xd7 33 ♕f6! d4 34 ♗xh6 c4 35 ♗g5 ♕c5 36 ♖xe7+! 1-0

The white king stops Black's pawns after 36...♖xe7 37 ♕xe7+ ♕xe7 38 ♗xe7 ♚xe7 39 ♚f1, but Black's cannot do the same: 39...♚f7 40 h5 ♚g7 41 f4 ♚h6 42 g4 d3 43 ♚e1 c3 44 f5 exf5 45 e6, etc.

Kasparov – Vallejo Pons
Linares 2002

1 e4 c5 2 ♘f3 e6 3 d4 cxd4 4 ♘xd4 a6 5 c4 ♘f6 6 ♘c3 ♕c7 7 a3 b6 8 ♗e3 ♗b7 9 f3 ♘c6 10 ♗e2 ♖b8 11 b4 ♗e7 12 0-0 0-0 13 ♖c1 ♘e5 14 f4 ♘g6 15 ♗d3 ♗a8 16 ♕e2 ♚h8 17 e5 ♘g8 18 ♕h5 a5 19 ♘db5 ♕c6 *(D)*

20 ♖c2!

Not 20 ♘e4?? f5.

20...axb4 21 axb4 ♗xb4 22 ♘e4

White's pawn sacrifice at first seems to be based upon kingside attacking chances only, but proves to be more subtle than that.

22...f5 23 ♘g5 ♘h6 24 ♚h1

This move protects against exchanges by ...♗c5. Although material down, White proceeds for many moves as though nothing in particular is happening. Again, the key element is lack of counterplay for the opponent, who has

few weaknesses but whose pieces, although reasonably well placed, can't do much. I am not so concerned here with the objective assessment as with Kasparov's approach. Such a seemingly cavalier attitude towards mid-to-long-term material loss is something that he and other modern players are exhibiting more and more. The justification is usually there, but not always immediately apparent.

24...♗c5 25 ♗c1 ♕c8 26 h3 ♚g8 27 ♚h2 ♘e7

White was considering g4, so Black gets ready to play ...♕e8 and in some cases a later ...g6. My computer has liked Black since move 24, and continues to do so for another 10 moves.

28 ♘d6! *(D)*

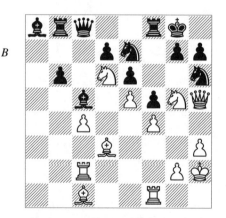

B

Finally a committal move. If Black captures, it opens up the long diagonal, so perhaps declining was best.

28...♗xd6?!

For example, 28...♕c6.

29 exd6 ♘c6

And here 29...♘g6!? deserved consideration.

30 ♗b2 ♘b4 31 ♖d2 b5!?

More Kasparov magic is seen in the line 31...♘xd3 32 ♖xd3 ♕xc4 *(D)*:

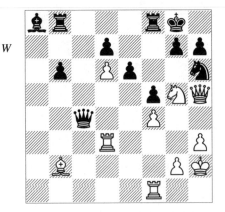

33 ♘xh7!! ♕xd3? (33...♚xh7 34 ♖g3; after 33...♕c2 34 ♖g3 ♕xb2 35 ♕xh6 White is much better) 34 ♕g6 ♖f7 35 ♘g5 and White is winning!

32 ♖c1 ♕e8

Or 32...♘xd3 33 ♖xd3 ♕e8 (33...bxc4 34 ♗xg7!) 34 ♕e2.

33 ♕e2

White's 'good' bishop is of course his bad one!

33...♘xd3 34 ♖xd3 ♘f7?!

This makes it fairly easy for White, but in any case Black's pieces are terribly placed, and he aims for opposite-coloured bishops.

35 ♖g3 ♘xg5 36 ♖xg5 ♖f7 37 ♕e5 ♕f8 38 cxb5

Next the queenside files come into play.

38...h6 39 ♖g3 ♚h7 40 ♗d4 ♗d5 41 b6 ♖f6 42 ♖cc3 ♖f7 43 ♖c7 ♗e4 44 ♖b3 ♗d5 45 ♖b5 ♗b7 46 ♖a5 ♕d8 47 ♖a7 ♗e4 48 ♕xe6! ♕h4 49 ♕xf7 ♕xf4+ 50 ♚g1 1-0

My notes here may not be precise or extensive, but the nature of this pawn sacrifice should be clear enough.

Against the highest-level opponent, we have this fairly simple example that has received a lot of publicity (*see following diagram*):

Kasparov is fighting against the Berlin Defence to the Ruy Lopez, an opening that helped Kramnik to defeat him in the BrainGames World Championship. He has conceded the two

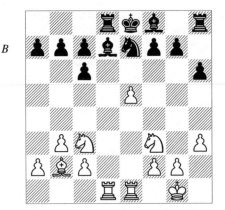

Kasparov – Kramnik
Astana 2001

bishops advantage but has space and a lead in development.

14...♘g6 15 ♘e4 ♘f4

It seems as though Black has secured all the key squares and is ready to develop. But Kasparov finds a shot:

16 e6! ♘xe6 17 ♘d4

This is another of Kasparov's pawn sacrifices in a queenless middlegame. It is also an example of opening lines for the knight-pair before Black can stabilize the position (by ...♘e6) and slowly exploit his bishop-pair advantage. I discussed that phenomenon in SOMCS.

17...c5 18 ♘f5

Now White has a tremendous bind and will quickly recover his material with a superior position. Since this well-known game has been analysed extensively elsewhere, I won't go into details:

18...♖h7 19 ♗f6 ♖c8 20 ♗xg7

According to Kasparov, 20 f4! is extremely strong.

20...♗xg7 21 ♘xg7+ ♖xg7 22 ♘f6+ ♚e7 23 ♘xd7 ♖d8 24 ♘e5 ♖xd1 25 ♖xd1 ♘f4?

Kasparov showed that 25...♘d4! was Black's last chance.

26 ♚h1 ♖g5 27 ♘g4 ♖d5 28 ♖e1+ ♚f8 29 ♘xh6 ♖d2 30 ♘e5 ♖xf2 31 ♖f5 ♚g7 32 ♘g4 ♖xg2 33 ♖xf4 ♖xc2 34 ♖f2 ♖c3 35 ♚g2 b5 36 h4 c4 37 h5 cxb3 38 axb3 ♖c5 39 h6+ ♚f8 40 ♘f6 ♖g5+ 41 ♚h1 1-0

Returning to lesser mortals, here's a typical long-term pawn sacrifice that depends upon dynamic factors, but is ultimately based upon a space advantage and an horrific bind:

Tkachev – Conquest
Ohrid ECC 2001

1 d4 ♘f6 2 c4 c5 3 d5 b5 4 ♘f3 ♗b7 5 ♕c2 bxc4 6 e4 e6 7 ♗xc4

Already a sort of pawn sacrifice, but acceptance would be dangerous.

7...exd5 8 exd5 ♗e7

Black should not capture the d-pawn by 8...♘xd5? 9 ♕b3 ♕e7+ 10 ♔d1 ♘b4 11 ♖e1 ♗e4 12 ♘c3 ♗c2+ 13 ♕xc2 ♘xc2 14 ♔xc2 and White is much better. But 8...♗xd5 9 ♗xd5 ♘xd5 is perhaps playable; then White has a choice between 10 0-0 and 10 ♗g5 f6 11 0-0 with definite but unclear compensation.

9 ♘c3 d6 10 0-0 ♘bd7 *(D)*

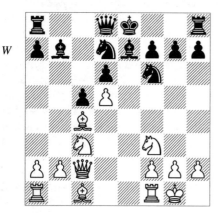

11 a4!?

An ambitious and far-seeing idea. This commits White to a long-term pawn sacrifice.

11...♘b6

11...0-0 12 a5 leaves Black very cramped.

12 ♗b5+ ♔f8 13 ♗c6! ♗xc6 14 dxc6 ♕c8

To pick up the pawn quickly. Otherwise moves like a5, ♗f4 and ♖ad1 might follow too rapidly for comfort.

15 b4!

Before this fine move it wasn't clear exactly what White would have for the pawn. Black's king was in the centre, to be sure, but his development was fine and the two passed central pawns could have become a force to be reckoned with. Now, however, b5 is threatened and White can drive away Black's pieces.

15...♕xc6

After 15...cxb4 16 ♘b5 a6 17 ♘bd4 the c-pawn will be a continual problem for Black.

16 b5 ♕b7 17 ♖d1 *(D)*

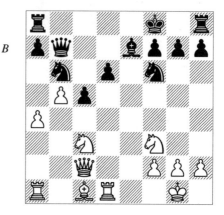

Tkachev is in no hurry, counting upon his queenside flank attack to counter any central ambitions on the part of his opponent. The text-move may be said to be a prophylactic against ...d5 and ...♘bd5 that also prepares moves like ♗f4 and ♗g5.

17...h5!?

To make room for the king by playing ...g6 and not having to worry about ♗h6+. Black may also be dreaming about ...h4 and ...♖h5, but he won't have time. Instead, 17...♘bd5?? loses to 18 ♘xd5 ♘xd5 19 ♕e4. More interesting is 17...d5 18 a5 ♘bd7 19 a6 (19 ♕a2!?) 19...♕b6 20 ♘xd5 ♘xd5 21 ♖xd5 ♘f6, which seems to win the b-pawn back, but 22 ♖e5! ♕xb5 23 ♘d4! ♕b6 24 ♘f5 gives White a substantial advantage by establishing that daunting knight on f5 that wins so many games.

18 a5 ♘c8!?

18...♘bd7 19 ♗f4 targets the d-pawn, but sacrificing it may have been as good as anything.

19 ♗g5! *(D)*

Now Black can hardly move!

19...h4!?

We see how bad things have become when Black has to return his material to activate his rook. The alternatives are depressing: 19...a6 20 b6 ♕c6 21 ♕b3! ♖b8 22 ♕c4! ♕b7, etc.; or 19...g6 20 ♕b2! hitting the dark-squared long diagonal, e.g. 20...♖h7 21 ♖e1 ♘g8 22 ♘e4! and Black's position is collapsing.

20 ♗xh4

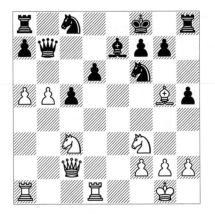

B

Now that White has his pawn back, things become pretty easy.

20...♖h5 21 ♗g3 ♔g8 22 ♖ab1 ♗f8 23 ♗h4 ♘g4

23...♗e7 24 ♖e1 ♕d7 25 ♖bd1 and Black is still tied up.

24 ♗g3 ♘f6 25 h3 d5 26 ♗e5 ♗e7 27 ♘a4!?

Or the fancy 27 ♘xd5! ♘xd5 28 ♕e4.

27...♘e4 28 a6!?

White begins a complex sequence that virtually wins by force, although 28 ♘c3 ♘xc3 29 ♕xc3 was a simple enough course.

28...♕d7 29 ♕xe4 dxe4 30 ♖xd7 exf3 31 ♗g3! c4

31...fxg2 32 ♔xg2 doesn't help.

32 ♗f4!? ♔f8 33 ♗e3! ♔e8 34 ♖c7

Preparing to sacrifice on a7 and push his pawns through.

34...♖h4

34...g6 35 ♗xa7! ♘xa7 36 ♘b6 is winning for White.

35 ♘c3

Or 35 ♗xa7!.

35...♗d8 36 ♖b7 ♗b6? 37 ♗xb6 ♘xb6

Also losing is 37...axb6 38 ♘d5.

38 ♖e1+ 1-0

There might follow 38...♔f8 39 ♖ee7 ♖f4 40 ♖xa7.

Pawn Sacrifices in Ultra-Solid Openings

In the opening, one might be inclined to think that positional pawn sacrifices will arise only out of situations that are dynamically unbalanced to begin with. Nevertheless, we are seeing them of late in the most solid and innocent of set-ups. Traditionally, English and Réti Opening lines involving ...c6 + ...d5 or ...e6 + ...d5 have been relatively immune to early pawn sacrifices by White because Black's pawn-structure is devoid of weaknesses. The next two games and notes indicate that modern players nevertheless will often sacrifice pawns in these openings, ignoring the material deficit in favour of long-term pressure. Characteristic of these pawn sacrifices is that they bring no immediate rewards.

In the next game one can see a few of many ways that White can make a positional gambit versus a black defence with ...c6, ...d5 and ...dxc4, such as we are about to see:

Dzhindzhikhashvili – Bagirov
USSR Ch (Baku) 1972

1 c4

An idea similar to those that follow arises in the popular line 1 ♘f3 d5 2 g3 c6 3 ♗g2 ♗g4. White can continue 4 c4 e6 5 0-0!?, sacrificing a pawn: 5...dxc4 6 ♘a3 (or Aseev's idea 6 ♘e5!? ♕d4 7 ♘xg4 ♕xg4 8 b3 with unclear play) 6...♗xa3 7 bxa3 ♗xf3 8 ♗xf3 b5 9 a4 a6 10 ♖b1 (10 ♗b2 ♘f6 11 ♗a3!?, to prevent castling, is another suggestion by Aseev) 10...♘e7 11 ♕c2 ♖a7 12 ♖d1 0-0 13 ♗a3 with the dark squares, two bishops, and sufficient compensation, Loginov-Aseev, St Petersburg 2002.

1...c6 2 ♘f3 d5 3 g3 ♘f6 4 ♗g2 dxc4 (D)

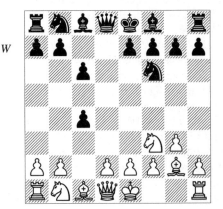

W

5 ♕c2

Another positional pawn sacrifice is 5 0-0 ♘bd7 6 ♕c2 ♘b6 7 ♘a3 ♕d5 8 ♘h4 ♕e6 9 e4 g6 10 b3! ♗g7 11 ♗b2 cxb3 12 axb3 0-0 13 d4 with unclear compensation, Salov-Beliavsky, USSR Ch (Minsk) 1987.

5...b5 *(D)*

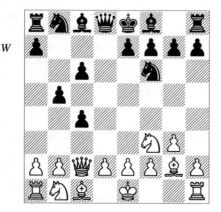

6 b3!?

This is a truly long-term positional sacrifice since Black's position has no serious weaknesses. It is based upon a few open lines and the particulars of the situation, especially the limited options that Black has as to how to develop his pieces. White will not concern himself with recovering the pawn, but try to develop a positional grip.

Equally positionally based was 6 a4 ♗b7 7 b3 cxb3 8 ♕xb3 in Salov-Anand, Linares 1993: 8...a6 9 ♗a3 ♘bd7 10 0-0 e6 11 ♗xf8 ♔xf8 12 ♖c1 with unclear compensation. The game concluded 12...♕b6 13 ♘a3 g6 14 ♕b2 ♔g7 15 ♘c4!? bxc4 16 ♕xb6 ♘xb6 17 ♖ab1 ♘fd7 18 a5 c5 19 axb6 ♖ab8 20 ♖xc4 ♖hc8 21 ♖a4 ♗xf3 22 ♗xf3 ♖xb6 23 ♖xb6 ♘xb6 24 ♖xa6 ♘c4 25 ♖a2 ♖d8 26 d3 ♘e5 27 ♔g2 c4 ½-½.

6...cxb3 7 axb3 ♗b7 8 ♗a3

This discourages ...e6, not only because Black won't be able to castle but because dark squares like c5 and d6 will be permanently weakened.

8...a6!? 9 0-0 g6 10 d4 ♗g7 11 ♘bd2 0-0 12 e4 a5 13 e5 ♘d5 14 ♘e4

White is achieving real pressure without worrying about his pawn deficit. In particular, his control of the c-file and c5 reduce Black's b7-bishop to a bystander, and the g7-bishop is also rendered ineffective.

14...b4?!

Bagirov suggests 14...♘a6.

15 ♗b2 ♘a6 16 ♖fe1 ♗b5 17 e6! f6 18 ♘c5

Now White has more than enough for the pawn.

18...♖a7

After 18...♘a6, 19 ♘b7 wins the a-pawn.

19 h4!?

Or 19 ♘d2, intending 19...♗h6 20 ♘c4. Regardless, White has a bind here.

19...♗h6 20 ♗h3?!

20 h5 is better.

20...♘c7 21 ♗g2 ♘d5 22 ♘h2!? ♗g7 23 ♘g4 ♔h8 24 ♗f3 ♘c3?! 25 ♕d2! ♖g8 26 ♗xc3 bxc3 27 ♕xc3 h5 28 ♘e3 f5 29 ♖ad1 ♘a6 30 ♘xa6 ♖xa6 31 ♘g2 a4 32 ♘f4

White has a large advantage.

Another surprising development has been the number of pawn sacrifices involving ...e6, ...d5 and ...dxc4. These take many forms; for example, a group of gambits of this type arises from an English Opening move-order:

Kosten – Goldin
Paris 1994

1 c4 e6 2 g3 d5 3 ♗g2

Now Black can combine ...c6 with ...e6 as in the Semi-Slav:

3...c6 4 ♘f3!?

4 ♕c2 is also played, but this is more ambitious.

4...dxc4 5 0-0 ♘f6

After 5...b5, 6 a4 ♗b7 7 b3! cxb3 8 ♕xb3 yields long-term compensation, according to Kosten.

6 a4 ♘a6 7 ♘a3 ♗xa3 8 ♖xa3 ♘b4 9 a5 0-0 10 b3 cxb3 11 ♕xb3

White has more than enough compensation consisting of the two bishops, control of the dark squares and a classical central advantage.

Alternatively, we see this sequence:

1 c4 e6 2 g3 d5 3 ♗g2 ♘f6 4 ♘f3 dxc4 5 0-0!?

5 ♕a4+ recovers the pawn but allows Black quick development.

5...a6 6 ♘c3 *(D)*

6...b5

This move is Black's natural response. Instead, 6...♗e7 7 b3!? cxb3 8 ♕xb3 0-0 9 d4 and

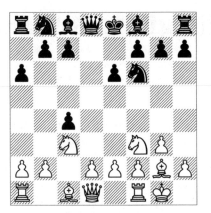

B

6...c6 7 b3 cxb3 8 ♕xb3 ♗d6 9 d4 0-0 10 e4 both give White space and active pieces. These are of course still unclear since Black is weakness-free.

7 d3! cxd3 8 ♘e5 ♖a7 9 ♗e3 c5 10 ♕xd3! ♕xd3

10...♕c7?! is weaker: 11 ♖fd1 ♗e7 12 a4! (Kuzmin-Beliavsky, Kiev 1978) with the point 12...♕xe5? 13 ♗f4.

11 ♘xd3 ♘bd7 12 a4 b4 13 ♘e4 ♘xe4 14 ♗xe4 ♗b7 15 ♗xb7 ♖xb7 16 ♖ac1

White is winning back the pawn with an advantage (Kosten's analysis).

The Catalan Opening also has a staid reputation. Yet a raft of new pawn sacrifices accompany this opening, some of which can be seen in the notes to the following game:

Kožul – Beliavsky
Bled 2001

1 d4 ♘f6 2 c4 e6 3 g3 d5 4 ♗g2 dxc4 5 ♘f3 *(D)*

B

5...♘c6

Slower but similar is 5...a6 6 0-0 ♘c6 7 e3 ♗d7 8 ♕e2 b5 9 a4 ♖b8 10 axb5 axb5 11 b3! (a nice idea, especially for a rapid game; White again aims for positional pressure based upon control of the c-file and c5) 11...cxb3 12 ♘bd2 ♗d6 13 ♗b2 0-0 14 ♘xb3 ♕e7 15 ♘e5 ♗xe5 16 dxe5 ♘d5 17 ♖fc1 ♖a8 18 ♘c5 with good play, Ki.Georgiev-Leko, Dubai rpd 2002.

6 0-0 ♖b8

In a sense this gains a tempo for Black over the ...a6 + ...b5 plan of the previous note.

7 e3 b5

Yet another variation of this patient gambit followed 7...♗d7 8 ♗d2 ♗e7 9 ♕c2 b5 10 b3! cxb3 11 axb3 ♘d5 12 ♖c1 0-0 13 ♘c3 ♘db4 14 ♕b1 f5 15 ♘e2 a5 16 h4 a4 17 ♘f4 with pressure for the pawn, Kožul-Barle, Maribor 1994.

8 ♕e2 ♗d6

White's basic strategy can also be seen after 8...♗e7 9 b3 cxb3 10 axb3 0-0 11 ♗b2 ♗b7 12 ♘e1!? (intending ♘d3, ♖c1, and ♘c5, perhaps in conjunction with e4-e5 and ♘d2-e4) 12...♘d5?! 13 ♕xb5 ♘cb4 14 ♕e2 and White had the better pieces in Kotsur-Dizdar, Dubai 2001.

9 ♖d1 0-0 10 e4 ♗e7 11 h4!?

Once more, White takes his time. He wants to establish space on the kingside and in the centre.

11...♘b4 12 ♘e1 c5!? 13 ♗f4 ♖b7 14 dxc5 ♖d7 15 ♘c3 ♗xc5 16 ♖xd7 ♗xd7 17 ♖d1 ♕b6 18 a3 ♘c6 19 e5 ♘d5 20 ♗xd5 exd5 21 ♘xd5 ♕b7 22 ♗e3 ♗xe3 23 ♕xe3

After the smoke has cleared White has regained his pawn and there is dynamic play with chances for both sides. White may be slightly better, and at any rate has the practical edge.

Can we say anything comprehensive about the multitudinous positional pawn sacrifices in this section? The ideas and strategic themes behind them are so varied as to defy systematic analysis. The only thing that is really evident to me is that top players today have fewer inhibitions than those in earlier times about remaining a pawn down, even when there is no prospect of recovery in sight. One should also note that the exchange of queens by no means guarantees an easier task for the side with the extra pawn.

2.4 Majorities and Minorities at War

In SOMCS, I posited that the old notion of the advantage of the queenside majority was losing its relevance and mentioned that modern games abound in positions where one side or the other happily accepts a pawn minority. I pointed out that "Such minorities may even constitute an advantage as late as the early stages of the endgame" and that a strong consideration is that the possession of a queenside majority tends to mean the ceding of a central majority. I now believe that the situation is more subtle than expressed there. In a sense, I underestimated the case for the pawn minority. Even in the endgame, for example, a centralized king pretty much neutralizes the advantage of a potential outside passed pawn, and in fact a central majority can often be the superior one. Ironically, however, it is not the inherent strength of White's majority that gives him chances, but the difficulty that Black has in *achieving* the queenside minority structure!

Daniel King wrote an extremely interesting article on this subject in *ChessBase Magazine*. He points out, first of all, that the most typical majority-versus-minority position, and indeed one of the most common pawn-structures arising in modern chess, is that with Black having four pawns versus White's three on the kingside and White having three pawns versus Black's two on the queenside:

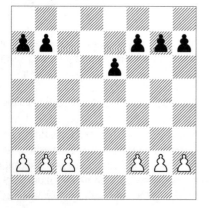

Obviously a white pawn could be on c3 or c4, black pawns on a6 or b6, or any number of variations (similarly on the kingside). But to emphasize how often this pawn-structure arises, consider these examples, several given by King and the rest by me:

Variations of the French Defence; for example:

a) 1 e4 e6 2 d4 d5 3 ♘d2 c5 4 exd5 ♕xd5 5 ♘gf3 cxd4 6 ♗c4 ♕d6 7 0-0 ♘c6 8 ♘b3 ♘f6 9 ♘bxd4.

b) 1 e4 e6 2 d4 d5 3 ♘d2 (or 3 ♘c3 ♘f6 4 ♗g5 dxe4 5 ♘xe4 ♘bd7 6 ♘f3 h6 7 ♘xf6+ ♘xf6 8 ♗h4 c5 followed by ...cxd4 or dxc5) 3...dxe4 4 ♘xe4 ♘d7 5 ♘f3 ♘gf6 6 ♘xf6+ ♘xf6 7 ♗d3 c5 8 dxc5 ♗xc5.

Variations of the Caro-Kann Defence; for example: 1 e4 c6 2 d4 d5 3 ♘c3 dxe4 4 ♘xe4 ♘d7 5 ♗c4 ♘gf6 6 ♘g5 e6 7 ♕e2 ♘b6 8 ♗d3 h6 9 ♘5f3 c5 10 dxc5 ♗xc5 (and many other lines in which Black plays the freeing move ...c5).

Variations of the English Opening; for example:

a) 1 c4 ♘f6 2 ♘c3 e6 3 e4 c5 4 e5 ♘g8 5 d4 cxd4 6 ♕xd4 ♘c6 7 ♕e4 d6 8 ♘f3 dxe5 9 ♘xe5.

b) 1 c4 c5 2 ♘f3 ♘f6 3 g3 b6 4 ♗g2 ♗b7 5 0-0 e6 6 ♘c3 ♗e7 7 d4 cxd4 8 ♕xd4 d6 9 ♖d1 a6 10 b3 ♘bd7 11 e4 ♕b8 12 ♗a3 ♘c5 13 e5 dxe5 14 ♕xe5.

Variations of the Sicilian; for example:

a) 1 e4 c5 2 c3 d5 3 exd5 ♕xd5 4 d4 ♘f6 5 ♘f3 ♗g4 6 dxc5 ♕xc5.

b) 1 e4 c5 2 ♘f3 d6 3 d4 cxd4 4 ♘xd4 ♘f6 5 ♘c3 a6 6 ♗e3 ♘g4 7 ♗c1 ♘f6 8 f3 e5 9 ♘b3 ♗e6 10 ♗e3 ♘c6 11 ♕d2 d5 12 exd5 ♘xd5 13 ♘xd5 ♕xd5 (or almost any line in which Black plays ...d5 and White plays exd5).

Variations of the Semi-Slav Defence (with a colour switch); for example:

1 d4 d5 2 c4 c6 3 ♘f3 ♘f6 4 ♘c3 e6 5 e3 ♘bd7 6 ♕c2 ♗d6 7 ♗d3 dxc4 8 ♗xc4 0-0 9 0-0 ♕e7 10 ♗d2 e5 11 dxe5 ♘xe5 (and other lines with ...dxc4, ...e5, and dxe5).

King mentions that such structures can also arise from the Queen's Indian Defence and Alekhine's Defence, and I don't doubt that there are others (the Colle Opening has a main line with dxc5 and e4, for example, after which ...dxe4 yields the structure mentioned; this is analogous with the Semi-Slav Defence).

King's comment: "There was perhaps a time when certain dogmatic thinkers would imagine that White had the advantage in such positions due to his 'queenside pawn majority', and occasionally it does occur that White succeeds in creating a dangerous passed pawn. However, first there is the middlegame to negotiate; and second, even in the endgame, in my experience, it is Black's central pawn majority which plays the more crucial role in the game." I would add that the variations above are all fully playable for Black (I will ignore the Semi-Slav case in order to refer to 'White' as having the queenside majority and 'Black' as having the queenside minority). That itself is a good sign for the minority.

However, I would add that White's play in all of these lines usually comes from piece play, and such play can be extremely effective indeed. The key thing to note is that White's advantage stems from his faster development and command in space, not from his structure. In fact, the results of many of the above opening variations is either equal or slightly better for White because Black has intentionally paid a price (said development and space) for what he feels is the *advantageous* queenside minority situation! It is also worth mentioning that White, by means of moves like ♘e5 or doubling on the e-file, will normally keep Black's majority under wraps indefinitely, so neither side has serious prospects for successful expansion.

The Effective Minority

Before moving on to my own examples, let's look at one that King supplies to illustrate the basic majority-minority theme. The following middlegame works out well for Black, although one should be aware that White normally does not allow his opponent such a free hand to advance in the centre:

Martinović – Yudasin
Krynica 1997

1 e4 c5 2 ♘f3 e6 3 c3 d5 4 exd5 ♕xd5 5 d4 ♘f6 6 ♘a3 ♘c6 7 ♘b5 ♕d8 8 dxc5

Establishing the basic structure. The subsequent exchange of queens is double-edged. If White can develop quickly and tie Black down, he will be well off. But the queen exchange also moves closer to an ending, in which Black will actually stand better in spite of the queenside majority.

8...♗xc5 9 ♕xd8+ ♔xd8 10 ♗f4 ♘e4 11 ♖d1+

It seems as though this line is satisfactory for Black because White cannot avoid simplification. Illustrating this was the game Deviatkin-Gagarin, Moscow 1996, which continued 11 ♘g5!? ♘xg5 12 ♗xg5+ f6 13 ♗f4 e5 14 ♗e3!? ♗xe3 15 fxe3 ♗e6 16 ♖d1+ ♔c8 17 c4? (this blocks off White's bishop; 17 ♗c4 ♗xc4 18 ♘d6+ ♔c7 19 ♘xc4; e.g., 19...b5 20 ♘d6 a6 21 e4) 17...♖d8 18 ♖xd8+ ♔xd8 19 ♗e2 a6 20 ♘c3 ♔c7 21 ♔f2 ♖d8 22 ♖d1 ♖xd1 23 ♘xd1 ♘a5 (or 23...f5, beginning to exploit the majority) 24 b3 ♔d6 25 ♘b2 ♘c6 26 a3 a5 27 ♗f3 ♗f5 28 ♔e1 ♗c2 29 ♗d1 ♗e4 30 ♗f3 ♗xf3! (straightening out White's pawns but establishing a space advantage that White can't match on the queenside) 31 gxf3 g5! 32 ♔e2 f5 33 ♔d3 h5 *(D)* (a massive pawn-front).

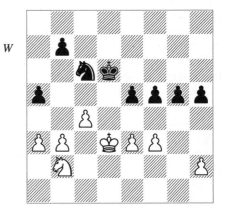

34 ♘d1 g4 35 ♔e2 e4!? (35...♔d8!, heading for e6, is *Hiarcs*'s suggestion and it's hard to argue with) 36 fxe4 fxe4 37 ♘c3 ♔e5 38 ♘a4 ♔d6 39 ♘c3 ♔e5 40 ♘a4 h4!? 41 ♘c5 ♘d8 42 b4? (42 ♔f2!) 42...axb4 43 axb4 ♘c6 44 ♘d7+

(44 ♘xb7 ♘xb4 intending ...g3 and ...♘d3) 44...♔f5 45 b5 ♘e5 46 ♘b6 g3 47 hxg3 hxg3 (or 47...h3! winning after 48 ♔f1 ♔g4) 48 c5 ♔g4 49 ♘d5 ♔h3 50 ♘f4+ ♔h2 51 ♔f1 ♘d3 52 ♘g2 ♘xc5 53 ♘e1 ♘a4 54 ♘g2 ♘c3 0-1.

11...♗e7 12 ♘bd4 ♘xd4 13 ♘xd4 ♖d8 14 ♗d3 ♘f6 15 ♗e3

Threatening ♘c6+. Instead 15 ♗e5 ♘g4! has the idea 16 ♗xg7 ♖g8.

15...♗b6 16 ♘c2 ♗xe3 17 ♘xe3 b6 18 f3 ♗b7 19 ♔f2 (D)

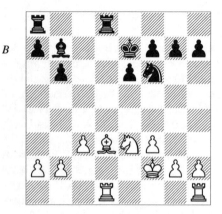

A fairly pure 4-3 versus 3-2 situation. Note that even were Black's back at g8, White would have no prospects of doing anything with his majority.

19...g6 20 ♗c4 ♘d7 21 ♗b5

21 ♖he1 ♘c5 is similar.

21...♘c5 22 ♖xd8?!

A little too eager to draw, White allows Black to gain time to take over the centre.

22...♖xd8 23 ♖d1 ♖xd1 24 ♘xd1 e5 25 b4?!

King suggests 25 ♔e3, although Black can still expand by 25...f5 and ...♔f6, ...h5, ...g5, etc.

25...♘e6 26 ♘e3 f5 27 ♗c4 ♘c7!?

27...♘f4 is more pointed, and in any case Black didn't have to retreat.

28 h4!?

To hold up the kingside, which is probably more important than creating a potential weakness.

28...♔f6 (D)

Black could also consider 28...f4! followed by ...e4.

29 a3 ♗c6 30 g3 h6 31 ♗d3 ♗d7!? 32 ♗c4 ♗e6 33 ♗xe6

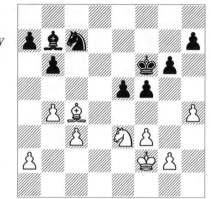

King analyses 33 ♗d3!? f4! at some length, ultimately favouring Black.

33...♔xe6 34 c4 ♘e8!? 35 g4 ♘d6 36 gxf5+ gxf5 37 c5 bxc5 38 bxc5 ♘b5 39 c6!

Since Black's own kingside pawns are weak, this is a good diversionary try. Black's knight is dominant after 39 a4 ♘d4.

39...f4 40 ♘c2?

White has defended well, but now 40 ♘c4 was still unclear, intending 40...♔d5 41 ♘a5, since 41...♔d6!? 42 ♘c4+ ♔xc6 43 ♘xe5+ should create enough trouble to draw.

40...♔d6

Now Black picks up the pawn and wins. Despite some inaccuracies, it was clear that Black held all the trumps after he started to expand in the centre.

41 ♔e2 ♔xc6 42 ♔d3 ♔d5 43 ♘b4+ ♔e6 44 ♘c6 ♔d6 45 ♘d8 ♔d5 46 h5 ♘d4 47 ♘f7 ♘xf3 48 ♘xh6 e4+ 49 ♔e2 ♔e6 50 ♘g4 ♔f5 51 h6 ♘g5 52 ♘f2 ♔g6 0-1

Development to the Rescue

Let's look at the opposite side of the coin. As noted above, White will very often stand better in these variations in spite of his queenside majority rather than because of it. This comes about because he tends to be quite a bit ahead in development by the time that Black manages to exchange his c- and d-pawns for White's d- and e-pawns. Here are typical examples of White gaining an advantage in the popular ...dxe4 variations of the French Defence, although it's worth keeping in mind that Black had opportunities to equalize.

Mikhalchishin – Chernin
Cienfuegos 1981

1 d4 e6 2 e4 d5 3 ♘c3 ♘f6 4 ♗g5 dxe4 5 ♘xe4 ♘bd7 6 ♘xf6+ ♘xf6 7 ♘f3 *(D)*

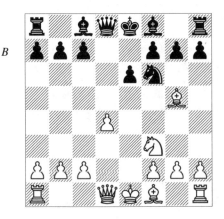

B

7...c5

A very high-level example of the same ideas was Anand-Ivanchuk, Linares 1992: 7...h6 8 ♗h4 c5 9 ♗b5+ ♗d7 10 ♗xd7+ ♕xd7 11 ♕e2 ♗e7 12 0-0-0 0-0 13 dxc5 ♕c6! 14 ♔b1 ♖fd8 (equal, according to Anand) 15 ♖he1 ♕xc5 16 ♘e5 ♖xd1+ 17 ♖xd1 ♖d8 18 ♖xd8+ ♗xd8 19 ♘d3 ♕c4 20 ♗g3 ♘d5 and we see that neither majority is having the slightest influence on the game.

8 ♗b5+ ♗d7 9 ♗xd7+ ♕xd7 10 ♕e2 cxd4

White's superior-quality piece positioning yielded a small but definite advantage in the game Leko-Korchnoi, Wijk aan Zee 2000: 10...♗e7 11 dxc5 0-0 12 ♘e5 ♕d5 13 0-0 ♗xc5 14 ♖fe1 ♘d7 15 ♘f3!, when 15...f6? 16 ♖ad1 ♕c6 17 ♕xe6+ ♕xe6 18 ♖xe6 worked out in White's favour.

11 0-0-0 ♗e7?!

According to Mikhalchishin, 11...♗c5 12 ♘xd4 ♗xd4 13 c3 is better, leading to a small edge for White, but 13...♖c8 14 ♗xf6 gxf6 15 ♕e4 e5 16 ♔b1 0-0 17 cxd4 (or 17 ♖d3 f5) 17...♖c4 is hard to crack.

12 ♖xd4 *(D)*

Now our disputed pawn-structure has arisen. As so often, White's pieces are better placed and this allows him to get a lead in development and in some cases to enforce a change in pawn-structure.

12...♕c7?

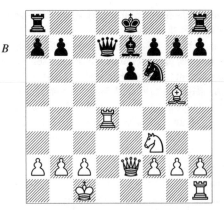

B

Mikhalchishin gives 12...♕c6 13 ♘e5 and stops there. Then 13...♕xg2! looks risky, but does hit both h1 and g5, so something like 14 ♕b5+ ♔f8 15 ♘d7+ ♔g8 16 ♖hd1 might follow with a lot of pressure but nothing clear.

13 ♕b5+!

13 ♖hd1 0-0 seems OK for Black.

13...♕c6 14 ♕xc6+ bxc6 15 ♖c4

Clearest, although 15 ♘e5 ♗c5 16 ♖c4 ♗xf2 17 ♖f1 is also advantageous.

15...c5

Black's queenside pawn structure not only includes two isolated pawns but also restricts the e7-bishop. Once past the middlegame, it is particularly debilitating to have to defend one's weak pawns with a bad bishop! But 15...♖c8 16 ♖d1 doesn't help Black either.

16 ♗xf6! gxf6 *(D)*

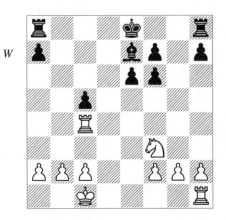

W

Now there's no mobile central majority, since ...e5 allows ♘h4 and ...f5 has no good follow-up, while encouraging a timely ♘e5.

17 ♖d1 ♖b8 18 ♖d3!

This is becoming a matter of master technique and is thus not germane. The lesson here is that in these 3-2 versus 4-3 positions, Black must be very careful not to fall too far behind in development or his structure will be irrelevant.

18...罝b4 19 ②d2 罝g8 20 g3 罝xc4 21 ②xc4 罝g4 22 f4 h5 23 查d2! h4 24 查e2 hxg3 25 hxg3 罝g6 26 罝a3 罝h6 27 查f3 罝h1 28 罝xa7 1-0

The main game below is another triumph for White, whereas the imbedded one shows Black's 4-3 majority in its best light. In none of the examples in this section did White's queenside majority play much of a role. I think that the reader will find that characteristic of most games with such a majority.

Beliavsky – Ehlvest
Erevan OL 1996

1 d4 e6 2 e4 d5 3 ②d2 dxe4 4 ②xe4 ②d7 5 ②f3 ②gf6 6 ②xf6+ ②xf6 7 ②d3 c5 8 0-0 cxd4 9 ②xd4 ②c5 *(D)*

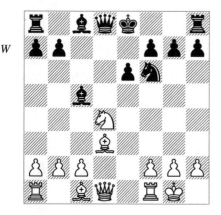

Once again we have 4-3 versus 3-2.

10 ②e3!?

A really excellent example of the majority/minority issue went 10 ②b3 ②d6! 11 豐f3 豐c7 12 h3 (12 豐h3 h5! is one of those useful ...h5 flank thrusts that we talk about in the section on flank pawns) 12...②d7 13 ②d4 ②e5!? (13...0-0 is a simple way to maintain Black's edge, in part because the threat of ...e5 eventually supported by ...f5 will be difficult to cope with) 14 ②b5 豐b8 15 罝e1 a6 16 ②c3 ②c6 17 ②e4 ②d7! 18 豐h5 豐c7 19 ②d2 g6 20 豐h6?

(20 豐h4 is better) 20...0-0-0 21 罝ab1 f5! (the majority awakens) 22 ②c3 ②c5 23 ②c4 ②g7 24 豐e3 ②d4 25 豐f4 (25 ②xe6+ ②xe6! 26 豐xe6+ 查b8 and Black is much better due to ideas like ...豐g3!, ...罝ae8, and ...②xf2+) 25...e5 *(D)*.

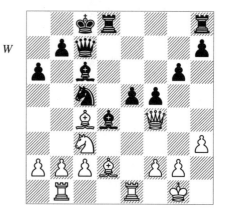

The ideal realization of Black's plans for his majority. As so often, the queenside majority hasn't got started. White now played 26 豐h6 and Chernin's suggestion of 26...b5! with the idea of ...f4 would have been extremely strong. The game was messy, although the mobility of Black's majority was ultimately of great importance: 26...查b8 27 ②e3 ②e4 (Chernin proposes 27...f4! 28 ②xd4 exd4 29 b4 dxc3 30 bxc5 f3!) 28 ②d3 ②c5 29 ②f1 ②e4 (or 29...②e6) 30 ②xe4 ②xe4 31 ②xd4 罝xd4, G.Kuzmin-Chernin, Irkutsk 1983. Black still has a nice advantage, although he went on to blunder and lose.

10...②b6 11 c3 0-0 12 罝e1 罝e8?!

Much better is 12...②d5 13 ②d2 ②xd4 14 cxd4 ②d7 with equality or 12...e5!? 13 ②b3 ②g4!?. So there isn't anything fundamentally wrong with Black's set-up.

13 ②b5 ②xe3 14 罝xe3 豐e7 15 豐f3 a6 16 ②d4 g6 17 罝ae1 罝d8 18 ②c4 *(D)*

White's pieces coordinate beautifully, and Black's natural counterplay via ...e5 and ...f5 is entirely prevented.

18...查g7 19 豐f4!?

Beliavsky calls this dubious and recommends 19 ②b3! with a large plus. But the text-move isn't bad at all.

19...②d7 20 g4!?

White counts upon his space. The attack could also have been continued by the still

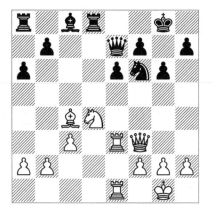

better 20 ♖g3! (threatening ♘f5+) 20...♔f8 21 ♖f3 ♔g7 22 ♕g5.

20...♖ac8 21 ♗b3 ♖c8?!

Beliavsky prefers 21...♖c5. Then White's advantage is kept to a minimum.

22 ♖e5 ♖c5?

Too late. Beliavsky suggests 22...♕d6!.

23 ♘f5+! gxf5 24 ♖xc5 ♕xc5 25 ♕g5+ ♔f8 26 ♕xf6

White's attack is winning.

26...♔g8

Immediate disaster follows 26...fxg4?? 27 ♖e5 ♕d6 28 ♖f5.

27 gxf5 ♕xf5 28 ♕xf5 exf5 29 ♖xe8+ ♗xe8

With Black's weak pawns all on the wrong colour, White has it fairly easy.

30 ♗d5 b6 31 f4!? ♔f8 32 ♔f2 ♔e7 33 ♔e3 a5 34 ♔d4 ♔d6 35 b3 f6 36 a3 h6 37 c4 ♗h5 38 b4 axb4 39 axb4 ♗d1 40 ♗g2 ♗a4 41 ♗f1 ♗e8 42 ♗d3 ♗g6!

A win by diversion results from 42...♗d7 43 ♔e3 ♔e7 44 ♗c2 ♗c8 45 ♔f2 ♔f7 46 ♔g3 ♔g6 47 c5. This is analysis by Beliavsky.

43 ♗c2 ♔c6 44 ♗a4+ ♔d6 45 c5+ bxc5+ 46 bxc5+ ♔c7 47 ♗b3 ♗h5 48 ♗c2 ♗g6 49 ♔c3! ♔c6 50 ♔b4 ♔c7 51 h3! ♔c6 52 ♗b3 ♔c7 53 ♗e6 ♔c6 54 ♔c4 ♔c7 55 ♔d5 ♗h5 56 ♗xf5 ♗f7+ 57 ♔d4 ♔c6 58 ♗e4+ ♔c7 59 ♔e3 ♗e6 60 ♗g2 ♗f7 61 ♔f2 ♗g6 62 ♔g3 ♔d7 63 ♗d5 ♔c7 64 ♔g4 ♔d7 65 ♔h4 ♔c7 66 ♗f3 ♗f7 67 ♗h5 ♗c4 68 ♗g6 ♗e2 69 ♗f5 ♔c6 70 ♗g4 ♗d3 71 ♔h5 ♔xc5 72 ♔xh6 ♔d4 73 ♗d7! ♔e4 74 f5 ♔e5 75 h4 ♔d6 76 ♗e6 ♔e7 77 ♔g7 ♗e2 78 ♗f7 1-0

This has been a relatively short section in which I have really only emphasized two different ideas:

a) The queenside minority and central majority is equal or superior to the queenside majority in most middlegames.

b) The side with the queenside majority tends to gain a lead in development while that structure is being established.

The relative importance of these two factors will tend to establish who gets the advantage.

3 The Pieces in Action

3.1 An Edgy Day and Sleepless Knight

The knight is in many ways the most mysterious piece. We can all sympathize with the beginner's first reaction: why can't it just move along linear files and diagonals like the other pieces? Even today, its nature is controversial; grandmasters, for example, seem to be of two minds about its strengths and weaknesses. Just when the bishop appears to have triumphed over its counterpart – and the phrase 'a bad bishop is better than a good knight' has often been heard of late – the knight shows surprising strength in a position from which it has no traditional advantages. And lengthy, time-consuming knight manoeuvres that never seem to end can result in the most amazing transformation of the game. I will dub these heroic wanderers 'sleepless knights', in honour of the fact that they never seem able to find rest at any particular spot. Their one-horse expeditions can end in absurd ruin or in triumph, but in either case do not always lend themselves to rational analysis. See the end of this section for entertaining and hopefully instructive examples.

In SOMCS I talked at considerable length about the degree to which masters have become more pragmatic in their treatment of knights. Most noticeably, modern players increasingly place and keep their knights on the edge of the board in defiance of the precept that they are poorly placed there ('knights on the rim are grim'). Of course, very few standard openings are dominated by such knight placements; but almost all of them include multiple instances in which the knights are best situated on the periphery of the board. Since dispatching one's knights in such a manner is so often a successful strategy, one must question whether the general rule against perimeter knights can get in the way of correct play. Rather than carry around a prejudice that doesn't have validity in many important types of positions, I have suggested that players are much better off assessing the situation on a case-by-case basis and using their experience, analysis and intuition to help them make decisions. In fact, this is what the great majority of masters do. Such a practical and fine-tuned approach contrasts with the 'rule and exception' model, which would be artificial and limiting in terms of understanding what's actually happening on the board.

Eccentric Knights in Double e-Pawn Openings

One criticism that was levelled at this idea was that the rule against knights on the edge applied to the types of positions, mostly double e-pawn, that were being played in the era when the rule was formed. Thus the idea that an attachment to the abstract principle limited the players of that age is unfair. One good answer to this is that if players today are less inhibited about placing knights on the rim they will almost by definition find and be willing to enter more positions of that type. But beyond that, one might legitimately ask whether the knight-on-the-edge rule *was* formed due to an old insight relating to double e-pawn openings. This doesn't seem likely; in fact the opposite seems to be true. In some of the best-established Open Games, knights go to and often stay on the edge of the board, and they did so in previous eras as well.

For example, we have the main line of the Two Knights Opening: 1 e4 e5 2 ♘f3 ♘c6 3 ♗c4 ♘f6 4 ♘g5 d5 5 exd5 ♘a5 6 ♗b5+ c6 7 dxc6 bxc6. Or what eventually became the main line of the Ruy Lopez, Chigorin's Defence with 1 e4 e5 2 ♘f3 ♘c6 3 ♗b5 a6 4 ♗a4 ♘f6 5 0-0 b5 6 ♗b3 ♗e7 7 ♖e1 0-0 8 c3 d6 9 h3 ♘a5 10 ♗c2 c5, etc. In the King's Gambit, we see the line 1 e4 e5 2 f4 exf4 3 ♘f3 ♘f6 4 e5 ♘h5 and a great number of other positions arising after the moves ...exf4, ...g5-g4, and now ...♘h5. The Evans Gambit includes various examples; e.g., 1 e4 e5 2 ♘f3 ♘c6 3 ♗c4 ♗c5 4 b4 ♗xb4 5 c3, and now 5...♗e7 6 d4 ♘a5, or 5...♗c5 6 0-0 d6 7 d4 exd4 8 cxd4 ♗b6 9 d5 ♘a5 10 ♗b2 f6 11 ♗d3 (and several other Evans positions). White too plays a variety of such moves in standard e-pawn openings; e.g., 1 e4 e5 2 ♘f3 ♘c6 3 ♗b5 a6 and now 4 ♗xc6 dxc6 5 0-0 ♕d6 6 ♘a3 or 4 ♗a4 ♘f6 5 0-0 b5 6 ♗b3 ♗c5 7 a4 ♖b8 8 c3 d6 9 d4 ♗b6 10 ♘a3. On the other side of the board, the move ♘h4 is a good one in the early middlegame of a great number of double e-pawn openings. The move appears in the context of playing for ♘f5, but often with the simultaneous goal of f4. Likewise with Black's use of ...♘h5. Indeed it could be argued that given the early predominance of 1 e4 e5 openings, warnings about knights on the rim stemmed more from a philosophical belief than what would have been best in actual practice. One possible influence was that such knight moves seemed almost forbidden in most 1 d4 d5 positions that they played at the time. More importantly, masters knew that knights on the edge were a definite disadvantage in endings. As noted elsewhere, this sort of generalization from endings to the middlegame has been a problem throughout the historical development of theory. In addition to the above influences, a very powerful factor was probably the too-inflexible belief in centralization that held sway for so many years. As a whole, then, abstract considerations appear to have become more powerful than the reality.

Today, while 1 e4 e5 has greatly declined in relative popularity, standard structures of all types lend themselves to support of knights on the edge of the board, and an impressive number of previously frowned-upon knight sallies have become respectable. This to some extent flies in the face of the principle of centralization, so dear to writers through the years. That principle deserves respect, of course, but not rigid adherence, and today's masters don't seem to fret over any hypothetical break with principle when breaching it. Even if a knight is well-placed towards the centre of the board 90% of the time in a particular pawn-structure, players are open to situations in which the best way to defend or make progress is to re-deploy to the periphery.

Statistics are not terribly meaningful with so many qualitative variables, but perhaps they have some limited value. We can look at all the cases in which white knights remained on h3, h4, a3, or a4 for 6 or more full moves (i.e., they were left there for more than temporary purposes), and then include the analogous positions for Black (knights on h6, h5, a6, a5). Going only up to move 30 (to minimize anomalies and endings), we find that the 20 top players from 1985-2002 moved to and *kept* their knights on the border in 17% of their games. In the period from 1901-1935, they did so in 11.5% of their games. But as suggested above, this latter figure goes down to well below 10% when one looks at positions arising from openings other than 1 e4 e5. Such numbers are naturally of limited significance, particularly since they ignore the range of positions in which these knight moves occurred; that has greatly expanded in modern times. But even ignoring qualitative issues these figures reflect a growing contemporary trend.

Knight Decentralization in Contemporary Play

Examples of knights effectively placed on the rim are strewn throughout the book before you (in the chapter on development, for example) and I have often pointed them out explicitly. With that in mind, I'll present a number of further examples, mostly but not all in specialized situations. That knight moves to the perimeter tend to be somewhat reactive in character is shown by the fact that the ones most familiar to us are played by Black. Using the same criteria as above for the 1985-2002 era, we find that about 65% of such edge placements are by Black. The reasons are not difficult to see. White more often establishes a specific pawn-structure with more space than Black does, and it is natural for Black to avoid the tempo-gaining advance of a large centre by developing to the side. In addition, one finds that with less space it is easier to run into the problem of one's pieces getting in each other's way. By developing knights to the edge of the board, one leaves paths free for the bishops' development. And finally, such knights won't block freeing pawn advances. Thus we often see the move ...♘a6 associated with breaking down a broad white centre, as in many variations of the King's Indian, Grünfeld, Pirc, Dutch, Slav, and others. In the Sicilian Defence we saw the decentralizing ...♘a5 in the Chapter 2 section on doubled pawns, the point being to drive back White's pieces by ...♘c4 and/or to clear the way for freeing moves like ...e5 and ...d5. The move ...♘h5 can also be a reaction to the opponent's space advantage. In the same chapter we saw some nice examples of ...♘h5 and allowing White to capture on h5 with either the bishop or knight, creating doubled pawns. This both increased Black's piece activity and allowed for ...f5 to attack White's centre. Probably the most extreme case of this, played while Black is completely undeveloped, short of space, and with no pressure whatsoever against White's centre, was seen in the variation 1 d4 ♘f6 2 c4 g6 3 ♘c3 ♗g7 4 e4 d6 5 f3 0-0 6 ♘ge2 c5 7 d5 e6 8 ♘g3 exd5 9 cxd5 ♘h5!? 10 ♘xh5 gxh5. Refer to that section for details.

There follows a tiny subset of the many other modern occurrences of knights on the rim. In my book on the Benoni, for example, I analysed a line similar to those above, although this time the knight is happy to stay on the edge for a while:

Zaichik – Romanishin
Tbilisi 1988

1 d4 ♘f6 2 c4 c5 3 d5 e6 4 ♘c3 exd5 5 cxd5 d6 6 ♘f3 g6 7 e4 ♗g7 8 h3 0-0 9 ♗d3 ♘h5!? (D)

This move is more or less absurd by classical standards, not only drawing a knight away from the central action, but doing so before Black's

pieces are developed. But from its post on h5 the knight:

a) performs the simple prophylactic function of preventing ♗f4,

b) opens up the path of Black's g7-bishop,

c) allows for ...f5, and

d) provides a handy path for the queen, which can actually go to h4 with effect if White's f3-knight strays to the queenside as it normally would like to do.

One might want to take special note of function 'b'. It is characteristic of many positions in chess that bishops, however strong in principle, exert little influence due to a knight that blocks them. The interesting question then arises of where that knight might move to avoid that problem. Instead of crowding the centre with more pieces or perhaps blocking another piece such as a rook, players are increasingly putting knights on the rim even if it means temporarily diminishing their influence. Such knights can either remain there to restrict enemy pieces or they can return to the centre after the disposition of its comrades becomes clarified. This pattern doesn't appear in all games with knights on the rim, of course, but it is worth keeping in mind when looking at examples throughout the book.

10 0-0

The move g4 would gain time, but not surprisingly it turns out that White has trouble keeping his kingside together. One line that shows the nature of Black's provocation is 10 ♗g5 ♗f6 11 ♗e3 ♘d7 12 g4?! ♘g7 13 g5 ♗e7 14 h4, Antwerpen-Hasselt, corres 1991. Here Black has replaced his fianchettoed bishop with a fianchettoed knight! As it turns out, since

White has exposed his kingside, that knight comes in very handy after 14...f5! intending ...fxe4 and ...♘f5.

10...♘d7 11 ♗g5

11 ♖e1 ♘e5 12 ♗e2 ♘xf3+ 13 ♗xf3 ♕h4 14 ♗xh5 gxh5 should look familiar inasmuch as it resembles the ...♘h5 and ♗xh5 or ♘xh5 doubled pawns lines that we examined in Chapter 2. Black has two bishops and activity in return for his several weaknesses.

11...♗f6 12 ♗h6

Or 12 ♗xf6 ♕xf6 with equality; once more the knight comes in handy, threatening to go to f4 in many lines.

12...♖e8!? 13 ♕d2 a6 14 g4 ♘g7

Again the fianchettoed knight isn't such a bad piece. Pretty soon White will be happy to exchange it off!

15 a4 ♕c7!? 16 ♔g2 c4 17 ♗c2 ♖b8 18 ♘d4 ♘c5 19 g5 ♕d7! 20 ♖h1 ♗d8 21 ♗xg7 ♔xg7 22 f4 ♗a5 23 ♖ae1 ♔g8 24 ♕d1!?

This has been criticized and 24 f5 recommended, but 24...♘xa4! (threatening ...♘xb2) is strong: 25 ♖a1 ♗xc3 26 bxc3 ♘c5 27 ♕f4 ♕e7 with advantage.

24...♕d8! 25 h4 ♕b6

Black's counterplay has come very quickly and White has trouble defending; for example, 26 ♕c1 ♘d3 27 ♗xd3 ♕xd4 28 ♗b1 ♗g4! and the bishop-pair is getting extremely annoying. Naturally this is just one game, and putting a knight at h5 has its disadvantages as well as advantages. From the notes, however, one can see both the logic and pragmatic value such a move can have.

It might be fun to revive a discussion begun in SOMCS about a variation that pits White's space advantage against Black's piece pressure, and particularly a border patrol knight on a5.

Burmakin – Morozevich
Omsk/Perm 1998

1 d4 ♘f6 2 ♘f3 g6 3 c4 ♗g7 4 g3 0-0 5 ♗g2 d6 6 0-0 ♘c6 7 ♘c3 a6 8 d5 ♘a5 9 ♘d2 c5 10 ♕c2 ♖b8 11 b3 b5 12 ♗b2 *(D)*

This is an old and established main line position; I quoted two examples played from it in SOMCS. The whole variation is a superb illustration of the usefulness of an offside knight,

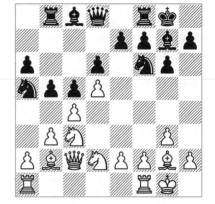

B

in this case one that is apparently stranded on a5. In fact, the knight has to justify itself there because no acceptable retreat exists, b7 being a truly awful square. Now the lines 12...e6, 12...e5, 12...♗h6 (to exert pressure against c4), and 12...bxc4 13 bxc4 ♗h6 have been played and analysed for years. Janjgava's 2003 book *King's Indian & Grünfeld: Fianchetto Lines* covers those moves in great depth, and briefly discusses 12...♖e8, 12...♘d7, and 12...♗f5 as well. But there's no mention at all of the next move:

12...h5!?

What's this? Black's game has been based upon queenside action, and now he pushes a flank pawn on the other side of the board? What's more, in contrast to 12...e6 or 12...e5, the move doesn't even establish a presence in the centre. At first this seems incomprehensible, but there is logic to it based upon our eccentric hero on a5. Since White's pieces are concerned with defending the queenside, they are at least partially immobilized by that knight. Black can therefore take the time to attack by, e.g., ...h4 and in many cases ...e5, ...♘h5 and ...f5. The f6-knight can also go to g4 with increased effect in certain lines. It's extraordinary that after so many games from the position after 12 ♗b2 (over 1600 in my largest database), chess-players can find an entirely new and perfectly legitimate middlegame strategy. Perhaps less surprising is the fact that 12...h5 is a flank pawn attack, one of the characteristic marks of contemporary chess.

In response to Black's advance on the other wing, White logically takes the opportunity to neutralize Black's standard exchange sacrifice involving ...bxc4 and ...罝xb2 by moving his rook off the a1-h8 diagonal:

13 罝ab1

The alternatives show what Black's up to:

a) 13 e4?! e5 14 ♘d1 h4 15 ♗c3 ♘h5 16 ♕d3 f5 was better for Black in Galicek-Reutsky, Olomouc 2002.

b) 13 罝ae1 has been tested recently and hasn't been particularly effective after 13...h4, and now: 14 ♘ce4?! ♘xe4 15 ♗xg7 ♘xd2 with the advantage; 14 ♘d1 hxg3 15 hxg3 e5 16 ♗c3 ♘g4!, Torbin-Smirnov, Kazan 2001; or 14 e4 e5 15 ♘e2 h3 16 ♗h1 ♘g4 17 ♘c1 ♗h6 18 f4 bxc4 19 ♘xc4 ♘xc4 20 ♕xc4 罝b4 with a small edge to Black, Navrotescu-Ardelean, Val Thorens 2001.

c) White has also tried 13 h3 bxc4 (Rogozenko thinks that 13...e5 is also satisfactory) 14 bxc4 e5 15 罝ab1 (Rogozenko-Magain, Istanbul 2000) and now Rogozenko wants to use that pawn again: 15...h4! 16 g4 ♘h7! intending ...f5, when I definitely prefer Black's chances.

13...♗f5!

This move prevents White's logical simplification by ♘ce4. It loses a tempo, but the tempo is one that limits White's own possibilities by forcing a pawn to e4. In fact, Black has done pretty miserably in games where he neglected this finesse.

14 e4

Much worse is 14 ♘ce4?! bxc4 15 ♘xf6+ (15 bxc4 ♘xe4 16 ♘xe4 罝xb2 17 罝xb2 ♗xb2 18 ♕xb2 ♘xc4) 15...♗xf6 16 e4 cxb3 and Black wins a pawn for little if any compensation.

14...♗d7 15 ♘d1!

An excellent reorganization that not only prepares ♘e3 and f4, but frees the b2-bishop to make useful moves like ♗c3. So Black needs to get his play underway.

15...e5 16 dxe6

Trying to undercut the attack referred to in the note to Black's 12th. This is the normal response to ...e5 in the main lines; the trade-off is that it cedes White's advantage in the centre. In another instructive game with 13 罝ab1 ♗f5!, Black achieved excellent play at this point after 16 f4 exf4 17 gxf4 bxc4 18 ♘xc4 ♘xc4 19 bxc4 罝xb2!? (19...罝e8 is safer, but the exchange sacrifice looks effective) 20 罝xb2 ♘g4 21 ♗f3 ♗d4+ 22 ♔h1 ♕h4!? (22...♗xb2! should be

quite good in view of 23 ♕xb2 ♕h4) 23 ♗xg4 ♗xg4 24 罝b3 ♗h3 with at least enough play for the material, N.Pert-Mason, British Ch (Scarborough) 1999.

16...♗xe6 17 f4 ♘c6!

The offside knight has done its work. Now we have a typical backward-pawn situation in which Black has activity as compensation.

18 a3!?

To stop ...♘b4, but it creates weaknesses.

18...♘d4

18...♘g4!? 19 ♗xg7 ♔xg7 threatens ...♘d4 and looks roughly equal.

19 ♕d3 bxc4 20 bxc4 (D)

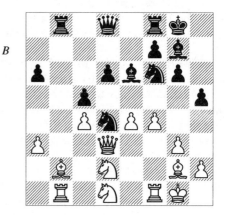

20...h4!

A full eight moves after 12...h5! This advance was always in the air, however. One might want to compare this with the more direct examples in the section on flank pawn attacks in Chapter 2.

21 ♘c3

Perhaps 21 f5, but that weakens the dark squares so that capturing on d4 will be increasingly unattractive.

21...h3!

Another point of ...h5-h4: to secure the g4-square.

22 ♗f3 ♘g4 23 ♗a1 ♕a5 24 罝xb8 罝xb8 25 ♘e2 ♘xf3+ 26 ♘xf3

In similar positions Kasparov has called the h3-pawn equivalent to a piece!

26...♗xc4! 27 ♕xc4 ♕xa3

Both attacking the a1-bishop and threatening ...♕e3+.

28 ♕c1

White has no defence; for example, 28 ♘g5 ♕e3+ 29 ♔h1 d5! 30 ♕xd5 罝f8, and White is curiously helpless against the threats of ...♕xe2 and ...♘f2+.

28...♕d3 29 ♘c3?

After 29 ♕d2 ♕xd2 30 ♘xd2 ♗xa1 31 ♖xa1, 31...♖b2 does more than win back the piece with an extra two pawns; it decimates the kingside, assisted of course by that h3-pawn.

29...♗d4+ 30 ♔h1 ♗xc3 31 ♗xc3 ♕e2 0-1

The increasingly popular Chigorin Defence to the Queen's Gambit is fertile territory for original handling of the knights, and for knights whose home seems to be on the perimeter. Witness this remarkable (and yet in some ways typical) knights-on-the-rim struggle versus the centralized bishop-pair:

Z. Szabo – Dobos
Budapest 1994

1 d4 d5 2 c4 ♘c6 3 ♘c3 ♘f6 4 ♘f3 dxc4 5 e4 ♗g4 6 ♗e3 e6 7 ♗xc4 ♗b4 8 ♕d3 0-0 9 a3 ♗xc3+ 10 bxc3 ♗xf3 11 gxf3 ♘h5! 12 ♕d2 ♘a5! *(D)*

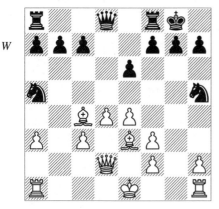

A two-knights-versus-two-bishops position has arisen with both knights on the rim. The move ...♘h5 both eyes f4 (perhaps after ...♕h4) and prepares to open lines after ...f5. The move ...♘a5 symmetrically prepares ...c5, after which the knight can exert pressure on the queenside.

The amazing thing about this example is that *neither* knight ever moves again, and yet Black gets a clear advantage!

13 ♗a2 c5 14 ♖b1

The pluses of White's position are impressive: two active bishops, two open files, and a large centre. Black has to force concessions quickly or he will be overrun.

14...♕f6!

Hitting f3 and clearing the back rank.

15 f4 ♖fd8 16 ♖g1

A good decision. 16 e5? ♕g6 hems in the e3-bishop and weakens White's light squares. 16 f5?! exf5! 17 ♗g5 ♕g6 18 ♗xd8 ♖xd8 gives Black terrific play. 16 f3 anticipates ...♕g6, but 16...cxd4 17 cxd4 ♘c6 favours Black.

16...♕h4 *(D)*

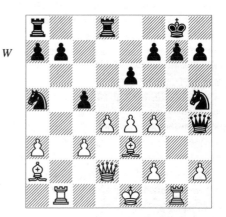

17 ♖g5?!

17 ♕d1! cxd4 18 cxd4 ♘c6! 19 ♖xb7 ♕xh2 20 ♔f1! (20 ♖f1? ♘xf4) 20...♘f6 (20...♕h3+ 21 ♔e1 ♕h2 repeats) leaves White with more problems than Black; e.g., 21 f5?! (21 ♖b5 g6 22 ♗b1 ♘xd4! 23 ♗xd4 ♖ac8; 21 d5 exd5 22 ♗xd5 ♘xd5 23 exd5 ♕h3+ 24 ♔e1 g6) 21...♕h3+ 22 ♔e1 ♘e5 23 fxe5 ♘xe4! 24 exf7+? ♔f8.

17...b6 18 ♔e2

Bronznik analyses 18 ♕d1 g6 19 ♕f3 c4! 20 ♖g2 f5! and Black's other central break comes into play.

18...♖ac8 19 d5 c4! 20 ♖bg1 g6?!

Black is undoubtedly winning, but according to Bronznik more accurate was 20...exd5! 21 exd5 g6.

21 ♖1g4?

Black's last move allowed 21 d6, which isn't exactly inspiring after 21...♘b3 22 ♗xb3 cxb3 23 e5!? ♖c4, but at least hangs on for a while.

21...♕h3 22 f5?

But also losing was 22 ♖g1 h6 23 ♖5g2 exd5 24 exd5 ♘f6.

22...exf5 23 exf5 h6 24 fxg6 hxg5 25 ♖xg5 0-1

After 25...f6 26 ♖g1 ♕xh2, Black is a rook up with the attack. Both 'out of position' knights have been happily sitting there for 13 moves! Quite a game.

When computers can play as undogmatically as in the next game, we humans are in trouble:

Leko – Fritz6
Frankfurt rpd 1999

1 e4 e5 2 ♘f3 ♘c6 3 ♗b5 a6 4 ♗a4 ♘f6 5 0-0 ♗e7 6 ♖e1 b5 7 ♗b3 d6 8 c3 0-0 9 h3 ♘a5 10 ♗c2 c5 11 d4 cxd4 12 cxd4 exd4!

Not usual in this exact position, and prepared by *Fritz*'s team.

13 ♘xd4

Now Black has both an offside knight and an isolated, weak d-pawn. But the bishop will be active on b7 and Black has a couple of nice open files to play with. This is all very Sicilian-like. But what is the computer doing playing with a backward pawn on an open file?

13...♗b7 14 ♘d2 ♖e8 15 b3 ♗f8 16 ♗b2 g6 17 ♖e2 ♗g7 18 ♕e1 ♖c8 19 ♖d1 ♘h5! *(D)*

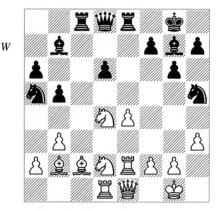

The two knights on the flank are a pleasing complement to Black's two fianchettoed bishops and symmetrically-placed rooks. This is a good example of the function mentioned in the very first game above, i.e., that knights move to the rim in order to unmask bishops and at the same not to crowd the centre or back rank. As explained there, such knights can either remain on the edge of the board to restrict enemy pieces or they can return to the centre after the disposition of the other pieces becomes clarified.

20 ♗b1 ♘f4 21 ♖e3 ♕f6 22 ♘2f3 ♘c6 23 ♔h2 ♘e5 24 g3?

A tactical oversight. Better was 24 ♘xe5 dxe5 25 ♘f3 ♕e6 leading to an unclear position.

24...♘d5! 25 exd5 ♘xf3+ 26 ♘xf3 ♖xe3 27 ♗xf6 ♖xe1 28 ♘xe1 ♗xf6

Black stands better due to his active bishop-pair. See Game 16 for further notes.

In case I am giving the impression that knight moves to the flank were forbidden in older times, I should make clear that it's a matter of the number and variety of positions in which such moves have become thinkable, even ones that looked absurd 30 years ago, much less 70 or 80. This is emphatically not the case with the 1...e5 examples above, nor, for example, with the flank move ♘h3 as used in the Dutch Defence. Those familiar with the opening will note that that in recent years ♘h3 has been a reliable counter to both the Dutch Stonewall and to certain Leningrad Dutch Variations. In fact, my database of top players from 1985 to 2002 reveals the score with ♘h3 versus the Dutch Defence as 61%-39%, with White performing at 120+ Elo points above rating expectations. But it's also true that many of the classical greats recognized the move's value; e.g., Rubinstein, Fine, Alekhine, Capablanca, Pillsbury, Spielmann, Sämisch and several others! They didn't do quite as well playing ♘h3, but this probably has to do with the spread of knowledge about how to handle the relevant positions and later refinement of both sides' precise move-orders. Nevertheless, looking at the following games, is there any serious difference in the basics of White's middlegame strategy?

a) Capablanca-Botvinnik, Hastings 1934/5: 1 d4 e6 2 c4 f5 3 g3 ♘f6 4 ♗g2 ♗e7 5 ♘c3 d5 6 ♘h3 c6 7 ♕b3 0-0 8 0-0 ♘a6 9 ♘f4 ♔h8? 10 ♘d3 ♘c7 11 ♗f4 ♘ce8 12 c5! ♘d7 13 e3 ♗f6 14 ♘e2! ♕e7 15 ♕c3 g5 16 ♗e5 ♘xe5 17 dxe5 ♗g7 18 f4 ♘c7 19 a4 ♗d7 20 ♘d4 with a large positional advantage (although Black held on to draw).

b) Rubinstein-Kmoch, Vienna 1922: 1 d4 e6 2 c4 f5 3 g3 ♘f6 4 ♗g2 d5 5 ♘h3 c6 6 ♕c2 ♗d6 7 0-0 0-0 8 b3 ♗d7 9 ♘c3 ♕e7 10 ♗f4 ♘a6 11 ♖ad1 ♗xf4 12 gxf4! ♔h8 13 ♔h1 h6 14 ♕d2 ♘h7 *(D)*.

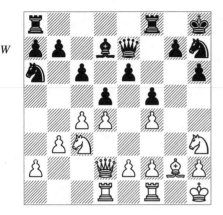

W

15 ♘g1! g5 16 ♘f3 ♖g8 17 ♘e5 ♖af8 18 ♕e3 ♕g7 19 ♖g1 ♖f6 20 ♕h3 ♘b8 21 ♘a4! ♗e8 22 ♘c5 b6 23 ♘cd3 with an overwhelming game. OK, Black played atrociously, but White's sleepless knights performed wonders.

c) Krasenkow-Przedmojski, Polish Cht (Lubniewice) 1998: 1 d4 e6 2 g3 f5 3 ♗g2 d5 4 c4 ♘f6 5 ♘h3 ♗d6 6 0-0 0-0 7 ♗f4 ♗e7!? 8 cxd5 exd5 9 ♗g5! c6 10 e3 ♕e8 11 ♘f4 ♗d6 12 ♘d3 ♘bd7 13 ♘d2 ♘e4 14 ♗f4 ♗e7 15 ♘f3 g5 16 ♗c7 h5 17 ♘fe5 ♘df6 18 f3 ♘d6 19 ♕b3 ♔g7 20 a4 (with a clear advantage; the rest of the game is pretty) 20...g4? 21 ♘f4 gxf3 22 ♗xf3 ♘de4 23 ♕d1! ♘g4 24 h3! ♘xe3 25 ♕d3 ♘xf1 26 ♗xh5 ♗d8 27 ♗xe8 ♗xc7 28 ♘h5+ ♔h6 29 ♖xf1 ♖xe8 30 ♕e3+ ♔xh5 31 ♖xf5+ ♗xf5 32 g4+ ♔h4 33 ♘f3+ ♔xh3 34 ♘e5+ 1-0.

d) Piket-Timman, Wijk aan Zee 1995: 1 d4 e6 2 c4 f5 3 g3 ♘f6 4 ♗g2 d5 5 ♘h3 ♗e7 6 0-0 0-0 7 ♕c2 c6 8 ♘d2 ♕e8 9 ♘f3 ♘e4 10 b3 ♘d7 11 ♘f4 ♗d6 12 ♘d3 ♕h5 13 ♘fe5! ♘xe5 14 dxe5 ♗e7! 15 f3 ♘c5 (Black probably intended 15...♘g5?, but then 16 h4! ♘f7 17 ♘f4) 16 ♗a3 b6 17 ♘xc5 bxc5 18 cxd5 cxd5 19 ♗xc5 with a large advantage for White.

e) Kasparov-Nikolić, New York rpd 1994: 1 d4 f5 2 g3 ♘f6 3 ♗g2 e6 4 c4 c6 5 ♘d2 d5 6 ♕c2 ♗d6 7 ♘h3 0-0 8 ♘f3 ♗d7 9 0-0 ♗e8 10 ♗f4 h6 11 ♗xd6 ♕xd6 12 ♘f4 ♘bd7 13 ♘d3 dxc4 14 ♕xc4 ♗h5 15 b4 ♘e4 16 ♖fd1 ♘b6 17 ♕b3 ♘d5 18 ♖ac1 f4 19 ♘c5 ♘xc5 20 bxc5 with a solid advantage.

I don't think that we can speak of any profound conceptual progress here. White's excellent score in this era reflects the lessons learned from Capablanca and Rubinstein. Of course even they would have considered many of today's other routine decentralizations as exotic and unsound.

Sleepless Knights

The rest of this section will be devoted to the topic of 'sleepless knights'. As explained above, these are knights that can't seem to find rest at any particular spot and seemingly unconcernedly rush from place to place at great cost of time, thus flouting the rules of development. For a good example of what I mean, we might hark back to the games with the French Advance Variation given at the end of Chapter 1. There, despite the potentially semi-open nature of the line indicated by either White's dxc5 and/or c4 and Black's ...f6, Black ignored his development. In the one case, he took time out to play ...♘ge7-g6-h8-f7, arriving just in time to avoid being overrun; and in the other case he found the effective strategy of ...♘ge7-g6-f8-h7-g5! It is no wonder that these plans weren't discovered until recently, because they require an ultra-specific attitude that pays attention to the minute particulars of the position rather than a preconceived notion of how White's pawn-chain must be attacked. When in the second case the knight had made its fifth move, Black hadn't even castled yet, and more significantly, he had abstained from both the traditional attack on the base of the pawn-chain at d4 and the modern one on the head of the pawn-chain on e5.

We can find examples of modern knight wanderings in the oldest of openings:

Xu Yuanyuan – Karaklajić
Beijing 1997

1 d4 d5 2 c4 e6 3 ♘c3 c6 4 ♘f3 ♘f6 5 cxd5 exd5 6 ♕c2 ♘a6 7 a3 ♘c7 8 ♗g5 ♘e6 9 ♗h4 g6

To fianchetto the bishop?

10 e3 ♘g7

No, the knight! It has taken an odd and time-consuming sojourn just to prepare ...♗f5, but this has been a standard Queen's Gambit strategy for some time now. However, this knight isn't finished yet by a long shot.

11 ♗d3 ♗f5 12 0-0 ♗e7 13 b4 a6 14 ♘e5 0-0 15 ♘a4 ♗xd3 16 ♘xd3 ♘f5 17 ♗xf6 ♗xf6 18 ♘ac5 ♕c7 19 a4 ♘d6!

It took six moves to get here, yet now the knight eyes c4 and guards against b5, White's only obvious break.

20 a5?!

I don't believe that it can be good for White to forego the dynamics of a potential b5 break here. He could, for example, feint at enforcing e4 for a while and maintain some sort of chances on both wings.

20...♖ae8 21 ♖fe1 ♖e7 22 ♖e2 ♖fe8 23 ♖ae1 ♗g7 24 ♘b2 ♘f5 25 ♘ba4

White is re-routing his knights as well. But one problem is that a knight would do nothing on b6 except leave the kingside defenceless (we saw something very similar in SOMCS). Not all knights on the edge are good.

25...h5 26 ♕d3 ♘h6! *(D)*

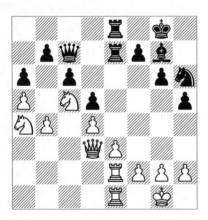

Except this one. Now the aim now is to create weaknesses with ...♘g4. This fellow's journey from one side of the board on a6 to the other one on h6 is very amusing: ...♘b8-a6-c7-e6-g7-f5-d6-f5-h6. And of course back to f5 on the next move!

27 f3

Mixed messages. White's knights are poorly placed to support e4. 27 h3 looks more logical, although Black has very nice attacking chances.

27...♘f5 28 ♘b3 ♕d6 29 ♘ac5 *(D)*

Now that's a pretty impressive path itself: ♘g1-f3-e5-d3-b2-a4-c5! And his companion hasn't done badly either: ♘b1-c3-a4-c5-b3. But obviously, Black's peregrinations have achieved a great deal more. Why? The answer

is in Dvoretsky's impressively original insight that we saw in SOMCS: the superfluous knight. It's hard to imagine a better example. White continually acts as though he wants to occupy c5 twice! In situations with multiple claimants to the same outpost (notice that a rook or queen could go there as well), it's often best to leave the piece occupying that square to its own devices. Otherwise the back-up piece (here the b3-knight) is reduced to standing by and becomes 'superfluous'. So if possible the opponent should not, by exchanging the forward piece, bail out the rear one(s) and make them more relevant.

29...h4 30 ♔h1 ♕f6!?

Baburin believes that this is mistimed and allows White to break out, but that doesn't seem correct. Unfortunately, Black doesn't get the tactics right. His first point is a real one: on a neutral move (say, 31 ♕d2?), 31...♘g3+! will win.

31 e4? *(D)*

Perhaps the other point of 30...♕f6 was 31 ♔g1! h3 32 g3 ♘xg3!? (32...♔h7! is better) 33 hxg3 ♕xf3, but then White can bail out by 34 e4! ♕xd3 35 ♘xd3 ♖xe4 36 ♘f4, and while that is not clear even after White captures the h-pawn, he should be no worse.

31...♘g3+?

Too bad. Probably Black couldn't resist delivering the *coup de grâce* by the sacrifice of the star piece of the game. This move is not disastrous, but Black misses what should have been the point of 30...♕f6: 31...♘xd4! (that knight again!) 32 e5 ♖xe5 with a winning game: 33 ♘xd4 (33 ♖xe5 ♖xe5 34 ♖xe5 ♕xe5 35 ♕xd4 ♕xd4 36 ♘xd4 ♗xd4 37 ♘xb7 ♗e3 and

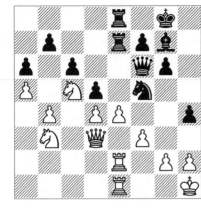

B

White can't even get his king out due to 38 g3 h3) 33...罝xe2 34 ②xe2 豐c3! 35 豐d1 豐xb4 36 ②b3 罝e3 and Black ends up with four passed pawns!

32 hxg3 hxg3 33 含g1 豐h4 34 罝c2 f5!

There is no mate, and 34...豐h2+ 35 含f1 豐h1+ 36 含e2 豐xg2+ 37 含d1 豐h3 38 e5 just wins for White.

35 ②d2!?

35 e5?? 盒xe5 36 dxe5 罝xe5 37 罝xe5 罝xe5 and ...豐h2+ will win. 35 含f1!? is another try. Chances are dynamically balanced here.

35...fxe4?

35...豐h2+ 36 含f1 豐h5! is a typical computer suggestion, when White needs a move and the situation is unclear.

36 fxe4 豐h2+ 37 含f1 罝f8+ 38 含e2 豐xg2+ 39 含d1

White has escaped now. In what looked like time-pressure, he later played inaccurately and allowed Black to draw. A fascinating positional and tactical game.

Kramnik – Karpov
Las Palmas 1996

1 c4 e5 2 ②c3 ②f6 3 ②f3 ②c6 4 d4 exd4 5 ②xd4 盒b4 6 盒g5 h6 7 盒h4 盒xc3+ 8 bxc3 ②e5 9 f4

A more extreme example of the knight as insomniac can be seen in Levenfish-Botvinnik, Leningrad 1934: 9 e3 ②g6 10 盒g3 ②e4 11 豐c2 ②xg3 12 hxg3 d6 13 盒e2 ②e5 14 罝d1 豐e7 15 豐e4 a6 16 罝h5 ②d7 17 豐f4 ②f6 18 罝a5 盒d7 19 g4 ②e4 20 盒f3 ②c5 21 ②b3 ②e6. Now this knight has made nine moves (and his cohort three) out of Black's first 21. But his

pieces are all well placed and he probably has a small advantage. The game was drawn quickly after 22 豐e4 罝b8 23 c5 盒c6 24 cxd6 盒xe4 25 dxe7 盒xf3 26 gxf3 含xe7 ½-½. For related examples, see the section on doubled pawns in Chapter 2.

9...②g6

After 9...②xc4?, 10 e4 has always been considered strong, and 10 ②f5 is recommended by Shamkovich.

10 盒xf6 豐xf6 11 g3 *(D)*

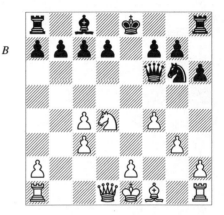

B

A very old and heavily analysed line of the English Opening in which one would be surprised to find radically new ideas. The battle is between more space (White) and better structure (Black).

11...②f8!

A truly remarkable idea. Black foregoes castling and developing to retreat his knight to the first rank! As far as I can tell, 11...②f8 was first played by Tukmakov. But in a time when this whole line with 4 d4 was very popular for White and the position after White's 11th was either reached or analysed numerous times, 11...②f8 was neglected. With Karpov's use of it in this high-profile game, players caught on.

12 盒g2

White would now seem to have ample time to take over d5 and get all his pieces out, when he is ready to play e4, and claim a big advantage. But appearances are deceptive.

12...②e6

Black has only one idea: c5 is the ideal blockading square and Black is headed there! With his lack of developing moves, he is challenging White: 'OK, what can you do to me?'.

13 0-0 0-0 14 e4

The original game went 14 ♕d2 d6 15 ♘b3 (otherwise ...♘c5 grants easy equality or better) 15...♖b8!? 16 f5 ♘g5 17 ♕d4 ♕xd4+ 18 cxd4 ♖e8, and by controlling the light squares Black equalized: 19 ♖ae1 b6 (19...♘e4!? looks fine) 20 ♗c6 (Ribli gave 20 e4 ♗a6 21 ♘d2 c5 22 d5 b5!) 20...♗b7! 21 ♗xb7 (a cute blunder is 21 ♗xe8?? ♘h3#) 21...♖xb7 22 d5 ♘e4 23 ♖c1 ♖bb8 24 ♖c2 ♘f6 ½-½ Vaganian-Tukmakov, Rostov 1993. Black is threatening moves like ...♘g4 and ...♖e3 and should be better in this position.

14...d6 15 ♕d2 ♘c5 (D)

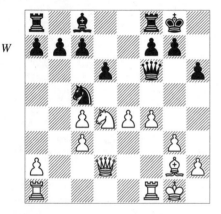

OK, time to discuss the knight's lack of sleep: ...♘b8-c6-e5-g6-f8-e6-c5! And it's only move 15. The irony is that the same knight often gets to c5 in only *two* moves by ...♘d7-c5.

16 ♖ae1

16 ♘b3 ♘a4 (yet another knight move!) 17 ♖ac1 ♗e6!? 18 ♕d4 c5! 19 ♕xf6 gxf6 20 ♖fd1 ♘b2 21 ♖xd6 ♘xc4 (that makes 9 knight moves out of 21) was positionally better for Black in G.Shahade-Akopian, New York 1998.

16...♖b8 17 ♖e3 ♗d7 18 ♘b3 ♘xb3!?

18...♘a4?! 19 e5 ♕e7 20 ♖fe1 is awkward, but 18...♖fd8 is OK after 19 ♕d4 (19 ♘xc5 dxc5 20 e5 ♕e7 with a small edge) 19...♕e7.

19 axb3 ♗c6 20 ♕d4 a6! 21 ♕xf6 ½-½

This is a case of useful doubled pawns for Black, because they restrain e5 and there is no knight for White to place on f5.

The next game is not very fancy or even exceptional, but I think shows how players are taking either side of certain complex modern

positions and creating chances. In many similar Nimzo-Indian lines this doubled-pawn structure is just torture for White to play, in part because Black defends the queenside and then can build up at leisure on the kingside. But that strategy is not foolproof.

Avrukh – Tyomkin
Beersheba 1997

1 d4 ♘f6 2 c4 e6 3 ♘f3 ♗b4+ 4 ♘c3 ♗xc3+ 5 bxc3 b6 6 ♗g5 h6 7 ♗h4 ♗b7 8 ♘d2 d6 9 f3 e5 10 e4 c5 11 ♗e2 ♘c6 12 ♘b3 ♕e7 13 a4 a5

This is one of those locked two-bishop-versus-two-knights positions that I've often talked about. It would seem that White could never make any progress, but Black's last does create a minor one weakness on b6, and one could argue that simply allowing a5 wasn't a bad idea.

14 ♖a2!

Already preparing White's 18th move?

14...0-0-0 15 ♖b2 ♔c7 16 0-0 g5 17 ♗f2 h5 (D)

18 ♘a1!

Much more pointed than the stereotyped developing of pieces by 18 ♕d2 ♖dg8 19 ♖fb1 ♘d7. Instead, the knight heads for e3.

18...♖b8 19 ♘c2 h4 20 ♘e3 ♗c8 21 dxc5 dxc5 22 ♖d2

22 ♘d5+ ♘xd5 23 cxd5 ♘d8 is also promising, but White has a more subtle way to employ the knight.

22...♖d8 23 ♖xd8 ♘xd8 24 ♕c1 ♗e6?!

Unfortunate, but a good move is hard to find.

25 ♘f5!

Completing the path ♘f3-d2-b3-a1-c2-e3-f5 and winning a pawn thereby.

25...♗xf5 26 ♕xg5 ♘e6

Or 26...♗d7 27 ♗xh4.

27 ♕xf5 ♘d7 28 ♖d1 ♖g8?

28...♖h8 would be tougher, at least protecting against ♕h5. The text-move is also tactically unsound.

29 ♗f1?!

White avoids the uncertainty of 29 ♗xh4! ♕xh4 30 ♕xf7 ♖xg2+ 31 ♔xg2 ♘f4+ 32 ♔f1, but it would have won for him.

29...♖g7?

The last chance was 29...♖h8!.

30 ♔h1 ♔c6 31 ♕h5 ♘f4 32 ♕h8 ♕f8 33 ♕xf8 ♘xf8 34 ♗xh4

and White won easily.

Valery Bronznik in his *Schach Ohne Abseits* ChessBase CD has collected a large set of paradoxical knight manoeuvres, quite a few relevant to our other themes. He starts this example at move 30, but the game as a whole game also provides a strong aesthetic impression:

Lukacs – G. Horvath
Hungarian Ch 1989

1 d4 ♘f6 2 c4 e6 3 ♘f3 b6 4 g3 ♗b7 5 ♗g2 ♗b4+ 6 ♗d2 ♗e7 7 ♘c3 0-0 8 0-0 c5 9 d5 exd5 10 ♘h4 ♘e4 11 ♘f5

The things that people are doing these days to get a knight to f5! On his video biography, Kasparov somewhat jokingly remarked that such a knight is worth a whole pawn. He was not referring to this position of course.

11...♗f6 12 cxd5 ♘xc3 13 ♗xc3 ♗xc3 14 bxc3 ♕f6 15 e4 d6 16 ♕d2 ♗c8

Black isn't too thrilled with the knight there either.

17 ♘e3 ♘d7 18 f4 ♗a6 19 ♖fe1 ♖ae8 20 ♘g4

Perhaps just 20 c4 was correct. One has to like White's position, but it's still not easy to see how he might go about trying to win.

20...♕d8 21 ♖e3?! ♗c8 22 ♘f2 b5 23 ♖ae1?!

More pointed would be 23 ♗f1 ♕a5 24 ♕b2 a6 25 a4.

23...f6

This is starting to look reasonable for Black, who has stopped e5 and can turn to the queenside.

24 ♗f1 ♕a5 25 ♕e2 c4

25...a6 26 c4 stabilizes the queenside in White's favour.

26 ♗h3!? ♘b6!?

The more natural move 26...♘c5 was perhaps better.

27 ♗xc8 ♖xc8 28 ♕d2 ♖c5 *(D)*

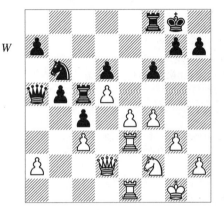

29 g4! ♕a6 30 ♘h1!

Sad to say, the computer finds this immediately. The knight is heading for c6!

30...♕c8?!

30...♘d7! 31 ♘g3 ♖c7 32 ♘f5 ♘c5 would achieve good counterplay, since this knight will land on d3.

31 h3 ♖e8 32 ♘g3 g6 33 ♘e2! ♕d7 34 ♘d4 ♖cc8 35 ♖d1 ♘a4 36 ♘c6

Completing the odyssey: ♘g1-f3-h4-f5-e3-g4-f2-h1-g3-e2-d4-c6!

36...a6 37 ♕d4 ♖f8 38 e5 fxe5 39 fxe5 dxe5 40 ♖xe5 ♖xc6?

Too desperate, but the position was awful anyway.

41 dxc6 ♕xc6 42 ♖e7 ♕f6 43 ♕xf6 ♖xf6 44 ♖d8+ ♖f8 45 ♖dd7 1-0

Goerge – Reicher
Bad Wildbad 1993

1 e4 g6 2 d4 ♗g7 3 c4 d6 4 ♘c3 ♘c6 5 ♗e3 e5 6 d5 ♘ce7 7 f3 f5 8 ♘ge2 ♘f6 9 g3 0-0 10 ♗g2 c5 11 ♕d2 a6 12 a4 ♖b8 13 0-0 ♗d7 14 h3 fxe4 15 fxe4 *(D)*

15...♘c8!?

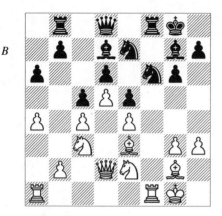

What's this?

16 g4 ᐃb6! 17 b3 ᐃa8! 18 ᐃg3 ᐃc7

OK, Black may not have had much to do, but development by ...ᐃc6-e7-c8-b6-a8-c7 is something else again! It's noteworthy that one of the modern main lines of the Benoni has similar ideas: 1 d4 ᐃf6 2 c4 c5 3 d5 e6 4 ᐃc3 exd5 5 cxd5 d6 6 ᐃf3 g6 7 g3 ᐃg7 8 ᐃg2 0-0 9 0-0 a6 10 a4 ᐃbd7 11 ᐃd2 ᐃe8 12 h3 ᐃb8 13 ᐃc4 ᐃb6 14 ᐃa3 ᐃd7 15 e4 *(D)*.

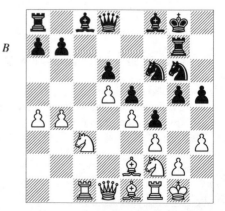

15...ᐃc7 (the knight can also retreat the other way after 15...ᐃe7 16 a5 ᐃa8! 17 ᐃc4 ᐃb5 18 ᐃb3 ᐃxc4 19 ᐃxc4 ᐃc7 and ...b5 next) 16 ᐃe3 ᐃc8! (from a7, the knight will support the crucial advance ...b5) 17 ᐃd3 ᐃa7 18 ᐃfc1 b5 19 b4 c4 20 ᐃf1 bxa4 21 ᐃxc4 ᐃb5 22 ᐃxa4 ᐃxe4 with complications that favour Black. The queen's knight travelled ...ᐃb8-d7-b6-c8-a7-b5, all moves of proven value and soundness.

19 g5 ᐃfe8 20 ᐃxf8+ ᐃxf8 21 ᐃf1 b5 22 axb5 axb5 23 ᐃf2 ᐃe7 24 ᐃf3 bxc4 25 bxc4 ᐃb3 26 ᐃd2 ᐃa6

Off on another trip! See where he ends up this time.

27 h4 ᐃb4 28 ᐃd1!

Avoiding 28 h5 ᐃc2 and ...ᐃd4.

28...ᐃa3 29 h5 ᐃd3

Black is better, because he can sacrifice a pawn with ...ᐃf4 (threatening g5), and even if the piece is captured Black gets the long diagonal for his bishop to terrific effect. At this point White sacrificed a piece unsoundly by 30 ᐃf5?, so the rest of the game is not of interest.

Let's wrap up with some fun. Fischer's knight tour in the next game is in a tactical context and thus not as relevant as the other examples. Still, it's interesting that in a variation known for the importance of each tempo Black can casually enjoy the scenery, as shown in the imbedded game even more dramatically.

Korchnoi – Fischer
Herceg Novi blitz 1970

1 d4 ᐃf6 2 c4 g6 3 ᐃc3 ᐃg7 4 e4 d6 5 ᐃe2 0-0 6 ᐃf3 e5 7 0-0 ᐃc6 8 d5 ᐃe7 9 ᐃd2

It's odd how accustomed we have become to strategies that are really exotic modern inventions. The black knight tour is absolutely standard in these King's Indian positions. But stepping back, it's amazing that in a line that is always characterized as a mad race to attack by both sides, Black can afford to make so many slow preparatory moves in the following line: 9 ᐃe1 ᐃd7 10 ᐃd3 f5 11 f3 f4 12 ᐃd2 g5 13 b4 ᐃf6 14 c5 ᐃg6 15 ᐃc1 ᐃf7 16 ᐃf2 h5 17 h3 ᐃf8 (beginning with this one) 18 cxd6 cxd6 19 a4 ᐃg7 20 ᐃe1 *(D)*.

20...♘h8! 21 a5 ♘f7 22 ♘b5 ♘h6! 23 ♕c2 g4 with an attack, Debarnot-Ree, Nice OL 1974. The crazy thing about this is that after all that re-routing (...♘c6-e7-g6-h8-f7-h6), the knight is still poorly placed on h6 by traditional standards: on the edge of the board with no good moves! It took quite an evolution of attitude for this manoeuvre to become something we play (or at least consider over the board) unreflectively and almost automatically.

9...c5 10 a3 ♘e8 11 b4 b6 12 ♖b1 f5 13 f3 f4 14 a4 g5 15 a5 ♖f6 16 bxc5 bxc5 17 ♘b3 ♖g6 18 ♗d2 ♘f6 19 ♔h1 g4 20 fxg4 ♘xg4 21 ♖f3 ♖h6 22 h3 ♘g6 23 ♔g1 ♘f6 24 ♗e1 (D)

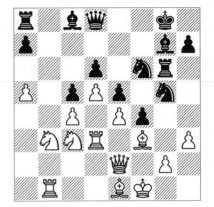

OK, it's just a blitz game and White has totally misplaced his pieces for a queenside attack. Nevertheless, his kingside is moderately well defended and Black faces a question of how to proceed. Just about anyone would think about attacking moves in the direction of the white king; e.g., 24...♘h5 (not a bad move, intending 25 ♖f1 ♘g3) or perhaps ...♘h4. Instead, Fischer plays:

24...♘h8!!

This must be one of the greatest moves ever made in a high-level blitz tournament! The point is (fairly) obvious once you see it, but who would think of it? Sort of a tactical version of Nimzowitsch's famous ♘h1 move.

25 ♖d3 ♘f7 26 ♗f3 ♘g5 27 ♕e2 ♖g6 28 ♔f1 (D)
28...♘xh3

Completing a remarkable journey: ...♘c6-e7-g6-h8-f7-g5-h3! Paradoxically, this has occurred in a variation in which it is normally the case that every tempo counts.

29 gxh3 ♗xh3+ 30 ♔f2 ♘g4+ 31 ♗xg4 ♗xg4 0-1

In this section, we first examined a number of new and creative situations in which knights reside happily and usefully on the edge of the board. The number of such situations is clearly on the increase, especially in games involving strong players, and it is obvious that worries about the knight's shorter range have been transcended by today's ever more pragmatic philosophy. Put simply: if moving a knight to the side of the board helps to win the game, put it there. Such knights often tie down the opponent's pieces to defence of a particular point and thus prove themselves of equal worth to the defending enemy pieces. In some structures, knights on the rim also unmask bishops and allow coordination of the rooks and queen.

In the rest of the section, we had some fun with examples of sleepless knights, i.e., those that can't seem to find rest anywhere and undertake exotic manoeuvres at apparent expense of time and development. The reader can guess that such wandering knights are to be found throughout the range of chess practice. They exemplify the sometimes paradoxical relationship between time and efficiency that keeps the mystery in our game.

3.2 The Behaviour of Bishops

Much of what I will say in this section was discussed in limited form in SOMCS; hopefully I can clarify it here and present appropriate examples. The first thing that one needs to know about the bishop is that in a majority of cases a bishop is superior to a knight, and a bishop-pair is better than a knight-pair with or without the presence of most other combinations of other pieces or pawns. The bishop-pair is very often full compensation for a pawn, and a bishop and pawn will frequently match up well against a rook. The reader may wish to refer to SOMCS for some related statistics.

This view of the bishop conforms with contemporary prejudices, and I suspect that one would be hard-pressed to find a top-50 grandmaster who would contest the general conclusion that bishops are better on the average. Kasparov, who once laughingly agreed with the statement that any bishop however bad is better than a knight, points out that Fischer believed the bishop to be so clearly better than the knight that he suggested 3¼ for a bishop's value. The bishop's superiority has of course been the majority belief among master players ever since the time of Botvinnik and (less definitely) before. But never as unanimously and unambiguously as among the younger players of the last two decades. Kasparov thinks, for example, that Petrosian found it difficult to accept the superiority of the bishop, something that his games often seem to reflect. He also notes that Smyslov was rather too willing to give up his bishops, citing four games from their Candidates match in which Smyslov ceded Kasparov the bishop-pair. Euwe and Kramer go further back in time when they say that "Formerly the knight was usually given preference, but nowadays it is the bishop. However, it is still not possible to assert that a bishop is in general stronger than a knight, or vice versa ... A century ago most players, in the romantic tradition, gave preference to the knight over the bishop. Today the opposite is more often the case, at least in certain types of common positions. How far this is due to subjective factors is difficult to decide. It is certain that in general two bishops are strong than two knights or than a knight and bishop, although there are some cases in which the knights will dominate."

Bishops Good and Bad

Of course a general statistical superiority has nothing to do with individual cases, the latter giving rise to different assessments of the respective minor pieces in countless actual positions with all types of characteristics. One of the elementary questions we may have about a bishop is whether it is well or poorly placed, and in particular whether it is 'good' or 'bad'. In SOMCS, the latter distinction was shown to be deceptive in many cases. A bishop hemmed in by its central pawns can serve many valuable functions. For one thing, it will often serve the defence better than a good bishop would, as is reflected in Suba's idea that 'bad bishops can defend good pawns'. An obvious and important example comes about in most Sicilian Defences, which have central pawns (normally a 2-1 majority) on d6 and e5 (e.g., Najdorf, Sveshnikov, etc.) or on d6 and e6 (Najdorf, Scheveningen, Paulsen, Taimanov, etc.); in both cases, a bishop on e7 is an excellent piece. In fact Black often transforms the latter structure into the former one, making the bishop 'worse' and the d-pawn backward (*see following diagram*).

This idea also crops up in many other openings, of course. I might add that bad bishops can not only protect good pawns but also good squares. SOMCS gave numerous disadvantageous examples of the exchange of one's bad bishop for a good one by moving a knight's pawn and then playing ...♗a6 or ...♗h6 (alternatively, ♗a3 or ♗h3, although White seems generally less interested in this particular type of exchange). This is a notoriously risky manoeuvre

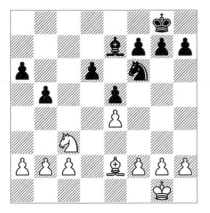

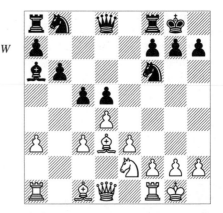

because, as shown there, the squares of the colour left behind (e.g., f6/h6/g7 or c6/a6/b7) tend to be weak. Notice that grandmasters are wary of playing ...♗a6 in a Queen's Gambit structure. Both ...♗a6 and ...♗h6 are particularly bad if they go there in two moves (e.g., ...♗b7 and ...♗a6) and/or are captured with tempo on that square (e.g., by an f1-bishop capturing on a6 instead of first going to d3 and then capturing). The main exception is when the recapturing knight gain access to a very useful square for that particular situation, such as c5 or f5. Thus as always one cannot generalize very well; each case has to be studied and calculated thoroughly.

Here's one of those ...♗a6 games in a variation made famous by Botvinnik-Capablanca, Rotterdam AVRO 1938. In this particular case White is in no position to exploit Black's queenside squares, but the prophylactic influence that a light-squared bishop has versus White's e4 break disappears. A great struggle ensues (both White and Black have ratings around 2650), with the most remarkable feature being the relative strengths and weaknesses of White's bad bishop.

Zviagintsev – Aleksandrov
Poikovsky 2002

1 c4 e6 2 ♘c3 d5 3 d4 ♗b4 4 e3 c5 5 a3 ♗xc3+ 6 bxc3 ♘f6 7 cxd5 exd5 8 ♗d3 0-0 9 ♘e2 b6

Intending ...♗a6, to exchange White's good bishop for Black's bad one.

10 0-0 ♗a6 (D)

11 f3

11 ♗xa6 ♘xa6 12 ♗b2 (note the voluntary relegation of this bishop to passivity) 12...♕d7

13 a4 ♖fe8 14 ♕d3 was the above-mentioned Botvinnik game, which in strategic terms went very similarly to the one before us. But this exact move-order is now considered inaccurate because of Botvinnik's suggestion 14...♕b7!, which discourages e4 and keeps the knight on a6 so that it protects c5 and doesn't get in the way of a potential rook on c8 by moving to c7.

11...♖e8 12 ♘g3 ♕d7

A rare and subtle move, eyeing the light squares and in particular a4. The logical continuation 12...♗xd3 13 ♕xd3 ♘c6 has also been also played, but it allows the remarkable rook swing by 14 ♖a2! ♖c8 15 ♖e2, intending ♗b2 and e4 in most lines. This is now a standard manoeuvre, and occurred recently in Yakovich-Campora, Santo Antonio 2001, which continued 15...♖e6 16 ♗b2 cxd4 17 cxd4 ♘a5 18 e4 ♖ec6 19 e5 (the obvious strategy, but it exchanges the bad {good?} bishop! Probably 19 ♘f5 with the idea 19...♘c4 20 ♗c1! was better, with the advantage) 19...♘e8 20 f4 ♘c4 21 f5 with an obscure attack. Here 21 ♗c1 fails to 21...♘xe5.

13 a4!?

Probably not the best line, but it leads to unique play. 13 ♖a2! prepares the previously-mentioned strategy of ♖e2 and e4-e5 and looks hard for Black to meet. For example, 13...♗xd3 14 ♕xd3 ♕a4 (14...♘c6 15 ♖e2) 15 e4 ♘c6 16 e5 ♘d7 17 ♖d2 ♘a5 18 ♖dd1 ♘c4 19 f4 ♘xa3 20 f5 with a serious attack.

Yet another idea is Zviagintsev's suggestion 13 ♗f5, advantageously preserving the two bishops. This is only possible due to the move 12...♕d7 and shows how move-specific the respective strategies can be.

13...♗xd3 14 ♕xd3

Even though Black has achieved his ideal goal of exchanging off White's light-squared bishop in minimal time (...♗a6 came in one jump and White had moved his bishop already before it was exchanged, so Black is two tempi up on the worst case), such positions are still difficult to handle in view of White's straight-forward idea of e4-e5.

14...♘c6 15 ♗b2! *(D)*

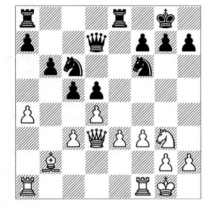

The very bad bishop protects the very good pawn on d4 so as to be able to play e4. It's interesting that my computer engine likes Black here in view of White's miserable-appearing bishop, slow development and Black's play down the c-file, including total control over the outpost on c4. Even the a4-pawn is weak. But this is where the modern faith in bishops appears. Black can dance around with his knights, but unless he can find a central break to disturb the equilibrium or find some squares on the king's wing, the side with the bishop can build up slowly until it becomes a superior piece.

15...c4

Black almost always feels compelled to play this move, even though it releases pressure on the centre. To see why, look at a line like 15...♘a5 16 e4 ♘c4 17 ♗c1, which illustrates Black's problems: White's bishop and rooks remain on the first rank, but e5 and f4-f5 will both free the bishop and aim every piece at the king. Black must also be careful not to allow e4 tactically; e.g., 15...♖ad8 16 e4! dxe4 17 fxe4 cxd4 (17...♘a5 18 ♖f4!) 18 cxd4 ♘xd4 19 ♖ad1 ♘e6 20 ♕c2 ♕e7 21 ♗xf6 gxf6 22 ♘h5 and White must come out on top.

16 ♕e2 h5!

This is natural and astute. Black plays prophylactically to prevent e4, which will be answered by ...h4 and the capture of the e-pawn. He sees the uselessness of ...♘a5-b3, which is an example of the weak knight on the 6th rank that was talked about in SOMCS.

17 ♖ae1 ♘e7!

Black understands the strategic threats very well. The knight move targets a4, but mainly serves to protect the kingside. The play seems about equal. 17...h4 18 ♘h1 would be similar to the game, but with less flexibility. Black lacks an aggressive plan other than grabbing the a-pawn, which makes his kingside even more vulnerable.

18 ♕c2!?

To stop ...♘f5, which constitutes Black's main hope of countering White's intended central advance. The normal-looking 18 e4?! allows Black's knights in after 18...h4 19 ♘h1 ♘g6 20 e5 ♘f4 21 ♕c2 ♘d3 22 ♖b1 ♘h5.

18...h4 19 ♘h1

Another knight in the corner. White intends ♘f2 and e4.

19...♘g6 20 e4!?

Very dynamic, although it does allow Black's knights to find good squares. Zviagintsev gives 20 ♗c1!, which is also very difficult to assess.

20...♘f4 21 ♘f2

Now d3 is covered; compare with the note to White's 18th.

21...dxe4 22 fxe4 ♘g4 23 ♘d1!? *(D)*

An amazing move, all the more so since 23 ♗c1 ♘xf2 24 ♗xf4 ♘d3 25 ♖e3 grants White some advantage with his big centre (and Black's vulnerable h-pawn). The knight has now completed the journey ♘g1-e2-g3-h1-f2-d1!

23...♘d3

A strange story: I originally got this exact game (same year, tournament and round, but unannotated) from the Internet and annotated it for this book with my notes. I later noticed that, apparently in some peculiar mix-up, the Internet version had given a completely incorrect sequence for the rest of the game! Since the false finish has ideas that are relevant to the actual game, I'll treat it as analysis and give a few hopefully instructive notes. Here are the mistakenly-given moves, so one should keep in mind that all the bad and dubious ones weren't

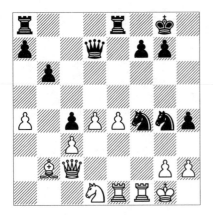

B

actually played: 23...♘e6 24 ♖e2? (24 e5! with ideas like ♖e4, ♕e4, and ♗c1, would be strong and justify the placement of the long-dormant bad bishop) 24...a6! 25 h3 ♘f6 26 ♖xf6?! (White should play 26 ♖ef2 instead, with the possible continuation 26...♘g5 {26...♖f8? 27 ♗a3} 27 e5 ♘fe4 28 ♖f5 g6 {28...b5 29 ♗c1!} 29 ♖xf7! ♘xf7 30 ♕xe4 ♗g7 31 ♘e3 and White has too strong an attack for Black to handle) 26...gxf6 27 ♘f2? (the natural move would have been 27 ♘e3!, when 27...♘g5 28 ♘g4 ♗g7 29 ♗c1 could follow, perhaps with e5 to come) 27...f5!? (27...♘f4! should be strongly considered, when after 28 ♖e3 f5 29 ♖f3 ♘h5, 30 ♖xf5?? has to be avoided due to 30...♕xf5 31 exf5 ♖e1+ 32 ♔h2 ♘g3; better is 30 e5 ♘g3 31 ♘h1! ♘e4 32 ♘f2, hoping for a repetition) 28 ♕d2 ♕c6?? and Black supposedly resigned in view of 29 d5! Later I received *New In Chess Magazine* with the real game and notes by Zviagintsev himself, to which we shall now return:

24 ♖e2

This threatens e5 and then h3.

24...a6

Alternatives include 24...b5 25 axb5 ♕xb5 26 ♗a3 with good play, and 24...♘xb2? 25 ♘xb2 ♖ac8 26 ♖f4 (threatening 27 h3 and then ♖xh4) 26...h3!? (26...g5 27 ♖f5 ♕d8 28 ♕d2 f6 29 e5!) 27 gxh3 ♘h6 28 ♖g2 (or 28 ♖e3) 28...♕xh3 29 ♖g3 ♕d7 30 e5 a6 31 ♕g2 g6 32 ♖f6, winning.

25 h3

25 ♗c1!? is a messy alternative; e.g., 25...b5 (25...♘xc1 26 ♕xc1 ♘f6 27 e5 ♘d5 28 ♘e3) 26 ♗g5 b4 27 h3.

25...♘f6 26 ♖xf6!

Zviagintsev didn't like 26 ♘f2 owing to 26...♘h5!. The text-move counts upon Black's damaged pawn-structure and White's control of the dark squares to compensate for the loss of the exchange. As noted elsewhere, the types of position in which a minor piece is considered long-term compensation for a rook have expanded dramatically with each passing decade. Here the paucity of remaining material doesn't discourage White from this decision.

26...gxf6 27 ♘f2 f5!

Zviagintsev gives 27...♘xb2 28 ♘g4 ♖e6 29 ♕xb2 "with an attack".

28 ♕d2!

Zviagintsev: "After the natural 28 ♘xd3 cxd3 29 ♕xd3 ♖xe4 30 ♖xe4 fxe4 31 ♕xe4 ♖e8 32 ♕xh4 ♕f5 Black has the advantage, although after 33 ♗a3 ♖e2 34 ♕g3+ ♕g6 35 ♕f3!, White has excellent chances of a draw."

28...♕e6!?

28...♕e7 would offer fewer winning chances after 29 exf5 ♕xe2 30 ♕g5+ ♔f8?! (30...♔h7 draws) 31 ♗a3+ (31 ♕h6+ ♔e7 32 ♗a3+ ♘c5 33 ♕xb6!?) 31...♘c5 32 f6 with a very interesting attack.

29 ♘xd3 cxd3 30 ♕xd3 fxe4 31 ♕e3 *(D)*

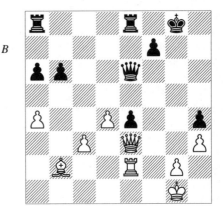

B

Zviagintsev merely says that White is "threatening ♖f2-f4 with an attack". At first sight, that seems incredibly slow, especially given the much-reduced material. White doesn't even have a pawn for the exchange, but Zviagintsev clearly just assumes that the (still bad) bishop is worth a rook. I have mentioned before how high-level annotators these days forget to mention that one player or the other is an exchange down, or even to refer to the precise material count (the number of pawns, for example) after an exchange sacrifice has occurred!

31...♕g6

Versus ♕g5+ and ♕xh4, but maybe giving up that pawn by 31...♖ad8!? was a good idea, intending 32 ♕g5+ (32 ♖f2!?) 32...♕g6 33 ♕xh4 ♖d5.

32 d5 b5 33 ♖f2 f5?

Instead of this, Zviagintsev suggests that 33...♕g3! 34 ♕d4 ♕e5 35 ♕e3 (intending c4, even after 35...♕xd5) 35...♕g3 "leads to a repetition of moves".

34 c4 bxc4

Also very complicated is 34...bxa4 35 ♕d4 ♖f8.

35 ♕d4

Zviangintsev thinks that White is clearly winning now, but I'm not sure.

35...♖eb8?

To get rid of the bishop. One better defensive try is 35...♖f8; for example, 36 ♕h8+ (36 d6 ♕h6 37 ♕xc4+ ♖f7 38 ♖xf5 ♕e3+ is drawn) 36...♔f7 37 ♕e5 (37 ♕xh4 ♔e8! with the idea 38 ♗a3 ♕f6) 37...♔g8 with a draw. In addition, moving the other rook by 35...♖ab8! would cover e5 and at least prevent what happens in the next note.

36 d6?

This seems to win eventually, but not as easily as Zviagintsev's proposal 36 ♕h8+ ♔f7 37 ♕e5! ♖xb2 38 ♖xf5+ ♔g8 39 ♖g5.

36...♖xb2?

36...c3! 37 ♕xc3 ♖xb2 38 ♖xb2 ♕xd6 39 ♖b7 ♕h6 is better according to Zviagintsev, although then 40 ♕c4+ ♔h8 41 ♕d4+ ♔g8 42 ♕d5+ ♔h8 43 ♕xf5 should probably win.

37 ♖xb2 ♕f7

Or 37...c3 38 ♕c4+ ♕f7 39 ♕xc3.

38 ♖b6 ♖c8

Black also loses after 38...♔h7 39 ♖c6! ♖a7 40 ♕c5.

39 d7 ♖d8 40 ♖h6 1-0

Top players are also extremely cautious about the analogous manoeuvre on the opposite wing by ...g6 and ...♗h6, since the kingside dark-square weaknesses can get exposed and/or occupied by enemy pieces after the exchange of bishops. SOMCS has two stark examples of this difficulty. For one thing, White can often break with f4, since the prophylactic influence

of the bishop on g7 is gone. Here's another example:

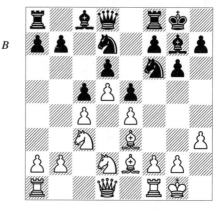

Onishchuk – Lupu
Bastia 2000

A basic King's Indian position has arisen. Black now manoeuvres to exchange his king's bishop.

12...♔h8 13 a3 ♘g8 14 ♕c2 ♗h6 15 ♘d1 a6 16 b4 ♗xe3 17 ♘xe3 (D)

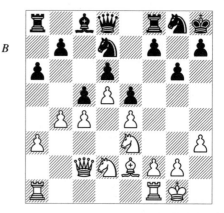

But with what result? Black has the 'better' bishop, to be sure (although it has nowhere to go). Yet he is cramped and the one break that is the redeeming feature of KID positions, ...f5, in this case only exposes his dark squares further after, say, exf5 and f4. The missing bishop on g7 would have at least strongly discouraged White from opening up the kingside in that manner. Its function in such a normal King's Indian, as explained in SOMCS, can be seen as indirect prophylaxis.

17...♕g5

For example, 17...♘h6 18 ♖ab1 f5 19 exf5 gxf5 20 f4, and the move ...e4 would only expose Black to a timely g4. In that event, his g7-bishop is no longer there to provide counterplay along the long diagonal, and the other bishop on c8 would be both formally and actually very bad.

18 ♕c3 ♘gf6

18...f5? is a mistake due to 19 f4.

19 g3 ♔g8 20 h4

White is clearly better on both sides of the board. 20 ♔h2 intending f4 is also not bad.

20...♕h6 21 ♔g2

Here too, 21 f4 exf4 22 ♖xf4 launches a nice attack.

21...b6 22 ♖ab1 ♖a7 23 ♖h1 ♘h5 24 ♗xh5 ♕xh5 25 g4 ♕h6 26 g5 ♕g7

26...♕h5?? 27 ♘df1 and ♘g3.

27 ♘g4

Where's that bishop when we need it?

27...f5 28 ♘h6+ ♔h8 29 ♖he1 ♘f6 30 bxc5 bxc5 31 ♖b6 ♘g4

After 31...♘e8, a possible although not necessary idea would be 32 f4!? exf4 33 ♕xg7+ ♔xg7 34 e5! ♖e7 (34...dxe5 35 ♖xe5 ♔h8 36 ♘b3 ♖c7 37 ♔f3, etc.) 35 e6, followed by ♔f3xf4 and winning at leisure.

32 ♖xd6 ♘xh6 33 gxh6 ♕xh6 34 ♕xe5+ ♖g7 35 ♘f3 ♕h5 36 ♕f4 ♔g8 37 e5

and we don't need to see any more.

Another simple strategy was seen in the next example:

Pelletier – Vigorito
Las Vegas 2002

1 c4 g6 2 ♘f3 ♗g7 3 d4 d6 4 ♘c3 ♗g4 5 e3 ♘c6 6 ♗e2 e5 7 d5 ♘ce7 8 0-0 ♗xf3 9 ♗xf3 f5 10 e4 ♗h6?! *(D)*

On the positive side, Black challenges the two bishops and tries to remedy the space disadvantage that he labours under. But again, the prophylactic role of a bishop on g7 will be missed.

11 c5!

Furthermore, protection of the e5-pawn has been weakened.

11...♔f7

Here 11...dxc5? 12 ♕e2! threatens both exf5 followed by ♕xe5 and in some cases ♕b5+;

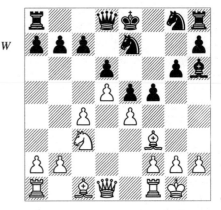

e.g., 12...♗xc1 (12...♕d6 13 exf5 with the point 13...gxf5? 14 ♘b5!) 13 ♖fxc1 f4 14 ♕b5+ ♔f7 15 ♕xb7 and Black can almost resign because of his pawn-structure. The alternative 11...♗xc1 12 ♖xc1 ♘f6 13 ♕b3 is also unpleasant.

12 exf5 ♘xf5 13 ♗e4!?

13 ♘e4 is natural and fine, but the bishop move is specifically directed against the h6-bishop.

13...♗xc1 14 ♕xc1!?

Not bad, emphasizing the dark squares, although 14 ♖xc1! ♘f6 15 ♕d3 is a more direct route to an advantage, hitting f5 and planning to play f4 next.

14...♘f6 15 f4!

The point. With a bishop on g7, ...exf4 would increase Black's activity, but here it would just open up lines against Black's king.

15...♖e8 16 ♗xf5 gxf5

At this point the straightforward 17 fxe5! ♖xe5 18 ♕c2 (or 18 ♕f4) is consistent and good for White; e.g., 18...♕d7 19 cxd6 (19 ♕b3!?) 19...cxd6 20 ♖f4 ♔g8 21 ♖af1, when apart from the weak f5-pawn, Black's king is exposed, especially on those long-abandoned dark squares. An example of the play (obviously with numerous alternatives for both sides) is 21...♘g4!? 22 ♕d3! ♖f8 23 h3 ♘h6 24 ♘b5! a6 25 ♘d4 ♖xd5 26 ♕g3+ ♔h8 27 ♕g5! ♘g8 28 ♘xf5 followed by g4. Then White has a large and probably winning advantage, because Black's pieces are stuck and he has weak pawns as well.

Of course many bad bishops can be activated by finding paths that get them outside or in front of the central pawn-structure. With

Black's pawns on d6 and e5 (but not c7), this might occur by ...♗e7-d8-b6 (or -a5) and with pawns on e6 and d5 (but not f7), we often see ...♗d7-e8-g6 (or -h5). Here's a simple example of the latter:

Shirov – Morozevich
Frankfurt rpd 2000

1 e4 e6 2 d4 d5 3 ♘c3 ♘f6 4 ♗g5 ♗e7 5 e5 ♘fd7 6 ♗xe7 ♕xe7 7 f4 a6 8 ♘f3 c5 9 ♕d2 ♘c6 10 0-0-0 c4!?

A very unusual plan for the French Defence as it releases the pressure on d4. It is also single-minded: Black plays for ...b5-b4 and an attack on the king. Notice that Black already had the bad bishop, but now it won't be getting out on the queenside. On the other hand, White is denied the ideal d3-square and (as in the Stonewall Dutch Defence in the next game) he must prove that his 'good' bishop isn't just biting on granite.

11 f5 ♘b6 12 fxe6 *(D)*

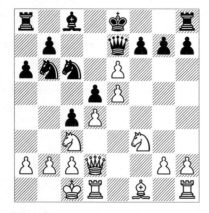

12...fxe6!?

A remarkable and probably correct recapture. Black foregoes the natural 12...♗xe6, when the bishop is developed but not very useful. One plan is 13 g3 (13 ♘e2 0-0 14 ♘f4!?) 13...0-0 14 ♗g2 f6 15 ♖he1 with a nice advantage. On the other hand, White seems to be much better after the f-pawn recapture as well.

13 h4 ♗d7 14 h5 0-0-0 15 h6!?

This looks like an innocent and almost automatic idea: White isolates Black's h-pawn on an open file, since 15...g6 would be a bit too much even for our featured light-squared bishop! But

this also allows Morozevich a standard mode of gaining activity in the French:

15...gxh6 16 ♖xh6 ♖dg8 17 ♕f4 ♗e8! 18 ♕f6 ♗g6

Now the bishop may be better than White's.

19 g4

Another possibility was to play 19 ♕xe7 ♘xe7 20 g4, although after 20...♔d7 and/or ...♖f8, Black's pieces are coordinating well.

19...♕e8 20 ♗g2?

It was time to admit that the bad bishop has become good and get rid of it: 20 ♘h4!, when White should still stand somewhat better in view of his space advantage.

20...♖f8

From now on Black's attack is deadly, with the bishop as a major player.

21 ♕h4

Finkel analyses 21 ♕g5 ♘b4 22 ♖d2 ♘a4 23 a3 ♘xc3 24 bxc3 ♕a4 25 cxb4 ♕xa3+ 26 ♔d1 ♖xf3 with a big advantage for Black.

21...♘b4! 22 ♖d2?

22 ♘e1 is a tougher defence.

22...♘a4! 23 a3

23 ♔b1 loses to the forcing continuation 23...♘xc3+ 24 bxc3 ♕b5! 25 cxb4 ♕xb4+ 26 ♔c1 c3!.

23...♘xc3 24 bxc3

24 axb4 ♕a4! wins immediately for Black.

24...♕a4! 25 cxb4 ♕xa3+ 26 ♔d1 ♖xf3 27 ♕e7

Or 27 ♗xf3 ♕xf3+ 28 ♔e1 ♕e3+ 29 ♔d1 ♖f8 and Black wins.

27...♖e3 28 ♕xe6+ ♔b8 29 ♕d6+ ♔a8 30 ♖e2 ♕a1+ 31 ♔d2 ♕c3+ 0-1

Not much of a game, but illustrative of the bishop-activation theme. White's own bishop on f1 turned into an onlooker even after it got to g2.

Here's an older example of the same issue in the Stonewall Dutch Defence, brilliantly resolved by one of the old masters:

Flohr – Goldberg
USSR Ch (Moscow) 1949

1 d4 e6 2 ♘f3 f5 3 g3 ♘f6 4 ♗g2 d5 5 0-0 ♗d6 6 c4 c6

This opening is a fertile ground for good-versus-bad bishop debates. At first sight one could hardly have a better example of a bad bishop for Black versus a good one (White's centre is defined by the dark-squared d-pawn). Let's consider Kramnik's query about the relative strengths of these bishops: is White's light-squared bishop so much better than Black's? And if not, why not?

a) White's 'good' bishop on g2 is restricted by the d5-pawn; it is not particularly effective in such a position.

b) Black's bishop is the 'bad bishop protecting a good pawn [or two]'.

How can the latter idea be relevant, since White is threatening neither b7 nor c6 (nor e6)? Because the standard white attack by c5, b4, a4 and b5 is more effective without that defensive bishop. Or consider an attack by f3 and e4, which can lead to a target on e6. That square that is defended if Black has his bad bishop, whereas the f3 + e4 attack almost always comes at the cost of counter play, e.g., by ...c5 or ...e5. Thus the whole idea arises infrequently in this opening.

Finally, an obvious point: the 'freeing move' ...e5 actually frees something, i.e., the bishop! This is especially true after the very common ...f4 attack for Black. Alternately, the c8-bishop sometimes gets out by ...♗d7-e8-h5, or ...b6 and ...♗b7, when after ...c5 the bishop can gain activity and/or protect crucial light squares. Finally, there is the set-up with ...c5 and ...♗d7, a modest but handy square; the bishop's placement is then non-ideal, but keeps an eye on the vulnerable e6 while monitoring queenside squares and clearing the back rank.

For all that I would prefer the bishop on g2, however unenthusiastically, to the one on c8. But one should not expect too much from that imbalance, nor be surprised if it turns against one.

7 b3 ♕e7 8 ♗b2 0-0 9 ♕c2 ♗d7 10 ♘e5 ♘a6 *(D)*

11 ♘xd7

An extraordinary decision! The e5-knight is a monster, and can even gain support from ♘d2-f3. Why on earth would Flohr give it up for a bishop? The first part of the answer is that after 11 ♘d2 ♗e8, as mentioned above, Black might bring the bishop to the useful square h5. Another point has to do with Dvoretsky's 'superfluous knight' concept: after ♘d2-f3, one

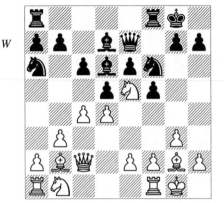

could argue that two knights aren't really needed to cover one square (e5). That may or may not be true if White then reorganizes with ♘d3-f4, but the whole issue is certainly not clear, especially if Black gets ...g5 in.

Aside from the above, there's a third potential reason for eliminating Black's light-squared bishop, already noted above. Although it doesn't come up in this game, White will often execute a central break by f3 and e4. In that case Black's bad bishop defends critical squares such as e6, d5 and f5.

11...♕xd7 12 ♘d2 g5 13 ♘f3 ♕g7 14 ♕c1 g4

14...♘e4!? would prepare ...f4. Then 15 ♘e5 f4 16 cxd5 cxd5 (16...exd5 17 ♗xe4 dxe4 18 ♕c2) 17 ♗xe4 dxe4 18 ♕c4 ♘c7 19 ♕c2! gains some advantage.

15 ♘e5

This knight isn't superfluous! And to capture it would risk positional disaster on the dark squares.

15...♘b8!? 16 ♗a3

This time White returns to the traditional exchange of the opponent's good bishop for his bad one. He thus wins crucial dark squares, and from now on that is the key to his advantage.

16...♗xa3 17 ♕xa3 ♘bd7 18 ♘d3 ♖fe8 19 ♖ac1 ♘f8 *(D)*

20 ♕b2!

Instead of trying to infiltrate by ♕d6 or some such, White calmly advances on the queenside and allows Black to do the same on the kingside.

20...h5 21 b4 h4 22 b5 hxg3 23 fxg3 ♕h6 24 ♘f4 ♖e7 25 e3 ♖h7 26 ♗h1 ♘h5 27 ♕f2 ♘d7 28 bxc6 bxc6 29 cxd5 ♘xf4

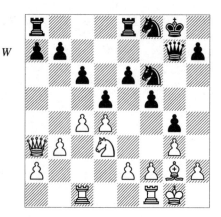

W

Not 29...exd5? which runs into 30 &xc6 (or 30 &xd5).

30 exf4 exd5

30...cxd5 31 &c6 threatens 32 &xd5, and 31...&b6 32 &e1 keeps Black hopelessly tied down, a cute (if unnecessary) white idea showing up in the line 32...&e8 33 a4 &he7 34 a5 &c4 35 &exe6! &xe6 36 &xd5 &h8 37 &xe6 &xe6 38 &xc4 with a winning game.

31 &fe1 &b6 32 &e5 &c4

Fairly desperate, but &e2 was threatened and Black was getting killed anyway.

33 &xf5

33 &xd5 &b8 34 &c5 &b2 35 &xc6! is more complicated, but also good.

33...&e8 34 &g5+ &g7 35 &e1??

A tactical oversight spoils the whole effort. Either 35 &xd5 cxd5 36 &xd5+ &h8 37 &xc4 or 35 &xg7+ would have won without too much trouble.

35...&xe1+ 36 &xe1 &xg5 37 &e8+?!

37 fxg5 is better: 37...&xg5 38 &e6+ &h7 39 &f7+ &h6 with equality.

37...&f8 38 &e6+ &f7 39 &xf7+ &xf7 40 fxg5 &e3

Black may well be winning now, but Flohr manages to draw.

41 &g2 &f5 42 &f2 &xd4 43 h4 gxh3 44 &xh3 &e6 45 g6+ &f6 46 &e3 &e5?!

46...c5! looks like a good try: 47 &g2 d4+ 48 &e4 &g5+!.

47 &d3 c5 48 &g4 ½-½

In the following game, Black's super-bad bishop not only protects a good pawn, but manages to become active with decisive effect after aeons of imprisonment.

Ljubojević – Beliavsky
Tilburg 1984

The French Winawer variation has all sorts of astonishing and paradoxical cases of good and bad bishops for both colours, often making lengthy trips to assert themselves as attackers or defenders. Even some standard variations contain positions that at first sight seem absurdly bad for Black based upon his light squared bishop's immobility. Yet these lines are played continually with perfectly good results for Black.

1 e4 e6 2 d4 d5 3 &c3 &b4 4 e5 c5 5 a3 &xc3+ 6 bxc3 &e7 7 &g4 0-0 8 &f3 &bc6 9 &d3 f5 10 exf6 &xf6 11 &g5 &f7 12 &xe7 &xe7 13 &h4 (D)

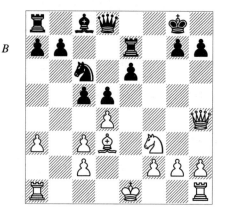

B

13...g6

Here 13...h6 is very often played and has had decent results. It certainly looks more logical to keep the pawns off light squares and avoid the serious holes on f6 and h6 that 13...g6 creates. But paradoxically, 13...g6 has quite a few advantages over 13...h6. These are the sorts of things that must be seen to be understood. As in the Stonewall Dutch, the combination of ...g6 and ...c4 can leave White's bishop 'biting on granite'. In the long run it should still prove superior to Black's, but there are hidden factors in the details. Stefan Kindermann and Ulrich Dirr's remarkable book *Französisch Winawer* shows how a wide variety of positions are playable in which this bishop is semi-permanently imprisoned. That contradicts the opinion of all theoreticians (and most if not all players) up until the last two decades or so.

14 0-0 c4 15 ♗e2 ♕f8

Both working along the f-file and covering kingside dark squares. It is a reasonable move, although the counterattacking line 15...♗d7 16 ♖fe1 ♕a5 has also done well and is probably easier to play.

16 ♖fe1 ♗d7 17 ♗f1

The role of Black's bad bishop and the surprising resilience of his defence is shown by lines like 17 ♗d1 ♔g7 18 ♕g3 ♕f6 19 ♖b1 b6 20 ♘e5 ♘xe5 21 ♖xe5 ♖f8 22 ♗g4 *(D)*.

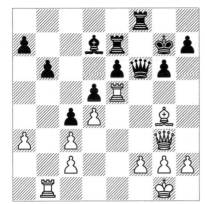

Isn't this almost the stereotype of an ideal position for White? He controls e5 in front of a backward pawn on an open file, and his bishop is purely good at the same time as Black's is bad. But one thing that we are learning is that defence of a key pawn will often fully justify a bishop's existence, and in similar games White has seldom been able to make progress in such positions. From the diagram, play continued: 22...♕f4 23 ♖be1 ♕xg3 24 hxg3 ♔f6 25 f4 h5 26 ♗f3 ♖fe8 27 ♔f2 ♗a4 28 ♖1e2 ♖d8 29 g4 hxg4 30 ♗xg4 ♖d6 31 ♗f3 ♔h7 32 g4 ♗d7 33 ♔g3 b5 (might as well put another pawn on a light square! But this move has a serious purpose, seen next) 34 ♖e1, and now Kindermann gives 34...♖a6! (34...♖h8!? was played in Van der Wiel-Brenninkmeijer, Dutch Cht 1987, and Black was still OK, but he needed to play the ...♖a6 idea soon thereafter) 35 g5+ ♔f7 36 ♗xd5 exd5 37 ♖e7+ ♔g8 38 ♖xh7 ♔xh7 39 ♖e7+ ♔g8 40 ♖xd7 ♖xa3 with equality.

17...♖ae8 18 ♕g5?!

Remarkably, Black was fine in spite of his bishop after 18 ♖e2 ♔g7 19 ♖b1 b6 20 ♖be1 h6 21 ♕g3 ♕f7 in Lanc-Draško, Tbilisi 1985.

18...♖f7 19 ♕d2 ♕d6 20 ♘e5 ♘xe5 21 ♖xe5 ♖ef8 22 ♖e2 ♕f4

Black is better!

23 ♕e1!?

Cirić gives 23 ♕xf4 ♖xf4 24 g3 ♖f3 25 ♗g2 ♖xc3 26 ♔f1 b5 27 ♔e1 a5 28 ♖d2 b4 29 axb4 axb4 30 ♖a7 ♖f7 31 ♗h3 as unclear; but 31...♔g7 32 f4 b3 is very strong.

23...g5

Another 25 moves from now and you realize that this makes room for Black's bishop on the kingside!

24 g3 ♕f5 25 ♗g2 g4! 26 ♕d2 ♕h5

With the idea ...♖f6-h6.

27 ♖e5 ♖f5 28 ♖ae1 ♖xe5 29 ♖xe5 ♖f5 30 ♖e2 *(D)*

After 30 ♖xf5? ♕xf5 simply ...♗a4 follows, winning a pawn! The ...♗a4 theme crops up just often enough to remind us that the bishop really isn't wholly passive.

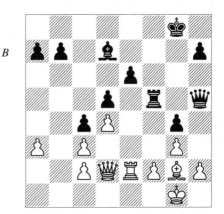

30...♔f7!

Watch this king, which walks all the way to the queenside and is ultimately an attacking piece!

31 ♕c1 ♔e7 32 ♕b1 ♗c6 33 ♕e1 ♕g6 34 h3 h5 35 hxg4?

35 h4 is essential, trying to block the position as far as possible.

35...hxg4 36 ♖e3 ♔d6 37 ♔f1 b6 38 ♔g1

Not 38 ♔e2? ♗a4 39 ♕b1 ♗xc2!.

38...♗d7 39 ♕e2 ♔c7 40 ♕d1 ♖f6 41 ♖e2 ♔b7 42 ♕c1 ♗a6

Now if the queens come off, the king is ready to attack on the queenside.

43 ♕b2 ♕h6 44 ♕b1 ♕f8 45 ♕c1 ♖f5 46 ♕b2 ♕f6 47 ♕b1 ♗e8 48 ♕e1 ♗f7 49 ♕b1

♕e7 50 ♕b2 ♕d6 51 ♖e1 ♖h5 52 ♖e2 ♗g6 53 ♖e1 ♖h8 54 ♖e5 ♕d7 55 ♔f1 ♗f5

Finally getting outside the pawn-chain. After over 50 moves, this has finally become a good bishop! And notice that White's own bishop hasn't even budged since move 25.

56 ♖e1 ♕h7 57 ♖e2? ♕h6 58 ♖e3 ♖h7 59 ♖e5 ♖f7 60 ♖e2 ♗e4!

This piece delivers the final blow.

61 ♗xe4 dxe4 62 ♔e1 ♕h1+ 63 ♔d2 e3+ 0-1

It's immediately over after 64 ♔xe3 (64 ♖xe3 ♖xf2+ 65 ♖e2 ♖f1; 64 fxe3 ♖f1) 64...♕d1!.

As I have said elsewhere, some common sayings are pretty useful, and the old saw that 'opposite-coloured bishops tend to favour the attacker' is both handy and true, especially with a few pieces off the board and some sort of realistic targets against which to direct the bishop's power. Although it's not usually expressed, it's also true that there is more likely to be a situation with mutual attacking chances when there are opposite-coloured bishops on the board. As usual, one must develop an instinct for which cases this might apply to and which not; that is normally gained by dint of experience. Nevertheless, this guideline is more useful than most since, crucially, it doesn't restrict one's thought. That one might look for some attacking chances when one has such a bishop is at worst harmless; no one is going to insist on attacking in a position with no such prospects just because there are opposite-coloured bishops. For the sake of comparison, I would remind you of the kind of rule-based thought that can and often does limit the imagination. One very well might (and many players do) dismiss worthwhile possibilities by adhering too closely to the notions of quick development in the opening, or of not moving knights to the rim, or of avoiding bad bishops entirely. That mode of thinking can lead to very good moves being missed and later explanations like 'I thought that I had to develop some pieces so that didn't even occur to me', 'Well I didn't consider that continuation because the knight looked funny out there' or 'I couldn't play with a bad bishop'.

Here's a crazy game that illustrates how in situations with opposite-coloured bishops one

can sometimes throw caution to the winds just to open lines:

Zviagintsev – J. Polgar
Las Vegas FIDE 1999

1 d4 ♘f6 2 c4 e6 3 ♘c3 ♗b4 4 ♘f3 c5 5 g3 cxd4 6 ♘xd4 0-0 7 ♗g2 d5 8 cxd5 ♘xd5 9 ♕b3 ♕b6 10 ♗xd5 exd5 11 ♗e3

This is a fairly well-known position from the Nimzo-Indian that also arises from the English Opening. Now Black creates opposite-coloured bishops.

11...♗xc3+ 12 ♕xc3 ♕g6

White's unchallenged pieces on the dark squares are obvious, but Black has opposite-coloured bishop attacking themes of her own planned; e.g., ...♗h3, ...♘d7, ...♖ac8, ...♘e5-c4 or similar moves.

13 h4!

Another of those darned flank thrusts! White would love to get h5-h6 in and take advantage of his unopposed dark-squared bishop.

13...h5?!

This is natural but turns out to be wrong. 13...h6 was probably best. Zviagintsev gives a pretty variation with 13...♗g4?! 14 h5! ♗xh5 15 f3! ♕xg3+ 16 ♔d2 ♗g6 17 f4! (threatening 18 ♖ag1) 17...♕g4 18 f5!, winning a piece in view of 18...♗xf5? 19 ♖ag1 ♕e4 20 ♖xg7+ ♔xg7 21 ♘e6+! ♔g6 22 ♘xf8# (the prettiest of three mates). As usual, a move like 13 h4 requires tactical justification.

14 g4! *(D)*

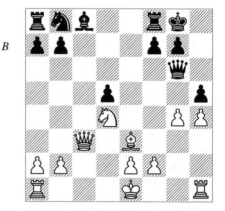

A beautiful move that illustrates what I said above. White is willing to make line-opening moves that he would shun were it not for the opposite-coloured bishops.

14...♗xg4

White was threatening to open the g-file by 15 gxh5, while 14...hxg4 is extremely strongly met by 15 h5 ♕e4 16 f3 ♕e5 17 h6.

15 f3 ♖c8

Otherwise the queen will still eye g7 after ♖g1.

16 ♕d2 *(D)*

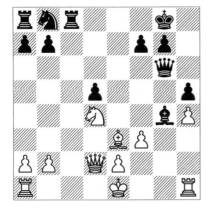

16...♘c6?!

A bit too desperate, trying to give away a piece for the sake of her own counterattack. 16...♗d7 17 ♔f2 ♕a6 18 ♖ag1 g6 was better, when White can still press after Zviagintsev's suggestion of 19 ♖g5.

17 fxg4 ♘e5 18 gxh5?

Plausible but giving Black a needed tempo. Better was 18 ♘f5! ♖e8 19 ♕xd5! ♗h7! (not 19...♘xg4 losing to 20 ♗d4) 20 ♖f1! ♖ad8 21 ♕b3, 'winning' according to Zviagintsev, although that seems exaggerated after 21...hxg4!. Instead, 21...♘xg4?! is fascinating, but 22 ♗d4 ♘h2! 23 ♖g1! ♕xf5 24 ♖xg7+ ♔h6 25 ♖xf7 ♘f3+ 26 ♕xf3 ♕xf3 27 ♗g7+ ♔g6 28 ♖xf3 ♔xg7 29 ♖c1 seems good enough to win.

18...♕e4

Now Black seems to have just enough counterplay. I give the rest of the game with no notes, since opposite-coloured bishops are no longer a factor. White is always a bit better, but not enough so to win.

19 ♖g1 ♘c4 20 ♕d3 ♘xe3 21 ♕xe4 dxe4 22 ♔f2 ♘c2 23 ♖ad1 ♖c5! 24 ♘xc2 ♖xc2 25 ♖d7 ♖xb2 26 h6 g6 27 h5 e3+! 28 ♔xe3 ♖e8+

½-½

Bishops in Complex Environments

The following game highlights several types of bishops in changing roles. White's extra pawn, serious weaknesses, and pathetically bad bishop end up being a match for Black's bishop-pair.

Solozhenkin – Aleksandrov
St Petersburg Chigorin mem 1997

1 d4 d5 2 c4 e6 3 ♘f3 ♘f6 4 ♘c3 c6 5 e3 ♘bd7 6 ♕c2 ♗d6 7 ♗e2 0-0 8 0-0 ♕e7 9 ♗d2 dxc4 10 ♗xc4 e5 11 h3 e4 12 ♘g5 ♘b6 13 ♗b3 ♘fd5!

A positional pawn sacrifice that looks good, even though Black may not regain the material in the foreseeable future.

14 ♘gxe4 ♗f5 15 f3 ♖ae8 16 ♕d1 *(D)*

'!' according to Solozhenkin. The move either consolidates the pawn advantage for the time being or grants White some positional trumps.

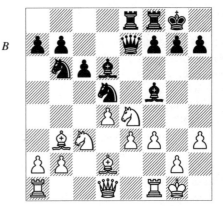

16...♗b8!?

A bold decision, trusting in the bishops. Very instructive is 16...♘xc3 17 bxc3! (17 ♘xc3 ♗d3 18 ♘e2 {18 ♖e1 ♗g3} 18...c5! gives Black more than enough play) 17...♗xe4 18 fxe4 ♕xe4 19 ♕f3! ♕xf3 20 ♖xf3 with the two bishops and the f-file, when Black's control of e4 may not yield enough counterplay; for example, 20...♘d5 (20...♘d7 21 ♖af1 ♘f6 22 ♖xf6! gxf6 23 ♖xf6) 21 ♖af1 ♖e7 22 c4 ♘f6 23 ♗e1 ♘e4 24 c5 ♗c7 25 ♗h4 g5 26 ♗e1 and White has ideas of ♖f5, g4, h4, etc.

17 ♘xd5 ♘xd5 18 ♗xd5 cxd5 19 ♘f2 ♕c7
20 f4 *(D)*

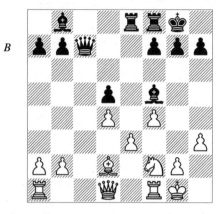

Uggh. Now White has an extra pawn, but his bad bishop looks awful and his centre is full of weak spots. For his part, Black has the bishop-pair and the open e-file; surely this constitutes *more* than enough compensation? It turns out that White's bishop is surprisingly effective, and this influences the assessment.

20...♕b6

Versus 21 ♗b4. This is more enterprising than the more strictly positional 20...♖e6 21 ♖c1 ♕b6 22 b3 ♖fe8 23 ♕f3 ♗e4 24 ♘xe4 ♖xe4 25 ♖c5 ♕e6, when White has some kind of theoretical advantage.

21 ♕a4!

Again thinking about ♗b4.

21...♖c8!?

Not bad, but in such positions, one should normally seize the initiative when one can. Apparently Black is reluctant to make an exchange sacrifice, which is an unusual feeling these days! I like the look of 21...♕xb2! 22 ♗b4 (22 ♕b4 ♕xb4 23 ♗xb4 ♖xe3 24 ♗xf8 ♔xf8 and the bishop-pair and pawn are more than enough for the exchange) 22...b5! (22...♗d7!?) intending 23 ♕xb5!? (similar positions result from 23 ♕a3 ♕xa3 24 ♗xa3 ♖xe3 25 ♗xf8 ♔xf8 and Black stands well, or 23 ♕a5 ♗c7! 24 ♕xb5 a5 25 ♕xd5 axb4 26 ♕xf5 ♖xe3 when Black threatens ...♕xd4, ...♖e2, and ...♗b6) 23...♖xe3 with the idea 24 ♘d1 ♕xa1 25 ♘xe3 ♕xd4 26 ♗xf8 ♕xe3+ 27 ♖f2 (not 27 ♔h1?? losing to 27...♗e4!) 27...♕c1+ 28 ♖f1 ♕e3+ with a draw. These are instructive lines with respect to the power of bishops.

22 ♗c3 ♖fe8 23 ♖fe1 ♗d6

23...♕e6 or 23...h5 should be considered.

24 ♖ac1 ♖e7 25 ♕d1

Solozhenkin actually likes White here because of the idea of ♕f3 hitting the d-pawn.

25...♖ce8 26 ♕d2

Black has compensation after 26 ♕f3 ♕b5 27 g4 ♗e4. It's odd, however, that any idea of his having the advantage has disappeared.

26...♕a6?!

26...h6! improves, according to Solozhenkin, although he assesses the position as slightly better for White.

27 a3! *(D)*

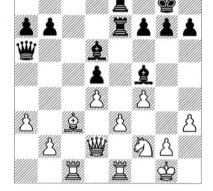

Ironically, putting another pawn on a dark square secures an advantage! Now that White's weaknesses are covered, 28 ♗b4 is threatened, to win the dark squares along the c-file.

27...♕b5!

27...♗b8 28 ♗b4 ♖e6 29 g4 ♗e4 30 f5 ♖h6 31 ♘xe4 dxe4 32 ♕g2 leaves Black struggling to justify his pawn deficit.

28 ♗b4 ♗xb4 29 ♕xb4

Also possible was 29 axb4 b6 30 g4 with some edge.

29...♕xb4 30 axb4 h5

Probably the best move, creating a flight square. 30...♖xe3!? ('??' according to Solozhenkin) is very interesting, because White keeps the advantage due to *Black's* bad bishop! The re-establishment of this conventional situation is typical when material is reduced and as one leaves the middlegame. Play might go 31 ♖xe3 ♖xe3 32 g4 (Solozhenkin assesses this as winning, although Black's bad position does hold together tactically) 32...♗d7 33 ♖c7 (33

Xc5 &e8 34 Xxd5 &f8 intending ...Xb3 in several lines) 33...&c6 34 ♘d1! Xe8 35 b5! &xb5 36 Xxb7 &c4!? 37 ♘c3 with a considerable advantage for White.

31 g4 hxg4 32 hxg4 &d7 33 Xc3

33 Xc7 &b5 34 Xxe7 Xxe7 35 ♘d1, again with a solid edge.

33...&c6 34 &g2 f6 35 &f3 &f7 36 Xh1 &e6 37 Xh7 &d6 38 f5

One of those knight retreats to the corner by 38 ♘h1! intending ♘g3 was another good idea.

38...&d7 39 ♘h3 &a4 40 b3 &c6 1-0

Black didn't want to suffer after 41 ♘f4 &d7 42 ♘g6 Xf7 43 Xc1, since he is a pawn down (doubled, to be sure) with the rook stuck on f7. This might have been worth fighting out, although Xh2-c2 is an effective plan, with either Xc7 or Xc8 to come.

Dvoretsky's recent book *School of Excellence 3: Strategic Play* contains many instructional gems. They generally aren't of the traditional hit-you-over-the-head sort, to be mindlessly absorbed, but require thoughtfulness and concentration upon the part of the reader. The following game says a great deal about modern bishop play and the application of general ideas thereto.

Ehlvest – Andrianov
Bukhara 1981

1 d4 ♘f6 2 c4 e6 3 ♘f3 b6 4 g3 &a6 5 ♕b3 d5 6 cxd5 exd5!? 7 ♘c3 &e7 8 &g2 0-0 9 0-0 c6 10 ♘e5 ♘fd7 11 f4 b5! 12 a3 ♕b6 13 &e3

Already the game is developing into a struggle featuring the good and bad bishops and their interpretation. The move 11...b5 is typical of the pragmatic but optically distasteful modern treatment (see Black's a6-bishop and the glaring hole on an open file on c5). With it, Black transforms a position with a standard white edge into something complex and multi-faceted.

13...♘xe5 14 fxe5 ♘d7 15 &f2 b4 16 axb4 &c4 17 ♕a4 &xb4 18 ♘xd5! cxd5 19 ♕xd7 &xe2 20 Xfc1 Xfd8 21 ♕c7 ♕e6 22 ♕c2 &b5 23 &e1 (D)

Dvoretsky uses this position (and the rest of the game) to make some points about chess

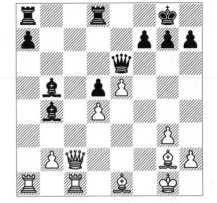

B

thinking and in particular the role of the bishops. Here he challenges the reader with the question "Should Black exchange bishops?" His answer is that "from a formal viewpoint, White's dark-squared bishop is 'bad' (his central pawns are on squares of the same colour as the bishop), whereas Black's is 'good' ... But in chess, formal logic is far from always valid. By standing at c3, the bishop securely defends the vulnerable pawns at b2 and d4, after which White can calmly strengthen his position – the opponent has no counterplay. (As grandmaster Mihai Suba pointed out, a bad bishop sometimes defends good pawns)."

23...&f8?

For the reasons given in the last note, Dvoretsky says that it was 'essential' for Black to pursue the initiative by 23...&xe1! 24 Xxe1 Xac8 25 ♕d2 ♕b6 26 b3 (26 Xac1?! Xc4! 27 Xxc4 dxc4) 26...&d7!, heading for e6 with a solid defence (27 &xd5? &b5). To be fair, I should admit that this suggestion is a good example of the virtues of exchanging when one has less space. In the section on exchanging in Chapter 1, I criticized Dvoretsky for his lack of such examples.

24 &c3 a6 25 ♕d2 &c4 26 &a5?!

Here Dvoretsky suggests 26 &f1 with "the unusual idea of exchanging [White's] g2-bishop for the opponent's 'bad' light-squared bishop". The idea is to get rid of the piece that is protecting all of Black's weak points. This voluntary ceding of White's optically attractive bishop is all the more surprising because it also contradicts the previously-mentioned advice not to exchange when you control more space. Nevertheless the move looks quite good. Dvoretsky provides the following abbreviated analysis: 26 ♗f1!? (D).

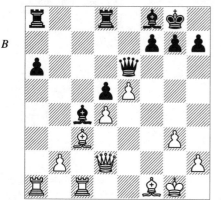

26...h5?! (26...♖dc8 27 ♗xc4 ♖xc4 28 ♖a5 "and then ♖ca1 or ♕g2") 27 ♗xc4 dxc4 28 ♖a5 ♖d5 29 ♖xd5 ♕xd5 30 ♕g2 "with an obvious advantage in the ending". How many average players, regardless of their experience, would be so free of textbook influence to consider playing this way and then to follow through? Such paradoxical exchanges are incidentally very typical of how Black can get in trouble in the French Defence. Furthermore, the analogous King's Indian positions with White's bad bishop on f3 and pawns on g2, e4, and d5 versus Black's good bishop on d7 or b7 with pawns on d6 and e5 are often difficult or lost for Black, who has trouble defending his good pawns.

26...♖dc8 27 ♗b4?

Ironically, Black's good bishop was worth less than White's bad one, the former having nothing useful to do or protect. As Dvoretsky has already pointed out, it is the protective function of White's dark-squared bishop that is so valuable.

Incidentally, one should note that almost none of what we're saying about these bishops would apply in the endgame. As I have often said, traditional rules tend to apply much better in the endgame than in the opening or middlegame. Indeed much of the misunderstanding and dogmatism of the textbooks arises from the fact that such 'principles' are derived from endgame positions and then incorrectly generalized to other situations.

27...♗xb4 28 ♕xb4 ♖ab8

At this point Dvoretsky meekly tries to defend the conventional wisdom by stating, "the negation of some obvious rule does not signify that the position is not subject to the laws of chess – it is simply that other, latent principles and rules are operating." In this case, the other 'latent principles and rules' include 'the initiative' and 'the possibility of being the first to mount an attack on the opponent's pawns'. I could launch into another speech here about how such an interpretation fails on the grounds of efficient explanation and is at best irrelevant due to linguistic confusion. Just ask yourself how a player would use those and a few hundred other such 'principles and rules' (??) to make assessments ('the possibility of being the first...' is a 'principle'?). But I have amply covered that ground elsewhere and won't bore the reader again. Abstractions apart, White's bad bishop that protected his good pawns is now gone while Black's remains, so time is now of the essence for White to neutralize the play against his b- and d-pawns.

29 ♕d2 ♖b3?!

Dvoretsky doesn't like exchanging rooks and suggests 29...♖b5! to triple by ...♕b6 and ...♖cb8. Then his earlier imaginative idea of 30 ♗f1! still looks right, holding some sort of balance after 30...♖cb8 31 ♗xc4 dxc4; e.g., 32 ♖c2 ♖b3 33 ♕e2?! ♖d3 34 ♖d1 ♖bb3! 35 ♖xd3! cxd3 36 ♕e4 h6 with equality.

30 ♖c3 ♖cb8 31 ♖xb3 ♖xb3 32 ♖c1 h6

32...f6!? is also of interest, since 33 exf6 ♕xf6 34 ♖f1! ♕e6 35 ♖e1? loses to 35...♖xb2!.

33 ♖c3 (D)

33...♕b6!?

Dvoretsky assigns this a '?', but that doesn't seem to correspond to his assessment of what happens next. He suggests that Black should keep the rooks on by 33...♖b4 ('!') 34 ♖f3 ♕b6 35 ♖f2, which is OK for White, since ♕f4 will divert Black from the queenside. Interestingly, he bemoans the fact that the bishop isn't on e6 protecting both d5 and f7. The irony there is that Suba's bad-bishops-protect-good-pawns maxim would then have reached its ultimate application, since normally bishops in front of the weaknesses they protect (here, on c4) are considered better than ones passively placed behind them.

34 ♖xb3 ♕xb3

Dvoretsky explains that the game is now level because Black's active queen cannot be driven back. Otherwise, White's bishop would give him the advantage, because it really is somewhat better than its rival now. He says "at last it is possible, without mistake, to apply the standard evaluation to the strength of the bishops." Unfortunately he doesn't seem to take note that we are now well and truly in an endgame, a stage at which that evaluation so normally applies that we might even dare to call it a ... rule? In this context, Euwe says: "In order to appraise the value of a bad bishop in any given position, it is important to consider how much material remains on the board. The weakness of the bad bishop is highlighted as the endgame approaches. And this brings us to the important conclusion that while the bad bishop can be quite strong in cooperation with other pieces, its strength wanes as opportunities for cooperation diminish with exchanges or unsuitable [placements] of other pieces."

35 ♔f2 a5 36 h4

36 ♗f3 followed by ♗d1 is better according to Dvoretsky. I'm not sure that there's much difference.

36...a4 37 ♗h3 ♗d3

Heading for e4.

38 e6?!

This is a mistake. 38 ♗g4! would equalize, still thinking about ♗d1.

38...♗e4?!

Much better was Dvoretsky's suggestion 38...f5!. That clever move would guarantee a considerable advantage by isolating White's e-pawn and preparing ...♗e4. After 39 ♗g2 ♗e4,

White would have trouble against moves like ...♕b6 and ...♔f8.

39 exf7+ ♔xf7 40 ♕f4+ ♔g8??

Time-pressure decides on the last move of the control. 40...♔g6 or 40...♔e7 draws.

41 ♗e6+ ♔h7 42 ♕xe4+! dxe4 43 ♗xb3 axb3 44 ♗e3 1-0

A tragedy, but what a wonderful game for understanding the middlegame and the bishops in particular. Dvoretsky consistently finds these sorts of subtle and intricate real-world battles that make his books stand out above the usual fare.

Restless Bishops

The knights aren't the only pieces that are increasingly to be found wandering around from one position to another at cost of time. It's impossible to do justice to the number of new bishop moves that seem to defy the rules of development. In any number of positions from modern practice, for example, fianchettoed bishops are returned to their original positions for a new task. Some simple examples are in double d-pawn and Indian openings in which Black first plays ...♗b7 or even ...♗a6 and then ...♗b7, yet after the exchange cxd5 and ...exd5 he reroutes that bishop to c8 and then, say, e6 (see the Tartakower Variation examples in Chapter 1). There are many King's Indian Defence variations in which after ...e5 and d5, Black will play ...♖e8 and ...♗f8. This is usually to defend against c5 and protect the d-pawn, but sometimes also to play ...♘h5, ...♗e7, ...♖f8, and ...f5! We also see White play ♗g2-f1 in a number of queen's pawn openings for the sake of protecting c4 and preventing ...b5. But what about the reverse process? Are there times when a player develops a bishop to a logical square and then re-routes it to a fianchettoed position? Here is a surprising example:

Schüssler – Miles
Reykjavik 1986

1 d4 ♘f6 2 c4 e6 3 ♘f3 b6 4 ♘c3 ♗b4 5 ♗g5 ♗b7 6 e3 h6 7 ♗h4 g5 8 ♗g3 ♘e4

So far so normal for a Nimzo-Indian Defence. Black will often aim to double two sets of pawns: one by the standard ...♗xc3 that we see in many Nimzo-Indians, and the other by ...♘xg3. Many hundreds of games have been played with that general strategy.

9 ♘d2

An example of what I said in the last note would be 9 ♕c2 ♗xc3+ 10 bxc3 ♘xg3, etc.

9...♘xg3

With this move-order, Black can accept the pawn sacrifice at the cost of some development and looseness by 9...♘xc3 10 bxc3 ♗xc3 11 ♖c1. That's rather risky.

10 hxg3 ♘c6!?

10...♗xc3 11 bxc3 ♘c6 is the normal plan.

11 ♕c2 *(D)*

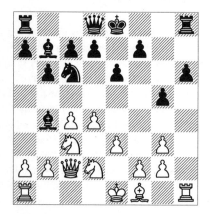

White wants to recapture on c3 with the queen. Black chooses to avoid this exchange, although in similar positions he has gone through with it and followed up by ...♕e7, ...0-0-0, and perhaps ...h5-h4. That strategy normally leads to a small advantage for White.

11...♗f8!

A new idea at the time, as far as I know. Black takes extra time to retain two bishops and with a complete reversal of direction tries a double fianchetto! He also protects his h-pawn thereby and so can defend against ideas of White's like doubling on the h-file. In fact, the idea of ...0-0-0 can be and has been safely replaced by ...0-0 in such positions. The reason that Miles doesn't play that way is that he wants to attack on the kingside!

12 a3

Not 12 ♗e2? ♘b4 and ...♗xg2.

12...♗g7 13 ♗e2 ♕e7

As discussed, 13...0-0 is also playable.

14 g4 0-0-0 15 0-0-0 ♔b8 16 ♔b1 ♖df8 17 ♗f3 h5!? *(D)*

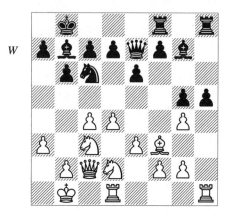

A typically creative Miles positional pawn sacrifice. The idea is to gain space and a pawn attack in return for White's extra pawn on h5, whose importance is yet to be decided. We have seen that the possession of two bishops is often worth a pawn, especially if they are supported by the initiative.

18 ♖xh5 ♖xh5 19 gxh5 f5 20 g4!?

Returning the pawn for positive play based on the passed h-pawn. White can't wait around; e.g., 20 b4? g4 21 ♗e2 ♕h4; but a defensive move like 20 ♘e2 was possible.

20...fxg4 21 ♗xg4 ♖xf2 22 ♕g6

22 ♕h7 appears more effective. Perhaps White saw nothing promising after 22...♖f6 or 22...♖h2.

22...♕f6!?

22...♖f6! intending 23 ♕xg5?! ♗h6 is a good idea, but Miles is confident in a two-bishop ending where the h-pawn is easily blockaded.

23 ♕c2

23 ♘de4 ♕xg6 24 hxg6 ♖f8 25 ♘xg5 ♘e7 gives Black plenty of counterplay.

23...♘d8 24 c5?! ♕f7 25 cxb6 axb6 26 ♘b5?! ♘c6

White's play hasn't been very pointed and Black stands very well now. I give the rest of the game without notes:

27 ♘c3 ♖g2 28 ♗e2 g4 29 ♕g6 ♕f6 30 ♕e8+ ♕d8 31 ♕g6 ♕h8 32 ♕f7 ♗h6 33 ♘f1 g3 34 ♕xd7 ♖g1 35 ♘b5 ♕c8 36 ♕h7 g2 37 ♕xh6 ♖h1 38 ♕f4 g1♕ 39 ♘g3 e5 40 dxe5 ♕xd1+ 41 ♗xd1 ♖xd1+ 42 ♔c2 ♕d8 43 ♘d6 cxd6 44 e6 0-1

A similar bishop manoeuvre takes place in the following game, which contains various other ideas of note.

J. Garcia Gutierrez – Kalinichenko
corr. 1988

1 e4 e6 2 d4 d5 3 ②d2 ②f6 4 e5 ②fd7 5 f4 c5 6 c3 ②c6 7 ②df3 ♕b6 8 g3 cxd4 9 cxd4 ♗b4+ 10 ♔f2

We talked about a variant on this line in Chapter 1 in which Black developed five pieces before White brought out more of his.

10...g5! *(D)*

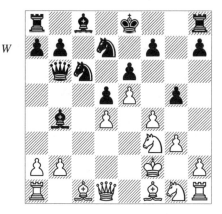

Another example of a purely pragmatic thrust whose justification is tactical. For many years, it either went unnoticed or was summarily dismissed in theoreticians' notes. Almost unquestionably this was due to its loosening nature and anti-positional appearance, which is accentuated after a few moves.

11 fxg5

There are several ways to stop the threat of ...g4 and ...②xd4. I won't even begin to delve into the considerably theory that has built up here, but it's amazing that if White defends by the solid 11 ♗e3, Black doesn't even need to challenge the massive centre by the dynamic 11...f6 12 ♗h3 h5!?, but can let White keep his centre completely intact by 11...g4. Then he obtains good play following 12 ②d2 (12 ②h4 ♗e7) 12...h5 (12...f6 is also played) 13 h3 f6!.

An excellent illustration of the themes in our main game is 11 h3 gxf4 12 ♗xf4 f6 13 ♔g2 ♗f8! (hitting b2, organizing a fianchetto to exert pressure against e5, and defending the king!) 14 ♖b1 ♗g7 *(D)*.

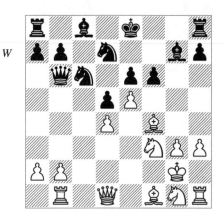

White can take aim at various loosely defended points in Black's position, but on the other hand his centre is in danger of crumbling: 15 ♗d3 (15 exf6 ②xf6 favours Black owing to the weakness of White's d-pawn; the natural follow-up would be ...0-0 and ...②e4) 15...0-0!? (15...②b4! is better, because it eliminates any hope that White has of attacking) 16 exf6 (16 ♕c2 looks strong, but 16...fxe5 17 ♗xh7+ ♔h8 18 dxe5 ②dxe5 gives Black sufficient counterplay) 16...②xf6 17 ♗d6 ♖d8 18 ♗c5 ♕c7 19 ②e2 ②e4 20 ♗a3?! (20 ♕c2 b6 21 ♗b4 ♗b7 is dynamically equal) 20...e5 21 dxe5 ②xe5 22 ②xe5 ♗xe5 (22...♕xe5! looks more promising) 23 ♖c1 ♕b6 24 ♖g1 ♕h6 25 ♖c2 ♗f5 26 g4 ♕g7 27 ♕e3 ♖e8 28 ♕f3 ♗d7 29 ②f4 ♗c6 30 ②h5 ♕h6 31 h4 ♔h8 32 g5 ♖g8 33 ②g3 ♕g6 34 ♖e1 ♗xg3 35 ♕xg3 ②xg3 36 ♗xg6 hxg6 37 ♔xg3 ½-½ Yudasin-Moskalenko, Sverdlovsk 1984.

11...②dxe5 12 ②xe5 ②xe5 13 ♔g2 ②c6

Here 13...②c4 is also possible.

14 ②f3 ♗d7 15 ♗f4

A traditional-looking position has arisen in which White has two active bishops and control over e5. Black's king has nowhere to go whereas White's is relatively safe. But there is one other consideration:

15...♗f8! 16 ♕d2 ♗g7 *(D)*

By this original manoeuvre, the bishop puts direct pressure on White's only weakness: his d-pawn. The g7-bishop also covers e5, so that an incursion on that square can be met by exchanges.

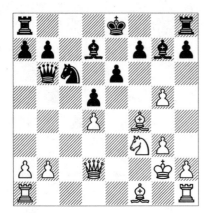

W

17 Rd1 Rc8 18 a3 Ne7!?

This move prepares ...Ba4 or, if the situation presents itself, ...Bb5. But it also takes pressure off d4. Instead, 18...0-0 is the natural way to get developed before undertaking operations; e.g., 19 Be2 Na5!? 20 Be5 Ba4! 21 Bxg7 Kxg7 and White will have to give up the exchange for active play. That will probably not be sufficient compensation.

19 Bd3 Bxd4?

Sacrificing the dark squares and bishop-pair for the sake of a centre pawn. This is risky at best, and probably just bad, so preferable is 19...Ba4 20 Rc1 Rxc1 (20...0-0!?) 21 Rxc1 Nc6 or 19...Bb5 20 Bb1!? Ng6. In both cases Black has full-fledged chances.

20 Nxd4 Qxd4 21 Qe2 Nc6 22 Bxh7 Kg7 23 Bb1 0-0 24 Rhf1!

This seems to encourage Black's expansion in the centre, but the two bishops will also have their say in things.

24...e5

24...Rfe8 is the move that Rhf1 anticipated. Then 25 Qh5 e5 26 Bd2 e4 (26...Be6 27 Rf6!

intending Rh6) 27 Bc3 d4 28 Rxd4! is everything White could have wished for.

25 Bc1?

Both sides underestimated 25 Rxd5! with the idea 25...Be6 (25...exf4 26 Rxd7 Ne5 27 Rxb7 f3+ 28 Rxf3 Nxf3 29 Qxf3 Qxg5 30 h4) 26 Rxe5! Nxe5 27 Qxe5 with two pawns, the dark squares, and an attack for the exchange. That should be easily enough to win with.

25...Nd4! 26 Qh5 Ba4

Black has grabbed back the initiative and threatens to eliminate White's attack permanently by ...Bc2.

27 Rd2!? Bb5

This isn't bad, but 27...Nb3! is obvious and more effective.

28 Bd3 Bxd3 29 Rxd3 Rc2+ 30 Kh3 Qg6!? 31 Qxg6+ fxg6 32 Rxf8+ Kxf8 33 Be3 Nf5! 34 g4

After 34 Bxa7 d4, moves such as ...e4 and ...Rxb2 are threatened, whereas 35 Rb3 e4 36 g4 loses to 36...d3 37 Rxb7 d2 38 Rd7 Ke8 39 Rd5 Ne7 40 Rd6 Nc8.

34...e4! 35 Rb3 Nxe3 36 Rxe3 Kf7 37 Kg3 Ke6 38 h4 Rxb2 39 h5 Rc2 40 hxg6 Rc7 0-1

The end might be 41 Kf4 Kg7 42 Rh3 Rxg6 43 Rh7 Rg8 44 Rxb7 Rf8+ and Black wins.

The subjects of good-versus-bad bishops, opposite-coloured bishops, and wandering/retreating bishops could consume a whole book, so I'll stop here. In this limited section we have seen that assessing the quality of a bishop and its role in development by employing abstract considerations is practically impossible. The role of bad bishops protecting good pawns has received some further attention, and it will be referred to elsewhere in this book.

3.3 The Minor Pieces Square Off

SOMCS went into so much detail about the pitting of minor pieces against each other that I will limit this section to some examples about situations that didn't receive much coverage there and a few more that struck my fancy. But I haven't really stinted on this crucial subject because there is vast amount of material on minor piece play throughout just about every part of this book, especially examples involving two knights versus two bishops in the section on doubled pawns. I have also tended to supply extra commentary to issues related to minor pieces.

Bishop and Knight Conflicts

In this section, for fun, let's first look at some older (but still modern-era) examples.

Geller – Spassky
USSR Cht (Moscow) 1959

1 ♘f3 ♘f6 2 c4 g6 3 d4 ♗g7 4 ♘c3 0-0 5 e4 d6 6 ♗e2 c5

Many years later, Spassky was on the other side of very similar issues: 6...♗g4 7 ♗e3 ♘fd7 8 0-0 ♘c6 9 d5 ♗xf3 10 ♗xf3 ♘a5 11 ♗e2 ♗xc3!? (turning it into a pure two bishops versus two knights game) 12 bxc3 e5 13 dxe6?! (this opening up of the game hurts White; better was 13 ♖b1 b6 14 ♕d2) 13...fxe6 14 f4 b6. As in our main game, White now has trouble making progress. Black doesn't miss his g7-bishop much, but White's doubled pawns are a real negative. 15 ♕e1 ♕e7 16 ♕g3 ♖ae8 17 ♖ae1?! ♕g7 18 ♗c1 (18 ♖c1) 18...♘c5 19 ♕e3 ♕d7! 20 h4 ½-½ Spassky-Züger, Zurich 1984. In fact, Black stands very well indeed as he can win either the c- or a-pawn after 20...♕c6! (or 20...♕a4) 21 e5 ♕a4 22 h5 ♘xc4 23 ♕g3 ♘e4 24 ♕g4 ♘cd2!.

7 0-0 ♗g4 8 d5 ♘bd7 9 h3 ♗xf3 10 ♗xf3 ♘e8 11 ♗e3 e6!? *(D)*

W

An idea that has got lost in the shuffle. Normally in such positions Black plays for ...b5 with moves such as ...a6, ...♖b8, and ...♘c7. He hasn't enjoyed much success thereby. Spassky's move initiates central action.

12 dxe6?!

Perhaps Geller doesn't see what's happening or reacts too quickly. He proceeds 'thematically' to open up the position for the bishops, but it turns out that the knights are given more freedom to find useful posts. A poor alternative is 12 ♗e2?! ♗xc3! 13 bxc3 ♕e7 with a solid game. But 12 ♖c1 or 12 ♕d2, both preventing the doubled pawns, retains a solid advantage. Then Black has no way to transform the central situation and secure posts for his knights. In many cases White can gradually increase his space advantage on both sides of the board after which the open lines will come of themselves. In general it will be very difficult to contest that expansion. We therefore see little of Black's set-up today.

12...fxe6 13 ♗g4 ♕e7 14 f4

This allows doubled pawns, but other moves aren't convincing given this new pawn-structure; e.g., 14 ♕d2 ♘e5 15 ♗e2 ♘c6! intending ...♘d4.

14...♗xc3 15 bxc3 ♘g7

Prophylaxis against f5.

16 ♕d2 ♘b6! 17 ♕d3 *(D)*

17 &e2 ♘h5 18 ♔h2 ♘f6 and ...♖ad8 is fine for Black.

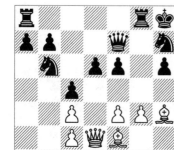

B

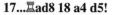

17...♖ad8 18 a4 d5!

Suddenly opening the position and dissolving White's doubled pawns. But Black establishes good squares for his knights thereby, and achieves active play.

19 cxd5 exd5 20 ♕b5!

For example, 20 e5 allows ...♘c4 and then ...♘f5. Now at least White is getting counterplay via a5.

20...d4 21 cxd4 ♕xe4 22 &f2 cxd4 23 a5 ♘c8!? 24 ♖ac1 ♘f5 25 ♕c4+ ♕d5 26 &xf5?!

Too hurried. 26 ♖fd1 has the idea 26...d3!? (26...♘ce7) 27 ♕xd5+ ♖xd5 28 &e2!.

26...♖xf5 27 &xd4 ♕xc4 28 ♖xc4 ♖xa5 29 ♖fc1 ♖ad5

Black is better, but Geller manages to hold on.

30 ♖xc8 ♖xd4 31 ♖1c7 b5 32 ♖xd8+ ♖xd8 33 ♖xa7 ♖b8 34 ♔f2 b4 35 ♔e3 b3 36 ♖a1 b2 37 ♖b1 ♔f7 38 ♔d4 ♔e6 39 g4 ♖b4+ 40 ♔c5 ♖xf4 41 ♖xb2 ♔f6 42 ♖b7 h6 43 ♖b6+ ♔g5 44 h4+ ♔xg4 ½-½

Purdy – Napolitano
corr. Wch 1950-3

Since I am dealing with over-the-board decisions, I have largely neglected to include correspondence games as examples. This creative contest continues the SOMCS discussion of doubled pawns and minor pieces in the Nimzo-Indian, and contains a great number of themes relevant to our purpose. Some of the notes are based upon Tim Harding's excellent ones in his terrific book *64 Great Chess Games: Masterpieces of Postal and Email Chess.*

1 c4 ♘f6 2 d4 e6 3 ♘c3 &b4 4 a3 &xc3+ 5 bxc3 c5 6 e3 ♘c6 7 &d3 e5

An alternative to the far more popular plan of ...0-0, ...b6, ...&a6, ...♘e8 (when necessary), ...♘a5, etc.

8 ♘e2 d6 *(D)*

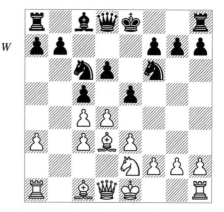

W

Here we have the classical approach to this position involving the direct blocking of White's e4-e5 idea. This strategy characterized early games around Nimzowitsch's time when the Nimzo-Indian began to catch on. I didn't say a great deal about it in SOMCS, since today so many strategies by Black in the Nimzo Indian involve opening the position quickly. Incidentally, for those of you who know this opening, Black seems to be a whole tempo up on the Hübner Variation (4 e3 c5 5 &d3 ♘c6 6 ♘f3 &xc3+ 7 bxc3 d6), since there Black voluntarily captures on c3 without the provocation by a3. The difference is that in our game White's knight has not been committed to the unfavourable square f3 and can keep open the options of kingside pawn advances from its position on e2.

9 e4 ♘h5!?

This is a rare move first tried by Smyslov. The idea is obviously to limit the effectiveness of White's f4 break, but also in some cases to bring Black's queen into play via h4 or f6. 9...0-0 leads to one of the main lines of the Nimzo-Indian Sämisch Variation. Alternatively, playable albeit dangerous is 9...exd4 10 cxd4 cxd4 11 0-0 ♕a5!? (11...0-0 12 &g5 h6 13 &h4 g5 14 &g3 ♘h5 15 ♘xd4!? ♘xg3 16 ♘xc6 bxc6 17 hxg3 ♕f6 is unclear, according to Kasparov) 12 ♗f4 ♕c5 (12...0-0!? 13 ♗xd6 ♖d8 14 ♗f4 b6 is double-edged) 13 ♘c1 ♘a5 14 ♗xd6! ♕xd6 15 e5 with a strong attack, Kasparov-Beliavsky, USSR 1983.

10 0-0

Botvinnik analysed 10 d5 ♘a5 11 f4 ♗g4 12 0-0 exf4 13 ♗xf4 0-0 as unclear.

10...g5!?

A bold flank thrust that at first hardly seems justified with Black's laggard development and off-centre knight, but the simple idea of ...♘f4 makes it reasonable.

11 ♗c2!?

White's idea looks even stranger: it drags the bishop away from the centre and protection of e4. 11 ♗e3 is probably objectively better, after which one plan for White is to play f3 and g3. A rook on a2 would also be handy to defend or attack from the kingside.

11...♘f4 12 ♗a4 (D)

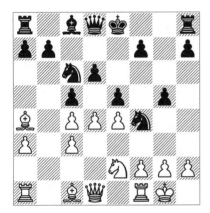

In one way White's is a typical manoeuvre, as he tries to rid himself of a bad bishop and perhaps damage Black's pawns. That definitely has its value. But the plan is also decentralizing, and it's probably a bit much to waste three tempi to give up the bishop-pair, weaken control of e4, and do so without even forcing Black to accept doubled pawns!

12...♗d7 13 ♘g3 cxd4?!

This is probably a mistake although that's not completely clear. Harding points out Black's moves 13-15 were a suggestion from the magazine *Československý Šach*. I doubt that they are very good because they justify White's retention of the dark-squared bishop by allowing

it free play. Bronstein-Smyslov, Budapest Ct 1950 is the fascinating stem game here. The early play looked about equal, White got in trouble in the late middlegame, and just when Black was taking over, Bronstein initiated an imaginative attack that was a thing of beauty and found success: 13...♕f6 (I like this move) 14 d5 ♘e7 15 ♗xd7+ ♔xd7 (now we have bishop and knight versus two knights; the bishop's prospects look pretty limited unless he could somehow get g3 and f4 in, and this is probably unrealistic) 16 ♖b1 ♖hb8! 17 ♕a4+ ♔d8 18 ♕c2 h5 19 ♘f5 ♘fg6 20 ♘e3?! (20 ♘xe7 {20...♘xe7 21 ♗d2 g4 22 f3!} 21 ♕e2 looks much better) 20...♕h8 21 a4 f6 22 a5 ♕e8 23 ♕d1 ♘f8! 24 ♕f3 ♕g6 25 ♘c2 ♘d7 26 ♘a3 a6 27 ♕e3 ♔c7 28 ♗d2 h6! 29 axb6+ ♘xb6 30 ♕d3 ♘d7 31 ♖a1 ♖b6 32 ♘c2 f5 33 f3? (33 exf5) 33...f4 34 ♖a5 g4 35 ♘b4!!? (D).

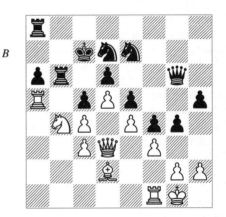

Perhaps this is not quite sound in some objective sense, but Black was beginning to dominate the board. Bronstein's knight sacrifice radically disturbs the peace: 35...gxf3 (35...cxb4 36 cxb4 gxf3 37 ♕xf3 ♘f6 {37...♖g8!} 38 ♖e1 ♕g4 39 ♕f2 ♘g6 40 c5 dxc5 41 bxc5 with very interesting play) 36 ♕xf3 ♕g4 37 ♕f2 cxb4 38 cxb4 ♖bb8 39 c5 ♘c8 40 ♖c1 ♔d8? 41 c6 ♖b5 42 h3 ♕g6 43 cxd7 ♔xd7 44 ♕e2 and White went on to win.

14 ♗xc6 bxc6 15 cxd4 ♕f6 16 ♗e3 h5 17 dxe5 dxe5 18 ♖b1 ♖d8 19 ♕c2 h4 20 ♘f5 ♗xf5 21 exf5 0-0

Harding: "Purdy observes that despite the kingside pawn advances, the black king is safer on g8 than in the centre."

22 ♖fd1 ♘h5?!

With the simple idea ...♘g7 and ...♘xf5. Still, I think that Black should force White to come after the a-pawn by 22...a6 rather than give it away so easily.

23 ♗xa7 ♘g7 24 a4?!

Not terrible, but I don't like the idea behind it at all. As pointed out by Suba and supported by several examples that I came up with in SOMCS, passed rook's pawns tend to be an advantage in the ending but a problem in the middlegame. Here White, who stands considerably better in my estimation, should attend to the business of simplification first by 24 ♗c5 ♖fe8 25 ♕e4! ♘xf5 26 ♖xd8 ♖xd8 27 h3 followed by ♖e1; for example, 27...♘d4 (27...♔g7 28 ♖e1 ♖e8 29 ♗b6 with ideas like ♗c7, and also a4-a5, since simplification has occurred) 28 ♖e1 ♘b3 29 ♗b6. This seems to establish a substantial advantage for White.

24...♘xf5 25 a5?!

Purdy questions whether to allow ...h3, giving Black at least speculative counterplay and perhaps more. He suggests 25 h3 and Harding agrees. White should retain a nice advantage in that case along the lines of the last note.

25...h3! 26 a6?

White should at least get some pieces off by 26 ♖xd8. This move is also tactically wrong.

26...♖a8 27 ♗c5 ♖fe8

Both the a6-pawn and ...hxg2 are threatened. Black has real chances now.

28 a7 e4! *(D)*

A dynamic move that is logical in every sense. Alternatively, Black might want to be sure to get 28...hxg2 in, but that doesn't seem necessary.

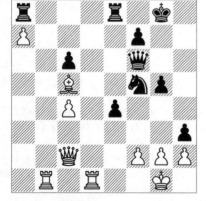

29 ♖b7!? ♘h4 30 ♕b3!?

The other move is 30 ♖dd7!?, as 30...♘f3+ 31 gxf3 ♕xf3 32 ♔f1 falls short. But 30...hxg2! keeps Black on top.

30...♕f5! 31 ♖dd7!?

Harding offers the line 31 ♖b8 ♕g4 32 g3 e3! 33 ♗xe3 ♕f3 (but 33...♘f3+! 34 ♔h1 ♘e1 looks like a draw) 34 ♔f1 ♘f5 35 ♔e1 ♘xe3 36 ♕xe3, which he thinks is slightly better for White. This doesn't pose Black even technical problems, however, since 36...♕xe3+ 37 fxe3 ♖exb8 38 axb8♕+ ♖xb8 can only favour him. Then White should probably play 39 g4.

After 31 ♖dd7!?, Harding goes into an exhaustive and fascinating multi-page analysis with the assistance of other analysts. Unfortunately the game is turning completely tactical and therefore beyond the book's scope. Therefore I'll just use his notes to indicate which moves were good or bad without the analysis. In any case, the end is most entertaining.

31...♘f3+?

Black (White?) will apparently draw after either 31...♕xc5 32 ♖xf7 e3!, 31...e3 32 fxe3! ♕xc5 33 ♖xf7 or 31...hxg2!, which is hell for White but perhaps ultimately drawing after John Timm's 32 ♕d1!!, the latter move leading to some endgame that becomes clear on about move 56 in one line! The text-move at the very least forfeits any winning chances, as Harding thoroughly demonstrates.

32 gxf3 exf3 33 ♔f1!

Purdy supplies the line 33 ♗e3 ♖ad8 34 ♕d1 ♕g4+ 35 ♔f1 ♕xc4+ with a draw.

33...♕xc5 34 ♕c3?

34 ♖xf7 is better.

34...♖f8 35 ♕d3! ♕e5! 36 ♕xf3 ♖ae8! 37 ♖b1 ♕xh2?

Black might still be able to achieve a draw after 37...♕e6!.

38 ♖b3 ♕e5 39 ♕xh3 ♕f4 40 c5!! ♕c4+ 41 ♔g2 ♖e4 42 ♕f5 ♕xb3 43 ♕xe4 ♔g7 44 ♕f5 g4 45 ♕xg4+ 1-0

The finish would be 45...♔h7 46 ♖d1!.

Harding concludes: "A wild game. In CC a simple style won't win a world title."

The next example is probably the most famous 'good knight vs bad bishop' game ever played. My discussion is not precisely aimed at the themes of this section; but I think that it's a worthwhile one because it questions the monumental status of Fischer's key minor-piece decision and puts it in a modern context.

Fischer – Petrosian
Buenos Aires Ct (7) 1971

1 e4 c5 2 ♘f3 e6 3 d4 cxd4 4 ♘xd4 a6 5 ♗d3 ♘c6 6 ♘xc6 bxc6 7 0-0 d5 8 c4! ♘f6 9 cxd5 cxd5 10 exd5 exd5? 11 ♘c3! ♗e7 12 ♕a4+! ♕d7?! 13 ♖e1! ♕xa4 14 ♘xa4 ♗e6 15 ♗e3

White is clearly much better here.

15...0-0 16 ♗c5 ♖fe8 17 ♗xe7 ♖xe7 18 b4! ♔f8 19 ♘c5 ♗c8 20 f3 ♖ea7 21 ♖e5 ♗d7 *(D)*

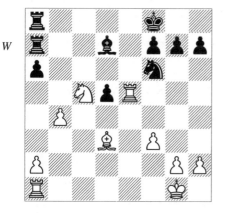

W

22 ♘xd7+!

The great attraction of the move is that Fischer counter-intuitively gives up a wonderful knight for a rather bad bishop (see the pawn on d5). His decision is open-minded and might even seem daring in the sense that White obviously stands better in any case. Fischer's point in exchanging is that he can clearly envisage an ending in which his active rooks, Black's weak d-pawn, and a potential passed pawn on the queenside give White all the trumps.

Fischer's 22 ♘xd7+! has been talked about and praised for years, perhaps as much as any individual move in the last century. Some have even given 22 ♘xd7+ a '!!' and included this game among the best ever played. I would disagree and will try to add some things from a different perspective. To my knowledge, very little has been said about either White's alternatives to 22 ♘xd7+ or Black's own defensive possibilities in his inferior position. It's a shame that, as far as I know, we never heard

Petrosian's own thoughts about this move. It wouldn't surprise me if he even anticipated it, based upon the concrete features of the position. For example, most annotators don't seem concerned that Black is threatening to improve his awful position considerably by ...♗b5, perhaps followed by ...a5. These are important freeing ideas, the consideration of which would lead White at least to make 22 ♘xd7+ a candidate move. Examining the alternatives, for example, White might not like the looks of 22 ♔f2 ♗b5 23 ♗c2? (23 ♖ae1 ♗xd3 24 ♘xd3 ♖c7 and Black has at least a lot more hope than in the original position) 23...a5, etc. So a natural move is 22 a4, which stops ...♗b5 and also makes a good start towards generating a passed pawn on the queenside. Apart from 22 ♘xd7+ this looks best to me; presumably Black would try 22...♗c6 (intending ...♘d7) 23 ♖ae1 (23 ♔f2 ♘d7 24 ♘xd7+ ♖xd7 25 b5 axb5 26 ♖c1 ♖d6 27 axb5 ♗d7 is again nice for White yet Black is still defending) 23...♘d7 24 ♘xd7+ ♗xd7 25 b5!? (there are two obvious alternatives: 25 a5 ♗e6 26 f4 {26 ♖xh7 ♖b8} 26...g6 and 25 ♖xd5 ♗xa4 26 ♖a5, which is attractive, but Black might be able to achieve a difficult pure rook ending after, for example, 26...♗b5!? 27 ♗xb5 axb5 28 ♖xb5 ♖e7 29 ♖b1 ♖e2 30 ♖g5 f6) 25...axb5 26 axb5 ♖a1 27 b6 f6 28 ♖5e2 ♖xe1+ 29 ♖xe1 ♖b8, and things aren't as clear as White would like; e.g., 30 ♖b1 ♔e7 (30...h6!?) 31 ♗xh7 ♔d6. All this is doubtless a case of 'long analysis, wrong analysis', but it serves to indicate the lack of clarity such continuations entail in the real world of concrete decision-making. Another tempting option is 22 g4, intending just g5, ♖xd5, etc. Then one idea is 22...♗b5! (22...h6 23 h4) 23 g5 ♘h5 24 ♖xd5 (24 a4 ♗xd3 25 ♘xd3 is better) 24...♘f4 25 ♖d4 ♘xd3 26 ♘xd3 a5.

These kinds of lines, and especially the idea of ...♗b5, probably influenced Fischer's decision, which is a quintessentially practical one leaving fewer complications and very little need for calculation. Why give such messy positions to Petrosian, a master of both defence and the endgame? This is especially true since it only takes one more move (22 ♘xd7+ ♖xd7 23 ♖c1) to see that White has a very large advantage indeed.

22...♖xd7 23 ♖c1 *(D)*

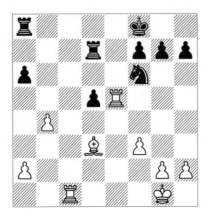

B

I suspect that Fischer himself would consider this position easily winning. He has a strong bishop versus a restricted knight with pawns on both sides of the board. In the meantime, Black is tied to the defence of the weak a6-pawn. In addition, White has much superior activity for his rooks and a passed pawn looms on the queenside. The first two of these advantages alone would probably suffice. It seems to me that this is another example of how strong players aren't thinking in terms of some theoretical preconception (in this case regarding good knights and bad bishops), but using their experience with similar positions and examining specific variations to which they then apply their judgement.

Thus I'm not convinced that Fischer's move, while obviously worthy of praise, is quite so wonderful as has been claimed. It does exhibit freedom from dogmatism, but in a form not atypical of that seen in many modern games. Furthermore, the decision to exchange is certainly the result of assessing the concrete possibilities for Black to free his game. Incidentally, it is often mentioned that some commentators at the time didn't even consider 22 ♘xd7+ as they watched the game. But this isn't very meaningful because they weren't sitting at the board looking as intensely as the players at actual variations regarding issues such as the counterplay via ...♗b5 and the specific sequence that follows 22 ♘xd7+. Listen to top grandmasters in the press room of any event and you will find that they both miss good moves and suggest horrendous ones quite frequently – the games aren't theirs, after all. At any rate, since many readers have seen this

game more than once, I will give its continuation without analysis. Indeed, you will see that the rest of the game looks fairly easy, especially for someone with Fischer's legendary technique.

23...♖d6 24 ♖c7 ♘d7 25 ♖e2 g6 26 ♔f2 h5 27 f4 h4 28 ♔f3 f5 29 ♔e3 d4+ 30 ♔d2 ♘b6 31 ♖ee7 ♘d5 32 ♖f7+ ♔e8 33 ♖b7 ♘xb4 34 ♗c4 1-0

In Praise of the Bishop-Pair

Moving into the present, this contest from the Women's World Championship illustrates the popular trade-off of a pawn for the bishop-pair.

Zhu Chen – Kosteniuk
Moscow wom Wch (2) 2001

1 d4 d5 2 c4 e6 3 ♘c3 c6 4 e4 dxe4 5 ♘xe4 ♗b4+ 6 ♗d2 ♕xd4 7 ♗xb4 ♕xe4+ 8 ♗e2 ♘a6 9 ♗c3 (D)

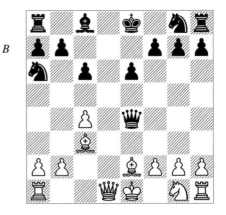

B

This long-term positional pawn sacrifice in order to acquire the advantage of the two bishops has become a main line, despite Black's lack of weaknesses. It is known as the Marshall Gambit and has recently become very popular. The moves 9 ♗a5 and 9 ♗d6 are also regularly played, which demonstrates that White's idea is positional pressure rather than a specific knockout. Ever since Kasparov started making this kind of pawn sacrifice on a regular basis, other leading players have joined in and found new contexts in which to do so. In this particular line, White has won a large majority of games, although it is likely that Black can hold his own with accurate play.

9...f6

A game between two top-notch non-humans is of illustrative interest here: 9...♘e7 10 ♗xg7 ♖g8 11 ♗f6 ♕f4 12 ♗c3 ♖xg2 13 ♘f3 f6? *(D)* (both engines like alternatives such as 13...♘f5 and 13...♘c5, judging that Black has a small advantage, but that reflects their innate materialism; Black indeed has to establish threats like ...♘e4 quickly, but even then the bishops are worth at least a pawn).

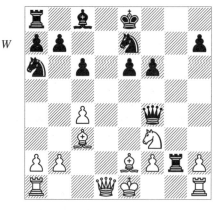

14 ♕d2! (as seen in a great many games from the last decade, two bishops in a queenless middlegame can be devastating, easily compensating for a lost pawn; Kasparov has been a leader in demonstrating this) 14...♕xd2+ 15 ♘xd2 e5 (15...f5 stops ♘e4, but now Black's weaknesses and development are awful; e.g., 16 ♗h5+ ♔f8 17 ♘f3 ♗d7 18 ♘e5 ♗e8 19 ♗f3 ♖g8 20 0-0-0 and ♖d6) 16 ♘e4 ♔f7 17 ♖d1 ♖g8 18 f4! (already decisive; Black never got any outposts for his knights) 18...♘f5 (18...♘g6 19 ♖d6 ♘xf4 20 ♖xf6+ ♔e7 21 ♗xe5 ♘xe2 22 ♗d6+ ♔d8 23 ♔xe2) 19 fxe5 fxe5 20 ♗xe5 (a classic two-bishop position) 20...♘b4 21 ♗c3 ♘c2+ (21...♘xa2 22 ♗d2!) 22 ♔f2 ♗e6 23 ♘f6 ♘ce3 24 ♗h5+ ♔e7 25 ♘xg8+ ♖xg8 26 ♖dg1 and White won easily in *Nimzo 8-Deep Fritz*, Cadaques 2001. An ideal demonstration of two-bishop compensation for a pawn when the queens are off the board.

10 ♘f3 ♘e7 11 ♘d2 ♕f4 12 g3 ♕c7 13 ♗h5+ ♘g6 14 f4 0-0 15 ♕e2 ♘e7 16 ♗f3 *(D)*

This is the sort of position that White is after. It reminds me of the two bishops compensation

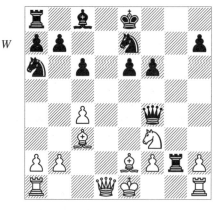

discussed in SOMCS in the line 1 c4 ♘f6 2 ♘c3 e6 3 e4 c5 4 e5 ♘g8 5 ♘f3 ♘c6 6 d4 cxd4 7 ♘xd4 ♘xe5 8 ♘db5 a6 9 ♘d6+ ♗xd6 10 ♕xd6 f6 11 ♗e3 ♘f7 12 ♕a3. White doesn't regain the pawn in that case either, but uses his bishops and a flank advance to increase the pressure gradually. Not surprisingly, the example of that line given in SOMCS was a game of Kasparov's.

16...♘f5 17 0-0-0 ♖b8 18 ♘b3 c5 19 ♖d2 ♘b4 20 ♔b1 b6 21 ♖hd1 a5 22 a4?!

An unnecessary weakness. 22 ♗e4! a4 23 ♘a1!? ♘c6 24 ♘c2 prepares g4, with the bishops growing ever stronger. This would have justified White's strategy.

22...♘c6 23 g4?!

The right idea, but premature, since White has trouble protecting f4.

23...♘fe7

Now Black has the advantage, so White speculates:

24 g5!? fxg5 25 ♕g2 e5!?

25...♖xf4! looks better, when 26 ♕xg5 ♘g6 27 ♗xc6 ♕xc6 28 ♖d8+ ♔f7 appears safe enough.

26 fxe5 ♗f5+ 27 ♔a1 ♘xe5 28 ♕xg5 ♘7g6

The bishops are still dangerous, but Black is a pawn up and only goes seriously wrong in the coming complications.

29 ♕g3 ♕e7 30 ♗d5+ ♔h8 31 ♘c1 ♖be8?
32 ♖e1

Because of the pin, White has regained the advantage.

32...♕c7?

The last chance was 32...♕d7! 33 b3 ♘c6 34 ♗e6! ♕xe6! 35 ♖xe6 ♖xe6 36 ♕c7, when White remains better, but it's still a game.

33 ♖de2 ♕d7 34 ♗xe5 ♘xe5 35 ♖xe5
♕xa4+ 36 ♘a2 ♖xe5 37 ♕xe5 ♗g6 38 ♕d6
♖e8 39 ♖xe8+ ♕xe8 40 ♘c3 h5 41 ♕xb6 a4
42 ♕e6 1-0

I find the next example fascinating because it
demonstrates the sophisticated understanding
needed to assess whether one should enter into
a bishops versus knights face-off.

Krasenkow – Rustemov
Panormo ECC 2001

1 d4 d5 2 c4 c6 3 ♘c3 ♘f6 4 ♘f3 a6
Remarkably popular, this ultramodern nondeveloping move threatens ...dxc4 and intends
an early ...b5. White has tried nearly everything
against it, but some of the world's leading players are still successfully defending with it.
5 c5 ♘bd7 6 ♗f4 ♘h5 7 e3!? (D)

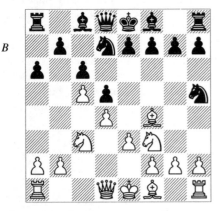

A clever idea that plans to surrender the
bishop-pair in order to open the e-file and secure the e5-square for the foreseeable future.
7...g6 8 ♗d3 ♗g7 9 0-0 0-0 10 h3!?
By threatening ♗h2, White forces the exchange. This is absolutely correct on principle,
but due to the particular sequence that ensues,
I think that White will achieve more by waiting. He might play the 'quasi-mysterious' rook
move 10 ♖e1! anticipating ...♘xf4, or something neutral like 10 ♕d2, when I think that he
retains some advantage.
10...♘xf4 11 exf4 ♕c7! (D)
A surprisingly uncomfortable move to meet
due to some specific tactical points. Black's
timing has been perfect.

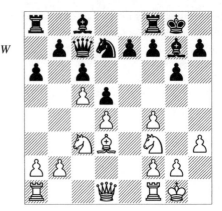

12 ♘e2
Rustemov doesn't like this, although he give
two rather depressing lines instead: 12 ♕d2
♗h6 13 g3 (13 ♘g5 looks better and equal)
13...e5!; and 12 ♖e1 ♕xf4 13 ♖xe7 ♗xd4 14
♘e2 ♕f6 15 ♖xd7 ♗xc5!. He also suggests a
third possibility, 12 f5, which is probably the
soundest move and should yield equal prospects.
12...b6 13 cxb6 ♕xb6 14 ♖c1 c5
The two bishops are coming into their own.
However, White seems to be able to stabilize
the centre and prevent them from becoming too
active.
15 b3
To stop both ...c4 and ...♕xb2.
**15...♗b7 16 ♗b1 ♖ac8 17 ♕d2 e6 18 ♕e3
♕d6 19 h4!? (D)**

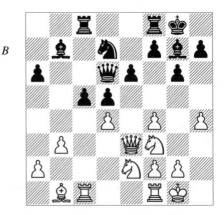

One of those when-in-doubt rook's pawn
moves! White feels that he has enough grip on
the position that a little softening-up of Black's
king position can be embarked upon. But this

costs time and in the end it even seems to help Black's own chances on the kingside.

19...罝c7 20 h5 罝fc8 21 hxg6 hxg6 22 dxc5 罝xc5 23 罝xc5 豐xc5 24 ②fd4

Obviously White doesn't want to exchange queens and let the two bishops mop up pawns in the ending.

24...e5!?

A remarkable idea, especially given that there were good alternatives. Black willingly isolates his d-pawn for the sake of activity, and in particular the b7-bishop will have trouble finding a useful occupation. But Rustemov sees that every other piece will coordinate beautifully to break down the dark squares.

25 豐h3

Alternatively, 25 fxe5 ②xe5 26 罝c1 豐a3 27 罝xc8+ 奧xc8 probably favours Black, since he can play ...奧d7 and ...②c6 and White has no particular plan.

25...豐e7 26 fxe5 ②xe5 (D)

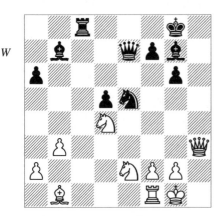

I admit that I find this position hard to understand. Black's b7-bishop looks just awful, White's bishop is good, the d-pawn is fully blockaded, and White can even reduce the material and achieve the sort of simplification that is supposed to favour him in isolated queen's pawn positions. But all this just shows a weakness in my instinctive judgement. In the end, despite all the other imbalances, there is only one really important explanation: the bishop-pair is always a force to be reckoned with and in this position makes all the difference.

27 罝d1

For example, simplifying just seems to help Black: 27 罝c1 罝xc1+ 28 ②xc1 ②g4! 29 ②ce2

f5 (or 29...奧c8) 30 豐c3 豐h4 31 豐g3 豐xg3 32 fxg3 宁f7 and the bishop-pair is too strong.

27...罝e8

Black also has a clear advantage following 27...②c6 28 豐d3 (28 ②xc6 豐xe2) 28...罝e8! *(D)*.

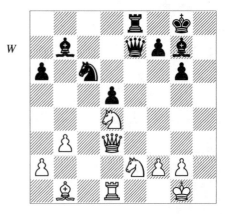

a) 29 豐d2 ②xd4 30 ②xd4 豐c5! threatens ...奧xd4 and either breaks down the blockade or allows Black to activate his bishops; e.g., 31 ②f3? d4! or 31 宁f1 奧c8 32 f3 (White is short of moves) 32...豐d6 33 宁g1 豐g3 34 ②e2 豐h4 35 豐f4 豐e7! 36 奧d3 奧f5!.

b) 29 ②xc6 豐xe2 30 ②a5 奧a8 31 豐xe2 罝xe2 32 b4 d4! 33 a3 奧d5 34 奧d3 罝a2 35 奧xa6 罝xa3 and the bishops, active rook and passed d-pawn count for more than White's b-pawn. In the meantime notice that White's knight is paralysed.

28 罝c1

It is not the immobility of White's bishop that is really hurting him, as shown by 28 奧d3 奧c8 29 豐e3 豐d8! (Black's pieces are in retreat! We have often seen how bishops often return to their original squares as they are decisively activated) 30 豐d2 豐b6 with a large advantage. Black prepares moves like ...奧g4 and ...②g4.

28...豐d8

28...②c6! is probably more accurate, with play resembling earlier notes.

29 罝d1 奧c8! 30 豐g3 ②g4 31 豐f3?!

This loses positionally, but ...奧e5 was a threat, and the bishops have become too strong; e.g., 31 奧d3 奧e5 32 f4 奧c7! 33 b4 罝e3 34 ②f3 奧b6, etc.

31...豐h4 32 豐g3 豐e7?!

A practical move in what may have been time-pressure for one or both sides. But much better and extremely strong was 32...♕xg3! 33 fxg3 (33 ♘xg3?? ♗xd4) 33...♗h6 *(D)* (the alternative 33...♗f8! is also good).

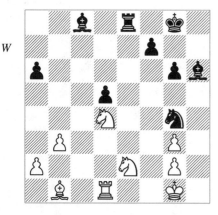

W

34 ♘f4 ♗f8! 35 ♗d3 (35 ♘xd5? ♗c5) 35...♗c5 36 ♘e2 ♘e5 37 ♗c2 ♗g4 and Black wins.

33 ♗d3

Finally the bishop comes out of his exile.

33...♗e5?

A much more serious error. Black is still much better after 33...♕a3 or 33...♕c5!.

34 f4?

White misses 34 ♘c6! ♗xg3 35 ♘xe7+ ♖xe7 36 ♘xg3.

34...♗xd4+ 35 ♘xd4 ♕c5

It's all over now.

36 ♗b1 ♘e3 37 ♕e1 ♗d7 38 ♖d2 ♘f5 39 ♕d1 ♘xd4 40 ♖xd4 ♗g4 41 b4 ♕c3 42 ♕d3 ♕e1+ 43 ♕f1 ♕e3+ 0-1

A tribute to the two bishops. I'm still left wondering how Black's position could have been so powerful when White's pieces were apparently ideally placed!

Benjamin – Anand
Groningen PCA 1993

There's one remaining situation involving minor-piece pairs that I didn't cover in SOMCS. Sometimes the knight-pair has no compensation from permanent weaknesses, outposts, blockaded positions, or activity, but their owner has a direct attack based upon a flank advance and space. This is obviously not a well-defined

area for discussion; nevertheless, the following game says something about the relationship of space and the two bishops in practice.

1 e4 c5 2 ♘f3 d6 3 d4 cxd4 4 ♘xd4 ♘f6 5 ♘c3 ♘c6 6 ♗g5 e6 7 ♕d2 ♗e7 8 0-0-0 0-0 9 ♘b3 ♕b6 10 f3 ♖d8 11 ♔b1 ♕c7

A fairly standard Sicilian position.

12 ♗xf6!?

Anand gives this an '!' and Stohl a '?!', so I'll compromise. It's an extremely original strategy that cedes the bishops for the sake of a barbaric pawn attack on the kingside.

12...♗xf6 13 g4 g6

Another point of White's exchange was prophylactic: the freeing move ...d5 is prevented. The text-move retains the bishop on the long diagonal for both attacking and defensive purposes at the cost of creating a weakness and target for White's attack. Stohl suggests 13...a6 14 g5 ♗e7 15 h4 (Anand offers 15 f4!?) 15...b5, and also mentions 13...♘e5!?.

14 h4 a6 15 g5 ♗g7 16 h5 b5 17 hxg6 hxg6 *(D)*

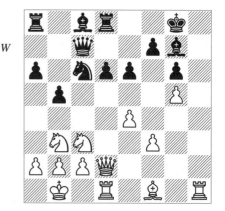

W

18 f4!

A big decision. With a bishop on g7, the attack by 18 ♕h2 b4 19 ♕h7+ ♔f8 tends to be useless (20 ♘e2 a5! with a counterattack). So White aims for f4-f5, however slow that looks. What's interesting is that Black's pieces are still on the first few ranks, so any attack that he undertakes will take time to develop. White tries to ensure this on his next move by placing his knight on the side of the board, sacrificing that piece's potential influence in a kingside attack to stop Black's main idea of ...a5-a4.

18...b4 19 ♘a4! ♖b8 *(D)*

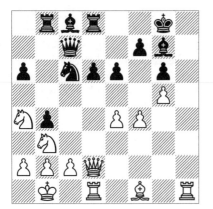

Oddly enough, both of White's knights will be divorced from his attack for the rest of the game! They have important defensive roles to play, and in an occasional line will recentralize to good effect, but most of the game now comes down to space and attack for two bishops.

20 ♕h2

Stohl initiates a very interesting discussion here about the idea that when one triples on a file, the queen should often stand behind at least one rook. This comes up in a lot of positions and I think is one of those handy 'mini-rules' that has a lot of validity in the theoretical sense. As explained in the discussion about opposite-coloured bishops, such a guideline strikes me as more useful than most others discussed in this book. It is essentially harmless: no one will forego an effective attack with the queen in front of the rook or vice-versa just because of such a modest suggestion. I have discussed the contrast between this and more sweeping rules elsewhere. Anyway, Stohl examines a number of lines with 20 ♖h4, intending ♕h2 and later ♖dh1 or ♖h7 and ♖xg7 if possible. He thinks that this is probably an improvement on the game, giving one line with 20...♘e7! 21 ♕h2 ♔f8! (21...♕c6? 22 ♖h7 ♕xa4 23 ♖xg7+ ♔xg7 24 ♕h6+ ♔g8 25 ♗b5!) 22 ♖h7 ♘g8 23 e5! dxe5 24 ♖xd8+ ♕xd8 25 f5! (a wonderful sequence!) with a strong attack based on the point 25...exf5?? (25...♗d7 26 fxg6! ♗xa4 27 ♗d3! and it's very hard to defend) 26 ♖xg7 ♔xg7 27 ♕xe5+.

20...♔f8 21 ♖d3 e5?

This gets Black into all kinds of trouble after White's next two moves. Benjamin's suggestion 21...♗d7! and Stohl's of 21...♘e7 22 ♖h3

♕c6! 23 ♖h7 ♘g8! both seem to hold and even give Black a small advantage in the long run. Thus the ♕h2 + ♖d3-h3 manoeuvre seems to take too long, and Stohl's idea of 20 ♖h4 was probably better. Overall, such variations show the long-term power of the bishops unless White can act quickly, in this case usually sacrificially.

22 f5 gxf5 23 ♖h3! ♘e7!

Forced in order to defend against ♖h7 and ♖xg7. It is fascinating how White's knights, totally out of play (with the one on a4 trapped) are hardly hurting his chances in any concrete variations!

24 ♖h8+?!

Stohl posits that 24 ♖h7 ♘g6! 25 ♗d3! was strong and extremely awkward for Black after 25...f4 26 ♘d2! ♗d7 27 b3 (D), when the d2-knight and potential bishop on c4 (or knight, if Black allows ♘b2-c4!) are suddenly very strong indeed.

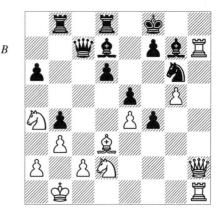

Thus the move 21...e5 falls short. The moral of the story seems to be that in the absence of direct tactical salvation, Black's normal solid Sicilian structure with pawns on e6 and d6 works well with the bishop-pair to beat off White's attack because White's minor piece are shut out of the key squares and diagonals. The corollary is that bishops should not be underestimated as defenders!

24...♘g8 25 ♖xg8+!

Not 25 ♕h7? ♗xh8 26 ♕xh8 ♕e7!.

25...♔xg8 26 ♕h7+ ♔f8 27 exf5 ♗xf5!

The only defence. Yet now the two bishops are finally gone and now it's just a question of tactics. Since we've covered the main strategic themes, I'll present the rest of the game with minimal notes.

28 ♕xf5 ♕c6 29 g6! ♖b7 30 ♖h7! ♕xa4 31 ♕g5?

31 ♖xg7! ♔xg7 32 gxf7 will ultimately draw by perpetual check.

31...♕e8 32 ♗xa6?!

Anand suggests 32 ♗g2!, after which Black can get an advantage, but perhaps not enough to win according to Stohl's analysis.

32...♖e7 33 ♗d3 e4! 34 ♗b5 ♖e5! 35 gxf7 ♖xg5 36 fxe8♕+ ♖xe8 37 ♗xe8 ♖g1+! 38 ♘c1 ♔xe8 39 a4?

Allows an immediate finish, but White was lost anyway.

39...bxa3 40 bxa3 ♗c3! 41 ♖h4 d5 0-1

After that too-limited sampling of this vast subject, I must emphasize that the fundamental imbalance of knights versus bishops is the most critical area for the theory of piece-play today. Mastery of this issue in many standard positions and structures has been of decisive importance at the very heights of competition. That was illustrated by Kramnik's revival of the Berlin Defence 1 e4 e5 2 ♘f3 ♘c6 3 ♗b5 ♘f6 4 0-0 ♘xe4 5 d4 ♘d6 6 ♗xc6 dxc6 7 dxe5 ♘f5 8 ♕xd8+ ♔xd8, which choice was arguably decisive in gaining him the world championship versus Kasparov. The queenless middlegame that arises pits Black's two bishops against White's space and development, with the value of Black's doubled c-pawns up for debate. We will undoubtedly see a more sophisticated understanding of this sort of trade-off in the years to come. In the meantime, I would recommend the games of Part 2 for study, as well as those in the section on doubled pawns in Chapter 2 because those pawns typically arise from an exchange of minor pieces.

3.4 Her Majesty as a Subject

I didn't talk that much about queens in SOMCS, and they generally play a small role in strategic middlegame literature. This is because the queen is often one of the last pieces out and is so powerful that it can go just about anywhere that it is needed. Thus consistent patterns are hard to discern. In books and articles, discussions of the queen normally centre about tactics, and specifically queen sacrifices. In this section, I will examine the validity of a few rules that have been posited about queen play.

The Relative Value of the Queen

Before that, I should note that in my and many others' opinion the relative value assigned to the queen has been overstated in a number of situations. That value has changed over the years, always in a negative direction. On the familiar point count scale where pawns are worth 1 point, knights and bishops 3, and rooks 5, queens tend to be assigned 9 points. When I was growing up, a number of elementary books gave their value as 10, and I remember being resistant to modifying my belief in this number for some time. Some books used the number $9^{1}/_{2}$. But I think that it's fair to say that for the last 30 years or so, the accepted number has been 9. Now we know that in every situation, the values of the pieces and pawns vary considerably, so one might justifiably consider these numbers to be meaningless. I am inclined to agree that they provide at best shaky grounds when playing a given game. But the scale nonetheless reflects a general belief among players about some sort of average value of the piece in question. So let's pursue that. Where does the number 9 come from? I would say that like so many other of our assessments and evaluations, it has to do with the endgame. In the case of two rooks versus a queen and pawn in the ending, for example, we can easily imagine a situation where two rooks (say, on the seventh rank) combine to capture a pawn that is defended by a queen and king. After these pieces are exchanged off, we are in a pawn ending with equal pawns on both sides. So 5+5 = 9+1. I would also say that in an ending with a queen on one side and three pieces on the other (with pawns, perhaps on both sides of the board), the queen will tend to hold her own, and probably in more cases than not be able to scarf up a pawn before the minor pieces coordinate and defend each other. It would be interesting to research that case.

But what about the middlegame? Here I would suggest that the traditional valuation is no longer respected. Very often we see situations in which three pieces are superior to a queen, this superiority coming right out of the opening and stretching well into the middlegame. Queen 'sacrifices' for three pieces are increasingly commonplace, and I think that most strong players prefer the pieces over the queen in a considerable majority of such situations. Several other commentators have made this point. It is unclear whether they would evaluate the pieces as worth, e.g., $9^{1}/_{2}$ on the average in that case, or keep them at 9 but devalue the queen to $8^{1}/_{2}$; and of course numerous other possible combinations exist, such as separate evaluations depending upon whether there are two bishops or two knights (this is very likely necessary, assigning a higher point value for the two bishops). All of that is beyond my precise expertise, but as I see it a relative shift in perceived relative value has indeed taken place.

Then there are more extreme cases. The queen is often sacrificed for material with lesser face value. A queen for two bishops and two pawns (again, in the opening or middlegame, not in the endgame) is a very common exchange today and I would suggest that the bishops hold their own (or perhaps better) as often as not. Interestingly, if you count the queen as $8^{1}/_{2}$ just for this case, that corresponds with

Fischer's evaluation of the bishop as $3\frac{1}{4}$, i.e., $8\frac{1}{2} = 2 \times 3\frac{1}{4} + 2$. Of course in such a case there are tremendously important issues such as whether the pawns are centre or flank pawns, how early in the game the trade takes place, and more. Remarkably, even the exchange of a queen for two bishops and a pawn is being made more often than one would ever guess. Here the queen is better in the great majority of cases, of course, but a few other factors can intervene to change the assessment. Of course the bishop-pair need other advantages to achieve a balance with the queen; e.g., better activity, superior pawn-structure and/or development, kingside threats and the like. But since sacrificing an exchange to get two bishops is fairly common today, this view of the material imbalance isn't outrageous. Furthermore, the bishops are often so effective in the middlegame that they can force the win of the exchange, thus returning us to material 'parity' at $\Xi+\hat{\mathbb{Q}}+\hat{\mathbb{Q}} = 9$ versus $\mathbb{W} = 9$. As one might suspect from what I've said thus far, several top players have also noted that the possession of $\Xi+\hat{\mathbb{Q}}+\hat{\mathbb{Q}}$ is indeed more desirable than having a queen in many cases (again excluding the endgame, and depending upon which pawn it is, what other pieces are out, etc.). A qualification to all this is that such judgements may stem less from the abstract theoretical truth than from the types of positions actually being played today. Regardless, I believe (and this is only opinion based upon observation) that as time has gone on, players have found the queen less valuable in the middlegame than it has traditionally been assumed.

Early Queen Excursions

Two traditional rules about the queen have been:

a) Don't move the queen out early;

b) Don't move your queen into the centre (meaning onto a square that is easy for the opponent's naturally centralized pieces to attack, as opposed to squares like e2/c2/e7/c7, which are often safe and often desirable posts).

Although common sense might indicate that such queen forays should be punished by loss of time and thus be avoided, that is not always the case. Often an early queen development comes with gain of space and staking out territory in the centre (e.g., 1 e4 d5 2 exd5 $\mathbb{W}$xd5 or 1 e4 e6 2 d4 d5 3 $\hat{\mathbb{Q}}$d2 c5 4 exd5 $\mathbb{W}$xd5). Furthermore, when the queen is attacked, the piece or pawn doing so may not be in an ideal position for that pawn-structure. Such a case could arise after 1 e4 c5 2 c3 d5 3 exd5 $\mathbb{W}$xd5 4 d4 $\hat{\mathbb{Q}}$f6, for example. Then an eventual move c4 will often be undesirable because it weakens squares like d4 and doesn't really assist development, whereas $\hat{\mathbb{Q}}$c3 can only be played after moves like 5 $\hat{\mathbb{Q}}$f3 $\hat{\mathbb{Q}}$g4 6 $\hat{\mathbb{Q}}$e2 e6 7 $\hat{\mathbb{Q}}$e3 cxd4 8 cxd4, by which time Black can argue that neither the bishop on e2 nor the one on e3 (a bad bishop, formally speaking) is as aggressively placed as White would like. Of course that is no great discovery, but the number of instances in which players are intentionally exposing their queens to tempo loss for the sake of other goals is on the increase.

It seems to me that most early queen moves are in positions with one's centre pawns on the second or third ranks, and possibly but not always with another pawn on the fourth rank. That is true in our Scandinavian and Sicilian examples, but also in fianchetto openings like the English Opening with 1 c4 e6 2 d4 b6 3 e4 $\hat{\mathbb{Q}}$b7 4 $\hat{\mathbb{Q}}$c3 $\hat{\mathbb{Q}}$b4 5 $\mathbb{W}$c2 $\mathbb{W}$h4 or the Trompowsky with 1 d4 $\hat{\mathbb{Q}}$f6 2 $\hat{\mathbb{Q}}$g5 $\hat{\mathbb{Q}}$e4 3 $\hat{\mathbb{Q}}$f4 c5 4 d5 $\mathbb{W}$b6. A popular variation of the Hyper-Accelerated Dragon Sicilian goes 1 e4 c5 2 $\hat{\mathbb{Q}}$f3 g6 3 d4 $\hat{\mathbb{Q}}$g7 4 c4 and now 4...$\mathbb{W}$a5+ or 4...$\mathbb{W}$b6 (D).

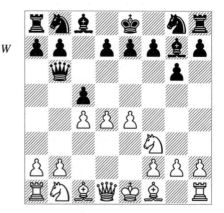

Other Sicilian Defences with the move ...$\mathbb{W}$b6 include 1 e4 c5 2 $\hat{\mathbb{Q}}$f3 e6 3 d4 cxd4 4 $\hat{\mathbb{Q}}$xd4 a6 5 $\hat{\mathbb{Q}}$c3 b5 6 $\hat{\mathbb{Q}}$d3 $\mathbb{W}$b6!? and 1 e4 c5 2 $\hat{\mathbb{Q}}$f3 $\hat{\mathbb{Q}}$c6 3 d4 cxd4 4 $\hat{\mathbb{Q}}$xd4 $\hat{\mathbb{Q}}$f6 5 $\hat{\mathbb{Q}}$c3 d6 6 $\hat{\mathbb{Q}}$c4 $\mathbb{W}$b6 (D):

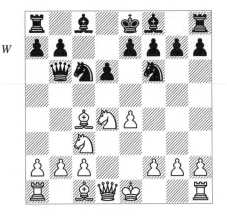

Benko developed this variation and it has been a favourite of Sicilian players for many years. Yes, the queen will lose a tempo to ♗e3 at some point (e.g., after 7 ♘b3 e6 8 ♗e3 ♕c7); but the idea is to force the d4-knight to retreat (note that Black's centre is strengthened after 7 ♘xc6 bxc6), when the lack of advanced pawns on Black's part means that the same knight will often want to return to d4 to support the attack after f4-f5 or g4-g5. In that case, Black has lost one tempo (...♕b6-c7) and White has lost two (♘b3-d4).

There are many other examples; e.g., the main-line Scotch Opening with 1 e4 e5 2 ♘f3 ♘c6 3 d4 exd4 4 ♘xd4 ♗c5 5 ♗e3 ♕f6; or the Czech Variation of the Pirc Defence with 1 e4 d6 2 d4 ♘f6 3 ♘c3 c6 4 f4 ♕a5 (D).

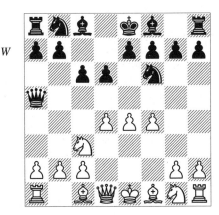

Notice that the openings mentioned so far (the Scotch excepted) are modern ones, i.e., they didn't really catch on until a few decades ago or less.

To unify the discussion, let me use as a modern test case an opening that has become remarkably popular: the 1 e4 d5 2 exd5 ♕xd5 variation of the Scandinavian Defence. This is an older opening that from early on was given as inferior by theoreticians of every stripe. Basically, it was considered a simple violation of both rules above, and therefore had to give White the advantage, presumably more than in a conventional opening. Quoting Curt Hansen from his excellent CD about the Scandinavian: "After the 1920s 2...♕xd5 was for many years only played very seldom at top level, and no serious grandmaster would have this variation as one of his main opening lines when defending against 1 e4." Yet it has become quite respectable in the last two decades, beginning with Larsen's revival of it, which really attracted attention after his defeat of Karpov at Montreal 1979. The same year one of the most important and instructive ideas in the whole opening appeared.

Djurić – Larsen
Copenhagen 1979

1 e4 d5 2 exd5 ♕xd5 3 ♘c3 ♕a5 4 d4 ♘f6 5 ♘f3 ♗f5 6 ♗c4 ♘bd7 7 ♕e2 e6 8 ♗d2 (D)

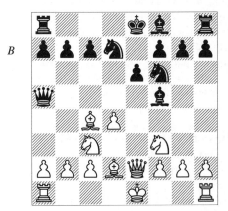

White was always considered better in such positions until the following breakthrough idea was discovered:

8...♗b4! 9 a3 0-0 10 0-0 ♗xc3 11 ♗xc3 ♕b6

Hansen: "This idea took so long to find because everybody seemed to have been focusing on Black's weak dark squares after the exchange of his dark-squared bishop. The realization that White's bishop is rather awkward on c3 (after ...♗b4xc3 and ♗d2xc3) was the new discovery, just as much as the concrete move ...♗f8-b4."

Because of the reverence for the combination of the two bishops and space, it took Larsen's special open-mindedness to appreciate the merits of Black's position. But once discovered, the concrete experience of playing both with and against it won the respect of players everywhere.

12 ♗b3 a5 13 ♗a4 c6 (D)

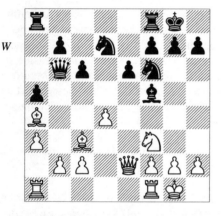

Here we have a now-standard two knights vs two bishops structure than can also occur in the Caro-Kann and Slav Defences, very often with equality. One idea is that White's dark-squared bishop is a poor one, and that Black's firm grip on d5 makes a pawn advance to that square (which would free the bishop) very difficult. Apart from that, Black's structure limits White's other bishop, and Black for his part can look to various plans (a well-timed ...e5 or ...c5, for example) to establish full equality. There are actually several other factors that help Black, including the fact that he can threaten to exchange one of White's bishops and either force concessions or succeed in doing so. This range of ideas is almost precisely that which arises in several Slav Defence variations.

14 ♗d2 h6 15 ♗e3 ♖fe8!

Naturally a move like 15...♕c7 is good, but Larsen makes a different useful move and enjoys the little trick that would now follow 16 d5? exd5.

16 c3?!

16 h3 would prevent Black's next move.

16...♗g4

After this I'm not sure that White can equalize.

17 ♖ab1 ♕c7! 18 h3 ♗h5 19 ♗c2?! e5

Black's strategy has worked to perfection. He no longer suffers from a space disadvantage and takes advantage of his active pieces on e8 and h5.

20 g4

20 dxe5 ♘xe5 21 ♗f4 ♗xf3 22 gxf3 ♖e7 (or 22...♘d5 and ...♕d8) clearly favours Black.

20...exd4

The safe route to a small edge. Black probably should avoid 20...♘xg4?! 21 hxg4 ♗xg4 when 22 dxe5 ♘xe5 23 ♗f4 ♗xf3 24 ♗xe5 ♗xe2 25 ♗xc7 ♗xf1 26 ♔xf1 is forced and the two bishops are presumably about equal to the rook and two pawns.

21 cxd4 ♗g6 22 ♗xg6 fxg6 23 ♕d3 ♘d5?

23...g5 might look loosening, but Black has all the positional trumps and would therefore have the advantage. Even 23...♔h7 is possible.

24 ♗xh6! gxh6 25 ♕xg6+ ♔f8 26 ♕xh6+ ♔g8 27 ♕g6+ ♔f8 28 ♕h6+

Moves like 28 ♖fe1 and 28 ♘g5 ♘7f6 29 ♖be1 intending ♖e5 are pretty threatening. Perhaps in the latter case White saw 29...♕g7 30 ♘e6+!? (30 ♕f5 is probably more testing) 30...♖xe6 31 ♕xg7+ ♔xg7 32 ♖xe6 ♖h8! with dynamic counterplay.

28...♔g8 ½-½

In contemporary chess a remarkable array of top players have used the 2...♕xd5 Scandinavian. After innovators like Larsen and Niels Fries Nielsen put it on the map, we have seen it played by the likes of Anand (versus Kasparov!), Khalifman, Morozevich, Hodgson, Van Wely, Rogers, Akopian, Speelman, Nisipeanu, Ye Jiangchuan and many more masters such as Guillermo Soppe, a specialist in this defence. The resilience of various lines for Black is remarkable: when one head is cut off, one or two more spring up. An extreme case of this would be the following line, considered decisively refuted for many years. Black's little-played idea and Stefan Bücker's analysis (from an article in *Kaissiber* magazine #6) may yet prove to be unsound and I could have chosen something more established, but I thought that the friskiness of

Black's queen would provide a counter-example to the 'rules' we established above.

1 e4 d5 2 exd5 ♕xd5 3 ♘c3 ♕a5 4 d4 ♘f6 5 ♘f3 ♗g4 6 h3 ♗h5 7 g4 ♗g6 8 ♘e5 ♘bd7!? *(D)*

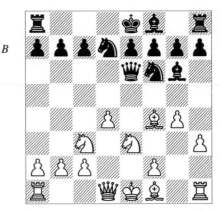

An almost absurdly provocative move that was thoroughly discredited by a Alekhine blindfold game and like so many ideas, only recently reinvestigated by the indefatigable Stefan Bücker. It is played in response to the problems that Black has encountered after 8...e6 (see next game).

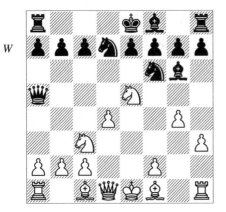

9 ♘c4

Greatly embarrassing the queen for squares. Instead, 9 ♘xg6 hxg6 10 ♗g2 is harmless after 10...c6 or Bücker's 10...0-0-0!?.

9...♕a6

Not 9...♕b4?? 10 a3 and the black queen is trapped.

10 ♗f4

The most logical move, threatening ♘d6+ with tempo and hitting c7. The stem game went 10 ♗d3!? ♕e6+ (10...0-0-0) 11 ♘e3 0-0-0 12 d5 ♕b6 13 ♘c4 ♕b4?? (Bücker suggests 13...♕a6 14 b4 ♘e4!) 14 a3 1-0 Alekhine-A.Schroeder, New York blindfold simul 1924. Another try is 10 d5 (cutting off e6) 10...♘e4! 11 ♘b5 (Kosmac-Hrelja, Krsko 1993), and now Bücker gives 11...♕xb5! 12 ♘d6+ ♘xd6 13 ♗xb5 ♘xb5.

10...♕e6+ 11 ♘e3 *(D)*

Harmless is 11 ♕e2 ♕xe2+ 12 ♗xe2 0-0-0 13 0-0-0 e6 14 ♗f3 c6 15 ♖he1 h5 16 g5 ♘d5 with equality, Sapi-Bellon, Montilla Moriles 1978.

11...♕b6!

Almost ridiculing White by continuing to make queen moves. In some sources the Alekhine game above is listed as 11...0-0-0?? 12 d5 ♕b6 13 ♘c4 ♕b4 14 a3 ♕c5 15 ♗e3 1-0. This may not be historically true, but it makes the point!

12 g5

12 ♘b5 looks dangerous, but 12...♖c8 13 g5 allows Black to equalize with 13...♗e4 14 ♖g1 ♘d5 15 ♘xd5 ♗xd5 16 c4 e5! (analysis by Bücker).

12...e5!

Black's play in this variation depends upon pure dynamism! In the stem game Topalović-Oreshković, Croatian Ch (Poreč) 1994, Black went a step too far by playing 12...♕xb2? 13 ♘b5 e5 14 ♘c4 (or 14 gxf6 exf4 15 ♘c4 ♕xc2 16 ♕xc2 ♗xc2 17 ♔d2!, as given by Bücker) 14...♗b4+ 15 ♔e2 with a winning game.

13 dxe5

The queen returns to e6 in Bücker's line 13 gxf6 exf4 14 ♘ed5 ♕e6+ 15 ♕e2 0-0-0.

13...♕xb2 14 ♘b5 *(D)*

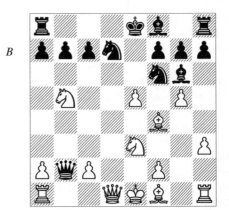

14...♕b4+

Black can also test the theory that when the queen has gone on a foray it is often better not to retreat to safety, but to stay in the enemy camp as a nuisance: 14...♗b4+! 15 ♔e2 ♘e4 16 ♘d5? (16 ♖b1 ♘c3+ 17 ♘xc3 ♕xc3 18 ♖b3 ♕c5 and White lacks compensation) 16...♗h5+ 17 f3 ♘xe5 18 ♗g2 ♘g6 19 ♗h2 0-0-0 20 ♖b1 ♕xa2! 21 ♘xb4 ♕c4+ and Black has a strong attack according to Bücker. This is probably just winning. That line features a queen that is not afraid to wander: ...♕d8-d5-a5-a6-e6-b6-b2-a2-c4.

15 ♕d2

If 15 c3 ♕xf4 16 ♘xc7+ ♔d8 17 ♘xa8, 17...♘e4 is too strong.

15...♘e4! 16 ♕xb4 ♗xb4+ 17 c3 ♗a5

Black is clearly better according to Bücker, who gives the sample line 18 ♘d5 c6! 19 ♘bc7+ ♔d8 20 ♘xa8 cxd5 21 0-0-0 ♘xc3 22 ♗d2 d4, winning.

Here's a more respectable version of that same variation. A dynamic struggle erupts into a slugfest as Black pits structure and development against White's space and flank attack. To maintain the balance, Black risks putting his king in the centre, even though that allows an immediate line-opening move against it. The queen's role is at first to support Black's pieces. Then at the key moment, instead of retreating to a safe square indicated by the pawn-structure, an active move seems to justify the whole middlegame strategy.

Egger – Soppe
Manila OL 1992

1 e4 d5 2 exd5 ♕xd5 3 ♘c3 ♕a5 4 d4 ♘f6 5 ♘f3 ♗g4 6 h3 ♗h5 7 g4 ♗g6 8 ♘e5 e6 9 ♗g2 c6 10 h4

White has obtained very good play against 8...e6 and 9...c6, so Black has become discouraged from playing this line. The dynamic response that comes next is probably the only chance for equality.

10...♘bd7!

This move challenges the centre just in time but risks being subject to a serious attack because it commits Black to his 11th move. Notice that Black now has more pieces out than

White, which explains his ability to survive what appears to be a risky situation.

11 ♘xd7

11 ♘c4 ♕a6 12 ♗f1 looks awkward for Black, but 12...b5 13 h5 (or 13 ♘e3 ♗b4!?) 13...♗xc2! 14 ♕xc2 bxc4 of Bertona-Soppe, San Luis 1999 favours Black, who as well as being a pawn up has his knights out and good prospects for his bishop and rooks.

11...♔xd7 *(D)*

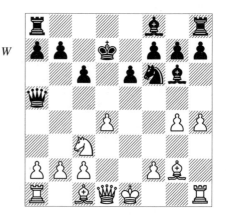

A typical idea these days: Black is more interested in exchanging pieces and preserving his pawn-structure than in finding a traditional spot for his king. It all depends upon tactical issues.

12 ♗d2

12 h5 ♗e4 13 f3 ♗d5 is solid.

12...h6

Played to defend against h5, obviously, but also to enforce some simplification and therefore protect Black's king.

13 g5 hxg5 14 hxg5 ♖xh1+ 15 ♗xh1 ♘e8 16 d5! *(D)*

Opening up lines against the king, which is necessary if White is going to have any pretensions of an advantage or perhaps even of avoiding a disadvantage; e.g., 16 ♘e4 ♕b6 17 ♘c5+ ♔c7 18 ♘b3 a5 19 a4 ♘d6 and Black has the better-placed pieces.

16...cxd5 17 ♘xd5 ♕a4!

The key queen move that makes sense of both ...♕a5 and ...♔d7, based only upon active play and move-to-move threats. Needless to say, this is all extremely risky on Black's part, yet White has some loose pieces as well.

18 ♘e3

B

Everything is getting tactical. White drops a piece after 18 b3?? ♕h4, but 18 ♘c3 ♕xc2 19 ♗f4 ǃ is critical. Play should continue 19...♗d6 20 ♗xd6 ♘xd6 21 ♘b5 (White needs to force the play) 21...♕c5 (21...♗d3ǃ? 22 ♘xd6 ♕xb2ǃ 23 ♖c1 ♕b4+ 24 ♕d2 ♕xd6 with equality) 22 ♘xd6 ♕xd6 23 ♕a4+ ♔e7 24 ♖d1 ♕e5+ 25 ♔f1 ♔f8!, when Black seems to be OK.

18...♘d6

Curt Hansen, upon whose thorough notes I am heavily relying, suggests 18...♔c7!? with the idea ...♖ad8.

19 c4!

This exchange helps to defang the attacking plans that Black might have had against White's exposed pawn-structure, e.g. by ...♕h4.

19...♕xd1+ 20 ♖xd1 ♗h5 21 ♖c1 ♖c8 22 c5 ♘b5 23 b4

An example has arisen of a queenside majority well supported by bishops. We have seen elsewhere, however, that with the kings centralized, this tends not to be much of an issue. White's real advantage, such as it is, is that Black normally would like to get his central majority moving with ...e5 and ...f5, and that idea isn't realizable.

23...b6 24 c6+

Hansen mentions that 24 ♗b7 ♖b8 25 c6+ ♔c7 doesn't really improve White's position, and in fact Black would have the more active pieces.

24...♔c7 25 ♖c4!?

This is meant to stop ...♘d4, which can be effective in a line like 25 a4 ♘d4 26 b5 ♘b3 27 ♖c4 ♘xd2 28 ♔xd2 ♖d8+ with equality, as given by Hansen.

25...♖d8?

Not the most accurate. Black can gain essential activity with Hansen's suggestion 25...♗e7 26 a4 ♘d6 27 ♖h4 ♗g6 28 ♘c4 ♘xc4 29 ♖xc4 ♗d6 with the idea ...♖h8. Then all of Black's pieces are well posted and he can begin to think about advancing his centre pawns.

26 ♖h4 ♗g6 27 a4 ♘d4 28 ♗c3! ♘c2+ 29 ♘xc2 ♗xc2 30 b5

Now White is better, because Black has to defend his pawns and has no counterplay. rest of the game is marked by inaccuracies and finally White loses the thread. I give minimal notes following Hansen's.

30...♗e7 31 ♗e5+

31 ♖f4 seems to give a considerable advantage, the first point being 31...♖d1+ 32 ♔e2 ♖xh1 33 ♖xf7 ♖xa4 34 ♗e5+.

31...♔c8 32 c7 ♖g8?

32...♖d1+ 33 ♔e2 ♗d6 wins the c7-pawn and effectively equalizes.

33 ♖d4?!

33 ♗c6! is much better.

33...f6 34 ♗g3 ♗b3 35 ♗c6 e5

Finally Black gets to play this move, and it wins.

36 ♖d7 ♗b4+ 37 ♔e2 ♗e6 38 ♖d1 ♔xc7 39 f4 ♗d6 40 fxe5 ♗xe5 41 ♗xe5+ fxe5 42 ♔e3 ♖d8 43 ♖c1? ♖d4! 44 ♗d5+ ♔d7 45 ♗xe6+ ♔xe6 46 ♖c7 ♖d7 47 ♖c8 ♔f5 48 ♖e8 g6 0-1

In many ways the variation we examine in the next game with 3...♕d6 is a more direct test of early queen development at the cost of time than 3...♕a5 is.

Biriulin – Melts
corr. 1988-90

1 e4 d5 2 exd5 ♕xd5 3 ♘c3 ♕d6 (D)

International Correspondence Master Michael Melts has specialized in this move and written a fascinating book about it. 3...♕a5 has always taken preference here, but 3...♕d6 is also logical because it covers key central squares like e5 and d4. At first glance the queen looks vulnerable to attack by ♗f4, but this proves hard to arrange and not always effective. A hallmark of the variation is that the queen tends to move forward instead of backward when attacked, often to grab pawns!

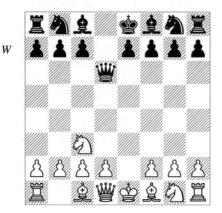

W

Before continuing, I think that Melts's comments are pertinent: "In many chess books we read that one of the main principles of the opening is 'Don't move your queen into the centre'." He then goes on to quote Suetin, who explains that nevertheless "Very characteristic of certain modern openings is the active role of the major pieces, if their manoeuvres disrupt the opponent's plans and assist the favourable coordination of one's own forces." Melts give a list of nine opening variations for which this is true, including:

a) 1 e4 e5 2 ♘f3 ♘c6 3 ♗b5 a6 4 ♗xc6 dxc6 5 0-0 ♛d6.

b) 1 e4 e6 2 d4 d5 3 ♘d2 c5 4 exd5 ♛xd5 5 ♘gf3 cxd4 6 ♗c4 ♛d6.

c) 1 e4 c5 2 ♘f3 d6 3 d4 cxd4 4 ♛xd4 ♘c6 5 ♗b5 ♛d7 6 ♛d3.

d) 1 e4 c5 2 c3 ♘f6 3 e5 ♘d5 4 d4 cxd4 5 ♛xd4 e6 6 ♘f3 ♘c6 7 ♛e4.

e) 1 d4 ♘f6 2 c4 g6 3 ♘c3 d5 4 ♘f3 ♗g7 5 ♛b3 dxc4 6 ♛xc4.

One can easily add to this list with lines like 1 e4 c5 2 c3 d5 3 exd5 ♛xd5 4 d4 ♘f6 5 ♘f3 ♗g4 6 ♗e2 e6 7 ♗e3 cxd4 8 cxd4 ♘c6 9 ♘c3 ♛d6 or 1 e4 c5 2 ♘f3 g6 3 d4 cxd4 4 ♛xd4 ♘f6 5 e5 ♘c6 6 ♛a4 ♘d5 7 ♛e4, or simple examples like 1 d4 d6 2 ♘f3 ♗g4 3 ♛d3. Recently White has been using the sophisticated move-order 1 c4 c5 2 ♘f3 ♘f6 3 ♘c3 e6 4 e4 ♘c6 5 ♗e2!?, which also arises in the Sicilian Defence via 1 e4 c5 2 ♘f3 e6 3 c4 ♘c6 4 ♘c3 ♘f6 5 ♗e2!?. White would like to play d4 in many variations, so Black came up with the simple prophylactic 5...♛b6!?. The queen looks awkward there, but as Suetin says, it disrupts the opponent's plans.

None of this is very shocking, of course, but it does indicate that a move like 3...♛d6 in the Scandinavian, previously dismissed by nearly all strong players, deserves the more open-minded attention that it has been receiving recently. GM Ian Rogers, for example, got a good game with it in a rapidplay game against Kasparov himself in Batumi 2001.

4 d4 ♘f6 5 ♗c4 c6

This move guards against a sequence with ♘b5 and ♗f4 while beginning to block d5 and giving the queen more room in some cases. It seems that every time a strong master plays this line as Black, some variation with ...a6 instead of ...c6 is tried. I feel that 5...c6 is more interesting (and thematic) and would love to see more tests of it. Be that as it may, more evidence that wandering around with the queen in the opening can be reasonable is offered by the line 5...a6 6 ♘ge2 ♛c6!? (a fork!) 7 ♗b3 (7 ♛d3!? ♛xg2 8 ♖g1 ♛h3 has been played and seems sound enough for Black) 7...♛xg2 8 ♖g1 (D).

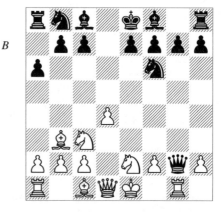

B

8...♛xh2 (a decision that relates to the discussion of whether a pawn-grabbing queen should stick around for nuisance value or beat it back home; here 8...♛f3 and 8...♛h3 have been played, and both seem better to me than 8...♛c6, but all these lines are relatively unexplored) 9 ♗f4 ♛h5. White has an enormous lead in development but Black's position is reasonably sound. Govbinder-Melts, Internet 1998 went 10 ♗xc7 ♗g4 11 ♛d2 ♘bd7 12 0-0-0 ♖c8 13 ♗g3 ♛a5 and the queen took up her traditional post, but only by means of making 7 moves out of Black's first 13!

6 ♘ge2 ♗f5 7 ♗f4 ♛b4

The first foray, gaining a tempo.

8 ♗b3 e6 9 0-0 ♘a6!?

This is the most fun, developing a knight to the rim and thus both preventing the dangerous ♗c7 by White (trying to trap the queen in some lines) and giving Black's rooks an unobstructed view down the d-file. Remember that avoiding interference with other pieces is one motivation for developing knights to the edge of the board. According to Melts, the moves 9...♛a5, 9...♘bd7 and 9...♗e7 have all proven playable, a game with the latter continuing 10 ♘g3 ♗g6 11 ♖e1 ♘bd7 12 ♘a4!? (12 ♗c7!? ♗d8!?) 12...♛a5 13 c4 0-0 with equality, Margulis-Schiller, San Francisco 1999.

10 ♘g3 ♗g6 11 a3 ♛a5

Back to the 'normal' Scandinavian square!

12 ♛e2 ♗e7 13 ♖fe1 0-0 14 ♘ge4 ♖ad8

A basic sort of position that looks much like the normal 3...♛a5 Scandinavian but with Black having avoided some difficult lines.

15 ♖ad1

15 ♘xf6+ ♗xf6 16 ♗e5 gives Black an easy life after 16...♖xe5 17 dxe5 (17 ♛xe5?! ♛xe5 18 dxe5 ♖d4!? {18...♘c5 looks good} 19 ♖ad1 ♖fd8 20 ♖xd4 ♖xd4 and Melts likes Black) 17...♖d4 (or 17...♘c7 18 ♖ad1 ♘d5) 18 ♖ad1 ♖fd8 19 ♖xd4 ♖xd4 20 ♛e3 c5 intending ...♘c7 with equality.

15...♘d5 16 ♘xd5 cxd5

Worth considering is 16...exd5!? with the idea ...♖fe8.

17 ♘g5 ♗f6 *(D)*

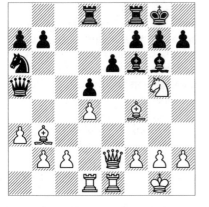

18 h4?

This creates a real weakness and White has no hope whatsoever for a kingside attack. Better was 18 c3 ♛b6 19 ♗a2 ♖c8 20 ♘f3 ♗h5 21 ♖d2 ♘c7 intending ...♘b5-d6. White probably has a slight edge, but it's not much.

18...h6 19 ♘f3?!

Since this move leads to more weaknesses and the loss of a pawn in short order, 19 h5 ♗f5 (19...hxg5 20 ♗d2) 20 ♘h3 should be tried, but White's pieces don't coordinate well and Black holds some advantage after 20...♛b6.

19...♗h5 20 g3

This exacerbates the light-square problem, but 20 ♗g3? ♗xf3 21 ♛xf3 (21 gxf3 ♛b6) allows 21...♗xd4!.

20...♛b6 21 ♔g2

21 ♗e3 ♘b8! prepares simply ...♘c6 and ...♘xd4, and there is little that White can do.

21...♘b8!?

More straightforward is 21...♗xd4! with an extra pawn and powerful centre.

22 ♗e5?!

22 ♗xb8 ♖xb8 23 ♛e3 is a better defensive chance.

22...♗e7! 23 ♛e3 ♘c6 24 ♛f4 ♖d7

24...♘xe5 25 ♛xe5 ♗g6 is also very good because ...♗e4 can follow.

25 g4 ♗g6 26 g5 h5

26...f6! 27 gxf6 ♗xf6 makes White's kingside too difficult to defend.

27 ♛c1?

27 ♔g1 ♗e4 28 ♖xe4! dxe4 29 ♛xe4 ♘a5 30 ♖d3 leaves White well short of full compensation, but was a fighting try.

27...♗e4 28 ♗a4 f6 0-1

Once the f-file is open, the game is over.

One can make comparable points about the early deployment of the queen in many other openings, several of which are mentioned in the introductory note to this last contest. I think that, just as in other parts of the game, players are taking a closer look at what they can get away with in this area and what benefits might accrue. I haven't touched upon the related idea of queens moving to the flank to capture pawns or otherwise harass the opponent, but similar considerations apply. One might wish to refer to SOMCS for examples. In general, these phenomena are reflections of the growing spirit of experimentation that pervades contemporary chess, and I'm sure that we'll be seeing more of them in the near future.

Part 2: Modern Games and Their Interpretation

In Part 2 I've picked out various games that exemplify important ideas of modern chess. They often deal with a particular type of position discussed in the book. The choice of such games has been a purely subjective one, since every issue of *New In Chess*, *ChessBase Magazine*, *Informator*, *ChessPublishing*, *Chess Today*, and just about any international or national magazine has a few or very many games that are temptingly representative of numerous ideas at the same time. My goal has been to give a flavour of how the strategic themes that I've outlined in both this book and SOMCS are realized in actual practice, warts and all. I haven't for the most part chosen well-known or famous games, although a few were irresistible. Nor have I emphasized the spectacular. Nevertheless, it *is* nice to have some pretty tactics here and there; in some cases they can remind us of how so much of contemporary chess comes down to justifying apparently anti-positional and committal strategies from which there is no turning back.

Instead of taking the modern era as a whole, I have predominantly chosen my examples from the last 10-15 years, with an occasional whimsical exception. That in a sense gives us the peak of the evolutionary trail and by default embraces earlier developments. We live in interesting times, however cursed that makes us; again and again I have included games with top-notch ideas that simply wouldn't have got more than a glance as recently as the 1970s and even 1980s, much less in the 1940s to 1960s (as creative as those times of course were).

The selection of representative games resembles what I did at the end of SOMCS, but there I took all my games from two Informators and didn't annotate them in any depth. Here I try to give comments and analysis for the game as a whole, and I have also imbedded other important games in the notes that I think illustrate related themes. My idea has been to present instructive games combined with illustrative examples pertinent to the game continuation. Most of the time the main contest is both the most thematic and entertaining, but once in a while the subsidiary games contain ideas that are more interesting than the main contest; in those cases I may have opted for organizational convenience or perhaps the imbedded games have been rapidplay games containing too many flaws. On that subject, however, I believe that some games with short time-limits can highlight the basic tendencies of the players involved because we see their instinctive responses. Remember that this book's emphasis is on how modern ideas and strategies are reflected in actual play, regardless of their success. Naturally I believe that the use of these ideas leads to superior results, even on a very low level of play, but not in every game! At any rate, those of an investigatory bent might first want to have some fun getting an overall impression of the flow of the game and then pick out what seems of interest to go over more seriously. Finally, one should note that while I sometimes try to dig into the details of the opening, these examples by no means constitute an opening survey and woe to the player who treats them as such!

Game 1
Topalov – Rozentalis
Batumi Echt 1999

1 c4 e6 2 ♘c3 ♘f6 3 e4 d5 4 e5 ♘e4 5 ♘f3 ♗e7 *(D)*

This relatively innocent position has arisen many times over the years. The conventional moves here are 6 d4, perhaps best met by 6...c5, and 6 ♕c2. Instead Topalov comes up with:

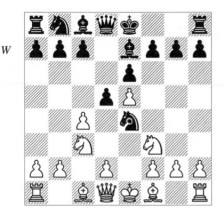

W

6 h4!?

A lovely advance that develops nothing and weakens the kingside! But this turns out to be a very clever waiting move, one which also eliminates one of Black's thematic ideas in this position, i.e., ...♘g5, which would get rid of the important central defender on f3. Apart from that typically modern prophylactic function, there are positive aspects of the move including among others the possibility of anchoring a piece on g5 and (you never know) attacking the kingside by ♖h3-g3.

But surely Black can utilize the extra tempo handed him? To gain some insight into that question, it's instructive to compare two alternatives to 6 h4. The first is 6 d4, which is probably best met by 6...c5, when White really can't do anything about the liquidation of the centre. The second is 6 ♕c2, to which an active solution is 6...♘c6!? intending 7 ♘xe4 (7 ♗e2 ♘g5!) 7...♘b4 8 ♕b1 dxe4 9 ♕xe4 ♗d7 and ...♗c6, with plenty of compensation for a pawn. Compare the analysis of 6...0-0 in the next note.

6...♘xc3

This leaves White with a comfortable space advantage. The alternatives are fascinating:

a) Topalov gives 6...♘c6 7 d4 f6 8 ♗d3 with a small advantage. Then the most natural line is 8...♘xc3 9 bxc3 fxe5 10 ♘xe5 ♘xe5 11 dxe5 g6 (11...dxc4 12 ♕h5+ ♔f8 13 ♗xc4 favours White) 12 h5! with an edge. Thus the 6 h4 move comes in handy after all!

b) White can also play with originality once Black has committed to 6...c5; for example, 7 ♕b3 (7 ♗d3 may also be good now that both ...♘g5 and ...♘c5 are ruled out; then 7...♘xc3 8 dxc3 dxc4 9 ♗xc4 ♕xd1+ 10 ♔xd1 should still

favour White somewhat) 7...0-0 8 cxd5 ♘xc3 9 dxc3 ♕xd5 (9...exd5 10 ♗g5 and 0-0-0) 10 ♕c2 ♘c6 11 ♗g5 (thanks again to 6 h4) 11...♖d8 12 ♗xe7 ♘xe7 13 ♗e2 with a comfortable advantage.

c) 6...0-0 7 ♕c2 ♘c6 8 ♘xe4 ♘b4 9 ♕b1 dxe4 10 ♕xe4 ♗d7 is similar to the pawn sacrifice in the note above with 6 ♕c2 ♘c6, but in this case White gets another chance to use the all-purpose 6 h4: 11 ♘g5! g6 (11...♗xg5 12 hxg5 g6 13 a3 ♘c6 14 d4 is good for White) 12 a3 ♗c6 13 ♕b1 ♘a6 14 b4 and after Black retreats one of his threatened pieces, there simply follows 15 d3.

7 dxc3 dxc4 8 ♕a4+

8 ♕xd8+ ♗xd8 9 ♗xc4 is also somewhat better for White, but Topalov wants the attack.

8...♗d7 9 ♕xc4 ♗c6 10 ♕g4 ♗xf3 *(D)*

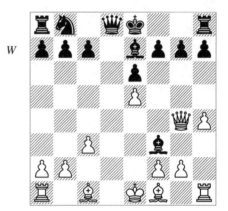

W

11 gxf3!

With this we have seen a whole set of modern characteristics in one game: flank advance to the neglect of development, 'good' dislocated doubled pawns, possession of the two bishops versus weaknesses in one's own position, and general dynamism. Note that 11 ♕xf3 is well met by 11...♕d5 with equality. The rest of the game is in good part a tribute to the power of the two bishops.

11...♗f8!?

Now for some backwards development to throw into the mix! But this doesn't seem to work out. Rozentalis suggests 11...g6 12 h5 ♕d5!, although after 13 hxg6 (or even 13 ♗e3 with the point 13...♕xe5? 14 hxg6 fxg6 15 f4! {15 0-0-0 is obviously good as well} 15...♕f5 16 ♕xf5 exf5 17 ♗d4 ♖f8 18 ♖xh7 and ♗c4 or

♞g7 with a large advantage) 13...♕xe5+ 14 ♗e3 fxg6 (14...hxg6 15 ♕e4! ♜h5 16 ♜xh5 ♕xh5 17 ♕xb7 is winning for White) 15 f4 ♕f5 16 ♕xf5 exf5 17 ♗d4 ♜f8 18 ♜xh7 ♞d7 19 ♗c4 the two bishops and threat of ♗g7 form a wicked combination.

12 f4 ♞d7 13 ♗e3 c6 14 0-0-0 ♕a5

After 14...h5, Rozentalis gives 15 ♕h3 (to preserve the idea of f5) 15...g6 16 ♗c4! threatening ♗xe6.

15 f5!! *(D)*

An amazing move! It's as though White's pawns and pieces have magically coordinated ever since move 6. The duller option is 15 ♚b1 0-0-0 with equality according to Rozentalis, although 16 ♗c4 probably retains some advantage.

15...♕xa2

15...♞xe5 16 ♕e4 exf5 17 ♕xf5 threatens f4 and is extremely hard to meet; e.g., 17...g6 18 ♕f6 ♜g8 19 ♗g5!, winning in view of 19...♕c7 20 ♗f4 or 19...h6 20 ♗c4! with the idea 20...hxg5 21 ♜he1.

16 fxe6 ♕xe6

Losing outright are 16...♞xe5?? 17 exf7+ ♕xf7 18 ♕e4 ♕e7 19 ♗g5 and 16...fxe6?? 17 ♗c4.

17 ♕f4!

Rozentalis argues that White's position is winning, and indeed the bishops are on the loose for real now.

17...♜d8

Just as bad is 17...♕xe5 18 ♗h3 or 17...♞xe5 18 ♗h3 ♕e7 (18...♕f6 19 ♜he1 ♗e7 20 ♕g3 h6 21 ♗d4) 19 ♜he1 f6 20 ♕g3!, following analysis by Rozentalis. This is totally winning;

21 f4 is White's biggest threat, but not the only one.

18 ♗c4 ♕e7 19 ♜he1 h5

The situation is clear after 19...♞xe5 20 ♗d4 ♞xc4 21 ♜xe7+ ♗xe7 22 ♜e1.

20 ♕g3

20 e6! fxe6 21 ♗xe6 is another win.

20...♞xe5 21 ♜xd8+ ♚xd8 22 ♗f4 ♞xc4 23 ♜xe7 ♚xe7

23...♗xe7 24 ♕d3+.

24 ♕d3! 1-0

Either the knight will fall or some horrible sequence with ♕d6+ and ♕b8+ will follow. A wonderful game, somewhat lost in the avalanche of more conventional brilliancies we are seeing these days.

Game 2

Dautov – Lputian

Istanbul OL 2000

This game illustrates a number of modern themes such as an early flank attack, the treatment of two bishops versus two knights, and pure pragmatism.

1 d4 d5 2 c4 e6 3 ♞c3 ♗e7

Black attempts to avoid the main lines of the Exchange Variation of the Queen's Gambit. By playing this move-order, he avoids 3...♞f6 4 cxd5 exd5 5 ♗g5.

4 cxd5 exd5 5 ♗f4 c6 6 e3 ♗f5

For some years, this position seemed to solve most of Black's problems in such a pawn-structure since White would usually like to play ♗d3 and force Black's c8-bishop to develop more passively on e6. Instead, the exchange of bishops after ♗d3 is pretty lame. The dilemma led Botvinnik to find a unique and counter-intuitive solution:

7 g4!?

A 'beginner's move' that violates the principle of early flank moves and apparently weakens the defence of the side of the board on which the white king will eventually reside. The point is, quite simply, to gain space.

7...♗e6

7...♗g6 is sometimes played, but after 8 h4, the greedy 8...♗xh4? (8...h5 is better) is supposed to be a mistake due to 9 ♕b3 b6 10 ♜xh4! ♕xh4 11 ♞xd5!. For some reason this line isn't given in *ECO*, where Miles is quoted suggesting 10 ♘f3 ♗e7 11 ♘e5 with an advantage.

8 h4 *(D)*

White continues to neglect development and even offers a pawn. 8 h4, often dismissed as too loosening, has been used over the years by Botvinnik, Kasparov and Karpov, among others. Recently this direct advance has received a lot more attention, and has produced many games with original positional ideas and dynamic tactics.

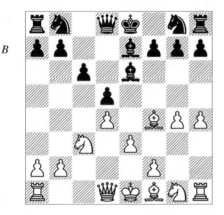

8...c5

The traditional central response to a flank attack: Black asks White what exactly those pawns are doing. Other moves are equally unclear; for example:

a) 8...♘f6 led to a difficult tactical struggle in Ki.Georgiev-Lputian, Istanbul OL 2000. I will just give some uncommented moves, because there are unclear options at every juncture: 9 g5 ♘e4 10 ♗d3 ♕a5 11 ♔f1! ♘xc3 12 bxc3 ♘d7 13 ♘e2 0-0-0 14 a4 h6 15 gxh6 gxh6 16 ♘g3 ♘b6 17 ♘f5 ♗f8 18 ♕c2 ♘c4 19 ♖g1 ♗d6 20 ♗xh6 ♗xf5 21 ♗xf5+ ♔b8 22 ♗g5 and White was a pawn to the good with the two bishops.

b) 8...♗xh4 is obviously critical. White gets excellent compensation for the pawn after 9 ♕b3 b6 10 ♘f3 ♗e7 11 ♘e5; e.g., 11...♘f6?! 12 g5 ♘fd7 13 g6! (a lovely justification of g4 and h4) 13...♘xe5 14 ♗xe5 ♘f6! (14...fxg6 15 ♗xg7 ♖g8 16 ♖xh7 with a clear plus) 15 ♖xh7 0-0! 16 ♗g3! fxg6 (16...♗f5 17 0-0-0 ♗xg6 18 ♖h2 and White stands much better; he will double on the h-file) 17 ♖h2 ♔f7! 18 0-0-0 ♖h8?! (Yusupov suggests 18...♘d7! 19 e4 ♗e7 with

just an edge for White; this was the last chance) 19 ♖xh8 ♕xh8 20 e4! ♕h5 (20...dxe4 21 ♗c4 ♕h3 22 ♘xe4 with a large advantage) 21 ♖e1! ♘d7 22 exd5 ♗xd5 (22...cxd5 23 ♖xe6 ♔xe6 24 ♘xd5 turns out to be too strong) 23 ♘xd5 cxd5 24 ♗g2 ♖c8+ 25 ♔b1 ♖e8 (25...♖c4 26 ♕b5) 26 ♗xd5+ ♔f8 27 ♖h1 ♕f5+ 28 ♔a1 ♔e7 29 ♕a3+ ♔d8 30 ♕d6 ♕c2 31 ♗c6 ♕f5 32 ♕c7+ ♔e7 33 ♗d6+ 1-0 Gulko-Lputian, Glendale 1994.

c) We saw the move 8...♘d7 in Chapter 2, Section 1 exemplified by the eccentric game Vaiser-Timoshchenko, Tashkent 1987. Another revealing display of the advantages of the space grab comes from Beliavsky-Geller, USSR Ch (Moscow) 1983: 9 h5 ♕b6 10 ♖b1 ♘gf6 11 f3 (restricting the knight) 11...0-0 12 ♗d3 c5 13 ♘ge2 ♖ac8 14 ♔f1 (14 g5!? ♘e8 15 ♕c2 is also good) 14...cxd4 15 exd4 ♗d6 16 ♕d2 ♘e8 17 ♔g2 ♕d8 18 ♖be1 (Black is completely tied up) 18...♘b6 19 ♗b1 ♘c4 20 ♕d3 f5?! (but Beliavsky points out that 20...g6 21 b3 ♘a3 22 hxg6 fxg6 23 ♕e3 ♕f6 24 ♗e5 {in fact, 24 ♗h6! is even better} 24...♗xe5 25 dxe5 ♕f7 26 ♖h6 gives White a clear advantage) 21 ♗c1 ♘f6 22 ♘g3! ♗xg3 23 ♖xe6 fxg4 (desperation) 24 ♔xg3 ♘e4+ 25 ♘xe4 ♖xf3+ 26 ♕xf3 gxf3 27 ♘g5 ♘d6 28 ♗xh7+ ♔f8 29 ♖f1 1-0.

9 ♗e5! *(D)*

A subtle, strange, and effective move. White would like to weaken Black's pawn-structure by provoking ...f6, which will also protect the h4-pawn. This pragmatic idea changed the status of the whole variation, which had previously been at least equal for Black.

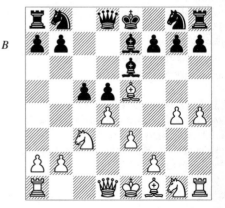

9...♗f6

Or:

a) 9...♘f6? 10 g5 ♘g4 can be met by the paradoxical 11 ♗xb8! ♖xb8 12 ♕d2!, threatening simply to trap the knight by f3: 12...♕c7 13 ♗b5+ ♔f8 14 f3 a6 (14...♕g3+ 15 ♔f1) 15 ♗d3 and White is clearly better. This comes from analysis by Dautov.

b) Dautov also shows that 9...f6?! 10 ♗xb8 ♖xb8 11 ♘h3! intending ♘f4 is now effective with the pawn on f6: 11...♕b6 12 ♗b5+ ♔f7 13 ♕f3! cxd4 14 ♘g5+ ♔f8 15 ♕f4 ♖d8 16 ♘xe6+ ♕xe6 17 ♕xd4 with a definite advantage.

c) It's hard to believe, but 9...♔f8 is probably the best move. Then 10 ♘h3! ♘c6 (10...♗xh4 11 ♘f4) 11 ♘f4 favours White somewhat because of the weak d5-pawn.

10 ♗xb8!

What's this? White exposes his kingside and then exchanges off one of his only two developed pieces, giving Black the two bishops into the bargain! But it's one of those easy-once-you-see-it moves that gives immediate positional results.

10...♖xb8

The flank pawns show their worth in the entertaining line 10...cxd4? 11 g5! dxc3 (11...♗e7 loses to 12 ♕xd4) 12 gxf6 cxb2 (12...♕xf6 13 ♗b5+) 13 fxg7 ♕a5+ 14 ♔e2 bxa1♕ 15 ♕xa1, winning for White.

11 g5 ♗e7 12 ♗g2!

Now d5 is a serious weakness. 12 ♕a4+!? ♔f8 13 ♕xa7?! ♖a8 14 ♕xb7 ♖b8 15 ♕a6 cxd4 16 exd4 ♖xb2 gives Black way too much play.

12...h6 *(D)*

To get Black's knight out before the pressure on d5 grows too strong.

13 ♘ge2!

13 f4? hxg5 14 hxg5 ♖xh1 15 ♗xh1 ♕a5 saves the g-pawn but at the cost of development.

13...hxg5 14 hxg5 ♖xh1+ 15 ♗xh1 ♗xg5

Now 15...♕a5 is a tempo behind after 16 ♘f4. Dautov analyses 16...♖d8 17 ♘xe6 fxe6 18 ♕h5+ ♔f8 19 ♕g4 ♕b6 20 0-0-0 and White is clearly better.

16 ♕a4+ ♔f8

White wins after 16...b5? 17 ♕xa7 b4 18 ♘xd5.

17 dxc5

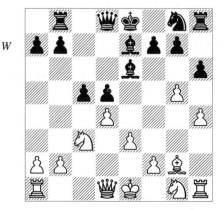

The dust has cleared and White has several pluses, not least of which is the double threat of ♕xa7 and 0-0-0. And this all came from 9 ♗e5!. Not for any profound reason, but simply because each of Black's replies had concrete drawbacks.

17...♘e7

17...a6? is too slow: 18 ♖d1 ♘e7 19 e4.

18 ♕xa7 ♘c6 19 ♕b6 ♕f6

A tricky move, but Black's exposed king and the weakness on d5 prove more important than Black's piece play.

20 ♕c7

20 ♘xd5!? is a bit complex, even though 20...♗xd5 21 ♗xd5 ♗h4 22 ♘f4 ♖e8, as given by Dautov, still gives White the advantage after the absurd computer sequence 23 0-0-0 ♗xf2 24 ♘g2!.

20...♖c8 21 ♕h2!

Avoiding 21 ♕xb7!? ♘e5! with complications.

21...♘b4 22 ♖d1 ♔g8

Dautov observes that 22...♖xc5 allows favourable simplification by 23 ♕d6+ (or 23 ♘d4) 23...♗e7 24 ♕xe7+ ♗xe7 25 a3 ♘c6 26 ♗xd5 with White on top.

23 a3 ♘c2+ 24 ♔d2 ♘d4

The knight is trapped after 24...♕g6 25 f4 ♗h6 26 ♕g1!.

25 ♘xd4

White wins more quickly after 25 f4! ♘b3+ (25...♘xe2 26 fxg5) 26 ♔c2 ♗h6 (useless is 26...♘xc5 27 fxg5 ♕g6+ 28 ♔d2 ♕d3+ 29 ♔e1 ♕xe3 30 ♕g3) 27 ♔xb3 d4+ 28 ♘d5.

25...♕xd4+ 26 ♔e1 ♕xc5 27 ♗xd5 ♕b6

Losing is 27...♗f6 28 ♘e4 ♕a5+ 29 b4 ♕xa3 30 ♘xf6+ gxf6 31 ♕g3+ ♔f8 32 ♕d6+;

27...&xd5 28 &xd5 &e7 29 &h3 is clearly better for White.

28 &xe6 &xe6 29 &g2 &f6

29...&h4 30 &e4! &xe4 (or 30...&h3 31 &e2 &f6 32 &h1 &e6 33 &xe6 fxe6 34 &c1) 31 &xe4 &e8! 32 &d4 f5 33 &c5 &xe3+ 34 &f1 &e5 35 &xb7 &f6 36 b4 and White wins.

30 &xb7 &xc3+ 31 bxc3 &xc3 32 &b8+ &h7

Also futile is 32...&c8 33 &d8+ &xd8 34 &xd8+ &h7 35 a4.

33 &h2+ &h6 34 &xh6+ gxh6 35 &a1 h5

No better is 35...&c5 36 a4 &a5 37 &d2 h5 38 &c3 &g6 39 &b4 &a8 40 a5.

36 a4 &c6 37 a5 &a6 38 &f1 &g6 39 &g2 &g5 40 &h3 f6 41 f4+ &g6 42 e4 1-0

Game 3
Shirov – Kramnik
Novgorod 1994

This game explores the issues of flank attack versus central play, bishops versus knights, and delayed development.

1 e4 c5 2 &f3 &c6 3 &b5 g6 4 &xc6 dxc6 5 h3 e5 6 d3 f6

This seems an odd move until one sees Black's follow-up.

7 c3 &h6 8 &e3 &f7 9 0-0

White's moves are reasonable, but he isn't establishing outposts for his knights, something that would require more active play to disturb the pawn-structure.

9...g5! *(D)*

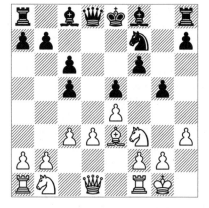

One has to admit that Black has discarded all pretence to obeying the classical rules of play!

With only one piece developed (versus White's three) and on an odd square at that, Black moves his g-pawn for a second time to launch a flank attack! How often in the older books have we seen some comment like: 'This flailing out on the flank when undeveloped is totally unjustified'?

10 &e2

'10 d4 is the natural solution', our confident hypothetical annotator would doubtless add, 'so as to refute a premature flank attack by a central counterattack'. But amazingly, that advance probably doesn't even equalize! Black continues 10...cxd4 (or he can use the move-order 10...g4, since 11 &h4?! cxd4 12 cxd4 gxh3 13 g3 exd4 14 &xd4 &g8 15 &c3 &g4 gave Black the initiative and a pawn in Oral-Krakops, Guarapuava U-18 Wch 1995; instead, 11 hxg4 cxd4 12 cxd4 transposes to 10...cxd4) 11 cxd4 g4 12 hxg4 &xg4 13 &bd2 &g8! 14 &b3 (Kramnik gives 14 &h1 &d7 with an edge for Black) 14...&d7 (perhaps even better is 14...&h3! 15 &h4, when 15...exd4 gives Black a clear advantage, while 15...f5 also looks good) 15 dxe5 &e6 16 &c3 fxe5?! (16...&h3! again favours Black) 17 &fd1 &c7 was roughly equal in Kalegin-Goldin, Elista 1995.

10...h5 11 &e1

A sensible move, lessening the impact of ...g4, but it starts to make White's development advantage look rather feeble.

11...&e6

11...g4 12 h4 f5!? is also an interesting possibility.

12 a3 a5 13 &d2 b6

Kramnik makes the astonishing suggestion of 13...&h7!? 14 &c2 &h8! *(D)*.

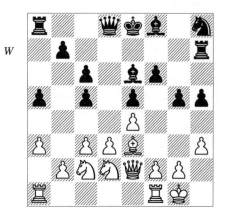

This absurd-looking idea prepares ...♘g6-f4 (which would be the fifth knight move!) and perhaps ...♖d7, to attack d3 and restrain d4. White is therefore virtually forced to play 15 d4, when Kramnik continues his analysis with 15...cxd4 (15...g4! is probably better due to White's 19th move alternative; then 16 h4 cxd4 17 cxd4 ♘g6 retains some advantage for Black) 16 cxd4 ♘g6 17 ♖fd1 g4!? 18 dxe5 fxe5 19 ♘c4 (19 ♘f3!) 19...♕f6. It is hard to imagine a more flippant dismissal of everything that the textbooks say.

14 ♘c2 ♖a7!

Another 2nd-rank rook idea.

15 d4?

White should play 15 ♖fd1! ♖d7 16 ♘f1, when 16...♗b3 and 16...h4 (to stop ♘g3) are both dynamically balanced.

15...cxd4 16 cxd4 ♖d7 17 dxe5 ♘xe5

Kramnik assesses this as giving an edge for Black. With his pressure along the d-file and specifically d3, along with two bishops and a pseudo-outpost on e5, that may be a slight understatement. The game continued:

18 ♖fd1 ♗e7

18...♖hh7!? is another aesthetically pleasing and effective Kramnik suggestion.

19 ♘f1 ♗c4 20 ♖xd7 ♕xd7 21 ♕d2 ♗d3!?

Or 21...c5 with an edge.

22 ♕c3

22 f3 g4! puts White's kingside in serious danger.

22...♗xe4 23 ♘g3 ♗d5! 24 ♗xb6 h4 25 ♘e2 g4 26 ♘f4 ♗e4?

A mistake. Kramnik points out that Black's strategy would be crowned by 26...♖g8! 27 ♘xd5 cxd5 28 hxg4 (28 ♔h1 ♔f7! 29 hxg4 ♕xg4 30 ♘e3 ♕e6 with a large advantage for Black) 28...♕xg4 29 ♘e3 ♕e6 30 ♗d4 h3 31 ♗xe5 fxe5 32 ♕xa5 d4 and Black is much better.

27 ♖e1! ♕f5 28 ♘e6 ♖g8 29 ♘cd4 ♘f3+! 30 ♔f1??

Nor is 30 ♔h1? ♘xd4 31 ♕xd4 good due to 31...♗xg2+! 32 ♔xg2 ♕f3+ 33 ♔f1 (33 ♔h2 g3+) 33...gxh3 34 ♘c7+ ♔f8 35 ♘e6+ ♔f7, which is analysis by Kramnik yielding Black a completely winning game. Correct is 30 ♕xf3!, which leads to a small white advantage after 30...gxf3 31 ♘xf5 ♗xf5 32 ♘d4! ♖xg2+ 33 ♔h1 ♗d7 34 ♘xf3.

30...♗d3+

Now Black is clearly winning.

31 ♖e2 ♗xe2+ 32 ♔xe2 ♕e4+ 33 ♕e3 ♘xd4+ 34 ♘xd4 ♕xe3+ 35 ♔xe3 gxh3 36 gxh3 ♖g5!? 37 ♘xc6 ♗c5+ 38 ♗xc5 ♖xc5 39 ♘d4 a4 40 ♔d3 ♖c1! 0-1

In view of 41 ♘f5 ♖h1.

Game 4
Lautier – Shirov
Manila IZ 1990

This game has a bit of everything: flank attacks, doubled pawn advantages, a positional exchange sacrifice and a tactical one, and above all dynamism!

1 d4 ♘f6 2 ♘f3 g6 3 g3 ♗g7 4 ♗g2 0-0 5 0-0 d6 6 c4 ♘c6 7 ♘c3 a6 8 h3

I talk about this modern opening in both SOMCS and in Chapter 2 of this book. In those cases White played 8 d5 ♘a5 9 ♘d2 c5. Here he plays a popular and less committal line. Thus he avoids chasing the c6-knight to the side of the board, acknowledging that it would be satisfactorily placed there.

8...♗d7 9 ♗g5 h6 10 ♗e3 ♖b8 11 ♘d5 b5!?

Black's first flank foray. This is more interesting and ambitious than 11...e6 12 ♘xf6+ ♕xf6, when White is somewhat better. But it commits Black to the following strange and risky position:

12 ♘xf6+ exf6

So Black captures away from the centre, accepts doubled pawns, and gives White a 2 to 1 central majority! All in all, an eccentric bargain whose value lies almost purely in the possibilities of activity, ultimately on both wings. In the meantime, White also has a chance to weaken his opponent's pawn-structure further.

13 cxb5 ♖xb5!

At first this seems like a poor attempt to gain activity at the expense of creating a further weakness on a6. Moreover, it proves not to be one of those dynamic rook-lifts to h5, as one sees from Black's next move. But after 13...axb5 instead, White has 14 d5! ♘e5 (or 14...♘e7 15 ♘d4 with a clear advantage) 15 ♘d4 ♘c4 16 ♗c1 with b3 next and wonderful pressure down the c-file.

14 ♕d2 g5!

Yet another flank advance, this time an ungainly protection of the h-pawn. It's not obvious at first how this is better than 14...♔h7 15 d5 ♘e7 16 ♘d4, when White is comfortably better. But Shirov has a subtle idea; compare this with the game continuation.

15 d5

Critical. Otherwise Black can contest the d5- or f5-squares for his knight by ...♘e7, giving him some time to advance on the kingside. For example, a game four years later saw both sides willing to copy this game and White tried 15 ♘e1?! ♘e7 16 f3 (16 d5 ♕c8 17 ♔h2 f5) 16...f5 17 ♗f2 f4! 18 gxf4 gxf4 19 ♕xf4 ♖xb2 with a considerable advantage for Black, Kekki-Norri, Helsinki 1994.

15...♘e7!

Preparing to go tactical. It's hard to resist 15...♘e5, threatening both ...♘xf3+ and ...♘c4. But White simply allows the latter; for example, Ftačnik suggests 16 ♘d4!? ♘c4 17 ♕c3 ♘xe3 18 fxe3! (threatening ♘f5 and ♖ac1) 18...♖c5!? 19 ♕d3 f5 20 ♘xf5 with a clear plus.

16 ♘d4

Everything is going smoothly. White is thinking about a line like 16...♖b8 17 f4! and f5 with everything going his way.

16...♖xd5!

This exchange sacrifice, which had to be anticipated when Black played 11...b5, changes the whole nature of the game. If one is fully objective, Black is probably still worse as he will still have a split and weakened pawn-structure; but he will also have gained the bishop-pair and can concentrate on blasting open lines for them.

17 ♗xd5 ♘xd5 (D)

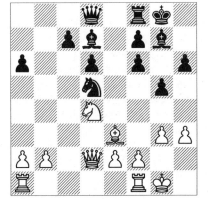

 W

18 ♘f5

It makes a lot of sense to simplify, but this also returns a pawn. The straightforward 18 ♔h2 protects the h-pawn and may be a better choice. Nevertheless, complications will follow 18...♕a8!? (or 18...♕c8 19 ♘f5 ♗xf5 20 ♕xd5 ♗xh3 21 ♖fc1 ♖e8 22 ♕a5 ♖e7; on the other hand, 18...♘xe3? 19 fxe3! wins the f5-square for White and it can even be reinforced by g4) 19 ♘c2 c5 20 f4 ♖e8; this is unclear, with Black having a lot of possibilities due to the bishops.

18...♗xf5 19 ♕xd5 ♗xh3 20 ♖fd1

20 ♖fc1 is an obvious alternative. White probably wanted to save that square for the queen's knight.

20...♖e8 21 ♖ac1

Again it looks as though White is consolidating his advantage.

21...f5 22 ♖d2

This is objectively good, but Black continues to mix things up. 22 ♕c6 is met in the same way.

22...♖xe3!?

A second exchange sacrifice! It's rare to see two rooks versus two bishops.

23 fxe3 ♕e7 24 ♔f2!

24 ♕d3 ♗e5 25 ♔h2 seems to batten down the hatches. Actually, after 25...♗g4, the idea of ...h5-h4 is still a problem. Probably White should then give back one of the exchanges by 26 ♖c4 intending ♖xg4 (26 ♖dc2 c5 27 ♖d1 h5 28 ♔g2 h4 29 gxh4 gxh4 is unclear), when Black should nevertheless try 26...h5 with the idea ...h4.

24...♗e5 25 ♖h1??

Natural enough, but a huge mistake. Instead, White had a strong idea in 25 ♖dc2! c5 26 b4.

25...♗xg3+!

It's interesting how Black maintains his attack with so little material (soon to be the lone queen).

26 ♔xg3

Fatal would be 26 ♔f3 g4+ 27 ♔xg3 ♕xe3+ 28 ♔h4 ♕f2+ 29 ♔h5 ♕f4! 30 ♔h4 ♕g5+ 31 ♔g3 f4+ 32 ♔h2 ♕h4.

26...♕xe3+ (D)

27 ♕f3

Not 27 ♔h2? ♕f2+ 28 ♔xh3 g4#.

27...♕xd2 28 ♕a8+

White will also lose after 28 ♖xh3 g4 29 ♕a8+ ♔g7 30 ♖e1 ♕xe2.

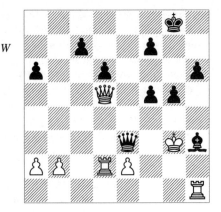

28...♔g7 29 ♔xh3

The alternative 29 ♖xh3 can be answered by 29...♕xe2, after which White is overwhelmed by pawns; e.g., 30 ♕g2 ♕e5+ 31 ♔f2 ♕xb2+ 32 ♔g1 ♕a1+ 33 ♔h2 ♕e5+ 34 ♕g3 f6!.

29...♕xe2 30 ♕d5?

The defensive 30 ♕g2 is better, although White is in trouble after 30...♕h5+ (or 30...♕e5) 31 ♔g3 ♕g4+ 32 ♔f2 ♕d4+ 33 ♔e1 ♕e3+ 34 ♔d1 g4.

30...♔g6?

This is good enough to take the point, yet 30...♕f2! threatens ...g4# and wins immediately.

31 ♕d4?

But as Ftačnik shows, 31 ♕g2 g4+ 32 ♔h2 ♕e5+ 33 ♔g1 h5 34 ♕h2 f4 is winning for Black.

31...f4! 32 ♖g1 f5 0-1

A typically dynamic and almost chaotic encounter, the type Shirov and so many new generation players revel in.

Game 5
Beshukov – Volkov
Antalya 2002

This game is not terribly exciting until the end, but features early flank attacks on both wings, the avoidance of castling, a rook-lift, and breakdown of the blockade, all without seeming particularly unusual.

1 e4 e6 2 d3 d5 3 ♕e2 ♘f6 4 ♘f3 c5 5 g3 ♗e7 6 ♗g2 b5

The opening is fairly normal although this an earlier flank attack than Black normally tries.

7 ♗g5 h6 8 ♗f4 ♘c6 9 c3 a5 10 h4

White plays his own flank move, ruling out ...g5. He also gains some space thereby.

10...♗b7

10...♗a6 would be a natural way to target d3, but Black has other ideas in mind.

11 0-0 b4 12 c4

12 ♘bd2 looks a little better, although White would still need a plan, since 12...0-0 13 e5?! ♘h5 14 ♗e3 d4 15 cxd4 cxd4 16 ♘xd4 ♘xd4 17 ♕xh5 (17 ♗xd4 ♘xg3 18 fxg3 ♕xd4+) 17...♗xg2 18 ♔xg2 ♘c2 19 ♖ac1 ♘xe3+ 20 fxe3 ♕xd3 favours Black.

12...dxc4 13 dxc4 ♘d7! *(D)*

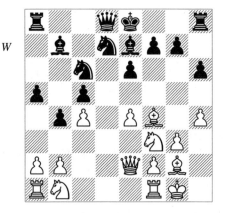

A remarkable move! Black takes the pressure off e4, eliminates his option of ...♘h5 (which could have been played immediately), and foregoes the natural ...0-0. The function of the move is both prophylactic and attacking.

14 ♖d1

Thanks to 13...♘d7, 14 e5 can now be answered by 14...g5!.

14...g5

Anyway. Black keeps his king in the centre in order to attack on both wings.

15 hxg5 hxg5 16 ♗e3 e5

Now d4 becomes a juicy outpost.

17 ♘bd2 ♘d4 18 ♕d3

18 ♗xd4 cxd4 19 a3 bxa3 20 bxa3 ♖a6! and ...♖ah6 ensures a deadly attack.

18...♖a6

A clever rook-lift! But it's surprising what role it plays.

19 ♘e1

White plans to exchange the dominating knight and then blockade the resultant passed pawn in classic Nimzowitschian style.

19...g4! 20 ♗xd4 cxd4 21 ♕e2 ♖g6!

We expected this piece to rush over to attack White's king. Instead, this odd and passive-looking manoeuvre ensures this rook's ultimately decisive role!

22 ♘d3 *(D)*

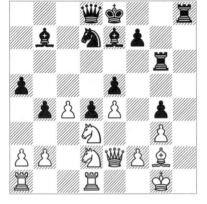

22...♕a8!

The point. The move ...f5 will follow shortly.

23 a3 bxa3 24 bxa3 f5 25 ♖ab1!? ♗c6 26 ♖b5

Anything to divert the attack. Black's threat is illustrated in the line 26 ♖a1 ♖gh6 27 ♖db1 fxe4 28 ♘xe4 (28 ♗xe4 ♖h1+) 28...♖h2 with ...♖xg2+ next; e.g., 29 ♖e1 ♖xg2+ 30 ♔xg2 ♘f6 31 f3 gxf3+ 32 ♕xf3 ♗xe4 33 ♖xe4 ♕xe4.

26...♗xb5

26...♗d6, preparing ...♖gh6, is also good.

27 cxb5 f4! 28 gxf4 g3 29 f3 exf4 30 ♘xf4 d3!

Quite aesthetic. The blockade is finally broken down.

31 ♘xd3 ♕a7+ 32 ♔f1 ♖gh6 33 b6?!

If 33 ♔e1 instead, 33...♕g1+ 34 ♘f1 ♗xa3 35 f4 ♘c5 is one good course among several.

33...♕xb6 34 ♘c4 ♖h1+ 35 ♗xh1 ♖xh1+ 36 ♔g2 ♖h2+ 37 ♔f1

Or 37 ♔xg3 ♕b8+.

37...♕h6 38 ♕e3 ♕h3+ 39 ♔e1 ♕g2 0-1

Game 6
Stein – Benko
Stockholm IZ 1962

Although we are mostly concerned with the last few decades, it can be fun to look back upon earlier games of modern chess that express the freedom of thought we are now seeing. This game is an example, a continually surprising struggle in which Stein attacks directly while Benko takes his positional style into hypermodern territory reminiscent of Petrosian and Bronstein. The following notes are based upon my own in Benko's autobiography.

1 e4 e6 2 d4 d5 3 ♘c3 ♘c6!?

A favourite move of the German player Reefschläger, and in my opinion quite playable.

4 ♘f3 ♘f6 5 e5 ♘e4 6 ♗d3 ♘xc3!?

Ulf Andersson once played 6...♗b4 here, but Benko isn't concerned with normal development.

7 bxc3 ♗e7 8 h4!

A powerful flank move which gains space, prepares to occupy g5 in some lines, and even plans ♖h3-g3 if the opportunity arises. White is unconcerned with castling.

8...h6 *(D)*

Black's last two moves are probably necessary, to prevent ♘g5 and ♕g4 or ♕h5.

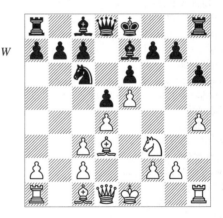

9 h5

Gligorić tried another plan versus Benko two years later: 9 ♘h2!? b6 (9...♘a5!) 10 ♕g4 ♗f8 11 ♘f1! h5?! (this may not be necessary; I like the idea of continuing on the queenside, having the courage to ignore White's kingside action) 12 ♕g3 ♘e7?! (12...♘a5 is equal) 13 ♗g5 ♕d7 14 ♘e3 ♗b7 (14...c5 would force White to make a decision and is nearly equal) 15 ♕f3?! (15 0-0) 15...♘c6 16 ♖h3 ♗e7 17 ♖g3 g6 (17...♘a3!?) 18 ♗f6 ♖g8 19 ♔f1 0-0-0 20 ♔g1 ♘a5 21 ♕f4 ♗xf6 22 ♕xf6 ♖h8? 23 ♖d1 ♖df8 (this is equal) 24 c4 dxc4 25 ♘xc4 ♘c6? (25...♕xd4 is one option) 26 c3 and White is on top, Gligorić-Benko, Belgrade 1964. But obviously the fundamental concept of Black's play was sound.

9...₺a5!

Again development is ignored, and a knight goes to the rim as well. The first idea is obviously that ...₺c4 is possible sometimes, but the move also stops c4 and prepares ...c5 if the occasion calls for it.

10 ₺d2!?

This not only moves one of White's two developed pieces to a passive square, but also blocks the development of his other pieces! However, it is quite a reasonable move that prevents ...₺c4 and prepares ₩g4. An alternative is 10 ₖh3, to threaten the kingside by ₖg3. In response to this idea, yet another undeveloping move, ...ₖf8!, would challenge White to find a plan, and it's not evident that there is anything effective.

10...c5 11 ₩g4

Here 11 0-0!? would be reminiscent of the main-line Winawer discussed in SOMCS. White has already advanced one pawn in front of his king, yet he intends to advance the others by f4, g4 and f5.

11...ₖf8!

Backwards, ever backwards! Black has only one piece out, and it's a knight on the edge of the board!

12 ₖh3!?

White abandons castling in favour of attack. This turns out badly because the rook gets in the way of White's ideal plan of f4, g4, f5, etc.

12...c4!

Black is crazy! He takes away the best square for his now useless-looking knight. Just as surprisingly he is giving up his queenside play by, for example, moves like ...ₖc8, ...cxd4, and ...₺c4. Why would he make this move, which is so often suicidal in the Winawer French? It turns out that Black is cutting off White's pieces from the defence of the queenside. However slowly Black reorganizes to attack on that wing, he feels that he stands solidly enough to counter any type of kingside attack by his opponent. It turns out to be an excellent and far-seeing move.

13 ₖe2 ₖd7 14 a4!?

To prevent ...ₖa4 and in some cases prepare ₖa3.

14...₺c6 *(D)*

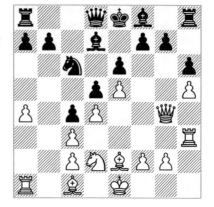

Another retreat! Black is in no hurry, because it is very awkward to try to enforce a kingside pawn advance by f4-f5 or g4-g5.

15 ₖf3 ₩a5 16 ₩f4 ₺d8

This passive retreat was made possible by Black's 15th, of course. How can it be good and where will Black's pieces go, including the rooks? But just with the ideas of ...ₖxa4 or ...b5, he is starting to get the advantage. Ingenious play.

17 ₖg3 b5?!

17...ₖxa4 is probably better, because tactical ideas such as 18 ₺b3 ₩b5 and 18 ₖxc4 fail. A possible follow-up might be ...₩b5-d7 and the eventual advance of the queenside pawns. Benko has another reasonable idea, to advance by ...b5-b4, although of course that will also allow White's kingside pieces finally to coordinate with his queenside.

18 ₩e3 ₺c6

A tacit draw offer in view of 19 ₩f4 ₺d8, etc.; Black is understandably afraid to open the position without supporting pieces.

19 f4!?

Eschewing the draw. But Benko's coming breakthrough justifies his bizarre-looking strategy and his excellent positional sense.

19...ₖb8 20 ₖf2

Another try is 20 ₖd1 b4 21 cxb4 ₺xb4 22 ₖf1, which is about equal.

20...b4 21 ₖb2 ₩c7 22 cxb4?

22 ₖg1 is more patient and wiser.

22...₺xb4

Now White has major problems.

23 ₩c3 ₺c6

Probably 23...₩a5! is still better, preventing ₖa3. Benko seems to have a considerable advantage at this point, but he has trouble converting it into victory, perhaps due to time-pressure.

24 ♗a3 ♗xa3 25 ♖xa3 ♕b6

Attacking the d-pawn and contemplating ...♕b2.

26 ♘f3 0-0

After all that, Black castles on move 26! It would have made little sense to do so earlier.

27 ♖h3!

27 ♕e3? is poor due to 27...♘e7.

27...♕b2 28 ♖h1

Preventing ...♕c1. Stein manages to resist successfully for the moment, but Black is still in control.

28...♕xc3 29 ♖xc3 ♖b2 30 ♖a1 ♖fb8 *(D)*

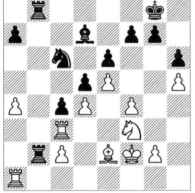

31 ♔e3 ♘a5 32 ♘e1!

32 ♘d2 is met by 32...♖8b4, keeping the pressure on.

32...♖b1 33 ♖ca3 ♖xa1 34 ♖xa1 ♖b4

Winning the a-pawn.

35 ♔d2 ♔f8!?

He should have just grabbed the pawn. After 35...♖xa4, Benko was probably afraid of 36 ♖b1, but 36...♔f8! 37 ♖b8+ ♔e7 is good, because 38 ♖g8 ♗b5! threatens ...c3+ and poses White too many problems.

36 ♔c3 ♖b8?

A mistake near the time-control. Black can still win a pawn with 36...♘c6! intending ...a5 and ...♘e7. Black has the concrete plan of meeting 37 a5 with 37...♖b5. Following the text-move, both sides made mistakes in the next few moves heading for the time-control.

37 g3 ♔e7 38 ♘g2 ♘c6 39 ♘e3 a5 40 g4 ♘a7 41 ♗f3 ♘c8 42 ♗xd5!? ½-½

A very aggressive sacrifice, after which Black agreed to the draw. Whether White is objectively equal in this obscure position may be debated; but in any case the number of modern themes appearing in this game is impressive, along with the uninhibited and creative attitude of the players.

Game 7
Gelfand – Bacrot
Cannes 2002

1 d4 d5 2 c4 c6 3 ♘c3 ♘f6 4 ♘f3 e6 5 e3 ♘bd7 6 ♕c2 ♗d6 7 g4 *(D)*

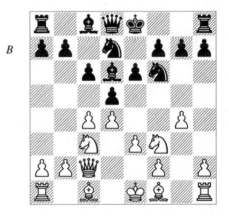

This move of Shabalov's in such a traditionally slow line exemplifies the modern obsession with flank attacks. Introduced around 1991, it immediately caught on at the top levels and is today established as an important weapon, played by leading grandmasters and doing very well a decade later. The fact that it took most of the last century for this move and its strengths even to be noticed says something about the reliance on older preconceptions and intuition (7 g4 is surely counter-intuitive!) as opposed to concrete analysis.

7...♗b4!?

Moving a piece twice in the opening and lessening control over the key e5-square. This is a rather amazing response to White's previous move, which caught on widely only after the obvious sequences like 7...♘xg4 8 ♖g1, 7...h6, and others were played, and after the prestigious Kramnik himself gave it his stamp of approval. The idea is to control e4 and in many cases prepare ...♘e4. 7...♗b4 is now

Black's most popular move. One has to marvel that only very infrequently has Black responded to 7 g4 by playing for either ...c5 or ...e5, the traditional central solutions to a flank attack. See both SOMCS and Chapter 2 of this book for further exposition of this theme. Two further examples to chew on:

a) 7...h6 featured in a recent game between two of the world's top-10 players. 8 ♗d2 b6 9 cxd5 exd5 10 ♖g1 ♕e7 11 0-0-0 ♗b7 12 ♗d3 c5 13 ♘h4!? (this isn't the only way to play it, but it's dynamic and difficult to meet) and now:

a1) 13...♗xh2 looks a bit suicidal, but after 14 ♘f5 ♕f8 15 ♖g2 ♗b8, it's anybody's guess what's going on; e.g., 16 e4 cxd4 (16...g6 17 ♘e3!?; for example, 17...dxe4 18 ♘xe4 cxd4 19 ♘xf6+ ♘xf6 20 ♗b5+ ♔d8 21 ♗c3) 17 ♘xd5 (17 ♘xd4 ♗e5! 18 ♗e3 dxe4 19 ♗b5 ♖c8 20 ♘f5 g6) 17...♘xd5 18 exd5 ♗e5 19 ♔b1 ♗xd5 20 ♖gg1 with a mess.

a2) 13...g6 14 ♗xg6! fxg6 15 ♘xg6 ♕h7 16 ♘xh8 ♕xh8 17 h4 0-0-0 18 g5 hxg5 19 hxg5 ♘e4 20 ♘xe4 dxe4 21 ♗c3 ♕g8 22 dxc5 ♗xc5 23 ♗f6 ♖d7 24 ♔b1 (24 b4 ♖c7 25 bxc5 ♖xc5 26 ♕xc5+ bxc5 27 ♖xd6 probably wins but is unnecessarily complicated) 24...♗a6 25 b4 ♗d3 26 ♖xd3 exd3 27 ♕c3 ♔b7 28 bxc5 and White has a large advantage, although the game Bareev-Ivanchuk, Dubai rpd 2002 went back and forth before White eventually won.

b) A lightweight example of the most direct and critical line is 7...♘xg4 8 ♖g1 ♕f6 9 ♖xg4 ♕xf3 10 ♖xg7 ♘f6 11 h3! (it's surprising that White can afford the time to stop ...♗xh2 and especially ...♘g4) 11...e5? (once again, the traditional counter to what might appear to be overextended flank play; better is 11...dxc4 12 ♗g2 ♕h5 13 e4 ♗f8 14 ♖g5 ♕h4 15 e5 ♘d5 16 ♘e4 ♗d7 17 ♖g4 ♕d8 18 ♕xc4 when White has good attacking chances and positional pressure) 12 dxe5 ♗xe5 13 ♖g5! ♘d7 (13...♗d6?? 14 ♗g2 and the queen is trapped!) 14 cxd5 cxd5 15 ♖f5 ♕h1 16 ♗d2 d4 17 exd4 ♗xd4 18 0-0-0 (Black's position is a complete wreck) 18...0-0 19 ♗h6 ♖e8 20 ♖g5+ ♔h8 21 ♖xd4 ♕xf1+ 22 ♖d1 ♖e1 23 ♗g7+ ♔g8 24 ♗e5+ 1-0 Tisdall-Sidselrud, Norway 2002.

8 ♗d2 ♕e7

Who wouldn't want White's position after 8...a5 9 g5 ♗xc3 10 ♗xc3 ♘e4 11 ♖g1 ♕e7 12 ♗d3 ♘xc3 13 ♕xc3 ♕b4 14 ♔e2! ♕xc3 15

bxc3 dxc4 16 ♗xc4, as in Krasenkow-Pekarek, Bundesliga 1992/3?

9 ♗d3 b6?!

One idea of this move is to work upon the weakened long diagonal after an eventual ...c5. Quite a few players have employed this strategy, as did Ivanchuk above, although it tends to be too slow. This is a case where 9...e5 makes a lot of sense and had initial success although it's likely that White retains a very small advantage. Games with 7 g4 tend to be highly tactical. Here is a more positional struggle, which was played with a short time-control and so is somewhat flawed, but contains some nice ideas: 9...h6 10 cxd5 exd5 11 ♖g1 ♗xc3 12 ♗xc3 ♘e4 13 0-0-0 0-0 14 h4! ♖e8 (14...♘xc3 15 ♕xc3 ♘f6 is the natural solution to the h4 thrust, but then 16 ♘e5! ♘e4 17 ♕c2 ♕xh4 18 f3 drives back the knight and White has more than enough for a pawn because of the h-file, aggressive pieces, and pseudo-outpost, i.e., ...f6 cannot disturb the e5-knight due to ♘g6) 15 g5 h5 16 ♔b1 a5 (16...♘f8 17 ♘e5 ♗f5 18 ♗e1 and f3 follows) 17 ♗e1 ♕e6 *(D)*.

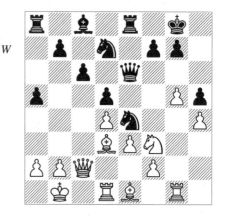

18 ♘d2! ♘d6 (18...♘xd2+ 19 ♗xd2 ♘f8 20 f4! and f5 will follow, even after 20...g6 21 ♖df1) 19 f3! b5 (19...♕xe3?? 20 ♗g3 threatens both ♗xd6 and ♖ge1) 20 e4 ♘c4 21 ♗f2 ♘db6 22 ♘b3 (or 22 e5) 22...♘a4 23 ♘c5 ♘xc5 24 dxc5 ♗d7 25 ♗d4 ♕h3 26 ♕g2! (a move that wouldn't occur to many players: the two bishops will be dominant in an ending) 26...♕xg2 27 ♖xg2 ♖ad8 28 b3 ♘e5 29 ♗xe5 ♖xe5 30 ♖gd2 ♖de8 31 ♗c2 g6 32 exd5 cxd5 33 f4 ♖e3 34 ♖xd5 and White went on to win in Gelfand-Piket, Monaco Amber rpd 2002.

10 cxd5 ②xd5 11 ②xd5 cxd5 12 ③c1! (D)

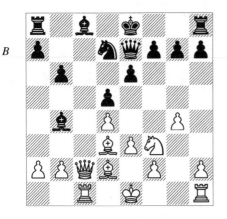

A pragmatic decision. This time White refrains from castling queenside. The idea is that he is better on both sides of the board, so leaving the king in the centre is acceptable.

12...④xd2+ 13 ⑤xd2!?

13 ⑨xd2 e5!? creates some interesting counterplay due to the pawn on g4; e.g., 14 dxe5 (14 ⑨c2 ⑨b4+ 15 ⑤e2 e4!? 16 ④xe4 ④a6+ 17 ④d3 ④xd3+ 18 ⑤xd3 ⑨b5+ with complications) 14...0-0 15 ⑨c3 f6 16 exf6 (16 ⑨c6 ②c5!; 16 ⑨c2 ②xe5! 17 ④xh7+ ⑤h8) 16...②xf6 17 h3 ②e4 18 ⑨d4 ⑤h8 19 ④e2 ④a6!. Whether these lines are good enough for Black is not clear, but the text-move maintains a simple bind at the cost of keeping the king exposed.

13...0-0 14 ⑨c7

Perhaps White gets the advantage after 14 ④xh7+ ⑤h8 15 ④d3, but 15...e5 16 dxe5 ②xe5 17 ②xe5 ⑨xe5 gives some counterplay due to White's king position.

14...⑨b4+ 15 ⑤c2 ②f6 16 ⑤b1 ②e4

16...②xg4 is no improvement thanks to 17 ③hg1 e5 18 ②xe5! with the point 18...②xe5? 19 ③xg7+!.

17 ②e5?!

Much safer and objectively better is 17 ④xe4! dxe4 18 ②e5; e.g., 18...④a6 19 ⑨c6 ⑨d2 20 ⑨xe4 ⑨xf2? (20...③ac8 21 f3) 21 ③c2 ⑨h4 22 ③c7 and Black is stuck for good moves.

17...②xf2 18 ③hf1 ②xd3 19 ②xd3 ⑨b5

19...⑨d2 loses to 20 ②e5 f6 21 ⑨c6 ③b8 22 ⑨d6, with the idea 22...③a8 23 ③xc8.

20 ②e5 f6 (D)

Now Black seems to be getting the advantage.

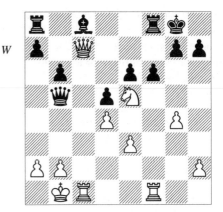

21 g5!?

An amazing piece sacrifice that refuses to cede the initiative. It has highly unclear consequences. White avoids 21 ②c6 ⑨d3+ 22 ⑤a1 ④a6! 23 ③fe1 ⑨d2.

21...fxe5 22 ③xf8+ ⑤xf8 23 ⑨d8+ ⑤f7 24 g6+! ⑤xg6

Avoiding 24...hxg6?? 25 ③c7+.

25 ③g1+ ⑤f7 26 dxe5!

White is a piece and a pawn down, but this *zwischenzug* keeps his options open for moves like ③c1-c7+ or ⑨h8, without allowing things like 26 ⑨h8 ⑨d3+ 27 ⑤a1 g5!.

26...⑨d3+!

Wells mentions 26...⑨c4!?, which is a fascinating attempt to win that deserves analysis. Black covers the dangerous c1- and f1-squares, but still has trouble getting his pieces out, and it's remarkable how White succeeds in attacking after 27 ⑤a1 (to stop ...⑨e4+ and ...⑨xe5) 27...h6 (27...a5!? 28 h4! ⑨b5 29 ⑨h8 g6 30 ⑨f6+; 27...⑨b5 28 ⑨h8 g6 29 ③c1! ⑤e7 30 ⑨xh7+ ⑤e8 31 ⑨xg6+; 27...⑨d3? 28 ⑨c7+ ⑤e8 29 ⑨c6+ ⑤d8 30 ③c1!) 28 h4! (these slow moves are the most fun) 28...h5 (28...g6 29 h5 g5 30 ⑨f6+ ⑤e8 31 ⑨xh6 and ⑨xg5, when the h-pawn becomes a factor) 29 e4!? (29 a3 g6 30 e4! is also promising) 29...b5 30 exd5 exd5 (30...⑨xd5 31 ③f1+) 31 e6+ and White wins.

27 ⑤a1 ⑨xe3!

This saves the game, covering c1. Bad is 27...g5? 28 ⑨c7+ ⑤g6 29 h4! g4 30 ③xg4+ ⑤h5 31 ③g5+ ⑤xh4 32 ③g1!.

28 ⑨c7+ ⑤e8 29 ⑨c6+

Alternatively, 29 ⑨xg7 ④a6! 30 ⑨h8+ ⑤d7 31 ③g7+ ⑤c6 32 ⑨xa8+ ⑤c5 33 ⑨f8+ ⑤d4 draws!

29...♔e7 30 ♕d6+ ♔f7 31 ♕c7+ ♔e8 32 ♕c6+ ½-½

A short but great battle. After a paradoxical opening, the game turned into a dynamic fight for the initiative.

Game 8
Kasparov – Portisch
Nikšić 1983

Moving back a few years, let's see how Kasparov implements his philosophy of 'splitting the board in two', as well as the kind of dynamic line-clearing that has so influenced his contemporaries. The following game was almost instantly a classic, partly because of the impression created by White's low-fuel attack. But it also showed a different philosophy of attack from what most players were used to.

1 d4 ♘f6 2 c4 e6 3 ♘f3 b6 4 ♘c3 ♗b7 5 a3 d5 6 cxd5 ♘xd5 7 e3 ♘xc3 8 bxc3 ♗e7 9 ♗b5+ c6 10 ♗d3 c5 11 0-0 ♘c6 12 ♗b2

White's fairly uninspiring piece disposition proves to have a touch of poison.

12...♖c8 13 ♕e2 0-0 14 ♖ad1 ♕c7

14...cxd4 is the normal move now, with 15 cxd4 ♗f6 the most common continuation. But 14...♕c7 had been played by Polugaevsky, with the idea of meeting 15 e4 with 15...♘a5 and queenside pressure.

15 c4!

This seems pretty obvious now, but in many similar positions played before this, advancing the c-pawn had weakened White's centre and in particular c4 itself. Also, the move e4 was supposed to be consistent with White's whole strategy. Portisch responds naturally:

15...cxd4

15...♗f6? 16 d5 ♘e5? is a tactical mistake due to 17 ♘xe5 ♗xe5 18 ♗xh7+! ♔xh7 19 ♕h5+ ♔g8 20 ♗xe5. Kasparov showed that 15...♘a5 also allows 16 d5! exd5 17 cxd5 c4 (17...♗xd5 18 ♗xh7+ ♔xh7 19 ♖xd5 and White is clearly better) 18 ♗f5 ♖cd8 19 e4, when there is no pressure on White's centre and he has a large advantage.

16 exd4 ♘a5?!

Natural, attacking c4, but after White's next move we discover that this is not one of those well-placed knights on the rim, e.g. one that ties White to the defence or exerts enough pressure

on the relevant central squares. In the end, it just hangs out there in space.

17 d5! *(D)*

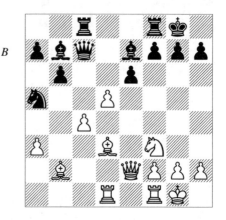

The same idea as in the last note, except that this time White's centre is traded away and Black gets counterplay down the c-file.

17...exd5

After 17...♘xc4 18 ♕e4! g6 19 ♗xc4 ♕xc4 20 ♕e5 f6 21 ♕xe6+ White wins the pawn back with a big attack. Kasparov gives the attractive line 21...♖f7 22 ♖c1 ♕a6 23 d6 ♖xc1 24 ♖xc1 ♗d8 25 ♘g5! fxg5 26 ♖c7!! ♗xc7 27 ♕e8+ ♖f8 28 ♕e5, winning.

18 cxd5 ♗xd5 19 ♗xh7+ ♔xh7 20 ♖xd5 ♔g8

The material is even, and Black is well poised to counter any cheap designs on the kingside by using his centre files.

21 ♗xg7!!

Or is he? Kasparov says that ♗xg7 represents 'a totally different style' and I have to agree. This attack is not only conducted a piece down with reduced material on the board, but White has to operate without his f1-rook! 21 ♘g5? is useless due to 21...♕c2!.

21...♔xg7 22 ♘e5! *(D)*

'Splitting the board in two' is Kasparov's comment. This is a slow way to pursue an attack, yet the added pressure on f7 makes the difference. The obvious 22 ♘d4? can be answered with 22...♖h8! 23 ♘f5+ ♔f8. Here the knight on f5 isn't sufficient because of the lack of attacking pieces.

22...♖fd8

The most natural idea, clearing f8 for the king. Black has a number of plausible defences,

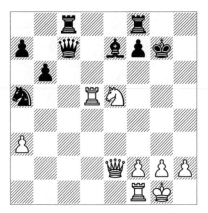

B

but the exposed black king and especially the f7-square are real problems for him. Following Kasparov's analysis, we can see how this works out:

a) 22...f5 23 ♖d7 (23 ♖d3 ♕c5 24 ♘d7) 23...♕c5 24 ♘d3 and White wins material.

b) 22...♖cd8 23 ♕g4+ ♔h7 24 ♘d7! threatens ♖h5#, and 24...f5 25 ♘xf8+ ♖xf8 26 ♖xf5 ♖xf5 27 ♕xf5+ ♔g7 28 ♖e1 leaves Black's king helplessly vulnerable, not to mention the three connected passed pawns.

c) 22...♕c2 23 ♕g4+ ♔h7 24 ♖d3 ♖c3 25 ♕f5+ ♔g8 26 ♖g3+ wins the queen on c2.

d) 22...♖h8 23 ♕g4+ (23 ♖d7 ♕c5 24 ♕g4+ ♔f8 25 ♕f4 also wins) 23...♔f8 24 ♕f5 f6 25 ♖e1 ♘c6 (25...♕c1 26 ♖dd1) 26 ♘d7+ ♔f7 27 ♖xe7+! and it's over.

23 ♕g4+ ♔f8 24 ♕f5! f6

White has so few attackers that one might expect something to hold. One try is 24...♗d6 25 ♕f6! ♘c4 (25...♔g8 26 ♕g5+ ♔f8 27 ♕h6+ ♔g8 {27...♔e8 loses to 28 ♖e1} 28 ♘g4! ♗xh2+ 29 ♔h1 is winning for White) 26 ♘g6+ ♔e8 27 ♖e1+ ♔d7 28 ♖e7+ ♔c6 29 ♖xc7+ ♔xc7 30 ♕xf7+ ♔b8 31 h4 and White wins. Another is 24...♗xa3 25 ♘d7+ ♖xd7 26 ♖xd7 ♕c4 27 ♖fd1 and Black's pieces are too far away on the queenside: 27...♘c6 28 ♕h3 (threatening mate on h8 and capture on a3) 28...♗b2 29 ♖7d2!, attacking b2 and c8.

25 ♘d7+

The tempting move 25 ♘g6+?! is less good: 25...♔g7! 26 ♘f4 ♖xd5 27 ♕g6+? (27 ♘xd5! ♕c5 28 ♘xe7 ♕xf5 29 ♘xf5+ gives White an extra pawn) 27...♔h8 28 ♕h6+ (28 ♘e6 ♖g5!) 28...♔g8 with a draw.

25...♖xd7

25...♔g7 26 ♖e1 is devastating.

26 ♖xd7 ♕c5 27 ♕h7

Kasparov also mentions 27 ♕h3.

27...♖c7 (D)

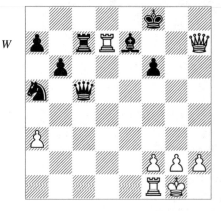

W

28 ♕h8+!

Black has a wonderful response to 28 ♖d3? in 28...♕xf2+!! 29 ♔xf2 (29 ♖xf2? ♖c1+ wins for Black) 29...♗c5+ 30 ♔g3 ♖xh7 31 ♖xf6+ with a draw.

28...♔f7 29 ♖d3

Now White is threatening moves like ♖g3 and ♖h3.

29...♘c4 30 ♖fd1! ♘e5?

But 30...♗d6! 31 ♖d5! ♕c6 (31...♕xa3? 32 ♖xd6! ♘xd6 33 ♕h7+, winning) 32 h4 ties Black up and prepares to promote the h-pawn.

31 ♕h7+ ♔e6

Also losing is 31...♔f8 32 ♖d8+.

32 ♕g8+ ♔f5 33 g4+! ♔f4 34 ♖d4+ ♔f3 35 ♕b3+ 1-0

In view of 35...♕c3 36 ♕d5+ ♔e2 37 ♕e4+.

Game 9
Kveinys – Speelman
Moscow OL 1994

1 e4 d6 2 d4 ♘f6 3 ♘c3 g6 4 ♗c4 ♗g7 5 ♕e2 ♘c6 6 e5 ♘d7 7 ♘f3 ♘b6 8 ♗b3!? 0-0 9 h3 ♘a5

This complex variation of the Pirc (or Alekhine) Defence is an older continuation. Well, if you consider the late 1960s (or early 1970s?) old!

10 0-0 h6!? 11 ♘e4 ♘xb3 12 axb3 f6

The play now becomes a mess, which is typical for these original and dynamic players.

13 c4 fxe5 14 dxe5 *(D)*

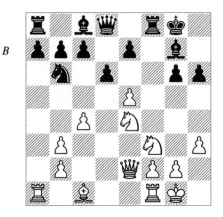

14...♘d7!?

Speelman mentions 14...g5!?, which is certainly appropriate in such a position! 14...dxe5 is positionally disastrous after 15 ♖d1 ♕e8 16 ♖a5!; for example, 16...♘d7 17 b4 b6 18 ♖ad5 ♘f6 19 ♖xe5! ♘h5 20 ♘c3! ♗xe5 21 ♘xe5, a no-brainer exchange sacrifice because White's ♘b5 must be stopped, allowing White to get a pawn back with complete domination after ♗xh6.

15 ♗d2 b6?!

Speaking of exchange sacrifices, Speelman mentions 15...♖xf3!? 16 ♕xf3 ♘xe5, although the weakness of Black's kingside may prevent him from gaining full compensation.

16 e6! ♘f6 17 ♘xf6+ ♖xf6 18 ♘d4 ♗b7

Speelman provides the nice-looking variation 18...c5 19 ♕e4 ♖b8 20 ♘c6 ♗b7 21 ♖xa7! ♕e8 22 ♖xb7 ♖xb7, when 23 ♘e5! gives White a slight advantage. But 19...d5! spoils the fun in this line, so White should play 19 ♘b5! and retain some advantage.

19 ♗c3! a6 20 f4!? *(D)*

As it turns out, 20 ♘c2 is better.

Black has two wonderful bishops, but White has good pieces as well and the threat of an overwhelming position after f5 or perhaps g4 and f5. Speelman comes up with an active solution.

20...♕f8 21 ♘c2 c5!

The point. White had foreseen 21...♖xf4 22 ♖xf4 ♕xf4 23 ♗xg7 ♔xg7 24 ♖f1 with good prospects, but instead Black sacrifices the exchange and gets two bishops. This turns out to be enough in the great complications that ensue.

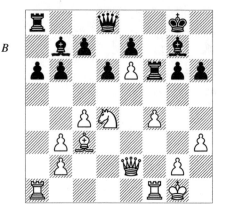

22 ♗xf6 ♕xf6 23 ♖ab1

23 b4 would be a more aggressive possibility, because 23...♕xb2? (23...cxb4 is better) 24 bxc5 dxc5 25 ♖ab1 is obviously good for White.

23...♖f8 24 b4 ♕f5 25 ♔h2 ♕e4!

Offering White another two-bishops queenless middlegame, but with the cost that Black will pick up at least a pawn for his exchange.

26 ♖be1

26 ♕xe4 ♗xe4 27 ♖f2 cxb4 28 b3 ♗c3 ties White up.

26...♖xf4 27 ♕xe4 ♖xe4 28 bxc5 ♖xc4 29 ♘e3

Both players had to calculate accurately. Here the attractive 29 cxd6 ♖xc2 30 ♖g1 exd6 31 e7 fails to equalize after 31...♗c6 32 e8♕+ ♗xe8 33 ♖xe8+ ♔f7 34 ♖a8 ♗e5+ 35 ♔h1 a5, when Black's advantage is evident.

29...♖xc5 30 b4! ♖e5 31 ♘c4 ♖g5 32 ♖e2 ♗d5 33 ♖f4!? b5 34 ♘b6 ♗b3 35 ♘d7?

White makes a fatal mistake in time-pressure. He could still hold on by 35 ♘c8! ♖e5! (35...♗e5 36 ♘xe7+ ♔g7 37 ♖xe5) 36 ♘xe7+ ♔h7 37 ♖d2 ♖xe6 38 ♘c6 ♗c4 39 ♖f7 and Black is only very slightly better.

35...♖f5! 36 ♖xf5 gxf5 37 ♔g3 ♗c4 38 ♖e3 ♗d4 39 ♖a3 ♗xe6 40 ♘b8 ♗e5+!? 41 ♔f2 ♔f7

Now Black has a large advantage. With powerful central passed pawns supported by two bishops, he went on to win. (A postscript: I saw this game annotated by a strong player who never mentioned that Black had given up an exchange. We have become so used to this material imbalance that it's beginning to go unnoticed!).

Game 10
Kasparov – Shirov
Horgen 1994

I've tried to avoid the most famous games of modern chess because they have already been so thoroughly talked about. There is plenty of material elsewhere. Nevertheless, this over-exposed game is loaded with modern ideas, even if one can be distracted by the unusual and brilliant fashion in which they are executed.

1 e4 c5 2 ♘f3 e6 3 d4 cxd4 4 ♘xd4 ♘f6 5 ♘c3 ♘c6 6 ♘db5 d6 7 ♗f4 e5 8 ♗g5 a6 9 ♘a3 b5

The Sveshnikov Variation, itself a symbol of the radical steps taken by defenders to insert dynamism into the game at the cost of positional concessions. Here we see disadvantages that the great majority of advanced players as late as the 1960s and 1970s still blanched at: the combination of the backward pawn on d6 and that glaring hole on d5 was a bit much even for experimental types. Then there were the concrete and intimidating difficulties posed by both of White's logical next moves.

10 ♘d5

The other reasonable move and main line today is 10 ♗xf6 gxf6 11 ♘d5 *(D)*.

B

Now the extent of Sveshnikov's heresy becomes clear: Black is slightly behind in development and has lost control of d5 (which can be reinforced in various ways, e.g. by a later ♘c2-e3). His queenside is subject to potentially devastating pawn breaks such as c4 or a4 which can put the light squares permanently in White's hands. He has also taken on doubled

pawns that are unsupported, and the only freeing move, ...f5, can further expose the light squares after exf5. For all these points, thousands of games have proved the viability of Black's position, which received crucial support at world-class level from Kramnik. Now the opening is in as good a shape as it has ever been and recently supplied Leko the critical edge in his qualification for the world championship reunification matches. Today's tournament players are getting so thoroughly familiar with this position that, as I have indicated about other opening ideas, they have likely forgotten the wholesale scepticism with which Black's set-up was once viewed. This reflects again the predominance of the concrete over the general. Naturally, Black must have his own advantages in this position or it wouldn't be playable. They are, among others, the bishop-pair (which presently looks inferior to the knight-pair), and the long-term idea of recapturing the centre by use of his central majority, as crazy as that looks. It's just that those advantages and others are self-evident neither to the classically-educated player nor even to the top-level modern pragmatists of some few decades ago. Also, it took the most concrete demonstration imaginable that White's numerous ideas such as c4, c3 + ♘c2-e3, ♗d3 + ♕h5, or even ♗xb5 (long considered a near-refutation) were ultimately answerable. Thus the theoretical justification for Black's play was post-facto, i.e., the play came first and then the abstract explanation. A close look at ideas from the radical breakthroughs in the 1940s to this day shows that they share that pragmatic and non-general character, a trend that has greatly accelerated in every decade since then.

10...♗e7

This move avoids the doubled pawns in the last diagram, but forfeits thereby the opportunity to strike quickly at White's centre with ...f5.

11 ♗xf6 ♗xf6 12 c3 ♗b7 13 ♘c2

Here we see the elementary ideas of a4 and ♘ce3 approaching, albeit no hint yet of actually developing other pieces!

13...♘b8

Yet another paradoxical move, undeveloping. The idea is to redeploy the knight on d7, from where it can go to either b6 or c5. Black's disdain for both key squares *and* development is astonishing. The best alternatives are 13...0-0 and 13...♘e7, challenging the d5-knight, but once again allowing ♘xf6 and doubled pawns after 14 ♘xf6+ gxf6 15 ♗d3 with a small edge.

14 a4

Single-mindedly concentrating upon gaining light squares, e.g. c4 for a bishop or knight.

14...bxa4 15 ♖xa4 ♘d7 16 ♖b4!?

What?? This could belong to a discussion of rook-lifts and play along the fourth rank, but that is usually done after getting the pieces out!

16...♘c5 (D)

I really don't want to query this natural move, since Shirov can hardly be faulted for making the most active and challenging one, even if he saw Kasparov's next move. Black has a shortage of choices. An oddball line is 16...♗c6? 17 ♖c4! ♗xd5 (after 17...♗b5 18 ♘c7+ ♔e7 19 ♘e3 ♗xc4 20 ♗xc4 White wins due to the continuation 20...♖c8 21 ♘f5+ ♔f8 22 ♕d5) 18 ♕xd5 0-0 (18...♖b8 19 ♖b4) 19 ♖c6! with a clear plus, targeting a6 and d6. Needless to say, this game inspired further attempts by both sides and wonderful analysis (a good source is John Nunn's *Understanding Chess Move by Move*). The best move here was found to be 16...♖b8!, with complications that are better left to a book on theory. After Shirov's 16...♘c5, I have to give a diagram, even though this position has been overexposed:

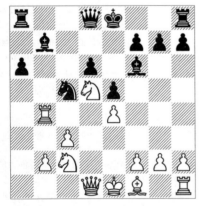

17 ♖xb7!!

Yet another modern theme: the exchange sacrifice. The move is shocking, because material is somewhat reduced and White doesn't have much development, the two bishops, or other traditional compensation for the exchange.

The exception is his powerful knight on d5, but Black has plenty of time to reorganize around it. Kasparov's next move reveals the real, underlying idea.

17...♘xb7 18 b4!

Terrific! White restricts the b7-knight from coming into play via c5; e.g., 18 ♗c4 0-0 19 0-0 ♘c5 20 f3 ♗g5 followed by ideas like ...♘e6, ...a5, and ...♘c7, swapping White's most dominant piece. Let's take stock for a moment. I will follow John Nunn's description of the play thus far, with a few additional comments. He points out that White has violated:

a) The rule that one should castle quickly. OK, it's rare but not unheard of to go 18 moves without castling, but in fact he waits until move 25 to do so!

b) The rule that one shouldn't move the same piece twice in the opening; White has moved his knights seven times and in fact they are the only pieces developed. Furthermore, his next two moves are knight moves!

c) The rule that one should develop one's rooks to central files. Instead he has played ♖xa4, ♖b4 and ♖xb7.

18...♗g5 19 ♘a3! 0-0 20 ♘c4

That makes seven moves by the same knight. This puts pressure on the d6-pawn and threatens a jump to b6 in some lines. Of course it's impossible to look into his head, but one suspects that Kasparov wasn't thinking 'I'd better get some pieces out', but undogmatically treated the position purely in terms of concrete positional strategy. Nunn also makes a strong point that I have not emphasized enough with respect to modern play: White's play here is not *illogical*, i.e., he isn't intentionally breaking rules nor playing chaotically. That way of thinking just doesn't enter the picture. But Kasparov is following a logical and consistent strategy; in Nunn's words, his moves 'form a seamless whole'.

20...a5 21 ♗d3 axb4 22 cxb4 ♕b8

This is a reasonable move, trying to initiate action on the a-file after ...♖a2, ...♕a7, etc. Nunn shows that the alternatives 22...♖a2?! and 22...♗h6?! leave White with a good position. Instead, he recommends the strange move 22...♖b8!? with the idea ...♕d7 and ...♘d8. This is a bit slow, and White has plenty of ideas, e.g. ♕h5, 0-0, g3 and f4. At any rate, very few players would find this plan as Black over the board!

23 h4! ♗h6?!

Nunn queries this move and suggests the odd-looking idea 23...♗d8 intending ...♗c7 and ...♘d8. This is probably a genuine improvement, but again, who would rush their bishop to the awful c7 when it could remain active on h6? Kasparov himself gives 23...♗d8 24 g3 ♕a7 (24...♗c7! – Nunn) 25 0-0 ♕d4 26 ♕b3 with a clear advantage.

24 ♘cb6 ♖a2 25 0-0 ♖d2 26 ♕f3?!

Time-pressure may have influenced the next few moves. White could play 26 ♕b1! (Nunn), threatening ♘c4, which is not preventable. Then White would re-establish material equality and retain most of his positional advantages.

26...♕a7 27 ♘d7

Also not best. The position is absurdly complicated, but White could keep up the pressure by 27 ♗b5! ♘d8 28 ♘d7 ♘e6 29 ♘e7+! (29 ♘xf8 ♔xf8 30 ♕c3 is also good, according to Nunn) 29...♔h8 30 ♘xf8 ♖xe7 31 ♘xe6 ♕xe6 (31...fxe6? 32 ♖a1 g6 33 ♗c4) 32 ♗c6 with a modest advantage, according to Kasparov.

27...♘d8?

Black is also losing after 27...♖d8? 28 ♘e7+ ♔h8 29 ♕xf7 ♖xd3 30 ♘f8 and 27...♘c5? 28 bxc5 ♕xd7 29 c6 ♕a7 30 c7. The best move is 27...♖a8!, when the play is very complicated, with probably only a very slight advantage for White.

28 ♘xf8 ♔xf8 29 b5!

With a powerful passed pawn to add to his other advantages, White is now winning.

29...♕a3

29...♕d4 is an interesting move to which White replies 30 ♗e2! with the ideas of 31 ♕a3 and 31 ♕f5! ♖xe2 32 ♕d7.

30 ♕f5! ♔e8

The same idea applies: 30...♖xd3 31 ♕d7 g6 32 ♕xd8+ ♔g7 33 ♕f6+ ♔g8 34 ♘e7+ ♔f8 35 b6! ♕a6 36 ♘c6 ♔g8 37 ♖b1, etc.

31 ♗c4 ♖c2 32 ♕xh7! ♖xc4 33 ♕g8+ ♔d7 34 ♘b6+ ♔e7 35 ♘xc4 ♕c5 36 ♖a1! ♕d4

Or 36...♕xc4 37 ♖a7+ ♔e6 38 ♕e8+ and wins.

37 ♖a3!

Instead 37 ♖a8? ♘e6! 38 ♖e8+ ♔f6 39 ♖xe6+ ♔xe6 40 ♕c8+ ♔f6 would be unclear.

37...♗c1 38 ♘e3 1-0

After 38...♗xe3 39 ♖xe3, White is not only the exchange ahead; he has the b-pawn and attacking prospects as well.

It's amazing how often seemingly irrational dynamism, impossible for the normal human to assess, pervades modern games. The purely positional factors tend to be of less importance in such slugfests, of course, but they still lurk below the surface and are important for the understanding of most of them. The next two games provide wild and enjoyable examples.

Game 11
Serper – Nikolaidis
St Petersburg 1993

1 c4 g6 2 e4 ♗g7 3 d4 d6

A Modern Defence. That opening could be the sole source of information for a book on modern chess strategy. Here it quickly transposes to another opening.

4 ♘c3 ♘f6

Now it's a King's Indian Defence. White decides upon a slightly unconventional line that received a lot of attention in the early 1990s.

5 ♘ge2 ♘bd7 6 ♘g3 c6 7 ♗e2 a6

This idea of enforcing ...b5 was widely recommended, but I think that systems based upon ...e5 are better.

8 ♗e3 h5

To chase the knight away and gain space.

9 f3 b5

Continuing a flank attack policy on both wings. This is in the spirit of the times, but it's healthy to be reminded that sometimes the centre wins!

10 c5

10 a3?! bxc4! 11 ♗xc4 d5! is assessed as unclear by Serper (notation marks his), but the positions after 12 ♗b3 or 12 ♗a2 are very comfortable for White and it's not clear how Black should play.

10...dxc5 11 dxc5 ♕c7 12 0-0 h4

Black pursues his flank strategy on both wings while White makes relatively traditional moves.

13 ♘h1

This looks like a poor placement, but White is happy to be chased back because the knight has more possibilities on f2 than on g3 (from where it had no other square to go to!). This idea crops up in other King's Indian and Benoni variations.

13...♘h5

A knight on the edge of the board, trying to grab the dark squares. In fact, Black on the move would come close to winning outright with ...♗e5.

14 ♕d2 e5

Otherwise f4 was going to yield a big advantage.

15 ♘f2 ♘f8?!

A good positional idea, planning ...♘e6-d4, which would give him the advantage (...♗e6, ...♖d8, and ...♘f4 might follow). However, Black has used a lot of time and Serper is alert to his own tactical possibilities. He suggests instead 15...♘f4 16 ♘d3 ♗h6 17 a4 with an edge, when Black's position is dangerously cramped and he has weak dark squares on the kingside. Then perhaps best would be something like 17...♘xd3 18 ♗xd3 ♗xe3+ 19 ♕xe3 b4 20 ♘e2 a5 21 ♖fd1 ♘f8 22 ♗c4 ♗e6 23 ♗xe6 ♘xe6, although after 24 ♖d6 White still has some advantage.

16 a4 b4 *(D)*

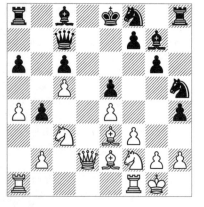

17 ♘d5!!

A courageous sacrifice that at first looks 'standard', since we see so many ♘d5 sacrifices today. White's idea is to create two connected and (hopefully) mobile passed pawns in the centre on the fifth rank, which certainly will be worth a lot. But in most of the sacrifices with ♘d5, Black's king is directly attacked and he lacks counterplay. Here, by contrast, we see a powerful black pawn-mass (...f5 and ...f4 or

...e4 are themes), and the h5-knight can leap into the fray by means of ...♘f4. In the meantime, can White's two pawns advance beyond Black's well-protected central light squares? Considering that White could have retreated safely by 17 ♘a2 a5 18 ♘c1 ♘e6 19 ♕d6!?, for example, Serper's decision is all the more admirable.

17...cxd5 18 exd5 f5

Natural, stopping ♘e4, although 18...♗f5 might have done the same. Both sides' decisions in this game were excruciatingly difficult. In what follows, I am heavily dependent upon Serper's notes in *Informator* and Christiansen's analysis in his entertaining book *Storming the Barricades*.

19 d6!

It's not worth the extra material to pause for 19 ♕xb4?! ♖b8 20 ♕a3 e4!.

19...♕c6

After 19...♕d7 20 c6! ♕xc6 21 ♖fc1 Black can practically resign, since ♖c7 with tempo follows any queen retreat. Now is White's attack at a halt?

20 ♗b5!! *(D)*

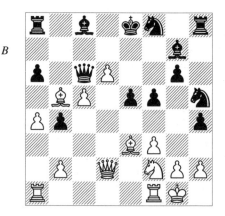

20...axb5 21 axb5

No it isn't, despite Black's growing material advantage.

21...♕xb5

The alternative 21...♕b7?! leads to messy play but should ultimately lose: 22 c6 ♕b8 (22...♕xb5 23 d7+! is winning for White), and now best is 23 ♕d5! (Serper argues that 23 b6 '!' wins, but the position after 23...♘f6 is not as convincing as the 23 ♕d5 line) 23...♖xa1 24 ♖xa1 *(D)*.

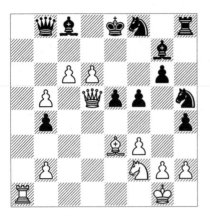

B

For example, 24...♘f6 (24...♗e6 25 d7+ ♔d8 26 ♗b6+ ♔xb6 27 ♕d6 and Black gets mated!) 25 ♕xe5+ ♔f7 26 ♖a7+ ♗d7 27 c7! ♕c8 (27...♕e8 28 ♕xe8+ ♔xe8 29 c8♕+ ♗xc8 30 ♖e7+ ♔d8 31 ♗b6#) 28 b6, etc.

22 ♖xa8 ♕c6 23 ♖fa1!

There is no end to the attack as White commits to sacrificing another piece.

23...f4 24 ♖1a7! ♘d7

A tactical trick here is 24...fxe3? 25 ♕d5!! exf2+ 26 ♔xf2 and Black's material is irrelevant (26...♖xd5 27 ♖xc8#).

25 ♖xc8+! ♕xc8 26 ♕d5!

The attack is too much, even if White is starting to run out of pieces!

26...fxe3

26...♘hf6 27 ♕e6+ ♔f8 28 ♘e4! has in mind the nice continuations 28...fxe3 29 ♘g5 ♕e8 30 ♖a8, and 28...♕e8 29 ♕xe8+! ♘xe8 (29...♔xe8 30 ♖a8+ ♔f7 31 ♘g5#) 30 ♖xd7 fxe3 31 c6 and wins.

27 ♕e6+ ♔f8 28 ♖xd7!?

A beautiful shot that eventually wins by force. In what was doubtless beginning to be serious time-trouble for both sides, it certainly wasn't easy to see that there was another way to win after the obvious 28 ♘e4 e2 29 ♔f2 ♘hf6!, and now the not-so obvious 30 ♔e1!! (instead of 30 ♘xf6? ♕xc5+ or 30 ♔xe2 ♘xe4 31 fxe4 ♕c6 32 ♔f3 ♕b5!).

28...exf2+ 29 ♔f1 ♕e8

The tactical try 29...♘g3+ 30 hxg3 ♕xd7 31 ♕xd7 hxg3 fails to 32 ♕e7+ ♔g8 33 ♕e8+ ♔h7 (33...♗f8 34 ♕xg6+ ♗g7 35 ♕xg3 and White wins) 34 d7 intending 34...♗f6 35 c6!. And even getting the queens off by 29...♕a6+ 30 ♔xf2 ♕e2+! 31 ♔xe2 ♘f4+ 32 ♔f1 ♘xe6

loses immediately to 33 c6 ♔g8 34 ♖e7!. White had to see all or most of this and trust his intuition when playing 28 ♖xd7!?, as well as anticipate much of what follows:

30 ♖f7+!!

Only move! Instead, 30 ♕xe8+? ♔xe8 31 ♖e7+ ♔f8! 32 c6 fails to 32...♘g3+!! 33 ♔xf2 (33 hxg3 hxg3 34 ♔e2 ♖h1) 33...♘f5 34 ♖xg7 ♘xd6!. The tactics just keep coming.

30...♕xf7 31 ♕c8+ ♕e8 32 d7 ♔f7 33 dxe8♕+ ♖xe8 34 ♕b7+

Still trailing in material, White also had to see that his c-pawn was now more important than Black's pieces and tricks.

34...♖e7

34...♔g8 35 c6 is hopeless for Black.

35 c6! c4!

Now ...♖xb7 followed by ...♗e5 is threatened, and it seems as though ...e3-e2+ is a problem. But not really:

36 c7 e3 37 ♕d5+! ♔f6

Or 37...♖e6 38 ♕xe6+.

38 ♕d6+ ♔f7 39 ♕d5+

Repeating moves to make the time-control.

39...♔f6 40 ♕d6+ ♔f7 41 ♕xe7+ ♔xe7 42 c8♕ ♗h6

42...♗d4 loses to 43 ♕c4.

43 ♕c5+ ♔e8

After 43...♔f7, 44 ♕c4+ and 45 ♕xh4 wins.

44 ♕b5+ ♔d8 45 ♕b6+ ♔d7 46 ♕xg6 e2+ 47 ♔xf2 ♗e3+ 48 ♔e1! 1-0

And not 48 ♔xe2?? ♘f4+. A superb game in which the centre triumphed over the flank!

Game 12
Nunn – Nataf
French Cht 1998/9

This primarily tactical game illustrates a typically 'anti-positional' but dynamic Sicilian variation and emphasizes the pragmatic dynamism that we see everywhere in chess today. It provides more than the usual dose of the latter.

1 e4 c5 2 ♘f3 ♘c6 3 d4 cxd4 4 ♘xd4 e5 5 ♘b5 d6

Once a rare line played mainly by beginners, this move caught on heavily in the late 1980s and continues to score well. It was certainly inspired by the success of the Sveshnikov Variation, which goes 4...♘f6 5 ♘c3 e5 6 ♘db5 d6 instead. But it is amazing that Black can so blithely cede the d5-square and assume a weak and backward d-pawn when White can reinforce his grip by c4, something he can't do in the Sveshnikov.

6 c4 ♗e7

Again, this passive move seems a poor trade-off for the active play that we have seen in the Sveshnikov. But it is a case of 'bad bishops protect[ing] good pawns' (Suba), i.e., if the pawn that holds up your entire structure is guarded by a bad bishop, are you about to complain? Black's d6-pawn, despite being backward, is in fact his most important one, and it is also the second centre pawn (versus one for White) that constitutes Black's fundamental advantage in the Sicilian Defence.

Regarding move-order, by the way, Black would like to avoid 6...♘f6 7 ♗g5, which creates doubled pawns after 7...a6 8 ♗xf6 gxf6 9 ♘5c3.

7 ♘1c3 a6 8 ♘a3 f5!? (D)

A sort of beginner's move that tries to break down White's centre and operate along the f-file. However, it creates more light-squared weaknesses (in addition to d5) and looks utterly anti-positional. Again, however, we see the influence of pragmatism as opposed to abstract thinking.

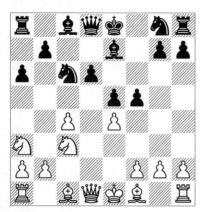

9 ♗d3!?

Logical enough. The threat is exf5, so White is developing with tempo to emphasize his light-square advantage. But today 9 ♗d3 is very rarely played, because Black's reply has driven it from mainstream practice. Today, almost everyone plays 9 exf5 ♗xf5 10 ♗d3, although 10 ♘c2 is a particularly interesting alternative.

9...f4!

A noteworthy move that uses a tempo to make the e7-bishop even worse and releases the pressure on e4! However, it also serves two important practical functions. First, the c1-bishop is cut off from play, and what may not be immediately evident is that White's a3-knight can't swing to its ideal destination on e3 (controlling f5 and d5). The main alternative is 9...fxe4, which is still theoretically unclear.

10 g3!?

Ultimately this doesn't work out, although it's almost impossible to ascertain whether it should have done. Black has done well in the few games from this position, an extremely dynamic and entertaining example being 10 ♘c2 ♘h6!? 11 b3 0-0 12 ♘d5 ♗g5 (Black's development is bizarre but difficult to refute) 13 ♗e2 ♗e6 14 ♗b2 ♔h8 15 ♕d3 ♖c8 16 ♗c3 b5!? (D) (more or less insane).

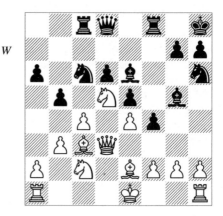

17 cxb5 ♗xd5 18 exd5 ♘a7 19 ♗d2 (there may be better options, but the obvious 19 bxa6 leads to a probable draw after 19...♕c7: 20 ♕c4 ♕b6 21 ♕d3 ♕c7) 19...e4!? 20 ♕xe4 ♖e8 21 ♕d3 ♘xb5 22 ♖c1 (22 0-0 ♖xc2; 22 a4 ♖xc2 23 axb5 f3! and Black wins) 22...♕e7 23 ♔d1? (23 ♔f1) 23...♖c3! 24 ♖e1 (24 ♗xc3 ♘xc3+ 25 ♔d2 ♘xe2 26 f3 ♘xc1 27 ♖xc1 ♕a7! 28 ♘d4 ♘f5! and Black wins) 24...♖xd3 25 ♗xd3 ♕f7 26 ♖xe8+ ♕xe8 27 a4 ♘g4 0-1 Fluvia Poyatos-Moiseenko, Aviles jr Ech 2000.

10...♘f6!?

The introduction to mad complications. This should definitely be classified as a tactical pawn sacrifice but it does have a few positional aspects. Vitally, it wins the important e5-square.

11 gxf4 exf4 12 ♗xf4 0-0 13 ♗g3

Nataf gives 13 ♕d2?! ♘g4! intending 14 0-0-0?? ♖xf4 15 ♕xf4 ♗g5, winning; and 14 ♗g3? ♘xf2!! 15 ♗xf2 ♖xf2 16 ♔xf2 ♗g5!!, a spectacular portent of things to come. But possibly White could have played 14 ♘d5, allowing 14...♘xf2!? because of the defensive line 15 ♔xf2 ♗g5 16 ♖af1! ♗xf4 17 ♘xf4 g5 18 ♖hg1 ♔h8 19 ♔e1. According to Nunn, 14...♗h4 is better, when 15 0-0 ♘d4 16 f3 ♘e5 is promising for Black. There are of course alternatives, and in fact I'm more concerned with the dynamic aspects of the game rather than the literal soundness of the sacrifice.

13...♘g4! *(D)*

'!', if only for the amazing ideas that it introduces.

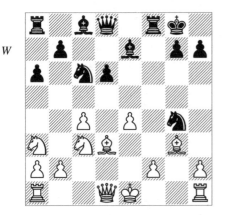

14 ♗e2?!

Nataf approves of this with an '!', but it doesn't work out so well and there may be a much better alternative ('f' below). He presents a number of lines here (I use my own notational marks):

a) 14 h3?? ♘xf2! 15 ♗xf2 ♖xf2 16 ♔xf2 ♗h4+ 17 ♔e2 ♘d4+ 18 ♔e3 (18 ♔d2 ♕g5#) 18...♕g5+ 19 ♔xd4 ♕c5#.

b) 14 ♘c2? ♘xf2! 15 ♗xf2 ♖xf2 16 ♔xf2 ♗h4+ and Black wins, since 17 ♔e2 runs into 17...♗g4+.

c) Also losing is 14 ♕d2? ♘xf2! 15 ♗xf2 ♖xf2 16 ♔xf2 (16 ♕xf2 ♗h4) 16...♗g5! (but not 16...♗h4+?? 17 ♔g2, since the mate that applied to the above lines by ...♕g5+ no longer exists) 17 ♕c2 ♗h4+.

d) Nataf offers 14 0-0!? but gives no further moves. I think that Black gets at least a

dangerous attack after 14...♘ge5 (finally using that important square) 15 ♗e2 (15 f4 ♕b6+) 15...♗h3 16 ♕d5+ ♔h8 17 ♖fd1 ♗h4! 18 c5 (18 ♕xd6? ♗xg3 19 hxg3 ♕b6) 18...♗xg3 19 hxg3 ♕g5 (introducing various ideas including 20...♖xf2) 20 ♕d2 ♕g6! 21 ♕e3 (21 ♕xd6?? ♕f7, and ...♖ad8 threatens as well as ...♕xf2+) 21...dxc5 intending ...♘d4 and Black has excellent attacking chances.

e) Nunn gives 14 ♖f1 ♘d4 15 ♗e2 ♘xe2 16 ♕xe2 ♘e5 with 'good compensation'.

f) Neither Nataf nor Nunn mentions 14 f4!, which is loosening, but on the other hand stops both ...♘e5 and any idea of a sacrifice on f2. It seems to me that this is a critical test of Black's pawn sacrifice. Play might continue 14...♕b6 (14...h5 15 ♗e2!; 14...♗h4 threatens ...♘xh2 and ...♖xf4, but 15 ♕d2 covers everything; then 15...♘b4 16 ♗c2 leaves Black with less than nothing for the pawn) 15 ♕d2 ♗e6 (15...♘b4 16 0-0-0 ♗e6 17 ♔b1) 16 h3 ♘f6 (16...♘d4? 17 0-0-0 ♘f6 18 ♗f2) 17 0-0-0, when Black doesn't seem to have enough play; for example, 17...♘h5 18 ♗h2 ♖ad8 19 ♗e2 ♘f6 20 ♗g1 ♕c7 21 ♘d5 and White wins. However, those are hardly comprehensive lines and both sides have alternatives.

14...♘xf2!! *(D)*

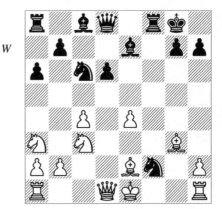

A remarkable move in view of the reduced material that is supporting the attack. From here on out it's just a question of whether Black will mate or White can work his way out.

15 ♕d5+

White has trouble defending after this move, but after 15 ♗xf2 ♖xf2! White has nothing better than 16 ♕d5+ ♔h8, transposing to the note to Black's 16th move. Instead, 16 ♔xf2? loses to 16...♗h4+ 17 ♔g2 (17 ♔e3 ♕g5+ 18 ♔d3 ♘b4+! 19 ♔d4 ♕c5#) 17...♕g5+.

15...♔h8! 16 ♗xf2?!

Nunn assigns this a '?' and suggests 16 ♖f1 ♘g4 with Black 'slightly better'. At this point it must have been nearly impossible to assess the precise worth of Black's forthcoming attack.

16...♘b4!?

Objectively inferior. Nunn says that 16...♖xf2 17 ♔xf2! ♘b4 transposes, finding the beautiful line 18 ♕f7 ♗h4+ 19 ♔f3 ♘c6!! 20 ♕f4 g5 21 ♕e3 ♗h3! 'and the king is trapped'. But here 18 ♕d4? ♗h4+ simply wins for Black, so the line in the next note isn't available and thus 16...♖xf2! wins!

17 ♕h5?

This seems to lose. The position is explosive, and it takes a computer to see through the rubble:

a) 17 ♕d2? ♖xf2! 18 ♔xf2 ♗g5! (but not 18...♗h4+? 19 ♔g2!) 19 ♕d4 ♗h4+ transposes to line 'b1'.

b) Nataf gives 17 ♕d4 a '?', but I consider it the best defence. 17...♖xf2! and now:

b1) 18 ♔xf2? ♗h4+ 19 ♔f3!? (19 ♔g2 loses to 19...♕g5+) 19...♗h3! and Black intends either ...♕f8+ or ...♕e8-g6, or in some cases ...♕e7 and ...♖f8. There might follow 20 ♘d5 ♕g5 21 ♘f4 ♖f8 22 ♕xd6 ♗g4+ 23 ♔e3 ♖xf4! 24 ♕xf4 ♗f2+. This is all very pretty, but...

b2) 18 ♖g1! ♖f7 19 0-0-0 seems to defend, although Black is still much better.

17...♖xf2!

The familiar idea, at first sight less likely to work this time because the queen on h5 covers some key squares. Nevertheless, Black finds his way through.

18 ♔xf2 ♗h4+ 19 ♔g2

Some beautiful lines follow the alternatives: 19 ♔e3 g6! 20 ♕f3 (20 ♕h6 ♗g5+ wins for Black) 20...♕g5+! 21 ♕f4 ♕c5+! 22 ♔d2 (22 ♔f3 ♕f2#) 22...♗g5 and Black wins; and 19 ♔g1 g6 20 ♕f3 ♕g5+ 21 ♔f1 ♗h3+! 22 ♕xh3 ♖f8+ 23 ♗f3 ♕e3 – compare the game.

19...g6! 20 ♕f3

20 ♕h6? loses to 20...♗g5.

20...♕g5+ 21 ♔f1 ♗h3+! 22 ♕xh3 ♖f8+ 23 ♗f3 ♕e3! *(D)*

24 ♕xh4

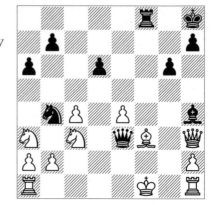

Versus ...♕f2#. Otherwise 24 ♘d1 ♖xf3+ 25 ♕xf3 ♕xf3+ 26 ♔g1 ♘d3, etc.

24...♘d3!!

The culmination of an incredible combination. Instead, 24...♖xf3+? loses to 25 ♔g2, because if now 25...♘d3, then 26 ♖hf1 and the attack is over. And the obvious 24...♕xf3+ 25 ♔g1 ♕e3+ 26 ♔g2 ♕f3+ only draws.

25 ♘d5

25 ♕g3? ♖xf3+ 26 ♔g2 ♘f4+! is winning for Black (27 ♕xf4 ♕f2#).

25...♕xf3+

25...♖xf3+ 26 ♔g2 ♕e2+ 27 ♔g1 g5 is an even better line, but the text-move is more pleasing.

26 ♔g1 ♘f2!

Threatening both mate on h1 and win of the queen by ...♘h3+.

27 ♔f1

27 ♘f6 ♘h3+! (27...♖xf6? 28 ♕xf6+ ♕xf6 29 ♖f1! is unclear) 28 ♕xh3 ♕xh3 29 ♖f1 ♔g7! 30 ♘d5 ♕g4#.

27...♕xh1+ 28 ♔e2 ♕xa1 0-1

Black cannot prevent the move ...♕xb2. Such a game would probably have made a '25 Greatest Brilliancies of Chess' book half a century ago, but today such chaotic adventures are seen on a fairly regular basis. That is in fact one of the most enjoyable facets of contemporary play.

Game 13
Voiska – Alexandrova
Warsaw wom Ech 2001

1 c4 c5 2 ♘f3 ♘c6 3 g3 g6 4 ♗g2 ♗g7 5 ♘c3 e6

This is a very common English Opening position, usually arrived at by the move-order 2 ♘c3 ♘c6 3 g3 g6 4 ♗g2 ♗g7 5 ♘f3 e6.

6 d4!? *(D)*

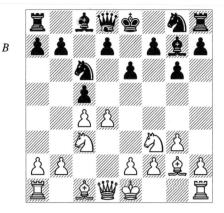

Today this is a mainstream and respectable move. For years, White struggled to find any sort of answer to 5...e6 that promised interesting play, and this is a sound continuation that does so. But as far as I know, 6 d4 was played only once before the 1980s in the isolated game Lengyel-Bilek, Budapest 1964. White went wrong in two more moves and got the worse game. But why after so many years of games with this line did no one else come up with 6 d4 until recently? Some leading players and numerous grandmasters didn't. For example, Petrosian suffered a critical loss in this line against Fischer in the 1970 USSR vs RoW match and in my database never won with White in several other contests. In general White tended to approach this position passively and ceded the centre to Black; his plans included d3, b3, e3, and a3. Given the poor performance of other reactions to 5...e6 (47%-53% in Black's favour), 6 d4 would at least have been a very handy practical weapon. Did players up to recent times lack good positional instincts? Of course not. What then? Were they somewhat wedded to the instinctive belief that such a move has to be, if not completely unsound, easily and quickly subject to neutralization? That's a different matter. Most reasonable people will agree that White should not or cannot give up a crucial centre pawn at this juncture. For one thing Black can always play an early ...d5, taking the initiative in the centre and activating his

pieces while White fiddles about trying to regain the pawn. And that pawn recovery may not even happen, because after ...cxd4 and White's ♘b5, Black can play ...♕b6. Then, White's only apparent resource would be to keep Black's king in the centre by ♘d6+. But that, as strong players know by dint of experience with other openings, would actually speed up Black's development (and the king is normally very comfortably placed on e7). As if all that weren't bad enough, Black might be able to capture by 6...♘xd4 7 ♘xd4 ♗xd4 without creating a target on d4; he might then cover the dark squares by means of ...♗e5. Thus, by all reasonable thinking according to general principle, and employing not just traditional but deeply ingrained instinctive reasoning, 6 d4 has to be wrong. It should at the very most barely equalize purely because White gets the first move in chess. I myself worked on the English Opening for years (with a 4-volume set devoted to it) and, fully aware of d4 sacrifices in similar positions, I didn't believe that 6 d4 was sound, nor did any other theoretician that I know of.

What happened? I don't think that there is much of a mystery here. Modern chess, and in a more extreme fashion the chess of the last few decades, has increasing turned to specific and unprejudiced analysis of positions, taking the pragmatic attitude that anything might work if you give it a chance, ugly or counter-intuitive as it might be. This approach has clearly been assisted, often in an indispensable way, by the introduction of computer analytical engines. Thus players have used an unnatural method to find some of these new ideas. But that's not the whole point, because in doing so they have opened their minds to accept the pragmatic analytical approach described throughout this book. And computers still don't, as far as I know, come up with or at least recommend 5...e6 6 d4 (*especially* not intending 6...♘xd4 7 ♘xd4 cxd4 8 ♘e4, the way this line was conceived and achieved its original successes). The less so do they find the move 7 d4 in the next paragraph.

Here is a side note dedicated to the creative grandmaster Tony Miles, who recently died. With both experience and imagination assisting him, Miles discovered the outrageous idea 1 c4 c5 2 ♘c3 ♘c6 3 g3 g6 4 ♗g2 ♗g7 5 ♘f3 e5 (also a main line move with a long and top-level tradition behind it) 6 a3 a5 (6...♘ge7 7 b4 is a positional gambit) 7 d4!!? *(D)*.

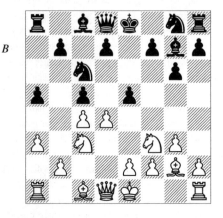

White's idea is that after both 7...cxd4 8 ♘b5 and 7...♘xd4 8 ♘xd4 cxd4 9 ♘b5, the move e3 will follow in order to expose the d6-square. For example, 7...cxd4 8 ♘b5 d6 9 e3 ♗g4 (9...♘h6 10 exd4 0-0 11 d5 with a clear advantage for White, Miles-Heyken, W.German Cup 1990) 10 h3 ♗xf3 11 ♗xf3 ♘ge7 12 exd4 exd4 13 ♗f4 ♗e5 14 ♗h6 ♘f5 15 ♕d2 a4 16 0-0 ♘a5 17 ♖ae1 ♘xc4 18 ♕b4! ♘xh6 19 ♗xb7 with great complications, Miles-Kudrin, Los Angeles 1991, a game eventually won by White.

I'm not going to enter into the theory of 7 d4, but you can already see that what I've said above also applies to this move. I don't think that the particulars work out as well for White as 6 d4 does in our main game, but the fact that 7 d4 has appeared in grandmaster practice again suggests how many new moves are being examined without particular prejudice, motivated only by the belief that they might work.

6...cxd4

This isn't a book on theory, but it's relevant to see that White has good compensation in a fascinating position after 6...♘xd4 7 ♘xd4 cxd4 (7...♗xd4 8 ♘b5 ♗e5 9 0-0 ties Black up) 8 ♘e4! *(D)*.

A surprising move as opposed to the natural 8 ♘b5 (which is also played). Black's usual reply to 8 ♘e4 is 8...d5 (8...♕c7?! 9 c5! ♘e7 10 ♗f4 ♕a5+ 11 ♗d2 ♕c7 12 ♘d6+ ♔f8 13 ♖c1 with tremendous pressure was Chernin-Parameswaran, Bangalore 1981, the first modern game with the 6 d4 and 8 ♘e4 idea) 9 cxd5

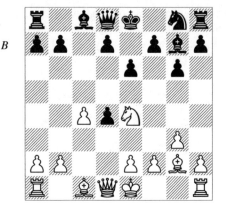

exd5 10 ♕a4+ ♔f8 and way back in 1988 I recommended 11 ♘c5 here, a move that seems to have got lost in the shuffle. I still think that White is a little better in this position: his pieces are very well placed and Black has to take care of his king.

7 ♘b5 d5

The main move these days. Black can get a disadvantage quickly after 7...e5?! 8 ♘d6+ ♔e7 9 ♘g5! ♘h6 10 ♘ge4, while 7...♕b6 8 0-0 ♘ge7 9 ♘d6+ ♔f8 10 b3!? has the ideas of ♗b2 or ♗a3 and makes it difficult for Black to come up with a plan.

8 cxd5 ♕a5+

Almost always played. 8...exd5 gives White a comfortable isolated pawn position after 9 0-0 ♘ge7 10 ♘bxd4 0-0 11 ♗e3, although this is only a bit better for him.

9 ♕d2

9 ♘d2!? is also promising, and has enjoyed some success after 9...♕xb5 10 dxc6, when 10...bxc6? 11 a4! with the idea of ♘c4 is much better for White.

9...♕xb5 10 dxc6 ♕xc6 11 0-0 ♕b6

After 11...♕d6, one theoretical line goes 12 ♖d1 e5 13 e3 ♘e7 (13...♗g4 14 h3 ♗xf3 15 ♗xf3 with an edge) 14 exd4 exd4 15 ♘xd4 0-0 16 ♘c6! ♕f6 17 ♘a5 and White is slightly better.

12 b3 ♘f6

12...♘e7 13 ♗a3 *(D)* launches a serious attack on the dark squares and along the c-file.

From this position, some entertaining examples are:

a) 13...e5!? 14 ♖ac1 ♗d7 15 ♘g5 f5 (versus ♘e4) 16 ♗c5 ♕a6 17 ♗xe7 ♔xe7 18 ♕b4+ ♔f6 (on 18...♔e8, 19 ♖c7 e4 20 ♘f7! ♗xf7 21

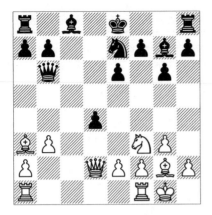

B

Ξxd7+ $\dot{\Xi}$g8 22 Ξc1! is winning) 19 Ξc7? (19 f4! should win quickly) 19...$\pounds$f8 20 $\pmb{\mathbb{W}}$d2 $\pmb{\mathbb{W}}$d6 21 Ξfc1 h6?! 22 $\pounds$xb7 Ξd8 23 $\bigtriangleup$f3!? (or 23 Ξ1c6 hxg5 24 Ξxd6+) 23...$\pmb{\mathbb{W}}$b4 24 $\pounds$c6? (24 $\pounds$d5! is clear and good) 24...$\pmb{\mathbb{W}}$xd2 25 $\bigtriangleup$xd2 $\pounds$b4?? 26 $\pounds$xd7 $\pounds$xd2 27 Ξ1c6+ $\dot{\Xi}$g5 28 h4+ $\dot{\Xi}$h5 29 $\dot{\Xi}$g2 g5 30 $\pounds$xf5 gxh4 31 Ξg7 hxg3 32 $\pounds$g4+ 1-0 Stryjecki-Kludacz, Krakow 1999.

b) 13...$\bigtriangleup$c6 14 Ξac1 e5 15 $\bigtriangleup$g5 f5 (Brückner-Rührig, W.German Ch (Bad Neuenahr) 1987), and White could play 16 $\bigtriangleup$xh7! Ξxh7 17 $\pmb{\mathbb{W}}$g5 $\bigtriangleup$b4 18 $\pounds$c6+ bxc6 19 $\pmb{\mathbb{W}}$xg6+ $\dot{\Xi}$f8 20 Ξxc6 with a considerable plus.

c) 13...$\bigtriangleup$d5 14 Ξac1 $\bigtriangleup$c3 15 e3 dxe3 16 fxe3 $\pmb{\mathbb{W}}$a6 (16...$\bigtriangleup$d5 17 $\pounds$c5) 17 $\pounds$b2 $\bigtriangleup$e4 18 $\pmb{\mathbb{W}}$c2 $\bigtriangleup$f6 (18...$\pounds$xb2 19 $\pmb{\mathbb{W}}$xb2 0-0 20 $\bigtriangleup$e5) 19 $\bigtriangleup$g5 e5 20 $\pmb{\mathbb{W}}$c5 $\pounds$e6 21 Ξxf6! $\pounds$xf6 22 $\pounds$f1 Ξc8 (22...$\pmb{\mathbb{W}}$b6 23 $\pounds$b5+ $\pounds$d7 24 $\pounds$xd7+ $\dot{\Xi}$xd7 25 $\pmb{\mathbb{W}}$d5+) 23 $\pounds$b5+ Ξc6 24 $\bigtriangleup$e4 $\pounds$e7 (24...$\pounds$g7 25 $\pounds$xe5) 25 $\pmb{\mathbb{W}}$xe5 f6 26 Ξxc6 fxe5 27 Ξxa6+ $\dot{\Xi}$f7 28 Ξxa7 $\pounds$d5 29 $\pounds$c4 1-0 Miles-Kosten, Palma de Mallorca 1989.

13 $\pmb{\mathbb{W}}$xd4!?

Anticipating Black's next move. Nogueiras-J.Alvarez, Santa Clara 1999 featured the more aggressive 13 $\bigtriangleup$e5!?: 13...$\bigtriangleup$e4 14 $\pounds$xe4 $\pounds$xe5 15 $\pounds$a3 f5 16 $\pounds$g2 $\pounds$d7?! (16...$\dot{\Xi}$f7) 17 Ξac1 Ξc8 18 Ξxc8+ $\pounds$xc8 19 Ξc1 $\dot{\Xi}$f7 20 $\pounds$c5 $\pmb{\mathbb{W}}$a6 21 f4! $\pounds$f6 22 $\pounds$xd4 $\pmb{\mathbb{W}}$d6 23 e3 $\pounds$xd4? 24 $\pmb{\mathbb{W}}$xd4 $\pmb{\mathbb{W}}$xd4 25 exd4 Ξd8 26 Ξc7+ $\dot{\Xi}$f6 27 $\dot{\Xi}$f2 and White won.

13...$\bigtriangleup$h5

13...$\pmb{\mathbb{W}}$xd4 14 $\bigtriangleup$xd4 $\bigtriangleup$d5 15 e3 and White has a small advantage, since his c1-bishop is more effective than its counterpart; for example, 15...0-0 16 $\pounds$a3 Ξd8 17 Ξac1 $\pounds$d7 18 $\pounds$xd5 exd5 19 Ξc7 $\pounds$xd4 20 exd4 $\pounds$c6 21 Ξe1

Ξe8 22 Ξee7 Ξxe7 23 $\pounds$xe7 with an edge according to Voiska. Such positions are trickier to defend than they look, since White can grab more space and tie Black's king down.

14 $\pmb{\mathbb{W}}$d1! *(D)*

A very nice exchange sacrifice! Surely Black expected the swap of queens when she went into this line, and 14 $\pmb{\mathbb{W}}$xb6 axb6 15 Ξb1 Ξxa2 leaves Black better.

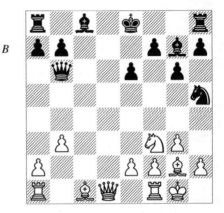

B

14...0-0

Black decides not to take the material and she's almost certainly right: 14...$\pounds$xa1 15 $\pounds$e3 $\pmb{\mathbb{W}}$b4 16 $\pmb{\mathbb{W}}$xa1 f6 (or 16...0-0 17 $\pounds$h6 Ξe8 18 h3 {18 $\bigtriangleup$e5!?} 18...$\pmb{\mathbb{W}}$e7 19 g4 $\bigtriangleup$f6 20 $\bigtriangleup$e5 Ξd8 21 $\pounds$g5 $\dot{\Xi}$g7 22 $\pmb{\mathbb{W}}$c1 $\dot{\Xi}$g8 23 $\pmb{\mathbb{W}}$f4 $\dot{\Xi}$g7 24 h4! intending h5-h6 and White is decisively better) 17 Ξc1 $\pmb{\mathbb{W}}$e7 18 g4 $\bigtriangleup$g7 19 g5! (the dark squares are collapsing, and White is only an exchange down) 19...e5 (or 19...$\bigtriangleup$h5 20 gxf6 $\bigtriangleup$xf6 21 $\bigtriangleup$e5 with ideas of $\bigtriangleup$g4, $\pounds$c5, $\pounds$g5, etc.) 20 gxf6 $\pmb{\mathbb{W}}$xf6 21 $\pounds$g5 $\pmb{\mathbb{W}}$f5 22 $\pounds$h3! $\pmb{\mathbb{W}}$xh3 23 $\pmb{\mathbb{W}}$xe5+ $\pmb{\mathbb{W}}$e6 24 $\pmb{\mathbb{W}}$xg7 Ξg8 25 $\pmb{\mathbb{W}}$c7, and White wins.

15 $\pounds$e3 $\pmb{\mathbb{W}}$a5 16 Ξc1 $\bigtriangleup$f6

Fatal is 16...$\pmb{\mathbb{W}}$xa2?? 17 g4 $\bigtriangleup$f6 18 Ξa1 $\pmb{\mathbb{W}}$b2 19 $\pounds$d4.

17 $\pounds$d4 Ξd8 18 $\pmb{\mathbb{W}}$c2 $\bigtriangleup$d5 19 $\pounds$xg7 $\dot{\Xi}$xg7 20 $\pmb{\mathbb{W}}$b2+ f6 21 Ξfd1

White has a clear advantage. Her pieces are all developed and Black has weaknesses.

21...$\pounds$d7 22 e4 $\bigtriangleup$e7 23 b4

23 e5 f5 24 Ξd6 $\bigtriangleup$c8 25 b4 $\pmb{\mathbb{W}}$a4 26 $\bigtriangleup$g5! $\dot{\Xi}$g8 (26...$\bigtriangleup$xd6? loses to 27 exd6+ $\dot{\Xi}$g8 28 $\pmb{\mathbb{W}}$f6 Ξf8 29 $\pmb{\mathbb{W}}$e7) 27 Ξd5!!, threatening both $\bigtriangleup$xe6 and Ξa5, winning the queen.

23...$\pmb{\mathbb{W}}$a4 24 g4

With a big advantage. The idea is g5. In a sense this is the culmination of the dark-square strategy beginning with 6 d4!

24...♗c6

Still worse is 24...♗b5?! 25 ♖e1 e5? 26 g5 ♘c6 27 gxf6+ ♔xf6 28 ♖xc6+! (Voiska); and 24...♖ac8 allows White to carry out her plan by 25 g5 ♘g8 26 ♖d6! ♗e8 27 e5! ♖xd6 28 exd6 ♖xc1+ 29 ♕xc1 with much the better game.

25 ♖e1! ♖d3?!

25...♖ac8 26 g5 ♘g8 27 gxf6+ ♘xf6 28 ♘g5 ♗d7 29 ♘xh7 and White will win.

26 g5 ♘g8 27 gxf6+ ♘xf6 28 ♘e5 ♖a3 29 ♖e2?

Most efficient was 29 ♖xc6! bxc6 30 ♘d7 and wins.

29...h5

29...♖d8 30 ♘g4.

30 ♘xc6!?

Signs of time-trouble are evident over the next few moves. 30 ♖xc6! bxc6 31 ♖d2, threatening ♘c4 and ♘d7, wins outright.

30...bxc6 31 e5!?

And here 31 ♖d2 is simple and decisive.

31...♘d5 32 ♗xd5 cxd5 33 ♖c7+ ♔h6 34 ♕d2+?!

34 ♕c1+! wins due to 34...g5 35 ♕b1! ♖h8 36 ♖f7. In spite of these slips, White retains just enough advantage to win.

34...g5 35 f4?

But this is getting serious. 35 ♖e7! ♕a6 36 ♕c2! is correct. Unquestionably both players were pressed for time.

35...♖f8 36 ♖f2 ♔g6 37 ♖e7 ♕c6 38 b5 ♕c5??

38...♕c8! 39 ♕b4 ♖e3 40 ♕d6.

39 ♖xe6+ ♔g7 40 ♖c6 ♕e3 41 ♕xe3

Or 41 ♖c7+ ♔h8 42 fxg5.

41...♖xe3 42 fxg5 ♖xf2 43 ♔xf2 ♖a3

Also losing is 43...♖xe5 44 ♖c7+ ♔g6 45 a4 ♔xg5 46 ♖xa7.

44 ♖a6 ♖h3 45 ♖xa7+ ♔g6 46 ♔g2 ♖h4 47 e6 d4 48 e7 ♖e4 49 b6 d3 50 ♖d7 d2 51 ♖xd2 ♖xe7 52 ♖b2 1-0

In spite of numerous technical difficulties at the end, this is a terribly instructive game.

Remember that the classical Open Games and middlegame formations were also evolving during the modern period from 1940-1990, and they continue to do so today. The number of

structures that are considered terribly passive or drawish has strikingly diminished. In practice, players have found ways to play originally in what seemed to be thoroughly researched territory. In 1 d4 d5 lines, for example, those familiar with Slav Defence theory can understand that the positionally-oriented players of that opening in the 1920s and 1930s would be taken aback by the wild and exotic paths this 'solid' opening has taken in so many variations. Pawns are gambited freely, pawn-structures are thoroughly compromised for long-term dynamic compensation, and no one flinches at things like severely delayed development or strange flank pawn advances. But there's always been the feeling that the bastion of 1 d4 d5 defences, the Orthodox Queen's Gambit Declined, was not subject to radical change. After all, this was the opening which prompted the 'death of chess' predictions from Capablanca and Lasker. It was said that the variations were too thoroughly worked out to provide enough opportunity for the strong player to avoid a draw against a well-prepared but inferior opponent. We have already seen in Chapter 1, Section 1 (The Surrender of the Centre) how the main lines of yesteryear have been replaced by new and more dynamic ones. But it's even true of a simple structure like the Queen's Gambit Exchange Variation; new ideas are possible. Here is a case in point:

Game 14
Khouseinov – Magomedov
Dushanbe 1999

1 d4 d5 2 c4 e6 3 ♘f3 ♘f6 4 ♘c3 ♗e7 5 cxd5 exd5 6 ♗g5 c6 7 ♕c2

To prevent ...♗f5 and to stay flexible.

7...♘a6

This flank development has become more popular of late.

8 a3

A common option is 8 e3, when 8...♘b4 9 ♕d1 (9 ♕b1 g6 and ...♗f5) 9...♗f5 10 ♖c1 ♕a5 (or 10...a5) is played. Black has had satisfactory results from these positions.

8...g6 9 e4!? ♘xe4! 10 ♘xe4 (D)

10...♘c7!!

An incredible move that more than justifies this variation. Apparently a suggestion of Lautier's and first tried in the mid-1990s, it shows

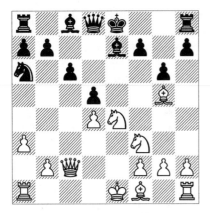

B

how creative sequences (beginning with 7...♘a6 and ending with 10...♘c7) can enliven even the most established variations. 10...♗f5 is the older move here, leading to lines like 11 ♗xa6 ♗xe4 12 ♕c3 ♗xf3! (12...bxa6? 13 ♕xc6+ ♔f8 14 ♗xe7+ ♔xe7 15 ♘e5 ♖c8 16 ♖c1) 13 ♗xb7 ♗xg5 14 ♗xc6+ ♔f8 15 ♕xf3 ♕e7+ 16 ♕e2 ♕xe2+ 17 ♔xe2 and White has good chances with his extra pawn despite the presence of opposite-coloured bishops.

11 ♕c5!?

A nice counter, even though it doesn't quite equalize. Everything else gives Black a modest edge or more:

a) 11 ♗xe7? ♕xe7 12 ♘e5 dxe4 with an extra pawn.

b) 11 ♗h6!? dxe4 12 ♕xe4 ♗f5 13 ♕e5 f6 14 ♕e3 ♘d5 15 ♕b3 ♕a5+ (15...♕d7 and ...0-0-0 is safe, with a lead in development and good play against the isolani) 16 ♗d2 ♕b6 17 ♕xb6 ♘xb6 (Black has a substantial edge) 18 ♗e2 0-0 (18...0-0-0! is much more natural) 19 0-0 ♖fe8 20 ♖fe1 ♗d6 21 ♗a5 ♘d5!? (21...♔g7 is probably better, to prepare to double rooks and play ...♘d5 without being pinned by ♗c4, but the move played also keeps a healthy edge) 22 ♗c4 ♔f8 23 ♗xd5 cxd5 24 ♗c3 ♖ac8 25 ♘d2 ♔f7, Sauleda-Voehringer, e-mail 1998. Black has a considerable advantage due to his two bishops and pawns on both sides of the board.

c) 11 h4!? dxe4 12 ♕xe4 ♘d5! (12...♗f5 13 ♕e5 ♖f8 is equal) 13 ♗c4 ♗f5 14 ♕e2 0-0 15 0-0 (Magomedov gives 15 ♗xd5 ♗xg5 16 hxg5 ♕xd5 17 0-0 ♖fe8 18 ♕d2 ♗e4, when Black is much better), and here Black can try 15...f6! (Lautier's 15...♖e8 gives a small edge) 16 ♗h6

♖e8 17 ♕d2 ♗d6 with a moderate but definite advantage.

11...dxe4 12 ♕e5 ♖f8 13 ♕xe4 ♗f5

According to Magomedov Black is a little better, and that seems fair.

14 ♕e3?

White shouldn't stay in the middlegame. Still, 14 ♕xe7+ ♕xe7+ 15 ♗xe7 ♔xe7 favours Black because of the isolani.

14...♘d5 15 ♕d2 ♗e4!?

15...♗xg5! is quite strong: 16 ♘xg5 (16 ♕xg5 ♕xg5 17 ♘xg5 f6 18 ♘f3 0-0-0 is a very bad ending: Black threatens ...♗e4 and ...♘f4 while his rooks rush to the central files) 16...f6 17 ♘f3 ♕d6 and Black is clearly better, with moves like ...0-0-0 and ...♘f4 to follow.

16 ♗h6 (D)

Magomedov analyses 16 ♗e2 ♗xf3 17 ♗xe7 ♕xe7 18 gxf3 ♕f6; this is winning for Black after ...0-0-0 and ...♘f4.

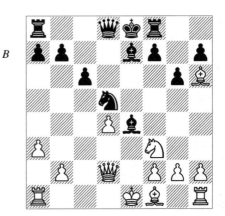

B

16...♗xf3?!

Sacrificing the exchange for obvious compensation, but probably not much more than that. Black should consider simply 16...♖g8, when he is considerably better without material investment.

17 ♗xf8!?

This gives up the crucial f4-square. But 17 gxf3 ♖g8 is probably even worse for White; e.g., Magomedov gives 18 ♗d3 ♕d6! 19 h4 ♗f8 20 ♗e3 f5.

17...♗g5 18 ♕c2?

A fatal mistake. After 18 ♕d3! ♗xf8 19 ♕xf3 ♕b6! 20 ♗c4 (20 ♗e2 is answered by 20...♗d2+!) 20...♗d2+ (20...♖e8+ 21 ♔f1 ♕xb2 22 ♖d1 ♖e6 with an edge) 21 ♔f1 ♕xb2 22

Ξd1 $\text{\wxd4}$ 23 $\text{\xd5}$ cxd5 24 g3, White is only somewhat worse.

18...$\text{\xf8}$ 19 gxf3 $\text{\wa5}$+ 20 $\text{\d1}$ Ξd8!

This position must already be lost for White.

21 $\text{\e2}$

Or 21 $\text{\wc5}$+ $\text{\wxc5}$ 22 dxc5 $\text{\b4}$+! 23 $\text{\e2}$ Ξd2+ 24 $\text{\e1}$ $\text{\c2}$#.

21...$\text{\f4}$!?

This is good enough, although 21...$\text{\b4}$! wins immediately. White can't protect the d-pawn due to 22 $\text{\wc3}$ Ξxd4+! 23 $\text{\wxd4}$ $\text{\wa4}$+.

22 $\text{\wc3}$ $\text{\we5}$! 23 $\text{\we3}$?

23 $\text{\c4}$ Ξxd4+ 24 $\text{\c2}$ $\text{\f6}$!, and White can resign anyway.

23...Ξxd4+ 24 $\text{\c2}$ $\text{\wf5}$+ 25 $\text{\b3}$ $\text{\wd5}$+ 26 $\text{\c3}$ $\text{\xe2}$+ 27 $\text{\wxe2}$ Ξd2 28 $\text{\we4}$ $\text{\f6}$+ 0-1

Game 15
Kan – Eliskases
Moscow 1936

While outside the basic idea of this section, it is nice to look occasionally at early games that reflect a number of the same themes that we have discussed regarding modern chess. Of course there are many such, even going back to the 19th century, although these occur infrequently relative to today and often in a context where the players had little choice as to the strategy they chose. In this game, played only a year after my original 'dividing point' for modern chess, Black's play is strategically way ahead of its time and would not be out of place on any level today. This game's setting reflects the evolving Soviet chess milieu from which stemmed the radical theoretical advances of the second half of the 1930s.

1 d4 $\text{\f6}$ 2 c4 g6 3 $\text{\c3}$ $\text{\g7}$ 4 e4 d6

Right away we have signs of modernity: the King's Indian Defence was relatively rare up to 1935, and in fact was played almost 8 times as much in the period 1936-70 as in 1900-35. In addition, the Sämisch Variation seen in this game (5 f3) was more popular after 1935.

5 f3 $\text{\bd7}$ 6 $\text{\e3}$ e5 7 $\text{\ge2}$ c6 8 d5 $\text{\b6}$

I won't comment upon the opening and early middlegame because it isn't very well played by modern standards, which is hardly surprising.

9 b3 cxd5 10 cxd5 $\text{\h5}$ 11 Ξc1 $\text{\d7}$ 12 $\text{\wd2}$ f5 13 $\text{\g3}$ *(D)*

White stands better here by virtue of his space and more pointed development. Now he challenges the h5-knight.

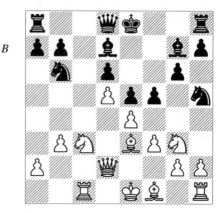

13...f4

The first interesting decision, allowing doubled h-pawns (which my dogmatic computer doesn't like and most players of the time didn't either!) and rendering the g7-bishop particularly problematic. But 13...$\text{\xg3}$ 14 hxg3, giving *White* the doubled pawns, probably would not appeal to many masters today: it not only opens the h-file, but makes counterplay particularly difficult. In the end, 13...f4 is probably the right choice.

14 $\text{\xh5}$ gxh5

Now the g-file is potentially useful, and as for h5, the saying that 'a weakness that can't be attacked isn't a weakness' applies, at least to some extent.

15 $\text{\f2}$ a6

Stopping $\text{\b5}$ and allowing a unique reorganization of Black's pieces. The advance ...b5 lurks in the background as well. White can take solace from the fact that he controls more space, his bishops are more active, and Black's queenside is compromised.

16 $\text{\d3}$ *(D)*

White looks better in almost every respect: two active bishops, pawn-structure, space in the centre and on the queenside, and then there's that g7-bishop of Black's. He should have a very large advantage and indeed has some, but the position is deceptive, and Black begins to manoeuvre behind the lines as in so many modern structures.

16...$\text{\f6}$!

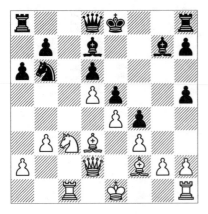

A flexible and interesting move which proves handy in several respects. The superficial idea is ...♗h4, which is unlikely to work. But Black wants the bishop able to influence the game, and notice that he is in no hurry to castle.

17 ♘e2 ♖c8 18 ♕b4 ♖xc1+ 19 ♘xc1 ♕c7 20 ♘e2 (D)

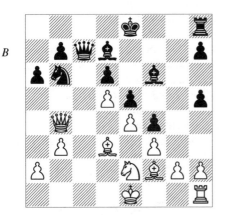

20...♘a8!

Considerably better than 20...♘c8, both because Black needs to be able to challenge the c-file by ...♖c8 and because the knight has greater chances of useful activation from the corner, as we shall see.

21 0-0 ♔e7!?

Again rejecting castling, to give d6 extra support and presumably to be better able to meet a break with g3.

22 ♖c1 ♕b8

Were Black's knight on c8, White could play ♗xa6 here.

23 ♕e1

23 a4 might be more pointed, to grab space.

23...♗g5!?

This prevents g3. It looks as though Black has no idea what he's doing and is living moment-to-moment. But now he also has the possibility of responding to ♗h4 with ...h6.

24 ♖c2 ♖c8 25 ♕c1 ♖xc2 26 ♕xc2 ♔f7!?

Neither Black's queen nor any of his pieces is particularly well placed, but he will now proceed to wander at length with his king, his dark-squared bishop, and his knight, coming out just fine in the end!

27 ♔f1 h4

Someday ...h3 may come in handy, and in the meantime this discourages g3.

28 h3!?

With this move, closing the kingside, White announces that he will try to win solely on the queenside. I'm not so sure. A hole on g3 is opened up on an open file and more importantly, White permanently forfeits the possibility of opening up a second front by g3 after, say, tying Black's pieces to the defence of the queenside.

28...♔g6 29 ♗e1 ♘c7!

One of the points behind ...♘a8. It may look as though the knight has designs upon the b5-square, but its eyes are elsewhere.

30 ♗b4 ♘e8 31 ♗e1

The bishop wasn't really doing much on b4, so White starts over.

31...♘g7! 32 ♗f2 ♘h5

Now we see part of Black's idea. The knight may not stand particularly threateningly on g3, but it will have great nuisance value that will help to coordinate Black's other pieces. These lengthy knight wanderings have been discussed in Chapter 3, Section 1. Here we have a case of ...♘b8-d7-b6-a8-c7-e8-g7-h5!

33 ♕c3 (D)

33...♗d8!

Here's the other part! Black wants at long last to free this bishop by ...b5 and ...♗b6, incidentally eliminating his opponent's best minor piece if he can.

34 ♔e1 ♔f7 35 ♕b4 b5! 36 ♕d2

To avoid ...a5 and ...b4. White looks a little disoriented, but it's hard to see how to make progress against Black's cramped game.

36...♘g3 37 ♔d1 ♗b6 38 ♗xg3! hxg3?!

38...♗e3! 39 ♕a5 hxg3 40 ♕xa6 b4 41 a4 bxa3 42 ♕xa3 ♗c5 43 ♕b2 ♕b6 gives Black compensation according to Bronznik; that is an

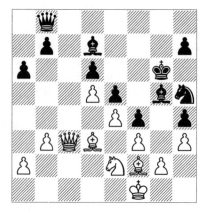

understatement. Now White is able to grab the initiative:

39 ♘xf4 exf4 40 ♕xf4+ ♚e8 41 ♕f6!

41 ♕xg3 ♚d8 42 ♕g8+ ♚c7 43 ♕xh7 ♕f8 followed by ...♕f4 is equal.

41...♕c7 42 e5?

42 ♕h8+ ♚e7 43 ♕xh7+ ♚d8 44 ♕g8+ ♗e8 45 ♕xg3 gives White four pawns for the piece, although Black does exert some pressure on the dark squares after 45...♕c5.

42...♕c5! 43 ♕h8+ ♚e7 44 ♕f6+ ♚e8 ½-½

A fascinating struggle in which Black resurrected what seemed like a position without redeeming value.

Game 16
Leko – *Fritz 6*
Frankfurt rpd 1999

It's valuable to present at least one computer example in this section. The following contest shows the computer relaxed and confident in a suspiciously modern setting. Generally these are a bastion of strength for humans.

1 e4 e5 2 ♘f3 ♘c6 3 ♗b5 a6 4 ♗a4 ♘f6 5 0-0 ♗e7 6 ♖e1 b5 7 ♗b3 d6 8 c3 0-0 9 h3 ♘a5 10 ♗c2 c5 11 d4 cxd4 12 cxd4 *(D)*

A normal Ruy Lopez has arisen in which Black would normally reinforce e5 in short order.

12...exd4

Called a strong theoretical novelty by Luther and found by his team, this move nevertheless surrenders the centre and leaves Black with a backward d-pawn on an open file, something you would think that a computer wouldn't like to do. The idea had been previously tried in

many games beginning with 12...♗b7 13 ♘bd2 exd4. But the drawback to 12...♗b7 is that White can play 13 d5 instead of 13 ♘bd2, as has occurred in at least as many games. The d-pawn advance can be awkward for Black: notice that the a5-knight has lost the ability to retreat to c6 and both black bishops are bad. 12...exd4 solves that problem.

13 ♘xd4 ♗b7 14 ♘d2

Now the game has transposed into a well-known position in which Black's chances are no worse. Luther mentions 14 ♘c3, when I think that Black is also OK.

14...♖e8 15 b3 ♗f8 16 ♗b2 g6

Re-routing. Again, one would think that a computer would develop with 16...♖c8 or perhaps recentralize by 16...♘c6, especially since ♘f5 isn't a threat yet.

17 ♖e2 ♗g7 18 ♕e1 ♖c8 19 ♖d1 *(D)*

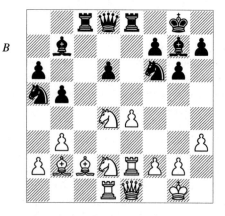

19...♘h5!

A scary position for humans, as the machine has grasped the essence of modernity! A backward isolated d-pawn on an open file, two fianchettoed bishops, and two knights on the rim (the one on a5 has been there for 11 moves and done its work, but of course the one on h5 is just *en route*). Leko on the other hand has developed all of his pieces to exert maximum influence in the centre and yet has serious difficulties.

20 ♗b1 ♘f4

The knights will return to the centre with effect.

21 ♖e3 ♕f6!?

As Luther says: "a typical computer move. The queen is not afraid to move onto the diagonal of the opponent's bishop."

22 ♘2f3 ♘c6

No more knights on the rim.

23 ♔h2

Hoping to drive the knight away by g3.

23...♘e5! 24 g3?

A tactical error. White should play 24 ♘xe5 dxe5 25 ♘f3 ♕e6 with complications, according to Luther.

24...♘d5! 25 exd5

No more backward pawn.

25...♘xf3+ 26 ♘xf3 ♖xe3 27 ♗xf6 ♖xe1 28 ♘xe1 ♗xf6

Two bishops and control of the open file will normally win, sometimes very easily. The rest of the game is played imperfectly by Black, but generally well enough.

29 ♗e4 h5 30 ♔g2 h4 31 g4 ♖c3 32 ♘f3 g5 33 ♘g1 ♖c5 34 ♘e2 b4 35 ♔f3 ♔g7 36 ♔e3 ♗d8 37 f4 ♗b6 38 ♔f3 ♔f6 39 fxg5+ ♔xg5 40 ♖d2 a5 41 ♖c2 ♖xd5 42 ♘f4 ♖e5 43 ♗xb7 ♖e3+ 44 ♔g2 ♖g3+ 45 ♔h2 ♔xf4 46 ♗g2 ♖d3 47 ♖e2 ♗e3 48 ♗c6 d5 49 ♗e8 ♔f3 0-1

An extremely interesting positional game reflecting the new pragmatism of computer play, in this case the willingness to play several classically anti-positional moves.

I have generally avoided correspondence games because it is over-the-board decisions that I am largely (although not exclusively) concerned with, i.e., whether players think in abstract or concrete terms and how typically modern their natural ideas are. It would be silly to make that a hard-and-fast rule if for no other reason than that any strategic vision that characterizes an age should be reflected in all forms

of the game (even blitz chess!). Thus correspondence games must also reflect the spirit of the times. Sanakoev's book *World Champion at the Third Attempt* covers many years of creative play. His play in the following game from three decades ago is surprisingly modern and would probably seem impractical to most strong players since Black accepts a dismal-looking, cramped position. But it takes a certain soundness in one's systems to play in the correspondence world championship, so we should not lightly dismiss this one. In fact, similar strategies are being seen more often today and may prove to be theoretically acceptable. The game is at any rate an illustration of how an elastic position can tie the opponent down to preventative measures and then explode into activity in the middlegame.

Game 17
Shmulenson – Sanakoev
corr. 1972-5

1 e4 c5 2 ♘f3 g6 3 d4 ♗g7 4 d5 d6 5 ♘c3 ♘f6 6 ♗b5+ ♘bd7 7 a4 0-0 8 0-0 a6 9 ♗e2 b6!?

An odd move that concedes White his space advantage for the foreseeable future. Instead, Black normally strives to claim territory of his own via 9...♘e8 and ...♘c7, often with ...♖b8, preparing ...b5 to stake out his own territorial claim.

10 ♘d2

The plan with 10 ♗f4 and 11 ♕d2 looks more challenging, but White follows a standard strategy of clamping down on Black's counterplay while he frees his f-pawn for a central advance.

10...♗b7!? *(D)*

An even more eccentric move: ...♗b7 is traditionally considered inappropriate because it bites on granite (the d5-pawn) and blocks the idea of ...♖b8 and ...b5. Playing so slowly is provocative, and a test of how much Black can get away with while reorganizing his pieces. Elasticity and prophylaxis become the central themes here.

11 f4 ♘e8

Only now, because White's centre can become overextended or at any rate a target after ...e6.

12 ♘c4 ♕b8

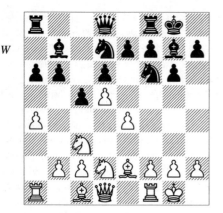

W

This not only indirectly supports ...b5 but also prepares ...e6 under the right circumstances. Still, Black's development looks artificial and passive at first glance.

13 ℤa3!? ♘c7 14 ℤb3!

This creative rook-lift spoils Black's plans by putting pressure on b6. Or does it?

14...b5!

A shocking decision that commits to exchanging Black's powerful king's bishop (arguably his only strong piece) in order to achieve queenside play. It also depends upon the speculative attack that Black is effectively forced to follow up with.

15 axb5 ♗xc3 16 ℤxc3

Maybe the paradoxical 16 bxc3 is a good idea, to maintain pressure on b5 even at the cost of creating weaknesses. But that isn't clear at all, and it's hard to believe that Black could possibly have enough play against 16 ℤxc3.

16...axb5 17 ♘e3 ℤa4! *(D)*

As Sanakoev comments, Black uses concrete threats to compensate for his disadvantages.

18 ℤa3

'!' according to Sanakoev, although Black seems to get plenty of counterplay. On the other hand, 18 ♗f3 e6! (Sanakoev suggests 18...♗a6 19 b3 ℤa1, but the direct central attack looks better) 19 dxe6 ♘xe6 both makes it hard for White to defend e4 and prepares ...♘d4. Much as in the Hedgehog structures that are so popular in modern times, Black's play has seemingly come out of nowhere. This is the 'coiled spring' effect of an elastic position, so called by Suba and commented upon by Marović.

18...ℤd4

Sanakoev thinks that this move is inaccurate. Instead, he prefers 18...ℤxe4 19 ♗d3 ℤxe3! (19...ℤa4 also looks fine; e.g., 20 ℤxa4 bxa4 21 c4 ♕a7) 20 ♗xe3 b4 and ...♘xd5, which certainly looks like enough for an exchange, especially since Black has two extra centre pawns. Thus Black's whole idea with ...b5 and ...♗xc3 seems justified.

19 ♕e1 ℤxe4 20 ♗d3 ℤd4?

"Black simply overlooks his opponent's brilliant reply." The obvious 20...ℤxe3 21 ♗xe3 b4 22 ℤa1 ♘xd5 again gives Black sufficient play.

21 ♘f5!!

A beautiful illustration of opposing dynamic ideas. This purely tactical shot should cancel out all of Black's positional gains in the centre and win the game.

21...b4

The immediate 21...gxf5 22 ♗xf5 is very similar, but ...b4 can be handy to have in.

22 ℤb3 gxf5 23 ♗xf5 ♘f6

23...ℤd8? 24 ♕h4 ♘f8 (24...♘f6 25 ♕h6 wins for White) 25 ℤh3 is too strong.

24 ℤh3 *(D)*

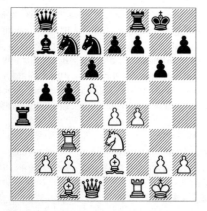

W

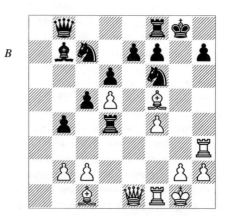

B

"What now?" asks Sanakoev. In spite of Black's inaccuracies, it's hard to believe that his active and logical destruction of White's centre can fail to hold the balance. White threatens 25 ♕g3+ ♔h8 26 ♗xh7 ♘xh7 27 ♕h4, among other things. Black finds the only idea:

24...♖c8!

An excellent defensive idea, even if not fully sufficient. 24...♖d8 is similar, but everything else fails immediately: 24...♗xd5? 25 ♕g3+ ♔h8 26 ♖xh7+! ♘xh7 27 ♕h4, 24...♗c8? 25 ♖g3+ ♔h8 26 ♕xe7 or 24...♘cxd5? 25 ♕h4 (Sanakoev gives 25 ♕g3+ ♔h8 26 ♕h4, but this may be a glitch, since then 26...♗c8 holds).

25 ♕g3+

25 ♖xh7 ♘xh7 26 ♕g3+ ♔f8 transposes.

25...♔f8 26 ♖xh7 ♘xh7 27 ♗xh7 ♔c8 28 ♕g8+ ♔d7 29 ♗f5+ ♘e6 30 dxe6+ ♔c6 31 ♕xf7 ♔b6 32 ♕xe7 ♗xg2!?

As good a try as any, since White's passed pawns are too strong for anything else to hold.

33 ♔xg2 ♖g8+ 34 ♔f2 ♕a8 35 ♖g1 ½-½

Here the players agreed to a draw. Unfortunately (or fortunately?) this game was played before the chess computer revolution, or Sanakoev would have realized that White was winning after 35...♖xg1 36 ♔xg1:

a) 36...♕f3 37 ♕d8+ ♔b7 38 ♗d3!; e.g., 38...♕g4+ (38...♕d1+ 39 ♔g2 ♕xc1 40 ♗e4+ ♖xe4 41 ♕d7+ and White picks up the rook by force!) 39 ♔f2 ♖xf4+ 40 ♗xf4 ♕xf4+ 41 ♔e1 ♕e3+ 42 ♗e2 ♕g1+ 43 ♔d2 ♕d4+ 44 ♔c1 ♕e3+ 45 ♔b1 ♕xe2 46 ♕d7+, etc.

b) 36...♖d1+ 37 ♔f2 ♕h1 38 ♕d8+ and Sanakoev says: "White gives perpetual check". However, the beasts (*Fritz, Hiarcs, Junior*, etc.) immediately discover that this isn't the case: 38...♔b7 (38...♔a7 39 ♗h3 is just as good) 39 ♗h3!! and astonishingly, the white king escapes to f3! But regardless of the flawed finish, this was a great battle and especially instructive for its unlikely dynamic counterplay from a cramped position.

Game 18
Hodgson – Adams
Wijk aan Zee 1993

Games with the Trompowsky Attack tend to ignore the classical rules more than those stemming from any other opening. This game is in that sense typical. A flank move on move 3 surrenders the two bishops, knights develop to the rim, doubled pawns are debated, and finally the two knights beat the two bishops in an open position without outposts.

1 d4 ♘f6 2 ♗g5

It's always fun to talk about the Trompowsky, since the bishop develops on only the second move and because it took so very long to catch on. Right away we have a violation of 'knights before bishops', and play extraordinarily often takes a radically untraditional path. One might say: 'Oh, but that's such an exceptional opening that it really doesn't help to make a case about modern play'. That sounds plausible until you realize how accepted 2 ♗g5 has become. My main database has just under 14,000 games with it – more than, for example, the Dragon Variation, the Scandinavian Defence, far more than the Classical French after 4 ♗g5 ♗e7, and about the same as the Najdorf Variation. And the Trompowsky is not just a favourite of certain lower-strength players. In my database of the top 20 players from 1985 to 2002, 2 ♗g5 occurred in their games in almost exactly the same percentage as in the chess population as a whole.

2...♘e4 3 h4!? (D)

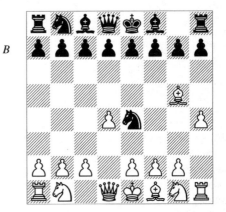

This rather amazing move offers to give up the bishop-pair and take on doubled pawns for ... an open file and a space advantage! Once again, this may look like a mere curiosity, and yet after 2...♘e4, about 850 of those Trompowskys are with this move, well over half as many as 3 ♗h4 and about a fifth as many as the popular 3 ♗f4. Granted, 3 h4 is currently still a bit much for the world's super-elite, but players like Hodgson (at 2565 for this game) are not exactly chopped liver, and a number of strong grandmasters have given it a whirl.

3...c5

There are several reasonable moves here, and I won't go into the theory.

4 d5 ♘xg5 5 hxg5 g6

White has ideas of g6 in this line, crippling Black's pawn-structure; this move puts an end to that notion while taking over the long diagonal.

6 ♘c3 d6 7 a4

A sort of waiting flank move (White still only has one piece out!), which in some cases intends a5, but also provides for a defence to his weakened squares along the a1-h8 diagonal.

7...♗g7 8 ♕d2 ♕b6!

A typical harassment move. Bringing the queen out before the other pieces is increasingly common, and typical of this variation.

9 ♖a2!? (D)

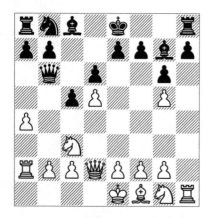

What can one say? Hodgson's play is typically creative, but also logical. This was one of the main points of 7 a4 (which therefore should probably get the '!?' instead), along with discouraging ...b5 at some point.

9...♘a6!

Black really isn't intending ...♘b4, but the knight is better placed here on the edge than on d7, where it can't go to f6 and gets in the way of the bishop. A very complex line results from 9...♕b4 10 ♘f3 with the idea ♖h4. Then, so early in the game, White would have committed both rooks to eccentric squares and forfeited castling, but the king is well placed in the

centre, e.g. for an ending. For example, 10...0-0 11 ♖h4 ♗xc3 12 ♕xc3 ♕xc3+ 13 bxc3 and we have a position whose assessment could be debated, but I like White's activity and space. If Black tries to stop e4 by 13...f5, then 14 e3 e5 15 a5 (15 ♘d2 b6 16 a5 and White has the edge) 15...♘d7 16 ♘d2 ♖d8 17 ♘c4 ♘f8 18 f4 is one possibility that probably favours White.

10 e4 0-0 11 ♗xa6!

Another remarkable move. White decides to pit his two knights against the bishop-pair, with no existing outposts nor particular prospects of one.

11...bxa6!

Better than 11...♕xa6 12 ♘ge2, when Black has to be careful about the attack following ♕f4-h4. Notice too that Black would have lost his chance to play ...♗xc3+ and after bxc3, ...♕b1+. As we have described in SOMCS, the doubled pawns on the a-file are often an advantage because of counterplay along the b-file. Here the two sides will try to prove each other wrong about their mutual decision.

12 ♘ge2 ♖b8 (D)

12...f6!? makes sense, to neutralize the ♕f4-h4 idea. But Adams isn't too worried about that.

13 ♕f4!?

This isn't as dangerous as in the ...♕xa6 case, because Black is able to play actively down the b-file and prevent any further pieces (such as the e2-knight) from joining White's attack. 13 a5 ♕b4 14 ♕f4 is probably more accurate, to prevent Black's next move. Black might then have more trouble finding a concrete plan.

13...♕a5

The queen doesn't do a great deal here, but the ideas of ...♖xb2 and ...♗b4 are irritating for White. Another move is 13...♕d8 (helping out on the kingside dark squares) 14 ♕h4 h5 15 gxh6 ♗f6 16 ♕g3 ♔h7 intending 17 f4 e5.

14 ♕h4 h5 15 gxh6 ♗f6!

15...♗xc3+ 16 ♘xc3! (16 bxc3 ♖b1+ 17 ♔d2 also favours White) 16...♖xb2 17 ♔d2! ♖xa2 18 ♕xe7, and to avoid ♕f6, Black has to play 18...♕d8 19 ♕xd8 ♖xc2+ 20 ♔xc2 ♖xd8 21 ♔b3! intending 21...♗d7 22 e5! dxe5 23 ♘e4 hitting all of Black's weaknesses.

16 ♕g3

White could also try 16 h7+ ♔h8 17 ♕h6 ♗g7 18 ♕e3 followed by ♔f1, g3, ♔g2 or even ♔d1. The whole position is incredibly hard to assess.

16...♗b4! 17 0-0!?

It's hard to give up fantasies of attack, but now White decides that it's time to pay attention to the queenside as well. 17 ♕e3!? is an interesting option to try to enforce f4. It might be met by 17...♔h7 (17...♗d4 18 ♕d2 ♗f6 19 ♘d1!) 18 f4 (18 ♕d2 ♗d7 19 ♘d1 ♖fb8 20 f3! ♕d8 is unclear) 18...e5!.

17...♔h7 18 ♘c1!?

18 f4 e5! 19 fxe5 ♗xe5 20 ♕h4 f6 looks fine for Black.

18...c4

Necessary to stop ♘b3; now Black has ceded d4, but that needn't be important.

19 ♕e3?

White misses Black's next. Better was 19 ♘1e2! ♔xh6 20 f4, intending e5; for example, 20...♕b6+ 21 ♖f2 ♖xb2?! (21...♕c7) 22 ♖xb2 ♕xb2 23 e5.

19...♕b6! 20 ♕xb6?!

20 ♕d2 ♖xb2 21 ♖xb2 ♕xb2 22 ♘1a2 intending ♖b1, but White's pieces aren't coordinating very well and Black must be better.

20...♖xb6?!

20...axb6! and a4 is too weak: 21 ♘d1 ♗d7 22 a5 bxa5 23 ♖xa5 ♖a4 24 ♖xa4 ♗xa4 and the bishops reign.

21 ♘d1! (D)

This is a very strange set-up with a rook on a2 and two knights on the bank rank! What's more, Black has two active bishops with opportunities for central breaks like ...e6 and ...f5. Of course White has play because of the weaknesses on a7, a6, and c4. But his position is so

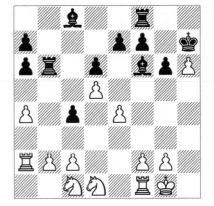

passive that it's hard to imagine those being influential factors. In fact, my computer engines, so often sensitive to pawn-structure defects, both like Black here. If you follow my advice from SOMCS, White should make some active change in the pawn-structure to secure himself outposts (or should already have done so). In what follows, he does no such thing, but slowly but surely makes his knights superior to two bishops on an open board! This is another illustration of how there are few reliable strategic rules or even recommended procedures in chess. The specifics of this position dominate, and I have to admit that what I've said elsewhere about knight and bishop-pairs just doesn't apply.

21...♗d7 22 c3 ♖fb8

To prevent White from playing ♘e3 and tying Black to the c-pawn.

23 f4 ♔xh6

23...e6?! is weak because of 24 ♘e3 ♖xb2 (24...♖c8 25 dxe6 fxe6 26 e5!) 25 ♖xb2 ♖xb2 26 e5! and Black is clearly worse.

24 ♖f2 ♗h4 25 ♖d2 ♗f6

25...g5!? is a hard move to make, but it creates complications, which are desirable here.

26 ♘e3 ♖c8 27 ♘e2 a5 28 ♘d4

Finally using that d4-square that we noticed earlier.

28...♔h7 29 ♔f2

Or 29 ♘f3!, to enforce e5. Suddenly Black's bishops look weak on the open board.

29...♔g8 30 ♘f3 ♗g7 31 g4 ♖c5 32 g5

Expanding on the kingside and making further breaks by Black even more weakening.

32...♖b8 33 ♔g3 f6?!

Impatient, but it would be hard to sit around watching White improve his position.

34 gxf6 exf6 35 ②h4 ☐e8 36 ☆f3 ☆f7 37 f5

37 ☐g2! f5 (37...g5!? fails to 38 ②hf5!) 38 exf5 gxf5 39 ②hxf5 is too good.

37...g5 38 ②g6 ☐b8 39 ☐a1 ☐b7 40 ☐h2

Now White can play a number of ideas, e.g. ☐ah1, ☐h7, and ②g4. The game ends more simply.

40...♗e8 41 ②g4 ☆g8 42 ☐ah1 ☐cc7

Or 42...♗xa4 43 ②h6+.

43 ☐h8+ ♗xh8 44 ☐xh8+ ☆g7 45 ☐xe8 ☐xb2 46 ②f8! ☆f7 47 ☐a8 ☐cb7 48 ②e6 1-0

A strange and unstereotyped game.

The theme of the next game is flank versus centre, although we also get to see the white king dance around in 19th-century style.

Game 19
Shabalov – Karklins
USA 1998

1 ②f3 ②f6 2 c4 e6 3 ②c3 ♗b4 4 g4!? *(D)*

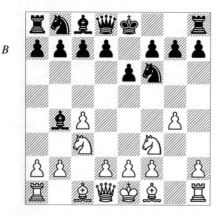

I've mentioned this move before, violating the strictures against flank pawn advances when undeveloped in the most extreme fashion!

4...h6

A fascinating juncture. Black avoids playing 4...②xg4 5 ☐g1 when the g-pawn falls. The first interesting thing here is that the thematic central counter to White's flank advance is disadvantageous: 4...d5 5 g5 ②e4 6 ♕a4+ ②c6 7 ②xe4 dxe4 8 ②e5 e3! (forced) 9 fxe3 ♕xg5 10 ②f3 (10 ②xc6 ♗d7! 11 ♕xb4 ♗xc6) 10...♕e7 11 a3 ♗d6 12 d4 ♗d7 13 ♕c2 and White was better in Krasenkow-Gild.Garcia, Groningen FIDE 1997. See SOMCS for the game's conclusion.

Furthermore, after 4...0-0 5 g5 ②e8, White was happy to forfeit castling by 6 ☐g1! in the recent game Vaïsser-A.Sokolov, France 2002. That game *again* saw the natural central response 6...d5 7 ♕b3 ♗xc3 (7...c5 8 cxd5 ♗xc3 9 ♕xc3 must favour White's bishops) 8 ♕xc3, and now 8...②d6!? was played, while Sokolov mentions 8...②c6 9 b4! d4 10 ♕b2 a6 11 e3 dxe3 12 dxe3 with an edge for White. Notice the space-grabbing advances on both flanks.

5 ☐g1!? c5 6 h4!? ②c6

For the third time, central play doesn't seem the best reaction to flank play: 6...d5 7 g5! hxg5 8 hxg5 ②e4 *(D)*.

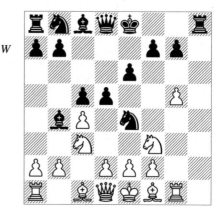

9 ♕c2 (9 g6!?) 9...②xc3 (9...♗xc3 10 dxc3 ②c6 11 g6 f5 12 cxd5 exd5 13 ♗f4) 10 dxc3 ♗a5 11 g6 f6 12 cxd5 exd5 13 ♗f4 and White stands clearly better (analysis by Bronznik).

7 g5! hxg5 8 hxg5 ②g8 9 g6! f5 10 a3 ♗a5 11 e4! ②f6

11...♕f6 is a reasonable possibility. White can fight for the advantage by 12 ♕e2 ②d4 (12...♗c7 13 ②b5 ♗b8 14 d4 cxd4 15 ♗g5 ♕xg6 16 exf5 ♕xf5 17 ②bxd4 ②xd4 18 ②xd4 ♕e5 19 ♗e3 with a small advantage) 13 ②xd4 cxd4 14 e5 ♕h4 15 ②b5 with an advantage in view of moves like ②d6+ and ②f7 or b4 and ♗b2.

12 ②g5! ②g4!?

This looks as though it should be almost decisive, sacrificing some material for a deadly-looking attack, but Shabalov has seen his way through it. Bronznik analyses instead 12...②e5 13 ☐b1! ②xg6 (13...♕e7 14 b4! cxb4 15 axb4 ♗xb4 16 ②b5 with the idea ☐xb4! and ♗a3; e.g., 16...☐b8 17 ☐xb4 ♕xb4 18 ♗a3 ♕a5 19

♗d6! and White wins) 14 b4 ♗b6 (or 14...cxb4 15 axb4 ♗b6 16 d4) 15 bxc5 ♖xc5 16 d4 'with more than enough compensation for the sacrificed pawn'.

13 ♘f7 ♕h4 14 ♖xg4 fxg4 15 ♘xh8 *(D)*

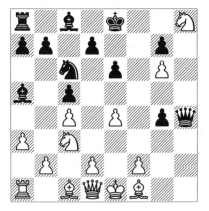

B

15...♘d4?

This isn't well enough calculated. At least 15...♕xh8! 16 ♕xg4 ♘d4 gives some compensation for the pawn, although not enough; e.g., 17 ♖a2!? ♕h1 (17...♘b3 18 ♔d1 ♕h1 19 ♕h3 ♕xh3 20 ♗xh3) 18 ♕g2 ♕h5 19 b4!? (19 ♗e2 ♘xe2 20 ♘xe2 is simpler) 19...cxb4 20 axb4 ♗xb4 21 ♘b5 ♘xb5 22 cxb5 intending ♗b2 or perhaps ♖c2 and ♗b2. 22...♕c5 23 ♔d1 doesn't help much.

16 ♘f7! ♘f3+

16...g3 17 ♗g2 gxf2+ 18 ♔f1 and White wins.

17 ♔e2 ♘d4+ 18 ♔e3! *(D)*

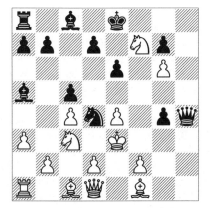

B

This king march, foreseen by Shabalov, effectively decides the game.

18...♗c7 19 ♘b5! ♘xb5 20 cxb5 d5 21 ♗g2 ♗d7

21...♕h5!? 22 ♕h1! ♕xg6 23 ♘h8! ♕g5+ 24 ♔e2 and White will drive the queen away.

22 a4 c4

22...d4+ 23 ♔d3 c4+ 24 ♔xc4 e5 25 ♔d3! and the king returns with his booty.

23 ♕h1

Again ignoring Black's petty threats.

23...♗b6+ 24 d4! cxd3+ 25 ♔xd3 ♕xf2 26 ♕h8+ ♔e7 27 ♗g5+ 1-0

Game 20
Salinnikov – Miroshnichenko
Ukraine 2000

Continuing with flank attacks, this game features an experimental and eccentric opening play followed by entertaining tactics.

1 e4 c5 2 ♘f3 d6 3 c3 ♘f6 4 h3!? ♘c6

It would be sad to fall for 4...♘xe4?? 5 ♕a4+.

5 ♗d3 *(D)*

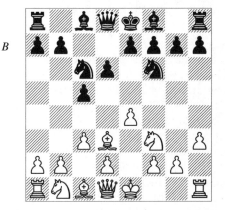

B

Showing to what extent players are willing to go to get original positions. In the last decade, this eccentric set-up has been a surprisingly popular alternative to the normal open lines with 3 d4. My TWIC database, for example, has more than 200 games with 4 h3, almost all of them followed by 5 ♗d3. Sometimes called 'The Kopec System', its point is to follow up with ♗c2 and d4.

5...e5

Black seems to aiming for a Ruy Lopez sort of position. But he should definitely also consider answering one strange move with another by 5...d5!?, moving the d-pawn twice within five moves, because 6 e5 ♘d7 7 e6!? (7 ♕e2 is sounder, when 7...♕c7!? should be fine after either 8 ♗b5 e6 or 8 e6 fxe6 9 ♘g5 ♘f6; and Black can always just play 7...e6) 7...fxe6 8 ♘g5 ♘f6 looks at least equal for Black; e.g., 9 ♕e2 (9 0-0 g6 10 ♗c2 e5; 9 ♕c2 g6) 9...e5 (9...g6 10 h4 e5 11 h5 e4) 10 ♗xh7?! (10 ♗c2 e4) 10...♘xh7 11 ♕h5+ ♔d7 12 ♘xh7 ♔c7 and Black is clearly better.

6 0-0 *(D)*

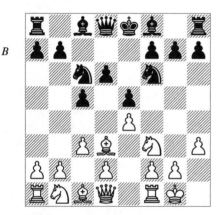

6...g5!

Is there nothing sacred? The natural 6...♗e7 had been played before numerous times, when among other ideas Black can continue with 7 ♗c2 0-0 8 d4 ♕c7 and try to play some kind of Chigorin Ruy Lopez without ...♘a5-c6.

Of course, once you see it, the idea behind 6...g5! is pretty obvious, if not the details and risks. This is one of those cases where the centre is secure and Black's development is satisfactory, so at least some traditional criteria for a flank attack are met. Nevertheless, one feels the influence of the times! Miroshnichenko even assigns 6...g5 a '!!', although White has some decent replies that produce a dynamic balance.

7 ♘xg5?

This is too cooperative, but White was either planning his sacrifice or missed the idea in the next note. Miroshnichenko suggests 7 ♗c4 g4!? (7...♖g8 8 d4 g4 9 ♘g5 ♖g7 seems fine in view of 10 ♕b3 cxd4!? 11 ♗xf7+ ♔e7 and Black stands better!) 8 ♘g5 d5 9 exd5 ♘xd5, but then 10 d4! is attractive. Thus 7...♖g8 is probably preferable.

7...♖g8 8 f4!?

Miroshnichenko gives the line 8 h4 h6 9 ♘f3 ♗h3 10 ♘e1 which temporarily saves the pawn, but there follows 10...♘h5!! hitting h4 and f4, and 11 ♕xh5 ♗g4 traps the queen!

8...exf4 9 ♘xf7!? ♔xf7 10 ♗c4+ d5!

Wild and unclear play results from 10...♗e6 11 ♗xe6+ ♔xe6 12 d4.

11 ♗xd5+

Not 11 exd5? ♘a5.

11...♘xd5 12 ♕h5+ ♔e6! 13 ♕f5+

Maybe 13 d4 should be tried, just to develop at all costs.

13...♔e7 14 ♕xh7+ ♖g7 15 ♕h4+ ♔d7?!

Not bad, but Black seems to win outright by 15...♔d6! 16 ♕xd8+ ♘xd8 17 exd5 ♗xh3 as given by Miroshnichenko.

16 ♕xd8+ ♔xd8 17 exd5 ♘e5 *(D)*

White's material situation isn't bad, yet he is practically lost in the face of Black's threats.

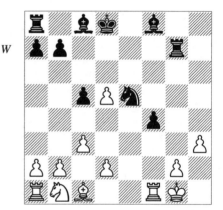

18 ♖xf4?!

18 g4 has several good replies like 18...♘d3!. The most dynamic solution would be 18...♗d6 19 d4 cxd4 20 cxd4 ♘xg4 21 hxg4 ♗xg4 with too much attack. 18 d4 ♘d3 gives Black a huge advantage, but the text-move leaves no hope at all. The game finished very prettily:

18...♗xh3! 19 d4

If White grabs the material by 19 ♖xf8+ ♔d7 20 ♖xa8 (20 ♖f2 ♘d3! decides) Black has mate in four by 20...♖xg2+ 21 ♔f1 (21 ♔h1 ♘f3!) 21...♖xd2+ 22 ♔g1 ♘f3+ 23 ♔h1 ♖d1#.

19...♖xg2+ 20 ♔h1 ♘d3! 21 ♖xf8+ ♔e7 22 ♖f3 ♘f2+ 23 ♖xf2 ♖xf2 24 ♗g5+ ♔d7 25 ♘d2 ♖e8 0-1

Since 26...♖ee2 follows. A creative and fun game.

Game 21
Kramnik – Leko
Tilburg 1998

(The analytical notes to this game are predominately by Leko and Adorjan, with all comments and occasional moves from the author.)

1 d4 ♘f6 2 c4 g6 3 f3 e5!?

This original and yet logical idea was mentioned in Chapter 1. It is amazing that after a century of Black playing 3...d5 or 3...d6 (or occasionally 3...c5), a previously unknown and effective move like this could be discovered.

4 dxe5

Two alternatives are 4 d5 e4! 5 ♘c3 exf3 (5...d6!?) 6 exf3 d6 7 ♕e2+ ♕e7 8 ♕xe7+ ♔xe7 with equality, and 4 ♗g5 h6 5 ♗h4 ♘c6!? (5...exd4 6 ♕xd4 ♗g7 7 ♕e3+ ♔f8 is also satisfactory, as Black develops quickly and has ...♔g8-h7 in reserve) 6 d5 ♘d4 7 ♘c3 c5! 8 e3 ♘f5 9 ♗f2 h5 intending ...♗h6 with counterplay.

4...♘h5

Knights to the edge!

5 ♘h3!

Both sides can play the flank game. 5 g3 does very poorly after 5...♘c6 (or 5...d6) 6 f4 d6 7 ♗g2 ♗e6! 8 exd6 ♗xd6.

5...♘c6 6 ♗g5 ♗e7 7 ♗xe7 ♕xe7 8 ♘c3! *(D)*

Too greedy is 8 f4? ♕b4+ 9 ♕d2 d6!.

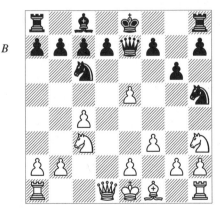

8...♕xe5!?

Not best, and perhaps leading to a small advantage for White. 8...0-0! is better:

a) 9 ♘d5 ♕xe5 10 ♕d2 ♘e7! 11 f4 ♕d6 12 g3 c6! 13 ♘xe7+ ♕xe7 14 ♗g2 d5! 15 cxd5 ♗xh3 16 ♗xh3 ♖ad8 17 ♗g2 ♘f6 and Black is better.

b) 9 g4 ♘g7 10 f4 ♕b4! 11 ♕d2 d6 is also good for Black.

c) 9 e4! ♕xe5 10 ♕d2 d6 11 f4 (11 ♘f2 f5) 11...♕d4! 12 ♕xd4 ♘xd4 13 0-0-0 c5! 14 g3 ♘f6 15 ♘f2 ♘g4! (or 15...♗d7).

9 g4! ♘g7

Black is again fairly happy with his fianchettoed knight, because it can support ...f5 and ...h5. White doesn't allow this, but weakens his position in preventing it. Leko also mentions 9...♘f6!?, which is probably also slightly better for White.

10 f4 ♕e7 11 ♘d5 ♕d8 12 ♕d3!?

12 ♗g2 keeps a small edge.

12...0-0 13 ♕c3 ♘e8!

It's hard to believe that Black's knight tour ...♘g8-f6-h5-g7-e8 can be effective, with the knight ending up so passively placed. But the key squares f6 and c7 are now defended and Black is ready to play ...♘e7.

14 g5 ♘e7 15 ♘f6+?

Correct is 15 ♘f2 ♘xd5 16 cxd5 d6, which is unclear with ...f6 to come.

15...♘xf6 16 gxf6 ♘f5 17 e4 ♖e8 18 ♘g5 c5!! *(D)*

Leko's annotation. By securing d4, Black actually gains the advantage, even though it looks at first as though White should simply be able to sacrifice the exchange and stand much better.

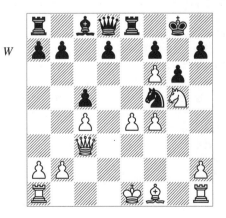

19 0-0-0 ♘d4 20 e5

The extremely natural exchange sacrifice 20 ♖xd4? cxd4 21 ♕xd4 fails to the counterattack 21...h6!, and now:

a) A pretty and surprising line follows the apparently suicidal 22 h4 hxg5!! 23 hxg5 d5! (intending to defend by ...♗g4-h5) 24 ♕f2 ♗g4 25 ♗e2 (Black wins after 25 ♕h4 ♗h5 26 ♗e2 ♕b6 27 ♗xh5 ♕e3+ 28 ♔b1 ♖xe4+ 29 ♔a1 gxh5) 25...♗xe2 26 ♕xe2 ♕c7, winning. One idea is 27 ♕h2 ♕xc4+ 28 ♔b1 ♖xe4+ 29 ♔a1 ♕e1+ 30 ♖xe1 ♖xe1#.

b) 22 ♘f3 b5!? 23 f5!? ♗b7 24 ♗d3 (24 fxg6 ♖xe4 25 gxf7+ ♔xf7 26 ♘e5+ ♖xe5 27 ♕xe5 ♗xh1 28 ♕h5+ ♔xf6) 24...bxc4 25 ♗c2 ♕b6 with a large plus for Black.

These lines seem counter-intuitive. It would certainly be hard to resist playing 20 ♖xd4 quickly and then thinking later!

20...d6 21 ♘f3!? ♗g4 22 ♘xd4 ♗xd1 23 ♘b5 dxe5 24 fxe5 ♗a4! 25 ♘d6 ♖e6! 26 ♗g2 ♖xd6!

After 26...♗c6 27 ♗xc6 bxc6 28 ♖d1 White has what he wants for the exchange. So Black gives it back and takes pleasure in the weaknesses in White's camp.

27 exd6 ♕xd6 28 ♗xb7 ♖e8 29 b3 ♕f4+ 30 ♔b2 ♖e3 31 ♖d1 h5 32 ♕a5 ♖e2+

Also advantageous is 32...♕xf6+!? 33 ♔a3 ♗e8 34 ♕xc5 ♖e2.

33 ♔a3 ♕f2 34 ♕d8+ ♗e8 35 ♖d2!

35 ♖a1? loses to 35...♕e3! 36 ♗c6 ♕c3!.

35...♖xd2 36 ♕xe8+ ♔h7 37 ♕xf7+ ♔h6 38 ♔a4 ♖xa2+ 39 ♔b5 ♕e3

39...♖b2!? is also good.

40 ♗d5 ♕xb3+ 41 ♔c6

Both kings march, but White's proves more vulnerable.

41...♖a6+!

Not 41...♕b8? 42 ♔d7!.

42 ♔d7 (D)

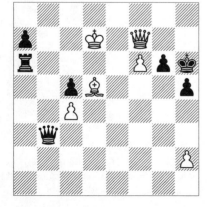

42...♕h3+! 43 ♗e6

Black switches to the winning endgame after 43 ♔e7 ♕xh2 44 ♕f8+ ♔g5 45 f7 ♕c7+ 46 ♔e8 ♕c8+ 47 ♔e7 ♕xf8+ 48 ♔xf8 ♖f6.

43...♕d3+ 44 ♔e8

Again the king hides successfully following 44 ♗d5 ♔g5! 45 ♕e7 ♖xf6 46 h4+ ♔f5 47 ♕xc5 ♔g4 and White has run out of resources.

44...♕d6 45 ♕e7 ♕xe6 0-1

There follows 46 f7 ♕c8+ 47 ♕d8 ♖e6+.

Bronznik brings attention to the next game as an example of flank pawn advances versus a classical centre. White keeps two centre pawns on the second rank and another on the third while dancing around with his pieces on the edge of the board. One should also notice the early commitment on White's part to forego castling, and the development of the rooks on wing files and across the ranks. White's play as a whole is almost a satire on rule-breaking. I don't think that this game proves anything about the superiority of flank play or central play, but it does demonstrate the legitimacy of a very flexible and latently dynamic set-up against even the solidest of positions. This reminds one of the Hedgehog systems as Black, certain Sicilian Defences with ...b5 and ...h5, and many variations of the English Opening as White. In addition, we get an example of both a queenside flank pawn advance (rare in my exposition of wing play) and a kingside pawn attack at the end.

Game 22
Nadanian – Ponomariov
Kiev 1997

1 ♘f3 d5 2 b4

A rather bold flank advance against Ponomariov, who is not only one of the world's best players but very much at home with the classical central development that he now pursues.

2...♗g4 3 ♗b2 ♘d7 4 b5!?

Essentially this is just a space-grabber, as opposed to the more conventional 4 e3 or 4 a3.

4...♘gf6 5 a4!?

An extremely ambitious move, both allowing doubled pawns and ignoring development. White is trying to create early queenside weaknesses or in some cases just to support the cramping b5-pawn.

5...♗xf3 6 gxf3 e5 7 ♖g1! (D)

This is really getting strange! But there is logic in the move, which prevents the development of the f8-bishop without playing ...g6, which in turn creates some weakness along the a1-h8 diagonal. '!' for originality.

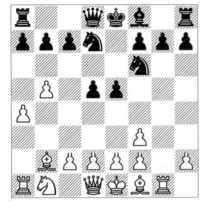

7...g6 8 e3 ♗c5

As Bronznik explains, Black is playing very 'regularly': grabbing the centre, developing his pieces, and preparing castling. He gives some analysis on the alternative 8...♗g7: 9 ♗a3 c5 10 bxc6 bxc6 11 ♘c3 c5 12 ♖b1 ♖b8 13 ♗h3, but perhaps this is mainly a whimsical attempt to get both rooks to the knight's files and both bishops to the rook's files on the third rank!

9 a5!? (D)

White pursues his seemingly bizarre quest on the queenside. It's hardly worth mentioning any more that he doesn't develop or move a central pawn.

9...0-0 10 a6! b6

10...bxa6 11 ♖xa6 is positionally nice for White.

11 ♖a4!

Not only a fourth-rank rook-lift, but this supports a potential f4. Oddly enough, my analysis engine gives White the tiniest of edges here, when one would expect the severest machine disapproval.

11...♕e7 12 f4!?

Perhaps this is a bit much. I think that it was time to get a piece out by 12 ♘c3, especially since 12...d4 13 ♘e2 looks surprisingly effective. Black's d4-pawn would be under pressure, whereas both f4 and ♘g3 are real prospects.

12...e4

Nadanian and Bronznik in combination give 12...d4 13 fxe5 dxe3 14 fxe3 ♘xe5 15 d4 (but maybe 15 ♗g2 gives White some advantage) 15...♘ed7 16 ♗g2! ♕xe3+ (16...♖ae8 17 dxc5 ♕xe3+ 18 ♔f1 ♘xc5 19 ♖h4! ♘fe4 20 ♗xe4 ♘xe4 21 ♗d4 is winning for White) 17 ♔f1 ♗d6 18 ♗xa8 ♖xa8 19 ♖g2 ♘d5 20 ♗c1 ♖e8 (more rook craziness follows 20...♕e7 21 c4 ♘e3+ 22 ♗xe3 ♕xe3 23 ♖aa2 with a large plus for White) 21 ♗xe3 ♘xe3+ 22 ♔e1 ♘xd1+ 23 ♔xd1 and Bronznik says that Black will have to fight for a draw. I wouldn't want to commit to an opinion about this still very complex position, but the line is certainly entertaining! Finally, I should add that Bronznik offers up the idea 12...♗d6 13 f5!, intending ♗g2 and ♘c3 with pressure on d5; this is also a difficult position to assess.

13 h4! (D)

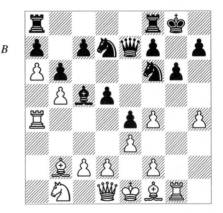

Now we have a truly remarkable situation. As Bronznik points out, White has made nine pawn moves out of thirteen, almost all on the flank. Of the four remaining moves, three have been by rooks, which incidentally has deprived him of castling rights! And of course White has allowed his pawns to be doubled. Ponomariov has by contrast played exclusively moves that secure the centre, develop pieces, and protect the king. For all of that, it is now difficult for Black to find any plan, and White has several ways to improve his position. In this regard, White's play may be said to have been primarily prophylactic.

13...♘e8 14 ♕h5

Bronznik mentions the alternatives 14 ♗g5!? and 14 h5!?. I think that both of these give White some advantage.

14...f5 15 ♕h6 ♘df6 16 ♗e2

Nadanian calls this clearly better for White, which seems correct.

16...♖f7

White answers 16...♕g7 with 17 ♕g5, and h5 is coming.

After the text-move (16...♖f7), according to both annotators, White would have gained a very large and probably winning advantage after 17 h5! ♕f8 18 ♕g5! (and even 18 ♕xf8+ ♔xf8 19 hxg6 ♖g7 20 ♖g5 hxg6 21 f3 is strong, with ♘c3 and fxe4 to follow, when the bishops are very effective). All in all, quite a demonstration of modern flexibility and neglect of development in favour of positional and prophylactic goals.

Game 23
Pelletier – Yusupov
Switzerland tt 2002

1 ♘f3 d5 2 d4 ♘f6 3 c4 e6 4 ♘c3 ♘bd7 5 ♗f4 dxc4

For a while, this looked like a sure equalizer versus ♗f4. In the line White chooses, for example, he has to give up his good bishop.

6 e3 ♘b6 7 ♗xc4 ♘xc4 8 ♕a4+ c6 9 ♕xc4 ♘d5 10 0-0!?

And now his other bishop!

10...♘xf4 11 exf4 *(D)*

White's opening has resulted in a classic case of two knights versus two bishops, and an example of the doubled f-pawn structure that we looked at in Chapter 2, Section 2. This is one of those cases where White hopes that his

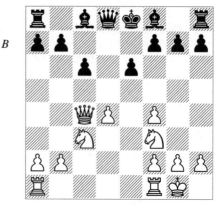

temporary lead in development and space advantage will translate into good squares for his knights before Black can get developed and free his bishops.

11...♗e7 12 ♖fe1 0-0 13 ♖ad1 a5

Pelletier feels that 13...♕b6 was better, with the idea ...♗d7, ...♖fd8, ...♗e8. That has a Laskerian look to it and has its points, because Black wants to consolidate and not allow White to open up the game. But Yusupov's plan is more active and looks adequate.

14 ♘e5 a4 15 a3 ♕a5 *(D)*

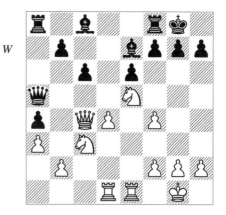

It's interesting to see how two such strong players approach this position. Now Yusupov has restrained White's queenside and put his queen on a comfortable square. He still has the problem of developing his other pieces, but that depends upon specific tactics.

16 ♖e3!?

16 ♕e2 and if 16...♕a6, 17 ♕e3 keeps a grip on the centre and potential for progress on both sides of the board.

16...♕a6

16...c5?! 17 d5 looks weak, but 16...♖d8!? is playable: 17 ♕e2 (17 f5? f6) 17...♕b6 (perhaps 17...f6 18 ♘c4 ♕c7 is safest) 18 ♖ed3, and here Pelletier assigns White a small advantage, but I'm not sure why.

17 ♕a2 b5?!

Loosening, and thus liable to give White's knights meaningful outposts. Pelletier gives 17...♖d8 18 f5!, but after 18...♗f6, it's not clear what White's up to, since 19 ♘xf7!? ♔xf7 20 fxe6+ ♔e7 apparently falls a little short. No wonder everyone loves the bishops: they are not only strong in open positions, but they can also be good defenders! Anyway, 17...♖d8 looks like the best move.

18 ♘e4 b4?

See the last note.

19 axb4 ♗xb4 20 ♕b1! f5!?

White threatens ♘g5 and this position is not easy; e.g., Pelletier analyses 20...♗e7 21 ♕c2 ♗b7 22 ♖h3 with the idea 22...h6? 23 ♘g5.

21 ♘c5 ♕b5 22 ♕c1!

White's position takes on a comic character: everything goes on dark squares! Of course, White has no dark-squared bishop to worry about.

22...♖d8 23 ♘cd3! ♗d6

One line after 23...♖xd4 24 ♘xb4 ♖xd1+ 25 ♕xd1 ♕xb4 is 26 ♕d8+!? ♕f8 27 ♕c7.

24 ♘c5 ♗e7 25 ♖c3 *(D)*

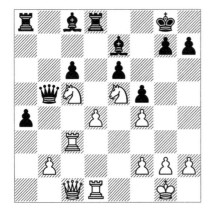

Now White has a large advantage (Pelletier), and an attractive-looking one at that.

25...♖d5 26 g3

Even the pawns shun the light squares.

26...♗d6 27 ♘f3

Pelletier prefers 27 h4.

27...h6 28 h4 ♖b8 29 ♖d2

This is getting silly, yet this last dark-square move reduces Black to near-zugzwang. He now sacrifices a pawn to gain activity.

29...♗a6!? 30 ♘xa6 ♕xa6 31 ♖xc6 ♕b7 32 ♕c4 ♔h7?! 33 ♖e2 ♕d7 34 ♕xa4 ♖db5 35 ♕a6 ♗c7 36 ♖exe6 ♖xb2 37 ♖xh6+! gxh6 38 ♖xh6+ ♔g8 39 ♕g6+ ♕g7 40 ♕e6+ ♕f7 41 ♖h8+ 1-0

A game with many themes, the most important of which might be that in this case Black with the bishop-pair had to keep lines closed until his pieces were fully developed. Thus the plan with 17...b5?! and 18...b4? has to be classified as a mistake.

Game 24

Nevednichy – M. Grünberg

Romanian Ch (Targoviste) 2001

1 e4 ♘f6

Alekhine's Defence (1...♘f6) used to be called the most hypermodern of openings. It teetered for years on the brink of respectability, but was usually looked down upon by the world's elite and even the middle-tier grandmasters. Recently it has achieved mainstream status and has been used by top stars and numerous leading grandmasters. It seems to me characteristic of the last two decades that literally every opening is being reinvestigated and that most of them are being found to be playable. One thing that has led to the revival of Alekhine is that Black has adopted the modern spirit of extreme flexibility. This game is an example.

2 e5 ♘d5 3 d4 d6 4 ♘f3 dxe5

Introducing two of the recent main lines, established as such only after many years featuring the moves 4...♗g4 and 4...g6. As so often, 4...dxe5 got a bad reputation on the basis of one notorious line.

5 ♘xe5 *(D)*

5...c6

Years ago the sacrifice 5...♘d7 6 ♘xf7 ♔xf7 7 ♕h5+ ♔e6 8 c4 chased just about everyone away from 5...♘d7. But for quite some time it also seemed to discourage Black from playing 4...dxe5 in other contexts. That has changed today; in fact, the most popular move after 4...dxe5 5 ♘xe5 has been 5...g6, which only caught on

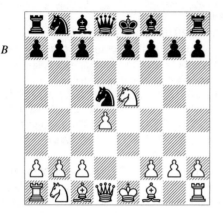

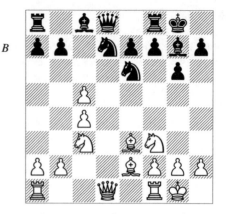

in the 1990s. Even 4...c6 5 ♗e2 dxe5 6 ♘xe5 g6 has received attention of late. I believe that the whole notion of ...dxe5 was rejected more from prejudice than concrete evaluation.

The move in the game (5...c6), was a favourite of Tony Miles and is an extreme example of keeping one's options open. Black waits for White to commit, and retains at least these options: ...g6, ...♗g4, ...♗f5, and ...♘d7, with even ...♘c7 being useful in some instances. The modern master is particularly enamoured of such flexibility. In SOMCS, I talked about how every move by the opponent gives one just that much more information about what he's doing. Such is Black's idea here.

6 ♗e2

Here 6 c4 ♘b4! threatens ...♕xd4 and equalizes. This wouldn't be true after 5...g6, for example.

6...♘d7

A safe move now that ♘xf7 definitely doesn't work. Black has a good deal of freedom here: both 6...♗f5 and 6...g6 have been played with satisfactory results.

7 ♘f3 g6 8 c4 ♘c7 9 0-0 ♗g7 10 ♘c3 0-0

These are all natural moves. Black is now intending ...c5 against most moves, and if d5, the idea ...e5 is generally acceptable, and sometimes Black will even play the Benko-like move ...b5.

11 ♗f4 c5 12 dxc5!?

For example, 12 d5 e5 13 ♗g5 f6 14 ♗e3 ♖f7 15 a3 ♗f8! (undeveloping, but both discouraging b4 and covering the blockade square d6) 16 ♖b1 ♘e8 intending ...♘d6-f5-d4 with equality. This was the ultra-modern course of Degraeve-Miles, Mondariz 2000.

12...♘e6 13 ♗e3 *(D)*

Now it looks as though White must be better after something like 13...♘dxc5 14 ♕c2 intending both b4 and ♖fd1.

13...♗xc3!

This move first occurred in W.Watson-Baburin, Kilkenny 1994. As discussed briefly in Chapter 2, Section 2 (Doubled Pawns in Action), a capture on c3 or c6 is probably the most common way of inflicting isolated doubled pawns in chess. But it's still surprising to see Black give his opponent the two-bishop advantage and weaken his kingside squares when he isn't very well developed. The real point here is that Black's pieces, especially the queen and knights, are so ready to take up ideal and/or active posts over the next few moves.

14 bxc3 ♘dxc5 15 ♘d4 ♕a5 16 ♕c2

16 ♘b3!? ♕c7 17 ♘xc5 ♘xc5 18 ♕d4 ♘e6 (after 18...b6? 19 ♗f4! ♕d8 20 ♗h6 ♘e6 21 ♕e4 White wins material) 19 ♕h4 b6 and either ...♗b7 or ...♗a6 is fine for Black.

16...♗d7

Not just connecting rooks, but covering a4. One feels that Black might even be better here.

17 h4

17 f4 f5 (Bosch).

17...♖ac8 18 h5 *(D)*

18...♘a4!?

18...♖fd8! is more natural than chasing after pawns, and at least equal. Black has ideas like ...b6 and ...♕a4, or simply ...♕c7.

19 ♖ac1 ♘b6 20 hxg6 hxg6 21 ♕b3! ♖fd8 22 ♖fe1!

Instead, 22 ♕b4 ♕xb4 23 cxb4 ♘xd4 24 ♗xd4 ♗e6 25 ♗xb6 axb6 looks equal after, for example, 26 ♖c2 (26 a3 ♖d2) 26...♖a8!.

22...♗a4?

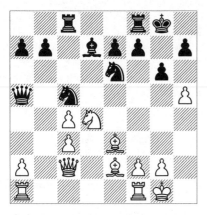

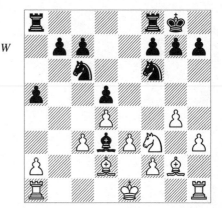

22...♕a6! is more accurate and forcing, leaving White only technically better after lines such as 23 c5 (23 ♕h4 ♘xc4 24 ♕xe7 ♕d6 25 ♕xd6 ♘xd6 26 ♘xe6 ♗xe6 27 ♗xa7 ♗xa2 with equality) 23...♘xc5 24 ♗xa6 ♘xb3 25 axb3 bxa6.

23 ♕a3?!

The subtle 23 ♕b1! ♗d7 24 ♘b5 (or 24 ♕b4) should give White a decent advantage.

23...♘xd4 24 cxd4 ♘xc4 25 ♗xc4 ♖xc4 26 ♕xe7 ½-½

Since the forcing continuation 26...♖dc8 27 ♗h6 ♖xc1 28 ♖xc1 ♖xc1+ 29 ♗xc1 ♕d5 is equal.

Game 25
Van Wely – Piket
Wijk aan Zee 2001

There follows a true slugfest that takes place from a relatively simplified position. This wonderful game features bishop versus knight-pairs, outpost struggles, paradoxical knight moves, and a surprising exchange sacrifice.

1 d4 ♘f6 2 c4 e6 3 ♘f3 ♗b4+ 4 ♗d2 a5 5 g3 d5 6 ♗g2 dxc4 7 ♕c2 ♘c6 8 ♕xc4 ♕d5 9 ♕xd5 exd5 10 ♘c3 ♗g4 11 e3 0-0 12 h3 ♗f5 13 g4 ♗xc3 14 bxc3 ♗d3 (D)

The opening seems a total success for Black. He has not only prevented castling but has strengthened his grip on the ideal outpost c4 while keeping control of e4, to which a knight may soon go. Given ideas like ...a4 and ...♘a5-c4, it's hard to believe that he doesn't stand better, much less that he has to be careful not to get into trouble.

15 ♘g1!

This undeveloping move is not only delightfully creative, but relates to our discussion about the modern role of the bishop-pair. Having just acquired them, White's concern is not with development or open lines, but with consolidation and denial of outposts to the enemy pieces. Also, an eventual advance by f3 and e4 would create the kind of big centre that the two bishops adore. Of course, Black still controls key squares and can hardly stand badly.

15...b5?!

It's hard to criticize the attacking plan that Black now follows, but getting rid of the bishops by 15...♘e4 is desirable: 16 ♘e2 (threatening ♘f4) 16...♗c4 17 f3 ♘xd2 18 ♔xd2 (Wells), and now 18...♘e7!? looks like a good equalizer, intending ...f5 and preparing 19 e4 ♘g6!. Another straightforward plan would be 15...a4 planning ...♘a5-c4; then the natural response 16 ♘e2 ♘a5 17 ♘f4 ♗c4 18 f3 ♖fe8 (18...h6 19 h4 and g5) 19 g5 ♘d7 20 e4 yields some advantage for White.

16 ♘e2 ♖fb8 17 f3 b4

Black seeks to infiltrate on the side where he is strongest.

18 ♔f2 b3 (D)

This is the culmination of Piket's strategy. Black's activity (and soon-to-appear passed a-pawn) promises to give him back the advantage that seemed to have slipped away.

19 ♘c1!

What's an exchange sacrifice among friends? Remember that the bishop-pair is sometimes worth the exchange by itself, and here White has an extra pawn for it. Instead, 19 axb3?! ♖xb3 and ...♖b2 is what Black wants.

19...b2 20 ♘xd3 bxa1♕ 21 ♖xa1 a4!?

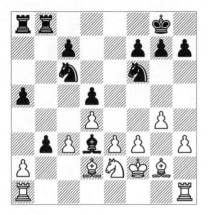

W

This is a little slow now, although the idea of ...♘a5-c4 is still tempting. 21...♘d8!? is an intelligent option, preparing ...♘e6 and ...c5, but also ...c6 if necessary.

22 e4 h6

A move that exposes the king in certain lines. Slightly more accurate would be the immediate counterattack by 22...♘a5 23 g5 (23 ♗g5 also seems to yield some advantage after 23...♖b6 24 ♘b4 dxe4 25 fxe4) 23...♘h5 (23...♘e8 24 exd5 ♘c4 25 ♗f4 ♘ed6; 23...♘c4 24 ♗f4 ♘e8 25 ♘b4) 24 exd5 ♘c4, although 25 ♗c1 f6 26 h4 with the idea of ♗h3 keeps the advantage.

23 h4 ♘a5 24 g5 hxg5 25 hxg5 ♘h5 26 exd5 ♘c4

Now 26...f6?? runs into 27 d6 ♖a7 28 ♖h1. It may still not be clear that Black is worse, since White's pawns are unimpressive and Black's knights are active. But most of the time bishops have to be exchanged or countered by a specific attack. Otherwise they tend to get out.

27 ♗c1 a3 28 ♘b4 ♖e8 29 ♗f1!

A typical pair of two bishops: they hang around on the first two ranks for a while behind their own pawns on f3 and c3, but then suddenly come out with decisive force.

29...♘b2 30 ♗d2

One could argue that the game is completely decided in view of the mobile pawns after c4-c5.

30...g6 31 ♗b5 ♖eb8 32 c4 ♖b6

After 32...♘g7 (to get to the strong outpost f5) 33 ♘c6 ♖b6 34 ♘e5 ♘f5 35 ♘d7 White regains the exchange with a winning position.

33 ♖e1 ♔f8 34 ♔g2 ♖ab8 35 ♘c6 ♖xb5 36 cxb5 ♖xb5 37 ♗b4+ ♔g7 38 ♗xa3 ♘c4 39 ♗c1 ♖xd5 40 ♖e7 ♖b5 41 ♖xc7

Easier was 41 ♘e5! ♘xe5 42 ♖xe5 ♖b1 43 ♖c5 ♖b7 44 a4, etc.

41...♖b1 42 ♘e5 ♖xc1 43 ♖xc4 ♘f4+ 44 ♔h2

...and the rest really was technique, although it took a while for White to win.

Game 26
Kasparov – Karpov
Linares 1992

1 e4 c6 2 d4 d5 3 ♘d2 dxe4 4 ♘xe4 ♘d7 5 ♘g5

It's easy to forget how sceptical people were of what is now this main line when it first appeared, especially after so many years of traditional developing moves at this point. The knight foray to g5 is a flexible and intensely pragmatic move that prepares a concrete response to any logical move by Black. In an odd sense, then, it is more of a prophylactic than an attacking move. That so many top players overlooked its possibilities is likely due to the flagrant violation of the fundamental rule of development: not to move the same piece twice (excluding recaptures) before bringing out one's pieces. Here White decentralizes the knight with no other pieces out, all for what seems to be a primitive attempt to play for tricks. But it is in fact a complex way of reorganizing White's pieces so that Black has no way to exchange them and must himself develop awkwardly.

5...♘gf6 6 ♗c4 e6 7 ♕e2 ♘b6

A positive result of 5 ♘g5: Black responds to the threat of ♘xf7 by placing his own knight on the less than ideal b6-square, where it doesn't coordinate well with the freeing move ...c5.

8 ♗b3 h6

And now a weakness is created, however small. Naturally Black doesn't want White to develop smoothly by ♘1f3.

9 ♘5f3

So White has now moved his knight four times, only to land it on a square that his g1-knight could have gone to immediately. By precluding the g1-knight from developing to its desired square, he also prevents the h1-rook from entering the fray! For all that, White's pieces command more space and he will be able to castle queenside quickly to frustrate Black's counterplay.

9...c5 10 ♗f4 ♗d6!?

Later 10...♘bd5 was played almost exclusively here.

11 ♗g3! *(D)*

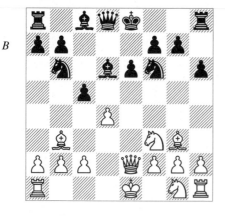

11...♕e7

The fine game J.Polgar-Epishin, Geneva rpd 1996 demonstrated that the opening of the h-file is worth the delayed development of White's knight: 11...♕c7!? 12 dxc5 ♕xc5 13 0-0-0 ♗xg3 14 hxg3 ♗d7 15 ♖h4! ♖c8 16 ♘e5 ♗b5 17 ♕e1 0-0 18 ♘gf3 ♘bd5 19 ♔b1 ♗c6 20 ♕d2 (now doubling of rooks on the h-file becomes a serious threat) 20...♖fe8 21 ♖dh1 ♕f8 22 g4 ♘e4 23 ♕e1 ♘d6 24 g5 ♘f5 25 gxh6! ♘xh4 26 h7+ ♔h8 27 ♘xh4 (threatening ♘hg6+) 27...♘f4 (27...♘e7 28 ♗xe6) 28 ♕b4! g5 (28...♕xb4 29 ♘hg6+ fxg6 30 ♘f7#) 29 ♕d4 ♕g7 (29...♕g7 30 ♘hg6+ fxg6 31 ♘f7#) 30 ♘f5+ exf5 31 h8♕+ ♕xh8 32 ♘xf7+ 1-0.

12 dxc5 ♗xc5 13 ♘e5 ♗d7

Black wants to castle queenside and avoid any kingside attacking nonsense.

14 ♘gf3

14 0-0-0 can be answered by 14...a5! (Kasparov) with an attack, rather than 14...0-0-0? 15 ♘xf7! ♕xf7 16 ♕e5.

14...♘h5 15 0-0-0

As always, Karpov has an answer to apparently attractive tactics: 15 ♘xf7?! ♘xg3 16 fxg3 ♔xf7! 17 ♘e5+ ♔e8! 18 ♕h5+ ♔d8 19 ♘g6 ♕g5 20 ♕xg5+ hxg5 21 ♘xh8 ♔e7 22 ♘g6+ ♔f6 with a large advantage for Black (Kasparov).

15...♘xg3 16 hxg3 0-0-0 17 ♖h5! *(D)*

A rook-lift that exerts pressure along the fifth rank and actually prepares to support a flank attack. Black must now attend to the threat of ♘xf7.

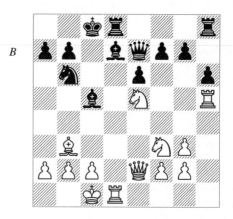

17...♗e8 18 ♖xd8+ ♔xd8 19 ♕d2+ ♗d6 20 ♘d3 ♕c7 21 g4!

The beginning of a positional assault on Black's kingside. White is operating on both flanks. Black, on the other hand, has accepted some awkwardness in his piece deployment in order to secure the two bishops, which at any moment can become active.

21...♔c8

21...f6 allows 22 ♘d4!.

22 g5 ♗f8

This looks passive, but we often see such bishops spring to life when the opponent's initiative dissipates. Again Karpov dodges a beautiful Kasparov trap: 22...♗b5 23 gxh6 ♗xd3 24 hxg7 ♖d8 *(D)*.

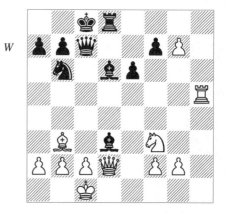

25 g3!! (25 ♖h8? ♗h7!! 26 ♘g5 {26 ♖xh7 ♗f4} 26...♗g8 and Black is clearly better!) 25...♗e4 26 ♖h8 (26 ♘g5? ♘c4!) 26...♗xf3 27

♗xe6+! fxe6 28 g8♕ ♖xg8 29 ♖xg8+ ♔d7 30 ♖g7+ (Kasparov) with a decisive advantage for White. This beautiful line illustrates how close both players are to disaster in these suddenly ultra-dynamic positions that have arisen since White's move ♖h5. Kasparov suggests 22...♔b8 23 gxh6 gxh6 24 ♔b1 with a small edge (24 ♖xh6?? ♗f4!).

23 ♖h4!

This serves the multiple purposes of preventing ...g6 and ...h5 while looking at ♖d4 and stopping ...♘c4.

23...♔b8 24 a4! ♗e7?!

Kasparov prefers 24...♘c8.

25 a5 ♘d5 26 ♔b1!

Intending c4. White disdains winning a pawn but losing the initiative by 26 ♗xd5?! exd5 27 ♘b4 ♗c6 28 ♘xd5 ♗xd5 29 ♕xd5 ♖d8.

26...♖d8!?

This allows a pretty attacking idea, but Kasparov indicates that other moves were not enticing either:

a) 26...♖f8 27 ♗xd5 exd5 28 ♘b4 ♗c6 29 gxh6 ♗xh4 30 ♘a6+! bxa6 31 ♕b4+. A nice tactic, probably both seen and avoided by Karpov.

b) 26...♖g8!? 27 ♖c4 (27 a6!?) 27...♕d6 28 ♖d4 hxg5 29 c4 ♗f6 30 cxd5 and Black is in no position to fight against the minor pieces.

27 a6 ♕a5 28 ♕e2!

Kasparov calls this 'winning', although that is not yet obvious to the casual observer and is probably an exaggeration.

28...♘b6?

This move has to be a mistake. Better seems 28...♘c7! 29 axb7 ♗e7, covering some key squares like e6, c5, and b4.

29 axb7

After 29 ♕e4! bxa6 30 ♕d4 White hits both d8 and g7.

29...♗xg5 30 ♘xg5 ♕xg5 *(D)*

31 ♖h5!

Back to the fifth rank! Black may have missed this pawn sacrifice.

31...♕f6

Karpov sees that he can't capture: 31...♕xg2 32 ♘c5 ♘d7 (Kasparov gives the cute line 32...f6 33 ♕xe6 ♕c6 34 ♕e7 ♗xh5 35 ♘a6#) 33 ♕a6! threatening ♕d6# and winning immediately due to 33...♘xc5 34 ♖xc5 ♕xb7 35 ♕d6+ ♔a8 36 ♕d8+ ♕b8 37 ♖c8.

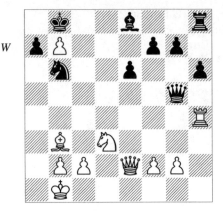

W

32 ♖a5!

It's fitting that the roaming rook provides the final element of the attack. The deadly ♘c5 and ♕a6 is threatened.

32...♗c6 33 ♘c5 ♗xb7 34 ♘xb7 ♔xb7 35 ♕a6+

Now it's just geometry.

35...♔c6 36 ♗a4+ ♔d6 37 ♕d3+ ♘d5 38 ♕g3+! ♕e5 39 ♕a3+ ♔c7 40 ♕c5+ ♔d8 41 ♖xa7 1-0

A great struggle; much of this game was hidden underneath the surface.

Somewhere in the midst of the years surrounding 1970 the Sicilian Defence seemed to take its final step in taking its place as the pre-eminent modern-style defence to 1 e4. It became clear that ultra-dynamic variations such as the Dragon and the Najdorf were not going to be refuted, with Fischer's play and prestige playing a large role in the latter case. At the same time, in the sometimes more positional variations of the Scheveningen and Classical Sicilians, Black's basic Sicilian structure (open c-file, central pawn majority, etc.) were proving to be resistant to the direct attacks by which they had been overrun in earlier times. Slowly the blitzkrieg tactics of a Tal were seen by Sicilian practitioners to be an inevitable danger rather than a threat to the viability of the defence as a whole. It is a process that continues to this day. The necessary corollary to this was that the underlying soundness of various now-standard structures of Black's had to be demonstrated. Games like the following helped to establish that and showed something rather different too: that Black was able to maintain a sort of general dynamic balance in positions with superficially weak pawn-structures.

Game 27
Hübner – Petrosian
Seville Ct (7) 1971

1 e4 c5 2 ♘f3 d6 3 ♘c3 e6 4 d4 cxd4 5 ♘xd4 ♘f6 6 ♗e3 ♗e7 7 f4 ♘c6 8 ♕f3!? e5! 9 ♘xc6

If White tries 9 ♘b3 in order to keep his outpost on d5 and saddle his opponent with a backward or isolated pawn down an open file, he runs into some of the most commonplace themes of a Sicilian Defence with ...d6 and ...e5: Black has an outpost on e5 worth at least that on d5 (because it is more supportable), White gets his own isolated pawn, and Black's 'bad' bishop on e7 turns out to be more than a match for White's good one: 9...♘g4 (9...exf4 10 ♗xf4 0-0 and ...♘e5 is a simple way to equality; 9...♘g4 tries for more) 10 ♘d5 (10 ♗d2 exf4 11 ♗xf4 0-0 12 0-0-0 ♘ce5! 13 ♕e2 ♗e6 14 h3 ♘g6! with the idea 15 ♗g3 ♘e3!) 10...♘xe3 11 ♕xe3 exf4 12 ♕xf4 0-0 (12...♗h4+ 13 g3 ♗g5 with equality) and now 13 ♘xe7+ is fairly meaningless, since Black's 'weak' d-pawn on an open file is not attackable after 13...♕xe7 14 0-0-0 (14 ♗c4 ♗e6) 14...♘e5 (D).

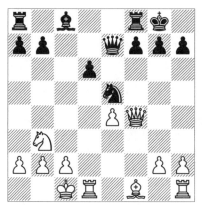

In this kind of position Black already has somewhat the better game, since his light-squared bishop will be strong on e6, his knight is better than White's, and he has the open c-file. All this is standard stuff now, but only really began to take hold in the 1950s in the USSR and didn't filter through to the everyday player for some years.

9...bxc6 10 fxe5 dxe5 11 ♗c4

Now Black has two isolated pawns, and indeed, c5 is a promising outpost square for White's pieces. On the other hand, the c6-pawn is very difficult to attack, d5 is now covered, and both of Black's bishops have active diagonals. It's probably about equal.

11...0-0 12 h3

This prevents ...♘g4 (or ...♗g4 in the event of ♖d1).

12...♗e6!

A move that apparently violates all principles, but that Petrosian would make without much trepidation. It may also be the only good one.

13 ♗xe6

According to Petrosian and Suetin, 13 ♗b3 can lead to 13...c5 14 ♖d1 ♕a5 15 ♗c1 (15 ♗d2 ♕a6), but then 15...c4! 16 ♗a4 ♗b4 is extremely strong.

13...fxe6 *(D)*

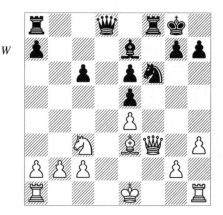

Black has now taken on two doubled pawns and four isolated ones. This is typical of Petrosian's provocative style. He is willing to lose all the long-term prospects for the sake of immediate queenside pressure. At first sight, one might not think that e6-pawn is fulfilling the usual doubled pawn function of covering outpost squares, since d5 is adequately protected by the c-pawn. But it is useful to gain the f-file with tempo (e.g., ...♘d5 is threatened), because that gives Black just enough time to attack the queenside effectively with moves like ...♖b8, ...♕a5 and ...♗b4. And it wouldn't be surprising if, after winning a queenside pawn, Petrosian might have been planning to neutralize

White's pressure by one of his patented exchange sacrifices via ...罝d4. Whether this works is of course a matter of timing and variations. If White gets a knight or bishop to c5 and his queen to c3 or c4, for example, all such reasoning is of no use.

14 豐e2 罝b8 15 0-0!

There's no easy way to guard the b-pawn; for example, 15 罝b1 奧b4. So White offers a positional pawn sacrifice to take over key queenside squares. Petrosian and Suetin give 15 豐c4 ♘h5!, when ....奧h4+ is in the air regardless of whether White captures the e-pawn.

15...罝xb2

Petrosian and Suetin call Black slightly better here, although they don't suggest how to meet their own later suggestions for White. Kasparov believes that White is a little better. Probably it's equal.

16 罝ab1

A revealing sequence is 16 豐c4 豐c8 17 奧xa7?! c5, when the e6-pawn is serving a valuable function. If nothing else, a knight wouldn't be able to get to d5. In the meantime, the a7-bishop is in danger.

16...罝b4!?

16...罝xb1 17 罝xb1 a5! is probably better (or at least easier), securing a post on b4 for the bishop and thus indirectly threatening the e4-pawn. Then play is dynamically balanced; for example, 18 豐c4 (18 豐a6?! 奧b4!) 18...奧b4! 19 豐xe6+ ♔h8 20 豐xe5 罝e8 with equality. Note that instead of 17...a5, 17...豐d7 allows 18 豐a6 when Black is very tied down; see the game.

17 豐a6!

This hits the key squares a7, c6, and b7 at the same time. 17 罝xb4 奧xb4 18 豐c4 奧xc3 19 豐xc3 豐c7 (19...豐d6! 20 豐c4 罝b8 intending 21 奧xa7 罝b4) 20 豐c4 罝e8 and Black is slightly better, according to Petrosian and Suetin.

17...豐c7 18 a3!

Black is doing well after 18 豐xa7?! 豐xa7 19 奧xa7 罝c4 or 18 奧xa7?? 罝a8 19 奧b6 豐xb6+!.

18...罝xb1 19 罝xb1 罝a8!

White gets the material back after 19...罝b8 20 罝xb8+ 豐xb8 21 豐xc6, forcing 21...奧f7. It's not immediately obvious how White would then make progress, but Black could only sit and wait.

20 a4! h6

Petrosian and Suetin prefer 20...♘d7 21 豐c4 ♘f8 22 豐a6 奧d6. Look at how passively placed every black piece is! And yet he is a pawn up, and Petrosian made a career out of such positions.

21 a5!?

Here the two grandmasters suggest 21 豐b7! 豐xb7 22 罝xb7 奧d8! 23 罝xa7 罝xa7 24 奧xa7 奧a5 25 ♘d1!, but this seems unduly pessimistic of Petrosian, who could continue 25...♘xe4 26 ♘e3 ♘d2! (preventing ♘c4; or even 26...♘d6) 27 ♔f2 ♔f7 and Black should be fine. So maybe the game was about equal all along? 21 a5!?, however, sets up an opportunity for Black.

21...♔h7! *(D)*

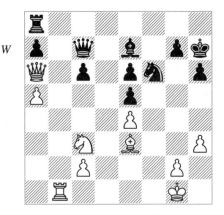

22 豐b7 豐xa5!

As shown in a separate section of SOMCS, Petrosian was one of the great exchange sacrifice geniuses, and certainly one of the first to play it for both attacking and defensive reasons.

23 豐xa8

Thus the value of 21...♔h7: no check!

23...豐xc3 24 豐xa7 ♘xe4

After 24...豐xc2? would follow 25 罝b7!.

25 罝f1

25 罝b7? 奧f6 just misplaces White's major pieces, and after 25 豐xe7 豐xe3+, 26 ♔h2? runs into 26...♘d2 27 罝b7?? ♘f1+ 28 ♔h1 豐g3 29 ♔g1 ♘e3. After the better 26 ♔h1, Black can give perpetual check in several ways, but it's hard to get winning chances; for example, 26...♘f2+ (26...♘d2 27 罝a1 豐d4 28 罝a7 e4 29 豐f7 e3 30 罝a8 豐e5 31 罝e8 豐a1+ 32 ♔h2 ♘f1+ 33 ♔g1 ♘g3+ draws) 27 ♔h2 豐f4+ 28 ♔g1 ♘xh3+ again with perpetual check.

25...奧h4

Even better is 25...♘g3! 26 ♖f7 ♕e1+ 27 ♔h2 ♘f5 28 ♗f2 ♕d2 with a big plus for Black according to Petrosian and Suetin.

26 ♖f7 ♗f6!?

This is a safe and pragmatic over-the-board decision that keeps an advantage, but the best way is 26...♕e1+ 27 ♖f1 ♕e2!.

27 ♔h2 ♕xc2

27...c5 28 ♖xf6! ♘xf6 29 ♕xc5 may well be only drawn; perhaps 27...h5!?.

28 ♕d7

Or 28 ♖f8 ♕b3 29 ♕a8 ♗e7! 30 ♖h8+ ♔g6 31 ♕e8+ ♔f6 and it's not clear how White should proceed.

28...♕b3 (D)

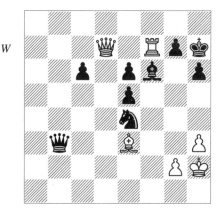

W

29 ♗f2

Black's now dominant position is illustrated by 29 ♖f8 ♗h4! 30 ♕e8 ♗g3+ 31 ♔h1 ♕b1+ 32 ♗g1 ♘f2+, when White can be very unhappy.

29...♕d5 30 ♕a7 ♕d2 31 ♕e3 ♕c2

The rest is pretty easy.

32 ♗e1 c5 33 h4 c4 34 ♖c7 ♕d3 35 ♕f3 ♕b1 36 ♕e3 ♘d6 37 ♕d2 ♘f5

37...e4! 38 ♕xd6 ♕xe1 wins instantly.

38 ♖xc4 e4 39 ♕c2?

A blunder, but White was lost anyway.

39...♕xe1 40 ♖xe4 ♗e5+ 0-1

The next game was the first one that I happened to open to recently when I got a new book on the French Defence. It is a calm enough encounter between players rated around 2500 at the time. I decided to include it for fun to illustrate the sort of positional battle that tends to go unnoticed these days. Apart from the games

of the very top players, I don't think that we really appreciate the creative nature of so much of 'ordinary' contemporary chess. For one thing, we are so used to modern ideas that just about anything that is purely strategic, however original, seems unremarkable. A draw without tactics certainly doesn't attract attention. This game has a traditionally strong centre and centralized pieces opposed by pure flank play. The game includes pawn-chains, a king in the centre, a knight on the rim, and an attack against the king initiated on the weak and cramped side of the side of the board.

Game 28
Marciano – C. Bauer
French Ch (Méribel) 1998

1 e4 e6 2 d4 d5 3 ♘d2 ♘c6 4 ♘gf3 ♘f6 5 e5 ♘d7 (D)

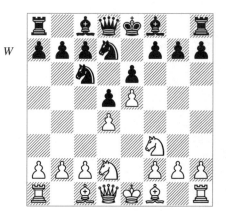

W

6 ♗d3

This is a main line of the so-called Guimard Defence to the Tarrasch Variation. 3...♘c6!? is perhaps not the strongest move, but it is the sort of thing that Nimzowitsch liked: to block the c-pawn and therefore break with all traditional advice for such positions. The alternative 6 ♗e2 allows Black to challenge the front of the pawn-chain by 6...f6. Similarly, 6 c3 can be met by 6...f6 when a natural follow-up is 7 ♗b5 (7 exf6 ♕xf6 8 ♗b5 ♗d6 followed by a quick ...e5) 7...fxe5 8 dxe5 a6 9 ♗xc6 bxc6 10 0-0 c5. So White puts his bishop on d3 where it will assist in an attack should ...f6 occur. One drawback is that this allows...

6...♘b4 7 ♗e2 c5

...with the traditional attack on the pawn-chain. The combination of ♘gf3 and ♗e2 is not too worrisome for Black, although since White has gained a tempo, he must be considered to have somewhat the better game.

8 c3 ♘c6 9 0-0 cxd4

9...♕b6 targets d4, but then 10 ♘b3 is held to favour White, particularly in view of Geller's move 11 dxc5! after 10...a5.

10 cxd4 ♘b6 *(D)*

Black commits to action and development on the queenside, since after this move his pieces will no longer support an attack on d4 (by ...♕b6) or e5 (by ...f6).

11 ♖e1 ♗d7 12 ♘f1!

To free the c1-bishop and leave the f1-knight with the option of going to g3 or returning to d2.

12...♗e7 13 ♗e3

After 13 ♘g3, 13...h5 is one idea, to gain a lot of space on the kingside for Black. Or he can continue as in the game.

13...a5 *(D)*

Black ignores the centre in favour of flank play. His first point is to grab as much space as he can on the queenside, deferring the question of castling until later.

14 ♖c1 a4 15 a3

This advance creates some weaknesses, although it's hard for Black to exploit them because of his cramped position. The alternative is to allow ...a3, which in turn frees b4 for Black's pieces; e.g., 15 ♘g3 a3 (15...♘b4 16 a3 ♘c6 loses time on the game, but is still reasonable) 16 b3 0-0 17 ♕d3 (17 ♕d2? ♗b4), and now 17...♖c8 18 ♗f4 ♘a7 19 ♖xc8 ♘bxc8 intending ...♗b5, ...♕a5, etc., is one strategy, but

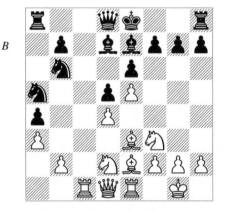

it's also possible to play 17...♘c8!?, casually re-routing the poorly-placed knight to support the b5-square. Then a sample line might be 18 ♘h5 ♘8a7 19 g3 ♘b4 20 ♕d2 ♗b5, which is unclear.

15...♘a5

This knight stays on the rim, tying White to b3 and c4, for the rest of the game!

16 ♘1d2! *(D)*

This shows the wisdom of not straying too far by ♘g3.

Black now has to decide how to improve his position. If he can't find a way to infiltrate on the queenside, then it seems that White will build up effectively on the opposite wing. By traditional theory, White ought to have a substantial edge here.

16...♗c6!

The introduction to a subtle plan.

17 ♗d3! h6 18 ♕e2

Extremely logical, covering c4, connecting rooks and putting an end to the idea of ...♗b5 to exchange the bad bishop. White's play has followed all the rules: protect the pawn-chain, centralize the pieces, take over the open file, and prevent the opponent's freeing moves. Now he is ready to take action.

18...♕d7 19 h3 ♖c8

Black refuses to castle into the attack, judging his king to be safer in the centre. He might even be contemplating the exotic ...♘a8-c7, to support the b5-square. But what then? And what about his rook on h8?

20 ♘h2!

Now the move ♕g4 is in the air and Black still hasn't achieved much on the queenside.

20...h5

This looks purely defensive and weakening, but it does more than prevent ♕g4 or ♕h5, as we shall see.

21 ♘hf3 (D)

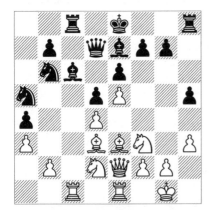

White was probably very satisfied here: by luring the pawn to h5, he can now play ♗g5 with a nice positional advantage (space, better bishop, and firm control of the centre).

21...♕d8! 22 ♖c3

Again, the classical way to progress, by doubling rooks.

22...♔d7!

As anticipated some moves ago, presumably even with 16...♗c6!. Black thus connects major pieces on his back rank and if need be, his king will be much safer on b8 than on g8 or even in the centre. One thing that bothers White is that there is a sort of mutual stand-off over c4, so that a move by his d3-bishop or d2-knight invites one of Black's knights into that square.

23 ♖ec1

White is superbly centralized and has put every piece to good use.

23...g5

Black hasn't even looked at the centre for a long time and has systematically shifted his forces to the queenside. Yet suddenly he throws out yet another flank pawn on the side of the board where he has almost no pieces! How can this be justified, especially with this central configuration? One idea is just to gain space (as was that behind ...a4); but he might also be able to open lines on the kingside or force White into a weakening of his kingside light squares. In the latter case, the sacrifice ...♘bc4 would be difficult to accept since the c6-bishop would become a very powerful piece. Thus the two flanks coordinate despite Black's pieces being passively placed. This reminds one of the philosophy behind the Hedgehog.

24 ♘e1!

The alternative of just blocking the kingside and restricting the e7-bishop by 24 g4 hxg4 25 hxg4 allows 25...♘bc4! (25...♔c7 26 ♔g2 ♔b8, castling by hand, is also possible) 26 ♘xc4 ♘xc4 27 ♗xc4 dxc4 28 ♖xc4 (D).

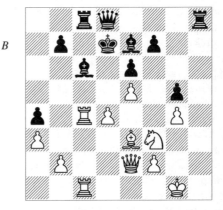

After 28...♕f8! threatening ...♕h6 (28...♖h3 29 ♖xc6! bxc6 30 ♔g2 yields unclear play), White must play 29 d5! exd5 30 ♕d3 ♕h6 31 ♔f1 ♕e6! but he still has trouble both defending his pieces and protecting the g4-pawn.

24...♕g8! 25 g3

To answer ...g4 with h4. This slightly weakens the light squares, however.

25...♖c7!?

As we shall see, 25...g4 26 h4 ♖c7 would simplify matters later. The idea of ...♖c7 is

...♗c8-b8, after which the attack can be continued by some combination of ...f6 and ...♘bc4, or Black can close the kingside and reorganize to contest the c-file.

26 ♗b5 ♕g6!?

26...g4 27 h4 ♖c8 deserves attention because it prevents ♘d3.

27 ♗d3

27 ♗xc6+ bxc6 helps Black on the light squares (queen on g6 and the idea of ...♘bc4), and 28 ♕a6 ♖a8! 29 ♕xb6 ♖b7 favours Black. However, 27 ♘d3!? is tactically possible, when 27...♘bc4 28 ♘xc4 dxc4 29 ♗xc4 ♘xc4 30 ♖xc4 leads to an unclear opposite-coloured bishop position after, for example, 30...♖cc8 31 ♘c5+ ♗xc5 32 ♖xc5 g4. In this line it would have been nice to have 25...g4 26 h4 already in.

27...♕g7 28 ♗b5

Offering the repetition. White is still optically better, but that may be an illusion because he has to be very careful about letting his light squares be occupied, and otherwise it's difficult to make progress without allowing Black counterplay. On a move like 28 ♔h2, an interesting idea is 28...g4 29 h4 ♔c8, intending ...♔b8 and ...♖hc8, followed by turning Black's attention back to the queenside! If White tries to open kingside lines, play can get very complex; e.g., 30 f3 ♔b8 31 fxg4 hxg4 32 ♘g2 (stopping ...♖xh4 tricks) 32...♖hc8! 33 ♘f4 ♘ac4 34 ♘xc4 dxc4 35 ♗xc4 ♗f3 36 ♕d3 ♕h8! 37 ♗f2 (also versus ...♗xh4; for example, White should avoid 37 ♔g1? ♗xh4 38 gxh4 ♕xh4 39 ♔f1 g3!, etc.) 37...♕h6! (threatening ...♗xh4 anyway) 38 ♘g2 ♘xc4 39 ♖xc4 ♕xc1! 40 ♖xc1 ♖xc1 with what should be a winning game, since the rooks coordinate so well with the light-squared bishop.

28...♕g6 29 ♗d3 ♕g7 30 ♗b5 ♕g6 ½-½

One should probably call some modern strategies 'hypermodern' because they really go beyond the limits of what I would normally characterize as 'modern'. The following ultra-flexible line for Black has been around for a few decades and is used by several 2500-2600 players. The average master will almost surely have difficulty handling the associated ideas, and even if in theory it only grants the usual slight edge for White, practice can be another

matter. It takes a knowledgeable and sophisticated strategic thinker (as in the next game) to achieve decent results as Black. That said, games with this strategic course have so many surprising elements that it is a treat to sit back and enjoy them.

Game 29
J. Shahade – Ehlvest
Philadelphia 1999

1 e4 g6 2 d4 ♗g7

An interesting move-order trick pointed out many years ago begins with 2...d6 3 ♘c3 c6!? 4 f4 (obviously 4 ♘f3 is a major option) 4...d5!? 5 e5 h5 6 ♘f3 ♗g4, which is an improved version of the next note. After a typical variation like 7 ♗e3 ♘h6 8 ♗e2 ♗xf3 9 ♗xf3 ♘f5 10 ♗f2 e6, it turns out that the bishop is much better placed on f8 than on g7 both because it isn't blocked by the monster on e5 and because it supports ...c5. So by playing this move-order, Black has in a sense gained two tempi by avoiding ...♗f8-g7-f8. In the meantime, he has lost only one tempo by playing ...d6-d5.

3 ♘c3 c6 4 ♘f3

4 f4 d5 is the Gurgenidze System, which is quite respectable. It goes 5 e5 h5!? (to restrain White's kingside expansion) 6 ♘f3 ♗g4 *(D)* (bishops before knights, with knights on the rim to come):

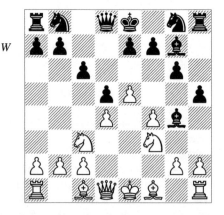

Now after 7 ♗e3 (for example) 7...♘h6, Black is intending to follow up with some combination of ...♘f5, ...e6, ...c5, and ...♕b6. All this was of course a late development of Caro-Kann/Modern Defence theory.

4...d5

A somewhat rare variation, but considered solid enough. It's as if Black wants the light and dark squares at the same time.

5 h3!

Prophylaxis. 5 e5 ♗g4 or 5 ♗e2 ♗g4 is reasonably easy for Black, who will exchange the bishop for knight, play the solid ...e6 and then aim for ...c5. Ideally, White's centre will be pried apart and Black's knights will find useful squares.

5...♘h6

Oddly enough, a standard move! Black's first idea is that if White plays ♗e3 soon, ...dxe4 and ...♘f5 chases the bishop and the knight stands well. 5...dxe4 with ...♘f6 is the more solid option.

6 ♗f4

Not the only move, but probably the best, developing and covering e5. White plays beginner's book chess, and it causes some real problems. For example, if 6...0-0 7 e5, White threatens to win a piece by 8 ♕d2 and 9 g4. Black's solution is outrageous:

6...f6!? *(D)*

It's astonishing that so many masters have willingly chosen to play this move and to take on any position resembling that in the diagram. Black cuts off his bishop and creates a serious weakness on e6, which makes ...dxe4 risky in view of the open e-file and ideas like ♗c4 and ♘c5. The initial point is a rather pathetic one: to provide an escape square on f7 for the knight. Beyond that, Black would like to stop ♘e5 and, sometime in the distant future, to play ...e5.

7 exd5

This tries to exploit Black's slow and skewed development. The other natural move is 7 ♕d2 ♘f7, and now:

a) 8 0-0-0 0-0 must be a little better for White, although Black has not done that terribly (at least strong players haven't). An inspiration for White was seen in the miniature Rogers-Hjorth, Sydney 1983: 9 ♔b1 e5!? (Black normally delays this; see our main game) 10 ♗g3! (10 ♗e3? c5!) 10...exd4 11 ♘xd4 dxe4 12 ♘xe4 f5 13 ♘c5 ♕f6?! 14 c3 (14 ♗c4!) 14...♖d8? (beginning with 9...e5, Black hasn't played very well, but he could still get a decent game with 14...b6! 15 ♘cb3 c5) 15 ♗c4! b6 16 ♘d3 ♗a6? 17 ♗b3 (17 ♗e5 also wins) 17...♘d7 (17...♗xd3+ 18 ♕xd3 ♘d7 19 ♕f3) 18 ♘b4! 1-0. Everything has fallen apart; for example, 18...♘c5 (18...♗b7 19 ♘e6) 19 ♘xa6 ♘xa6 20 ♕f4! (threatening ♗h4 and ♘e6, among others) 20...h6 (20...♘c5 21 ♗h4!) 21 ♘e6 ♖xd1+ 22 ♖xd1 g5 23 ♕c4 f4 24 ♕xa6 fxg3 25 fxg3 and there is no answer to things like ♖f1, ♖d7, and ♕b7.

b) 8 ♗h2 0-0 9 ♗e2 e6 10 0-0 ♘d7 11 ♖fe1 *(D)*.

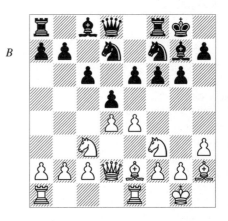

Notice how White has done everything right: set up a strong centre, got all of his pieces out, centralized the knights, and removed the king to safety. Black has shut out both of his bishops and huddled his pieces miserably on the first two ranks. And yet things aren't so dire for him because there are no obvious targets and his position has a degree of flexibility and elasticity (i.e., any attempt to force things by White can lead to a rapid mobilization of the enemy forces). Black's next move begins a flank attack from an undeveloped position: 11...b5 12 exd5 (Black was threatening ...b4, and 12 a3 ♘b6 is no improvement) 12...exd5 13 ♗d3 ♘b6 14 b3 ♗h6 (a sort of pseudo-activation with the purely pragmatic goal of exposing the queen to tempo loss) 15 ♕e2 ♗d7 (preparing ...♖e8; even the computer engines think that it's approximately equal here – what happened?) 16 ♕f1 ♘c8! (why think about developing when you can keep moving your knights? Now the idea is not only to take up a spot on d6 but to clear the way for queen moves like ...♕a5 or ...♕b6; finally, ...♘cd6, ...f5 and ...♘e4 is a theme) 17 ♘e2 ♘cd6 18 ♘f4 f5? (too loosening; perhaps Black overlooked White's reply; 18...♖e8 or perhaps 18...♕a5 is much more solid and equal) 19 c4! bxc4 20 bxc4 ♕a5 21 ♘e5 (21 ♘e6! causes real trouble) 21...♘xe5 22 dxe5 ♘e4 23 ♕e2 ♔h8?! (23...♖fc8! is very flexible, intending either ...♗g7, ...♕c5 or ...♖ab8, depending upon White's response) 24 e6 ♗e8?? (24...♗xf4! 25 ♗xf4 ♗xe6 is unclear, although White controls the dark squares and has a lot of compensation) 25 f3? (25 e7! wins; e.g., 25...♖f7 26 ♕b2+ ♗g7 27 ♕b7, etc.) 25...♕c5+ 26 ♕e3 ♕xe3+ (26...♗g7) 27 ♖xe3 ♗g7 28 ♖ae1 and White stood somewhat better in Sø.B.Hansen-Van Mil, Isle of Man 1995. An extremely interesting example of how a strategy can be so ugly-looking and yet playable. Here Black arrived at a position with equal chances before things went wrong.

7...cxd5 8 ♘b5 ♘a6

Now Black has two knights on the rim as well as no space. The good part is that the c8-bishop is free and f5 is available for occupation.

9 c4 ♗e6?!

A light-square strategy, deferring ...e5 for a while. This leads to fascinating play in the game but is probably dubious. 9...0-0 10 cxd5 ♕xd5 has been played a number of times; for example, 11 ♘c3!? (11 ♖c1 ♔h8 12 ♗c4 ♕e4+ 13 ♗e3 ♘f5 14 0-0 ♘xe3 15 ♕e2 ♗h6 16 ♖fe1, Gallagher-Efimov, Pula Echt 1997, and here Finkel suggests 16...e5! 17 ♗d3 ♕d5 18 ♘c3 ♕f7 19 fxe3 exd4 20 ♘xd4 ♘c5 with a slight advantage to Black) 11...♕f5 12 ♕d2 ♘f7 13 ♗d3 ♕e6+ 14 ♔f1 ♕d7 15 ♖e1 e6, Mi.Tseitlin-Teplitsky, Budapest 1993. Again White has made all the logical traditional moves, but Black can get a knight to d5 and stands no

worse, especially in view of White's king position.

10 ♘c3! dxc4 11 ♗xc4!?

11 d5! ♗d7!? 12 ♗xc4 looks like the right treatment, and calls 9...♗e6 into question. Nevertheless, the rest of this game illustrates the value of flank versus centre even when everything else seems to favour the opponent.

11...♗xc4 12 ♕a4+ ♕d7 13 ♕xc4 ♖c8 14 ♕b3 ♘f5 15 0-0

White was surely happy here: Black can't castle, his g7-bishop and a6-knight are ineffective, and ♖fe1 exerts pressure directly at Black's king. This is all true, and yet...

15...g5! *(D)*

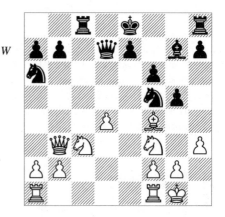

Out of nowhere, Black launches a flank attack of the type we saw in Chapter 2. It doesn't even seem to matter where his pieces are!

16 ♗e3!

This protects d4. 16 ♗h2 runs into 16...h5, when White can't stop ...g4; for example, 17 ♖ad1? (17 g4 hxg4 18 hxg4 ♘h4 19 ♘xh4 ♕xg4+ 20 ♘g2 ♕h3) 17...g4 18 hxg4 hxg4 19 ♘e1 ♘xd4 is winning for Black because of 20 ♖xd4 (20 ♕a3 ♖c5! and ...♖h5) 20...♕xd4 21 ♕xb7 ♖c5 22 ♘c2 ♕d7 23 ♕xa6 ♖ch5.

16...h5 *(D)*

17 ♕b5?!

White must fight for kingside equity by means of 17 ♘h2! with the following sample analysis: 17...g4 18 hxg4 hxg4!? (this leads to equality, but perhaps better is the safe solution 18...♘xe3 19 fxe3 hxg4 20 ♕c2 0-0!, a paradoxical idea that abandons the h-file but prepares ...f5; then Black gets equal play or better following 21 ♕f5 ♕xf5 22 ♖xf5 e6) 19 ♘xg4

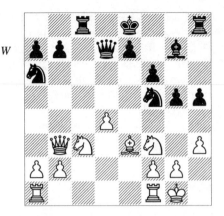

W

♘xd4 (19...♘d6) 20 ♗xd4 ♕xd4 (20...♕xg4 21 ♕xb7 ♖b8 22 ♕c6+! ♔f8 23 ♖fd1 ♕h4 24 g3 ♕h2+ 25 ♔f1 ♖xb2 26 ♗xa7 favours White!) 21 ♕xb7 ♕xg4 22 ♕xa6 ♖c5! 23 ♕a4+ ♕xa4 24 ♘xa4 ♖ch5 25 f4 f5 and even though the rooks are cut off, Black's strong bishop and temporary attack put the game into dynamic balance; for example, 26 ♖ad1 ♖h1+ 27 ♔f2 ♖xf1+ (or 27...♖1h4 28 g3 ♖h2+ 29 ♔f3 ♗xb2) 28 ♔xf1 ♖h4 29 g3 ♖h2 30 ♖e1 ♗xb2 31 ♘xb2 ♖xb2 with equality.

17...g4 18 ♕xd7+ ♔xd7 19 ♘e1

White has no hope after 19 hxg4 hxg4 20 ♘h2 g3 21 ♘f3 ♘b4!! 22 ♖ac1 (22 a3 ♘c2 23 ♖ac1 ♘cxe3 24 fxe3 ♗h6 is winning for Black) 22...♘xe3 23 fxe3 ♗h6 24 ♖fe1 ♘d3.

19...♖hg8!?

Black can also open the g-file by 19...gxh3 20 gxh3 ♗h6 21 ♗xh6 ♖xh6; this isn't bad, but 19...♖cg8 would make more sense than the text-move, when White is under direct pressure after 20 ♔h2 (20 hxg4 hxg4) 20...gxh3 (or 20...g3+ 21 ♔h1 gxf2 22 ♗xf2 ♗h6 intending ...♘e3) 21 ♔xh3 ♗h6 22 ♘c2 (22 ♗xh6 ♖xh6 23 d5 ♖hg6 24 ♖d1 ♖g4 25 ♔h2 ♘c5) 22...♖g4.

20 hxg4 hxg4 21 ♘c2 ♖h8 22 g3 ♘c7 23 d5

After 23 ♖ac1 e6 24 ♖fd1 ♘d5, Black's better pieces and the h-file give him an advantage.

23...♖h3 24 ♔g2 ♘b5! 25 ♖ac1

25 ♘xb5? ♖xc2 threatens ...♖xg3+ and ...♘xe3+, but 26 ♗f4 will lose to 26...♖h6!.

25...♘xc3 26 bxc3 ♖xc3 27 ♗xa7

Giving up material. There was no really good move; for example, 27 ♖h1? ♖xg3+! 28 fxg3 ♖xc2+ 29 ♖xc2 ♘xe3+, etc.

27...♗h6 28 ♘e3 ♗xe3 29 ♖xc3 ♗xa7

The rest needs no comment.

30 ♖b1 ♘d6 31 ♖b4 ♖h5 32 ♖d3 ♖g5 33 ♖a4 ♗c5 34 ♖a5 b6 35 ♖a7+ ♔e8 36 ♖d2 ♘e4 37 ♖e2 ♖e5 38 ♖a4 f5 39 ♖c4 ♖xd5 40 a4 ♔d7 41 ♖cc2 e6 0-1

Game 30
Bologan – Svidler
Tomsk 2001

More Sicilian madness. We have to see a good deal of this dynamic opening because it is modern and on the strategic cutting edge. The short game before you has the usual flank action, king in the centre, outpost in front of the backward pawn, and yes, an exchange sacrifice. And yet in all seriousness it isn't that far out of the ordinary.

1 e4 c5 2 ♘f3 d6 3 d4 cxd4 4 ♘xd4 ♘f6 5 ♘c3 a6 6 ♗e2 e5 7 ♘b3 ♗e7 8 g4

Here we come.

8...h6 9 f4!? (D)

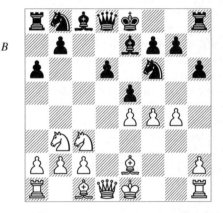

B

A different theme from ones we're used to seeing. If this sort of thing can work, the Sicilian should be out of business!

9...b5!?

Surely 9...exf4 10 ♗xf4 ♘c6 is the natural solution? Then Shirov-Van Wely, Tilburg 1997 continued 11 h3 (where's the flank advance? What's that bishop doing on e2 instead of g2?) 11...♗e6!? (11...♘e5 12 ♕d4 0-0 13 0-0-0 ♕c7 with equality) 12 ♕d2 d5!? (D).

This was assessed as 'clearly better for Black' in an old *Informator*. Wouldn't any Sicilian player agree that White has been fiddling about while Black has freed his game in classic style?

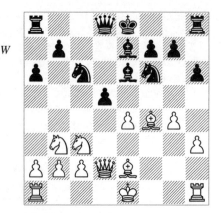

13 0-0-0 dxe4 14 ♕e3! (then again, maybe not; perhaps Black might have played 12...♘e5) 14...♕c8 15 ♘xe4!? (pessimism about this line was based on 15 ♗d6 ♗xd6 16 ♖xd6 0-0 17 ♘c5 ♘b4! of Rigo-Ribli, Hungary 1977, when Black was held to be better due to the ideas of ...♘bd5 and ...♘xa2+; nevertheless, White doesn't look badly off at all after 18 ♖hd1, 18 ♘xe6 fxe6 19 ♕d4 or 18 g5, and a move earlier 17 g5 was fairly promising as well) 15...♘xe4 16 ♕xe4 0-0 17 ♔b1?! (Shirov posits that it was time for 17 ♗c4 ♗xc4 18 ♕xc4; 17 ♗d3 f5 18 gxf5 ♗xf5 19 ♕g2!? is a wild alternative) 17...f5 18 ♕e3 ♘b4 and Black was somewhat better although Shirov went on to win.

10 g5 ♘fd7!? (D)

Svidler doesn't make a peep about the win of a pawn by 10...hxg5 11 fxg5 ♘h7, when it seems that 12 h4 ♘xg5 13 ♕d5 ♖a7 14 ♗e3 ♗e6 15 ♕d3 ♖d7!? 16 0-0-0 might be tried.

11 ♘d5

All kinds of possibilities arise after 11 h4!? or 11 0-0!? hxg5 (Svidler gives 11...exf4 12 g6! fxg6 13 ♗xf4 with advantage) 12 fxg5 ♗xg5 13 ♕d5 0-0!? 14 ♕xa8 ♗xc1 15 ♖axc1 ♕b6+ 16 ♘c5! dxc5 17 ♘d5 ♕g6+ 18 ♔f2 ♕h6 and according to Svidler, this is unclear!

11...♗b7 12 ♗d2!? ♘c6

12...♗xd5 13 ♗a5 maintains White's outpost in Svidler's line 13...♕c8 14 ♕xd5 ♘c6 15 ♗h5! g6 16 ♗g4 and White has promising play.

13 gxh6! ♗h4+ 14 ♔f1 gxh6 (D)

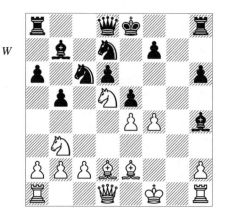

15 c4!?

This position is just a big mess. White has voluntarily committed his king to a most vulnerable square yet counts upon his activity to turn the balance. With this in mind, 15 ♗h5 also merited strong consideration.

15...bxc4 16 ♗xc4 exf4 17 ♖c1

Svidler assigns this an '!', and indeed, 17 ♗xf4 ♘ce5 looks very comfortable for Black, who would like to play ...♗xd5 and ...♕f6.

17...♖c8 18 ♗e2?

Apparently 18 ♖g1 is best, with tremendous complications. It's odd how White's knight remains undisturbed on d5 and the weak pawn sits on d6, but neither seems a problem for Black.

18...♘f6 19 ♗g4? (D)

This logical plan proves fatal for White. Now 19...♘xg4 20 ♕xg4 leaves White very active. But:

19...♘xd5! 20 exd5 ♘e5!

The good old exchange sacrifice. It pretty much wins!

21 ♗xc8

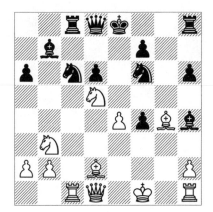

B

Or 21 h3 ♖xc1 22 ♗xc1 ♕b6 23 ♖h2, but Black has pawns and two bishops.

21...♗xc8

Threatening ...♗h3+. The two bishops are overwhelming against the exposed king.

22 ♖c3

Svidler shows one win after 22 h3: 22...♗f5 23 ♖c3 ♗e4 24 ♖g1 f3, etc.

22...♗g4 23 ♕c2 ♕d7 24 ♗xf4 ♕b5+

24...♗h3+! is even easier.

25 ♔g1 ♕xd5 26 ♗g3 ♖g8

26...♗d8! is also strong, looking at ...♗b6+.

27 ♕g2 ♗f3 28 ♖xf3 ♘xf3+ 29 ♔f2 ♖g5!
30 ♕h3

Or 30 ♕xf3 ♖f5.

30...♖f5 31 ♖d1 ♘g5+ 0-1

Game 31
Gulko – Hector
Copenhagen 2000

As discussed in the section on flank pawns in Chapter 2, energetic early attacks with the g- and h- pawns are not limited to dynamic openings such as the Sicilian Defence. Here's a case in which a middlegame that has always been characterized by positional manoeuvring was transformed by an unlikely and almost simplistic new strategy.

1 c4 ♘f6 2 ♘c3 e5 3 ♘f3 ♘c6 4 g3 ♘d4!? 5 ♗g2

The capture 5 ♘xe5 gives Black a powerful initiative after 5...♕e7, especially because 6 ♘d3?? allows 6...♘f3#! That detail provides the needed tactical justification for Black's strategy outlined in the next note.

5...♘xf3+ 6 ♗xf3 ♗b4

This variation has been popular for at least 20 years. The surprising loss of time and development incurred by 4...♘d4 and 5...♘xf3+ (moving a piece three times to exchange one that has moved once) is made up for by the fact that Black's c-pawn is free to advance to c6 and support ...d5. Furthermore, there may be situations in which ...♗h3 is a useful move. A typical example of modern pragmatism.

7 ♕b3 ♗c5 8 d3! (D)

As we shall see, this can introduce a completely different strategy from the traditional one with 8 0-0 0-0 9 d3. Delaying or foregoing castling opens up the idea of playing on the flanks.

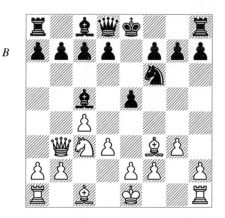

B

8...h6!?

Black's move is superficially directed against ♗g5, which would strengthen White's grip on the light squares. But since that really isn't much of a threat in the line 8...0-0 9 ♗g5 h6 10 ♗xf6 ♕xf6 (which is fully equal), we will have to look deeper. In fact, 8...h6 may be aimed at a later ♗g5, but it is also turning out to be a prophylactic move directed against White's ideas of g4 and h4! That leaves us in the odd situation that a radical strategy, which for years didn't even occur to White (and is so new as to have escaped inclusion in the recent theoretical works on the English Opening), is already fearsome enough that Black desires advance protection from it! We live in fast-changing times.

So granting for the moment that Black wants to avoid 8...0-0 9 g4! followed by g5 and h4 in the new spirit, let's look at a recent game with 8...c6, after which White shamelessly ignores the fact that Black hasn't castled and plays 9 g4 anyway! Vallejo Pons-Gelfand, Pamplona 1999/00 then continued 9...d6!? (Gelfand mentions the natural 9...d5; then a strategically interesting line would be 10 g5 dxc4 11 ♕xc4 ♘d7 12 h4 ♕e7 13 ♘e4! ♗b4+ 14 ♗d2 ♗xd2+ 15 ♔xd2!, when White has space and connected rooks, while his king is well placed for an endgame after, say, 15...♘b6 16 ♕c5) 10 g5 ♘g8 11 ♘a4!? (11 ♘e4) 11...♘e7?! (11...♕a5+! is better in view of 12 ♗d2? ♗xf2+, so 12 ♔f1 would have to be played with a very unclear position) 12 ♘xc5 dxc5 13 ♗e4! 0-0 14 h4 (14 f4!?) 14...♘f5 (D).

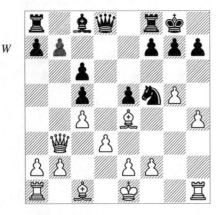

15 ♕c3! (Gelfand gives 15 ♗xf5 ♗xf5 16 ♕xb7 e4! with obscure counterplay) 15...♘d4?! (15...♘d6 16 ♕xe5 ♘xe4 17 ♕xe4 {or 17 dxe4} favours White, but not by so much) 16 e3 f5 17 ♗g2! ♕e8 (according to Gelfand, 17...♖e8 18 ♕d2 ♘e6 19 b3! gives White a clear advantage with his two bishops and pressure on e5) 18 ♕d2! f4!? (this looks a little desperate, but is actually a very interesting long-term piece sacrifice; 18...♘e6 19 b3! is still very strong for White) 19 exd4 f3 20 ♗f1 exd4+ 21 ♔d1 ♗g4! 22 b3 ♕g6 23 ♗a3 b6 24 ♔c2 a5!. White has a winning game, of course, but contrary to one's first impression, it actually takes great care to convert his advantage into victory. In fact, Vallejo Pons failed to handle the complications well and ended up losing. An unfair reward for his excellent strategic play.

We now return to 8...h6!? (D):

9 h4!?

What do we call this? A space-gaining flank thrust, of course, but also a kind of prophylactic waiting move! First, Black cannot play 9...d6?

due to 10 ♗xb7 and if 10...♖b8, then 11 ♗c6+. But White also strongly discourages 9...0-0? (preparing 10...d6) due to 10 g4, when g5 has obviously gained strength from the inclusion of h4. So Black's choices have been strangely limited to slightly less natural or at least more committal moves.

Incidentally, Gulko mentions the additional possibility of 9 g4, to which he only supplies the response 9...d6. Then the obvious continuation 10 g5 hxg5 11 ♗xg5 still promises a game with plenty of content. The seemingly small difference of move-order initiated by 8 d3 leads to vast stretches of unexplored territory!

9...c6

A later game Piket-Avrukh, Amsterdam 2001 went 9...♘h7?! 10 ♘e4! (10 g4 c6 11 ♘e4 ♗e7 is unclear; this was probably Black's idea) 10...♗e7 (10...♗b6!?) 11 ♕b5! c5?! (Black is already in terrible shape – he should probably just castle and give up the pawn; Piket gives the line 11...f5 12 ♘c3! threatening both ♕xe5 and ♗h5+; instead, 12 ♗h5+ ♔f8 13 ♘c3 ♘f6 is not so clear) 12 ♗e3 (12 ♘xc5 a6 13 ♘xb7 may also work, but it's not worth it) 12...a6 13 ♕a4 ♕c7 14 ♘c3! (White is already positionally winning) 14...♕d8 (14...♘f6 15 g4!) 15 b4! ♘f8 (Piket offers 15...cxb4 16 ♘d5 b5 17 cxb5 ♗b7 18 ♗b6 axb5 19 ♕xa8! and Black can resign) 16 bxc5 ♘e6 17 ♕b4 0-0 18 ♘d5 and White had a very large advantage and went on to win.

10 g4 (D)

White has managed to liven up one of the dullest lines of the English Opening. What's more, he may well stand better already!

10...d5

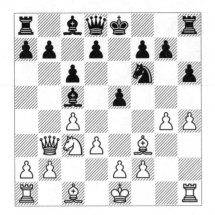

Gulko examines 10...d6 11 g5 (he calls 11 ♖g1 ♕b6 12 ♕xb6 ♗xb6 slightly better for White, but I'm not so sure about that) 11...hxg5 12 hxg5 (12 ♗xg5!?) 12...♖xh1+ 13 ♗xh1 ♘g4 14 ♘e4 ♗b6 (if 14...♕b6?, 15 ♕xb6 wins the d-pawn, because 15...axb6?? 16 ♘xc5 bxc5 17 f3! ♘h2 18 ♔f2 actually wins the knight!) 15 ♕a3 ♗c7 (15...♔e7 16 f4!?) 16 ♗d2 with a small advantage.

11 g5 hxg5

After 11...dxc4 12 ♕xc4 ♘d7, White can play 13 g6! fxg6 14 ♕e6+ ♕e7 15 ♕xg6+ ♕f7 16 ♗h5 ♕xg6 17 ♗xg6+ ♔e7 18 ♘e4 and the weakness of e5 together with White's better development guarantees him a substantial edge.

12 hxg5 ♖xh1+ 13 ♗xh1 ♘g4 14 cxd5! ♗xf2+ 15 ♔d1 ♗b6 16 ♔c2 (D)

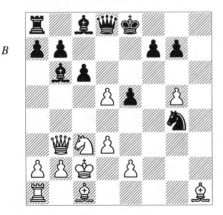

As always, a king march. What ever happened to castling?

16...♗d7

White already controls more squares and Black doesn't want to cede d5. White would

also have much the better game after 16...cxd5 17 ♗xd5 ♕e7 18 ♗d2.

17 dxc6

Although the advance 17 g6!? would split Black's pawns and doubtless increase White's advantage slightly, it's better to clarify matters first.

17...bxc6

As Gulko points out, 17...♗xc6? 18 ♗xc6+ bxc6 19 ♕c4 ♕d7 20 g6! gives White a substantial advantage. Then 20...♕e6 21 ♕xe6+ fxe6 22 ♗d2 0-0-0 23 ♖f1 ♘e3+ 24 ♗xe3 ♗xe3 25 ♖f7 ♖d7 26 ♘e4 would be a typical continuation.

18 ♗d2

Once again, 18 g6 could be considered. Both moves keep the advantage.

18...♗e3!? 19 ♖f1 ♕e7 20 ♘e4! ♗e6

According to Gulko, this move is dubious and 20...♗xd2 21 ♔xd2 ♗e6 22 ♕a4 ♖c8 is best, but then 23 ♖c1 wins a pawn, since 23...♗d5? 24 ♘f6+ gxf6 25 ♗xd5 hits g4 and c6.

21 ♕a4 (D)

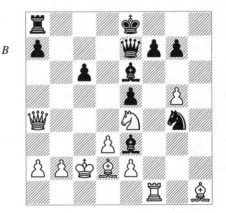

21...♔f8

White is winning. Gulko's analysis includes 21...♖c8?? 22 ♗b4 and 21...♖b8 22 ♗f3 ♗xd2 23 ♖h1! ♕b4 24 ♖h8+ ♔e7 25 ♕xa7+ ♖b7 26 ♕c5+ ♕xc5+ 27 ♘xc5 ♖b4 28 ♘xe6, when Black loses more material.

22 ♗f3 ♗xd2 23 ♖h1! ♘h6

It doesn't really matter at this point: the alternative 23...♔g8 24 ♔xd2 ♖d8 25 ♖h4 (or 25 ♕xc6) is also hopeless for Black.

24 ♔xd2 ♘g8 25 ♕xc6 ♕b4+

The alternative 25...♖c8 26 ♕d6 (or 26 ♕a4) 26...♗xa2? 27 ♖a1 ♗b3 28 ♖xa7 gives White a clear advantage, according to Gulko, which is an understatement!

26 ♕c3 a5 27 ♘c5 ♕f4+ 28 ♔d1 ♖e8 29 ♘xe6+ ♖xe6

At least a piece and then the king is lost after 29...fxe6 30 ♖f1!.

30 ♕c5+ ♖e7 31 ♖h8 1-0

This game was a wonderful technical performance by Gulko, who made the opening look like a forced win for White. We are getting used to the idea of only lightly supported flank advances on the side of the board opposite to where the other pieces are directed (in this case, the queen on b3, c3-knight and f3-bishop). It's also remarkable how once again Black's central counterattack failed so miserably against White's flank advance.

Game 32
Petrosian – Korchnoi
Moscow Ct (9) 1971

The first part of this game goes horrifically for Petrosian, who plays it with the apathy that characterized many of his openings over the years. But when you want to see an extraordinary strategic game you can hardly go wrong by leafing through those of Petrosian, the true giant of modern positional play.

1 c4 e5 2 g3 c6 3 b3 d5 4 ♗b2 d4 5 ♘f3 ♗d6 6 d3 c5 7 ♗g2 ♘e7 8 0-0 ♘ec6

This is reminiscent of a famous Petrosian-Fischer game from their Candidates match, although Black has lost a tempo with ...c6-c5.

9 e3!?

9 e4 is arguably better, since it would create a position like the one that arises later without loss of time.

9...0-0 10 ♘bd2 ♗e6 11 e4!? *(D)*

Both of White's bishops are now blocked off and ineffective while his opponent has a clear space advantage. Watch how Petrosian slowly solves this problem, and makes his knight useful as well. This is particularly impressive as White's standard breaks b4 and f4 are not available.

11...♘d7 12 ♘h4 g6

Now any idea of progressing on the kingside looks hopeless for White. Petrosian finds the kind of creative continuation that made him legendary in slow manoeuvring positions.

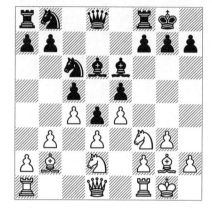

B

13 ♗f3! ♗c7!

Black activates his worst piece, and now both of his bishops are clearly superior to White's. Instead, 13...♗e7 14 ♘g2 would encourage White's remarkable idea of ♗e2 or ♗g4 followed by f4.

14 a3 ♗a5 15 ♗c1

At first it's not clear if this bishop is better on c1 than on b2. Later it becomes so.

15...♕e7

Black is playing good moves, but he has a hard time making progress. White now provokes ...f5 in order to open the long diagonal, a double-edged decision that leads to a sort of Benoni-like position.

16 ♗g4! f5 17 exf5 gxf5 18 ♗f3 ♘f6 19 ♗g2 ♖ad8 20 ♖a2!

Anticipating defence of the kingside as well as aggression by ♖e2. 15 ♗c1 is looking good!

20...♗c8 21 ♖e1 ♔h8?

Perhaps Black should side-step the pin by 21...♕c7.

22 b4! *(D)*

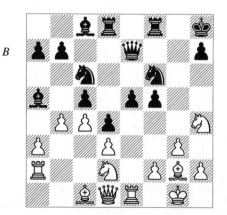

B

A lovely and perfectly timed sacrifice that ultimately shreds Black's pawn-structure.

22...cxb4 23 ♘b3 ♗b6

This seems to call White's strategy into doubt. Of course, 23...bxa3? loses to 24 ♘xa5 ♘xa5 25 ♗xa3, and 23...♗c7 24 axb4 ♘xb4 25 ♖xa7 obviously favours White.

24 ♗xc6!

The solution! White gives up his best bishop to make the knights maximally effective in an attack versus Black's centre.

24...bxc6 25 axb4 a6

Versus c5 and ♖xa7, but now Black runs into worse:

26 ♘f3 e4!?

26...♗c7 27 ♘xe5 ♗xe5 28 f4 is horrible.

27 c5 ♗c7 28 ♘fxd4

Black never gets compensation for this pawn. The rest of the game is still interesting but not relevant to our topic.

28...♕f7 29 ♖d2 ♗d7 30 ♗b2 ♔g8 31 ♘a5 ♗xa5 32 bxa5 ♖b8 33 ♗a1 ♖fe8 34 ♖de2 ♕h5 35 ♕d2 ♔g7 36 h4 exd3 37 ♕xd3 f4 38 ♘f3 ♖xe2 39 ♕xe2 ♕xc5 40 ♘e5 ♔f8 41 ♘xd7+ ♘xd7 1-0

A wonderful strategic demonstration.

Game 33
Shirov – Nisipeanu
Las Vegas FIDE 1999

Moving from statics to dynamics, this mighty struggle serves as an extreme example of the unbalanced complications that can arise from the Advance Variation of the Caro-Kann with 5 g4 that I discussed in Chapter 2. We see a mad flank pawn advance, a positional pawn sacrifice, brilliant and paradoxical attacking ideas, tough and ingenious defence from an elastic position, and above all a thoroughgoing dynamism that makes the game so remarkable and fun. The imbedded game between Grishchuk and Shirov is also of dramatic interest.

1 e4 c6 2 d4 d5 3 e5 ♗f5 4 ♘c3 e6 5 g4 ♗g6 6 ♘ge2 c5 7 h4

The currently most popular line is 7 ♗e3 ♘c6 8 dxc5 ♖c8, when Grishchuk-Shirov, Moscow Russia vs RoW rpd 2002 continued with wonderfully chaotic play: 9 f4!? (a novelty with this game, planning a pawn sacrifice that also leaves his king in the centre! There are always many fighting ideas in this opening; for example, 9 ♘d4 and 9 h4) 9...♕h4+ 10 ♗f2 ♕xg4 11 ♕d2! (Shipov points out that Black is all right with the queens off: 11 ♖g1 ♕h5 12 ♘g3 ♕xd1+ 13 ♖xd1 ♗xc2 14 ♖d2 ♗g6) 11...♘b4 12 ♖g1!? (Shipov prefers 12 0-0-0, giving the sample line 12...♗xc2 13 ♖g1 ♕h5 14 ♘g3 ♕h6 15 ♗b5+ ♔d8 16 ♘xd5! with complications that seem to favour White) 12...♕f5 (D).

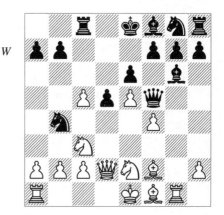

13 ♖c1! (remarkably, Grishchuk decides to forego castling and expose his king to checks for the sake of one tempo!) 13...♘xc2+ 14 ♔d1 d4?! (according to Shipov, Black has counterchances after 14...♗xc5 15 ♗xc5 ♖xc5 16 ♘g3 ♕g4+ 17 ♗e2 ♕h4 18 ♖xc2 ♗xc2+ 19 ♔xc2 ♘e7, although White's position still appears preferable after 20 ♘h5 ♔f8 21 ♗g4) 15 ♗xd4! ♘b4 16 ♘g3 ♕g4+ 17 ♗e2 ♕h4 18 ♘ce4 (suddenly everything is going White's way) 18...♘c6 19 ♘d6+ ♗xd6 20 exd6 ♘xd4 21 ♕xd4 ♘f6 22 ♗b5+ ♔f8 23 d7! ♘xd7! (generating some cheapo chances) 24 ♗xd7 ♖d8 25 ♔e1?! (25 c6! bxc6 26 ♖xc6 wins) 25...♕xh2 26 ♔f1 h5 (Black is still losing, but getting some unnecessary counterplay) 27 ♖g2 ♕h3 28 ♔g1 h4 29 ♘f1 ♖h5? 30 ♖xg6?! (30 ♕d6+ ♔g8 31 ♗xe6! wins outright) 30...fxg6 31 ♕d6+ ♔f7 32 ♖e1 ♕g4+ 33 ♔f2 ♖xd7 34 ♕xd7+ ♔f6 (D).

Now White missed the extremely pretty 35 ♖e4! ♕f5 36 ♕e8!!, which threatens ♕f8# and will leave White a clear piece up after the forced 36...g5. Indeed, after 35 ♕d8+ ♔f7 36 ♕d7+ ♔f6, Grishchuk tragically did very much what Shirov himself does in our main game: he tries too hard to win and eventually even

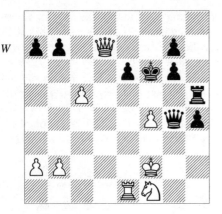

managed to lose after 37 ♘e3? ♛xf4+ 38 ♔e2 ♖e5 (achieving dynamic equality), making still further mistakes later.

7...h6 8 f4!

This rare idea had a poor reputation before this game, in which Shirov infuses it with new life. 8 ♗e3, the main move at the time, leads to terribly complex play that is still being debated. For more on the various themes involved, see Chapter 2.

8...♗e7 (D)

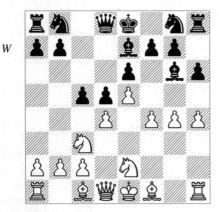

A very tempting move that seems to identify the weakness of 8 f4: White has opened the h4-e1 diagonal. I won't delve into the theory on other moves here.

9 ♗g2!

This constitutes a long-term pawn sacrifice of the highest order, encompassing both positional and tactical ideas. White decides that clearing f1 is more important than gaining a tempo by 9 h5 ♗h4+ 10 ♔d2 ♗h7. He also places his bishop on the apparently unpromising square

g2 (see White's remarkable 16th move), when h3 seems a more aggressive point from which to attack.

9...♗xh4+ 10 ♔f1 ♗e7

Played to cover d6 and avoid possible embarrassment after g5. White is surprisingly on top after 10...cxd4 11 ♘xd4 ♘c6 12 f5 ♘xd4 (12...♘xe5 13 ♗f4!) 13 ♛xd4 ♗h7 due to 14 ♘b5! ♗e7 (D).

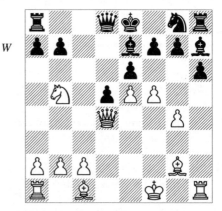

Now by the clever 15 ♛a4! ♔f8 16 fxe6 fxe6 17 ♖h3!, White launches an original and ultimately extremely advantageous attack, as analysed by Stohl in his thorough notes to this game in *Instructive Modern Chess Masterpieces*. Notice that neither of White's bishops nor his a1-rook are participating!

11 f5! ♗h7

11...exf5? 12 ♘f4 (according to Stohl, 12 ♘xd5 fxg4 13 ♘ef4 is also good) 12...♘c6 13 ♘xg6 fxg6 14 gxf5 is extremely strong for White. Black's centre collapses.

12 ♘f4 ♛d7 13 ♘h5!?

Nisipeanu felt that 13 ♘cxd5!? exd5 14 ♗xd5 was very strong, threatening 15 ♗xf7+, although Stohl then appears to believe that 14...♛c7! holds on and provides analysis to that effect. This would nevertheless have been a pragmatic over-the-board decision.

13...♗f8

Moving backwards, but 13...♔f8 14 fxe6 fxe6 allows 15 ♛f3+, so there really isn't any option. On the other hand, White's knight is apparently away from the action and he must do something to counteract the impending break-up of his centre.

14 dxc5 ♘c6

Stohl feels that 14...exf5? 15 ♕xd5! ♘c6 16 ♘b5! is extremely strong; e.g., 16...0-0-0 17 ♘d6+ ♗xd6 18 exd6 (or perhaps 18 cxd6!?, since the c-file can be very dangerous vis-à-vis Black's king) 18...fxg4 19 ♗d2, threatening b4-b5. At any rate the move played develops and attacks White's centre.

15 ♘b5! ♗xc5 *(D)*

Black feels that his better development and threats of ...♘xe5 will more than compensate for the loss of the g-pawn. At this point the complications begin to become so outrageous that I won't confuse the reader with too many of them. The main alternative is 15...♘xe5 16 ♕e2! and against most moves, such as 16...♘xg4, White plays 17 ♗f4!. When all is said and done, Stohl believes that White retains the advantage in all variations.

W

16 c4!! *(D)*

A magnificent move, which incidentally sacrifices a second pawn. Stohl relates that upon seeing this move Nisipeanu nearly fell off his chair! Surely any mere mortal would prefer to keep Black's king in the centre and inflict injury upon the enemy pawn-structure by 16 ♘xg7+ and in fact play that quickly, out of perceived necessity if nothing else. In the face of ...0-0-0 and ...♘xe5, White would seem to have no choice. Shirov's move still neglects development and even allows Black to castle on the queenside. His reasoning is that he finally activates his g2-bishop and perhaps prepares possible action on the queenside by means of ♗f4 and ♖c1 (Black of course has options everywhere, including ...d4). Nevertheless, is it really possible that being a pawn down with his king

on the awful square f1, and with Black having a lead in development (all the more so if he now plays 16...0-0-0), White can speak of equality, much less an advantage? The first key here is in the consideration of the concrete variations, any one of which might instantly refute White's play but may also bear out difficulties that Black faces. Without the ability to see accurately and fairly deeply into many potential sequences, one cannot play in this manner. But naturally there is a limit to any player's ability to calculate precisely and much must be left to a grandmaster's instinct. That consists of a feel for the dynamic possibilities and the assessment of the end positions of numerous lines under analysis. The game before you is a wonderful example of these qualities. Perhaps only Kasparov of the world's top players could also play in this way with confidence in both his instinct and calculations.

B

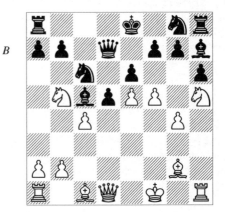

16...♘xe5!

A bold and accurate defence. The first thing to realize is that by c4, White has protected his b5-knight; this is non-trivial and affects nearly every variation. Stohl now enters into a lengthy, dense analysis of many wild possibilities to conclude that the text is 'the most demanding move'. By far the most important alternative is 16...0-0-0 17 cxd5 ♘xe5 (after 17...exd5 Stohl gives 18 ♗f4 or 18 ♕c2 b6 19 ♘d6+! with superior chances), when amazingly, White takes even more time out to play 18 a4! *(D)*.

We then arrive at a mess that requires analysis of four black replies. Stohl finds them all better for White, starting from the relatively easy 18...a6 19 ♕c2 b6 20 b4! on to variations

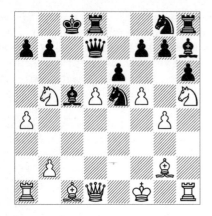

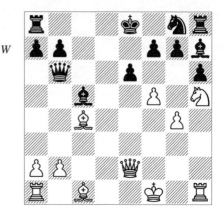

like 18...exf5 19 ♗f4 fxg4 20 ♖c1 b6 21 ♗xe5 ♛f5+ 22 ♗f4 g5 23 b4 gxf4 24 bxc5 "where White's play should be faster"! Wonderful stuff. But the very main line is 18...exd5 19 ♗f4! ♘c4 20 ♖c1 a6 (20...g6 21 b3! gxh5 22 bxc4 d4 23 ♛e1!, and now Stohl gives the very pretty variation 23...♖e8 24 ♛a5 b6 25 ♛a6+ ♔d8 26 ♗c7+ ♔e7 27 ♛b7! hxg4 28 ♗xb6! and 29 ♖e1+) 21 ♘c3 ♘e7 22 b3 ♗e3 23 ♘xd5! ♗xc1 24 ♘xe7+ ♛xe7 25 ♛xc1 ♖d4 26 bxc4 and White is better!

17 ♛e2 ♘xc4

Another remarkable variation given by Stohl is 17...f6 18 ♗f4! (18 fxe6? ♛e7! threatening ...♗d3) 18...dxc4 19 ♗xe5 fxe5 20 ♛xe5! ♛xb5 21 ♘xg7+ ♔f7 22 fxe6+ ♔f8 23 ♛f4+. I hope that the reader doesn't mind the intrusion of so many tactics into a book on strategy, but they do reflect the almost chaotically dynamic character of much of modern chess (take a look, for example, at the best games from *Informator*!). Besides, we are allowed to indulge ourselves once in a while.

18 ♗xd5! ♛xb5!?

Two other responses are 18...♘d6 19 ♘xd6+ ♛xd6 20 ♗xb7 ♖d8 21 ♗f4!, which is still rather unclear, and 18...♘d2+? 19 ♗xd2 0-0-0 20 ♘f4! exd5 21 ♖c1.

19 ♗xc4 ♛b6 *(D)*

20 fxe6?!

Natural, but it doesn't seem best. Stohl points out that 20 ♘xg7+ ♔f8 21 ♘h5, although apparently slow, threatens ♛e5 and is quite strong: 21...exf5? (another rook-lift follows 21...♛c6 22 ♖h3!, but this time White's pieces are classically active) 22 ♛e5 ♗d4 23 ♛d5 ♗g6 24 ♘f4 ♛f6 25 ♘xg6+ fxg6 26 g5!, winning. This

might have justified Shirov's entire conception. Now Black fights back:

20...0-0-0! 21 exf7 ♘e7 22 ♛e6+

As usual, there are alternatives; e.g., Stohl's 22 ♗f4 ♘d5 23 ♖h3!? leads to obscure complications, although it seems that Black is holding his own.

22...♔b8 23 ♗f4+?!

Remarkably, this natural check probably throws away any chances for a win, in spite of Shirov's powerful-looking move 25 which he must have anticipated would win. Stohl thinks that the best continuation was the exciting forcing line 23 ♘xg7 ♖d1+ 24 ♔g2 ♛xe6 25 ♘xe6 ♗e4+ 26 ♔g3 ♗d6+ 27 ♗f4 ♗xf4+ 28 ♔xf4 ♖xh1 29 ♖xh1 ♗xh1 30 f8♛+ ♖xf8+ 31 ♘xf8, when White has some winning chances, mainly based upon his aggressive king position.

23...♔a8 24 ♛xb6 axb6 25 ♗e5 *(D)*

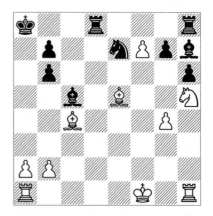

25...♖hf8!

The ingenious saving move! This must have shocked Shirov after his exhausting climb to apparent victory. Nisipeanu has played incredibly well on defence for the entire game and may well have anticipated this.

26 ⌾e2??

Black's point was 26 ♗xg7 ♗d3+! 27 ♗xd3 ♖xf7+, when 28 ♗f5 ♘xf5 29 gxf5 ♖xf5+ yields a perpetual check! At this point Shirov continues to play for the win without objective justification. Perhaps we see the difference here between him and the pragmatic Kasparov who, especially with as little time as Shirov had left, would doubtless have bailed out into the above variation.

26...♘d5 27 ♖hf1?!

27 ♘xg7 had to be tried, although Stohl demonstrates with exhaustive analysis that 27...♖xf7 28 ♘e6 ♖e7! would have led to a large advantage for Black, White's best option being 29 ♘xd8 ♖xe5+ 30 ⌾d2 ♘e3! 31 ♗b3 ♘xg4 32 ♖h3! ♗b4+ 33 ♖c3. Then Black still has several moves leading to an advantage, but it would still be a fight.

27...♘e3 28 ♗b5!

28 ♗xg7 ♘xc4 29 ♗xf8 ♗d3+ 30 ⌾e1 ♖xf8 is no contest. But the text-move also leads to an eventual loss.

28...♘xf1 29 ♖xf1 ♗g6 30 ♖f4?

Probably a product of Shirov's deteriorating time situation. Better is 30 ♗xg7 ♖xf7 31 ♖xf7 ♗xf7 32 ♗xh6, but according to Stohl, 32...♖xa2 or 32...♖d4 should suffice to win.

30...♗d6 31 ♗xd6 ♖xd6 32 ♗c4 b5! 33 ♗b3 ♗d3+ 34 ⌾e3 g5 35 ♖f2 ♗c4 36 ♗xc4 bxc4 37 ⌾e4 ♖d7 38 ♖f6 ♖fxf7 39 ♖xh6 ♖fe7+ 40 ⌾f5 ♖d5+ 41 ⌾g6 ♖e2 0-1

This was in my opinion one of the great games of the past five years or more. A terrible tragedy for Shirov, who played with stunning brilliance, but one must also admire Nisipeanu's accurate and inspired resistance.

Game 34
Timman – Topalov
Moscow OL 1994

It's always fun to see a dynamic slugfest in the King's Indian Defence, perhaps the most modern and paradoxical of major openings. In this game, as so often in the KID, both sides play on both sides of the board. There are numerous positional themes, and Topalov plays an early

positional pawn sacrifice that is truly long-term in nature.

1 c4 ♘f6 2 ♘c3 g6 3 e4 d6 4 d4 ♗g7 5 f3 0-0 6 ♗e3 e5 7 d5 ♘h5 8 ♕d2 f5 9 0-0-0 *(D)*

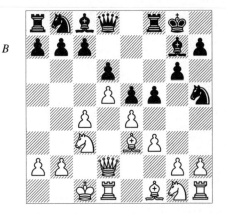

A typical Sämisch Variation structure. White has developed harmoniously and has ideas of breaking through on the queenside by ⌾b1, c5, and ♖c1. Black has a knight on the rim and a bad bishop! Of course it's not that easy, as we shall see.

9...a6!?

9...f4 just makes the bishop worse and it can't really get out after 10 ♗f2 ♗f6 11 ♘ge2 ♗h4 12 ♗g1. But 9...♘d7 is a pointed and flexible move, with the intention of coming to f6 in most lines and supporting a kingside attack.

10 exf5!?

A committal but perfectly logical move. White wants to get chances on the kingside as well as the queenside. Two common alternatives are 10 ⌾b1 and 10 ♗d3.

10...gxf5 11 ♘ge2!?

This allows a pawn sacrifice that looks unsound but creates enough dynamic counterplay to call that characterization into doubt. White of course has other moves like 11 ♗d3, which has its own complex theory.

11...b5! *(D)*

Striking on the side where his pieces aren't! Black's theoretical structural advantage is on the kingside as well. But during the early days of the King's Indian revival, especially in the 1950s and 1960s, players learned that Black often needed play on both wings so as not to get choked by White's extra space. Black may not get an immediate attack, but 11...b5 will either

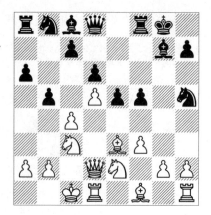

W

open one of the queenside files or gain critical squares.

12 ♘g3!

Trying to keep things closed by 12 c5 allows 12...b4 13 ♘b1 f4 14 ♗f2 ♗f5! and the bishop's diagonal cannot be blocked by a knight on e4, while ...e4 becomes a major theme.

12...♘f6

12...♘xg3? 13 hxg3 and White is winning on both sides of the board.

13 ♗g5

From here on out, I will borrow heavily from Igor Stohl's analysis in his wonderful *Instructive Modern Chess Masterpieces*, and hopefully give the reader some insight into the strategic themes.

13...b4

Making the sacrifice official. Black is in major trouble after 13...bxc4? 14 ♘h5 ♗h8 15 g4! (or 15 ♗xc4) as given by Stohl. Then 15...f4, in order to keep the g-file closed, allows White to control e4 after 16 ♘xf6+ (or 16 ♗xc4 ♘bd7 17 ♗d3) 16...♗xf6 17 h4!; e.g., 17...♗xg5?! 18 hxg5 ♕xg5 19 ♘e4 ♕g6 20 ♗xc4 ♘d7 21 ♗d3 ♕g7 22 ♖h5! with a winning attack.

Another idea is 13...♕e8!? 14 cxb5 axb5 15 ♗xb5 ♕g6, giving Black a couple of files, but I like White's active pieces.

14 ♘b1

An unclear option is 14 ♘ce2.

14...♕e8

Protecting the pawn is way too slow: 14...a5? 15 ♗d3 f4 16 ♘h5 (or even 16 ♕c2!) is extremely strong.

15 ♕xb4 h6 16 ♗d2?!

White has the good idea of guarding the queenside squares, but the specifics of the position are unfriendly. Stohl prefers 16 ♗h4! a5 17

♕d2 ♘a6 18 ♘c3, when the queenside is well protected and White's bishop will eventually get back to f2. There will of course be a whole game ahead, but White still has the pawn and he must be considered better.

16...a5! 17 ♕a3 ♘a6 18 ♘c3 ♗d7

Slow and patient. 11...b5 was played quite some time ago, but Black is still developing. Black realizes that the b-file really isn't enough to compensate him for the pawn, so he pursues a different idea. This is truly a positional sacrifice, with tactical play in mind only far down the road.

19 ♗d3 ♕g6 20 ♗b1!? ♘b4 21 ♖hg1! *(D)*

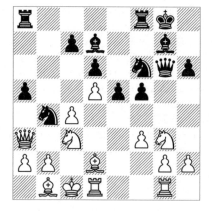

B

Suddenly White is attacking on his supposedly weak wing. His idea is clearly to enforce g4 at some point and go after the king. How can Black get counterplay?

21...h5

First, a prophylactic move directed against g4.

22 ♘ge2

Stohl's suggestion 22 ♘f1!? plans the devastating ♘e3 and g4. I won't go into all the details, but he gives the variation 22...♕f7 23 ♘e3 f4 24 ♘f5 ♗xf5! 25 ♗xf5 ♘fxd5! 26 ♗e4?! (26 ♘xd5) 26...♘b6! (Black sacrifices the exchange, as minor pieces are worth more than rooks here) 27 ♗xa8 ♖xa8 28 b3 and instead of his 28...♘d3+ 29 ♔c2 ♘c5, I like 28...e4!! (the King's Indian move!) intending 29 ♘xe4 (29 fxe4 ♗d4 30 ♖gf1? ♗c5!, winning!) 29...♘d3+ 30 ♔c2 ♗b2!, trapping the queen. These are typical tactics, of course, but notice how positionally based they are.

22...♕f7 23 ♘g3?

White changes his mind, but Black doesn't have to repeat. Stohl analyses the consistent and strong 23 g4! *(D)* to a white advantage.

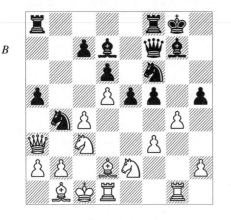

For example, 23...hxg4 (23...fxg4 24 ♖df1!?, or just 24 fxg4) 24 fxg4 fxg4 (24...♘xg4? 25 h3 ♘f6 26 ♗h6 ♘e8 27 ♖xg7+! ♘xg7 28 ♖g1) 25 ♘g3 with ♖df1 to come.

23...♘h7!

The odd thing is that retreat to the kingside helps the queenside attack.

24 ♘b5 ♖fc8 25 ♕b3?

It's positionally painful to surrender the dark squares (and open the a-file) by 25 ♗xb4?! axb4 26 ♕xb4 ♗h6+ 27 ♔c2 ♗e3!.

25...♗f8! *(D)*

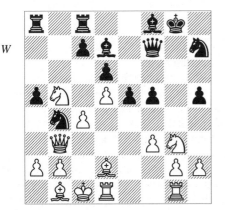

Finally, finally, Black's alternative to working on the b-file becomes clear. He will play ...c6 and open the more important c-file.

26 a3?! c6!

Perfect timing. Black is winning now, although the variations are very close to being

OK for White. They also provide a fascinating case for dynamic play.

27 ♘c3

The best try. Eventually losing are 27 ♘xd6 ♗xd6 28 axb4 cxd5, 27 axb4 cxb5 28 bxa5 ♖xc4+ 29 ♗c3 ♗h6+ 30 ♔c2 ♘f6, and 27 dxc6 ♖xc6! 28 ♘c3 (28 axb4 ♖xc4+ 29 ♗c3 axb4 30 ♘xd6 ♗xd6 31 ♖xd6 ♖xc3+!) 28...♖xc4! with the idea 29 ♘xf5? ♗xf5 30 ♗xf5 ♖xc3+! 31 ♕xc3 ♘a2+. This is again Stohl's analysis.

27...cxd5 28 cxd5

Or 28 axb4 axb4! 29 ♕xb4 d4 with an attack and a large advantage.

28...♖ab8 *(D)*

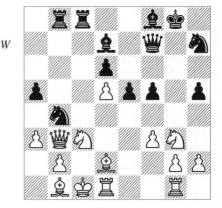

Finally the picture of what Black has been aiming for all along: the rooks will win practically by themselves.

29 axb4 axb4 30 ♕c2 bxc3 31 bxc3 ♖c4 32 ♕d3 ♖a4! 33 ♗e3 f4! 34 ♕xh7+ ♕xh7 35 ♗xh7+ ♔xh7 36 ♘e4 ♖a1+ 37 ♔d2 ♖b2+ 38 ♔d3 ♗b5+ 39 c4 ♖a3+ 40 ♘c3 ♗e8! 0-1

An appealing picture. The move ...♗g6+ is too strong.

Game 35
Nimzowitsch – Olson
Copenhagen 1924

How better to conclude this book than with a game by the great genius of middlegame strategy? This was one of Nimzowitsch's favourite games; he spoke of it as a "triumph of mind (the dynamic effect) over mere material". It seems unlikely that the game was played in a tournament setting: we have record of Nimzowitsch's participation in only one tournament in 1924, a

Copenhagen international event in which Olson didn't play (Nimzowitsch won with 9½ points out of 10!). In fact, Nimzowitsch-Olson is by no means a great game. Nimzowitsch's play is delightful but hardly rigorously correct, and his opponent fails to put up any resistance at the end. But it *is* undeniably a modern game in every sense of that word, as much so today as in 1924. White plays a thoroughly experimental opening, launches an extraordinarily early flank attack, creates a giant hole in his centre just begging for occupation by his opponent, and defies numerous conventional principles of development! Lastly, with a positional pawn sacrifice based upon a surprising retreat, he demonstrates a dynamic philosophy that would do a player of any era proud.

1 f4 c5 2 e4 ♘c6 3 d3 g6 4 c4!?

An unusual and already rather brash move, since it leaves a permanent hole on d4 that provides an outpost for Black's pieces. To this day, some commentators might brand this type of move as dubious and anti-positional, and I suspect a great many more would have done so at the time the game was played. Nimzowitsch, however, characteristically adorns 4 c4 with an '!'.

4...♗g7 5 ♘c3 b6

Obviously this can't be a bad move, but 5...d6 is more natural, opening a path for the queen's bishop.

6 ♘f3 ♗b7 7 g4!? *(D)*

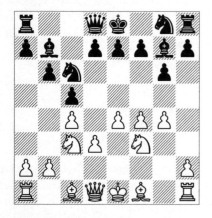

It's truly amazing that Nimzowitsch was living and playing in the time of players like Lasker, Rubinstein, Capablanca, Alekhine, and the young Euwe. The most important games of

these players were dominated by respectable openings, mostly classical and often symmetrical ones, to the extent that the complaints about the death of chess expressed by Lasker and Capablanca were based on the remarkably narrow notion that to be playing truly 'correctly', one somehow had to play 1 e4 or 1 d4 and even respond symmetrically to those moves. (It was also claimed that those openings had been 'worked out'!). For a world-class player merely to conceive of setting up such a structure, regardless of the opponent, shows that Nimzowitsch had freed himself of 'the dead dogmas', a phrase that he used in his introduction to this very game. Why is a move like 7 g4 so offensive to classical sensibilities?

a) It is the fifth pawn move out of the seven moves that White has made.

b) It launches a flank advance when White has barely begun to develop his pieces.

c) It has no apparent connection to the fight for the centre, much less for the crucial d4-square that White surrendered on the fourth move.

d) It attacks nothing and defends nothing.

e) It advances a pawn in front of White's king, assuming that he castles kingside (which he does).

What then could justify 7 g4? First, some concrete and pragmatic considerations:

a) White's king's bishop is better placed on g2 than e2.

b) The g4-pawn supports a potential f5, cramping Black, while discouraging Black's thematic thrust ...f5.

c) While in general moving pawns in front of one's king can expose it to attack, that is simply not a real concern in this particular position.

But beyond all that, 7 g4 grabs space, just as the ubiquitous early flank advances that we saw in Chapter 2 did. That tends to restrict the opponent's options for development, and what Nimzowitsch called "the collective mobility" of White's pawns gives him certain attacking chances. Is 7 g4 therefore an unusually strong move? Probably not, but it is a playable one and, more significantly, a thinkable one.

7...e6 8 ♗g2 ♘ge7 *(D)*

A standard set-up that we often see today. Black has various good ideas in store such as ...d5 and ...f5.

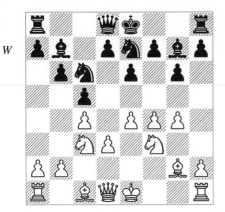

9 ♘b5!?

Or '!' if we listen to Nimzowitsch. This foray may not be objectively better than the alternatives but it has its points, and again it's remarkable to see one of the best players in the world making what are apparently time-wasting and decentralizing beginner's moves!

9 0-0 is a satisfactory alternative, and 9 ♗e3 is also noteworthy, because 9...d5 (9...0-0 10 d4!? is obscure) 10 e5 d4 (10...0-0 11 ♘b5!?) 11 ♘b5 (11 ♘e4!?) 11...0-0 12 ♗f2 gives White promising and double-edged play.

9...d6

9...d5 would presumably be answered by something like 10 e5 0-0 11 ♘d6, although this is probably only equal.

10 0-0 a6 11 ♘a3!? (D)

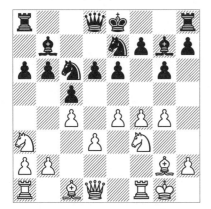

The point! Nimzowitsch makes the extravagant and preposterous claim that by provoking ...a6 he has made the necessity for Black to defend b6 the basis for a future combination! This in fact occurs, but hardly due to such farsighted

preparation. The student of modern chess might note, however, that White is perfectly willing to place his knight on the edge of the board, and that it can potentially both defend d4 and support b4 from c2.

11...0-0 12 ♕e2 ♕d7 13 ♗e3 ♘b4!?

"Otherwise there follows 14 ♖ad1 and d4 with advantage for White", says Nimzowitsch. Of course, Black needn't cooperate; for example, 13...f5! is a more challenging continuation.

14 ♘c2!

An excellent positional pawn sacrifice that makes particular sense if you anticipate White's 17th move.

14...♗xb2

Justifying Nimzowitsch's comment to move 9. This capture turns out to be surprisingly risky, so it may be that 14...♘xc2 15 ♕xc2 ♘c6 was preferable.

15 ♖ab1 ♗c3 16 ♘xb4 ♗xb4 (D)

After 16...cxb4 17 ♗xb6, White has an attractive centre and some advantage. Black should probably counter immediately with 17...f5.

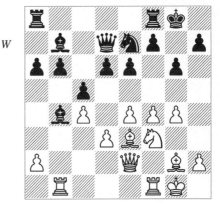

17 ♗c1!

Correct or not, this retreat gets credit for imaginativeness! The bishop is headed for b2 and the long diagonal. White also could have played 17 f5, which similarly tries to exploit the absence of Black's dark-squared bishop from the kingside.

17...f6?!

Black tries to block things, but this weakens his kingside without challenging White's centre. 17...f5! would have been more aggressive.

18 ♗b2 e5? (D)

This is a huge mistake. Better was 18...b5, when White does seem to have compensation for the pawn; for example, 19 g5 fxg5 20 ♘xg5 h6 21 ♘h3 and the situation is unclear because the b4-bishop is still out of play.

19 g5!?

Quite a good move, although Nimzowitsch mentions that 19 f5 would also be thematic in terms of his 7 pawns holding up the opponent's 8. Then 19...g5 20 h4 would condemn Black to a long and laborious defence.

19...♘c6?

The critical line is 19...fxg5 20 ♘xg5 (threatening ♗h3) 20...♘c6, when Nimzowitsch likes 21 f5, although then 21...♕e7 is unclear. So 21 ♗h3! ♕e7 22 ♗e6+ ♔g7 23 ♗d5 ♖f6 (23...♘d8 24 ♗xb7 ♘xb7 25 ♕g4) 24 ♕g4 looks like the most promising course. Certainly White has more than enough compensation for the pawn.

20 gxf6 ♕g4?

But 20...♖ae8 21 fxe5 dxe5 22 ♘g5! threatens both 23 f7+ and sometimes ♗h3; for example, 22...♘d8 (22...♔h8 23 ♗h3 ♕d6 24 ♕f2) 23 ♕e3 ♕d6 24 ♕h3 h5 25 ♕f3 with a winning game.

21 fxe5 dxe5 22 ♕e3 ♕h5

Trying to protect e5. 22...♖xf6 23 ♘xe5 ♖xf1+ 24 ♖xf1 ♘xe5 25 ♗xe5 is hopeless. White wins outright with ideas like ♗h3 and ♕h6.

23 ♘g5 ♗c8

This leads to a pretty finish. 23...♘d8 24 ♗xe5 hardly improves much.

24 f7+ ♔g7

Black would lose quickly after 24...♔h8 25 ♕f4.

25 ♕f4 ♔h6 (D)

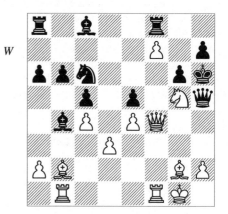

26 ♘e6+! exf4 27 ♗g7# (1-0)

Bibliography

This abbreviated list consists of important sources for *Chess Strategy in Action* (apart from those already given in *Secrets of Modern Chess Strategy*). I have depended more upon databases than for the previous volume; but I have also gleaned ideas and examples from books and magazines, just a few of which are presented below.

Periodic Publications

ChessBase Magazine (up to 89). My biggest intellectual debt in the preparation of this book has been to Peter Wells, whose original and profound middlegame articles in CBM have made me reconsider various subjects. CBM was also my source for some unique contributions by Curt Hansen and Daniel King.
The Week in Chess, webmaster Mark Crowther
New in Chess Magazine; New in Chess
Informator (up to 86); Šahovski Informator
ChessCafe (website); especially Richard Forster's *Late Knight* column
Kaissiber (magazine); Stefan Bücker

Books and CDs

Bangiev, A.; *Philidor Defence*; ChessBase 2002
Bronznik, V.; *Abseits von Schach*; ChessBase 2002
Benko, P. & Silman, J.; *Benko's Life, Games, and Compositions*; Siles Press 2003
Christiansen, L.; *Storming the Barricades*; Gambit 2000
Gligorić, S.; *I Play Against Pieces*; Batsford 2002
Hansen, Cu.; *Scandinavian* (CD); ChessBase 2002
Harding, T.; *64 Great Chess Games: Masterpieces of Postal and Email Chess*; Chess Mail 2002
Kasparov, G.; *My Story* (VHS); GM Video 2000
Korchnoi, V.; *My Best Games Volume 1: Games with White*; Edition Olms Zürich 2001
Korchnoi, V.; *My Best Games Volume 2: Games with Black*; Edition Olms Zürich 2001
Marović, D.; *Dynamic Pawn Play in Chess*; Gambit 2001
Melts, M.; *The Scandinavian Defence: the Dynamic 3...Qd6*; Russell Enterprises 2001
Nimzowitsch, A.; *Mein System*; Kurt Rattmann 1999
Nunn, J.; *Understanding Chess Move by Move*; Gambit 2001
Rowson, J.; *The Seven Deadly Chess Sins*; Gambit 2000
Stohl, I.; *Instructive Modern Chess Masterpieces*; Gambit 2001
Yermolinsky, A.; *The Road to Chess Improvement*; Gambit 1999

Finally, I'd like to thank the many correspondents who conveyed their ideas to me via e-mail, and the reviewers of *Secrets of Modern Chess Strategy* who offered their constructive criticisms.

Index of Players

When a page number appears in **bold**, the named player had White.

Index of Openings